PROBLEMS IN ELECTRONICS
WITH SOLUTIONS

Problems in Electronics with Solutions

F. A. BENSON
D.Eng., Ph.D., F.I.E.E., F.I.E.E.E., F.Illum.E.S.
Professor of Electronic and Electrical Engineering,
University of Sheffield

FIFTH EDITION

LONDON
CHAPMAN AND HALL

First published 1958
by E. & F. N. Spon Ltd.,
Second edition, 1961
Third edition, 1963
Fourth edition, revised and enlarged, 1965
Fifth edition, revised and enlarged, 1976
published as a Science Paperback by Chapman and Hall, Ltd.,
11 *New Fetter Lane, London EC4P 4EE*

Softcover reprint of the hardcover 1st edition 1976

ISBN-13: 978-0-412-14770-8 e-ISBN-13: 978-94-009-5770-1
DOI: 10.1007/978-94-009-5770-1

Distributed in the U.S.A.
by Halsted Press, a Division
of John Wiley & Sons, Inc., New York

Library of Congress Catalog Card No. 76-22643

CONTENTS

PREFACE TO THE FIFTH EDITION

Many changes have been made in this edition, first to the nomenclature so that the book is in agreement with the International System of Units (S.I.) and secondly to the circuit diagrams so that they conform to B.S.S. 3939. The book has been enlarged and now has 546 problems. Much more emphasis has been given to semiconductor devices and transistor circuits, additional topics and references for further reading have been introduced, some of the original problems and solutions have been taken out and several minor modifications and corrections have been made. It could be argued that thermionic-valve circuits should not have been mentioned since valves are no longer considered important by most electronic designers except possibly for very high power or voltage applications. Some of the original problems on valves and valve circuits have been retained, however, for completeness because the material is still present in many syllabuses and despite the advent and prolification of solid-state devices in recent years the good old-fashioned valve looks like being in existence for a long time. There are still some topics readers may expect to find included which have had to be omitted; others have had less space devoted to them than one would have liked.

A new feature of this edition is that some problems with answers, given at the end of each chapter, are left as student exercises so the solutions are not included.

The author wishes to thank his colleagues Professor P. N. Robson, Drs. J. Allison, A. P. Anderson, K. Barker, J. C. Bennett, B. Chambers, R. Hackam and G. S. Hobson and Mr. R. W. J. Barker for providing questions and solutions on certain topics which they have produced for tutorial classes and the University of Sheffield for permission to use some of the questions set in examination papers. The author takes full responsibility, however, for any mistakes which have crept in.

F. A. BENSON

Department of Electronic and Electrical Engineering
The University of Sheffield
1976

PREFACE TO THE FIRST EDITION

This book is based largely on problems which the author has collected over the last ten years, many of which have been given to undergraduate engineers. The purpose of the book is to present the problems, together with their solutions, in the hope that they will prove of value to other teachers and students. It is thought that the book covers almost the complete undergraduate electronics courses in engineering at Universities, but it has not been written to match any particular syllabus, and it should also be found useful by postgraduate students and research workers as a reference source. In fact, a few questions of postgraduate standard are included.

Within the author's knowledge, there is no other problem book on electronics with solutions which covers such a wide field as the present one. The few problem books which are available, while being excellent in some ways, suffer from certain disadvantages. In some, answers are given but not solutions, in others there are no questions at all on electronics, or if there are they form only a small part of the whole. In other instances, where solutions are given, the questions and solutions are not separated. Descriptive questions are given in some problem books; and, while it may be argued that these should be included to assist readers engaged in private study, the answers to these can easily be found in standard textbooks. The purpose of a problem book should surely be the application of theory rather than the teaching of it.

Textbooks form other useful sources of problems; and in fact, most textbooks give some worked examples too, but these are generally used merely to illustrate points which have just previously been made in the text and do not encourage students to think for themselves.

The author is very much in favour of problem papers and tutorials as a method of education, because it is well known that young students encounter many difficulties when they first try to apply their theoretical knowledge to practical problems.

The 282 problems are divided up into 23 sections and the solutions are separated from the problems so that the students shall not see solutions by accident. The answer is also given, however, at the end of each problem for convenience. A thorough grasp of the principles involved in any particular problem cannot be obtained by merely reading through the solution. Students should not therefore consult the solutions until they have either repeatedly tried hard and failed to obtain the stated answer, or successfully solved the problem and wish to compare the method of solution with that given. Wherever possible the problems are based on practical data, so as to familiarize the student with practical orders of magnitude.

At first it was thought that, because of the enormous range of subjects to be included, two books might be published, one featuring the elementary topics and the other the more advanced ones. It was finally decided that one volume rather than two was much more desirable; but, to keep the price of the book at a figure reasonable for students, it was necessary to limit the number of examples to about the same as already given in the author's existing book *Electrical Engineering Problems with Solutions.* It was also obvious at the outset that, because of length limitations, it would not be possible to include step-by-step mathematics, but only the electrical steps in the solutions. It is therefore assumed that the reader knows the necessary mathematics. It has been felt desirable to include a few problems of importance which are just standard textbook material but, in such cases, the solutions simply give references to suitable textbooks. Some topics which readers may expect to find included, e.g. kinetic theory of gases, sound equipment, polyphase rectifiers, vacuum techniques, have had to be omitted, and others have had less space devoted to them than one would have liked.

The author cannot possibly claim that all the problems in the collection are original, but it is impossible to acknowledge the sources of those which are not. Most of the problems are new, however, and in many cases they have been carefully formulated to try to encourage thought and understanding; but some, which require only numerical substitutions in formulae are included, in the hope that they will develop the student's sense of magnitudes.

To avoid repetition, all the general data required have been collected together and are given at the beginning of the book.

While great care has been taken to try to eliminate errors some will inevitably have crept in, and the author will be glad to have any such brought to his notice.

The author is indebted to Dr. J. Allison, B.Sc. (Eng.) for providing some experimental figures for use in several questions on transmission lines. He also expresses appreciation to a number of his former students who have confirmed the answers to many of the problems. The encouragement given and many helpful suggestions made by Professor A. L. Cullen, B.Sc. (Eng.), Ph.D., M.I.E.E., M.I.R.E., throughout the preparation of the manuscript are also gratefully acknowledged.

Electrical Engineering Department F. A. BENSON
The University of Sheffield, 1957.

GENERAL DATA

Charge on an electron (e)	$= 1.602 \times 10^{-19}$ C
Mass of an electron (m)	$= 9.107 \times 10^{-31}$ kg
Planck's constant (h)	$= 6.624 \times 10^{-34}$ Js
Boltzmann constant (k)	$= 1.38 \times 10^{-23}$ JK^{-1}
Permittivity of free space (ϵ_0)	$= 8.855 \times 10^{-12}$ Fm^{-1}
Excitation potential of argon	= 11.6 V
Ionization potential of mercury	= 10.4 V
Ionization potential of neon	= 21.5 V
Resistivity of copper	$= 1.7 \times 10^{-8}$ Ωm
Resistivity of nickel	$= 9.39 \times 10^{-8}$ Ωm

Section 1

PROBLEMS

CHAPTER ONE

CIRCUIT ANALYSIS

1. A series L, C, R circuit, with $R = 4\ \Omega, L = 100\ \mu$H and $C = 200\ \mu\mu$F is connected to a constant-voltage generator of variable frequency. Calculate the resonant frequency, the value of 'Q' and the frequencies at which half the maximum power is delivered.

[*Ans.* 1126 kHz; 177; 1129 kHz; 1122 kHz]

2. The graph shows the variation of current through a series L, C, R circuit when connected to a 5-V constant-voltage generator of variable frequency. Find the values of 'Q', R, L and C.

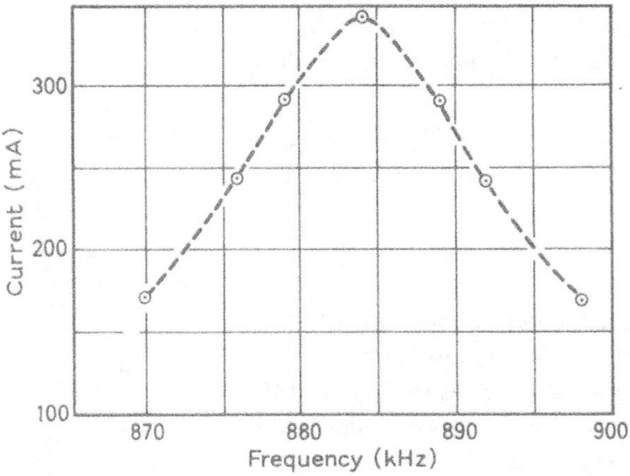

[*Ans.* 55.25; 14.53 Ω; 144.5 μH; 224 $\mu\mu$F]

3. A coil of inductance 88 μH is placed in series with a 4.8-Ω resistor. The combination is connected in parallel with a 375-$\mu\mu$F capacitor. Calculate the frequency of the circuit for which the effective impedance is a pure resistance.

[*Ans.* 876.4 kHz]

4. Determine the 'Q' factor of the parallel damped circuit shown below.

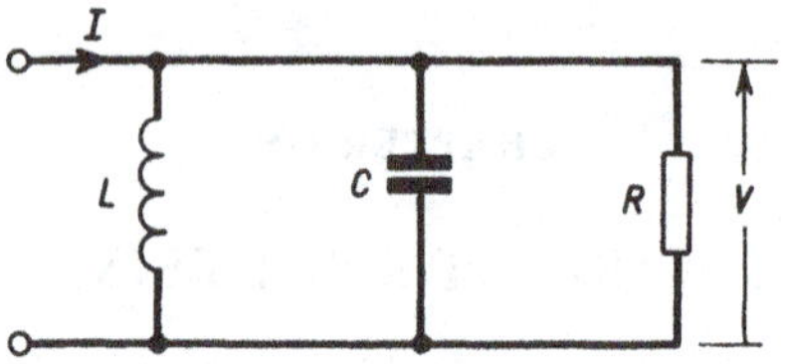

[*Ans.* $R/\omega_r L$]

5. A parallel resonant circuit is tuned to a frequency of 1 MHz and contains a 200-$\mu\mu$F capacitor. When a source of constant voltage is injected in series with the circuit the current falls to 0.707 of its resonant value, for a frequency deviation of 5 kHz from the resonant frequency. Calculate the circuit 'Q' and the parallel resonant impedance.

[*Ans.* 100; 79.6 kΩ]

6. A parallel resonant circuit employs a 50-$\mu\mu$F capacitor and has a bandwidth of 250 kHz. Calculate the maximum impedance of the circuit.

[*Ans.* 12 740 Ω]

7. Reduce the two circuits shown at (a) and (b) to the simple coupled circuit of (c) by assigning suitable values to Z_p, Z_s and M.

What are the coefficients of coupling for the circuits (a) and (b)?

[*Ans.* (a) $Z_p = j\omega(L_1 + L_m)$,
$Z_s = j\omega(L_2 + L_m)$, $M = L_m$;
(b) $Z_p = (C_1 + C_m)/\omega C_1 C_m$,
$Z_s = (C_2 + C_m)/\omega C_2 C_m$,
$M = 1/\omega^2 C_m$; coefficients of coupling are
$L_m/\sqrt{[(L_1 + L_m)(L_2 + L_m)]}$ for (a) and
$\sqrt{[C_1 C_2/(C_1 + C_m)(C_2 + C_m)]}$ for (b)]

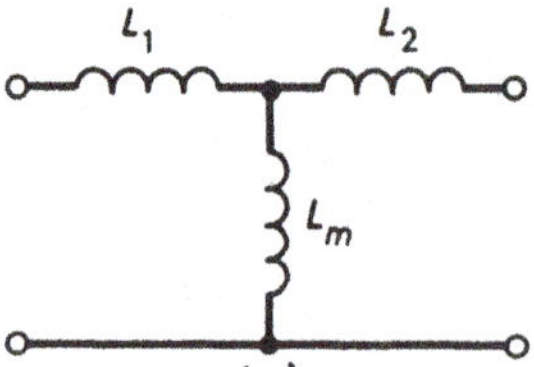

(a)

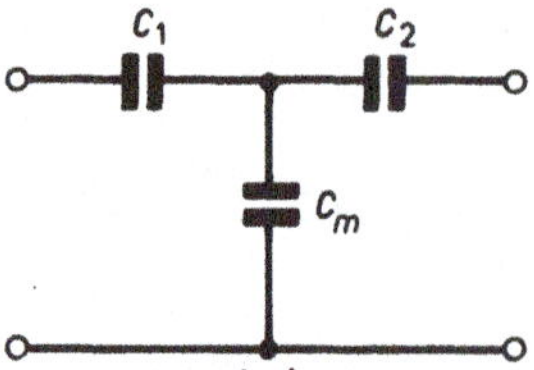

(b)

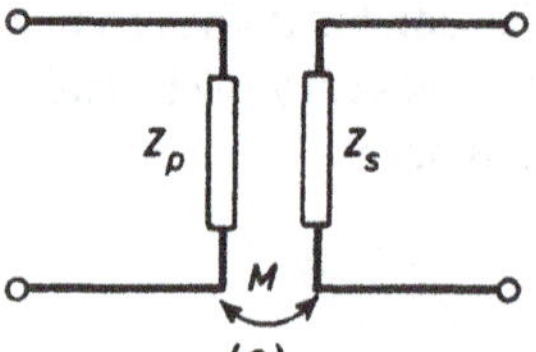

(c)

8. The two resonant circuits shown are tuned to the same frequency $\omega_r/2\pi$ and coupled together. Obtain an expression for the secondary current I_s in terms of the voltage V, the circuit Q's, Q_p and Q_s, the coefficient of coupling k and the ratio of the actual frequency to the resonant frequency, α.

Show that I_s reaches its maximum value when the circuits are in resonance and when $\omega_r M = \sqrt{(R_p R_s)}$ and that the value of k for critical coupling is $1/\sqrt{(Q_p Q_s)}$.

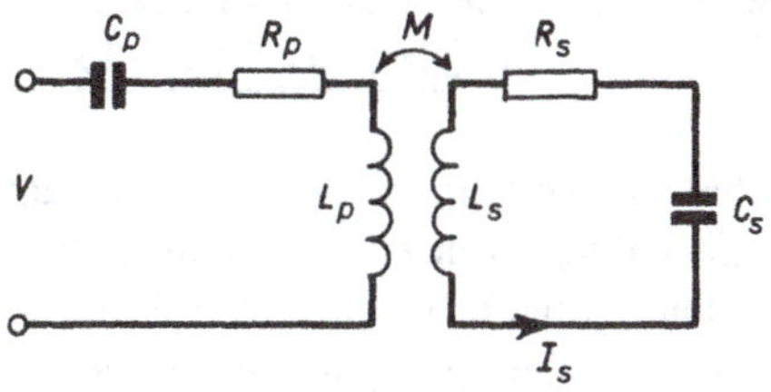

[*Ans.* $I_s = -jVk/\alpha\omega_r\sqrt{(L_pL_s)}\{k^2 + 1/Q_pQ_s - (1 - 1/\alpha^2)^2 + j(1 - 1/\alpha^2)(1/Q_p + 1/Q_s)\}$]

9. Two series circuits, each consisting of a 300-μH inductor and a 1000-$\mu\mu$F capacitor, are magnetically coupled so as to have a mutual inductance of 60μH. A voltage of 10 V having a frequency of $1/\pi$ MHz is injected into one circuit. Determine the current in the other circuit and the coefficient of coupling (k).

[*Ans.* $-$j0.273 A; 0.2]

10. Evaluate the input impedance of the circuit shown, at a frequency of 1 MHz. The coefficient of coupling is 0.1.

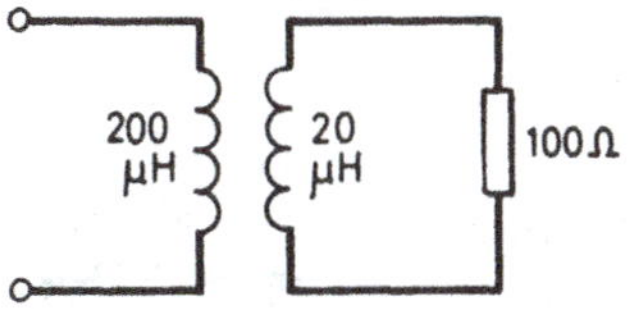

[*Ans.* (6.1 + j1249.1) Ω]

11. A voltage of 100 V at a frequency of $[10^6/2\pi]$ Hz is applied to the primary of the coupled circuit illustrated. Calculate the total effective resistance and reactance referred to the primary.

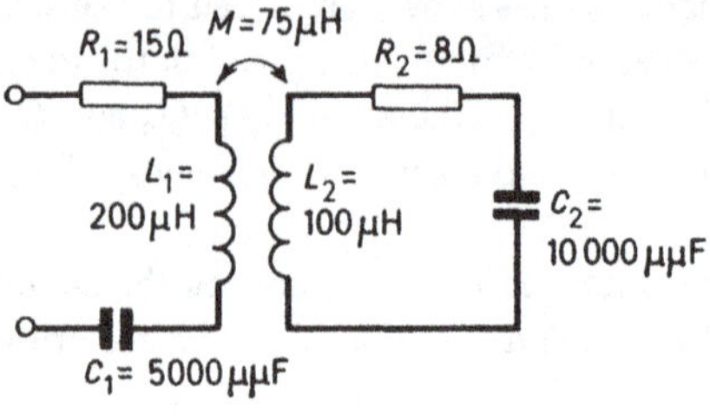

Determine also the primary and secondary currents.

[*Ans.* 718 Ω; 0; 0.139 A; 1.306 A]

12. A transformer has a tuned primary winding and an untuned secondary. The inductance of each winding is 1 mH and the mutual inductance between them is 0.5 mH. The primary winding is tuned with the secondary open-circuited, and resonates at a frequency of 500 kHz. If the secondary circuit is now short-circuited find the change of tuning capacitance required to keep the same resonant frequency. Neglect the resistances of the windings.

[*Ans.* 34 μμF]

13. In the circuit illustrated $\omega L_2 = 1/\omega C_2$. Determine the value of the input impedance, if C_1 is chosen to make it purely resistive. The frequency is 1 MHz.

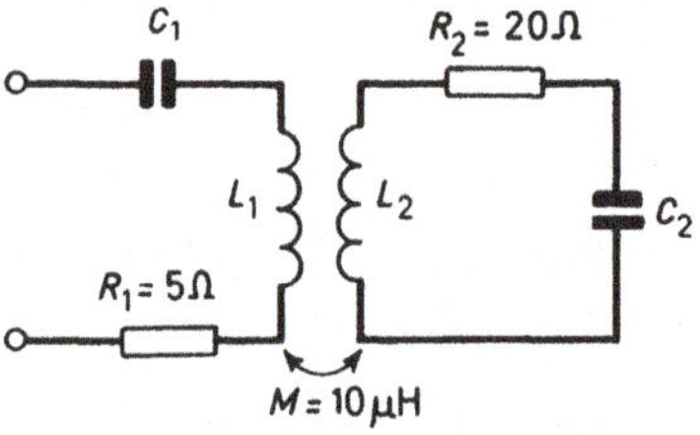

[*Ans.* 202.4 Ω]

14. In the circuit illustrated $e_1 = 169.7 \sin 1885t$ volts and $e_2 = 141.4 \sin (1885t + 45°)$ volts. Calculate the primary and secondary currents and draw a complete phasor diagram for the circuit.

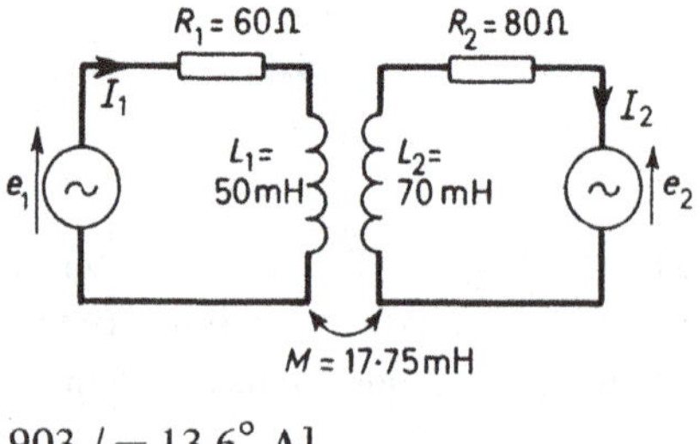

[*Ans.* $I_1 = 1.168\ \angle{-45.6°}$ A; $I_2 = 0.903\ \angle{-13.6°}$ A]

15. Determine the equivalent impedance of the two magnetically-coupled parallel circuits illustrated.

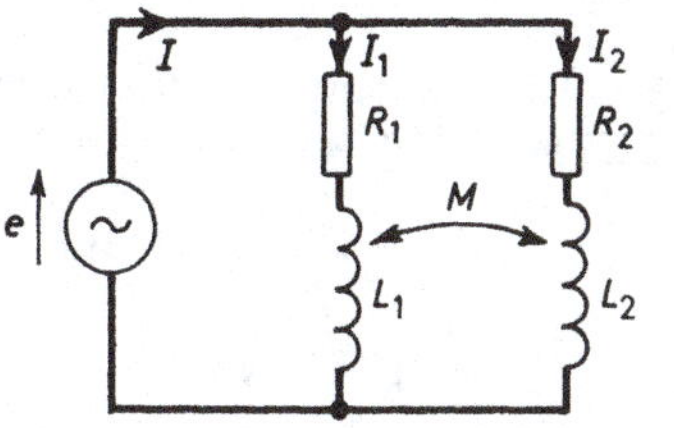

[*Ans.* $(Z_1Z_2 - Z_m^2)/(Z_1 + Z_2 - 2Z_m)$

where $Z_1 = R_1 + j\omega L_1$

$Z_2 = R_2 + j\omega L_2$

and $Z_m = \pm j\omega M$]

16. Experiments carried out on a variometer, whose two coils were series-connected, showed that the inductance values obtainable varied from 40 mH to 360 mH. Assuming that the self-inductances of the two coils are equal, determine the range of inductance values obtainable if the coils are reconnected in parallel. Neglect resistances.

[*Ans.* 10 to 90 mH]

17. Calculate the current flowing in resistor R_6 of the network, involving several coupled circuits, as shown. The angular frequency $\omega = 2 \times 10^6$ rad s^{-1}.

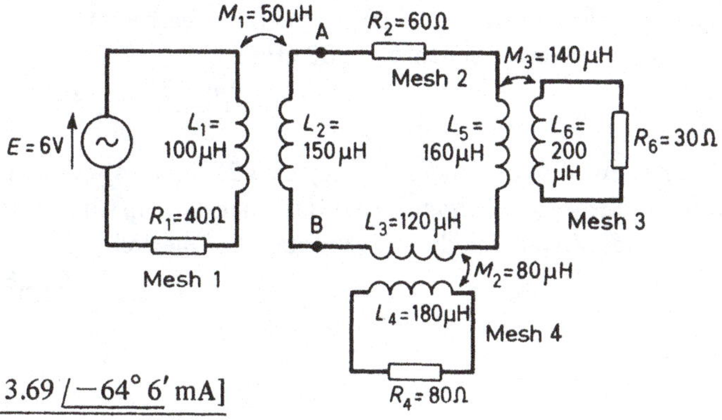

[*Ans.* 3.69 $\angle -64^\circ 6'$ mA]

18. For the circuit shown, calculate the total loop impedances, the mutual impedance, the apparent impedance of the primary loop and the currents in the two loops.

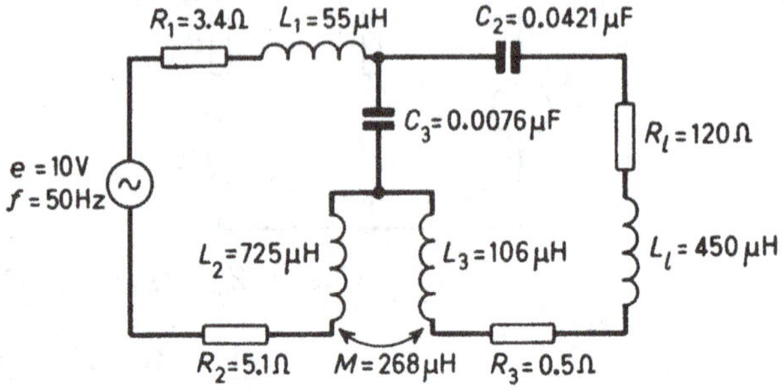

[*Ans.* $(8.5 - j174)\ \Omega$; $(120.5 - j320)\ \Omega$;
$j503\ \Omega$; $(271 + j522)\ \Omega$;
$0.017 \angle -62.6^\circ$ A; $0.0251 \angle -83.2^\circ$ A]

19. A wavemeter consists of a variable capacitor, having a range of 50 to 1000 $\mu\mu$F, and two coils of inductances 300 and 100 μH respectively. If the coils are fixed so that their mutual inductance is 25 μH, what range will the wavemeter have when the coils are used (*a*) in series aiding (*b*) in series opposing, (*c*) in parallel aiding and (*d*) in parallel opposing?

[*Ans.* (*a*) 283 to 1265 m; (*b*) 249 to 1115 m;
(*c*) 122 to 546 m; (*d*) 107 to 481 m]

20. A coil has an inductance of 5 mH, a self-capacitance of 5 $\mu\mu$F and a high-frequency resistance of 100 Ω. Determine the effective resistance and inductance of the coil at a frequency of 500 kHz.

[*Ans.* 177 Ω; 6.67 mH]

21. A coil is tuned to a certain frequency by a 250-$\mu\mu$F capacitor. To tune the coil to the second harmonic of this frequency a capacitance of 55 $\mu\mu$F is required. Determine the self-capacitance of the coil.

[*Ans.* 10 $\mu\mu$F]

22. Two coils, of inductances 50 μH and 200 μH respectively, are magnetically coupled. Find the effective value of the mutual inductance between them, at a frequency of 2 MHz, their self-capacitances being 5 and 7 $\mu\mu$F respectively, and the coefficient of coupling being 0.05.

[*Ans.* 6.3 μH]

23. Derive the conditions which must be satisfied for the two circuits illustrated to present identical impedances at all frequencies.

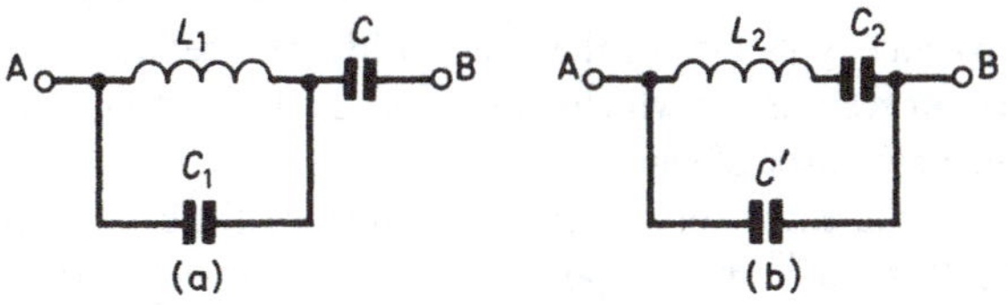

[*Ans.* $C' = CC_1/(C + C_1)$; $L_2 = L_1(C + C_1)^2/C^2$; $C_2 = C^2/(C + C_1)$]

24. Prove that if $R = \sqrt{(L/C)}$ the impedance of the circuit shown is independent of frequency, and determine the value of this impedance.

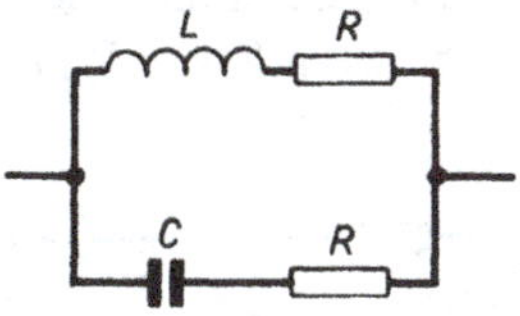

[*Ans.* R]

25. A non-inductive resistor of resistance R ohms is connected in parallel with a coil of inductance L henrys and negligible resistance. Calculate the values of R and L so that the impedance of the parallel combination, at a given frequency, is the same as that of a single coil of resistance r ohms and inductance l henrys.

[*Ans.* $R = \{r + (\omega^2 l^2/r)\}$; $L = \{l + (r^2/\omega^2 l)\}$]

26. Prove that the load impedance which absorbs the maximum power from a source is the conjugate of the impedance of the source.

A loudspeaker is connected across terminals A and B of the network illustrated. What should its impedance be to obtain maximum power dissipation in it?

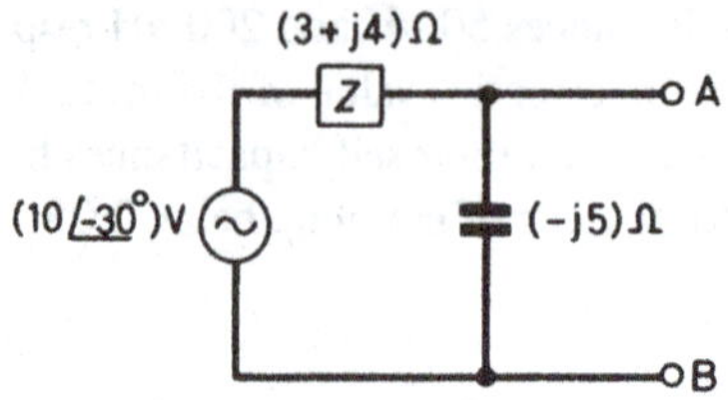

[*Ans.* (7.5 + j 2.5) Ω]

27. Derive an expression for the relationship between the series resistance ρ and the shunt resistance r which may be used alternatively to represent the losses in a capacitor of capacitance C.

For a particular capacitor at a certain frequency the product ρC was found to be 25×10^{-10} and the power factor was known to be 0.001. Determine the frequency at which the measurement was carried out.

[*Ans.* $\omega^2 C^2 \rho r = 1$, where $\omega = 2\pi \times$ frequency; 63.7 kHz]

28. The diagram shows a phase-shifting network. R and C are always adjusted so that the magnitude of their total impedance in series is 5000 Ω. The supply frequency is 1000 Hz. Determine the values of R and C which produce a phase shift of 30° between V_i and V_o. Does V_o lag or lead with respect to V_i?

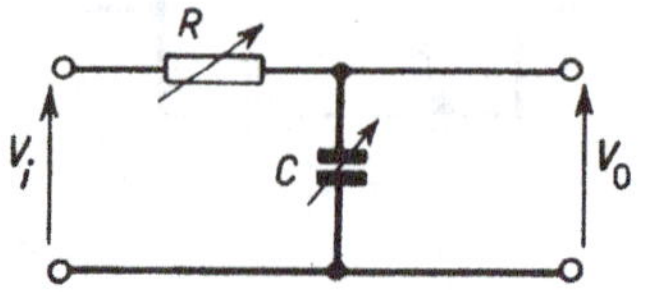

[*Ans.* 2500 Ω; 0.037 μF; lags]

29. Find the voltages V_1, V_2 and V_3 in the circuit illustrated using (*a*) mesh analysis, (*b*) nodal analysis.

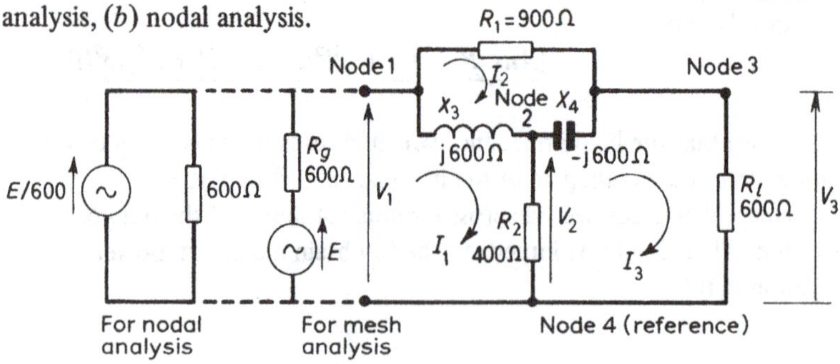

[*Ans.* $V_1 = E(0.499 + j0.214)$

$V_2 = E(0.143 - j0.143)$

$V_3 = 0.284E$]

30. Write down the nodal equations for the circuit illustrated.

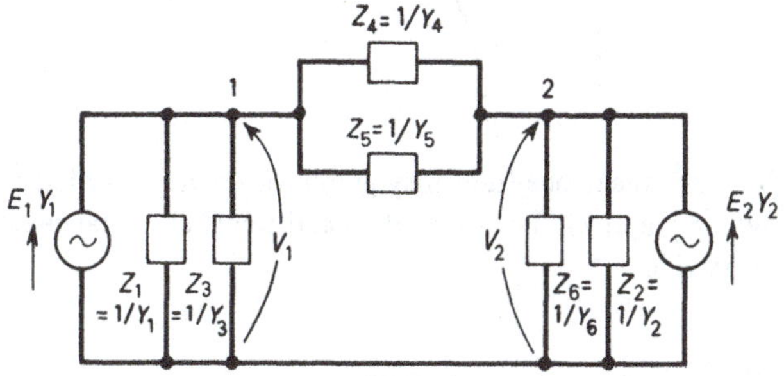

[*Ans.* $-E_1Y_1 + V_1(Y_1 + Y_3 + Y_4 + Y_5) - V_2(Y_4 + Y_5) = 0;$

$-E_2Y_2 + V_2(Y_2 + Y_4 + Y_5 + Y_6) - V_1(Y_4 + Y_5) = 0$]

31. Write down the nodal equations for a linear network with n independent nodes if $I_1, I_2, \ldots I_n$ are the generator currents and $V_1, V_2, \ldots V_n$ are the various node voltages. The node admittances are $Y_{11}, Y_{22}, \ldots Y_{nn}$ and the mutual admittances are Y_{12}, Y_{21}, etc.

Give the solution for any node voltage V_k in determinant form and define the open-circuit transfer and input impedances.

[see Solution for answers]

32. Sketch the reactance-frequency graphs for the network illustrated assuming that:

(*i*) the two parallel LC circuits have different values of the product LC, and then

(*ii*) that the left-hand coil has become open-circuited.

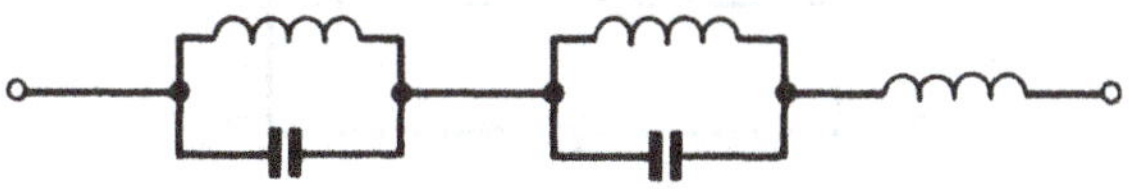

Draw a network of interconnected coils and capacitors which will be an inverse network of the one illustrated here.

[see the Solution for the graphs and network]

33. (*a*) Devise two networks whose reactance-frequency graphs are as shown.

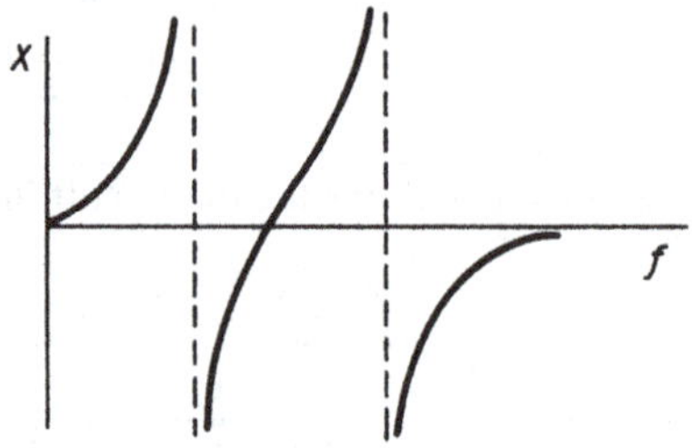

(*b*) Draw the reactance-frequency graph for the network illustrated. Show how the graph will be altered if an additional capacitance C_3 is connected across *AB*.

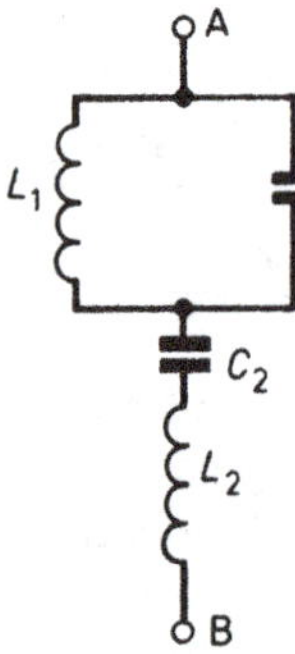

[*Ans.* see the Solution]

34. Sketch the form of the reactance-frequency graph for the network shown.

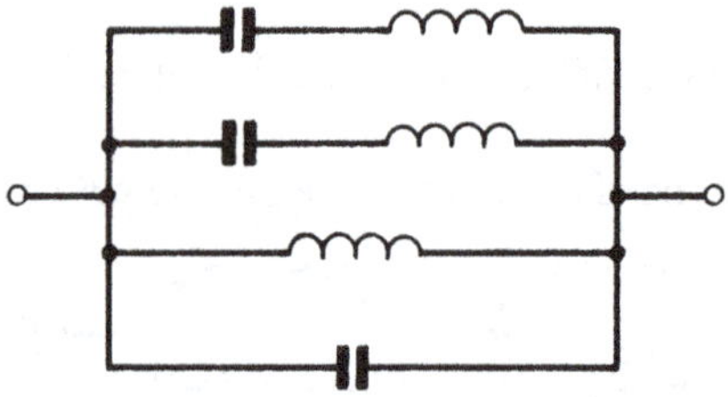

Deduce the reactance-frequency graph of the inverse network; hence draw two forms of the inverse network.

[*Ans.* see the Solution]

35. For the two-terminal network illustrated at (a) sketch the reactance-frequency graphs for:

(*i*) the portion of the network to the right of *AA*,
(*ii*) the portion of the network to the right of *BB*,
(*iii*) the whole circuit.

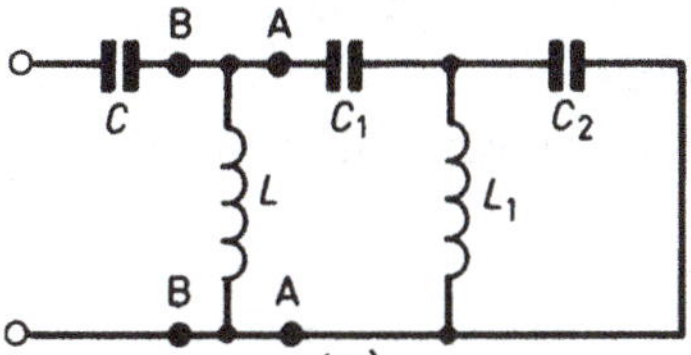

(a)

Sketch the reactance-frequency graphs for the circuit shown at (*b*) and its inverse network. Hence deduce two inverse networks for the arrangement (*b*).

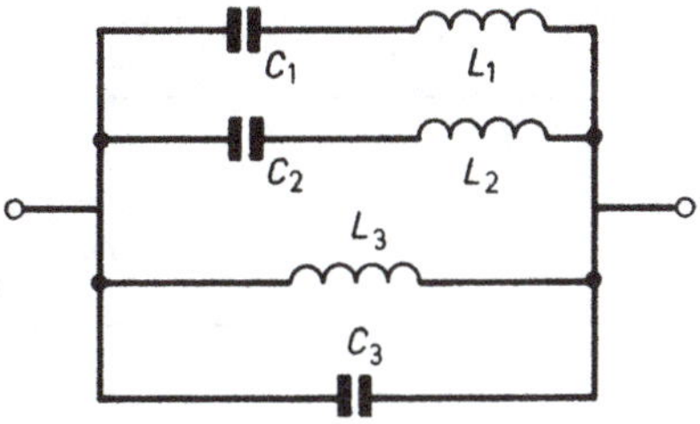

(b)

[*Ans.* see the Solution]

36. (*a*) Illustrate the direct method of constructing linear signal flow graphs by considering the equations

$$t_{11}x_1 + t_{12}x_2 + t_{10}x_0 = 0$$
$$t_{21}x_1 + t_{22}x_2 + t_{20}x_0 = 0$$

where x_0 is the known independent variable or source node in the flow graph.

(*b*) For the signal flow graph illustrated evaluate the ratio V_3/V_0 by (*i*) writing down and solving the three equations represented by the graph, (*ii*) using the general flow graph equation

$G = \Sigma \dfrac{G_k \Delta_k}{\Delta}$ where G_k is the gain of the kth forward path

$\Delta = 1 -$ (sum of all individual loop gains)

+ (sum of the gain products of all possible combinations of 2 non-touching loops) –
(sum of the gain products of all possible combinations of 3 non-touching loops)

+ (sum of the gain products of all possible combinations of 4 non-touching loops) etc.

and Δ_k = value of Δ for that part of the graph not touching the kth forward path.

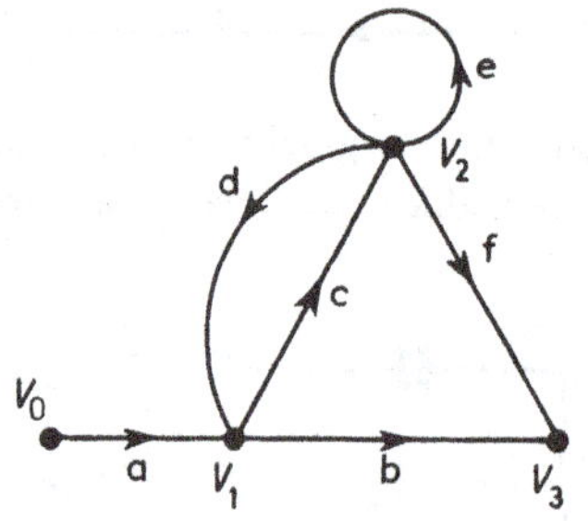

[*Ans.* (*b*) $\dfrac{acf + ab\,(1 - e)}{1 - e - cd}$]

37. (*a*) Employing *h* parameters draw a signal flow graph for a single-stage, common-emitter, transistor amplifier** with a load impedance Z_1.
(*b*) For the signal flow graph illustrated evaluate the ratio V_6/V_1.

** The application of signal flow graph techniques to transistor circuit analysis has been illustrated in a book by Abrahams and Coverley.* The circuits of some single and cascaded amplifiers, differential amplifiers and feedback amplifiers have been analysed by these authors. Some flow-graph techniques useful in the modelling and analysis of linear systems have been presented by Lorens.† A good introduction to signal flow graphs has been given by Chirlian.‡

* J. R. Abrahams and G. P. Coverley, *Signal Flow Analysis*, Pergamon, 1965, Chapter 5.

† C. S. Lorens, *Flowgraphs*, McGraw-Hill, 1964.

‡ P. M. Chirlian, *Electronic Circuits: Physical Principles, Analysis and Design*, McGraw-Hill, 1971, Chapter 12.

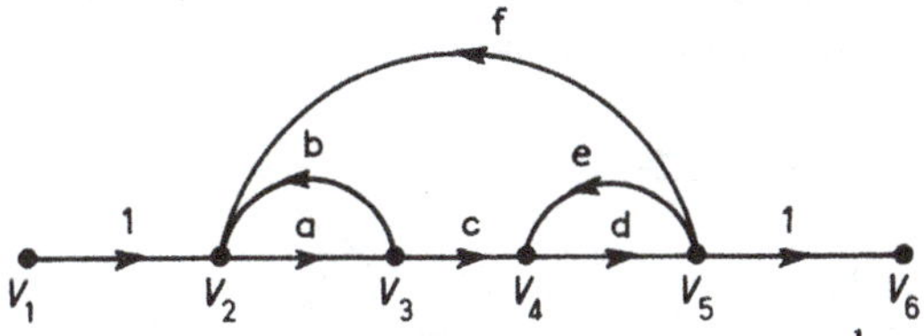

[*Ans.* (*b*) $\dfrac{\text{acd}}{1-(\text{ab}+\text{de}+\text{acdf})+\text{abed}}$]

38. For the signal flow graph illustrated evaluate the ratio V_2/V_0 by (*i*) writing down and solving the two equations represented by the graph, (*ii*) using the general flow-graph equation $G = \Sigma \dfrac{G_k \Delta_k}{\Delta}$ (see Problem 36(b)).

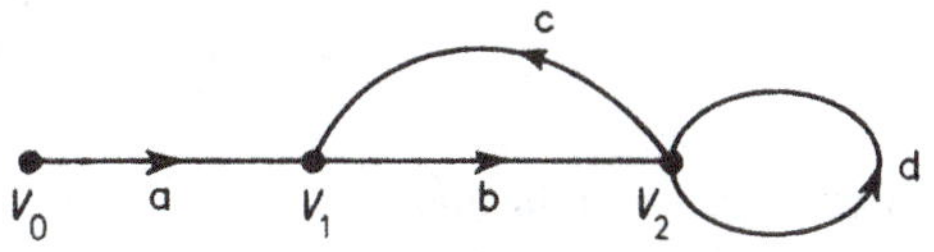

[*Ans.* ab/(1 − d − bc)]

39. A bridge network is illustrated. Draw the three paths that connect nodes 1 and 3 and the three residual networks that correspond to these three paths.

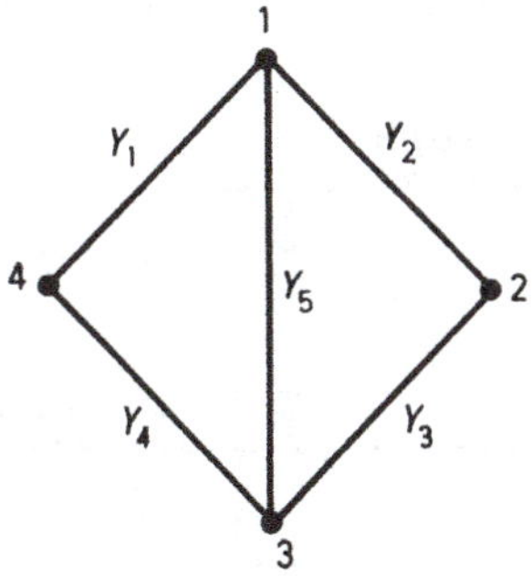

Write down the path values and path co-factors and then the network determinant. Show that the triple-product terms in the network determinant each serve to identify the individual trees of the bridge network.

[*Ans.* see the Solution]

40. For the network shown draw the three unique trees. Write down the tree values and hence the network determinant.

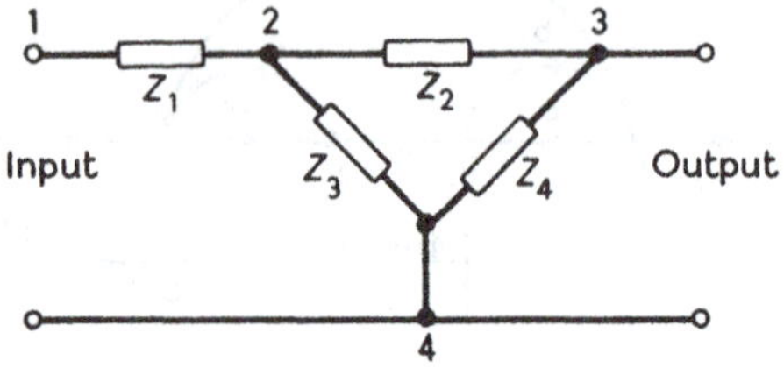

Compute the voltage attenuation between the input and output terminals for this network.

[*Ans.* $Y_1Y_2Y_3$; $Y_1Y_2Y_4$; $Y_1Y_3Y_4$; $Y_1(Y_2Y_3 + Y_2Y_4 + Y_3Y_4)$; $\dfrac{Y_1Y_2}{(Y_1 + Y_3)(Y_2 + Y_4) + Y_2Y_4}$]

41. For the circuit illustrated in Question 40 determine the network determinant by using the method of 'expansion in paths'. Calculate, also, using the topological approach, the input impedance of the network.

[*Ans.* $Y_1Y_3(Y_2 + Y_4) + Y_1Y_2Y_4$; $\dfrac{Y_1Y_2 + Y_1Y_4 + Y_3Y_2 + Y_3Y_4 + Y_2Y_4}{Y_1Y_2Y_3 + Y_1Y_3Y_4 + Y_1Y_2Y_4}$]

42. Find the ratio of polynomials for the driving-point impedance of the network shown.

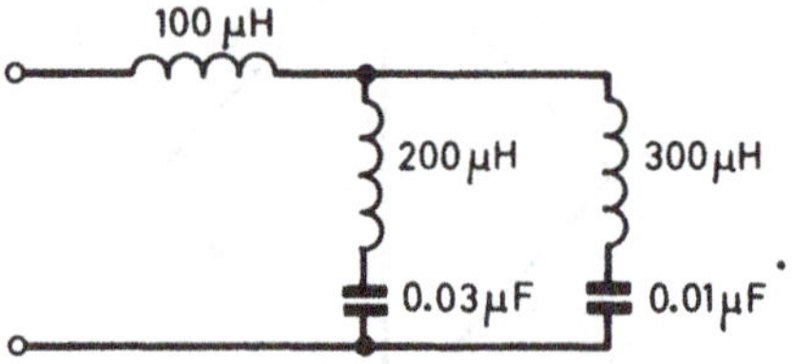

[*Ans.* $\dfrac{1}{j\omega}\left\{\dfrac{33\omega^4 - 13\omega^2 \times 10^{12} + 10^{24}}{-15\omega^2 \times 10^4 + 4 \times 10^{16}}\right\}$]

43. Determine the poles and zeros of the input impedance $Z(s)$ of the circuit illustrated and plot them on the complex frequency plane. Use the plot to evaluate the impedance at a value of frequency $s = j2$.

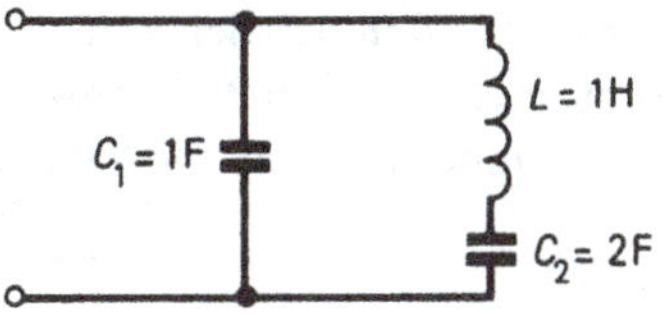

[*Ans.* 0; $\pm j\sqrt{(3/2)}$; $\pm j1/\sqrt{2}$;0.68]

44. Determine the poles and zeros for the input impedance of the circuit illustrated and plot them on the complex frequency plane.

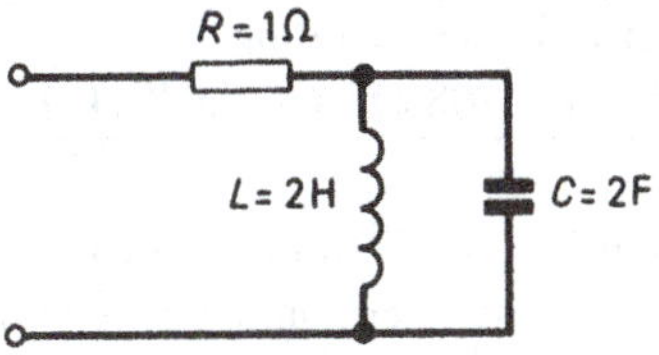

[*Ans.* $\pm j/2$; $-1/4 \pm j\sqrt{(3/4)}$]

ADDITIONAL PROBLEMS

45. An air-cored inductor takes 40 mA when a 10-V., 50-kHz supply is connected across it. A capacitor, *C* farads, is connected in series with the inductor and when the frequency of the supply is varied the current through the circuit rises to a maximum of 1 A. If the supply frequency is then 100 kHz calculate:

(*a*) the resistance of the inductor,
(*b*) the inductance,
(*c*) the capacitance,
(*d*) the '*Q*' factor at resonance.

Assume that the resistance of the coil is constant.

[*Ans.* (*a*) 10 Ω; (*b*) 796 μH; (*c*) 0.00318 μF; (*d*) 50]

46. A coil, a variable capacitor and a thermal milliammeter are connected in series with a constant-voltage supply of frequency 500 kHz. When the capacitor is set to 720 and 500 pF the current is 70.7 per cent of the value at resonance. Calculate the inductance and resistance of the coil. Assume the meter resistance is 20 Ω.

[*Ans.* 172 μH; 77 Ω]

47. A 40-μF capacitor is placed in parallel with a coil of inductance 0.2 H and effective resistance 10 Ω. Evaluate the resonant frequency of the parallel circuit, the dynamic impedance and the 'Q' factor.

[*Ans.* 55.7 Hz; 500 Ω; 7]

48. An intermediate-frequency transformer has identical primary and secondary circuits; each winding is tuned by a capacitor of 150 $\mu\mu$F. If the transformer has a bandwidth of 9 kHz centred on a frequency of 470 kHz and there is critical coupling, find (*a*) the inductance of each winding, (*b*) the coefficient of coupling, (*c*) the mutual inductance between the windings, (*d*) the 'Q' factor of each winding.

[*Ans.* (*a*) 768 μH, (*b*) 0.019, (*c*) 14.6 μH, (*d*) 52.2]

49. Two identical coils have each an inductance of 1000 μH and a 'Q' factor of 50. The coefficient of coupling between them is 0.01. Each coil is tuned by a 500-$\mu\mu$F capacitor. A source of 1 V at a variable frequency is placed in series with one circuit.

Determine the frequency at which the current in the second circuit is a maximum and this value of current.

[*Ans.* 225 kHz; 14.1 mA]

50. A 3-mH coil, supplied with current at 500 kHz, is brought near to a short-circuited coil of inductance 1 mH and a 'Q' factor of 30 at this frequency. Find the change in effective inductance of the 3-mH coil if the coefficient of coupling between the coils is 0.1.

[*Ans.* 0.03 mH]

51. Prove that if $R = \sqrt{(L/C)}$ the impedance of the circuit illustrated is independent of frequency and determine the value of this impedance.

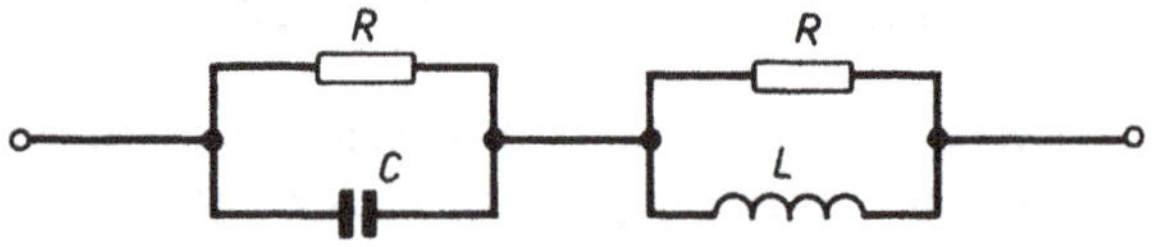

[*Ans.* R]

52. Determine the values of L_3, L_4 and C_2 in terms of L_1, L_2 and C_1 if the arrangements shown at (*a*) and (*b*) are equivalent.

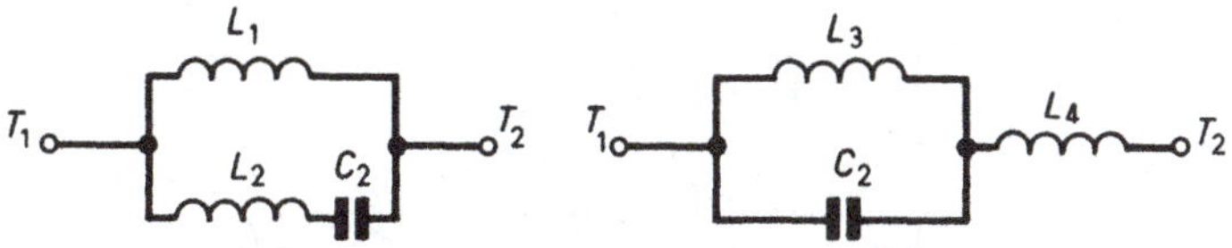

(a) (b)

[*Ans.* $L_3 = L_1^2/(L_1 + L_2)$, $L_4 = L_1L_2/(L_1 + L_2)$, $C_2 = C_1(L_1 + L_2)^2/L_2^2$]

53. Calculate the currents I_1, I_2 and I_3 in the network illustrated using the nodal method of analysis.

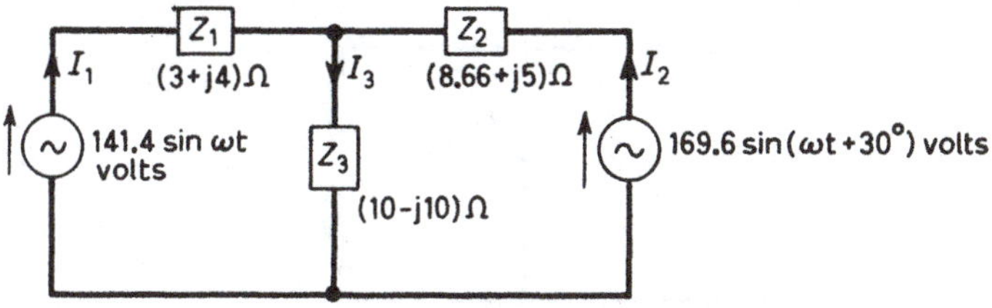

[*Ans.* $I_1 = (1.1\,\angle{-21^\circ})$ A; $I_2 = (6.4\,\angle 52^\circ)$ A; $I_3 = (6.8\,\angle 43^\circ)$ A]

54. Sketch two different networks of interconnected coils and capacitors each of which has a reactance-frequency graph of the form illustrated below.

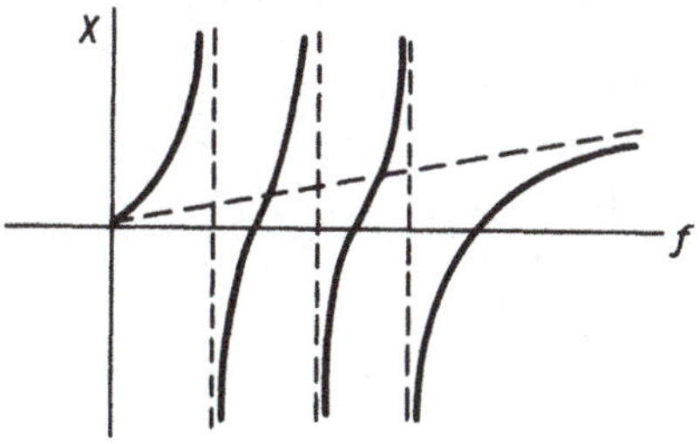

Draw the reactance-frequency graph of the inverse of the network whose reactance-frequency graph is shown above.

[*Ans.*

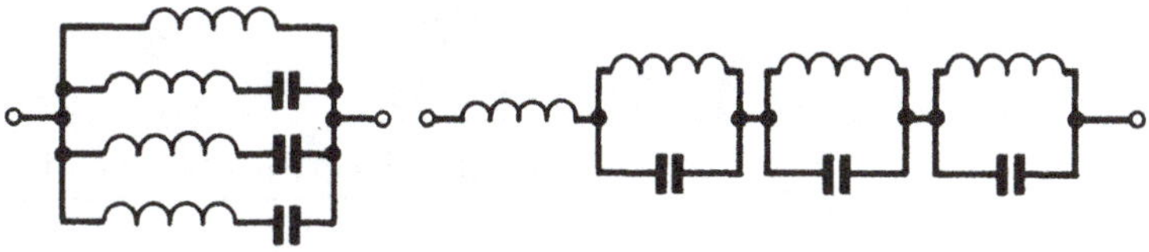

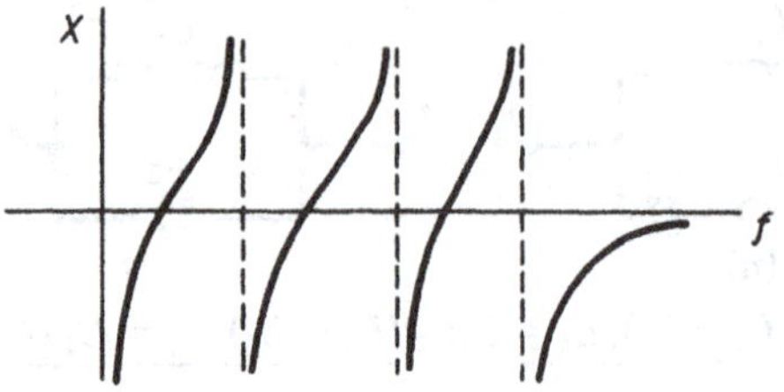

]

55. Sketch the variation of reactance with frequency for the loss-free two-terminal network illustrated.

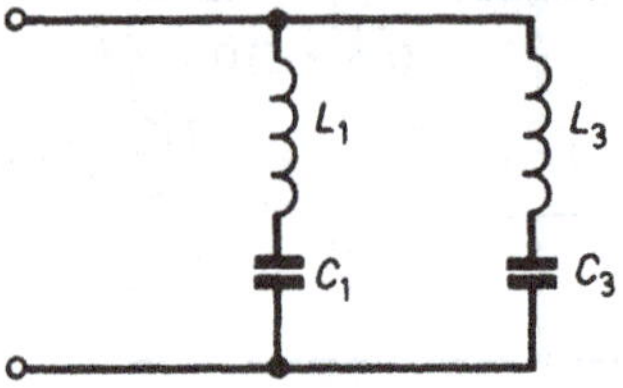

Express the reactance in the form

$$X = \frac{k}{\omega} \frac{(\omega^2 - \omega_1^{\,2})(\omega^2 - \omega_3^{\,2})}{(\omega^2 - \omega_2^{\,2})}$$

and derive expressions for k, ω_1, ω_2 and ω_3 in terms of L_1, C_1, L_3 and C_3.

[*Ans.*

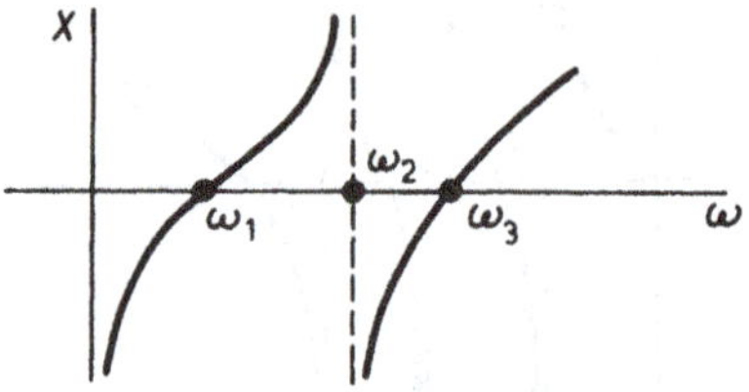

$$X = \frac{L_1 L_3}{\omega (L_1 + L_3)} \left[\frac{(\omega^2 - 1/L_1C_1)(\omega^2 - 1/L_3C_3)}{\omega^2 - (C_1 + C_3)/C_1C_3(L_1 + L_3)} \right]$$

Hence $k = L_1L_3/(L_1 + L_3)$

$\omega_1 = 1/\sqrt{(L_1C_1)}$

$\omega_3 = 1/\sqrt{(L_3C_3)}$

$\omega_2 = 1/\sqrt{\{(L_1 + L_3)\, C_1C_3/(C_1 + C_3)\}}$]

56. For the signal flow graph illustrated determine the overall gain V_4/V_1.

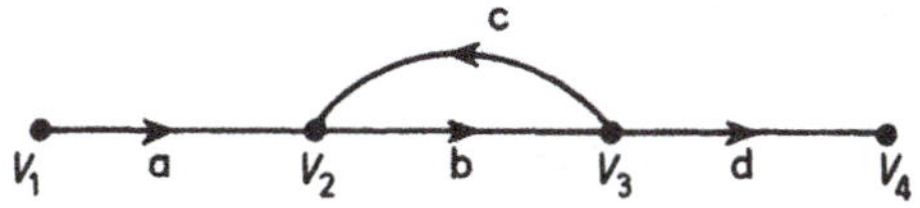

$$\left[Ans.\ \frac{abd}{1-bc}\right]$$

57. A general bridged-T network is illustrated. Use topological analysis to yield the voltage transmission ratio

$$T=\frac{Y_4(Y_1+Y_2+Y_3)+Y_1Y_2}{(Y_1+Y_3)(Y_2+Y_4)+Y_2Y_4}$$

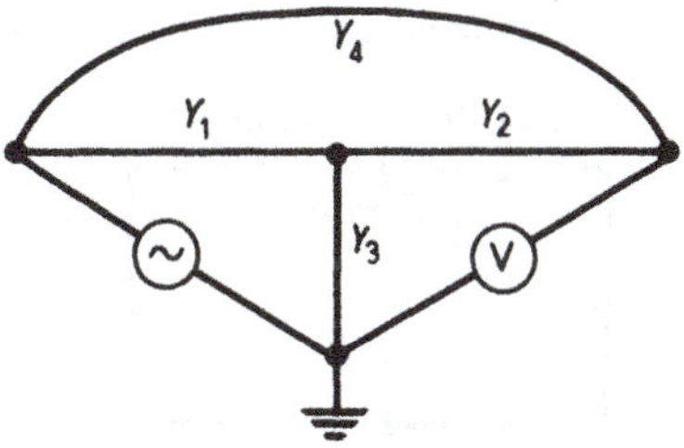

58. For the circuit illustrated show that the transfer function V/E is $8(s+1)/(s^3+3s^2+14s+16)$. Hence find the locations of the poles and zeros of the function.

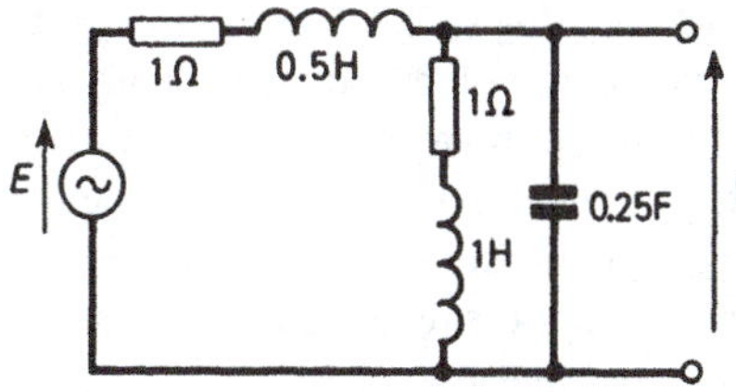

[*Ans.* Poles $s=-1.36$, $s=-0.82-j3.33$,

$s=-0.82+j3.33$, Zero at $s=-1$]

CHAPTER TWO

TRANSIENTS AND OSCILLATORY CIRCUITS

59. For the series circuit shown, prove that the current after closing the switch S is oscillatory, of gradually decreasing amplitude and of frequency 159 Hz. Plot the current-time wave from the instant the switch is closed.

The 0.5-Ω resistor is now replaced by a 10-Ω one. Obtain the new expression for the current which flows after closing the switch and plot the current-time wave.

Repeat the calculation for the case where the resistor has a value of 20 Ω.

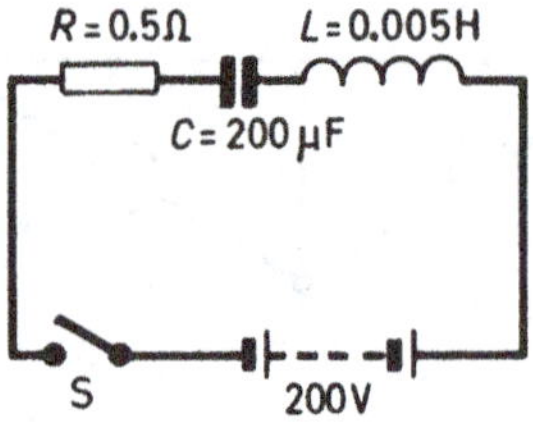

[*Ans.* $40\,000t\,e^{-1000t}$ amperes; $11.54\,(e^{-268t} - e^{-3732t})$ amperes]

60. Derive an expression for the current which flows in the circuit shown, immediately after closing switch S. At the instant at which S is closed the applied voltage is zero. Plot curves showing the variation of the two components of the current wave, and of the resultant current, with time. (Observe that after a time corresponding to about three complete cycles of the supply voltage the transient term has become relatively small.)

If the resistance in the circuit is reduced to zero show that the current never becomes negative, and that the voltage and current waves pass through zero values simultaneously.

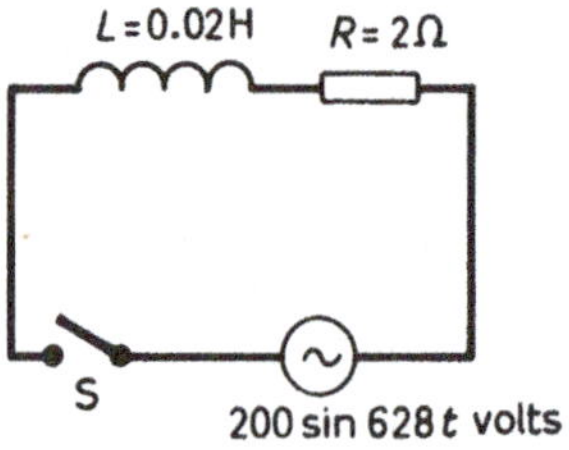

[*Ans.* $15.52\,e^{-100t} + 15.71\sin(628t - 81°)$ A]

61. Derive an expression for the current which flows in the circuit shown, immediately after closing the switch *S*. At the instant at which *S* is closed the applied voltage is zero. Plot graphs showing how the two components of the current wave, and the resultant current, vary with time. Observe that (*a*) about 0.05 s after closing *S* the amplitude of the transient wave is less than 10 per cent of its maximum amplitude of 41.3 A; (*b*) the frequency of the transient current is 159 Hz.

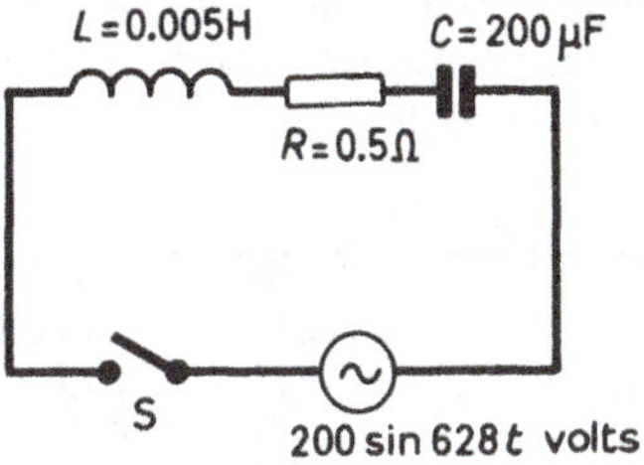

[*Ans.* $41.5\,e^{-50t}\cos(1000t + 173.5°) + 41.3\cos(628t - 6°)$ A]

62. Repeat Question 61 for the case where $R = 0.25\ \Omega$ and the supply frequency is 159 Hz, the other constants remaining the same.

[*Ans.* $-\,800\,e^{-25t}\sin 1000t + 800\sin 1000t$ A]

63. Repeat Question 61 for the case where $R = 10.1\ \Omega$ and the supply frequency is 50 Hz, the other constants remaining the same. Assume that when the switch is closed the applied voltage is at its maximum positive value.

[*Ans.* $-\,131.6\,e^{-1151t} + 125\,e^{-868t} + 11.4\cos(314t + 54.7°)$ A]

64. An inductor-capacitor-resistor series circuit has the following constants: $C = 2.5\ \mu$F, $L = 2$ mH, $R = 40\ \Omega$. The applied voltage, which is sinusoidal, has a peak value of 100 V and the frequency is 1000 Hz. The mains switch is closed when the voltage is at half its peak value and the capacitor is initially uncharged. Derive an expression for the current at a time *t* after closing the switch.

[*Ans.* $1.73\,e^{-10^4 t}\sin(10^4 t - 61°\,44') + 1.54\sin(6283t + 80°\,23')$]

65. A 2.5-μF capacitor, a 2-mH coil and an 80-Ω resistor are connected in series with a switch. The capacitor is initially charged to a voltage of 100 V. Derive expressions for the current, the capacitor voltage and the charge on the capacitor at a time *t* after closing the switch. Calculate, also, the maximum value of the current.

If the 80-Ω resistor is replaced by a 40-Ω one derive an expression for the current at a time t after closing the switch.

[*Ans.* $1.77\{e^{-5858t} - e^{-34\,142t}\}$A; $\{120.8\, e^{-5858t} - 20.8\, e^{-34\,142t}\}$V; $10^{-4}\{3.02\, e^{-5858t} - 0.52\, e^{-34\,142t}\}$C; 1.02 A; $5\, e^{-10^4 t} \sin(10^4 t)$ A]

66. A steady voltage of 100 V is applied to the circuit shown. The capacitor is initially uncharged. Derive expressions for the currents i_1 and i_2 at time t after closing the switch.

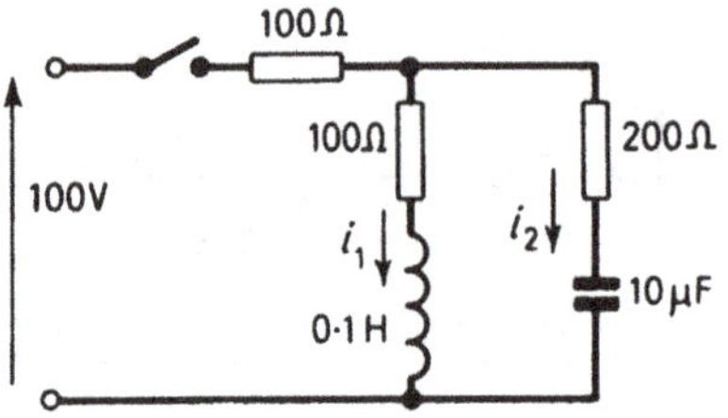

[*Ans.* $i_1 = \{-0.395\, e^{-1575t} - 0.105\, e^{-424t} + 0.5\}$A;
$i_2 = \{0.168\, e^{-1575t} + 0.1653\, e^{-424t}\}$A]

67. In the circuit illustrated, $R_1 = 20\ \Omega, R = R_2 + R_L = 100\ \Omega, L_1 = 2$ H, $L = L_2 + L_L = 4$ H and $M = 2$ H. A sinusoidal voltage of peak value 100 V and frequency 50 Hz is suddenly applied to the primary at the instant when it is a maximum. Derive expressions for the currents i_1 and i_2 at any time t after the voltage is applied.

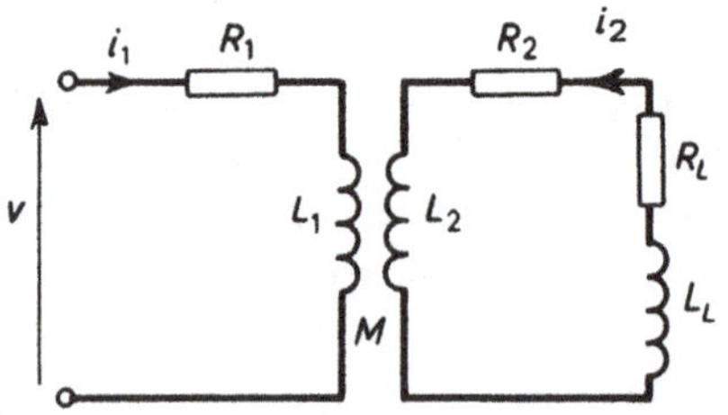

[*Ans.* $i_1 = \{-0.2176\, e^{-61{\cdot}9t} + 0.173\, e^{-8{\cdot}1t}$
$+ 0.287 \cos(314t - 81°\ 3')\}$A;
$i_2 = \{-2 \cos 314t + 0.182\, e^{-61{\cdot}9t} + 0.041\, e^{-8{\cdot}1t}$
$+ 0.1146 \cos(314t - 81°\ 3') - 1.81 \sin(314t - 81°\ 3')\}$A]

68. Find the Laplace transforms of:

(*a*) $y(t) = e^{-at}t^{n-1}/(n-1)!$ and

(*b*) $y(t) = e^{-bt}\sin at$.

Obtain the Laplacian subsidiary equation for a series circuit containing resistance (R), inductance (L) and capacitance (C) and show how the transient response of such a circuit may be investigated no matter what the form of the applied voltage.

Calculate the current in the series circuit, at time t, from the subsidiary equation if there is no initial current and no initial charge on the capacitor and the applied voltage E is constant. Assume that $R = 2\sqrt{(L/C)}$.

[*Ans.* $1/(s+a)^n$; $a/\{(s+b)^2+a^2\}$;
$(Ls + R + 1/Cs)\bar{I} = \bar{V} + LI_0 - Q_0/Cs$; $Et\,e^{-\alpha t}/L$ where $\alpha = R/2L$]

69. (*a*) Use the Laplace-transformation procedure to solve the following simultaneous differential equations:

$$\left.\begin{aligned}(D^2+2)x - Dy &= 1\\ Dx + (D^2+2)y &= 0\end{aligned}\right\}\; t>0$$

given that at $t=0$, $x = x_0$, $y = Dx = Dy = 0$.

(*b*) A voltage $v(t)$ is applied to the primary circuit of the figure illustrated at time $t=0$ with zero initial conditions. Show how the secondary current $i_2(t)$ can be found by the Laplace-transformation method. Neglect the primary resistance.

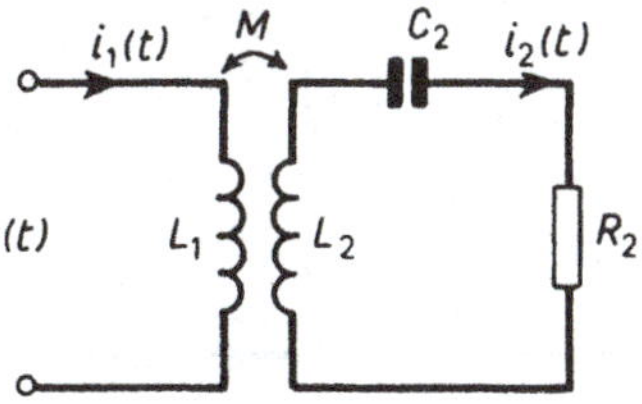

[*Ans.* (*a*) $x = \frac{1}{2} + \frac{1}{3}(2x_0-1)\cos t + \frac{1}{6}(2x_0-1)\cos 2t$;
$y = \frac{1}{3}(2x_0-1)\sin t - \frac{1}{6}(2x_0-1)\sin 2t$;

$$\bar{\imath}_2 = \frac{-Ms\bar{v}}{(L_1L_2-M^2)s^2 + R_2L_1s + L_1/C_2}\Bigg]$$

70. (*a*) An oscillatory circuit tuned for a wavelength of 300 m has a coil inductance 150 μH and an effective resistance of 10 Ω. Calculate the logarithmic decrement.

[*Ans.* 0.033]

(*b*) Prove that in an oscillatory circuit for which the logarithmic decrement is 0.1 there are 47 oscillations in a wave train before the amplitude of the current has fallen to 1 per cent of its initial value.

71. Find the exact natural frequency of free oscillations in an oscillatory circuit in which the capacitance is 0.055 μF, the inductance is 2 μH and the resistance is 1 Ω.

Determine also the minimum value of the circuit resistance which would make the discharge of the capacitor unidirectional.

[*Ans.* 478 kHz; 12.1 Ω]

ADDITIONAL PROBLEMS

72. A series RLC circuit with $R = 5\ \Omega, L = 0.1$ H and $C = 500\ \mu$F has a constant voltage of 10 V applied at time $t = 0$. Evaluate the resulting current transient.

[*Ans.* $0.72e^{-25t} \sin 139t$]

73. In the network illustrated the switch S is closed at time $t = 0$. Determine the resulting currents i_1 and i_2.

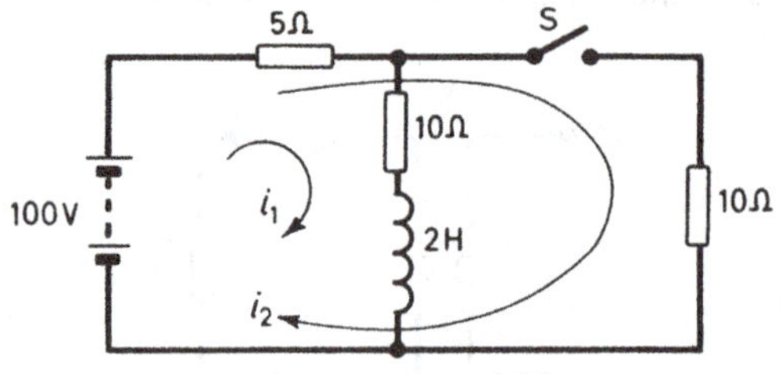

[*Ans.* $i_1 = 1.67e^{-6.67t} + 5; i_2 = -0.55e^{-6.67t} + 5$]

74. A series *RL* circuit with $R = 10\ \Omega$ and $L = 0.2$ H has a constant voltage of 50 V applied at time $t = 0$. Find the resulting current using the Laplace transform method.

[*Ans.* $5 - 5e^{-50t}$]

75. In a series *RC* circuit the capacitor has an initial charge of 25×10^{-4}C. At time $t = 0$ a constant voltage of 100 V is applied to the circuit.

Use the Laplace transform method to find the current.

[*Ans.* $5e^{-2\times10^3 t}$]

76. A series *RL* circuit has initial energy stored in the inductance. Show that the time constant is equal to twice the ratio of the energy stored at any instant of time to the rate at which energy is being dissipated at that instant.*

* Readers may wish to repeat this question for an *RC* circuit in which energy is stored in the capacitance.

CHAPTER THREE

WAVEFORM ANALYSIS

77. Find the Fourier-series representation of the output-voltage wave of a single-phase half-wave rectifier.

Hence, deduce the corresponding expression for a full-wave rectifier.

Determine the r.m.s. value of the full-wave rectifier waveform from the Fourier-series formula.

$$\left[Ans.\ E\left\{\frac{1}{\pi}+\frac{1}{2}\sin\theta-\frac{2}{\pi}\sum_{n=2,4,6\ldots}\frac{\cos n\theta}{(n^2-1)}\right\};\right.$$
$$\left. E\left\{\frac{2}{\pi}-\frac{4}{\pi}\sum_{n=2,4,6\ldots}\frac{\cos n\theta}{(n^2-1)}\right\}; E/\sqrt{(2)} \right]$$

78. Show that the Fourier series for the square waveform illustrated is

$$y=\frac{4E}{\pi}\left(\cos x-\frac{\cos 3x}{3}+\frac{\cos 5x}{5}-\frac{\cos 7x}{7}+\ldots\right)$$

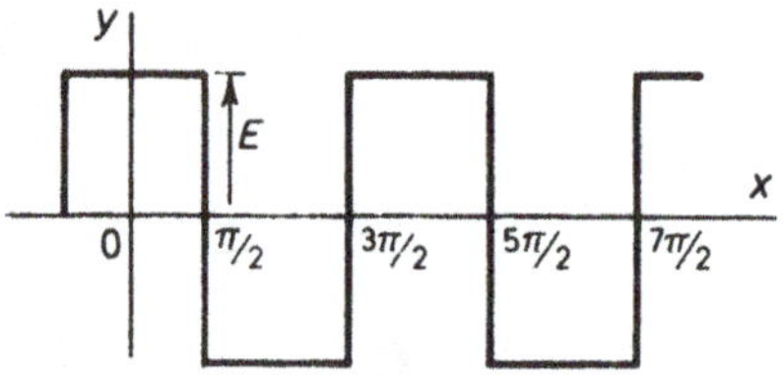

79. Show that the Fourier series for the sawtooth waveform illustrated is

$$y=\frac{2E}{\pi}\left(\sin x-\frac{\sin 2x}{2}+\frac{\sin 3x}{3}-\frac{\sin 4x}{4}\ldots\right)$$

Find, graphically, the result of adding the first four terms and determine, graphically, some of the coefficients of the Fourier series.

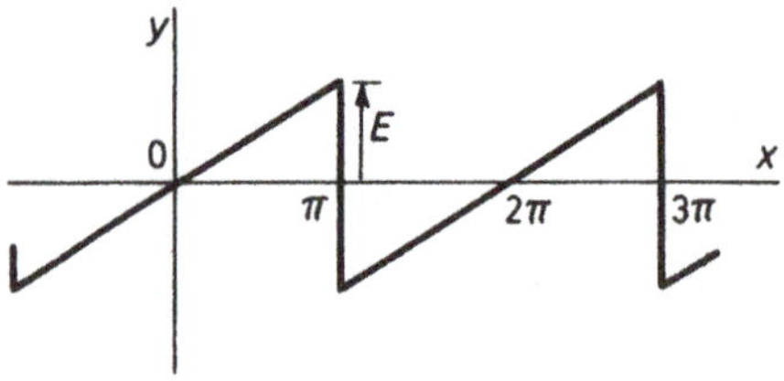

80. Show that the Fourier series for the short square pulse illustrated is

$$y = E\left\{n + \frac{2}{\pi}\left(\sin n\pi \cos x + \frac{\sin 2n\pi \cos 2x}{2} + \frac{\sin 3n\pi \cos 3x}{3} + \ldots\right)\right\}$$

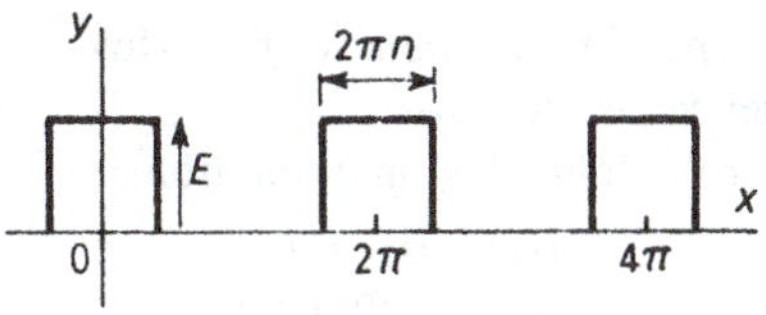

81. Show that the Fourier series for the short triangular pulse illustrated is

$$y = E\left[\frac{n}{2} + \sum_{N=1}\left\{\frac{2}{N\pi}\sin N\pi n - \frac{2}{N^2\pi^2 n}\left(N\pi n \sin N\pi n - 2\sin^2\frac{N\pi n}{2}\right)\right\}\cos Nx\right]$$

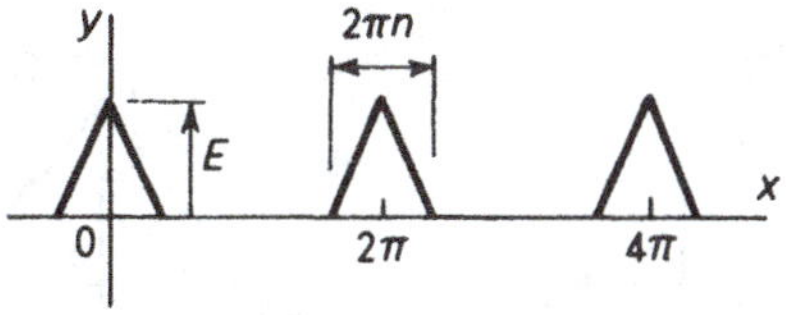

82. Find the Fourier series for the waveform illustrated which is produced by an m-phase rectifier.

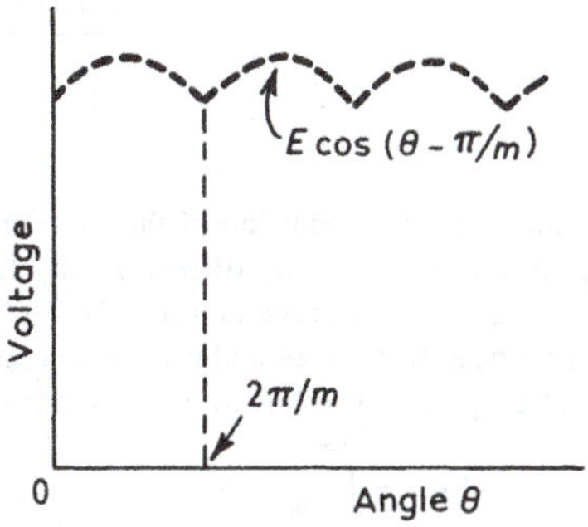

Hence, show that the percentage of sixth harmonic in a six-phase rectifier waveform is 5.71 per cent.

$$\left[Ans.\ (mE/\pi)\sin(\pi/m)\left\{1 - \sum_{n=1}^{n=\infty}\frac{2}{(m^2n^2-1)}\right\}\cos mn\theta\right]$$

83. One of the Fourier transform pair‡ can be written

$$g(\omega) = \frac{1}{2\pi} \int_{-\infty}^{+\infty} f(t)\, e^{-j\omega t} dt$$

Write down the corresponding formula for $f(t)$. How are these formulae related to the Fourier series formulae?

Calculate $g(\omega)$ for the following time function:

$$f(t) = 0, t < 0$$
$$f(t) = e^{-\alpha t}, t \geqslant 0$$

Show how this spectrum can be used to calculate the response of an amplifier of complex gain $G(\omega)$ to a step voltage input.

[*Ans.* $f(t) = \int_{-\infty}^{\infty} g(\omega) e^{j\omega t}\, d\omega$; $1/2\pi(\alpha + j\omega)$]

84. Evaluate the Fourier transforms of the two time waveforms shown at (*a*) and (*b*).

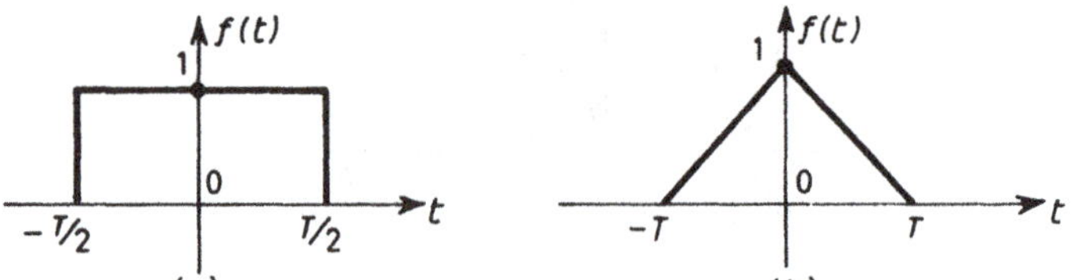

(a) (b)

$$\left[Ans.\ T\left\{\frac{\sin\omega T/2}{\omega T/2}\right\},\ T\left\{\frac{\sin\omega T/2}{\omega T/2}\right\}^2\right]$$

‡ As pointed out by Goodyear* the definition of the Fourier transform most commonly adopted in communication theory differs slightly from that given here by the omission of the factor $1/2\pi$. In this case a factor $1/2\pi$ has to be included in the expression for the time function. In the remainder of this chapter, therefore, the Fourier transform $g(\omega)$ of a signal $f(t)$ will be defined as $2\pi g'(\omega)$, thus:

$$g(\omega) = \int_{-\infty}^{\infty} f(t) e^{-j\omega t}\, dt$$

and

$$f(t) = \frac{1}{2\pi} \int_{-\infty}^{\infty} g(\omega) e^{j\omega t}\, d\omega$$

Scott† has also mentioned that the factor 2π is treated differently by authors.

* C. C. Goodyear, *Signals and Information*, Butterworths, 1971, p.33.

† R. E. Scott, *Linear Circuits* (complete), Addison Wesley, 1960, p.706.

ADDITIONAL PROBLEMS

85. Show that the Fourier series for the waveform illustrated is:

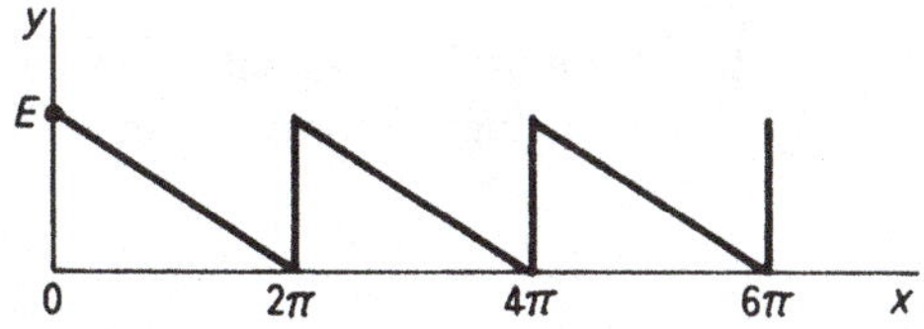

$$y = \frac{E}{2} + \frac{E}{\pi}\left(\sin x + \frac{1}{2}\sin 2x + \frac{1}{3}\sin 3x + \ldots\ldots\right)$$

86. Show that the Fourier series for the waveform illustrated is:

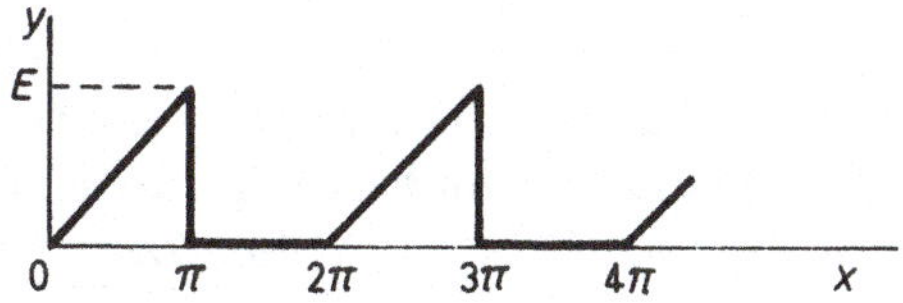

$$y = \frac{E}{4} - \frac{2E}{\pi^2}\cos x - \frac{2E}{(3\pi)^2}\cos 3x \ldots\ldots$$

87. Show that the Fourier transform of the function

$$f(t) = \begin{Bmatrix} 1 + \cos(\pi t/T) & \text{for } -T \leqslant t \leqslant +T \\ 0 & \text{for } |t| > T \end{Bmatrix}$$

is given by
$$-\frac{2(\pi/T)^2 \sin(\omega T)}{\omega(\omega^2 - (\pi/T)^2}$$

88. Evaluate the Fourier transforms of the waveforms illustrated. Sketch for each case the spectrum obtained.

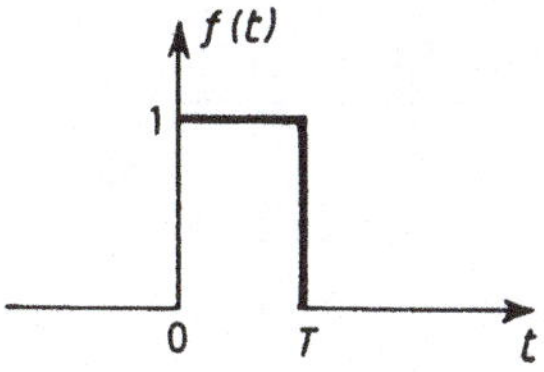

(a)

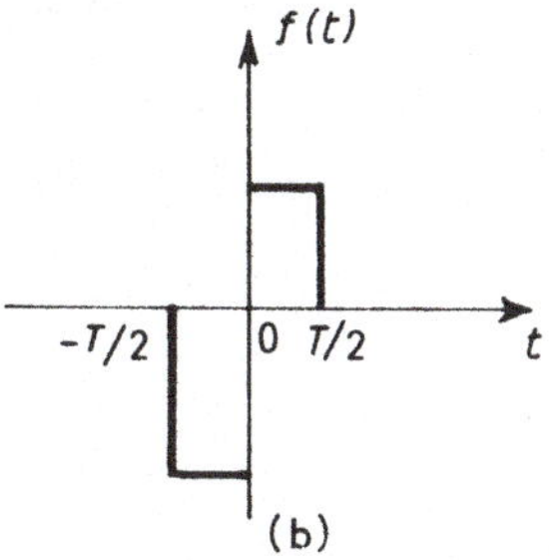

(b)

[*Ans.* (*a*) $\dfrac{T \sin\omega T/2}{\omega T/2} e^{-j\omega T/2}$; (*b*) $\dfrac{-jT \sin^2 \omega T/4}{\omega T/4}$]

89. Find the Fourier transform of the function shown by: (*a*) straightforward integration, (*b*) differentiating the waveform to produce three impulse functions.

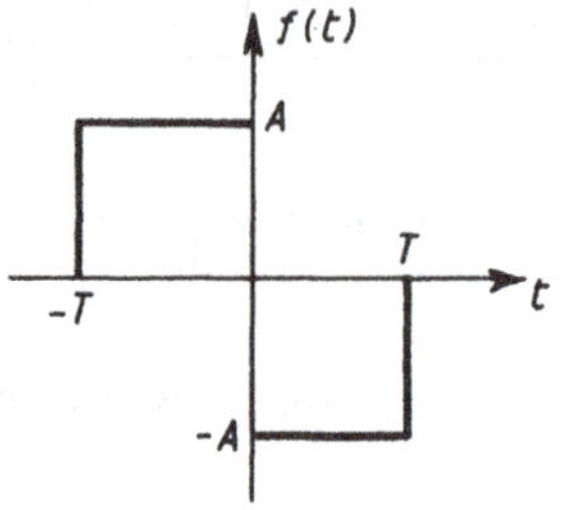

Plot graphs showing: (1) the amplitude spectrum, (2) the phase spectrum, and (3) the energy density spectrum for the above waveform.

[*Ans.* j2*A* (1 − cosωT)/ω]

90. Use the Fourier integral $g(\omega) = \int_{-\infty}^{\infty} f(t)e^{-j\omega t}\,dt$ to derive an expression for the spectral amplitude $g(\omega)$ corresponding to the pulse waveform defined by

$$f(t) = 0 \quad \text{for} -\infty < t < 0$$
$$f(t) \quad Ve^{-\alpha t} \text{ for } 0 < t < \infty$$

Draw a graph showing the variation of the amplitude with frequency and find

(*a*) the value of $g(0)$

(*b*) the frequency at which the amplitude is 3 dB below the value of $g(0)$

If the pulse is developed as a voltage across a resistor *R* show that the energy dissipated is $V^2/2\alpha R$ joules.

[*Ans.* (*a*) V/α; (*b*) $\alpha/2\pi$]

CHAPTER FOUR

SOLID STATE ELECTRONICS AND SEMICONDUCTOR DEVICES

91. The allowed orbit radii and energy levels of the Bohr atom are given by:

$$r_n = \frac{\epsilon_0 h^2 n^2}{\pi m Z e^2}$$

and

$$W_n = \frac{-me^4 Z^2}{8\epsilon_0{}^2 h^2 n^2}$$

where Z is the atomic number, e and m are the electron charge and mass respectively, h is Planck's constant, n is the principal quantum number for the orbit and ϵ_0 is the permittivity of free space.

Show that these equations may be written as $r_n = 0.529n^2/Z$ angstrom units and $W_n = -(13.6Z^2/n^2)$ eV.

92. (*a*) What are the first four permissible energy levels for a hydrogen atom?

(*b*) An electron in a hydrogen atom makes a transition from energy level 2 to the ground state. Determine the energy released by the electron. What is the frequency of the resulting radiation from the atom?

[*Ans.* (*a*) −13.6 eV; −3.4 eV; −1.51 eV; −0.85 eV,
(*b*) 10.2 eV; 2.465×10^{15} Hz]

93. The motion of the fifth electron in the outer shell of a group V impurity atom in a semiconductor may be considered to be a circular orbit around a single positive nuclear charge of $+e$ and through a material with a dielectric constant of the bulk material.

Show that the electron only requires about 0.1 eV of energy to be freed for conduction in the crystal if the dielectric constant is 11.7. Estimate also the radius of the ground-state orbit and thereby justify the assumption that the electron moves in a medium with the bulk dielectric constant. The lattice constant of the material is 5.42 Å.

[*Ans.* 6.16 Å]

94. Calculate the velocity of an electron in the ground state of hydrogen. At what fraction of the velocity of light is the electron travelling? Take the velocity of light as $3 \times 10^8\ \text{ms}^{-1}$.

[*Ans.* $2.19 \times 10^6\ \text{ms}^{-1}$, 7.3×10^{-3}]

95. The resistivity of intrinsic germanium at 300 K is $0.47\Omega\text{m}$. The electron and hole mobilities in germanium are $0.36\ \text{m}^2\text{V}^{-1}\text{s}^{-1}$ and $0.17\ \text{m}^2\text{V}^{-1}\text{s}^{-1}$ respectively. Calculate from this information the intrinsic density of electrons and holes.

[*Ans.* $2.5 \times 10^{19}\text{m}^{-3}$]

96. The material used in Question 95 is doped with antimony impurity atoms so that there is one impurity atom per 10^6 germanium atoms. Calculate the electron and hole densities at 300 K. It may be assumed that all antimony atoms are ionized at this temperature. The density of germanium atoms is $4.4 \times 10^{28}\text{m}^{-3}$. What is the resistivity of this doped material?

[*Ans.* $4.4 \times 10^{22}\text{m}^{-3}$, $1.42 \times 10^{16}\text{m}^{-3}$, $4 \times 10^{-4}\Omega\text{m}$]

97. From the information given in Question 95 determine the diffusion coefficients both for holes and electrons in germanium at 300 K.

[*Ans.* $4.4 \times 10^{-3}\text{m}^2\text{s}^{-1}$, $9.3 \times 10^{-3}\text{m}^2\text{s}^{-1}$]

98. Show that a semiconductor has a minimum conductivity at a given temperature when the electron density n is $n_i\sqrt{(\mu_h/\mu_e)}$ where n_i is the intrinsic density and μ_h and μ_e are the mobilities of holes and electrons respectively. What is the hole density p in this condition?

Find the intrinsic and minimum conductivities for germanium when $n_i = 2.5 \times 10^{19}\text{m}^{-3}$, $\mu_h = 0.19\ \text{m}^2\ \text{V}^{-1}\text{s}^{-1}$ and $\mu_e = 0.38\ \text{m}^2\text{V}^{-1}\text{s}^{-1}$.

For what values of n and p (other than $n = p = n_i$) does this crystal have a conductivity equal to the intrnsinc conductivity?

[*Ans.* $n_i\sqrt{(\mu_e/\mu_h)}$, $2.28\ \text{Sm}^{-1}$, $2.12\ \text{Sm}^{-1}$, $1.25 \times 10^{19}\text{m}^{-3}$, $5 \times 10^{19}\text{m}^{-3}$]

99. A *p-n* junction consists of a region of *p*-type germanium with a conductivity of 10^4S and a region of *n*-type germanium with a conductivity of 10^2 S. The mobilities of electrons and holes in germanium are $0.36\ \text{m}^2\text{V}^{-1}\text{s}^{-1}$ and $0.17\ \text{m}^2\text{V}^{-1}\text{s}^{-1}$ respectively. The intrinsic density of holes and electrons in germanium at 300 K is $2.5 \times 10^{19}\ \text{m}^{-3}$. Calculate the contact potential that would appear across the juntion at 300 K.

[*Ans.* 0.35 V]

100. The diffusion length for both electrons and holes in germanium is 1×10^{-3} m. Use this information and that given in the previous question to find the saturation current density at 300 K. Evaluate also the ratio of the saturation hole current to electron current.

[*Ans.* 0.25 $\mathrm{Am^{-2}}$; 100]

101. Obtain an expression for the contact potential developed across a p–n junction. The hole and electron densities in the p-type material are p_p and n_p respectively and in the n-type material are p_n and n_n.

[*Ans.* $kT \log_e (p_p/p_n)/e = kT \log_e (n_n/n_p)/e$]

102. Calculate the voltage that would have to be applied across the p–n junction described in the last two questions to cause a forward current density of 10 $\mathrm{Am^{-2}}$ to flow.

[*Ans.* 0.33 V]

103. A sample of germanium has a donor density of $10^{20}\ \mathrm{m^{-3}}$. The electron effective mass ratio is 1.57 and a donor may be regarded as a scattering centre whose radius is 500 Å. What is the mean free path and mean time between collisions at 300 K? Calculate also the electron mobility.

[*Ans.* 1.27×10^{-6} m; 1.36×10^{-11} s; 1.52 $\mathrm{m^2\,V^{-1}\,s^{-1}}$]

104. Intrinsic germanium has a conductivity of 3.56 $\Omega^{-1}\,\mathrm{m^{-1}}$ at 310 K and 0.42 $\Omega^{-1}\,\mathrm{m^{-1}}$ at 273 K. A sample of n-type germanium has 10^{21} ionized donor atoms per cubic metre at these two temperatures. Calculate the conductivity of the doped sample. The electron mobility is 0.36 $\mathrm{m^2\,V^{-1}\,s^{-1}}$ and the hole mobility is 0.17 $\mathrm{m^2\,V^{-1}\,s^{-1}}$ in germanium.

[*Ans.* 57.6 $\Omega^{-1}\,\mathrm{m^{-1}}$]

105. A thermistor which is made of intrinsic silicon has a resistance of 500 Ω at 290 K. Estimate its approximate resistance at 325 K, assuming a gap energy for silicon of 1.08 eV and that the carrier mobilities do not vary appreciably over this range of temperatures.

[*Ans.* 50 Ω]

106. Derive a formula for the Hall coefficient of a semiconductor specimen possessing n electrons and p holes per unit volume. The electron and hole densities are n and p respectively and the corresponding mobilities are μ_n and μ_p.

Hence, find the values of the coefficient for (*a*) an intrinsic semiconductor with carrier density n_i; (*b*) a highly-doped *n*-type material.

[*Ans.* $(p\mu_p^2 - n\mu_n^2)/e(p\mu_p + n\mu_n)^2$; (*a*) $(\mu_p - \mu_n)/n_i e(\mu_p + \mu_n)$; (*b*) $-1/ne$]

107. A sample of semiconductor 30 mm long, 6 mm wide and 1 mm thick, has a resistance of 500 Ω. Placed in a magnetic field of 0.5 T normal to the plane of the slab, it develops a Hall voltage of 5 mV when the current through the sample is 10 mA. Determine the Hall mobility and the density of carriers on the semiconductor assuming it to be extrinsic.

To what value would the Hall voltage be changed if a specimen of copper, of similar dimensions and carrying the same current, were placed in the same field, assuming that the concentration of conduction electrons in copper is about $8.5 \times 10^{28}\,m^{-3}$?

[*Ans.* $10^{-2}\,m^2\,V^{-1}\,s^{-1}$; 6.25×10^{21}; 0.37 nV]

108. A certain semiconductor has, under equilibrium conditions, a hole concentration *p* of $10^{20}\,m^{-3}$ and an electron concentration *n* of $2 \times 10^{19}\,m^{-3}$. Determine (*a*) the net impurity concentration (*b*) the type of impurity which dominates and (*c*) the intrinsic carrier density.

[*Ans.* (*a*) $8 \times 10^{19}\,m^{-3}$; (*b*) acceptors in majority; (*c*) $4.5 \times 10^{19}\,m^{-3}$]

109. The variation of the resistivity, ρ, of intrinsic germanium with temperature, *T*, is found to be as follows:

T(K)	385	458	556	714
ρ (Ωm)	0.028	0.0061	0.0013	0.00027

Determine the value of the gap energy, E_g, in germanium assuming it not to be a function of temperature. As an approximation, assume that hole and electron mobilities, μ_n and μ_e, vary as $T^{-3/2}$.

[*Ans.* 0.8 eV]

110. A *p-n* junction diode is to be used as a voltage controlled capacitor. Its incremental capacitance is found to be 200 pF at a reverse bias voltage of 2 V. What reverse bias voltage is required to reduce its capacitance to 100 pF? Assume a contact potential of 0.85 V.

[*Ans.* 10.6 V]

111. The channel of an *n*-channel silicon junction field-effect transistor has a conductivity of 20.9 Sm^{-1} and is 5μm thick when the gate voltage is zero. Find the pinch-off voltage for the device assuming an electron mobility of 0.13 $m^2 V^{-1} s^{-1}$ and a relative permittivity of 12.

When the gate voltage is zero, the drain-source resistance is 50 Ω. What voltage is required on the gate to increase this to 250 Ω?

[*Ans.* 4.71 V; 3.01 V]

112. In a certain *n-p-n* bipolar transistor, the emitter has a donor concentration of 10^{24} m^{-3} and the base has an acceptor concentration of 10^{22} m^{-3}. Assuming electron and hole mobilities of 0.4 $m^2 V^{-1} s^{-1}$ and 0.2 $m^2 V^{-1} s^{-1}$, estimate the ratio of electron to hole currents at the emitter base junction.

[*Ans.* 200 : 1]

113. A germanium junction diode has a saturation current of 1 μA compared to 10^{-8} A for a similar sized rectifier made of silicon. Compare the forward voltages dropped across the diodes at room temperature when each carries a current of 100 mA.

[*Ans.* 288 mV; 407 mV]

114. The saturation current of a particular Schottky barrier diode is 3 μA. The diode is connected in series with a resistor across a d.c. source of 0.2 V, in such a way that the diode is forward biased. Find the value of the resistor such that 0.1 V is dropped across it at room temperature.

[*Ans.* 650 Ω]

115. A particular *n*-channel MOST has the following properties

width of gate	= 0.84 mm
channel length	= 5 μm
oxide thickness	= 150 nm
electron mobility	= 0.02 $m^2 V^{-1} s^{-1}$
relative permittivity of oxide	= 3.7
drain-source voltage at saturation	= 10 V

Estimate the transconductance of the device at saturation.

[*Ans.* 7.34×10^{-3} S]

116. A boron drive-in diffusion into silicon lasts for 1 hour at a temperature of 1150° C, at which temperature the diffusion coefficient of boron impurities in silicon, D_B, is 10^{-16} $m^2 S^{-1}$. The background concentration of donor impurities in the silicon before drive-in is 10^{22} m^{-3} and the junction depth afterwards is 1 μm. What concentration of boron atoms were pre-deposited on the surface of the silicon slice before drive-in?

[*Ans.* $2.1 \times 10^{16} m^{-2}$]

ADDITIONAL PROBLEMS*

117. A shell of prinicipal quantum number n can contain n sub-shells. A sub-shell can contain $2(2\ell + 1)$ electrons where ℓ is a positive integer or zero but must never be greater than $(n - 1)$. Show that a shell cannot contain more than $2n^2$ electrons.

118. Show that when holes are injected as minority carriers into a region of n-type material the injected hole concentration decays with distance as e^{-x/L_p} where L_p is the diffusion length for holes.

Prove that the relationship between L_p and the minority carrier recombination time τ_p is:

$$L_p = \sqrt{(D_p \tau_p)}$$

where D_p is the hole diffusion constant.

119. A rod of p-type germanium 6 mm long, 1 mm wide and 0.5 mm thick has an electrical resistance of 120 Ω. What is the impurity concentration? What proportion of the conductivity is due to electrons in the conduction band? The mobilities of holes and electrons μ_h and μ_e may be taken as $0.19\ m^2 V^{-1} s^{-1}$ and $0.39\ m^2 V^{-1} s^{-1}$ respectively and the intrinsic density n_i as $2.5 \times 10^{19} m^{-3}$.

[*Ans.* $3.29 \times 10^{21} m^{-3}$; 1 in 8.4×10^3]

120. The resistivities of the p- and n-sides of a particular silicon junction diode are 0.0001 Ωm and 0.01 Ωm respectively. Calculate the magnitude of the contact potential at 300 K assuming hole and electron mobilities of $0.05\ m^2 V^{-1} s^{-1}$ and $0.13\ m^2 V^{-1} s^{-1}$ and an intrinsic density in silicon of $1.38 \times 10^{16} m^{-3}$.

[*Ans.* 0.8 V]

121. Pure silicon has a resistivity of 2000 Ωm at 300 K and a density of conduction electrons of $1.4 \times 10^{16} m^{-3}$. Calculate the resistivities of samples

* Some interesting problems on solid state devices and their solutions are given by P. N. Robson in Chapter 8 of the following book: R. L. Ferrari and A. K. Jonscher (Eds.), *Problems in Physical Electronics*, Pion, 1973.

containing acceptor concentrations of 10^{21} and $10^{23}\,m^{-3}$. Assume that the hole mobility remains the same as in pure silicon and that it equals 0.26 of the electron mobility.

[*Ans.* 0.135 and 0.00135 Ωm]

122. Compare the drift velocity of an electron moving in a field of 10 000 Vm^{-1} in pure germanium with that of one that has moved through a distance 10 m in this field in a vacuum. The free electron mass is 9.1×10^{-31} kg and $\mu_e = 0.39\ m^2 V^{-1} s^{-1}$ in germanium.

[*Ans.* $3.9 \times 10^3\ ms^{-1}$ in germanium; $5.93 \times 10^6\ ms^{-1}$ in vacuum]

123. The resistivity of intrinsic germanium at 300 K is 0.47 Ωm. Assuming μ_e and μ_h are 0.30 and 0.18 $m^2 V^{-1} s^{-1}$, calculate the intrinsic carrier density n_i at 300 K.

[*Ans.* $2.38 \times 10^{19}\ m^{-3}$]

124. Germanium is doped with 1×10^{-2} atomic per cent of antimony. Assuming that at 300 K all antimony atoms are ionized, compare the electron and hole densities. Assume that the electron density is determined only by the donors. From this information calculate the resistivity of the material at 300 K if the electron and hole mobilities are 0.38 and 0.18 $m^2 V^{-1} s^{-1}$. Assume that the density of germanium atoms is $4.2 \times 10^{28}\ m^{-3}$.

[*Ans.* $4.52 \times 10^{24}\ m^{-3}$; $1.25 \times 10^{14}\ m^{-3}$; 0.36×10^{-5} Ωm]

125. The Hall coefficient of a specimen of doped silicon is found to be $3.66 \times 10^{-4}\ m^3 C^{-1}$; the resistivity of the specimen is 9.93×10^{-3} Ωm. Find the mobility and density of charge carriers, assuming single carrier conduction.

[*Ans.* $2 \times 10^{22}\ m^{-3}$; $0.035\ m^2 V^{-1} s^{-1}$]

126. A specimen of semiconductor is 1 mm thick and 10 mm wide. A magnetic flux density of 0.5 T is applied parallel to the 1 mm edge and Hall voltage contacts are attached to measure the voltage across the width of the sample. The current flowing lengthwise through the sample is 10 mA. If the Hall coefficient of the material is $3.66 \times 10^{-4}\ m^3 C^{-1}$, compute the voltage measured between the Hall contacts.

[*Ans.* 1.83 mV]

127. A specimen of a semiconductor has a Hall coefficient of $3.66 \times 10^{-4}\,m^3C^{-1}$ and a resistivity of $8.93 \times 10^{-3}\,\Omega m$. In a Hall effect experiment a magnetic flux density of 0.5 T is used. Find the Hall angle.

[*Ans.* 1.1°]

128. A bar of intrinsic germanium at 3000 K has 2.5×10^{19} electrons m^{-3} in the conduction band. Find the net current density when an electric field of 500 Vm^{-1} is applied to the bar.

[*Ans.* 1.06 kAm^{-2}]

129. A current density of $10^3\,Am^{-2}$ flows through a 0.05-Ωm, *n*-type germanium crystal. Calculate the time taken for electrons to travel 5×10^{-5} m.

[*Ans.* 2.5 μs]

130. A germanium *p-n* junction has a bulk resistivity of 4.2×10^{-4} and $2.08 \times 10^{-2}\,\Omega m$ for the *p*- and *n*-type material respectively. If $\mu_e = 0.3$ and $\mu_h = 0.15\,m^2V^{-1}s^{-1}$ for this material, and $n_i = 2.5 \times 10^{19}\,m^{-3}$ at 300 K, calculate the height of the potential barrier at the junction.

[*Ans.* 0.3 eV]

131. The lifetimes of the *p*- and *n*-type material of the junction of problem 130 are 75 and 150 μs respectively, and the sample has a cross-sectional area of $10^{-6}\,m^2$. Assuming that there is a large thickness of semiconductor on each side of the junction, calculate the saturation current. What proportion of the saturation current is carried by holes?

[*Ans.* 0.51 μA; 98 per cent]

132. A sample of germanium is doped to the extent of 10^{20} donor atoms m^{-3} and 7×10^{19} acceptor atoms m^{-3}. At the temperature of the sample, the resistivity of intrinsic germanium is 0.6 Ωm. If the applied electric field is 200 Vm^{-1} find the total conduction current density. The electron and hole mobilities in germanium may be assumed to be 0.38 and 0.18 $m^2V^{-1}s^{-1}$ respectively.

[*Ans.* 524 Am^{-2}]

133. The resistivity of a doped silicon crystal is $9.27 \times 10^{-3}\,\Omega m$ and the Hall coefficient is $3.84 \times 10^{-4}\,m^3C^{-1}$. Assuming that conduction is by a single type of charge carrier, calculate the density and mobility of the carrier.

[*Ans.* $1.6 \times 10^{22} m^{-3}$; $0.041\ m^2V^{-1}s^{-1}$]

134. A silicon junction goes into avalanche breakdown when the electric field reaches $6 \times 10^7 Vm^{-1}$. If the doping concentrations on the *n* and *p* sides of the junction are $10^{20} m^{-3}$ and $10^{22} m^{-3}$ respectively, calculate the approximate width of the depletion layer and the applied voltage at the onset of avalanche breakdown. Assume a relative permittivity of 12.

[*Ans.* 0.4 mm; 12 kV]

135. A thin *p*-type germanium specimen of dimensions 20 × 10 mm is located in a plane normal to the earth's magnetic field. Calculate the potential difference which must be applied between the faces 20 mm apart if a Hall voltage of 10 mV is to arise. The earth's magnetic field strength may be taken as 44 μT and the mobility of holes in germanium as 0.18 $m^2V^{-1}s^{-1}$.

[*Ans.* 2.52 kV]

136. In a particular *p*-channel silicon JFET, the width of the channel with no gate voltage applied, is 2 μm. If the resistivity of the channel is 0.1 Ωm, find the pinch-off voltage of the device, V_p. It may be assumed that the hole mobility for silicon is 0.05 $m^2V^{-1}s^{-1}$ and its bulk relative permittivity is 12.

Also find the channel half-width when the gate voltage equals $V_p/2$ and the drain current is zero.

[*Ans.* 3.8 V; 0.59 μm]

137. A particular linearly graded *p-n* junction in silicon has a cross-sectional area of 1 mm^2 and a capacitance of 300 pF when the applied reverse bias voltage is 10 V. Calculate (*a*) the change in capacitance for a 50 per cent reduction in bias voltage (*b*) the maximum field in the depletion layer with the 10-V reverse bias applied. Assume a relative permittivity for silicon of 12.

[*Ans.* (*a*) 78 pF, (*b*) $4.2 \times 10^7 Vm^{-1}$]

138. A *p-n* junction diode has a forward current of 0.8 A when 0.3 V is applied in the forward direction at an ambient temperature of 35° C. Find:

(*a*) the saturation current

(*b*) the dynamic resistance for a forward voltage of 0.2 V
(*c*) the dynamic resistance when a reverse voltage of 1 V is applied.

[*Ans.* (*a*) 10 μA, (*b*) 1.43 Ω, (*c*) 6×10^{19} Ω]

139. A 10-kΩ resistor is made up of two strips connected in parallel, each 40 μm thick and 6 mm long. One strip is of intrinsic germanium and is 0.5 mm wide. Determine the width of the other strip if it is made of germanium doped with arsenic, there being 10^{21} atoms of arsenic per cubic metre of host material. At the working temperature the intrinsic carrier density for germanium is 2.5×10^{19} m^{-3} and the electron and hole mobilities are 0.4 m^2 V^{-1} s^{-1} and 0.2 m^2 V^{-1} s^{-1} respectively.

[*Ans.* 0.215 mm]

140. A boron diffusion is to be made into an *n*-type, 0.005-Ωm, silicon epitaxial layer. The impurity concentration at the silicon surface is maintained at 5×10^{25} atoms m^{-3} throughout. The diffusion takes place at 1100° C at which temperature the diffusion coefficient of boron is 4.3×10^{-17} m^2 s^{-1}. A junction is to be formed 5 μm below the surface. For what length of time should the diffusion be carried out? An electron mobility in silicon of 0.15 m^2 V^{-1} s^{-1} may be assumed.

[*Ans.* 5.7 h]

141. A four-point probe method is to be used to evaluate the doping profile of a *p*-type impurity in a silicon epitaxial layer. When the four equi-spaced probes are placed on the surface of the slice a probe current of 10 mA produces a voltage at the inner probes of 0.22 V. What is the sheet resistance of the slice?

Successive layers, 1 μm thick, are to be removed from the epitaxial layer by anodic oxidation, monitoring the resistance by the four-point probe method, keeping the probe current fixed at 10 mA. After the first layer is removed, the voltage reasured is 0.55 V. What is the mean resistivity and the average impurity concentration of the removed layer, assuming a hole mobility of 0.05 m^2 V^{-1} s^{-1}.

[*Ans.* 100 Ω per square; 1.67×10^{-4} Ωm; 7.5×10^{23} m^{-3}]

142. The slope of the voltage-current curve obtained by a four-point probe measurement on a 12 μm thick *n*-type epitaxial layer is 800 Ω. Find (*a*) the sheet resistance (*b*) the resistivity and (*c*) the approximate donor concentration of the layer. Assume an electron mobility of 0.13 m^2 V^{-1} s^{-1}.

Use the answers to estimate the resistance along the length of an isolated strip of the layer which has surface dimensions 200 × 10 μm.
[*Ans.* (*a*) 3620 Ω per square; (*b*) 4.35 Ωm; (*c*) 1.1 × 10^{21} m^{-3}; 72.4 kΩ]

143. An isolation diffusion is made through an *n*-type epitaxial layer, 10 μm thick, having an impurity concentration of 10^{22} atoms m^{-3}. The effective acceptor concentration at the surface of each diffused region is 5 × 10^{25} atoms m^{-3} and is maintained constant throughout the diffusion. Calculate the minimum time for the diffusion at 1200° C when the diffusion coefficient has a value 3.0 × 10^{-16} $m^2 s^{-1}$.

[*Ans.* 3-4 h]

CHAPTER FIVE

VALVE AND TRANSISTOR CHARACTERISTICS AND EQUIVALENT CIRCUITS

144. A diode has the following I/V characteristic:

I(mA)	0.52	1.17	1.90	2.78	3.85	5.15	6.50
V(V)	25	50	75	100	125	150	175

This diode is placed in series with a resistor of 20 000 Ω and a battery of 200 V. A resistor of 60 000 Ω is connected between the electrodes of the diode. Determine the current through the diode.

[*Ans.* 3 mA]

145. The anode-voltage/anode-current characteristic of a certain diode is given by the following figures:

Voltage V_a (V)	0	5	10	15	20	25	30	35
Current I_a (mA)	0	3.1	8.9	17.0	26.8	38	51.4	66

Plot the dynamic characteristic curve if the load has a resistance of 2500 Ω. Hence find the load current, and the voltage across the load when the supply voltage is 50 V.

[*Ans.* 14.5 mA; 36.25 V]

146. The linear parts of the control characteristics of a certain thyratron are given by the following expressions:

$V_a = [-120\ V_g - 160]$, when the temperature is 40° C

and $V_a = [-\ \ 70\ V_g - 130]$, when the temperature is 70° C,

where V_a is the anode voltage in volts, and V_g is the grid voltage in volts.

Evaluate, for an anode voltage of 400 V, the change in critical grid voltage when the temperature of the valve rises from 40° C to 70° C.

The thyratron is used as a controlled rectifier on a sinusoidal a.c. supply of peak value 350 V. Determine the striking angles for a d.c. grid bias of -4 V (*a*) when the temperature is 40° C, and (*b*) when it is 70° C.

[*Ans.* 2.8 V; 66° 5′; 25° 22′]

147. Three triodes having amplification factors of 10, 20 and 30, and with mutual conductances 2, 5 and 3 mS respectively, are operated in parallel. Calculate the equivalent mutual conductance, the anode resistance and the amplification factor of the combination.

[*Ans.* 10 mS, 1818 Ω, 18.18]

148. A certain thoriated-tungsten filament operating at 1900 K gave a saturation current of 85 mA. Calculate the corresponding current for a pure-tungsten filament of the same area operating at 2500 K. The Dushman constants are:

For thoriated tungsten

$$A = 3 \times 10^4 \text{ Am}^{-2}(\text{K})^2, b = 30\,500 \text{ K.}$$

For pure tungsten

$$A = 602 \times 10^3 \text{ Am}^{-2}(\text{K})^2, b = 52\,400 \text{ K.}$$

[*Ans.* 21.8 mA]

149. Calculate the space-charge-limited current density between parallel plates 2 mm apart when the voltage across them is 200 V.

[*Ans.* 1.65×10^3 Am^{-2}]

150. Two diodes each have an anode 4 mm in diameter and 20 mm long, but one of them has a filament 0.1 mm in diameter, while the other has an indirectly-heated cathode 1.5 mm in diameter. Calculate the space currents flowing in each valve when the annode voltage is 25 V.

[*Ans.* 17 mA; 41 mA]

151. Explain the conditions under which the current in a thermonic diode is given by the law $I = kV^{3/2}$. Show that the shape of the electrodes only affects the constant k.

152. In a cylindrical diode the electric-field intensity at the cathode surface is 10^6 Vm^{-1}, and the cathode temperature is 2600 K. Determine the percentage increase in the zero-external-field thermionic-emission current because of the Schottky effect.

[*Ans.* 18.4 per cent]

153. (*a*) A low-mu, plane-electrode triode has a grid-anode spacing of 1.9×10^{-3} m, a grid-wire spacing of 1.27×10^{-3} m and a grid-wire radius of 6.4×10^{-5} m. Estimate the amplification factor.

(*b*) In a cylindrical-electrode triode with an amplification factor of 20 the anode radius is 1.05×10^{-2} m. The evenly-spaced grid wires are each of 4×10^{-4} m radius, and are arranged to form a squirrel cage around a grid-wire circle of radius 5×10^{-3} m. Determine the total number of grid wires.

(*c*) Derive the Vodges-Elder expressions* for the amplification factors of both high-mu, plane-electrode and cylindrical-electrode triode valves.

[*Ans.* (*a*) $\simeq 8$, (*b*) $\simeq 10$, (*c*) see the solution for the expressions]

154. The characteristics of a junction transistor are given in the following Table:

Collector Voltage V_{ce} (volts)	Collector Current (I_c) in mA		
	$I_b = 0$	$I_b = 40\ \mu A$	$I_b = 80\ \mu A$
1	0.2	1.90	3.7
4	0.3	2.05	4.0
7	0.4	2.20	4.3

The transistor is connected in a common-emitter stage with a collector load of 1500 Ω, to supply voltage of 6 V and a d.c. bias of 40 μA. Plot the characteristics, draw the appropriate load line† and calculate the power dissipated in the transistor.

What will be the total voltage swing at the collector for an a.c. input signal current of 40 μA peak in the base?

[*Ans.* 6 mW; $\simeq 4.9$ V]

* See F. B. Vodges and F. R. Elder, 'Formulas for the Amplification Constant for Three-element Tubes,' *Phys. Rev.*, **24**, 683–9, 1924

† Readers may like to see a discussion of the application of load lines to transistor amplifiers in the book: R. Lowe and D. Nave, *The Electrical Principles of Telecommunications*, MacMillan, 1973, Chapter 7.

155. The output characteristics of a certain *p-n-p* transistor for common-base and common-emitter connections are illustrated in the figures. Determine, from these curves, the values of $\alpha = (\delta i_c/\delta i_e)_{V_{cb}}$ and $\beta = (\delta i_c/\delta i_b)_{V_{cb}}$.

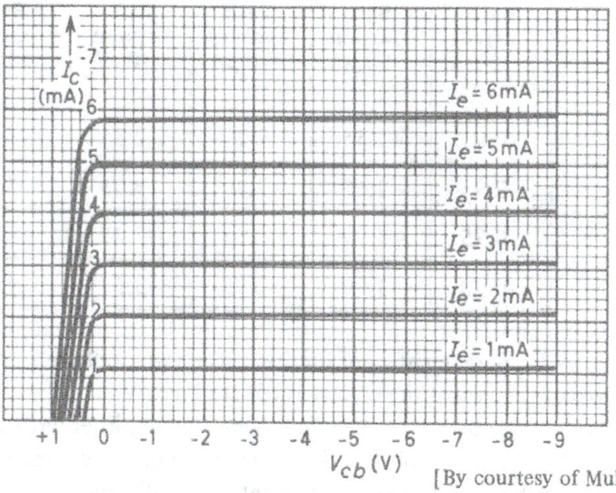

[By courtesy of Mullard Ltd]

Show how β may be expressed in terms of α and vice-versa.

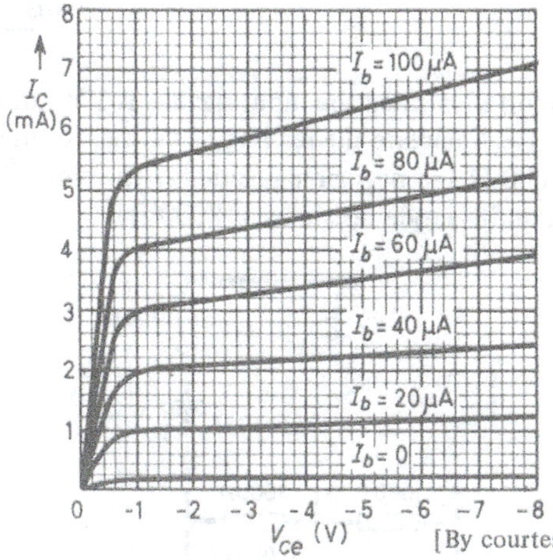

[By courtesy of Mullard Ltd]

[*Ans.* 0.98; $\simeq 57$; $\beta = \alpha/(1-\alpha)$; $\alpha = \beta/(1+\beta)$]

156. For a transistor used in the common-emitter configuration the relationship between collector current and collector voltage, with various fixed values of base current, are given in the following Table.

Collector Voltage (V)	Collector Current (mA)				
	Base Current −30 μA	Base Current −50 μA	Base Current −70 μA	Base Current −90 μA	Base Current −110 μA
−2	−0.9	−1.55	−2.2	−2.85	−3.55
−4	−0.92	−1.65	−2.4	−3.05	−3.77
−6	−0.95	−1.77	−2.55	−3.25	−4.0
−8	−0.98	−1.90	−2.75	−3.5	−4.2

Draw the static characteristics of the transistor and use these to determine the current gain when the collector voltage is −5 V.

The transistor is to be used as a common-emitter amplifier with a load resistance of 1800 Ω and a collector battery voltage of −9 V. Draw the load line and use this to find the base current for a collector voltage of −4 V.

[*Ans.* 37; 82 μA]

157. In the circuit illustrated the input signal *e* is 1 V r.m.s. and the frequency is 2000 Hz. Calculate the reading of the a.c. voltmeter if it has a resistance of 10 000 Ω and negligible reactance. The amplification factor of the valve is 20 and its anode resistance is 8000 Ω.

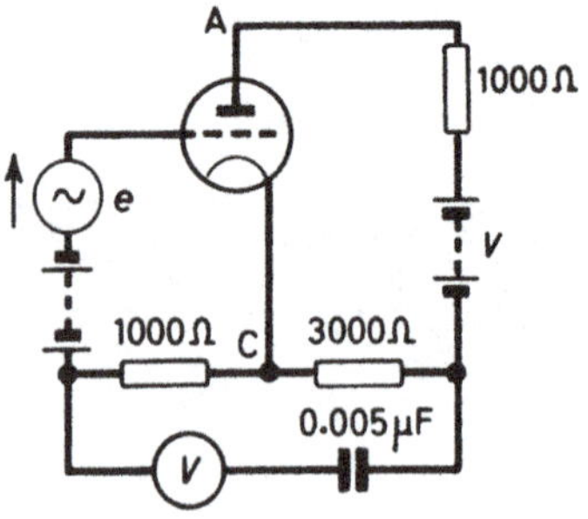

[*Ans.* 2.06 V]

158. Draw the equivalent circuit for the network illustrated, and write down the equations from which the various alternating currents and voltages may be calculated. Assume that, with the reference potentials shown, the voltage e_2 is 30° ahead of the voltage e_1, and that the r.m.s. values of e_1 and e_2 are 1 V and 2 V, respectively.

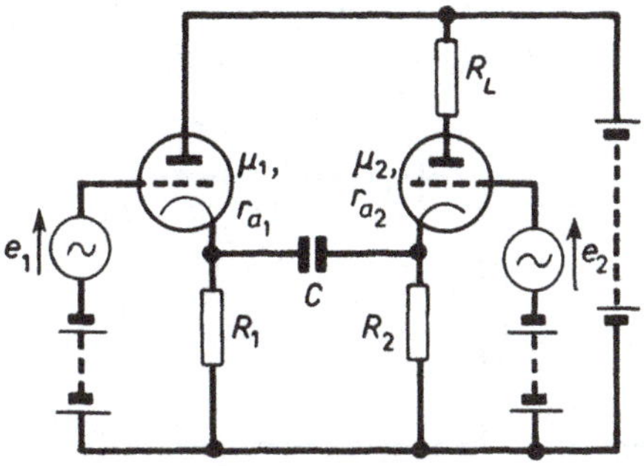

159. Derive the current-source equivalent circuit for a triode valve, where the valve is replaced by a current generator which supplies a current $g_m V_g$ flowing from anode to cathode within the valve and the anode resistance r_a is connected across the generator terminals. g_m is the mutual conductance of the valve and V_g the grid-cathode voltage.

160. Two triode valves have amplification factors of 20 and 40, and anode resistances of 5000 and 10 000 Ω, respectively. The two anodes are joined together, and a load of resistance 20 000 Ω is connected between the anodes and the h.t. supply line. An alternating voltage of 4 V is applied between the grid and cathode of the first valve, and a voltage of 2 V, of the same frequency and phase, is applied between the grid and cathode of the second valve. Calculate the alternating voltage across the load resistor and the alternating component of the anode current in each valve.

[*Ans.* 68.6 V; 2.3 mA; 1.1 mA]

161. The hybrid parameters of a certain transistor are:

$$h_{ib} = 35\ \Omega,\ h_{fb} = -0.976,\ h_{ob} = 1.0\ \mu\text{S and } h_{rb} = 7 \times 10^{-4}.$$

Calculate the values of $r_{11}, r_{12}, r_{21}, r_{22}, \alpha, r_e, r_b, r_c$ and r_m.

[*Ans.* 718.2 Ω; 700 Ω; 976 kΩ; 1 MΩ; 0.976; 18.2 Ω; 700 Ω; ≃ 1MΩ; 975.3 kΩ]

162. Draw an equivalent circuit for the transistor common-base configuration using the parameters r_e, r_b, r_c and r_m. Repeat for the common-emitter and common-collector configurations.* Show that $r_b = r_{12}$, $r_e = r_{11} - r_{12}$, $r_c = r_{22} - r_{12}$, $r_m = r_{21} - r_{12}$ and $\alpha = r_{21}/r_{22}$.

163. Show that the arrangement illustrated, which is frequently used as a transistor equivalent circuit, does not, in general, satisfy the reciprocity condition.

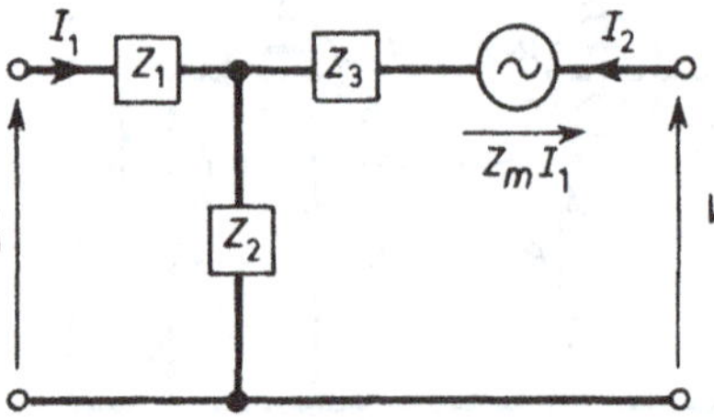

Determine the condition that must be satisfied for reciprocity to apply.

[*Ans.* $Z_m = 0$]

164. A transistor has a current amplification factor of 0.96 at low frequencies and the alpha cut-off frequency is 5 MHz. Determine the current amplification factor at 10 MHz and calculate the frequency at which the current amplification factor falls to 0.6.

[*Ans.* 0.43; 6.25 MHz]

165. The current amplification factor α of a common-base junction transistor, operating at a frequency f is given by:

$$\alpha = \alpha_0 \left\{ \frac{1}{1 + j(f/f_\alpha)} \right\}$$

where α_0 is the low-frequency value of α and f_α, called the alpha cut-off frequency, is that frequency where $\alpha = \alpha_0/\sqrt{2}$.

Derive a corresponding expression for the current amplification factor when the transistor is used in the common-emitter configuration and give the corresponding cut-off frequency in terms of α_0 and f_α.

$$\left[\textit{Ans.}\ \frac{\alpha_0}{(1 - \alpha_0) + j(f/f_\alpha)}; f_\alpha(1 - \alpha_0) \right]$$

* Small- and large-signal models of transistors have been given in the book W. H. Cornetet and F. E. Battocletti, *Electronic Circuits by System and Computer Analysis*, McGraw-Hill, 1975, including the Ebers-Moll model because of its applicability to computer programs (see J. J. Ebers and J. L. Moll, Large-Signal Behaviour of Junction Transistors, Proc. I.R.E., December, 1954, p.1761.

166. Derive an equivalent circuit for the *n*-channel FET illustrated.

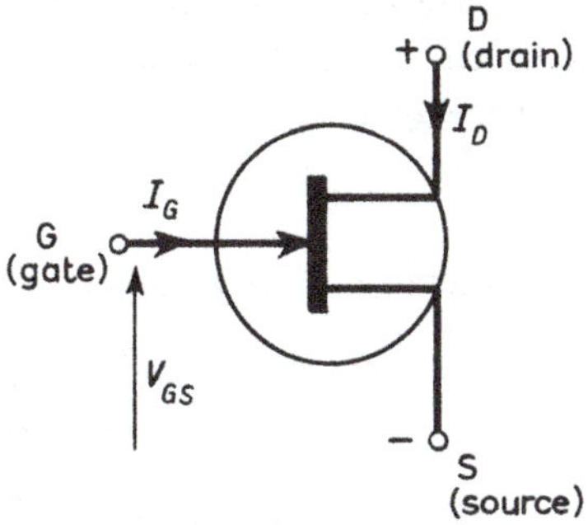

[*Ans.* see the Solution]

ADDITIONAL PROBLEMS

167. In tests on a certain thyratron, with a steady value of negative grid voltage applied to the valve, the anode voltage was gradually raised until the valve conducted. The corresponding grid and anode voltages at the point of conduction were:

Grid voltage (V)	−8.7	−8.0	−7.0	−6.0	−5.0	−4.0	−3.0	−2.0	−1.0	−0.5
Anode voltage (V)	191	176	152	131	109	88	66	46	34.2	33.8

Plot the control characteristic, and estimate the control ratio over that portion of the graph which is approximately linear.

[*Ans.* 21.8]

168. A thyratron just becomes conducting with 200 V on the anode when the negative grid voltage is held at −8 V. The control ratio is 35. Find the minimum anode voltage for conduction when the grid is held at −20 V. Determine also the critical grid voltage, when the anode voltage is 340 V.

[*Ans.* 620 V; −12 V]

169. A certain filament operating at 2100 K was thought to give a saturation current 10 000 times as great as that when the operating temperature was 1600 K. If this had been true what would the work function of the filament material have been?

[*Ans.* 5 V]

170. A diode with parallel-plane electrodes 4×10^{-2} m apart has an anode voltage which is 8 V negative with respect to the cathode. Calculate the maximum distance which an electron can travel from the cathode surface if it leaves it with an energy of 2 eV.

[*Ans.* 1×10^{-2} m]

171. Find h_{re} and h_{ie} in terms of the common-base h parameters.

$$\left[Ans.\ h_{re} = \frac{h_{ib}h_{ob} - (1 + h_{fb})\,h_{rb}}{h_{ib}h_{ob} + (1 - h_{rb})(1 + h_{fb})};\quad h_{ie} = \frac{h_{ib}}{h_{ib}h_{ob} + (1 - h_{rb})(1 + h_{fb})}\right]$$

172. A transistor has a current gain α of 0.985 in the common-base configuration and the common-base collector leakage current I_{co} is 4 μA. Determine the current gain β in the common-emitter configuration and the common-emitter collector leakage current I_{co}'.*

Another transistor has $h_{fe} = 85$; find h_{fb}.

[*Ans.* 65.7; 267 μA; $-$0.988]

173. Draw the equivalent circuit of the arrangement shown and find the r.m.s. a.c. anode current in the valve. The valve constants are $\mu = 20$ and $r_a = 5000\ \Omega$.

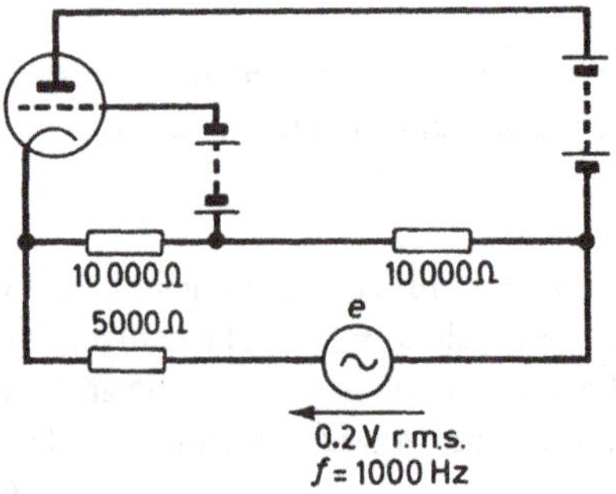

[*Ans.* 35.9 μA]

* The relation between I_{co}' and I_{co} is given in many textbooks, see, for example, S. M. Bozic, R. M. H. Cheng and J. D. Parsons, *Electronic and Switching Circuits*, Arnold, 1975, Section 1.10.

174. Show that the common-emitter transistor arrangement at (*a*) can be represented by the equivalent circuit at (*b*).

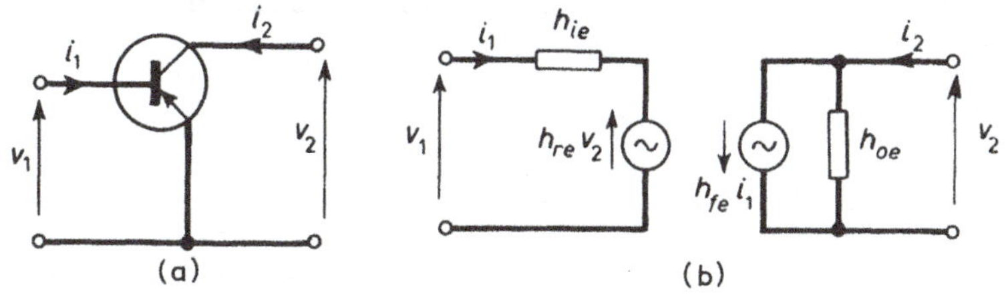

It should be noted that h_{oe} is an admittance.*

175. Develop the small-signal a.c. h-parameter equivalent circuit for the arrangement shown assuming that h_{re}, h_{oe} and the fixed bias components can be neglected.

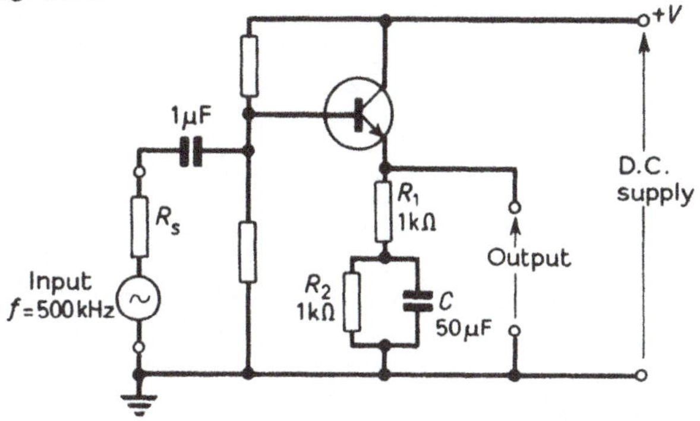

Hence, verify the following expressions for the input resistance R_i and the output resistance R_0:

$$R_i \simeq h_{ie} + (1 + h_{fe})R_1$$

and
$$R_0 \simeq \frac{(R_s + h_{ie})R_1}{R_s + h_{ie} + (1 + h_{fe})R_1}$$

176. Measurements on a junction transistor at 30 kHz gave values of 0.98 and 40 for the magnitudes of the current amplification factors in the common-base and common-emitter configurations respectively. Calculate

* In some books the resistor symbol is labelled $1/h_{oe}$ instead of h_{oe}.

the phase angle of the common-emitter current amplification factor at 30 kHz and evaluate the cut-off frequency for both configurations.

[*Ans.* 77°; $f_\alpha = 395$ kHz; $f_\beta = 6.8$ kHz]

CHAPTER SIX

RECTIFICATION AND VOLTAGE AND CURRENT STABILIZATION

177. A high-vacuum diode, with an internal resistance of 150 Ω, supplies power to a 1000-Ω load from a 300-V r.m.s. source. Find:

(*a*) the mean load current,
(*b*) the r.m.s. alternating load current,
(*c*) the d.c. power supplied to the load,
(*d*) the input power to the circuit,
(*e*) the rectification efficiency,
(*f*) the ripple factor.

[*Ans.* (*a*) 177 mA; (*b*) 184 mA; (*c*) 13.8 W; (*d*) 39.1 W; (*e*) 35.3 per cent; (*f*) 1.21]

178. A gas diode, for which the striking and extinction voltages may both be taken as 10 V, supplies power in a half-wave rectifier circuit to a 1000-Ω load from a 300-V r.m.s. source. Calculate:

(*a*) the mean load voltage,
(*b*) the d.c. power supplied to the load,
(*c*) the input power to the anode circuit,
(*d*) the rectification efficiency,
(*e*) the ripple factor.

[*Ans.* (*a*) 130 V; (*b*) 16.9 W; (*c*) 43.7 W; (*d*) 38.7 per cent; (*e*) 1.225]

179. Calculate the regulation and efficiency for a half-wave rectifier circuit, from no load to 80 mA. The transformer r.m.s. secondary voltage is 230 V and the internal resistance of the diode is 500 Ω. Find also the current at which maximum power is obtained.

[*Ans.* 40 V; 40.6 to 24.9 per cent; 103.5 mA]

180. A full-wave single-phase rectifier employs two diodes, and the internal resistance of each of these may be assumed constant at 500 Ω. The transformer r.m.s. secondary voltage from the centre tap to each end is 300 V and the load has a resistance of 2000 Ω. Evaluate:

(*a*) the mean load current,
(*b*) the r.m.s. alternating load current,
(*c*) the d.c. output power,
(*d*) the input power to the circuit,
(*e*) the rectification efficiency,
(*f*) the ripple factor,
(*g*) the regulation from no-load to the given load.

[*Ans.* (*a*) 108 mA; (*b*) 120 mA; (*c*) 23.3 W; (*d*) 36 W; (*e*) 64.8 per cent; (*f*) 0.482; (*g*) 54 V]

181. A moving-iron ammeter and a simple moving-coil ammeter are placed in series with the load in a half-wave rectifier circuit. The reading on the a.c. instrument is 5 A. What is the reading of the other ammeter?

Calculate the instrument readings if the other half-wave is also rectified. Assume sinusoidal waveforms.

[*Ans.* 3.18 A; 7.07 A; 6.37 A]

182. A metal rectifier has the voltage-current characteristic shown. A sinusoidal alternating voltage, with a maximum value of 2 V, is applied to the rectifier, in series with a non-inductive resistor of value 80 Ω and a moving-coil ammeter of negligible resistance. Calculate the reading of the instrument.

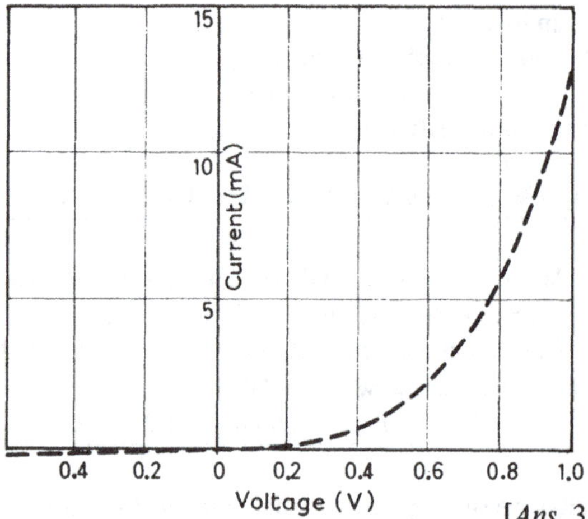

[*Ans.* 3.32 mA]

183. The rectifying element of a single-phase half-wave rectifier circuit has a resistance of 10 Ω in the forward direction and its resistance in the reverse direction may be taken as infinite. A resistor and a capacitor in parallel form the load and the capacitance is so great that the voltage across it is practically constant during both the charging and discharging periods. The resistance of the load is such that current flows through the rectifying element for one-sixth of each cycle of the a.c. supply voltage.

Determine the resistance of the load and the efficiency of rectification.

[*Ans.* 585 Ω; 89.4 per cent]

184. The grid voltage of the thyratron shown in the diagram is such that conduction begins 60° after the start of each cycle. Calculate:

(*a*) the r.m.s. value of the load current,
(*b*) the r.m.s. value of the voltage across the thyratron,
(*c*) the total power delivered by the a.c. supply.

The drop in the valve during conduction is 10 V.

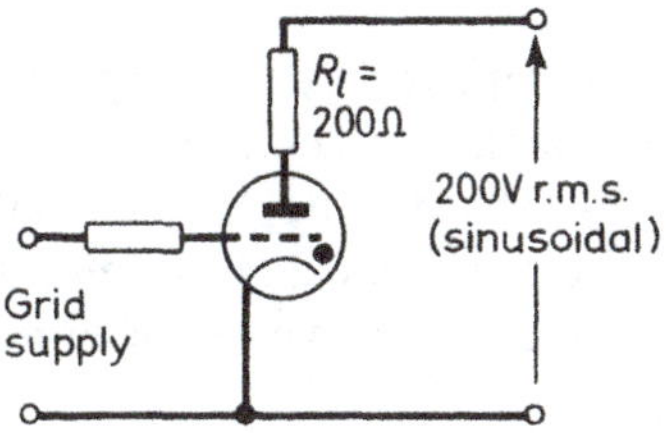

[*Ans.* (*a*) 0.63 A; (*b*) 155 V; (*c*) 77 W]

185. A single-phase full-wave rectifier circuit, employing a single L-type filter, is to supply 120 mA at 300 V with a ripple that must not exceed 10 V. Design a suitable filter if the supply frequency is (*a*) 50 Hz, (*b*) 60 Hz.

[*Ans.* A 10-H choke and a 4-μF capacitor are suitable in both cases]

186. A full-wave rectifier is used to supply power to a 2000-Ω load. Two 20-H chokes and two 16-μF capacitors are available for filtering purposes. Calculate, approximately, the ripple factors for the following cases:

(*a*) one choke only in series with the load,
(*b*) two chokes in series with the load,
(*c*) one capacitor only in parallel with the load,
(*d*) two capacitors in parallel with the load,
(*e*) a single, L-type filter using one choke and one capacitor,
(*f*) a single, L-type filter using two chokes in series and two capacitors in parallel,

(*g*) a double, L-type filter, each section consisting of one choke and one capacitor.

The supply frequency should be taken as (*i*) 50 Hz, (*ii*) 60 Hz.

[*Ans.* (*i*) (*a*) 0.074; (*b*) 0.037; (*c*) 0.090; (*d*) 0.045; (*e*) 0.0037; (*f*) 0.0009; (*g*) 2.95×10^{-5}
(*ii*) (*a*) 0.062; (*b*) 0.031; (*c*) 0.075; (*d*) 0.0375; (*e*) 0.0025; (*f*) 0.0006; (*g*) 1.42×10^{-5}]

187. Outline the design of a power supply, from a single-phase full-wave rectifier, using a π-section filter, to give a d.c. output of 250 V at 50 mA and with a ripple factor not exceeding 0.01 per cent. The supply frequency should be taken as (*i*) 50 Hz, (*ii*) 60 Hz.

[There is no unique solution to this problem]

188. In a full-wave rectifier circuit, employing a 20-H choke in a π-section filter, what would be the power dissipated in a resistor R which replaced the choke and gave the same ripple factor, with an output current of 100 mA? The supply frequency should be taken as (*i*) 50 Hz, (*ii*) 60 Hz.

Repeat the calculation for the case where the output current is only 10 mA.

[*Ans.* (*i*) 125.7 W; 1.257 W; (*ii*) 150.8 W; 1.508 W]

189. In the circuit shown the load voltage of 33 V is regulated in the current range 15 to 65 mA. The Zener diode regulates over the large range of current 8 to 120 mA. Determine:

(*a*) the minimum value of R to permit regulation over the whole range of load current,
(*b*) the Zener current to satisfy (*a*).
(*c*) the limits between which the supply voltage may vary without loss of regulation in the circuit if the load current is set at 55 mA.

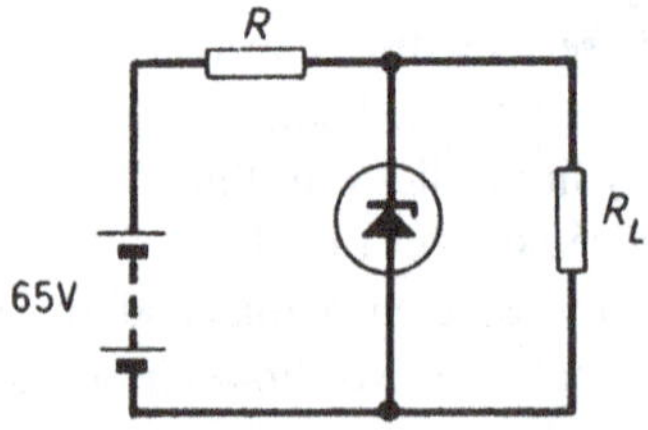

190. For the series stabilizer illustrated draw a small-signal equivalent circuit using h parameters and derive expressions for the stabilization ratio and the output impedance.

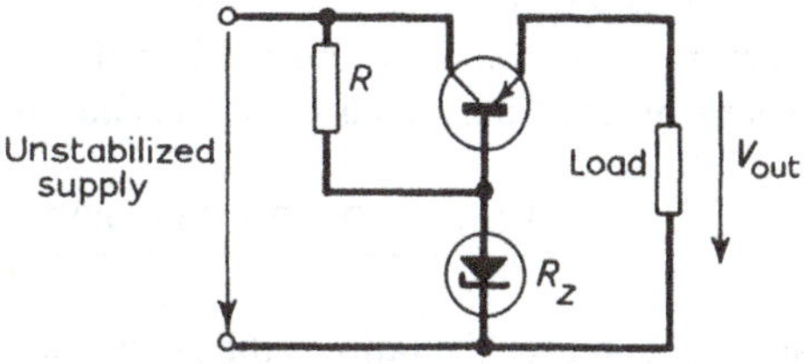

$$\left[Ans.\ \frac{R_z + R'}{R_z + h_{rb}R'},\ \text{where } R' = \frac{R}{1 + h_{ob}R};\ h_{ib} + \frac{(1 + h_{fb})(1 - h_{rb})}{h_{ob} + 1/R + 1/R_z}\right]$$

191. A Zener diode, which is designed to produce a voltage of 6.5 V when operated at a current of 3 mA, and an operational amplifier are to be used to produce a stabilized power supply. The power supply is to operate from a nominal 30-V unstabilized supply and it is to deliver a stabilized output of 15 V. Draw a circuit for the stabilized power supply indicating suitable values for the additional components used.

If the operational amplifier has an open-loop voltage gain of 3×10^4 and an output resistance of 200 Ω determine the output resistance of the stabilized supply.

[*Ans.* see the Solution]

192. The d.c. input voltage to a simple glow-discharge stabilizer is V_i, and the limiting resistor has a resistance R. The resistance of the load is R_L. Discuss how the values of V_i and R are chosen when the tube and load are specified.*

A certain tube has a maximum allowable current of 40 mA, and a minimum specified current of 5 mA. The working voltage of the tube is 150 V, and may be assumed constant. If the input voltage V_i varies by 10 per cent, plot curves showing (*a*) the relation between the maximum and minimum values of load current $I_{L\max}$ and $I_{L\min}$, if $I_{L\max} + I_{L\min} = 30$ mA, and (*b*) the relation between the minimum value of V_i and $(I_{L\max} - I_{L\min})$.

* Similar calculations can be made for a Zener-diode shunt stabilizer (as will be clear from Problem 189), e.g. see J. A. Chandler, 'The Characteristics and Applications of Zener (Voltage Reference) Diodes,' *Electronic Engineering*, **32**, 78, 1960.

193. Two glow-discharge tubes in series, each having a running voltage of 100 V, are connected to a d.c. supply of voltage 400 V. They supply a load taking a current of 20 mA. The normal tube current is 30 mA. Calculate the resistance of the series resistor.

If the specified current range of each tube is 10 to 50 mA, find the range of input voltage over which stabilization is effective, and the range of load resistance.

[*Ans.* 4 kΩ; 320 V to 480 V; 5 kΩ to ∞]

194. Derive an expression for the ratio of the percentage change of output voltage to the percentage change of input voltage for the simple parallel-valve voltage stabilizer shown, if the load resistor R_l is constant. Hence show that stabilization in such a circuit is impossible without a reference voltage and that the larger the value of the mutual conductance of the valve the better the stabilization.

Assume that the valve characteristics are linear and that the heater voltage of the valve remains constant.

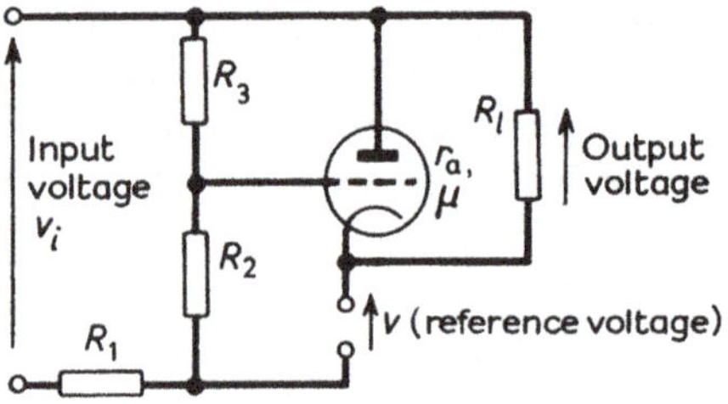

$$\left[\textit{Ans.} \; \frac{1}{1 + \dfrac{v}{V_i}\left[\dfrac{R_1(\mu R_3 - r_a)}{r_a(R_2 + R_3)} - 1\right]} \right]$$

195. The diagram shows one form of thermionic-valve voltage stabilizer. Derive an expression for the ratio of the percentage change of output voltage to the percentage change of input voltage of the stabilizer if the load resistor is constant. Hence, show that theoretically, perfect stabilization is obtained when

$$R_3\mu_2(r_{a_1} + \mu_1 R_4) = (R_2 + R_3)(R_4 + R_5 + r_{a_1})$$

where μ_1 and μ_2 are the amplification factors of valves 1 and 2 respectively and r_{a_1} and r_{a_2} are the corresponding anode resistances.

Make the same assumptions as in Problem 194.

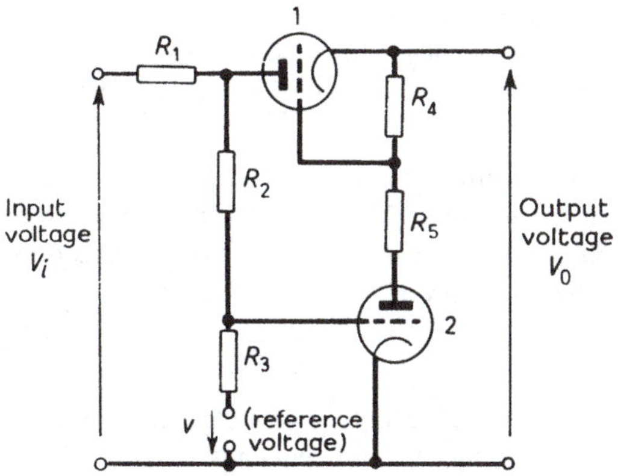

[*Ans.* $1/(1 - Av/BV_i)$

where $A = \mu_2\{(R_1 + R_2 + R_3)(R_1 + r_{a_1} + \mu_1 R_4) - R_1^2\}$

$-R_3\mu_2(R_1 + r_{a_1} + \mu_1 R_4)$

$-R_1(R_4 + R_5 + r_{a_2})$

and $B = R_3\mu_2(r_{a_1} + \mu_1 R_4) - (R_2 + R_3)(R_4 + R_5 + r_{a_2})$]

196. The voltage/current characteristic of a certain barretter is given by the following figures:

Voltage (V) .	80	100	120	140	160	180
Current (A) .	0.476	0.495	0.498	0.500	0.502	0.514

A number of valve heaters having a total resistance of 100 Ω are connected in series with this barretter. Find the current through the circuit when the input voltage is 200 V.

When the input voltage changes by ± 10 per cent calculate the corresponding current variation.

[*Ans.* 0.5 A; 0.004 A]

ADDITIONAL PROBLEMS

197. A full-wave power supply unit consists of a centre-tapped transformer and two diodes whose forward resistances may be considered equal and constant at 300 Ω. If the unit supplies a mean current of 100 mA to a 2-kΩ load, calculate:

(*a*) the r.m.s. transformer voltage,

(*b*) the diode peak current,

(*c*) the diode dissipation,
(*d*) the a.c. input power neglecting transformer losses.

[*Ans.* (*a*) 255 V-0-255 V; (*b*) 157 mA; (*c*) 0.75 W; (*d*) 21.5 W]

198. A controlled rectifier has a voltage drop when conducting of 5 V. It is connected in series with a 125-V r.m.s. mains supply and a 20-Ω resistive load. The rectifier begins conduction at 35° and is turned off at 125°. Determine the load power.

[*Ans.* 292 W]

199. In a half-wave circuit using a silicon controlled rectifier (SCR) conduction begins at an angle $\theta = \pi/6$ and ends at $\theta = \pi$. The peak value of the applied voltage is 1000 V. Find the mean load voltage.

What is the effect of (*a*) changing the control so that conduction begins at $\theta = \pi/3$ (*b*) using a triac in place of the SCR.

[*Ans.* 297 V (*a*) 239 V; (*b*) 594 V, 478 V]

200. A 20-V d.c. supply of negligible output impedance is connected through a 470-Ω resistor to a Zener diode in shunt with a 1-kΩ load resistor which carries a current of 6 mA. A 5 per cent change in supply voltage causes a 0.1 per cent change in load voltage. Calculate the slope resistance and the reverse breakdown voltage of the diode. Assume that the slope resistance of the diode is independent of current.

[*Ans.* 2.86 Ω; 5.93 V]

201. In the circuit illustrated if the output load resistance is constant show that the incremental variation of output voltage with a change in input voltage is equal to $x\,(x + R + xR/R_L)^{-1}$ where x is the incremental impedance of the Zener diode.

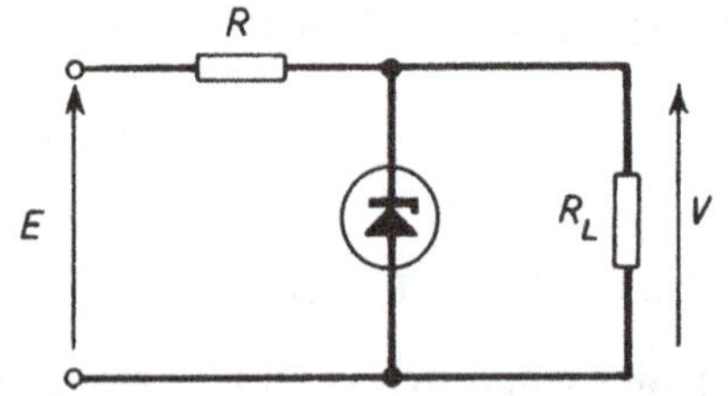

202. The transistor in the series stabilizer illustrated has the following parameters:

$$h_{ib} = 2\ \Omega,\ h_{rb} = 2 \times 10^{-3},\ h_{ob} = 50\ \mu\text{S},\ h_{fb} = -0.98.$$

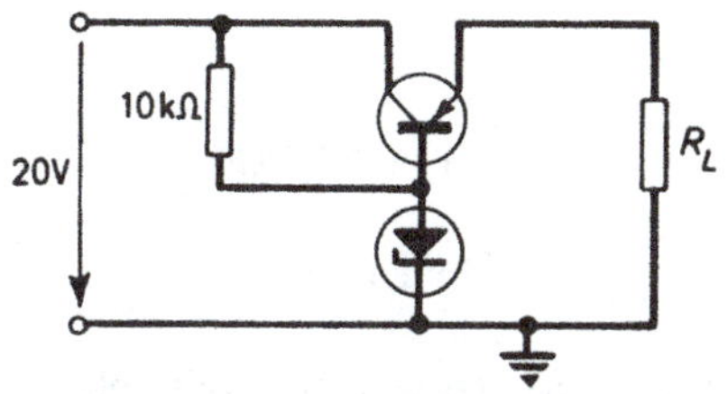

The Zener diode has a dynamic resistance of 10 Ω and a reference voltage of 10 V. Evaluate the load current when R_L is 490 Ω, the output impedance and the stabilization ratio.

[*Ans.* 20 mA; 2.2 Ω; 287]

203. The equivalent circuit of a series-valve stabilizer is illustrated. Find the change in output voltage for a 10 per cent change of input voltage if $R_1 = 10$ kΩ, $R_2 = 1$ MΩ, $R_3 = 16$ MΩ, $V_i = 2700$ V, $v = 100$ V, $\mu = 300$, $r_a = 100$ kΩ and $R_l = 260$ kΩ.

Calculate also the change in output voltage produced by a 10 per cent change of R_l.

Make the same assumption as in the Problem 194.

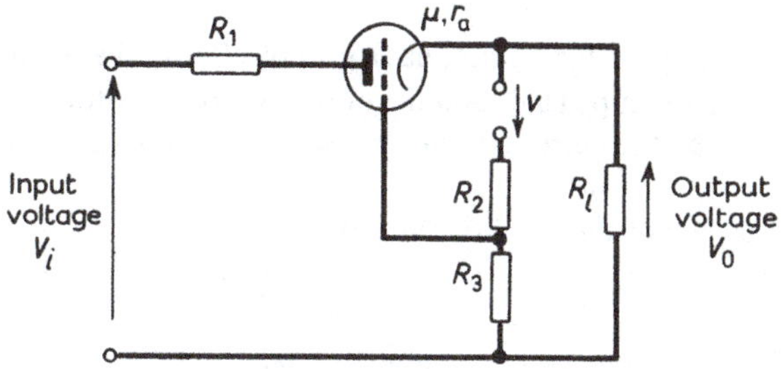

[*Ans.* 14 V; 3.5 V]

204. The anode voltage V_a, the grid voltage V_g and the anode current I_a of a triode are related by the expression

$$V_a = r_a I_a - \mu V_g - c r_a^*,$$

where c is a constant which is normally small.

Show that a 10 per cent change of the heater voltage of the triode in Question 203 causes the output voltage of the stabilizer to change by about 4.2 V (assume that c is originally zero, and that it changes by 0.8 mA for a 10 per cent change of heater voltage).

* See F. A. Benson, G. V. G. Lusher and M. S. Seaman, 'Variations of Triode Characteristics with Heater Voltage,' *Electrical Journal*, **151**, 481, 1953.

CHAPTER SEVEN

AMPLIFIERS

205. A certain triode operates with an anode voltage of 250 V and a grid voltage of −8 V. The anode current is then 9 mA. If the valve is used with a load having a resistance of 10 000 Ω, what is the value of the supply voltage required?

If the h.t. supply voltage is fixed at 430 V, calculate the resistance of the load to keep the valve working at the same operating point.

[*Ans.* 340 V; 20 kΩ]

206. A voltage amplifier employs a valve operating with an anode current of 9 mA and a negative bias of 8 V. Find the value of the resistance of a cathode resistor to give the required bias.

Determine also a suitable value for the cathode by-pass capacitance, if the signal frequency is (*a*) 1000 Hz, or (*b*) 100 Hz.

[*Ans.* 889 Ω; 2 μF; 20 μF]

207. A low-frequency amplifier has a gain of 60 dB. The input circuit is of 600 Ω resistive impedance and the output is arranged for a load of 10 Ω. What will be the current in the load when an alternating voltage of 1 V is applied at the input?

Express the gain of the amplifier in nepers.

[*Ans.* 12.9 A; 6.9 nepers]

208. A triode valve with an amplification factor of 20 and an anode resistance of 8000 Ω is used as an amplifier with an inductive load of inductance 0.8 H and resistance 1000 Ω. Determine the gain and phase shift of the amplifier at a frequency of 300 Hz and sketch the phasor diagram of the arrangement. The input voltage is 5 V.

By calculating the gain and phase shift of the amplifier at a frequency of 2000 Hz, show that both frequency distortion and phase-shift distortion occur.

[*Ans.* $3.92 \angle{-133^\circ}$; $14.97 \angle{-143.8^\circ}$]

209. By analysing the equivalent circuit of the RC-coupled amplifier correlate the sinusoidal and pulse responses of the amplifier.

210. A triode amplifier operating at a frequency of 10 000 Hz has a resistive load of 90 000 Ω. Calculate the voltage gain. The valve has an amplification factor of 60 and an anode resistance of 40 000 Ω. The inter-electrode capacitances are $C_{ga} = 3.0\ \mu\mu F$, $C_{gc} = 3.0\ \mu\mu F$ and $C_{ac} = 3.6\ \mu\mu F$.

Find the gain of this stage when it forms the first section of a two-stage amplifier. The two stages are identical. Make any reasonable assumptions.

[*Ans.* 41.6; 39.1 $\angle 160.2°$]

211. A valve with an amplification factor of 80 and an anode resistance of 50 000 Ω has a load resistor of 100 000 Ω connected between the anode and the positive h.t. supply terminal. Between the cathode and the negative h.t. terminal is a resistor of 2000 Ω with a 1-μF capacitor connected in parallel. An alternating voltage v_i is applied between the grid and the negative h.t. terminal, and the output voltage v_o is measured across the anode load. Calculate the maximum and minimum values of the ratio v_o/v_i.

At what frequency is the magnitude of v_o/v_i equal to 0.707 of its maximum value?

[*Ans.* 53.3; 25.6; 121.2 Hz]

212. The first stage of a resistor-capacitor coupled amplifier employs a valve with an amplification factor of 20 and an anode resistance of 7700 Ω. The resistance of the load is 50 000 Ω, the coupling capacitor has a capacitance of 0.01 μF, and the grid leak (including the resistive component of the input impedance of the next stage) has a resistance of 500 000 Ω. The input capacitance of the next stage is 200 μμF. Evaluate the gain of the stage at intermediate frequencies.

Find also the frequencies at which the gain falls to $1/\sqrt{(2)}$ of its intermediate-frequency value and calculate the frequency range over which the gain is greater than 14.

[*Ans.* −17.1; 31 Hz; 121 000 Hz; 44 to 84 960 Hz]

213. A two-stage resistor-capacitor coupled amplifier is to be designed with an overall mid-frequency gain of at least 6000 and with the gain only 5 per cent below the mid-frequency value at a frequency of 100 kHz. Pentodes are available which have

$$C_{gc} + C_{ac} = 10.5\ \mu\mu F$$

and g_m is 5.2 mS. It may be assumed that 10 $\mu\mu$F of stray capacitance shunts the equivalent circuit of one stage. Determine the value of the load resistance required and the actual overall gain at mid frequency.

[*Ans.* 17.2 kΩ; 7992]

214. By considering an RC-coupled amplifier employing pentodes show that it is not possible to increase bandwidth without a commensurate sacrifice in gain and vice-versa.

Calculate the maximum figure of merit (gain X bandwidth) for a pentode which has g_m = 5.7 mS, C_{gc} = 6.6 $\mu\mu$F and C_{ac} = 2.6 $\mu\mu$F.

[*Ans.* 98.6]

215. Three non-identical RC-coupled amplifier stages are cascaded. The bandwidth limits f_1 and f_2 for the individual amplifiers are given in the Table below.

Amplifier	Frequency f_1 (Hz)	Frequency f_2 (kHz)
1	100	250
2	80	350
3	50	550

Obtain equations from which the overall bandwidth limits could be calculated.

[See the solution for the equations]

216. The circuit illustrates one method of extending the upper limit of the frequency range of an RC-coupled amplifier where an inductor L counteracts the effect of C_g in reducing the load impedance at high frequencies.

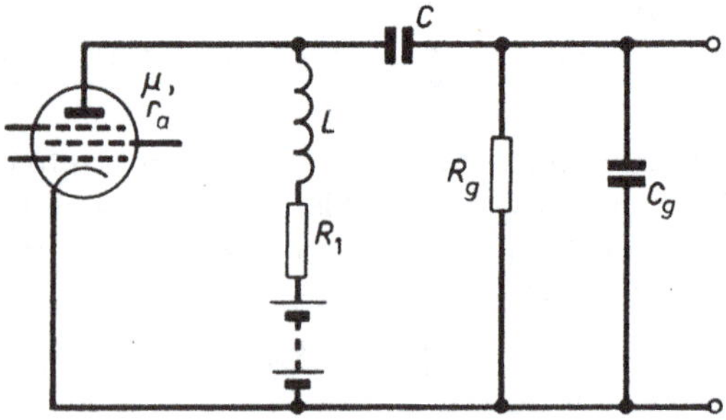

Analyse the circuit to find a desirable relation between L, C_g and R_1.

[*Ans.* For best flatness of the response curve $L = 0.414\,C_gR_1^2$ but a single value of L is not satisfactory for simultaneous flat gain and constant time delay and a compromise is necessary.]

217. Assuming the characteristic curves for a triode valve to be equidistant straight lines, prove that the maximum possible anode-circuit efficiency for a class-A amplifier, coupled to a resistive load through an ideal transformer, is 50 per cent.

Show also that the theoretical maximum efficiency for the simple series-fed, class-A, power amplifier is 25 per cent.

218. A transformer-coupled amplifier has the following constants:

Amplification factor of valve = 10.

Anode resistance of valve = 8000 Ω.

Ratio of secondary to primary turns of transformer = 3.

Effective leakage inductance of transformer referred to primary = 0.5 H.

Total effective shunt capacitance of transformer referred to primary = 1000 μμF.

Total effective resistance of transformer referred to primary = 15 000 Ω.

Resistance of primary winding of transformer = 3500 Ω.

Inductance of primary winding of transformer = 70 H.

Obtain a curve showing how the gain of the amplifier varies with frequency.

219. Determine the mean current, fundamental gain and second-harmonic distortion for a triode valve which has the anode-current/anode-voltage characteristics shown in the figure, when it is operating with a grid bias of −8 V, an anode supply voltage of 400 V and a load resistor of 8000 Ω. The peak input signal is 6 V.

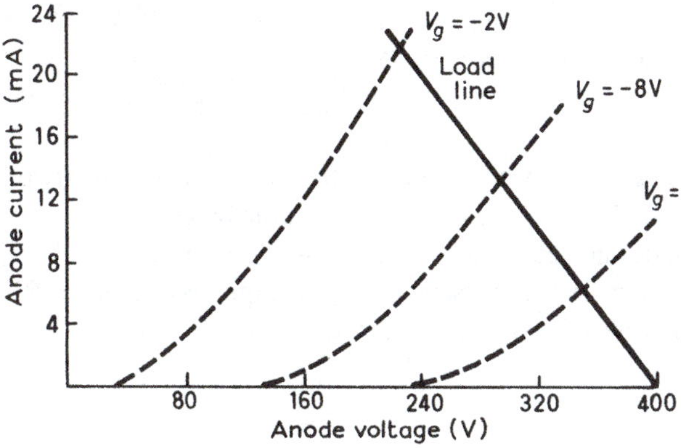

[*Ans.* 13.575 mA; 10.2; 4.9 per cent]

220. The following figures refer to a certain 25-W triode valve which delivers power to a resistive load by means of a choke-capacitor coupling.

Grid voltage $V_g = 0$.

Anode voltage V_a (V) . .	24	60	100	150	180
Anode current I_a (mA) . .	10	30	68	120	154

Grid voltage $V_g = 10.7$ V.

Anode voltage V_a (V) . .	123	150	200	250
Anode current I_a (mA) . .	10	25	66	120

Grid voltage $V_g = -21$ V.

Anode voltage V_a (V) . .	220	250	300	350
Anode current I_a (mA) . .	10	27	67	119

Grid voltage $V_g = -32$ V.

Anode voltage V_a (V)	312	350	400
Anode current I_a (mA)	10	29	68

The h.t. supply voltage is 300 V. Determine the approximate resistance of the load for maximum undistorted power output. Calculate this maximum value of power and the efficiency.

[*Ans.* 1.95 kΩ; 4 W; 16 per cent]

221. (*a*) Show that in a push-pull amplifier circuit employing two identical valves all even harmonics are suppressed in the output.

(*b*) Two triodes in a push-pull amplifier each have an anode-voltage/anode-current characteristic passing through the quiescent point (250 V, 30 mA) which is given by the following figures:

Anode voltage (V) . .	150	175	200	225	250	275	300	325
Anode current (mA) .	0	3	9	18	30	43	58	73

Draw the two curves with one inverted, and then obtain the composite characteristic. Find, from the curves, the anode resistance at the quiescent point of (*i*) each valve, (*ii*) the composite valve.

[*Ans.* (*i*) 2000 Ω; (*ii*) 1000 Ω]

222. (*a*) Show that the maximum possible efficiency of a class-B audio-frequency amplifier, for sinusoidal signals, is 78.5 per cent.

(*b*) A class-B amplifier operates from a 500-V, h.t. supply. The relation between the maximum permissible peak anode current (in amperes) and the minimum anode voltage is $I_{max} = 10^{-3}\ V_{min}$. If transformer losses are neglected, what is the maximum a.c. power which can be obtained, and what is the efficiency?

(*c*) Show that for a class-C amplifier where the angle of flow is 120° the maximum efficiency is 89.6 per cent.

[*Ans.* (*b*) 31.25 W; 39.3 per cent]

223. The anode current in a class-C amplifier may be regarded as triangular pulses having a peak value of 2.5 A and an angle of flow of 90°. The grid voltage varies sinusoidally and the anode-current/grid-voltage characteristic is linear. If the h.t. supply is 2.5 kV and the r.m.s. current delivered to a 750-Ω load is 0.8 A, what is the efficiency of the amplifier?

If the peak-to-peak amplitude of the anode voltage is 4 kV find the instantaneous anode voltage when anode current commences to flow.

[*Ans.* 61.9 per cent; 1086 V]

224. A triode valve with an amplification factor of 50 and an anode resistance of 30 000 Ω has for its anode load a parallel resonant circuit, of 'Q' = 45, which contains a resistor R of 15 000 Ω. The circuit resonates at 20 000 Hz. A second coil L_2 is coupled magnetically to the resonant-circuit coil L, the mutual inductance M between the coils being 1 mH. Calculate the voltage between the terminals of L_2 when a voltage of 1 V at a frequency of 20 500 Hz is applied between the grid and cathode of the valve.

[*Ans.* 3.485 V]

225. An amplifier has a gain of 20, without feedback. If 10 per cent of the output voltage is fed back by means of a resistive negative-feedback circuit, determine the actual amplification.

[*Ans.* 6.67]

226. A certain audio-frequency amplifier has a nominal gain of 120 and gives an output voltage of 60 V to its output transformer, with 10 per cent second-harmonic distortion. How much feedback must be used to reduce the distortion to 1 per cent? Find also the additional gain required ahead of the feedback amplifier in order to give the same output voltage.

[*Ans.* Feedback factor = −0.075; 10]

227. A multistage amplifier, when operated without feedback and with normal supply voltage, has a gain of 24 000. When the supply voltage falls by 25 per cent the amplification is only 16 000. Show that if a negative-feedback potentiometer across the output is used to feed back 1/1000 of the output voltage to the input, the amplification is nearly independent of variations in supply voltage.

[*Ans.* Gain for normal supply voltage = 960; gain when supply voltage falls by 25 per cent from its normal value = 941]

228. An amplifier employing pentodes with anode slope resistance r_a and mutual conductance g_m has three identical resistor-capacitor coupled stages, each coupling circuit having capacitance C and resistance R_g. The anode load resistance in each stage is R_l. A fraction β of the amplifier output voltage is fed back to the input without phase-shift.

Use Nyquist's criterion to find the maximum value of β which may be employed without causing instability.

Assume that R_g and r_a are large compared with R_l and neglect inter-electrode and stray capacitances.

[*Ans.* $8/(g_m R_l)^3$]

229. Show that the output impedance of a cathode-follower stage, which employs a valve with a mutual conductance of 4 mS, is about 250 Ω but the input impedance is high.

230. Draw the equivalent circuit of the feedback arrangement illustrated in the diagram and use Millman's network theorem* to find the overall gain. Obtain also, expressions for the output and input admittances of the network. If a pentode is used in the circuit, for which the anode resistance r_a is 1 MΩ and the mutual conductance g_m is 2 mS, and $Y_1 = Y_f = 2 \times 10^{-6}$ S and $Y_g = 0.2 \times 10^{-6}$ S, show that the gain is approximately unity. Under the same conditions, prove that the value of the output impedance is approximately $[2/g_m]$, and that the input impedance is approximately Y_1.

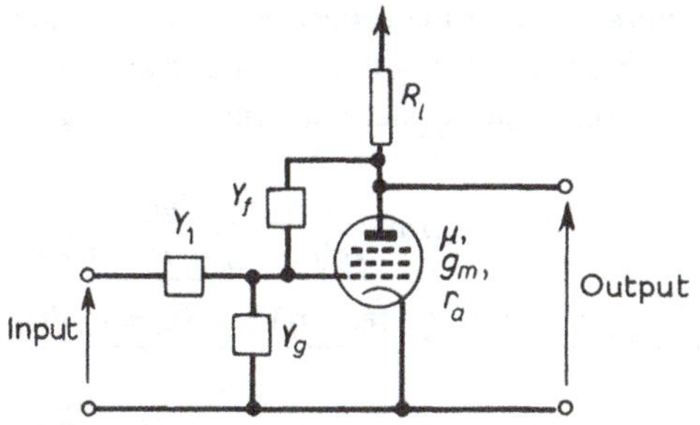

Compare the results with the corresponding ones for a cathode follower.

[*Ans.* $Y_1(Y_f - g_m)/\{(Y_1 + Y_f + Y_g)(Y_a + Y_l) + Y_f(Y_1 + Y_g + g_m)\}$
$= A$ say, where $Y_l = 1/R_l$ and $Y_a = 1/r_a$;
$Y_a + Y_f(Y_1 + Y_g + g_m)/(Y_1 + Y_f + Y_g)$;
$Y_1\{Y_g + (1 - A)\,Y_f\}/(Y_1 + Y_g + Y_f)$]

231. (*a*) Show that, for an amplifier which possesses voltage feedback, the output impedance is reduced in a ratio numerically equal to the voltage gain without feedback. Repeat the calculation for a circuit provided with current feedback, and thus prove that the output impedance is increased in the same ratio as the reduction in gain.

(*b*) Plot a Nyquist diagram† for a single-stage amplifier having a resistive load and negative voltage feedback, and investigate the stability of the circuit.

232. A junction transistor has the following constants: $r_{11} = 550\ \Omega$, $r_{12} = 500\ \Omega$, $r_{21} = 1.9$ MΩ, $r_{22} = 2$ MΩ. Determine the input resistance of a

* J. Millman, 'A Useful Network Theorem,' *Proc. I.R.E.*, **28**, p. 413, 1940. See also, F. A. Benson, *Electric Circuit Problems with Solutions*, Chapman and Hall, 2nd Edition, 1975, p. 183 or F. A. Benson and D. Harrison, *Electric-Circuit Theory*, Arnold, 3rd Edition, 1975, pp. 123–125.

† See H. Nyquist, 'Regeneration Theory,' *Bell System Tech. J.*, **11**, 126, 1932.

common-base amplifier stage using this transistor as the load resistance varies from zero to infinity.

If the resistance of the source at the input of the amplifier is zero find the output resistance of the arrangement.

Calculate, also, the maximum possible voltage gain.

[*Ans.* 75 to 550 Ω; 2.72×10^5 Ω; 3454]

233. Derive expressions for the voltage amplification, the current amplification, the input resistance, the output resistance and the power gain of a common-base transistor-amplifier stage in terms of the transistor parameters r_b, r_c, r_e and r_m.

[*Ans.* $\dfrac{(r_m + r_b)R_l}{r_b(r_c - r_m + R_l + r_e) + r_e(r_c + R_l)}$;

$(r_m + r_b)/(r_b + r_c + R_l)$; $(r_e + r_b) - r_b(r_b + r_m)/(r_b + r_c + R_l)$;

$r_c - \dfrac{r_b(r_m - R_g - r_e)}{R_g + r_e + r_b}$

$\dfrac{(r_m + r_b)^2 R_l}{(r_b + r_c + R_l)\{r_b(r_c - r_m + R_l + r_e) + r_e(r_c + R_l)\}}$

where R_g is the internal resistance of the source

and R_l is the load resistance]

234. Derive expressions for the voltage and current gains and the input and output resistance of the following transistor amplifiers in terms of the transistor parameters r_b, r_c, r_e and r_m:

(*a*) a common-emitter circuit, (*b*) a common-collector circuit.

[*Ans.* (*a*) $\dfrac{R_l}{r_b + \{(r_b + r_e)(r_c + R_l)/(r_e - r_m)\}}$;

$(r_e - r_m)/(r_e + r_c - r_m + R_l)$;

$r_b + \dfrac{r_e(r_c + R_l)}{r_c + r_e - r_m + R_l}$; $(r_c - r_m) + \dfrac{r_e(r_b + r_m + R_g)}{r_b + r_e + R_g}$

(*b*) $\dfrac{r_c R_l}{r_b(r_c - r_m + r_e + R_l) + r_c(r_e + R_l)}$;

$r_c/(r_e + r_c - r_m + R_l)$;

$$r_b + \frac{r_c(r_e - R_l)}{r_e + r_c - r_m + R_l}; r_e + \frac{(r_c - r_m)(r_b + R_g)}{r_b + r_c + R_g}$$

where R_g is the internal resistance of the source and R_l is the load resistance]

235. A junction transistor whose parameters are $r_{11} = 820\,\Omega$, $r_{12} = 800\,\Omega$, $r_{21} = 1.98\,\text{M}\Omega$ and $r_{22} = 2\text{M}\Omega$ is used in a single-stage, common-emitter amplifier, with a load resistance of 430 Ω.

Calculate the voltage gain, the current gain and the input resistance.

[*Ans.* $-15.2; \simeq 99; \simeq 2755\,\Omega$]

236. Derive the following expressions for the single-stage common-emitter transistor amplifier:

$$\text{Voltage gain} = \frac{-h_{fe} R_l}{h_{ie}(1 + h_{oe} R_l) - h_{re} h_{fe} R_l}$$

$$\text{Current gain} = \frac{-h_{fe}}{1 + h_{oe} R_l}$$

$$\text{Input resistance} = h_{ie} - \frac{h_{re} h_{fe} R_l}{1 + h_{oe} R_l}$$

where h_{ie}, h_{fe}, h_{re} and h_{oe} are the hybrid parameters and R_l is the load resistance.

A certain transistor has the following parameters:

$h_{ie} = 500\,\Omega$, $h_{re} = 2.5 \times 10^{-4}$, $h_{oe} = 12.5 \times 10^{-6}$ S, $h_{fe} = -11.5$.

It is used as a single-stage amplifier with a load resistance $R_l = 16$ kΩ. Determine the current gain, voltage gain and input resistance and, if the source resistance is 460 Ω, show that the output resistance is 64.5 kΩ.

[*Ans.* 9.6; 285; 538 Ω]

237. (*a*) Using equivalent circuits employing the a, r_b, r_c and r_e transistor parameters determine the current gain of the first stage of a two-stage RC-coupled, common-emitter transistor amplifier at low, intermediate and high audio frequencies. Hence, derive expressions for the two frequencies f_1 and f_2 where the gain falls to $1/\sqrt{(2)}$ of its intermediate frequency value.

(*b*) Draw equivalent circuits employing h parameters for an RC-coupled common-emitter transistor amplifier at intermediate and high audio frequencies. Hence, determine the voltage gains in these two frequency bands and obtain an expression for the gain-bandwidth product.

[see the Solution for the expressions]

238. A transistor biasing circuit giving a measure of stabilization of the working point is illustrated. Obtain a relationship between the stability factor S, the parameters R_b and R_c and the current amplification α of the transistor.

In a typical case $R_c = 10$ kΩ, $R_b = 100$ kΩ and $\alpha = 0.98$. Determine S.

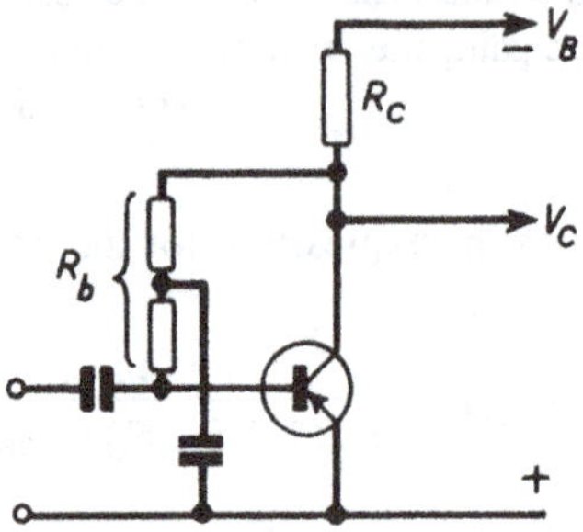

$$\left[Ans.\ S = \frac{R_b + R_c}{R_c + (1-\alpha)R_b}; 9.2\right]$$

239. A transistor bias stabilization circuit is illustrated. Show that the stability factor S is given by $(R_b + R_e)/\{R_e + R_b(1-\alpha)\}$ where $R_b = R_1R_2/(R_1 + R_2)$.

In a typical circuit $R_1 = 50$ kΩ, $R_2 = 20$ kΩ, $R_e = 2.5$ kΩ and $\alpha = 0.98$. Find S.

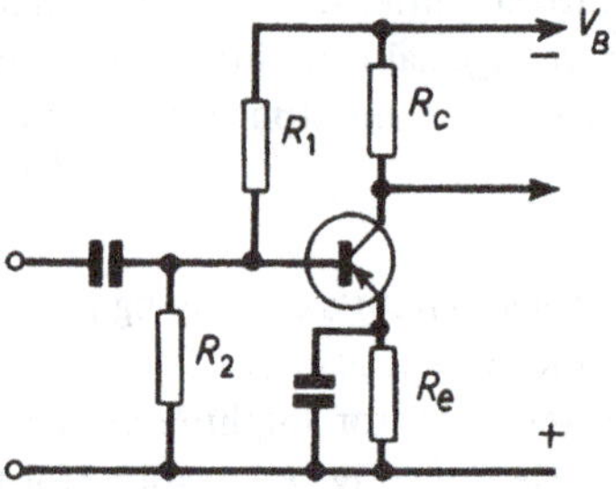

[*Ans.* 6]

240. For the field-effect transistor in the circuit illustrated $g_m = 5$ mS and $r_d = 30$ kΩ. Find the voltage gain v_o/v_s.

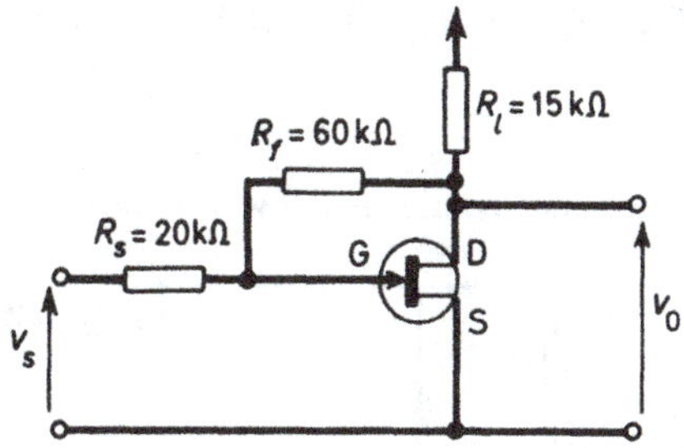

[*Ans.* 2.7]

241. Find the amplitude and phase of the output voltage of the amplifier shown at the frequencies of the input signal. The hybrid parameters of the transistor are: $h_{ie} = 1$ kΩ, h_{re} negligible, $h_{fe} = 120$ and $h_{oe} = 40$ μS.

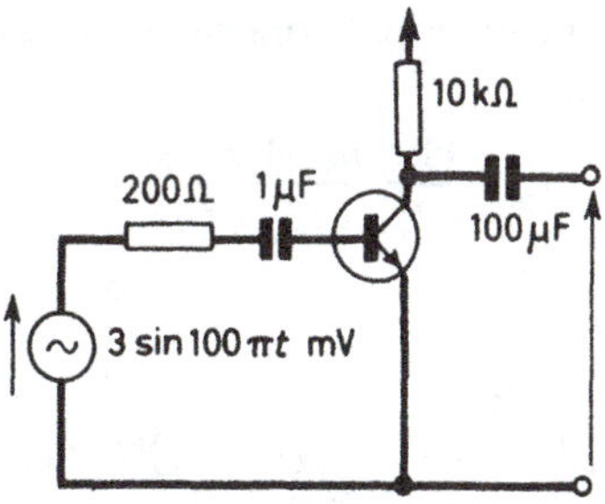

[*Ans.* 0.76 V; 200.6°]

242. The common-base h parameters for the transistor of Problem 236 are:

$$h_{ib} = 40\ \Omega,\ h_{rb} = 2.5 \times 10^{-4},\ h_{ob} = 10^{-6}\ \text{S},\ h_{fb} = -0.92.$$

If the transistor is used in a single-stage common-base amplifier with the same load and source resistances as in Problem 236 determine the current gain, voltage gain and input resistance and show that the output resistance is 685 kΩ.

[*Ans.* 0.905; 331; 43.5 Ω]

243. Repeat Problem 242 for a single-stage common-collector amplifier with the same load and source resistances and show that the output resistance in this case is about 77 Ω.

The common-collector h parameters for the transistor are:

$h_{ic} = 500\ \Omega, h_{rc} = 1, h_{oc} = 12.5 \times 10^{-6}\ \text{S}, h_{fc} = -12.5.$

[*Ans.* 10.4; 0.997; 167 kΩ]

244. The circuit shows an emitter-follower amplifier

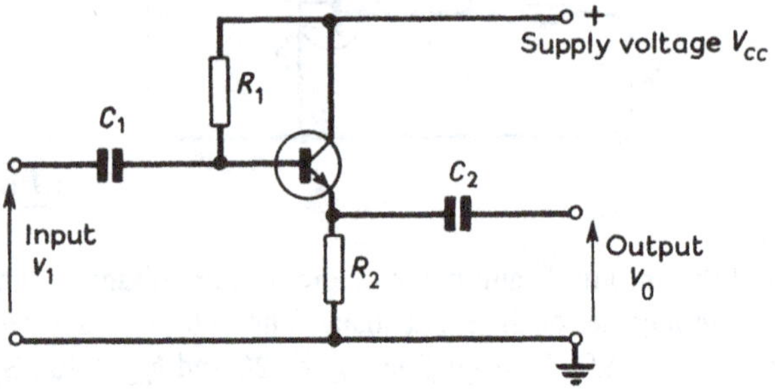

Draw the equivalent circuit using h parameters and analyse it to show that the input resistance is

$$h_{ie} + \frac{(1 - h_{re})(1 + h_{fe})}{h_{oe} + G_2 + G_l}$$

and the voltage gain is

$$\frac{1 + h_{fe}}{h_{ie}(G_l + G_2 + h_{oe}) + (1 - h_{re})(1 + h_{fe})}$$

where $G_2 = 1/R_2$ and the load on the amplifier due to the following circuits is assumed to be equivalent to a single component of admittance G_l.

245. Show that the equivalent h parameters of the Darlington connection illustrated at (a) can be represented by single equations in terms of the h parameters of the individual transistors. Extend the analysis to the 3-stage circuit at (b) and then to n stages.

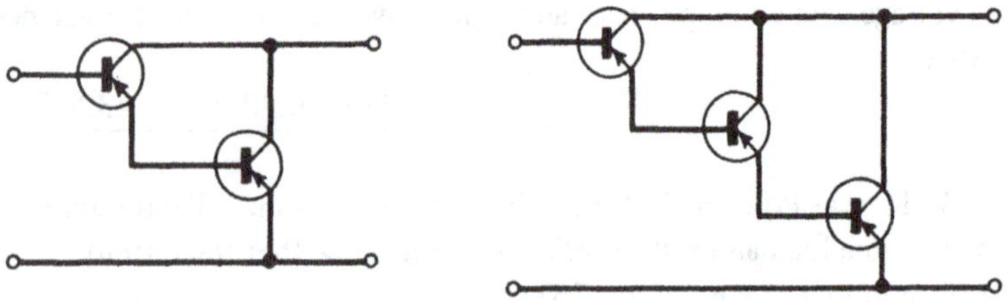

(a) (b)

246. A two-stage transistor amplifier is illustrated. The parameters of the transistors are as follows:

	T_1	T_2
h_{ie}	800 Ω	2400 Ω
h_{fe}	−24	−50
h_{re}	8×10^{-4}	25×10^{-4}
h_{oe}	20×10^{-6} S	45×10^{-6} S

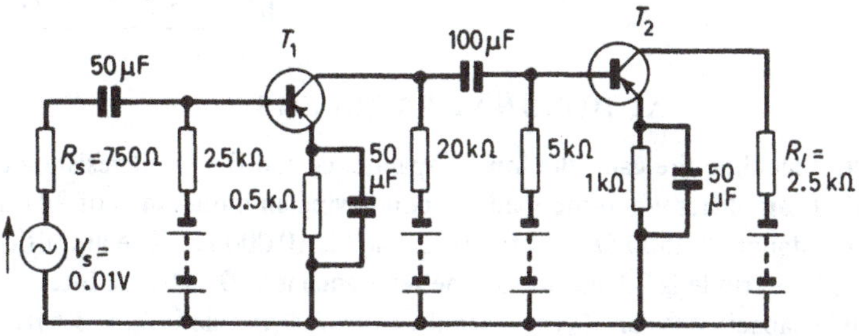

Calculate the overall current gain and the input resistance of the amplifier as presented to the generator terminals.

It may be assumed that for a common-emitter stage with a load of resistance R_l the current gain is

$$-h_{fe}/(1 + h_{oe}R_l)$$

and the input resistance is:

$$h_{ie} - \{h_{re}h_{fe}R_l/(1 + h_{oe}R_l)\}.$$

[*Ans.* 463; 623 Ω]

247. (*a*) A rectangular voltage pulse is applied to the input of an RC-coupled amplifier. Determine the transient performance of the amplifier for the cases of (*i*) a pentode amplifier (*ii*) a common-emitter transistor amplifier. Derive expressions for the output voltage during the rise time and after the constant-voltage portion of the pulse.

State the conditions for small distortion of the pulse. What is the relationship between sinusoidal and pulse responses of an R-C coupled amplifier?

(*b*) An RC-coupled amplifier has n identical stages. Show that the optimum number of stages to provide a specified overall gain A with minimum overall rise time is $n = 2 \ln A$.

248. A complementary transistor emitter-follower pair is used as a class-B output power amplifier* supplying a load R_L, consisting of a loudspeaker of purely resistive impedance 8 Ω. If the d.c. supplies, $\pm V_{cc}$, to the amplifier are ± 30 V calculate the maximum possible undistorted power in the load, assuming an ideal amplifier and a sinusoidal signal.

The two transistors with their heat sinks have a maximum total dissipation of 30 W. Given that maximum collector dissipation occurs when the peak collector current is $2V_{cc}/\pi R_L$ to what voltage would the d.c. supplies need to be reduced in order that the amplifier could safely supply power to two 8-Ω loudspeakers in parallel?

[*Ans.* 56 W; 24.4 V]

ADDITIONAL PROBLEMS

249. Calculate the gain, the input capacitance and the input resistance of a triode amplifier when the load is a coil having an inductance of 20 mH and a resistance of 2500 Ω, and the frequency is 10 000 Hz. The amplification factor of the triode is 20 and the anode resistance is 7700 Ω. The interelectrode capacitances are $C_{ga} = 3.4$ μμF, $C_{gc} = 3.4$ μμF and $C_{ac} = 3.6$ μμF. μμF. [*Ans.* 5.4 $\angle -160.4°$; 24.2 μμF; −2.564 MΩ]

250. The circuit illustrated provides an anode-load impedance that rises with decrease of frequency and can compensate for the reduction in gain at low frequencies caused by capacitor C.

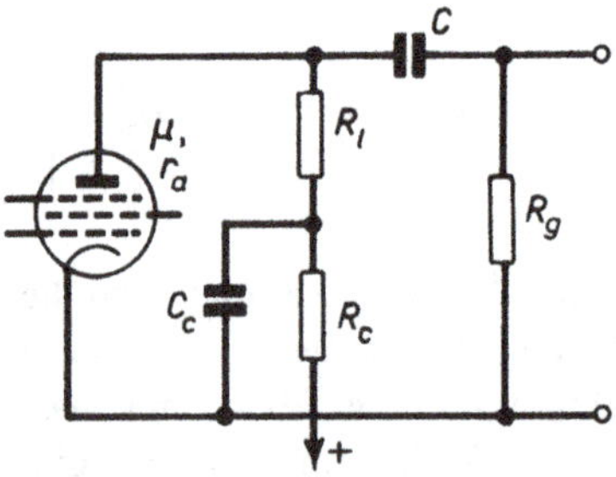

Assuming that R_g and r_a are large with respect to R_l, that the shunting effect of C and R_g on the load is negligible and that R_c is large compared with the reactance of C, show that if $C_cR_l = CR_g$ the low-frequency gain is independent of frequency.

* Transistor power amplifiers with output circuits and push-pull arrangements are discussed in many books. See, for example, S. Seely, *Electronic Circuits*, Holt, Rinehart and Winston, 1968, Chapter 6.

251. A triode in an amplifier has an anode resistance of 8000 Ω and an amplification factor of 16. It is coupled to the following stage by a transformer with a step-up ratio of 3. The secondary of the transformer is loaded with a resistance of 450 kΩ. Calculate the stage gain at a frequency where the primary reactance is 5 kΩ.

[*Ans.* 24.3]

252. A triode valve operates from a 300-V supply and its load is a resistor of 2000 Ω coupled through an ideal transformer of ratio 1:1. When a sinusoidal voltage is applied between the grid and the cathode of the valve, the maximum and minimum values of anode current are 150 mA and 20 mA. When the alternating grid voltage is zero, the anode current is 80 mA. Determine the power delivered to the load, the efficiency and the approximate percentage of second-harmonic current.

[*Ans.* 4.23 W; 0.17; 3.85 per cent]

253. The anode current of a triode can be expressed as $[I_a + B_o + B_1 \cos \omega t + B_2 \cos 2\omega t + B_3 \cos 3\omega t + B_4 \cos 4\omega t]$ when the input voltage to the grid is sinusoidal, and of the form $v_g = V_4 \cos \omega t$. Obtain a 5-point schedule by the Espley* method for determining B_0, B_1, B_2, B_3 and B_4 in terms of the anode currents for $\omega t = 0, \pi/3, \pi/2, 2\pi/3$ and π.

[*Ans.* $B_0 = (I_{max} + 2I' + 2I'' + I_{min})/6 - I_a$

$B_1 = (I_{max} + I' - I'' - I_{min})/3$

$B_2 = (I_{max} - 2I_a + I_{min})/4$

$B_3 = (I_{max} - 2I' + 2I'' - I_{min})/6$

$B_4 = (I_{max} - 4I' + 6I_a - 4I'' + I_{min})/12$

where I_{max}, I', I_a, I'' and I_{min} are the anode currents for $\omega t = 0$, $\pi/3, \pi/2, 2\pi/3$ and π respectively]

254. Two power triodes, each having characteristics as defined by the figures in the following tables, operate in class-A push-pull. Draw the composite characteristics if the quiescent point is at $V_a = 200$ V, $V_g = -20$ V. Draw also the composite load line for an anode-to-anode load of 5 kΩ.

Determine the power output of this push-pull amplifier when the peak input to each valve is 20 V.

* D. C. Espley, 'Harmonic Production in Thermionic Valves with Resistive Loads,' *Proc. I.R.E.*, 21, 1439–1446, 1933.

Grid voltage $V_g = 0$.

Anode voltage V_a (V) . .	0	40	80	120
Anode current I_a (mA) . .	0	13	32	52

Grid voltage $V_g = -20$ V.

Anode voltage V_a (V)	0	40	80	120	160	200	240
Anode current I_a (mA)	0	0	0	5	15	30	47

Grid voltage $V_g = -40$ V.

Anode voltage V_a (V)	0	40	80	120	160	200	240	280	320
Anode current I_a (mA)	0	0	0	0	0	3	9	19	33

[*Ans.* $\simeq$ 1.53 W]

255. A pentode in a tuned-amplifier circuit has an anode resistance of 500 kΩ and a mutual conductance of 5 mS. In its anode circuit is a 20-μH coil with a '*Q*' of 50, and this is tuned to parallel resonance at 1592 kHz. The output voltage is fed to a second stage of input resistance 500 kΩ through a coupling capacitor of negligible reactance. Calculate the gain of the stage at resonance.

[*Ans.* 48]

256. An amplifier employing a pentode with an amplification factor of 1000 and a mutual conductance of 5 mS has a 200-kΩ load resistor. Calculate the voltage amplification (*a*) without feedback, (*b*) with 5 per cent negative voltage feedback.

Determine also the effective constants of the valve when feedback is used.

[*Ans.* 500; 19.2; $\mu' = 19.6$; $r_a' = 3.92$ kΩ; $g_m' = 5$ mS]

257. The hybrid parameters for a transistor used in the common-emitter configuration are:

$$h_{ie} = 1.5 \text{ k}\Omega,\ h_{re} = 10^{-4},\ h_{fe} = 70,\ h_{oe} = 100\ \mu\text{S}.$$

The transistor has a 1-kΩ load resistor in the collector lead and is supplied from a signal source of resistance 800 Ω.

Calculate the input resistance, the output resistance, the voltage gain and the current gain for the stage.

[*Ans.* 1.5 kΩ; 10.3 kΩ; 27.7; 63.6]

258. The collector-current/collector voltage characteristics of a junction transistor in the common-emitter configuration with base current as parameter are given in the Table.

V_{CE} (V)	I_c (mA)		
	$I_b = 40\ \mu A$	$I_b = 80\ \mu A$	$I_b = 120\ \mu A$
0.5	0.6	1.8	2.4
2	0.8	2.8	4.8
6	1.0	3.0	5.0
12	1.3	3.3	5.3

The transistor is to be used as a common-emitter amplifier with a battery supply of 12 V and a collector load resistance of 2 kΩ. The quiescent operating point is $V_{CE} = 6$ V, $I_c = 3$ mA.

If the base current is changed 40 μA by a peak input signal of 100 mV, determine the current gain, the voltage gain and the power gain. Express the power gain in decibels.

[*Ans.* 46; 36; 1656; 32.2]

259. The collector characteristics of a certain transistor, when used in the common-emitter configuration may be assumed linear between the points given in the following table.

I_b (μA)	I_c (mA)	
	$V_c = -0.4$ V	$V_c = -10$ V
20	0.9	1.5
60	2.8	4.2
100	4.8	6.6
140	6.6	9.8

By drawing the output characteristics and superimposing the load line for the low-power transformer-coupled a.f. amplifier illustrated, estimate:

(*a*) mean input power,
(*b*) a.c. output power,
(*c*) efficiency,
(*d*) current gain } between base and collector
(*e*) voltage gain }

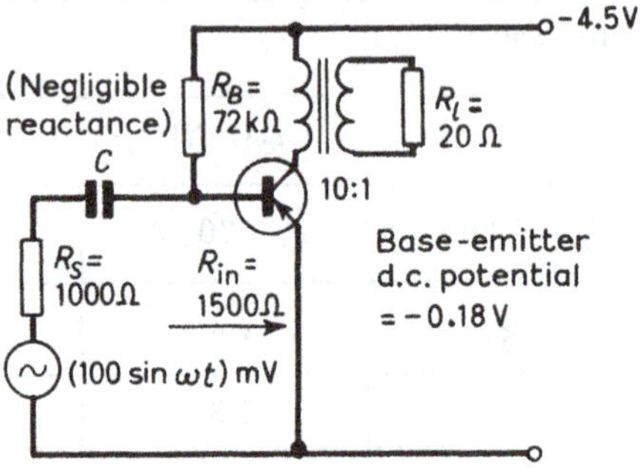

[*Ans.* 1.2 μW; 3 mW; 20 per cent; 45; 56]

260. In a single-stage, push-pull, class-A, transistor amplifier with an ideal transformer and a resistive load, the transistor characteristics may be represented by:

$$i_{c_1} = 300\,(v_{be_1} - 0.1) + 10\,(v_{be_1} - 0.1)^2$$

and

$$i_{c_2} = 250\,(v_{be_2} - 0.11) + 9\,(v_{be_2} - 0.11)^2,$$

where the collector currents are in milliamperes and the base-emitter voltage in volts.

The base bias voltage is − 350 mV at each transistor and the peak sinusoidal signal voltage is 100 mV to each base. Determine the percentage second harmonic distortion at the output.

[*Ans.* 0.009 per cent]

261. Compute the input resistance, output resistance, current gain and power gain for a common-base transistor amplifier having $r_e = 25\ \Omega$, $r_b = 500\ \Omega$, $r_c = 500\ \text{k}\Omega$, $a = 0.96$, $R_l = 25\ \text{k}\Omega$ and $R_s = 100\ \Omega$.

[*Ans.* 67.9 Ω; 116 kΩ; 0.914; 307]

262. Calculate the input and output resistances of a common-collector transistor stage with emitter load resistance of 5 kΩ. The working point is such that the equivalent – T parameters are as follows:

$$r_e = 40\ \Omega, r_b = 500\ \Omega, r_c = 1\ \text{M}\Omega, \alpha = 0.98.$$

[*Ans.* 201.5 kΩ; 50 Ω]

263. Show that the output resistance R_o for the common-base amplifier is:

$$R_o = r_{22} - \{r_{12}r_{21}/(R_s + r_{11})\}$$

Hence, using the junction transistor whose characteristics are given in Problem 232, plot a curve of R_o against R_s. If R_s varies from zero to infinity what are the limits of R_o?

[*Ans.* 270 kΩ and 2 MΩ]

264. Show that the input resistance R_i for the common-base amplifier is:

$$R_i = r_{11} - \{r_{12}r_{21}/R_l + r_{22})\}$$

Hence, using the junction transistor whose characteristics are given in Problem 232, plot a curve of R_i against R_l. Plot a similar curve for a transistor which has parameters $r_e = 25\ \Omega$, $r_b = 300\ \Omega$ and $\alpha = 0.98$ and prove that R_i must lie between 31 Ω and 325 Ω.

265. Find the voltage gain v_0/v_s and the output resistance for the transistor feedback amplifier stage shown. The transistor parameters h_{fe} and h_{ie} are 100 and 1200 Ω respectively and h_{re} and h_{oe} are negligible.

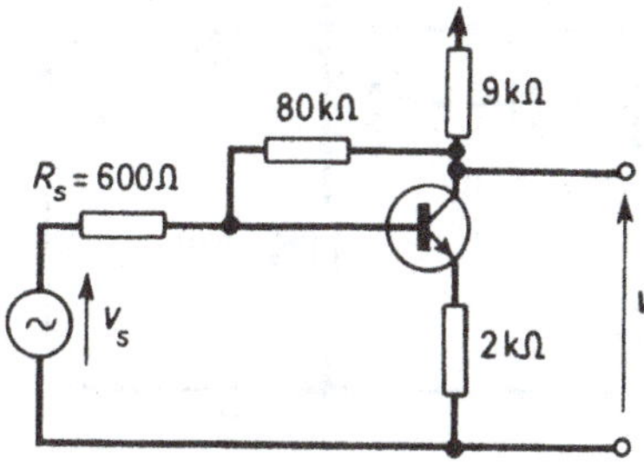

[*Ans.* 3.75; 7.9 kΩ]

266. A Darlington amplifier is illustrated.* Sketch as a function of frequency:

* The emitter follower and Darlington circuit are analysed in the following book which readers may like to consult. A. van der Ziel, *Introductory Electronics*, Prentice-Hall, 1974.

(*a*) the voltage gain v_0/v_s
(*b*) the current gain i_0/i_1
(*c*) the input impedance of the amplifier
(*d*) the phase shift from input to output.

Find the frequency at which the voltage gain drops by 3 dB from its higher frequency value.

The transistors are identical with $h_{ie} = 1$ kΩ and $h_{fe} = 120$. Both h_{re} and h_{oe} may be neglected.

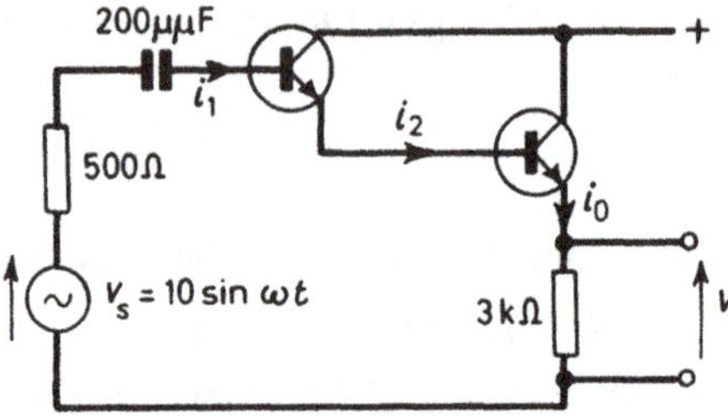

[*Ans.* 18 Hz]

267. The parameters of the FET in the circuit illustrated are $\mu = 40$, $r_d = 10$ kΩ. Determine (*a*) the voltage gain (*b*) the output resistance of the stage if $R_i = 0$.

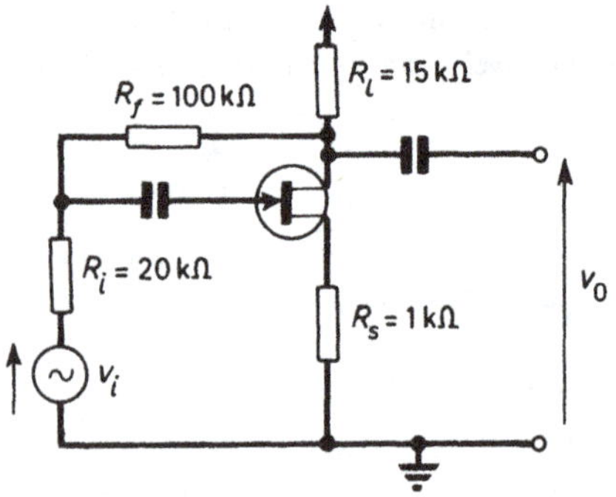

[*Ans.* (*a*) − 2.9, (*b*) 10.4 kΩ]

268. For the circuit shown using an *n*-channel JFET, with $g_m = 5$ mS and $r_d = 100$ kΩ evaluate

(*a*) the current gain I_l/I_s
(*b*) the voltage gain v_0/v_s

(*c*) the ratio I_l/v_s
(*d*) the ratio v_0/I_s
(*e*) the input resistance seen by the source,
(*f*) the output resistance seen by the load.

Neglect all capacitive effects.

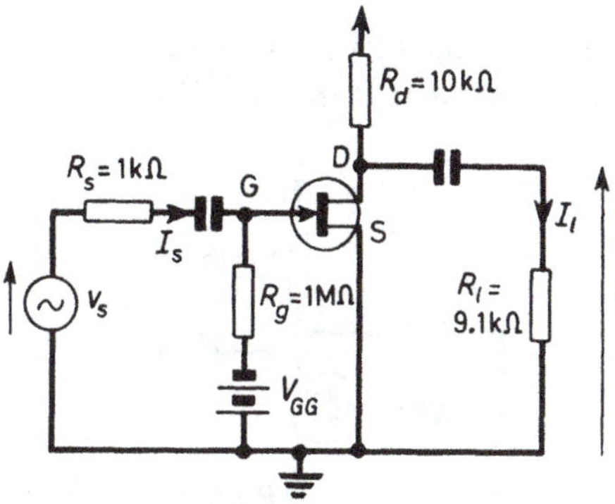

[*Ans.* (*a*) – 2500; (*b*) – 22.7; (*c*) – 2.5 S; (*d*) – 22.7 × 10^6 Ω; (*e*) 1 MΩ; (*f*) 9.1 kΩ]

269. A voltage amplifier employs a field-effect transistor with a 60-kΩ load resistor. When the resistance of the load is reduced to 65 per cent of its original value the gain decreases to 80 per cent of its initial value. The mutual conductance is 5 mS. For both values of the load find (*a*) the voltage gain and (*b*) the output resistance.

[*Ans.* (*a*) – 139, – 111, (*b*) 27.8 kΩ, 22.3 kΩ]

270. A field-effect transistor is used as a voltage amplifier with a load resistor of 40 kΩ and a gain of 40 is obtained. If the load resistance is halved the voltage gain drops to 30. Calculate the output resistance and the mutual conductance of the transistor.

[*Ans.* 20 kΩ, 3 mS]

271. A field-effect transistor is used as a voltage amplifier and with a 40-kΩ load resistor a gain of 40 is obtained. If the resistance of the load is halved the voltage gain drops to 30. Calculate the output resistance and the mutual conductance of the transistor.

[*Ans.* 20 kΩ; 3 mS]

272. A field-effect transistor is used as a voltage amplifier with a 45-kΩ load resistor. When the resistance of the load is halved the output resistance is reduced to 91 per cent of its original value. Find the voltage gain for both values of the load. The mutual conductance is 6×10^{-3} S.

[*Ans.* 26.7; 24.3]

273. The parameters of the FET shown are $g_m = 4$ mS and $r_d = 10$ kΩ. Find (*a*) the output resistance of the stage if $R_i = 0$ (*b*) the voltage gain taking into account R_i and R_f.

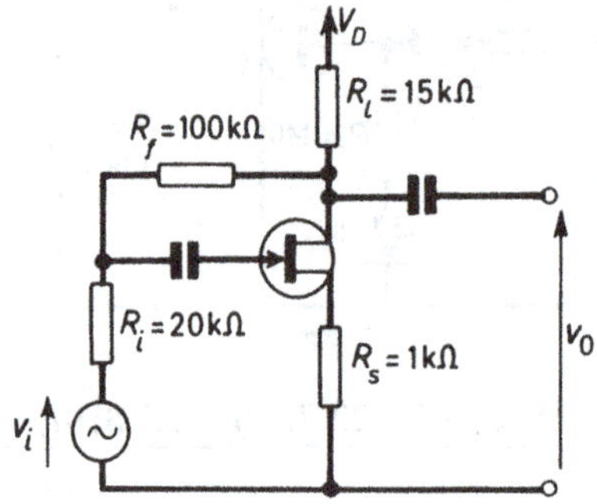

[*Ans.* 10.3 kΩ; − 3]

274. The transistor in the emitter-follower circuit shown has the following parameters: $h_{ie} = 2$ kΩ, $h_{fe} = 100$, $h_{oe} = 10^{-4}$ S and $h_{re} = 0$. It is desired to operate the transistor with a base current of 10 mA, a collector-emitter voltage of 5 V and a supply voltage V_{CC} of 10 V.

Determine suitable values for R_1 and R_2. What value of load resistor has to be placed across the output terminals in order to reduce the small-signal output voltage to one half of the open-circuit value? The input voltage V_1 is kept constant and the capacitors C_1 and C_2 may be assumed to have negligible reactance.

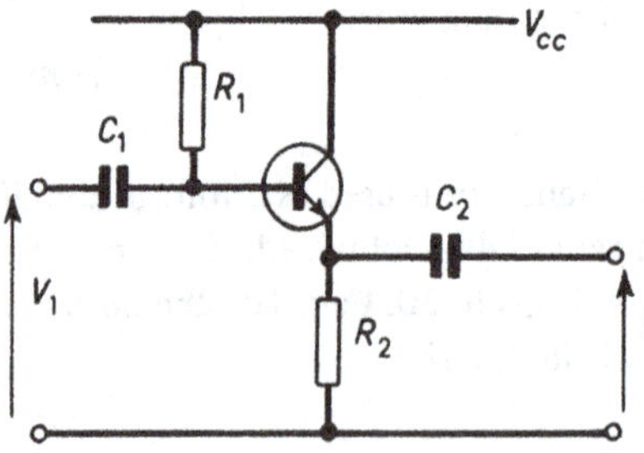

[*Ans.* 86 kΩ, 500 Ω, 19 Ω]

275. For the circuit illustrated show that the voltage gain V_0/V_s is

$$\frac{-h_{fe}R_l}{R_s + h_{ie} + (1 + h_{fe})(1 - \beta)R_e}$$ assuming that $h_{oe}(R_l + R_e) < 0.1$.

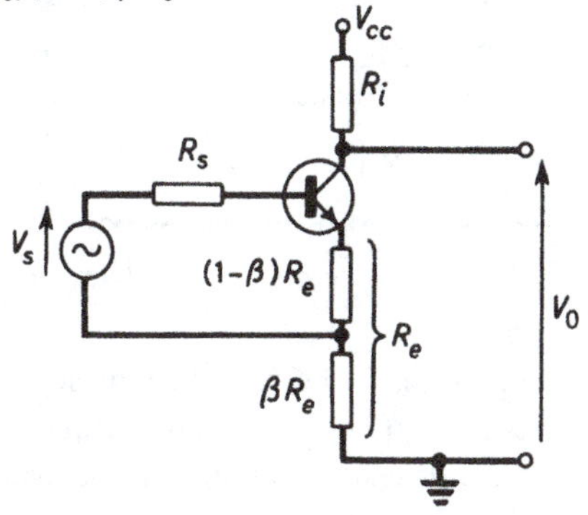

276. Calculate the overall voltage gain for the two-stage amplifier illustrated (supply voltages are not shown). The transistors are identical and have the following parameters:

$$h_{ie} = 1.1\ \text{k}\Omega,\ h_{re} = 2.5 \times 10^{-4},$$
$$h_{fe} = 50,\ h_{oe} = 24 \times 10^{-6}\ \text{S},$$
$$h_{ib} = 21.6\ \Omega,\ h_{rb} = 2.9 \times 10^{-4},$$
$$h_{fb} = -0.98,\ h_{ob} = 0.49 \times 10^{-6}\ \text{S}.$$

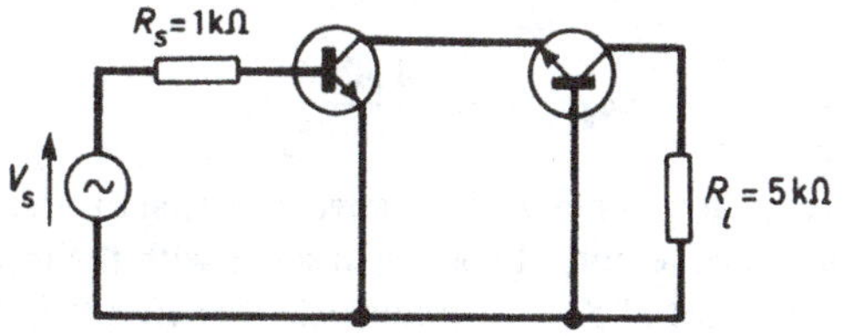

[*Ans.* 117]

277. Show that the exact expression for collector current to base current amplification for the circuit illustrated is

$$A_i = \frac{h_{fe}r_{oe} - R_e}{r_{oe} + R_L + R_e},\ \text{where}\ r_{oe} = 1/h_{oe}.$$

Given that the transistor parameters are $h_{fe} = 50$, $r_{oe} = 15$ kΩ, $h_{ie} =$ 800 Ω, $R_L = 12$ kΩ and $R_b \gg R_L$, find R_e to make $V_2 = -V_3$ and calculate V_2/V_1.

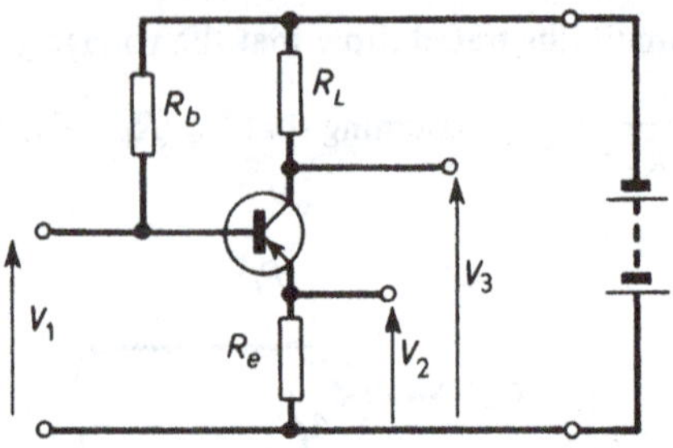

[*Ans.* 11.4 kΩ; 0.997]

278. Specify the frequencies f_1 and f_2 at the low- and high-frequency ends where the gain falls to $1/\sqrt{(2)}$ times its intermediate-frequency value for each stage of a four-identical-stage amplifier if the overall bandwidth is to extend from 100 Hz to 450 kHz.

[*Ans.* 44 Hz; 1023 kHz]

279. A transistor amplifier has five identical stages in cascade. If the overall gain at 100 kHz is 0.5 dB down on the mid-band gain calculate the upper 3-dB cut-off frequency for an individual stage.

[*Ans.* 472 kHz]

280. A three-stage transistor amplifier has an overall voltage gain A_v which may be represented by

$$A_v = -\frac{1000}{(1 + j\,10^{-5} f)^3}$$

where f is the frequency in hertz. A resistive potential divider feeds back a fraction $\beta = 1/150$ of the output voltage in series with the input.

Sketch the polar plot of βA_v for frequencies between 0 and infinity. Show that the amplifier is stable and calculate the percentage increase in stage gain to induce instability.

[*Ans.* 6.67 per cent]

281. Calculate the mid-band current gain of a two-stage common-emitter transistor amplifier if each stage has a 1-kΩ load resistor and a 100-kΩ resistor is connected between the base and negative supply to determine the operating point. The constants of the *p-n-p* transistors are $r_e = 30\ \Omega$, $r_b = 1\ \text{k}\Omega$, $r_c = 1\ \text{M}\Omega$ and $\alpha = 0.98$.

[*Ans.* 638]

282. Determine the d.c. operating point and stability factor S for the circuit illustrated if $I_{co} = 10\ \mu A$ and $\alpha = 0.972$.

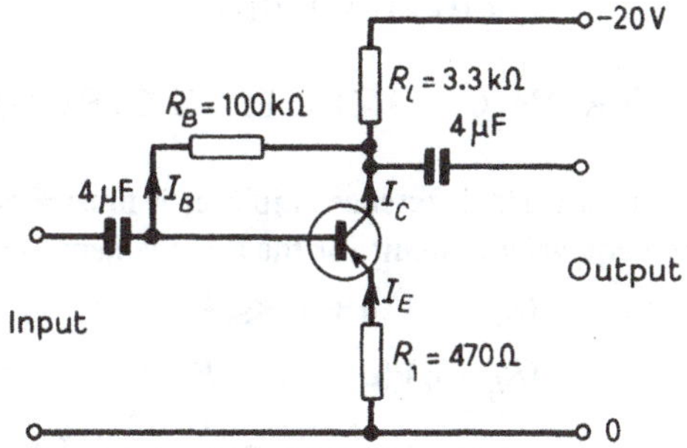

[*Ans.* $V_{CE} = -8$ V, $I_B = 80\ \mu A$, $I_c = 3.12$ mA; $S = 15.8$]

283. A common-emitter stage of the type shown has a collector load R_L of 2.7 kΩ. The supply voltage is 6 V and when conducting normally V_{BE} may be taken as 0.3 V. If the transistor has $\beta = 49$ and the operating value of the emitter current is to be 1 mA, calculate a suitable bias resistor R_B and hence determine the stability factor S.

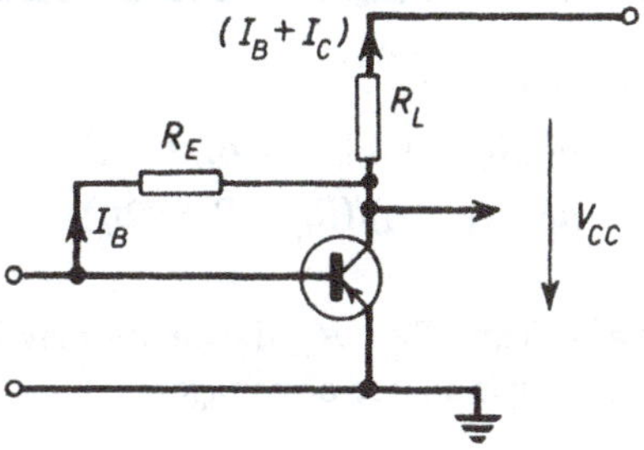

[*Ans.* 150 kΩ; 26.8]

CHAPTER EIGHT

ELECTRONIC COMPUTING CIRCUITS

284. A common-cathode difference amplifier is illustrated in the diagram. Draw the equivalent circuit for the arrangement and prove that, if

$$(R_{l_1} + r_a)/(\mu + 1) \ll R_c$$

and

$$(R_{l_2} + r_a)/(\mu + 1) \ll R_c$$

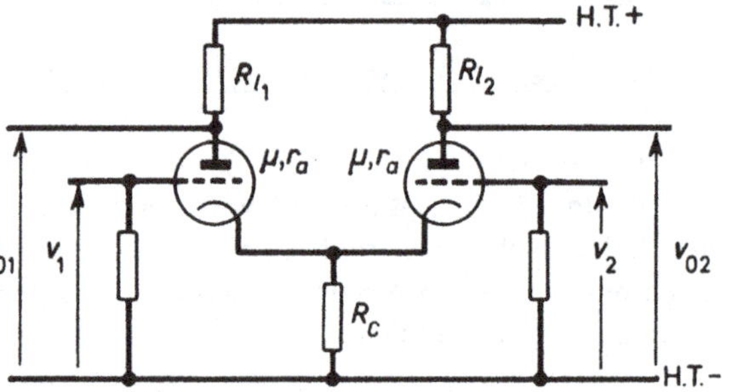

the output voltages v_{o1} and v_{o2} are

$$-\mu R_{l_1}(v_1 - v_2)/(R_{l_1} + R_{l_2} + 2r_a)$$

and

$$\mu R_{l_2}(v_1 - v_2)/(R_{l_1} + R_{l_2} + 2r_a)$$

respectively.

Show also that if $v_2 = 0$ and $R_{l_1} = R_{l_2}$, the circuit may be used to produce push-pull signals from a single source of voltage.

285. An emitter-coupled difference amplifier is illustrated. Show that $(v_{o_1} - v_{o_2})$ is proportional to $(v_1 - v_2)$.

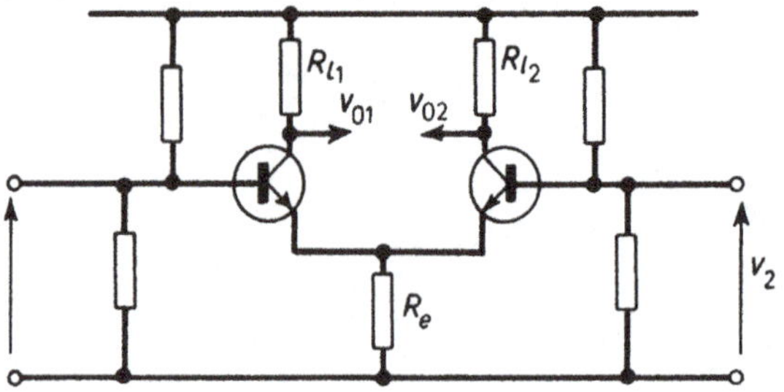

286. Cascode types of difference amplifier are shown in the diagrams. Analyse the operations of the circuits and show that the output voltage in the case of (*a*) is $v_0 = \mu(v_1 - v_2)/2$.

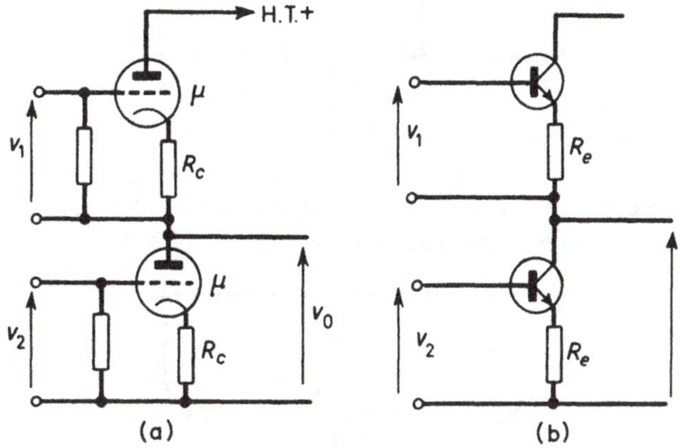

287. Simple feedback summing amplifiers are illustrated in the diagrams. Show that the output voltages v_0 are nearly equal to $-(v_1 + v_2 + v_3)$ if the voltage gains of the amplifiers without feedback are large. Assume the resistances R_1, R_2, R_3, R_f and R_b are equal, that R_g is large and i_b is negligible.

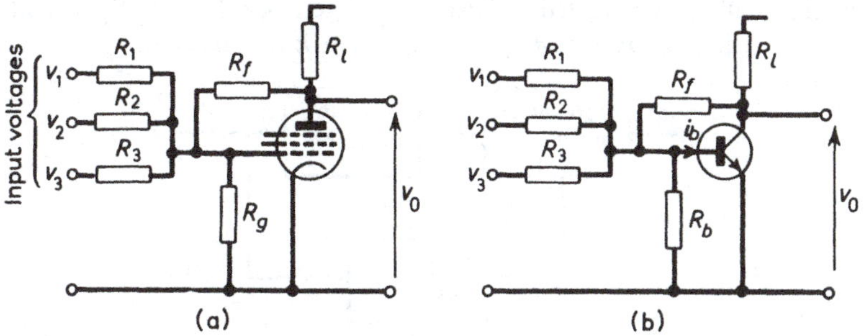

288. An arrangement for the addition of voltages in the cathode circuit of a chain of identical valves is shown in the diagram. Draw the equivalent circuit and apply Millman's network theorem* to show that the output voltage $\simeq \mu \Sigma e_n / n(\mu + 1)$ where n is the number of stages.

* J. Millman, 'A Useful Network Theorem,' *Proc. I.R.E.*, **28**, 413, 1940. See also, F. A. Benson, *Electrical Engineering Problems with Solutions*, Spon, 1954, pp. 17–18 and pp. 104–109.

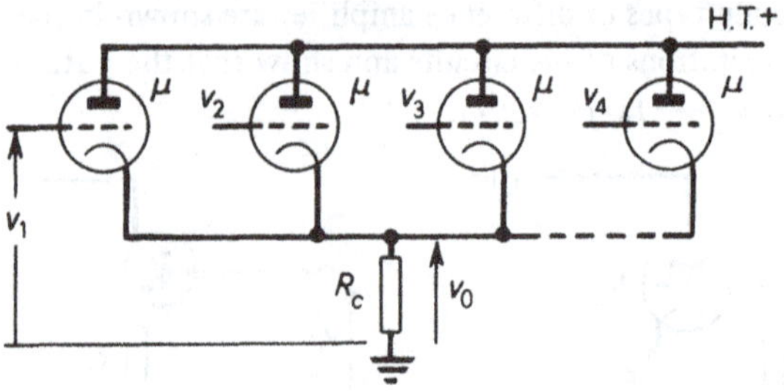

The corresponding common-emitter summing chain is illustrated in the diagram below. Analyse the circuit to show that $v_0 \simeq (\Sigma\, v_n)/n$.

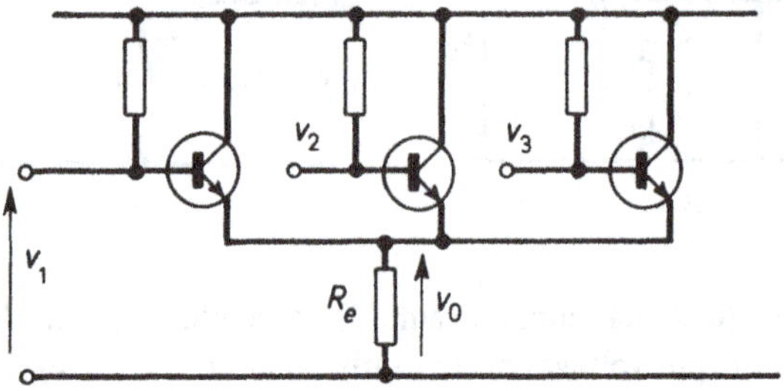

289. A difference amplifier, an ordinary amplifier of gain A and a squaring circuit are connected as illustrated in the block diagram. Show that, if A is large, the output voltage v_o is $k\sqrt{(v_i)}$ where k is a constant.

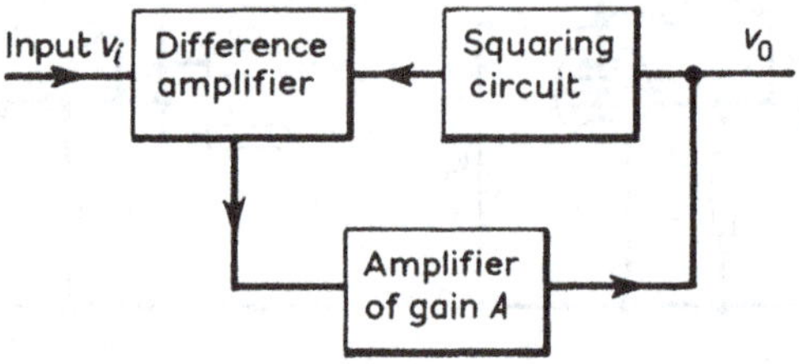

290. A difference amplifier, an ordinary amplifier of gain A and a multiplying circuit are connected as illustrated in the block diagram. Show that, if A is large, the output voltage v_o is $k\, v_{i_1}/v_{i_2}$ where k is a constant.

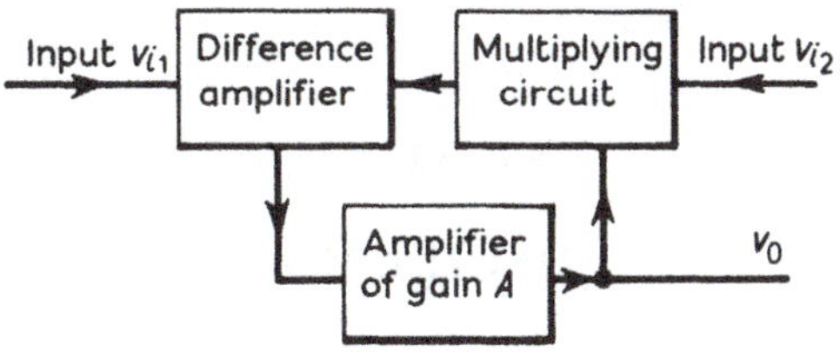

ADDITIONAL PROBLEMS

291. For the summing amplifier shown, what is the percentage error involved in the output sum if the amplifier is assumed ideal except for a finite voltage gain of 80 dB?

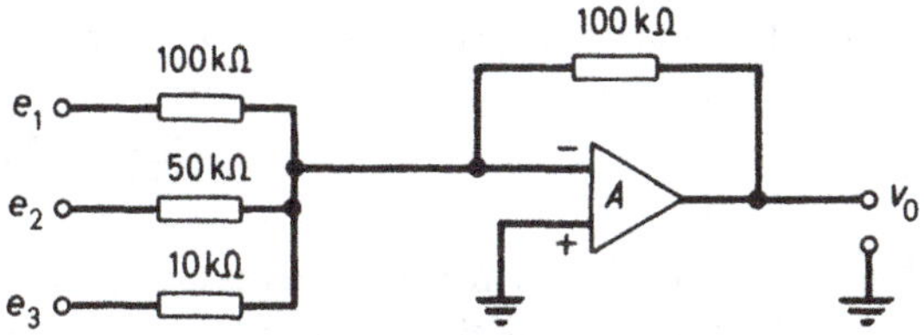

[*Ans.* 0.14 per cent]

292. Two matched FET's with $g_m = 5$ mS and drain conductance of 150 μS when at a working point of $V_{DS} = +5$ V, $I_D = 1$ mA and $V_{GS} = -2$ V form a differential amplifier between + 25 V and − 25 V supply lines as illustrated. Calculate (*a*) R_2 and R_3, (*b*) the gain for a single input signal (i.e. $v_2 = 0$) if $1/R_3$ is negligible.

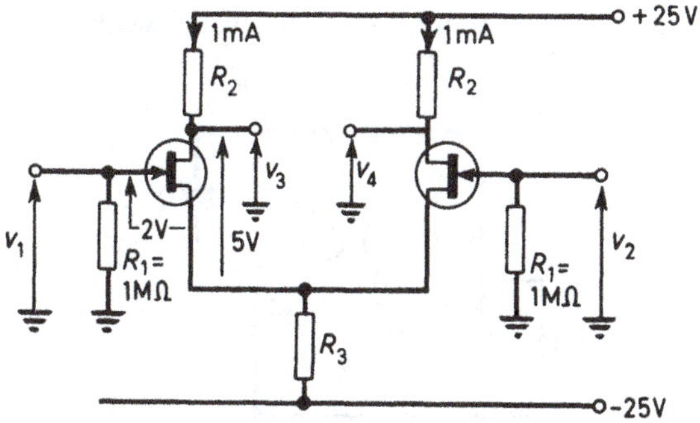

[*Ans.* (*a*) 18 kΩ, 13.5 kΩ, (*b*) −24.4]

CHAPTER NINE

OSCILLATORS

293. A certain triode with an amplification factor of 9 has an anode resistance of 11 000 Ω when the anode and grid voltages are 90 V and −6 V respectively, and an anode resistance of 9000 Ω when the anode and grid voltages are 135 V and −9 V respectively. A tuned-anode circuit has $L = 175\ \mu H$, $C = 220\ \mu\mu F$ and $R = 18\ \Omega$. The grid coil has an inductance of $60\ \mu H$. With the higher anode voltage, what coefficient of coupling is required between the coils to make the circuit oscillate? How much must the coupling be if the anode voltage is dropped to 90 V and the bias adjusted accordingly?

[*Ans.* 0.228; 0.237]

294. Using a certain triode, having an amplification factor of 5 and an anode resistance of 1800 Ω, it is desired to generate a frequency of 25 Hz in a tuned-anode circuit. Two coils, each of 0.6 H inductance and 11 Ω resistance, are available, the maximum attainable coupling between them being 32 per cent. Can the required oscillations be produced with this arrangement?

What is the lowest frequency at which the circuit will oscillate?

[*Ans.* No; 48.3 Hz]

295. A tuned-drain FET oscillator is shown. Determine the frequency of oscillation and the condition for maintenance of oscillation.

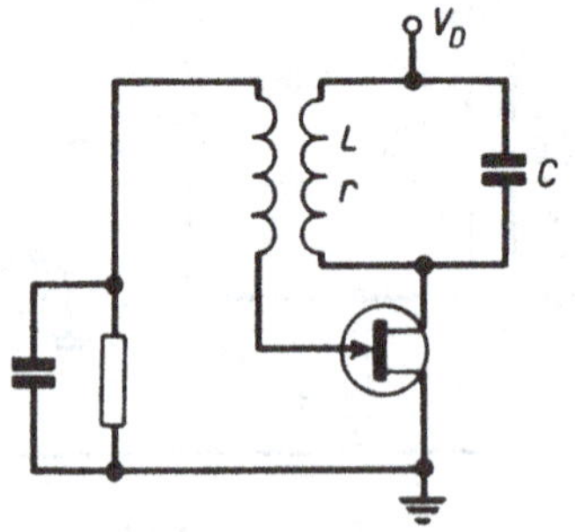

[*Ans.* $\frac{1}{2\pi}\sqrt{\{(r_a + r)/r_aLC\}}$; $M = (L + r_arC)/\mu$]

296. The circuit illustrates a tuned-collector oscillator. Assuming low-frequency sinusoidal operation derive an expression for the angular frequency of oscillation. The collector resistance is high enough to be ignored. The bias components R_b and C_b can be assumed to have a negligible effect on the a.c. equivalent circuit. Neglect the resistance of coil L_2.

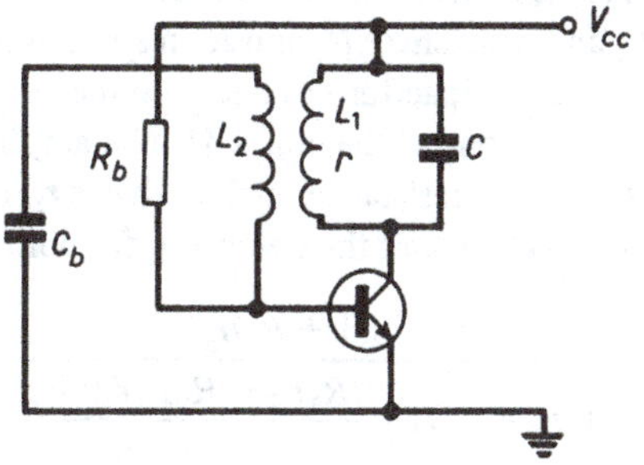

[*Ans.* $\sqrt{(R/\{L_1CR + L_2C(1-\alpha)r\})}$ where $R = r_e + r_b(1-\alpha)$]

297. A triode, with an amplification factor of 9 and an anode resistance of 11 000 Ω, has a tuned-grid circuit with constants of values $L = 180\ \mu$H, $R = 26\ \Omega$ and $C = 0.0012\ \mu$F. The coil in the anode circuit has an inductance of 50 μH and a coupling of 30 per cent to the grid circuit. Will the circuit oscillate?

[*Ans.* No]

298. Prove that for all valve oscillators

$$[Z + r_a/(1 + \mu N)] = 0$$

where Z is the impedance of the whole external circuit connected between the anode and cathode of the valve, N is the complex ratio $[V_g/V_a]$ between the grid and anode voltage phasors, μ is the amplification factor of the valve and r_a the anode resistance of the valve.

Use this theorem to determine the frequency of oscillation of a simple tuned-anode oscillator. Determine also the condition necessary for continuous oscillation.

[*Ans.* $\frac{1}{2\pi}\sqrt{\left(\frac{r_a+R}{r_aLC}\right)}$; $M = (L + r_aRC)/\mu$ (R, L and C are the oscillatory circuit constants, and M is the mutual inductance between grid and anode coils)]

299. In a certain Hartley oscillator the inductance of each coil is 20 mH and the capacitor has a capacitance of 0.1 μF. Determine the frequency of oscillation if there is no mutual inductance between the coils. Neglect losses. Find also the coefficient of coupling which will reduce the frequency to 2 kHz,

[*Ans.* 2.517 kHz; 0.584]

300. In a class-A Hartley oscillator the two sections of the coil have inductances L_1 and L_2 and resistances R_1 and R_2 respectively, the latter being in the grid circuit. The capacitor has a capacitance of C. The mutual inductance between the sections of the coil is M. The amplification factor of the valve is μ and the anode resistance of the valve is r_a. Derive expressions for the frequency of oscillation, and the condition for continuous oscillations.

[*Ans.*

$$f=\frac{1}{2\pi}\sqrt{\left(\frac{1+R_1/r_a}{C\left[(L_1+L_2+2M)+\dfrac{(R_1L_2+R_2L_1)(1+\mu)-\mu MR_1}{r_a}\right]}\right)};$$

$$(r_a+R_1)(R_1+R_2)-\omega^2(L_1-\mu M)(L_1+L_2+2M)+(L_1-\mu M)/C$$
$$=R_1(R_1-\mu R_2)-\omega^2(L_1+M)(L_1+M-\mu L_2-\mu M) \text{ where } \omega=2\pi f]$$

301. The coil in the tuned circuit of a Colpitts oscillator has an inductance L and a resistance R. The two capacitors have capacitances C_1 and C_2. The valve has an amplification factor μ and an anode resistance r_a. Determine the frequency of oscillation, and the condition for steady oscillations.

$$[\textit{Ans. } f=\omega/2\pi=\frac{1}{2\pi}\sqrt{\left(\frac{1}{L}\left\{\frac{1}{C_2}(1+R/r_a)\right\}\right)};$$

$$(1+\mu)/\omega^2C_1C_2=r_aR+L/C_1]$$

302. Show that for maintenance of oscillations in a transistor Colpitts oscillator circuit

$$C_1/C_2=\{r_m\pm\sqrt{[r_m^2-4(r_c-r_m)(r_b+r_e)]}\}/2(r_b+r_e),$$

where C_1 and C_2 are the tuned-circuit capacitances and r_b, r_c, r_e and r_m are the usual transistor parameters. It must be assumed in deriving the expression that the frequency of oscillation is given by $1/2\pi\sqrt{(LC)}$ and $r_e \ll r_m$, where L is the inductance of the tuned circuit.

Determine, also, the exact frequency of oscillation for the circuit and show that changes of the transistor parameters r_c and r_e are important when considering frequency stability.*

[*Ans.* $(1/2\pi)\sqrt{(1/LC + 1/xC_1C_2)}$, where $C = C_1C_2/(C_1 + C_2)$ and $x = r_br_c + r_br_e + r_cr_e - r_br_m$]

303. The essential parts of a transistor Hartley oscillator are as illustrated.

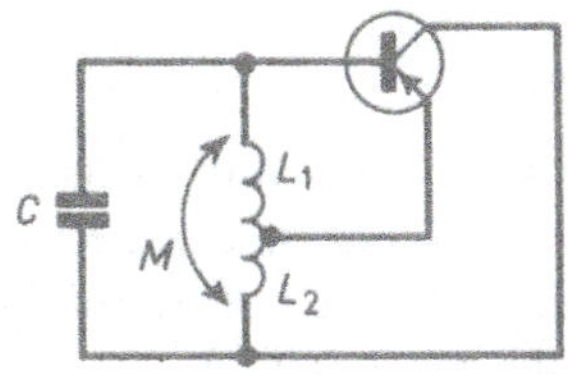

Show that the frequency of oscillation (f) is given by:

$$f = \frac{1}{2\pi}\sqrt{\left\{\frac{1}{C(L_1 + L_2 + 2M) - (L_1L_2 - M^2)/k}\right\}}$$

where $k = (r_b + r_e)r_c + r_b(r_e - r_m)$, r_b, r_c, r_e and r_m being the usual transistor parameters.

Prove, also, that for maintenance of oscillations the oscillator requires that:

$$(L_2 + M)/(L_1 + M) \geqslant r_m/(r_b + r_e)$$

304. A crystal-oscillator circuit is illustrated. Determine the frequency of oscillation if the equivalent circuit of the crystal is assumed loss-free.

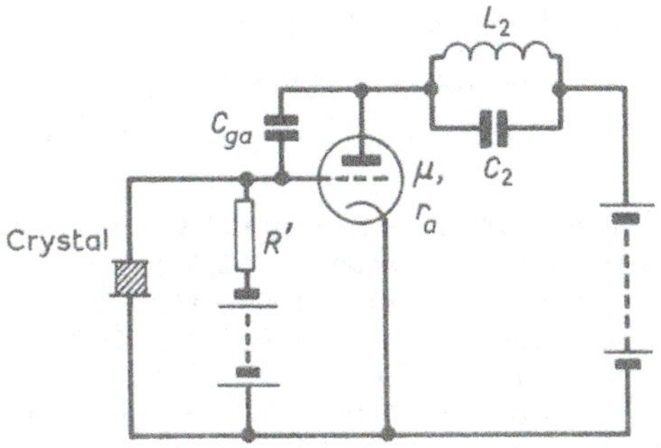

* Analyses of the transistor Colpitts oscillator using h parameters have been given by many authors. See, for example, R. J. Maddock, *Intermediate Electronics Book 1*, Butterworths, 1969, pp. 282–286.

[*Ans.* $\frac{1}{2\pi}\sqrt{\left(\frac{1}{LC}\left[\frac{1+(1+C_1/C_{ga}+C/C_{ga})/\mu}{1+(1+C_1/C_{ga})/\mu}\right]\right)}$

where L, C and C_1 are the crystal constants.

305. In a certain Wien-bridge type of oscillator* the frequency-selective network employs 120-kΩ resistors and 0.001-μF capacitors. Find the frequency of oscillation.

[*Ans.* 1326 Hz]

306. A three-section ladder phase-shift oscillator* has three similar phase-advancing sections, each consisting of a 100-kΩ resistor and a 0.0005-μF capacitor. Calculate the frequency of oscillation, and show that the attenuation ratio of the network is 29.

[*Ans.* 1300 Hz]

307. Repeat the calculation of Question 306 for a similar oscillator having three phase-retarding sections.

[*Ans.* 7800 Hz]

308. A fourth similar section is added to the phase-shift network of Question 306. Calculate the new frequency of oscillation and the attenuation ratio of the network.

[*Ans.* 2663 Hz; 18.39]

309. Show that the period of oscillation of the simple discharge-tube relaxation oscillator of the type illustrated is

$$CR \log_e\{(V-V_e)/(V-V_s)\}$$

where V_s is the striking voltage of the tube and V_e is the extinction voltage.

* A good account of such oscillators is given by T. P. Flanagan, 'Resistor-Capacitor Oscillator Design,' *Marconi Instrumentation*, 3, p. 82, May, 1952. An oscillator using the Wien-bridge network and valves has been described by F. E. Terman, R. R. Buss, W. R. Hewlett and F. C. Cahill, 'Some Applications of Negative Feedback with Particular Reference to Laboratory Equipment,' *Proc. I.R.E.*, 27, 649, 1939.

The ladder phase-shift networks were first fully described by E. L. Ginzton and L. M. Hollingsworth, 'Phase-shift Oscillators,' *Proc. I.R.E.*, 29, 43, 1941.

Complete circuit diagrams of some transistor R-C oscillators of the Wien-bridge type and employing ladder networks have been given in the Mullard Reference Manual on Transistor Circuits, 1st Edition, 1960.

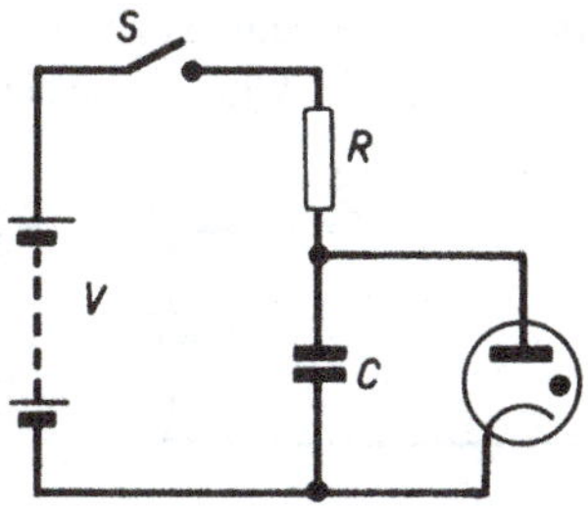

310. In a certain thyratron relaxation oscillator the capacitor has a capacitance of 0.01 μF and the resistor has a resistance of 500 kΩ. The supply voltage is 250 V. The thyratron has a control ratio of 30 and its extinction voltage is 20 V. Find the grid bias required to give an oscillation amplitude of 100 V.

What is the period of oscillation under these conditions?

[*Ans.* -4 V; 2.83×10^{-3} s]

311. In a symmetrical multivibrator each valve has an anode voltage of 110 V with the coupling capacitor removed, and the static cut-off grid bias is 20 V with full anode voltage. The h.t. supply voltage is 250 V. Calculate the frequency of oscillation when each capacitor has a capacitance of 0.005 μF and each grid resistor has a resistance of 50 kΩ.

[*Ans.* 1027 Hz]

312. Determine the beat frequency when a signal of 300-m wavelength is combined with the output of a 1.3-MHz oscillator.

If a second signal of 400-m wavelength is now received to what frequency must the oscillator be tuned to provide the same beat frequency as before?

[*Ans.* 300 kHz; 1050 kHz]

313. A voltage source with a frequency range of 50 to 10 000 Hz is required. Calculate the ratio of the maximum/minimum values of capacitance required (*a*) in a single feedback type of oscillator, (*b*) using the beat-frequency method, where the oscillator with the lower frequency operates at 100 kHz.

[*Ans.* 4×10^4; 1.2]

314. A possible equivalent circuit for a tunnel diode is illustrated. Derive an expression for the input impedance and calculate the frequencies for which the real and quadrature components are zero if $R = 1.5\ \Omega$, $L = 0.01\ \mu H$, $C = 50\ \mu\mu F$ and $r = -25\ \Omega$. What is the significance of the results?

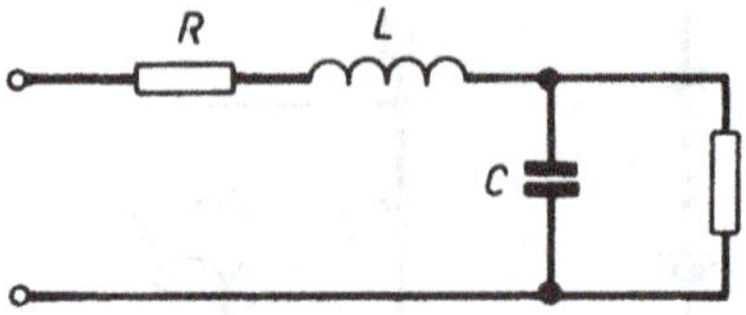

ADDITIONAL PROBLEMS

315. A triode, with an amplification factor of 8 and an anode resistance of 6000 Ω, has a tuned anode circuit of $L = 200\ \mu H$, $R = 8\ \Omega$ and $C = 0.0005\ \mu F$. The grid coil has an inductance of 35 μH. The maximum available coupling is 40 per cent. To the tuned circuit is coupled a tuned antenna having a resistance of 24 Ω. Determine the maximum permissible mutual inductance between the antenna and the tuned circuit if oscillations are to be maintained.

[*Ans.* 5.94 μH]

316. A tuned-collector oscillator employs a collector coil of inductance 1.5 mH and resistance 100 Ω tuned to a nominal frequency of $(10^6/2\pi)$ Hz by a shunt capacitor. The base coil has inductance 0.15 mH and resistance 10 Ω with a coupling coefficient k of 0.01. If the parameter h_{ie} for the transistor is 1 kΩ and h_{oe} can be neglected evaluate the actual frequency of oscillation and the minimum value of h_{fe}.

[*Ans.* 158 kHz; 14.2]

317. Determine approximately the condition necessary for maintaining oscillations in a tuned-grid circuit, using a triode with an amplification factor of 10 and an anode resistance of 10 000 Ω, when the tuning capacitance is 0.01 μF and the grid-coil resistance is 100 Ω.

[*Ans.* Mutual inductance = 1 mH]

318. In a class-A Hartley oscillator the two sections of the coil have inductances of 45 mH and 15 mH, the latter being in the grid circuit. The capacitor has a capacitance of 0.2 μF. The amplification factor of the valve is 20. Neglecting losses, calculate the critical mutual inductance for maintaining oscillations.

[*Ans.* 13.42 mH]

319. A triode valve has a coil in its anode circuit of inductance L_2 and resistance R_2. In the grid-cathode circuit of the valve is a second coil of inductance L_1 and resistance R_1. There is no magnetic coupling between the coils, but a capacitor of capacitance C is connected between the anode and grid of the valve. The valve has an amplification factor μ and an anode resistance r_a. Determine the condition for maintenance of oscillations in this circuit, and the corresponding frequency. Neglect valve-electrode capacitances.

[*Ans.* $r_a(R_1 + R_2) + R_1R_2(1 + \mu) + L_2/C = \omega^2 L_1 L_2(1 + \mu)$;

$$f = \omega/2\pi = \frac{1}{2\pi}\sqrt{\left(\frac{1 + R_2/r_a}{C[L_1 + L_2 + (R_1L_2 + R_2L_1)(1 + \mu)/r_a]}\right)}$$]

320. Indicate, by means of a sketch, how the circuit illustrated may be utilized in conjunction with a suitable transistor amplifier to form an oscillator and show that the frequency of oscillation f is given by:

$$f = \sqrt{(1 + 2n + 3n^2)}/2\pi nCR$$

provided the gain exceeds $-(8 + \frac{12}{n} + \frac{7}{n^2} + \frac{2}{n^3})$

Assume the input impedance to the amplifier is infinite and the output impedance zero.

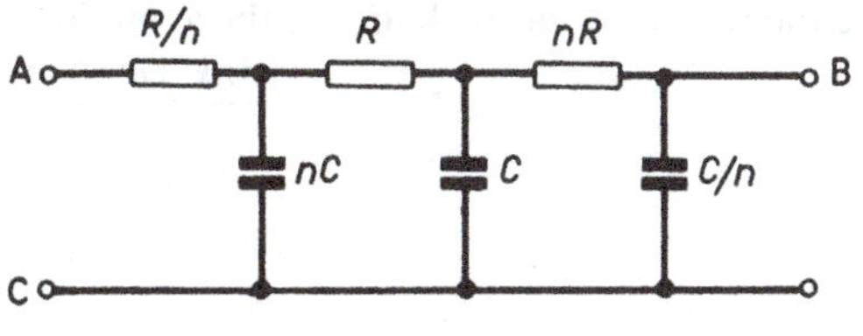

If this oscillator circuit is now rearranged so that the amplifier input terminals are connected to points A and B and the output terminals to points A and C, utilise the results from the first calculation to determine the frequency of oscillation and minimum gain for maintenance of oscillations if $n = 2$, $C = 0.01$ μF and $R = 100$ kΩ.

[*Ans.* 328 Hz; 0.94]

321. A crystal to be used in an oscillator circuit has the following parameters (see Problem 304):

$L = 0.33$ H, $C = 0.065$ $\mu\mu$F, $C_1 = 1$ $\mu\mu$F and $R = 5.5$ kΩ.

What is the series-resonant frequency? Find by what percentage the parallel-resonant frequency exceeds the series-resonant frequency. Evaluate the 'Q' factor for the crystal.

[*Ans.* 1.09 MHz; 3.3; 410]

322. A glow-discharge tube relaxation oscillator is supplied at 200 V. The striking and extinction voltages of the tube are 160 V and 120 V, respectively. Calculate the resistance to be used with a 0.04-μF capacitor for a frequency of oscillation of 100 Hz.

Determine also the percentage change in frequency if the supply voltage drops by 1 per cent.

[*Ans.* 360.7 kΩ; $-$3.66 per cent]

323. A voltage amplifier has three identical stages each having a voltage amplification A at frequency f hertz where

$$A = 50/\{1 + j(f/f_o)\}$$

where $f_o = 10^4$ Hz.

Voltage feedback is provided by a resistive network connected to feed back a fraction β of the output voltage. The feedback is negative at low frequencies. By using the Nyquist diagram,* or otherwise, calculate the largest value of β which can be used without the amplifier becoming unstable.

What will be the frequency of oscillation if the amplifier is unstable?

[*Ans.* 1/15625; 17.3 kHz]

* Readers who wish to read about the condition for stability and the Nyquist criterion should see, for example, J. Millman and C. C. Halkias, *Integrated Electronics: Analog and Digital Circuits and Systems*, McGraw-Hill, 1972, Section 14–9.

CHAPTER TEN

NOISE

324. Calculate the r.m.s. value of the noise voltage developed across a 1000-Ω resistor at a temperature of 290 K in a frequency band of 10 MHz.

Show that this noisy resistor can be regarded, as far as the effect of thermal-agitation noise is concerned, as a noise-free resistor in parallel with a generator supplying a constant current of 12.66×10^{-9} A.

[*Ans.* 12.66 μV]

325. Evaluate the r.m.s. component of noise current in a 20-kHz bandwidth due to a random current of 1 mA.

[*Ans.* 2.53×10^{-9} A]

326. The emission current of a temperature-limited diode is 10 mA. Determine the r.m.s. value of the fluctuation components of the current in a 20-kHz bandwidth.

[*Ans.* 7.98×10^{-9} A]

327. A resistor of R_1 ohms is placed in parallel with a capacitor of C farads. Find the noise voltage across the combination in the frequency band 0 to ∞.

[*Ans.* $\sqrt{(kT/C)}$ where k is Boltzmann's constant and T is the absolute temperature]

328. It is convenient to interpret the noise in a triode as being due to a noisy resistor in series with the grid of a noise-free valve. Calculate the value of this noisy resistor for a triode with a mutual conductance g_m equal to 2.6 mS.

[*Ans.* 961 Ω]

329. The noise of a pentode can be supposed to be due to a noisy resistor in series with the control grid of a noise-free valve. Estimate the value of this noisy resistor for a pentode in which the anode current is

10 mA, the screen-grid current is 2.5 mA and the mutual conductance g_m is 9 mS.

[*Ans.* 716 Ω]

330. The positive-ion control-grid current in a valve containing some gas is 0.01 μA. The mutual conductance of the valve is 5 mS, the anode current is 1 mA and the shunt resistance of the grid circuit is 100 kΩ. Calculate the value of the equivalent noise-generating grid resistor.

[*Ans.* 2003.2 Ω]

331. A network consists of a resistor R_1 at temperature T_1 in parallel with a further resistor R_2 at temperature T_2. What is the maximum noise power per unit bandwidth available from this network? Under these conditions calculate the value of the load resistance connected across the network.

[*Ans.* $k(T_1R_2 + T_2R_1)/(R_1 + R_2)$; $R_1R_2/(R_1 + R_2)$, where k is Boltzmann's constant]

332. The following statement often simplifies noise calculations on a network when there are several elements present, all at different temperatures:

"The effective noise temperature of a complex two-terminal network is equal to the summation over all the elements of the product (temperature of element) × (fraction of total power dissipated in that element when the network is regarded as a passive load)."

Verify this statement in the case of a network consisting of two resistors R_1 and R_2 at temperatures T_1 and T_2 respectively when they are connected (*a*) in series, (*b*) in parallel. The Johnson formula may be assumed.

Use the statement to show that the effective temperature of a length l of transmission line at temperature T_1 terminated by its matched load at temperature T_2 is $T_1\{1 - \exp(-2\alpha l)\} + T_2 \exp(-2\alpha l)$ where α is the voltage attenuation constant.

333. Three resistors, having resistances R_1, R_2 and R_3 ohms are maintained at temperatures T_1, T_2 and T_3 respectively. They are initially all connected in parallel. Show, starting from the Johnson noise generated in each resistor, that this parallel combination is equivalent to a single resistance R at temperature T where

$$R = R_1R_2R_3/(R_1R_2 + R_2R_3 + R_1R_3)$$

and $T = (T_1R_2R_3 + T_2R_1R_3 + T_3R_1R_2)/(R_1R_2 + R_2R_3 + R_1R_3)$.

Calculate the values of R and T if the resistors are now connected in series.

[*Ans.* $R_1 + R_2 + R_3$; $(T_1R_1 + T_2R_2 + T_3R_3)/(R_1 + R_2 + R_3)$]

334. To perform some noise measurements on a receiver a resistor contained in a variable-temperature bath is used to replace the antenna. The resistor is matched to the input impedance of the receiver. Show that the noise power per unit bandwidth delivered to the receiver is kT watts where k is Boltzmann's constant and T is the temperature of the bath.

The noise output from the receiver is first measured with the bath at room temperature (300 K) and is then found to have doubled itself when the temperature of the bath is raised to 900 K. Prove that the noise figure of the receiver is about 3 dB.

335. A signal generator whose output impedance is 500 Ω is calibrated in terms of the power it will deliver to a matched load (i.e. the maximum available signal power). It is connected to a receiver with a bandwidth of 10 kHz and whose first stage consists of a triode with negligible shot noise and which has a 1-kΩ resistor connected between cathode and grid.

What will be the signal-generator reading when it is adjusted so that the signal output from the receiver is equal to the noise output?

The temperature should be taken as 300 K.

[*Ans.* 6.2×10^{-17} W]

336. A galvanometer is stated by its manufacturer to have a sensitivity of 75×10^6 mm A^{-1}. The effective mirror-scale distance is 1 m. The specific couple of the suspension is 10^{-10} Nm rad^{-1}.

Calculate the r.m.s. deflection due to thermal agitation at 300 K. Estimate also the minimum detectable current.

[*Ans.* 0.0129 mm; 0.172 mμA]

337. The input circuit of an amplifier consists of a resistance R shunted by a capacitance C. The voltage gain (G) of the amplifier is constant up to the frequency f where $2\pi fCR = 1$ and is zero above this frequency. Show that the mean square output voltage from the amplifier due to thermal noise in the input impedance is $kTG^2/2C$ volts^2 where T is the ambient temperature and k is Boltzmann's constant.

ADDITIONAL PROBLEMS

338. What is the noise power available from a parallel combination of a 50-kΩ resistor at 293 K and a 100-kΩ resistor at 473 K over a bandwidth of 2 MHz?

[*Ans.* 0.00972 $\mu\mu$W]

339. What is the noise voltage associated with a parallel combination of a 20-kΩ resistor and a 0.1-μF capacitor over a bandwidth of 50 Hz?

[*Ans.* 0.123 μV r.m.s.]

340. What direct current is required in a diode whose emission is temperature-limited to give a noise current of 20 $\mu\mu$A r.m.s. over a bandwidth of 5 MHz?

[*Ans.* 250 mA]

341. A resistor (R ohms) at temperature T, an inductor (L henrys) and a capacitor (C farads) are connected in series. Show that the mean square noise voltage per unit bandwidth appearing across the capacitor is given by

$$\frac{4\,kTR}{(1 - 4\pi^2 f^2 LC)^2 + 4\pi^2 f^2 C^2 R^2}$$

where k is Boltzmann's constant and f is the frequency.

Write down an expression in the form of an integral for the *total* mean square noise voltage appearing across the capacitor. Show, using the equipartition law, that if this integral was evaluated, the answer must be kT/C.

$$\left[\textit{Ans.}\ \int_0^\infty \frac{4\,kTR\,df}{4\pi^2 f^2 C^2 R^2 + (1 - 4\pi^2 f^2 LC)^2}\right]$$

342. A galvanometer has a 50-turn rectangular coil of area $1 \times 10^{-4}\,\mathrm{m}^2$. The coil is situated in a radially directed magnetic field of strength $1\ \mathrm{Wb\,m^{-2}}$. The specific couple of the suspension is 10^{-10} Nm rad^{-1}.

Assuming the usual optical system, calculate the deflection of the light spot on a scale one metre distant from the mirror attached to the coil when a current of 10^{-10} A passes through the coil.

At what current is the deflection equal to the r.m.s. random deflection due to thermal fluctuations at a temperature of 300 K?

[*Ans.* 10^{-2} m; 0.129 $\mu\mu$A]

CHAPTER ELEVEN

TRANSMISSION LINES AND NETWORKS

343. Calculate the attenuation constant, the wavelength (or phase) constant, the characteristic impedance, the velocity of propagation and the wavelength for a line having a resistance of 10.4 Ω km^{-1}, a capacitance of 0.00835 μF km^{-1}, an inductance of 3.67 mH km^{-1} and a conductance of 0.8 μSkm^{-1} at a frequency of 796 Hz.

[*Ans.* 0.00785 neper km^{-1}; 0.0287 rad km^{-1}; 711 $\angle -14° 14'$ Ω; 174 300 kms^{-1}; 219 km]

344. A line having the constants given in the preceding problem is 300 km long, and is terminated by its characteristic impedance. A 2-V generator with an internal resistance of 600 Ω is connected to the sending end. Determine the voltage and current at the receiving end.

[*Ans.* 0.1036 $\angle -499° 30'$ V; 0.0001458 $\angle -485° 16'$ A]

345. Repeat the calculations of Question 343 for the case where loading coils, each of resistance 7.3 Ω and inductance 246 mH, are added at intervals of 7.88 km.

[*Ans.* 0.0036 neper km^{-1}; 0.085 rad km^{-1}; 2038 $\angle -1° 19'$ Ω; 58 800 kms^{-1}; 74 km]

346. Repeat the calculations of Question 344 for the case where the line length is reduced to 100 km and the load impedance is (353.5 + j353.5) Ω.

[*Ans.* 0.472 V; 944 mA]

347. An alternating voltage of 10 V and of frequency 1000 kHz is connected to the sending end of a transmission line which can be represented by a resistance of 70 Ω with a shunt capacitance of 0.001 μF at the receiving end. An inductive load of inductance 0.002 H and resistance 100 Ω is connected across the receiving end of the line. Determine the load current. The internal resistance of the supply is 10 Ω.

[*Ans.* 0.71 mA]

348. A transmission line of length l has resistance, inductance and leakage conductance per unit length R, L and G. Its capacitance is negligible.

It is short-circuited at both ends and at time $t = 0$ a voltage distribution $V = V_0 \sin(\pi x/l)$ is set up on it.

Calculate the subsequent variation of voltage.

[*Ans.* $V = V_0 \sin(\pi x/l) e^{-\gamma t}$ where $\gamma = R/L + \pi^2/LGl^2$]

349. A transmission line, of length 5 m, is tested at a frequency of 20 MHz. When the far end of the line is short-circuited the impedance measured at the sending end is 4.61 Ω resistive, and when the far end is open-circuited the impedance becomes 1390 Ω resistive. Calculate the characteristic impedance of the line, the attenuation constant in dBm^{-1}, the velocity of propagation and the permittivity of the dielectric.

[*Ans.* 80 Ω; 0.1; 2×10^8 ms^{-1}; 2.25]

350. A loss-free transmission line of characteristic impedance 70 Ω is terminated by an impedance $R + jX$. The standing-wave ratio (expressed so as to be a quantity greater than unity) is 2, and the position of the first voltage maximum is one-twelfth of a wavelength from the termination. Calculate R and X.

[*Ans.* $R = 80$ Ω; $X = 52$ Ω]

351. A transmission line of length l, having a propagation constant P and a characteristic impedance Z_o, is terminated in an impedance Z_r. The input impedance is given by:

$$Z_1 = Z_o \left[\frac{Z_r \cosh Pl + Z_o \sinh Pl}{Z_r \sinh Pl + Z_o \cosh Pl}\right]$$

Develop from this expression the theory of the cartesian-grid form of circle-diagram, for solving transmission-line problems, explaining clearly how 'u' circles, 'v' arcs and 'n' arcs are derived.

Explain, also, how the Smith polar form of transmission-line calculator is developed.

352. A length of transmission line, 0.3 of a wavelength long and of characteristic impedance 75 Ω, is terminated by an impedance $Z = (37.5 + j52.5)$ Ω. Use both the cartesian-grid form of circle diagram and the Smith Chart to find the input impedance, assuming the line to be loss-free.

What is the voltage standing-wave ratio existing in the line?

Determine also the new input impedance for a loss in the line of 1.15 dB.

[*Ans.* (31.5 – j41.2) Ω; 0.315; (42 – j36) Ω]

353. At radio frequencies the resistance per unit length R of a concentric line of copper, with air dielectric, is given by:

$$R = 41.6\sqrt{(f)}[1/a + 1/b]10^{-9}\ \Omega\text{m}^{-1},$$

and the characteristic impedance $Z_o = 138 \log_{10}(b/a)\ \Omega$, where

a is the outer radius of the inner conductor in metres,

b is the inner radius of the outer conductor in metres,

and f is the frequency in hertz.

Calculate the input impedance of a quarter-wavelength, short-circuited line of this type at a frequency of 500 MHz, if $b = 0.01$ m and $b/a = 9.2$.

[*Ans.* 248 600 Ω]

354. Calculate the value of 'Q', for the line in Question 353.

[*Ans.* 1468]

355. Show that the input impedance of a short-circuited transmission line is equal to

$$[Rc(l/\lambda)/2f \cos^2\{2\pi(l/\lambda)\} + jZ_o \tan(2\pi l/\lambda)]$$

where l/λ is the line length in wavelengths, f is the frequency, c is the velocity of light, Z_o is the characteristic impedance and R is the resistance of both conductors of the line per unit length. Hence, prove that for such a line, where l/λ is 0.2, the ratio of the selectivity of the line reactance to the selectivity of a lumped reactance is 4.28.

356. Calculate the attenuation and the characteristic impedance, at a frequency of 8800 MHz, of an air-filled coaxial line having the following properties:

Diameter of inner conductor	$= 1.13 \times 10^{-3}$ m
Inner diameter of outer conductor	$= 7.94 \times 10^{-3}$ m
Resistivity of inner conductor	$= 1.78 \times 10^{-8}\ \Omega$m
Resistivity of outer conductor	$= 6.5 \times 10^{-8}\ \Omega$m

[*Ans.* 0.331 dB m^{-1}; 117 Ω]

357. Repeat the calculations in Question 356 for a line entirely filled with a dielectric having a permittivity of 2.25 and a power factor of 0.0004.

[*Ans.* 0.977 dB m^{-1}; 78 Ω]

358. A polythene-filled coaxial cable is terminated with a short-circuiting piston, and its input admittance is measured by the location of a point of minimum voltage, and the determination of the voltage standing-wave ratio, for a measuring line of characteristic impedance 75 Ω. The resulting admittance circle obtained by moving the piston over half a wavelength is as shown. Calculate the attenuation and apparent characteristic impedance of the cable at this frequency. Y_o is the characteristic admittance of the slotted line.

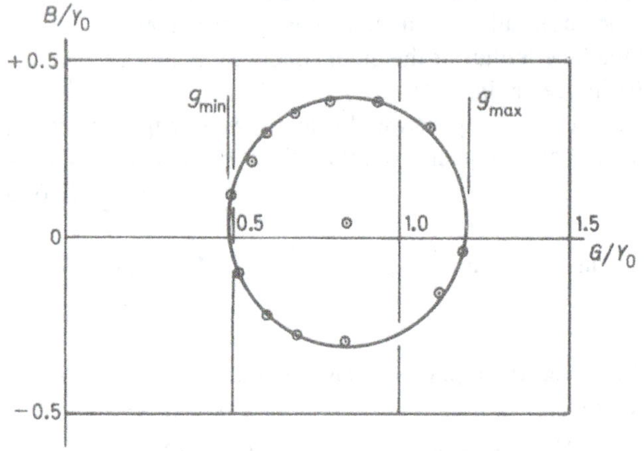

[*Ans.* 6.55 dB; 97.8 Ω]

359. Assuming that the zero-susceptance points were accurately located in Question 358, calculate, by using the two-point system of Blackband and Brown,* the values of attenuation and characteristic impedance which would be obtained by this method of measurement.

[*Ans.* 6.60 dB; 97.7 Ω]

360. It is desired to connect a transmission line of characteristic impedance 75 Ω to a load of impedance (150 + j0) Ω using a quarter-wavelength transformer. Determine the characteristic impedance of the transformer for perfect matching.

[*Ans.* 106 Ω]

* See W. T. Blackband and D. R. Brown, 'The Two-point Method of Measuring Characteristic Impedance and Attenuation of Cables at 3000 MHz,' *J.I.E.E.*, 93, Part IIIA, 1383, 1946.

361. A load of impedance (100 + j100) Ω is to be matched to an open-wire transmission line of characteristic impedance $500\underline{/0}$ Ω, using a short-circuited stub and a quarter-wave line inserted between the 500-Ω line and the load. Calculate the characteristic impedance of the quarter-wave line, and the minimum length of stub required. Assume that the stub and quarter-wave line have the same characteristic impedance, that the stub is at the load end of the quarter-wave line and that the lines are loss-free. The frequency is 100 MHz.

[*Ans.* 316 Ω; 1.23 m]

362. The diagram shows the arrangement of a double-stub tuner. The positions of the stubs on the transmission line are fixed, but the lengths l_1 and l_2 are adjustable. If the line and stubs have the same known characteristic impedance Z_o, and the load impedance Z_l is also known, explain how a Smith Chart can be employed to determine the shortest values of l_1 and l_2 which will give no reflected wave at the point *P*.

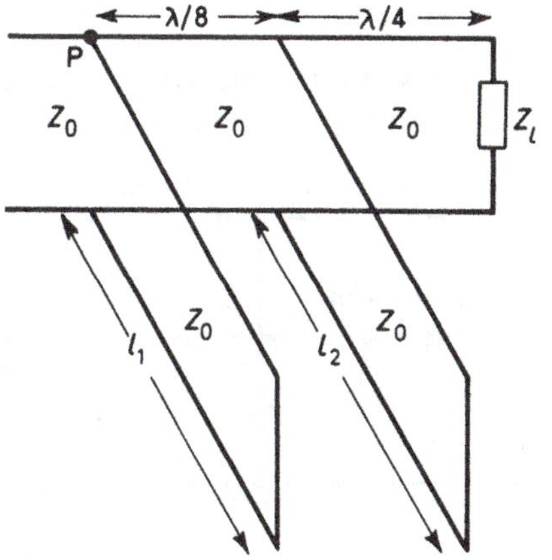

363. In a linear passive four-terminal network, the input voltage and current, V_1 and I_1, can respectively be expressed in the forms

$$V_1 = [AV_2 + BI_2] \text{ and } I_1 = [CV_2 + DI_2];$$

where V_2 and I_2 are the output voltage and current respectively. Find the values of A, B, C and D for the network shown.

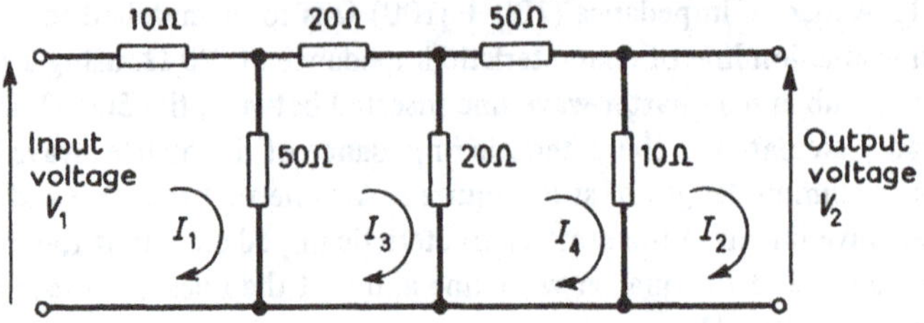

[*Ans.* $A = 20.8, B = 179\ \Omega, C = 0.68$ S, $D = 5.9$]

364. A symmetrical four-terminal network has an image impedance of 600 Ω resistive, and an image attenuation constant of 0.5 neper. The image phase constant is zero. A resistive load of 1000 Ω is connected between one pair of terminals, and the other two terminals are connected to a generator of e.m.f. 10 V and an internal impedance of 200 Ω resistive. Determine the current through the load.

[*Ans.* 5.44 mA]

365. Find the frequency at which the output of the twin-T network shown is zero, when the input voltage is finite.

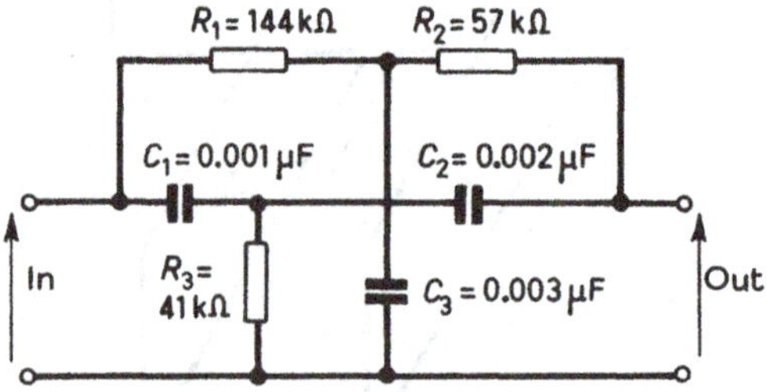

[*Ans.* 1240 Hz]

366. (*a*) Find the values of the resistors of the T-section attenuator which will have an iterative impedance of 600 Ω and a loss of (i) 10 dB, (ii) 20 dB.

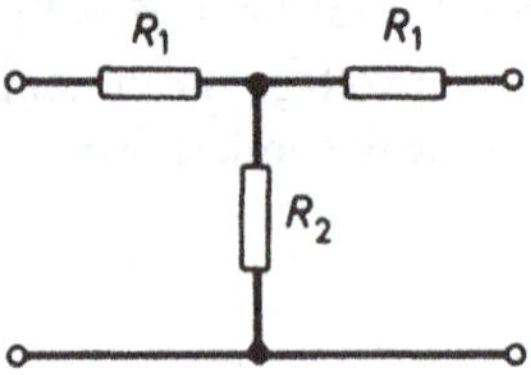

(*b*) In an H-type attenuator, matched to a transmission line of 600-Ω impedance, each of the series resistances is 240 Ω. Determine the attenuation and the value of the shunt resistance.

[*Ans.* (*a*) (i) $R_1 = 311.8\ \Omega, R_2 = 421.6\ \Omega$;
(ii) $R_1 = 491\ \Omega, R_2 = 121\ \Omega$; (*b*) 19.1 dB; 135 Ω]

367. Open- and short-circuit tests are performed on the four-terminal network illustrated. An impedance of (250 + j100) Ω is measured between terminals 1 and 2 with terminals 3 and 4 open-circuited. With 3 and 4 short-circuited the impedance between 1 and 2 is (400 + j300) Ω. An impedance of (200 + j0) Ω is measured between 3 and 4 with 1 and 2 open. Evaluate the impedances of the equivalent T-network.

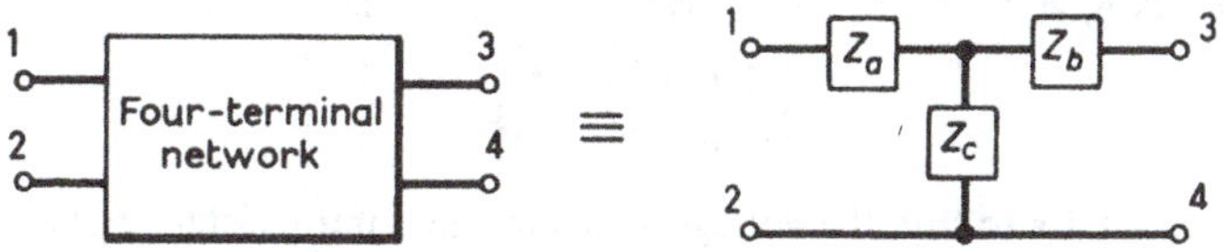

[*Ans.* $Z_a = (150 + j300)\ \Omega$; $Z_b = (100 + j200)\ \Omega$; $Z_c = (100 - j200)\ \Omega$]

368. Determine the Z, Y, A, B, C, D and image parameters Z_{i_1}, Z_{i_2} and θ of the network shown.

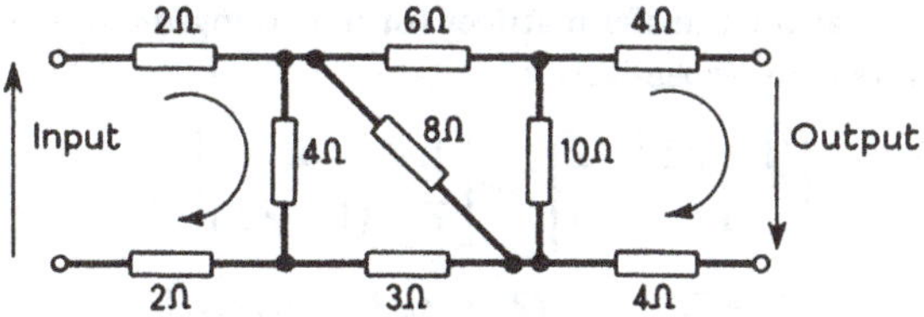

[*Ans.* $Z_{11} = 6.704\ \Omega$, $Z_{12} = 1.078\ \Omega$,
$Z_{22} = 13.006\ \Omega$, $Y_{11} = 0.1513$ S,
$Y_{21} = 0.0126$ S, $Y_{22} = -0.0784$ S,
$A = 6.222$, $B = 79.37\ \Omega$,
$C = 0.928$ S, $D = 12$,
$Z_{i1} = 6.66\ \Omega$, $Z_{i2} = 12.84\ \Omega$,
$\theta = 2.846$]

369. Starting with the equations relating the input voltage and current with the output voltage and current of a linear passive four-terminal network, show that the transfer matrices of the simple circuits (*a*) and (*b*) illustrated are given by

$$\begin{bmatrix}1 & Z\\0 & 1\end{bmatrix} \text{ and } \begin{bmatrix}1 & 0\\Y & 1\end{bmatrix}$$

respectively.

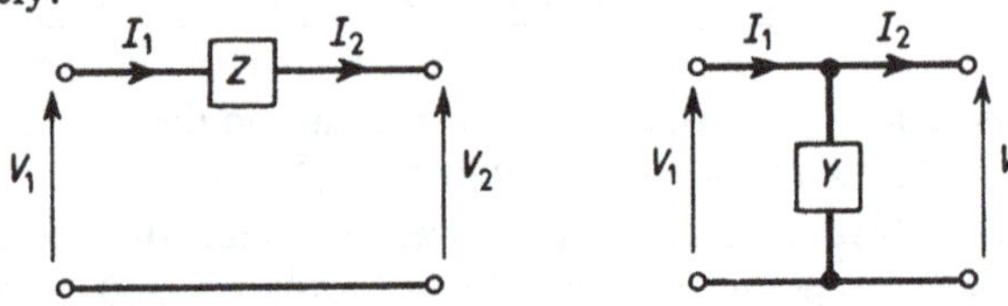

(a) (b)

Hence, show that the transfer matrix of a network which has general parameters A, B, C and D, and a load Z_l in cascade is

$$\begin{bmatrix}A+B/Z_l & B\\C+D/Z_l & D\end{bmatrix}$$

Use these results to find the voltage gain and the input resistance of a common-base transistor amplifier stage in terms of the transistor parameters r_{11}, r_{12}, r_{21} and r_{22} and the load resistance R_l.

$$\left[Ans.\ \frac{r_{21}R_l}{r_{11}R_l+r_{11}r_{22}-r_{12}r_{21}};\ r_{11}-r_{12}r_{21}/(r_{22}+R_l)\right]$$

370. Show that the transfer matrices for the arrangements (*a*), (*b*), (*c*) and (*d*) illustrated are respectively,

$$\begin{bmatrix}(1+ZY) & Z\\Y & 1\end{bmatrix},\quad \begin{bmatrix}1 & Z\\Y & (1+ZY)\end{bmatrix},$$

$$\begin{bmatrix}(1+Z_1/Z_{12}) & (Z_1+Z_2+Z_1Z_2/Z_{12})\\1/Z_{12} & (1+Z_2/Z_{12})\end{bmatrix},$$

$$\begin{bmatrix}(1+Z_{12}/Z_2) & Z_{12}\\\{1/Z_1+(1+Z_{12}/Z_1)(1/Z_2)\} & (1+Z_{12}/Z_1)\end{bmatrix}.$$

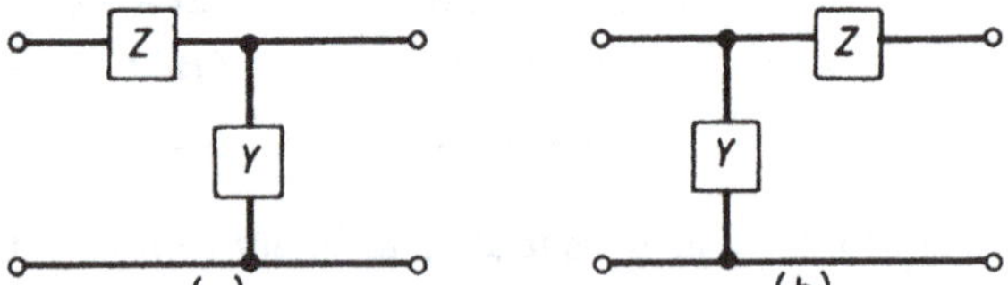

(a) (b)

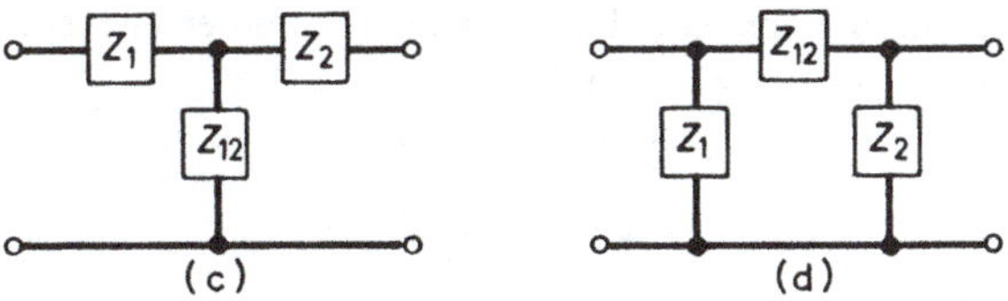

371. Use the results of Question 369 to find the ratios V_2/V_1 for the circuits shown.

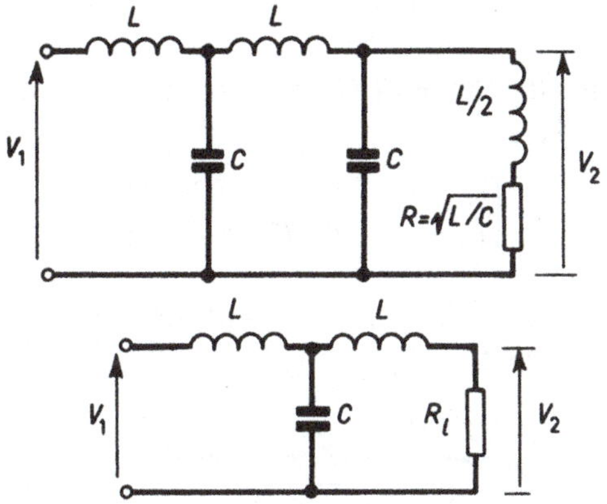

[*Ans.* $\dfrac{1}{1-3\omega^2LC+\omega^4L^2C^2+\mathrm{j}\omega L(2-\omega^2LC)/(\sqrt{(L/C)}+\mathrm{j}\omega L/2)}$;

$\dfrac{R_l}{(1-\omega^2LC)R_l+\mathrm{j}(2\omega L-\omega^3L^2C)}$, where $\omega = 2\pi \times$ supply frequency.]

372. (*a*) Show that the transfer matrix for a combination of two four-terminal networks in cascade is equal to the product of the transfer matrices of the individual networks.

(*b*) Two networks have general A, B, C, D parameters as follows:

	Network 1	Network 2
A	1.50	1.66
B	11 Ω	4 Ω
C	0.25 S	1 S
D	2.5	3.0

If the networks are connected in cascade in the order 1, 2, show that the transfer matrix of the combination is:

$$\begin{bmatrix} 13.5 & 39.0 \\ 2.92 & 8.5 \end{bmatrix}.$$

If the two networks are connected with their inputs and outputs in parallel, prove that the resulting admittance matrix is:

$$\begin{bmatrix} 43/44 & -15/44 \\ 15/44 & -73/132 \end{bmatrix}.$$

373. Show that the $[Z]$ and $[A]$ matrices of the symmetrical lattice network illustrated are:

$$\begin{bmatrix} (Z_1+Z_2)/2 & (Z_2-Z_1)/2 \\ (Z_2-Z_1)/2 & (Z_1+Z_2)/2 \end{bmatrix}$$

and

$$\begin{bmatrix} (Z_1+Z_2)/(Z_2-Z_1) & 2Z_1Z_2/(Z_2-Z_1) \\ 2/(Z_2-Z_1) & (Z_1+Z_2)/(Z_2-Z_1) \end{bmatrix}$$

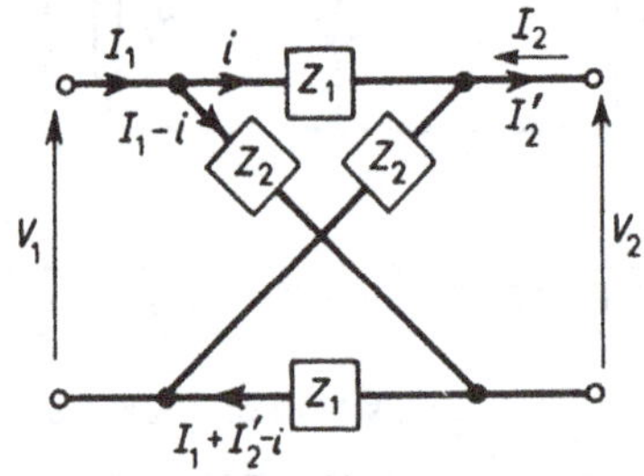

374. Derive the transfer matrices of the various elements of the circuit illustrated and then show that the transfer matrix for the whole arrangement is:

$$[A] = \begin{bmatrix} n(1+Z_1Y) & nZ_2(1+Z_1Y)+Z_1/n \\ nY & nZ_2Y+1/n \end{bmatrix}$$

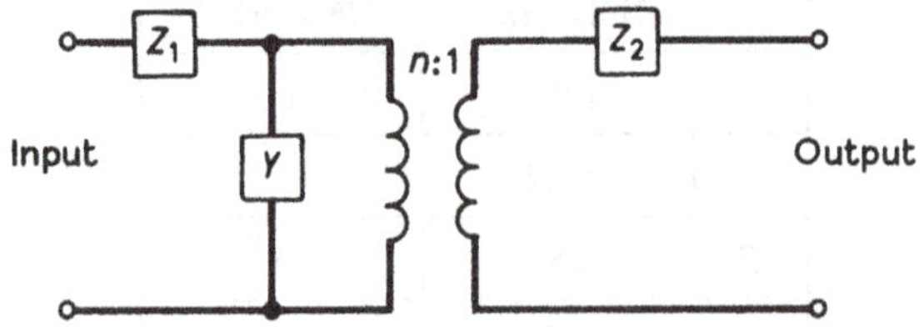

375. Determine, using matrix methods, the transfer matrix for the network illustrated.

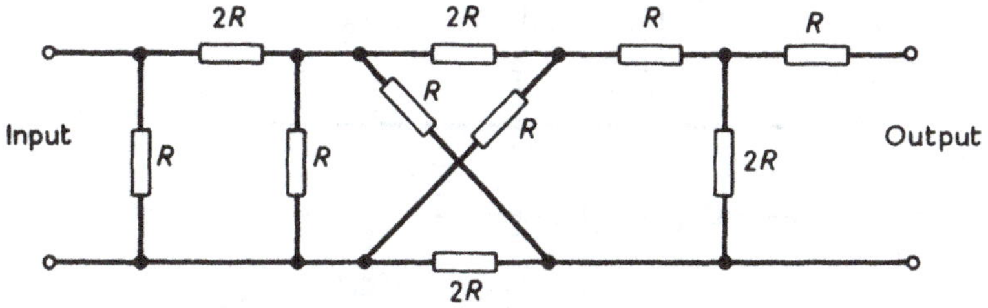

If the network is terminated by a resistance R_l evaluate:
(i) the input impedance of the network combined with the load,
(ii) the ratio of the output voltage across the load to the input voltage.

$$\left[Ans. \begin{bmatrix} 57/2 & 119R/2 \\ 79/2R & 165/2 \end{bmatrix}, \frac{57R_l + 119R}{79R_l/R + 165}, 2R_l/(57R_l + 119R)\right]$$

376. The symmetric T network illustrated is to be used as an equivalent circuit for a section of transmission line of electrical length θ and characteristic impedance Z_0. After determining the transfer matrix for the section of line prove that

$$Z_1 = Z_0(\cosh\theta - 1)/\sinh\theta$$

and

$$Z_2 = Z_0/\sinh\theta$$

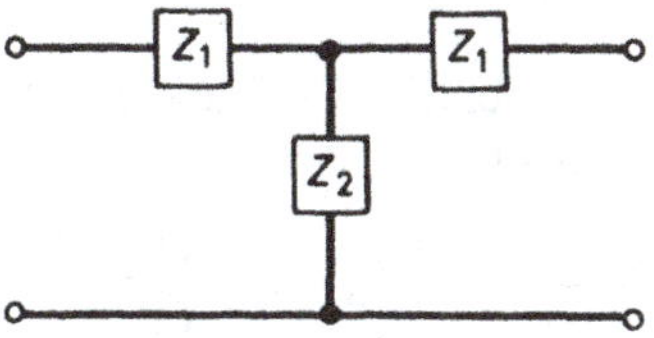

377. Determine the transfer matrices for the networks illustrated at (*a*) and (*b*). Show how either network can be incorporated in a transistor oscillator circuit and from the transfer matrices derive for each case expressions for the frequency of oscillation of the oscillator and state the condition for maintenance of oscillation.

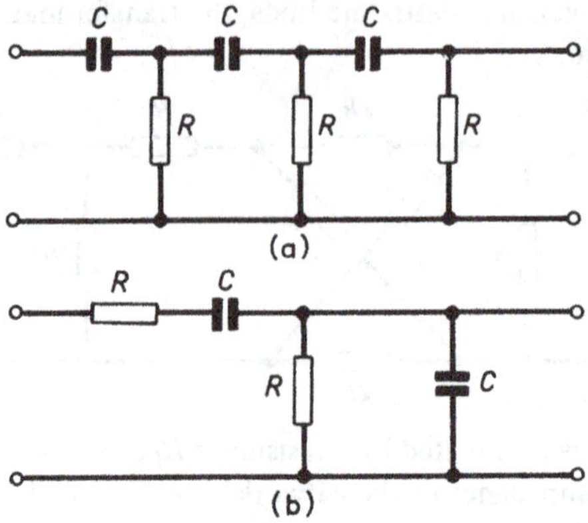

[*Ans.* (*a*) $1/2\pi\sqrt{(6)}\,CR$, Amplifier gain > 29;
(*b*) $1/2\pi\,CR$, Amplifier gain > 3]

378. A certain two-port microwave junction may be represented by the following equivalent circuit

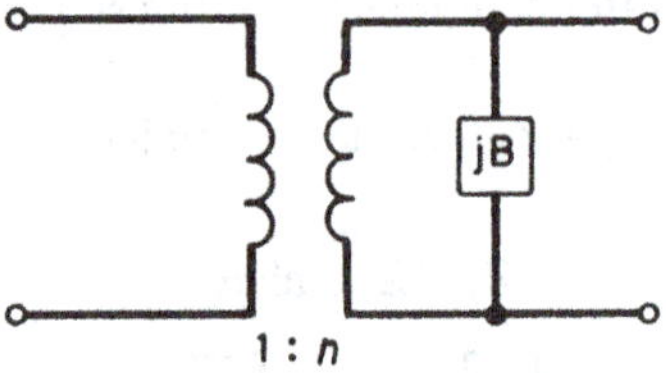

From laboratory measurements it was found that the scattering matrix elements S_{11} and S_{22} are given by:

$$S_{11} = -\frac{(1+j)}{(3+j)},\quad S_{22} = \frac{(1-j)}{(3+j)}$$

Determine the susceptance B and the turns ratio n of the ideal transformer. What is the value of the scattering matrix element S_{12}?

[*Ans.* 0.5 S, $\sqrt{(2)}$, $1/\sqrt{(2)}$]

ADDITIONAL PROBLEMS

379. (*a*) A loss-free line of length l is terminated with a resistance equal to half its characteristic impedance Z_0. Show that the magnitude of the input impedance to the line is

$$Z_0\sqrt{\{(1+4\tan^2\beta l)/(4+\tan^2\beta l)\}}$$

where β is the phase constant.

(*b*) Prove that for any transmission line the sending-end voltage is given by

$$V_s = \frac{I_R}{\sqrt{(1-\tanh^2\gamma l)}}(Z_T - Z_0\tanh\gamma l)$$

where γ = propagation constant
l = length of line
Z_T = terminating impedance
Z_0 = characteristic impedance
and I_R = the current in the terminating impedance.

The input impedance of a transmission line is found to be 800 Ω on open-circuit and 200 Ω with the distant end short-circuited. The line is connected to a matched telephone line of characteristic impedance 400 Ω. Calculate the input voltage to the transmission line required to supply 1.6 mW to the matched load of the telephone line.

[*Ans.* 1.39 V]

380. The propagation constant of a transmission line can be written

$$\gamma = \sqrt{\{(R + j\omega L)(G + j\omega C)\}}$$

where all the terms have their usual meaning.

Show that for a line with small but finite attenuation the phase velocity v_{ph} can be written

$$v_{ph} = \frac{1}{\sqrt{(LC)}}\left[1 - \frac{1}{8\omega^2}\left(\frac{R}{L} - \frac{G}{C}\right)^2\right]$$

Find the corresponding expression for the attenuation constant to the same order of approximation.

$$\left[Ans.\ \frac{R}{2}\sqrt{\left(\frac{C}{L}\right)} + \frac{G}{2}\sqrt{\left(\frac{L}{C}\right)}\right]$$

381. Show that the attenuation constant for guided waves is given by

$$\alpha = \frac{R_s\int_W |B_t|^2\,dl}{2Z\int_A |B_t|^2\,ds}$$

where R_s is the surface resistivity of the guide material, Z is the wave impedance, B_t is the transverse magnetic field of the wave, $\int_W dl$ is taken over the surface of the guiding structure and $\int_A ds$ is taken over the cross-section of the guide.

The magnetic field of a TEM wave in a coaxial cable is given by

$$B = \frac{\mu_0 I}{2\pi r} \exp\{j(\omega t - \beta z)\}$$

where the terms have their usual meanings. Calculate the attenuation constant in a coaxial cable having an inner conductor diameter of 1 mm, an outer conductor diameter of 5 mm and filled with dielectric of relative permittivity 2 at the frequency for which $R_s = 8 \times 10^{-3}\,\Omega$ per square.

[*Ans.* 0.1 dB m^{-1}]

382. A lossless transmission line of characteristic impedance 50 Ω has a voltage standing wave ratio of 2.4 when terminated by an unknown impedance. When the unknown impedance is replaced by a capacitor of impedance (− j50) Ω the nearest voltage minimum to the receiving end is shifted towards the receiver by 30°. What is the value of the unknown impedance?

[*Ans.* (91.5 − j45.4) Ω]

383. A lossless, coaxial, air-filled, transmission line of length 98 m is connected to a load of impedance (120 + j120) Ω. The line has the following constants:

$$\text{Inductance} = 6.4 \times 10^{-6}\,\text{Hm}^{-1}$$
$$\text{Capacitance} = 4 \times 10^{-11}\,\text{Fm}^{-1}$$

If the half of the line nearest the load is filled with an oil dielectric of relative permittivity 2.78, calculate the V.S.W.R. in each section of the line, assuming a signal wavelength of 4 m.

If the length of the oil-filled part of the line is reduced by 3 m due to an oil leak (leaving an air-filled section of length 52 m), calculate the effect on the V.S.W.R. in each section of the line.

Check the answers with the aid of a Smith Chart.

[*Ans.* 2.62, 2.45, 2.62, 3.65]

384. An air-spaced, cylindrical, concentric line of length 7.5 m and characteristic impedance 50 Ω is open-circuited at one end. The other end is connected to a source of 50 V at a frequency of 75 MHz and having an internal reactance of 20 Ω. A resistive load of 50 Ω is connected across the line at 1 m from the source and an inductance of 3.3×10^{-7} H is connected across the line at 7 m from the source.

Find (*a*) the current from the source

(*b*) the change in current from the source when a dielectric material of length 1 m of relative permittivity 4 is placed in the line at the source end.

[*Ans.* 0.684 $\angle -47^\circ$ A; 3.43 $\angle 149^\circ$ A]

385. For a uniform, air-spaced, coaxial transmission line with copper conductors and operating at high frequencies the following expressions are valid:

$$R = 41.6\sqrt{(f)}\left[\frac{1}{a}+\frac{1}{b}\right]10^{-5}\,\Omega\text{m}^{-1}$$

$$L = \frac{\mu_0}{2\pi}\ln\left(\frac{b}{a}\right)\text{Hm}^{-1}$$

$$C = \frac{2\pi\,\epsilon_0}{\ln\left(\frac{b}{a}\right)}\ \text{Fm}^{-1}$$

where *a* is the outer radius of the inner conductor and *b* is the inner radius of the outer conductor. Using these expressions show that, if the outer diameter of a coaxial line is fixed, the line has minimum attenuation when $b/a = 3.6$. Assume G is negligibly small.

386. (*a*) A TEM wave propagates down a coaxial cable filled with a dielectric of wave impedance Z_1. If at a plane boundary the medium changes to one of impedance Z_2, show that the power flow is continuous at the boundary.

Calculate the ratio of transmitted to incident power for $Z_2 = 2Z_1$.

(*b*) Determine the input impedance of the transmission system shown.

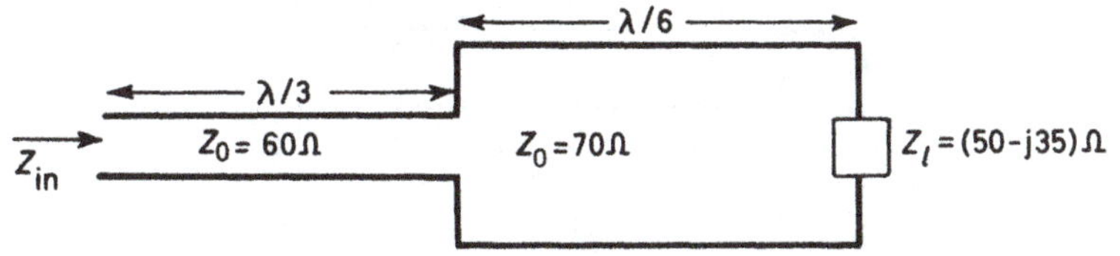

[*Ans.* (*a*) 8/9; (*b*) (42.6 − j22.8) Ω]

387. Show that the electric and magnetic field components of a plane wave travelling in free space can exist when the wave is guided between parallel conducting strips. Derive an expression for the characteristic impedance of this air-filled waveguide for the case when the strip width w is much greater than the spacing s. Compare the result with the impedance of free space.

Suppose that for a practical line the conductors are spaced by dielectric supports of equal dimensions to the line and a thickness t measured along the line ($t \ll$ the wavelength λ). By considering the additional capacitance of one support show that the reflection coefficient is $\simeq \pi t(\epsilon_r - 1)/\lambda$, where ϵ_r is the relative permittivity of the dielectric.

Ans. $\dfrac{s}{w}\sqrt{\left(\dfrac{\mu_0}{\epsilon_0}\right)}, \sqrt{(\mu_0/\epsilon_0)}$

388. An antenna array used at 40 MHz has an input impedance of (36 + j0) Ω. The transmitter supplying power to the antenna has an output impedance of (500 + j0) Ω and is located 100 m from the antenna terminals. A parallel-wire transmission line with $Z_0 = (500 + j0)$ Ω runs from the transmitter to the vicinity of the antenna.

(*a*) Design a quarter-wavelength transformer, using a parallel-wire transmission line on which the phase velocity is 97 per cent of the free-space velocity of light, to connect the antenna to the main line and provide an impedance match.

(*b*) What is the length of the main line?

[*Ans.* (*a*) $Z = 134$ Ω; $l = 1.82$ m (*b*) 98.18 m]

389. Derive an expression for the ratio V_0/V_i for the network illustrated and show that at a certain frequency the output voltage is zero. Determine this frequency if $C = 0.05$ μF and $L = 150$ mH.

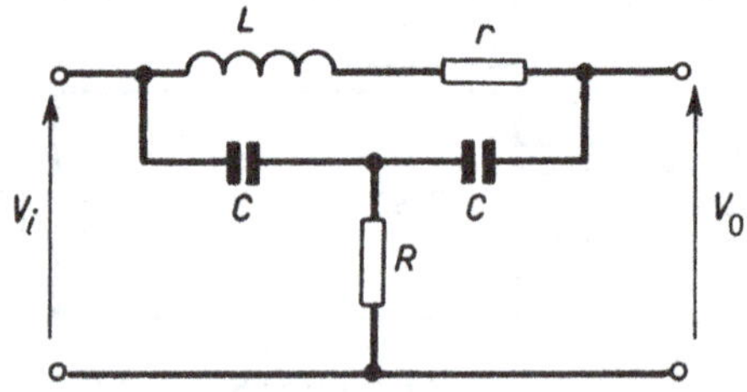

[*Ans.* $\dfrac{s^2C^2R(r + sL) + 2sCR + 1}{sC(r + sL)(1 + sCR) + 2sCR + 1}$

where s is the complex frequency variable;

$V_0 = 0$ when $f = \sqrt{(2/LC)}/2\pi$; 2598 Hz]

390. A field-effect transistor in the common-source circuit has a mutual conductance g_m, a drain resistance r_d and inter-electrode capacitances C_{gs} (gate-source), C_{gd} (gate-drain) and C_{ds} (drain-source). Assuming linear operating conditions show that the admittance matrix for the device is

$$\begin{bmatrix} j\omega\,(C_{gs} + C_{gd}) & -j\omega\, C_{gd} \\ g_m - j\omega\, C_{gd} & j\omega\,(C_{ds} + C_{gd}) + 1/r_d \end{bmatrix}$$

CHAPTER TWELVE

WAVEGUIDES

391. State Maxwell's equations, and use them to derive an expression giving the critical wavelength for the H_{mn} mode in a rectangular waveguide, of internal dimensions a and b m.

[*Ans.* $2/\{(m/a)^2 + (n/b)^2\}^{\frac{1}{2}}$ m]

392. Use Maxwell's equations to derive expressions for the E and H components of the two basic types of wave which can be propagated in rectangular waveguide. Sketch the field patterns for the normal H_{01} mode.

393. Calculate the critical and guide wavelengths in an air-filled rectangular waveguide, with internal dimensions 0.0762 m × 0.0254 m, for the normal H_{01} mode at a frequency of 3000 MHz.

[*Ans.* 0.152 m; 0.133 m]

394. Derive expressions for the field components of both the E and H waves in a circular waveguide, and show that the critical wavelengths for the E_0 and H_0 modes are 2.61a and 1.64a respectively, where a is the guide radius.

395. A cylindrical attenuator, operated in the E_0 mode at 1000 MHz, is required to provide 100 dB attenuation over a 0.1 m length. Calculate the radius of the cylinder required.

[*Ans.* 0.0206 m]

396. Calculate the attenuation per metre in an air-filled rectangular copper waveguide, with internal dimensions 0.0254 m × 0.0127 m for the H_{01} mode at a free-space wavelength of 0.031 m.

Repeat the calculation for a free-space wavelength of 0.032 m.

[*Ans.* 0.0801 dB m^{-1}; 0.0814 dB m^{-1}]

397. A rectangular copper waveguide, with internal dimensions 0.048 m × 0.016 m, carrying the H_{01} wave is filled with a dielectric which has a dielectric constant of 2.55, and a loss angle δ given by $\tan \delta = 0.0006$. Determine the total attenuation per metre, due to the losses in the wall metal and the dielectric, at a frequency of 3000 MHz.

[*Ans.* 0.399 $\mathrm{dB\,m^{-1}}$]

398. The following information was obtained from standing-wave measurements on a short-circuited, low-loss, waveguide component:

Position of first minimum = 0.03749 m

Position of second minimum = 0.05731 m

Distance between two points of equal field strength, on either side of a minimum, at which the value of the field strength is K times the minimum, is $w = 8.8 \times 10^{-4}$ m when $K^2 = 2.12$.

Find the guide wavelength, the voltage standing-wave ratio and the loss in the component.

[*Ans.* 0.03964 m; 15.25; 0.581 dB]

ADDITIONAL PROBLEMS

399. Calculate the attenuation in an air-filled rectangular waveguide, having internal dimensions 0.0254 m $\times$ 0.0127 m for the H_{01} mode at a free-space wavelength of 0.032 m assuming perfectly smooth walls. The resistivity of the wave-guide wall metal is 6.266×10^{-8} Ωm.

[*Ans.* 0.157 $\mathrm{dB\,m^{-1}}$]

400. An air-filled rectangular waveguide has dimensions $a = 2.286 \times 10^{-2}$ m and $b = 1.016 \times 10^{-2}$ m. Find (*a*) the cut-off frequency of the dominant mode and that of the next higher-order mode, (*b*) the attenuation constant associated with this next higher-order mode at a frequency mid-way between the two cut-off frequencies.

[*Ans.* (*a*) 6.56 GHz; 13.12 GHz; (*b*) 1570 $\mathrm{dB\,m^{-1}}$]

401. An air-filled rectangular waveguide has dimensions $a = 2$ cm, $b = 1$ cm. Assuming that only *TM* modes are excited find (*a*) the dominant mode and its cut-off frequency, (*b*) the phase velocity, phase constant, guide wavelength and the characteristic wave impedance, if frequency $f = 1.5 f_c$ where f_c is the cut-off frequency.

[*Ans.* (*a*) TM_{11}, 16.8 GHz;

(*b*) $4.03 \times 10^8\ \mathrm{ms^{-1}}$, 392 $\mathrm{rad\,m^{-1}}$, 1.6×10^{-2} m, 280 Ω]

CHAPTER THIRTEEN

FILTERS

402. A constant-k, low-pass filter is designed to cut off at a frequency of 1000 Hz, and the resistance of the load circuit is 50 Ω. Calculate the values of the components required, and the attenuation constant per section at a frequency of (*a*) 1500 Hz, (*b*) 2000 Hz.

An m-derived filter corresponding to this constant-k one is now to be designed to have a frequency of infinite attenuation of 1200 Hz. Determine the values of the components required for this filter and the new value of the attenuation constant per section at a frequency of 2000 Hz.

[*Ans.* $L = 15.92$ mH; $C = 6.37$ μF; 1.928; 2.64;
Each series $L = 4.4$ mH; Shunt $L = 5$ mH; Shunt $C = 3.52$ μF; 1.51]

403. (*a*) In a constant-k, band-pass filter the ratio of the capacitances in the shunt and series arms is 100:1, and the resonant frequency of both arms is 1000 Hz. Calculate the bandwidth of the filter.

(*b*) A constant-k band-pass filter terminated with a 600-Ω resistor has lower and upper cut-off frequencies of 120 kHz and 123 kHz, respectively. Calculate, for a T-section, the values of each series inductance, each series capacitance, the shunt inductance and the shunt capacitance.

[*Ans.* (*a*) 200 Hz; (*b*) 31.8 mH; 53.9 μμF; 9.7 μH; 0.177 μF]

404. A constant-k, high-pass filter is required for a cut-off frequency of 2500 Hz. The resistance of the load circuit is 600 Ω. Determine the values of the components required.

[*Ans.* $L = 19.1$ mH; $C = 0.053$ μF]

405. A wave filter can be built up of either T-sections of the type illustrated in diagram (*a*) or of π-sections as shown in diagram (*b*). Determine the iterative impedances of the two sections.

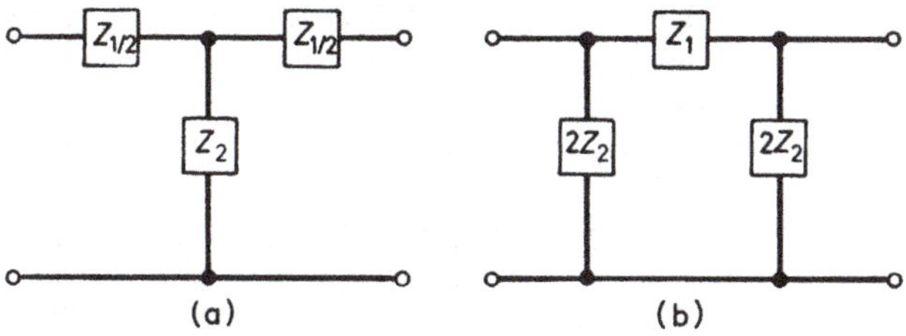

[*Ans.* $Z_{OT} = \sqrt{\{Z_1 Z_2(1 + Z_1/4Z_2)\}}$; $Z_{O\pi} = 2Z_2\sqrt{\{Z_1/(Z_1 + 4Z_2)\}}$]

406. Draw the series-derived *T*-section and the shunt-derived π-section corresponding to the prototype sections illustrated in the previous problem. Show clearly how the impedances in the series and shunt arms of the derived sections are determined.

407. Prove that, for a derived low-pass filter, a *T*-section of which is illustrated, the ratio of the frequency for infinite attenuation to the cut-off frequency is $\sqrt{(1 + L_{1m}/4L_{2m})}$.

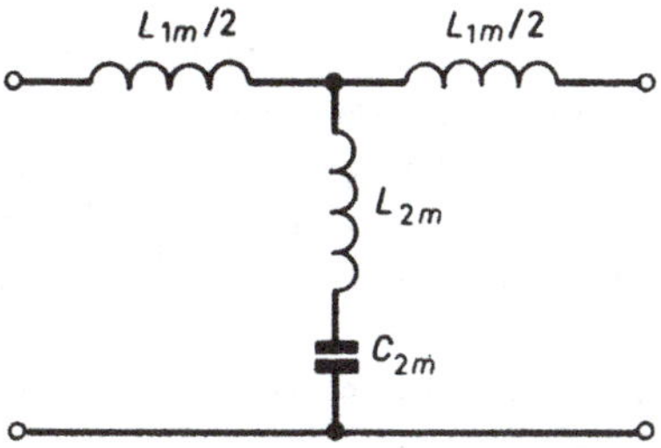

408. Show that the image impedances of the series-derived and shunt-derived half sections of a filter are respectively equal to the mid-series and mid-shunt iterative impedances of the corresponding full sections.

409. Design a constant-*k*, low-pass filter to have a cut-off frequency of 796 Hz and a load impedance of 600 Ω using (*a*) a *T*-section, or (*b*) a π-section.

[*Ans.* (*a*) Series inductances, 120 mH each, Shunt capacitance, 0.666 μF;

(*b*) Series inductance, 240 mH, Shunt capacitances, 0.333 μF each]

410. Design an m-derived, low-pass filter to have the same characteristics as that of the filter in the preceding problem, using (a) a T-section, or (b) a π-section. Take m as 0.6.

[*Ans.* (a) Inductance of each series arm, 72 mH, Inductance in shunt arm, 64 mH, Capacitance in shunt arm, 0.4 μF; (b) Inductance in series arm, 144 mH, Capacitance in series arm, 0.178 μF, Capacitance of each shunt arm, 0.2 μF]

411. A T-section of a constant-k, high-pass filter has a capacitance $2C$ in each series arm and an inductance L in the shunt arm. Derive expressions for the cut-off frequency and the iterative impedance Z_0 of the T-section and sketch curves showing the attenuation constant α, the phase constant β and Z_0 as functions of angular frequency ω.

$$\left[Ans.\ f_c = 1/4\pi\sqrt{(LC)};\ \sqrt{\left\{\frac{L}{C}\left(1-\frac{\omega_c{}^2}{\omega^2}\right)\right\}}\right]$$

412. A low-pass filter is required for which the cut-off must be sharp and the attenuation must be large over the whole attenuation band. These characteristics are to be achieved by constructing a filter with (i) a series-derived T-section with $m = 0.3$ (ii) a series-derived T-section with $m = 0.87$ (iii) a constant-k T-section and (iv) a series-derived half-section with $m = 0.6$ at each end of the filter.

Sketch the attenuation-frequency curve for this composite filter.

413. A low-pass filter has the following specification:

(i) the allowable deviation from ideal in the passband must be equal to or less than 0.5 dB,

(ii) the passband extends from 0 to 1 rad s^{-1},

(iii) the attenuation must be at least 18 dB at angular frequencies greate than 2 rad s^{-1},

(iv) the filter is to operate between two equal resistances of 1 Ω.

Use the equal-ripple approximation to derive a suitable network function $N(s)$ for this case.

[*Ans.* $\dfrac{k}{s^3 + 1.256s^2 + 1.5495s + 0.72}$ where k is a constant]

ADDITIONAL PROBLEMS

414. Each of the series arms of a low-pass filter *T*-section consists of an 18-mH inductor and the shunt arm contains a 0.1-μF capacitor. Indicate how the iterative impedance varies with frequency and calculate its value at frequencies of 1 kHz and 8 kHz.

[*Ans.* 588 Ω; j676 Ω]

415. Outline the design of a third-order Chebyshev low-pass filter with a cut-off frequency of 10^4 rad s^{-1} and an iterative impedance of 600 Ω. The ripple in the pass-band must not exceed 0.5 dB.

[*Ans.*

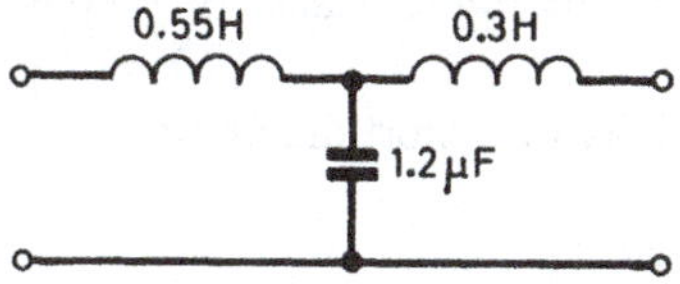

]

CHAPTER FOURTEEN

ANTENNAS

416. Evaluate the radiation resistance of a single-turn circular loop with a circumference of a quarter of a wavelength.

[*Ans.* 0.77 Ω]

417. Determine the radiation resistance of a dipole antenna 1/12 wavelength long.

Find also the directivity of a short dipole.

[*Ans.* 5.5 Ω; 1.5]

418. An antenna having a directivity of 90 is operating at a wavelength of 2 m. Calculate the maximum effective aperture of the antenna.

[*Ans.* 28.6 m^2]

419. If 100 kW of energy are radiated from an antenna of 100 m effective height, at a frequency of 60 kHz, what is the strength of the electric field at a distance of 100 km? Assume that no absorption effects are present.

[*Ans.* 0.03 Vm^{-1}]

420. A certain antenna has an effective height of 100 m and the current at the base is 450 A r.m.s. at a frequency of 40 kHz. Calculate the power radiated. The total resistance of the antenna circuit being 1.12 Ω, determine the efficiency of the antenna.

[*Ans.* 56.9 kW; 25.1 per cent]

421. An antenna array consists of 10 vertical antennas in a straight line spaced half a wavelength apart and equally energized in phase. Deduce the angular width of the forward beam in the horizontal plane.

[*Ans.* 23° 4′]

422. Calculate the voltage induced by a plane wave of field strength 0.01 Vm^{-1} and wavelength 300 m in a frame antenna 1 m square having

12 turns, the plane of the frame being in the plane of propagation of the wave.

[*Ans.* 25.14×10^{-4} V]

423. Develop the basic radar equation relating transmitted and received powers P_T and P_R respectively:

$$\frac{P_R}{P_T} = \frac{G_T G_R \sigma \lambda^2}{(4\pi)^3 r^4}$$

where G_T and G_R are the transmitter and receiver antenna gains respectively, σ is the target echoing area, λ is the operating wavelength and r is the radar range.

424. A one-dimensional microwave antenna has an aperture of width a which is illuminated by a uniform field distribution. Derive an expression for the antenna far-field radiation pattern in the vicinity of the boresight direction.

If the aperture width is 0.9 m, find the angular positions of the first three nulls and the amplitude of the first sidelobe in decibels relative to the main beam amplitude when the operating frequency is 10 GHz.

[*Ans.* $\dfrac{a \sin(\pi\theta a/\lambda)}{(\pi\theta a/\lambda)}$; 1.91°, 3.82°, 5.73°; – 13.46 dB]

425. A 0.1-m totally absorbing blockage is situated at the centre of the antenna aperture referred to in Question 424. Calculate the resulting change in received signal strength caused by the blockage at angles of (*a*) 0°, (*b*) 2.865°, relative to boresight. It may be assumed that the source of radiation is greater than $2a^2/\lambda$ from the antenna.

[*Ans.* (*a*) – 1.038 dB; (*b*) + 3.52 dB]

426. A ground station is to be designed to receive domestic television signals from a satellite which radiates 100 kW effective radiated power from a directional antenna at a frequency of 12 GHz. If the satellite is 40 000 km from the ground station, find the gain of the ground station antenna assuming the receiver to have the following characteristics:

(*i*) bandwidth = 5 MHz,
(*ii*) input noise figure above 300 K = 10 dB,
(*iii*) input signal-to-noise ratio = 20 dB.

[*Ans.* 46 dB]

ADDITIONAL PROBLEMS

427. For a rhombic antenna the approximate relationship between the angle of elevation of the main lobe and the height of the antenna is $\sin\theta = \lambda/4h$. If the antenna height is 20 m and the leg length is 100 m for what frequency range is the antenna suitable, how many wavelengths is the leg length at the extremities of this operating band and what is the angular range of elevation of the main lobe for this antenna?

[*Ans.* 6 to 24 MHz; 12.5 and 50 m; 9° to 38° 41′]

428. An array consists of three vertical half-wave dipole antennas with their centres lying on a common horizontal axis. The three elements are fed with equal-amplitude currents having a progressive phase difference of 90° and are spaced at quarter-wavelength intervals.

If the self-impedance of each dipole is $(73.1 + j0)\ \Omega$ and the mutual impedance is $(-12.5 - j30)\ \Omega$ between adjacent dipoles and $(5 + j17.5)\ \Omega$ between the first and third dipoles, calculate the percentage power radiated by each dipole and the power gain in decibels of the array referred to a half-wave dipole.

[*Ans.* 47 per cent; 35 per cent; 18 per cent; 4.97 dB]

429. A 0.1-m radar set is operating with a peak output power of 200 kW and a pulse length of 1 μs. Calculate the noise figure of the receiver if an aircraft of radar cross-section 80 m^2 is to be detected at a range of 200 km. The antenna gain G may be assumed to be 30 dB and the effective area A of the antenna is related to G by $A = G\lambda^2/4\pi$. Assume that satisfactory detection results when the signal-to-noise ratio is 6 dB or better.

[*Ans.* 2.05]

430. A satellite communication system operates at a wavelength of 0.06 m with a spherical balloon of equivalent echoing area 10 m^2 and identical antennas of 50 dB gain for transmission and reception. The transmitter power is 10 kW, the receiving antenna noise temperature is 20 K and the receiver noise temperature is 30 K. The distances from the balloon to the transmitting and receiving antennas are 2000 and 3000 km respectively.

Evaluate the signal-to-noise ratio of the receiver output assuming a receiver bandwidth of 10 kHz.

[*Ans.* 12.2 dB]

CHAPTER FIFTEEN

MODULATION, DETECTION AND FREQUENCY CHANGING

431. The tuned circuit of an oscillator in an amplitude-modulated transmitter employs a 50-μH coil and a 0.001-μF capacitor. If the oscillator output is modulated up to 10 kHz, what is the frequency range occupied by the carrier and sidebands?

[*Ans.* 702 to 722 kHz]

432. The antenna current of a transmitter is 8 A when the carrier only is transmitted, but it increases to 8.93 A when the carrier is sinusoidally modulated. Find the percentage modulation.

Determine the antenna current when the depth of modulation is 0.8.

[*Ans.* 70 per cent, 9.19 A]

433. A certain transmitter radiates 9 kW of power with the carrier unmodulated, and 10.125 kW when the carrier is sinusoidally modulated. Calculate the depth of modulation.

If another audio wave, modulated to 40 per cent is also transmitted, determine the radiated power.

[*Ans.* 0.5; 10.845 kW]

434. Several frequencies simultaneously modulate a carrier. Show that the total power of all the sidebands will always be less than half of the carrier power.

435. A signal voltage $E_s = 1.5 \sin(1000t)$ V and a carrier voltage $E_c = 5 \sin(4 \times 10^6 t)$ V are applied to a non-linear device whose current-voltage characteristic can be represented by the expression $I = [10 + 2V + 0.02V^2]$ mA. Determine the amplitude and frequency of the various components of the current, and evaluate the depth of modulation.

[*Ans.* $I = 10.2725 + 3 \sin 10^3 t + 10 \sin(4 \times 10^6 t)$
$- 0.25 \cos(8 \times 10^6 t) - 0.0225 \cos(2 \times 10^3 t)$
$+ 0.15 \cos(4 \times 10^6 - 10^3)t - 0.15 \cos(4 \times 10^6 + 10^3)t$ mA; 0.03]

436. If a radio-frequency carrier wave is amplitude-modulated by a band of frequencies, 300 Hz to 3.4 kHz, what will be the bandwidth of the transmission and what frequencies will be present in the transmitted wave if the carrier frequency is 104 kHz?

[*Ans.* 6.8 kHz; 100.6 to 103.7 kHz, 104 kHz, 104 to 107.4 kHz]

437. A sinusoidal carrier of frequency f_c and peak amplitude 1 V is amplitude modulated with the traingular-wave modulating signal $f(t)$ shown. It is assumed that $T_c \ll T_m$ where $T_c = 1/f_c$. Find the total sideband power and the powers associated with the four lowest frequency components of $f(t)$ in terms of the unmodulated average carrier power, P_c, when the modulated carrier voltage is applied to a 1-Ω resistor.

(Note: Expanding $f(t)$ in a Fourier series gives $f(t) = \frac{2}{\pi}\left\{\sin\left(\frac{2\pi t}{T_m}\right) - \frac{1}{2}\sin\left(\frac{4\pi t}{T_m}\right) + \frac{1}{3}\sin\left(\frac{6\pi t}{T_m}\right) - \ldots\right\}$)

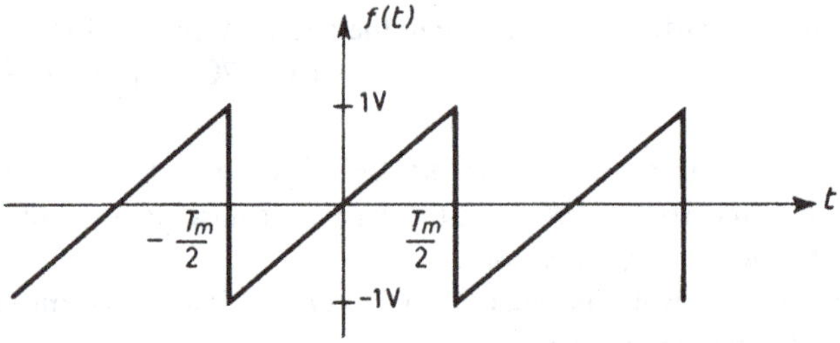

438. A balanced modulator employs two non-linear elements which have slightly different characteristics. If their characteristics are $i_1 = [I + aV + b_1V^2]$ and $i_2 = [I + aV + b_2V^2]$, find the output spectrum when the carrier frequency is f_c and the audio frequency is f_a.

[*Ans.* Output $= 2aE_a \sin \omega_a t + \left(\frac{b_1 - b_2}{2}\right)(E_c^2 + E_a^2)$

$-\left(\frac{b_1 - b_2}{2}\right)(E_c^2 \cos 2\omega_c t + E_a^2 \cos 2\omega_a t)$

$+ (b_1 + b_2)E_aE_c\{\cos(\omega_c - \omega_a)t - \cos(\omega_c + \omega_a)t\}$]

439. The following particulars refer to a certain anode-modulated, class-C amplifier:

D.C. anode-supply voltage, $E_a = 2000$ V.

Average anode current, $\bar{I}_a = 200$ mA.

Modulation voltage on the secondary side of the modulation transformer, $e_l = 1400 \sin 2000\,\pi t$ volts.

Anode-circuit efficiency = 0.8.

Determine:

(*a*) the depth of modulation *m*,

(*b*) the approximate maximum value of the anode-cathode voltage of the valve,

(*c*) the power delivered by the d.c. supply,

(*d*) the power delivered by the modulation transformer,

(*e*) the r.f. output power without modulation,

(*f*) the r.f. output power with modulation,

(*g*) the impedance into which the modulation transformer works.

[*Ans.* (*a*) 0.7; (*b*) 6460 V; (*c*) 400 W; (*d*) 98 W; (*e*) 320 W; (*f*) 398 W; (*g*) 10 000 Ω]

440. A frequency-modulated wave can be represented by the expression $i = I \sin(ct + M \sin at)$, where *M* is the frequency-deviation ratio, *a* is the angular frequency of the modulating signal and *c* is the angular frequency of the carrier. Show that the spectrum consists of a carrier and an infinite number of sidebands, all of whose amplitudes are various-order Bessel functions of *M*.

441. A frequency-modulated wave, resulting from modulation by an audio-frequency wave of frequency $f_a = 5000$ Hz, has a frequency deviation of 50 kHz. If this wave when radiated produces an unmodulated field of 0.001 Vm^{-1} at a certain point, what is the strength of the carrier and the sidebands at the same point when the wave is modulated?

[*Ans.* Carrier, $240 \times 10^{-6}\ Vm^{-1}$; sidebands, $50 \times 10^{-6}\ Vm^{-6}$; $260 \times 10^{-6}\ Vm^{-1}$, $50 \times 10^{-6}\ Vm^{-1}$, etc.]

442. A junction diode, whose capacitance is inversely proportional to the square root of the applied voltage, is used as the only capacitance element of an *LC* oscillator. The oscillator is frequency-modulated by superimposing a time-varying voltage on a steady bias voltage of 16 V which is applied to the diode.

In the absence of the modulating voltage the oscillation frequency is 50 MHz. Determine the modulation index and the percentage of second harmonic distortion when the modulating voltage is a 10-kHz sine wave of peak amplitude 100 mV (the third- and higher-order terms may be assumed negligible).

[*Ans.* 7.8; 0.117]

443. The calibration of a particular frequency modulator is effected by using a wave analyser to monitor the carrier component of the modulator output as the amplitude of the modulating signal $E_m \sin 2\pi f_m t$ is varied. As E_m is increased from zero the carrier component falls and becomes zero when $E_m = 3.46$ V. If $f_m = 3$ kHz, what is the conversion factor, k_f, for the modulator?

Sketch and label the output amplitude frequency spectrum for this modulator when the modulating signal is $2.11 \sin 4000\,\pi t$ V.

[*Ans.* 2085 Hz V^{-1}; for frequency spectrum see the solution]

444. In an amplitude-modulated system designed to transmit a 3-kHz baseband signal the input and output signal-to-noise power ratios of the envelope detector are 20 and 18 dB respectively. A frequency-modulated (F.M.) system is designed to carry the same amount of information. Determine the maximum peak frequency deviation for which full F.M. improvement can be realized and calculate this improvement.

Base the calculations on single sine-wave modulation at the highest baseband frequency. Also assume that the F.M. threshold occurs for an input signal-to-noise ratio of 12 dB and both systems have equal input signal powers and equal input noise power spectral densities. The relation $B_t = 6f_m + 2.13\, f_{fm}$ may also be assumed where f_{fm} is the maximum peak frequency deviation and B_t is the transmission bandwidth.

[*Ans.* 9.1 kHz, 16.4 dB]

445. Information is transmitted over a communication link via a phase-modulated carrier wave. The conversion factor, k_p, for the phase modulator in the transmitter is 1 rad V^{-1}. If the baseband signal is a sine wave of peak value $E_m = 3$ V, what is the maximum message frequency which may be transmitted if 40 kHz of spectral space are available? What values of E_m will cause complete suppression of

(*a*) the carrier component

(*b*) the third sideband pair components of the modulated waveform?

[*Ans.* 3.33 kHz; (*a*) 2.405, 5.520, 8.654, 11.792 - - - V,

(*b*) 6.380, 9.761, 13.015, 16.223 - - - V]

446. Show that the reactance-valve circuit illustrated, neglecting the effect of the alternating anode voltage on the valve current, is equivalent to a resistance $R_{AB} = \{1 + (R\omega C)^2\}/g_m$ in parallel with an inductance $L_{AB} = \{1 + (R\omega C)^2\}/g_m R\omega^2 C$, where g_m is the mutual conductance of the valve.

Find the equivalent resistances and reactances of the circuit for the three other combinations of resistance, inductance and capacitance elements which may be used for Z_1 and Z_2.

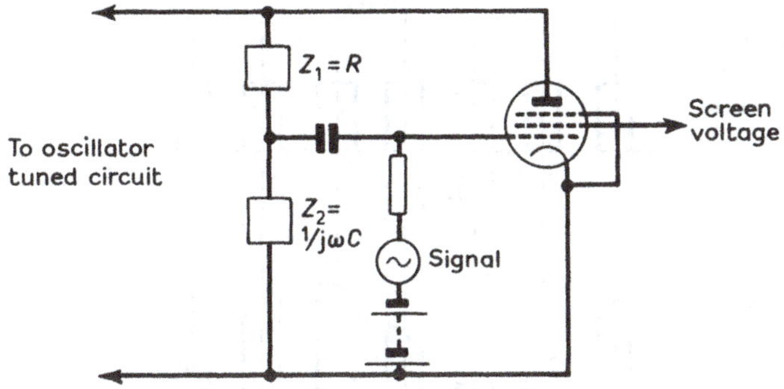

[*Ans.*

Z_1	C	R	L
Z_2	R	L	R
R_{AB}	$1 + (R\omega C)^2/g_m(R\omega C)^2$	$(R^2 + \omega^2 L^2)/g_m\omega^2 L^2$	$(R^2 + \omega^2 L^2)/g_m R^2$
X_{AB}	$C_{AB} = [g_m RC/\{1 + (R\omega C)^2\}]$	$C_{AB} = [g_m RL/\{R^2 + \omega^2 L^2\}]$	$L_{AB} = [(R^2 + \omega^2 L^2)/g_m R\omega^2 L]$

447. Pulse-amplitude modulation (P.A.M.) is defined as the process of varying the amplitude of a periodic, rectangular carrier pulse train, in synchronism with, and in direct proportion to, the amplitude of the modulating signal and the process is illustrated in the diagram.

Show that the unmodulated carrier pulse train $e_c(t)$ has a Fourier series expansion:

$$e_c(t) = \frac{E_c \tau_c}{T_c}\left[1 + 2\sum_{n=1}^{\infty}\left\{\frac{\sin(\omega_n \tau_c/2)}{\omega_n \tau_c/2}\right\}\cos \omega_n t\right]$$

where $\omega_n = 2\pi n/T_c$ and $n = 1, 2, 3 \ldots \infty$.

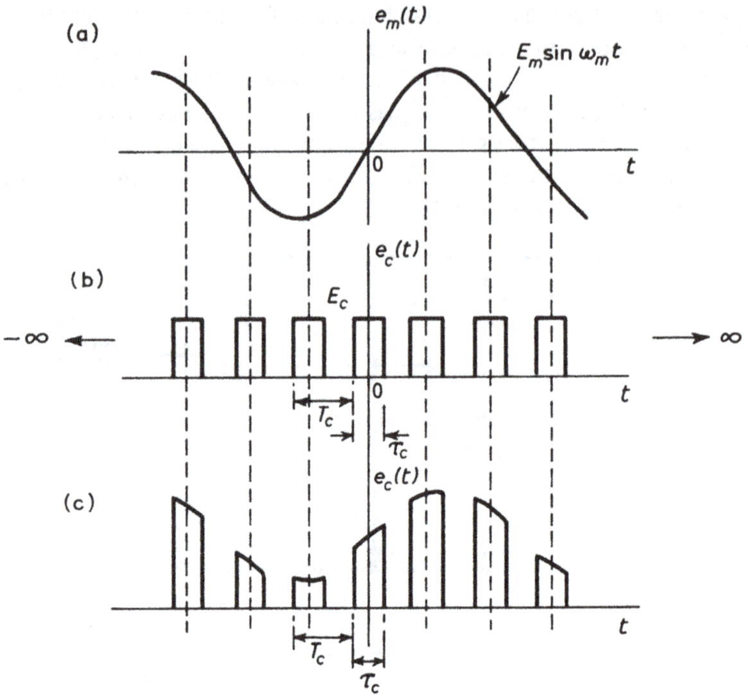

With a sinusoidal modulating signal $e_m(t) = E_m \sin \omega_m t$, E_c becomes $E_c + E_m \sin \omega_m t = E_c(1 + m_h \sin \omega_m t)$ where $m_h = E_m/E_c$.

Show that the above expressions give:

$$e_c(t) = \frac{E_c \tau_c}{T_c} \left\{ 1 + 2 \sum_{n=1}^{\infty} \left[\frac{\sin(\omega_n \tau_c/2)}{\omega_n \tau_c/2} \right] \cos\omega_n t \right\} (1 + m_h \sin\omega_m t)$$

$$= \frac{E_c \tau_c}{T_c} + \frac{E_c \tau_c m_h}{T_c} \sin\omega_m t + \frac{2E_c \tau_c}{T_c} \sum_{n=1}^{\infty} \left[\frac{\sin(\omega_n \tau_c/2)}{\omega_n \tau_c/2} \right]$$

$$x \left[\cos \omega_n t + \frac{m_h}{2} \sin(\omega_n + \omega_m) t - \frac{m_h}{2} \sin(\omega_n - \omega_m) t \right]$$

448. A diode detector employs a 220-kΩ resistor and a 100-μμF capacitor. Calculate the maximum value of the depth of modulation if peak clipping is to be avoided, and the maximum modulating frequency which the detector is designed to handle is 6000 Hz.

[*Ans.* 0.77]

449. Show that additive frequency changing can be obtained by applying the signal and oscillator voltages to a device with a non-linear current-voltage characteristic; and also show that a device having two control electrodes can be used as a multiplicative frequency changer.

450. An amplitude-modulated superheterodyne receiver has an intermediate frequency of 465 Hz and the desired-signal frequency is 700 kHz. Prove that undesired-signal frequencies of 351, 816, 1867 and 2797 kHz present at the input of the frequency changer, produce 2-kHz interference whistles if the current-voltage characteristic of the device has a third-power term.

451. (*a*) Design an oscillator tuned circuit containing only two preset components for a receiver covering the frequency band 550 to 1500 kHz, which has to gang with a signal circuit containing a 156-μH inductance coil. The intermediate frequency is 465 kHz.

(*b*) Design an oscillator tuned circuit containing three preset components for the receiver.

[*Ans.* (*a*) Padding capacitance = 288 $\mu\mu$F, Tuning inductance = 117.3 μH, (*b*) Padding capacitance = 601 $\mu\mu$F, Trimmer capacitance = 36.5 $\mu\mu$F, Tuning inductance = 77.4 μH,

ADDITIONAL PROBLEMS

452. An amplitude-modulated transmitter has an output of 24 kW when modulated to a depth of 100 per cent. Determine the power output (*a*) when the carrier is unmodulated (*b*) when after modulation to a depth of 60 per cent one sideband is suppressed and the carrier component is reduced by 26 dB.

[*Ans.* (*a*) 16 kW; (*b*) 1.48 kW]

453. A sinusoidal carrier of frequency f_c and peak amplitude 1 V is amplitude modulated with the square-wave modulating signal $f(t)$ having a peak value of 0.6 V as shown in the diagram. It is to be assumed that $T_c \ll T_m$ where $T_c = 1/f_c$. Find the total sideband power and the sideband powers associated with the four lowest frequency components of $f(t)$ in terms of the unmodulated average carrier power P_c, when the modulated carrier voltage is applied to a 1-Ω resistor.

(Note: Expanding $f(t)$ in a Fourier series gives

$$f(t) = \frac{2.4}{\pi}\left\{\sin\left(\frac{2\pi t}{T_m}\right) + \frac{1}{3}\sin\left(\frac{6\pi t}{T_m}\right) + \frac{1}{5}\sin\left(\frac{10\pi t}{T_m}\right) + \ldots\right\}\Bigg)$$

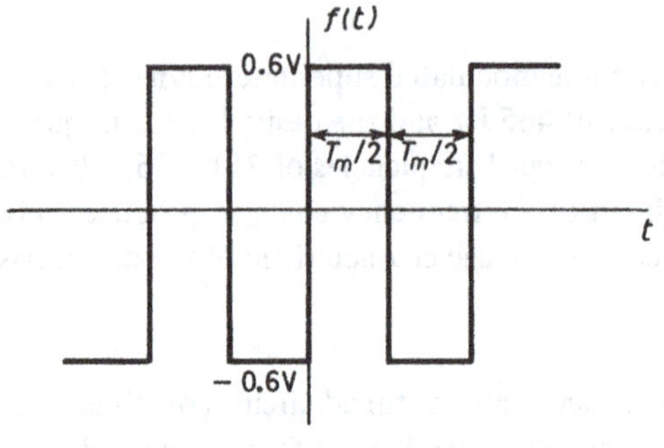

454. A sinusoidal carrier is amplitude modulated with the triangular modulating signal $f(t)$ given in the diagram.

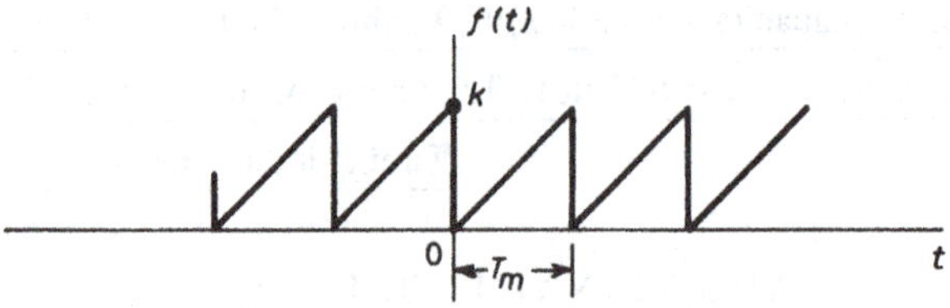

Show that the total average normalized power associated with the modulated carrier is

$$P = P_c\,(1 + k^2/3 + k)$$

where the total sideband power is given by

$$P_{sb} = P_c\,k^2/3$$

and P_c is the unmodulated average carrier power.

455. The modulation in a frequency-modulated transmitter is achieved by variation of the tuning capacitance of an oscillator operating at a mean frequency of 3 MHz. The coil used in the parallel tuned circuit of the oscillator has an inductance of 10 μH. If the modulated waveform is frequency-multiplied to give an output of 120 MHz with a maximum frequency deviation of 180 kHz determine the change in capacitance to be produced by the modulating signal.

[*Ans.* 1.68 $\mu\mu$F]

456. Pulse-width modulation (P.W.M.) is defined as the process of varying the width of the pulses in a periodic, rectangular carrier pulse train, in synchronism with, and in direct proportion to, the amplitude of the modulating signal. The leading edge or the trailing edge of the pulse, or both, may be shifted. Consider the case where both the leading and trailing edges of each pulse are shifted symmetrically about the pulse centre but the centre-to-centre spacing of the carrier pulses is held constant.

The expression for the unmodulated carrier pulse $e_c(t)$ given in Problem 447 still holds. The pulse width now becomes $\tau_c + \tau_m \sin \omega_m t = \tau_c (1 + m_\omega \sin \omega_m t)$ where $m_\omega = \tau_m/\tau_c$.

Show that:

$$e_c(t) = \frac{E_c \tau_c}{T_c} + \frac{E_c \tau_c m_\omega}{T_c} \sin \omega_m t$$

$$+ \sum_{n=1}^{\infty} \frac{2E_c}{n\pi} (\cos \omega_n t) \sin \left(\frac{\omega_n \tau_c}{2} + \frac{\omega_n \tau_c m_\omega \sin \omega_m t}{2} \right)$$

and that this can be expanded in terms of Bessel functions as:

$$e_c(t) = \frac{E_c \tau_c}{T_c} + \frac{E_c \tau_c m_\omega}{T_c} \sin \omega_m t$$

$$+ \sum_{n=1}^{\infty} \frac{2E_c \tau_c}{T_c} \times \left[\frac{\sin (\omega_n \tau_c/2)}{\omega_n \tau_c/2} \right] J_o \left(\frac{\omega_n \tau_c m_\omega}{2} \right) \cos \omega_n t$$

$$+ \left[\frac{\sin (\omega_n \tau_c/2)}{\omega_n \tau_c/2} \right] \times \sum_{p=2,4,6}^{\infty} J_p \left(\frac{\omega_n \tau_c m_\omega}{2} \right) \left[\cos (\omega_n + p\omega_m) t + \cos (\omega_n - p\omega_m) t \right]$$

$$+ \left[\frac{\cos (\omega_n \tau_c/2)}{\omega_n \tau_c/2} \right] \sum_{p=1,3,5} J_p \left(\frac{\omega_n \tau_c m_\omega}{2} \right) \left[\sin (\omega_n + p\omega_m) t - \sin (\omega_n - p\omega_m) t \right]$$

CHAPTER SIXTEEN

COMMUNICATION AND INFORMATION THEORY

457. The face of a colour television tube is divided into 5×10^5 independent incremental areas and each area is activated once during a picture scan. There are 64 colour shades for each incremental area and 16 brightness levels for each colour shade. If all colour-shade, brightness-level combinations are equally likely and statistically independent, calculate the required channel capacity to transmit 100 pictures per second.

If the signal-to-noise power ratio at the receiving end of a communication channel is 30 dB, what system bandwidth must the communication channel have in order to transmit the colour picture.

[*Ans.* 5×10^8 bits per second, $\simeq$ 50 MHz]

458. A network has a transfer function $H(\omega)$ given by:

$$H(\omega) = \exp(-a\omega^2 - \mathrm{j}b\omega)$$

where a and b are real positive constants. A unit delta function $\delta(t)$ is applied to the input terminals of the network. Show that the resulting output signal reaches its maximum value at time $t = b$ and the width of the signal at the $1/e$ points of the maximum value is $4\sqrt{(a)}$.

459. A discrete source produces symbols A and B. The probability of A occurring is 3/4; that of B occurring is 1/4. In an attempt to match the source to a binary channel the symbols are grouped in blocks of 2 and encoded as follows:

Grouped symbol	Binary symbol
AA	1
AB	01
BA	001
BB	000

Calculate the coding efficiency.

[*Ans.* 96 per cent]

460. A message source generates a number of discrete symbols such that the probability of occurrence of the nth symbol is P_n. Define and justify an expression for the self-information content of this symbol. Show how the entropy of the message is related to the self-information of the symbols contained in the message.

A message source generates eight different symbols A to H. The probabilities of these signals occurring are shown in the following table. Also shown is the Huffman binary code for this message source. One characteristic of the Huffman code is that it always calls for less than one binary digit per symbol more than the entropy. Verify that this statement is true for the code given in the table and calculate the coding efficiency.

Symbol	Probability	Huffman Code
A	0.50	1
B	0.15	001
C	0.12	011
D	0.10	010
E	0.04	00011
F	0.04	00010
G	0.03	00001
H	0.02	00000

Describe one possible code for the message which uses three binary digits per symbol, and calculate the coding efficiency in this case.

[*Ans.* 97.7 per cent, see the solution for the code and its coding efficiency]

461. The Hartley-Shannon law is often written

$$C = B \log_2 \left(1 + \frac{S}{N}\right) \text{bits per second.}$$

Define carefully the terms appearing in this equation and then show that it is a plausible relationship.

The transmitter power of a microwave data-link is increased by 3 dB. What quantitative effect could this have on the amount of information that might be transmitted over the link in a given time? Assume $S/N \gg 1$, and $B = 10$ MHz.

[*Ans.* C increased by 10^7 bits per second]

ADDITIONAL PROBLEMS

462. The letters A, B, C, D are transmitted, each letter being coded as a sequence of binary pulses. Each individual pulse interval is 5 μs. Calculate the maximum rate of transmission of information in symbols per second if:

(*i*) the different letters are equally probable,

(*ii*) the probability of occurrence of $A = \frac{1}{2}, B = \frac{1}{4}, C = \frac{1}{8}$ and $D = \frac{1}{8}$.

[*Ans.* 10^5, 1.14×10^5]

463. The telemetry system of a satellite sends out a binary symbol (say 0 or 1) every 10 ms. Measurements of temperature are to be transmitted as lying always in one of five ranges, denoted by T_1, T_2, T_3, T_4, T_5. If these levels are equally likely, at what rate can temperature readings be conveyed? Give the average entropy of the message.

Suppose now that the different temperature levels are not equally likely and the different probabilities are $Pr(T_1) = 1/16, Pr(T_2) = 1/4, Pr(T_3) = 1/2, Pr(T_4) = 1/8, Pr(T_5) = 1/16$. If these temperatures were still encoded without recognition of these probabilities what would be the maximum average transmission rate? What would be the new average entropy of the message assuming no intersymbol influence?

[*Ans.* 43 levels per second, 2.32 bits per level, 43 levels per second, 1.88 bits per level]

464. A Gaussian voltage pulse $v(t) = A \exp(-t^2/\tau^2)$ is received in the presence of white noise whose r.m.s. voltage per unit bandwidth is N. The signal and noise are passed through a filter whose transfer function $H(f)$ is also Gaussian:

$$H(f) = \exp(-\omega^2/\omega_c^2)$$

where ω_c is a constant.

Show that the peak signal-to-noise power ratio after the filter is:

$$4\sqrt{(2\pi)}\, A^2\, \omega_c\, \tau^2/N^2 (\omega_c^2 \tau^2 + 4).$$

465. A rectangular voltage pulse of unit amplitude and pulse length T is contaminated by white noise having a mean square voltage of V_n^2 per unit bandwidth. Calculate the output signal-to-noise power-ratio if both signal and noise are passed through a matched filter.

Rather than use a matched filter, it is decided to use a simple R-C low-pass filter. Show that the signal-to-noise ratio is now $\frac{2CR}{T}\left\{1-\exp\left(-\frac{T}{RC}\right)\right\}^2$ times that if the correct matched filter were used.

[*Ans.* T/V_n^2]

466. A standard voice telephone circuit is used to transmit the six symbols detailed below. The signal-to-noise ratio after transmission is 30 dB and the available bandwidth is 3 kHz. The probilities of the symbols occurring are as follows:

Source symbol	Probability
A	1/4
B	1/4
C	1/4
D	1/8
E	1/16
F	1/16

Show that the maximum rate at which symbols could be transmitted over this system is approximately 12 600 symbols per second.

CHAPTER SEVENTEEN

KINETIC THEORY OF AND CONDUCTION IN GASES

467. Calculate the root-mean-square speed of nitrogen molecules (N_2) at 273 K and 373 K. Take the mass of a proton as 1.67×10^{-27} kg and the atomic weight of nitrogen as 14.

[*Ans.* 492; 575]

468. What fraction of the molecules per cubic metre in a gas have speeds lying within ± 1 per cent of the most probable speed?

[*Ans.* 0.0166]

469. Show that the distribution function for gas molecules having x directed velocity components in the range v_x to $v_x + dv_x$ and with any velocity in the y and z directions is:

$$dN_x = N\left(\frac{m}{2\pi kT}\right)^{\frac{1}{2}} e^{\frac{-mv_x^2}{2kT}} dv_x$$

$$= Ne^{-\omega^2} d\omega/\sqrt{(\pi)}$$

where $\omega = v_x/v_p$ and v_p is the most probable speed.

470. Use the results of Problem 469 to show that the number of gas molecules that strike unit area of the container walls in unit time with a normal velocity greater than v is $Nv_p e^{-\omega^2}/2\sqrt{(\pi)}$.

471. Use the expression given in Problem 469 to show that the pressure exerted by a gas on the walls of its containing vessel is equal to NkT.

472. A metal may be thought to consist of a box containing many electrons. If these electrons behave like molecules of a gas and require an energy greater than ϕ in a direction normal to one face of the box to escape from it, show using the results of Problem 470 that the electron current emission from the box has a temperature dependence of the form $A\sqrt{(T)}$ $e^{-\phi/kT}$ where T is the absolute temperature and A is a constant for the metal.

473. For a gas having a Boltzmann distribution of energies the fractional number of particles having energy in the range E to $E + dE$ is given by:

$$2\pi \left(\frac{1}{\pi kT}\right)^{3/2} E^{\frac{1}{2}}\, e^{-E/kT}\, dE.$$

Use this expression to determine the most probable energy and the mean energy of the system.

Calculate the temperature to which a gas would have to be raised if its mean energy was 1 eV.

[*Ans.* $kT/2$; $3kT/2$; 7740 K]

474. A hypothetical distribution function of a group of N particles is given by:

$$dN_v = K\,v^2\,dv \qquad (V > v > 0)$$
$$dN_v = 0 \qquad (v > V)$$

(i) Sketch the form of the distribution function.
(ii) Find the constant K in terms of N and V.
(iii) Compute the average speed, the r.m.s. speed and the most probable speed in terms of V.

[*Ans.* (ii) $K = 3N/V^3$, (iii) $3V/4$, $\sqrt{(3)}\,V/\sqrt{(5)}$, V]

475. (*a*) Determine the minimum velocity which an electron must have to excite an argon molecule.

(*b*) An electron travelling with the same velocity as the one in (*a*) ionizes a mercury molecule by collision. If the excess energy is assumed to be shared equally between the colliding and liberated electrons, what is the final velocity of each?

(*c*) The mean free path of an electron in neon gas is 7.9×10^{-4} m at room temperature and a pressure of 1 torr. Find the minimum field strength for an electron, starting at rest, to acquire the ionization energy in its mean free path.

(*d*) A mercury atom is excited to an energy of 7.93 V. It returns to the normal 'ground' state in two steps, first falling to an energy level of 6.71 V and then to zero. Calculate the wavelengths of the emitted radiations.

[*Ans.* (*a*) $2.02 \times 10^6\ ms^{-1}$; (*b*) $0.459 \times 10^6\ ms^{-1}$; (*c*) $2.72 \times 10^4\ Vm^{-1}$; (*d*) 10 160 Å; 1848 Å]

476. In a discharge tube containing gas at a pressure of 5 torr the following readings of current I and electrode separation x were obtained with a constant voltage gradient:

x (m)	0.002	0.004	0.006	0.008	0.016
I ($\mu\mu$A)	1.8	3.3	6.0	11.0	200

Estimate the values of the primary ionization coefficient in the gas, the secondary emission coefficient at the cathode and the electrode spacing at which breakdown may be expected.

[*Ans.* 3 cm^{-1}; 0.0033; 1.91 cm]

477. In a uniform-field discharge gap at a certain gas pressure the effective value of γ for the cathode is 0.02. Breakdown is found to occur at 400 V when the gap is 5 mm long. Find the value of the first ionization coefficient and the multplication obtained with 200 V across a 2.5 mm gap in the same gas.

[*Ans.* 7.82 cm^{-1}; 8.06]

478. In a discharge tube with electrodes 20 cm apart the positive column of a glow discharge is about 15 cm long and a Langmuir probe of effective surface area 0.033 cm^2 is inserted at a point 12 cm from the anode. The following values were obtained for the probe potential relative to the anode V_p and indicated current I_p:

V_p (volts)	−6	−8	−10	−12	−14	−16
I_p (mA)	37.0	36.6	36.4	18.8	5.0	1.32

V_p (volts)	−18	−20	−22	−24	−26
I_p (mA)	0.30	0.02	−0.06	−0.08	−0.08

Estimate the electron temperature and concentration and find the voltage gradient in the plasma if the anode fall of potential is 5 V positive. If the random current density is six times the drift current density determine the mobility of the electrons in the plasma.

[*Ans.* 17 800 K; 3.3×10^{17} m^{-3}; 0.5 Vcm^{-1}; 6.8×10^6 cm^2 V^{-1} s^{-1}]

479. A cathode-ray tube has an anode voltage of 500 V and the distance from anode to screen is 20 cm. What is the maximum allowable pressure in the tube if not more than 10 per cent of the electrons in the beam are to be scattered in their passage from the anode to the screen?

The total collision cross-section for the gas in the tube at a pressure of 1 torr and an energy of 500 eV is 10^{-16} cm^2. Assume Loschmidt's number is 2.7×10^{19} molecules/cm^{-3} at N.T.P.

[*Ans.* 1.405×10^{-3} torr]

480. In a pulsed discharge experiment microwave beams of wavelengths 8 mm and 3 cm respectively are directed towards the discharge tube. It is found that transmission of the beams resumes at times 5.7 and 81 μs respectively after the end of the current pulse. Estimate the effective recombination coefficient of the plasma.

[*Ans.* $\simeq 10^{-8}$]

ADDITIONAL PROBLEMS

481. A hypothetical material with N electrons m^{-3} has a speed distribution function:

$$f(v) = Cv^2 \text{ for } 0 < v < v_0$$
$$= 0 \quad \text{for } v > v_0.$$

Find the mean square fluctuation of the speeds which is defined as the mean square speed minus the square of the mean speed.

If N is independent of temperature T and the mean square speed is equal to $3kT/m$ calculate the temperature dependence of C and v_0.

[*Ans.* $0.0375\, v_0{}^2; C = 3N\left(\frac{m}{5k}\right)^{\frac{3}{2}}\left(\frac{1}{T}\right)^{\frac{3}{2}}; v_0 = \sqrt{(5kT/m)}$]

482. A hypothetical distribution function has the following number of electrons with speed between v and $v + dv$:

$$dN_v = \frac{K}{(b^2 + v^2)^2}\, dv$$

where K and b are constants.

Calculate the mean speed, the r.m.s. speed and the most probable speed as functions of b. How many electrons have a speed of exactly 2b? How would b be expected to change if the electrons were heated?

[*Ans.* $2b/\pi, b, 0, 0$, increase]

483. A discharge tube, with electrodes 1 cm apart producing a uniform field, contains a gas for which

$$\alpha/p = 15\, e^{-350p/E}$$

where p is the pressure in torr and E the field in V cm^{-1}.

Find the maximum multiplication, the pressure at which it occurs and the average energy required per ion-pair, if the applied voltage is 100 V.

[*Ans.* 4.81; 0.29 torr, 64 eV]

484. A Langmuir probe of surface area 2.5 mm^2 can draw a saturated electron current of 18 mA from a glow-discharge plasma. When the probe is 2.2 V negative to the surrounding plasma the electron current is one-quarter of its saturated value. Find the electron concentration and temperature.

[*Ans.* 2.15×10^{17} m^{-3}; 18 200 K]

CHAPTER EIGHTEEN

MOTION OF ELECTRONS IN ELECTRIC AND MAGNETIC FIELDS

485. An electric field of $10^4\ \text{V m}^{-1}$ is parallel with but opposed to a magnetic field of $5\ \text{mWb m}^{-2}$. Electrons travelling with a velocity of $1.19 \times 10^7\ \text{ms}^{-1}$ enter the region of the fields at an angle of 30° with the direction of the electric field. Determine the motion of an electron.

[*Ans.* The electron path is helical]

486. A magnetic field B and an electric field E are at right-angles to one another as illustrated. Determine the path of an electron which starts at rest at the origin O.

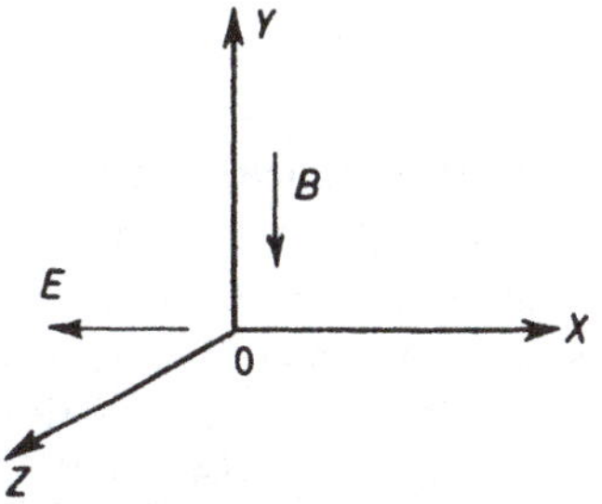

[*Ans.* The path is cycloidal: the path generated by a point on the circumference of a circle which rolls along the Z axis]

487. In a certain cathode-ray tube there is a magnetic field of $0.01\ \text{Wb m}^{-2}$ along the axis and an electric field of $10^4\ \text{Vm}^{-1}$ applied to the deflector plates which are 0.02 m long. Calculate how far from the axis an electron will be when it leaves the region between the deflector plates if it was travelling initially along the axis with a velocity of $10^6\ \text{m s}^{-1}$.

[*Ans.* 2.04×10^{-2} m]

488. A magnetic field B of $1\ \text{mWb/m}^{-2}$ and an electric field E of $5\ \text{kV m}^{-1}$ are at angle of 20° with each other as illustrated. Determine the path of an electron which starts at rest at the origin.

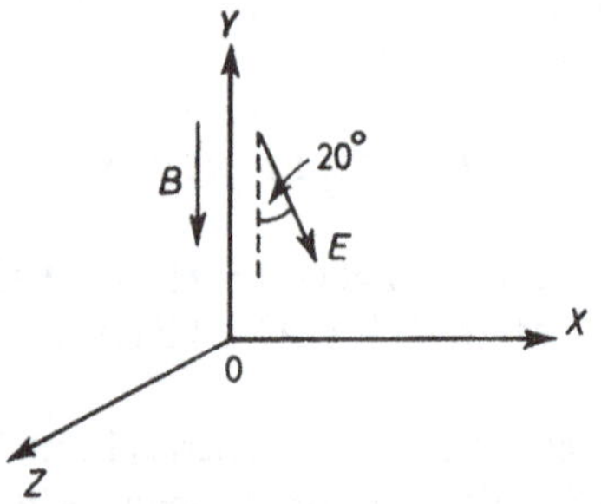

[*Ans.* The projection of the path in the *XZ* plane is a common cycloid]

489. A cathode-ray tube has plane-parallel deflector plates 1.5 cm long spaced 0.3 cm apart. The screen is 20 cm from the ends of the deflector plates. Before entering the space between the plates the electron beam is accelerated by a voltage of 1500 V. Determine the sensitivity of the tube. Neglect any fringing at the ends of the deflector plates.

[*Ans.* 28.9 V cm^{-1}]

490. A cathode-ray tube is constructed with internally-mounted plane-parallel magnetic poles 1.5 cm long and the ends of these are a distance of 20 cm from the screen. Before entering the field due to the poles the electrons are accelerated by a voltage of 1500 V. Determine the sensitivity of the tube. Neglect any fringing of the magnetic field.

[*Ans.* 0.042 Wb m^{-2} per metre]

ADDITIONAL PROBLEM

491. A beam of electrons enters the evacuated space between two parallel plates with a velocity u_o through a small hole at 'A' and, as a result of the applied voltage V, leaves through a similar hole at 'B' as shown.

Find the relationship between V and u_o and hence calculate V if $u_o = 10^7 ms^{-1}$.

The battery is now disconnected and a uniform magnetic field superimposed over the space between the plates parallel to them and at right angles to the plane in which the electron is moving. Calculate the flux density if the electron enters and leaves the space between the plates as before.

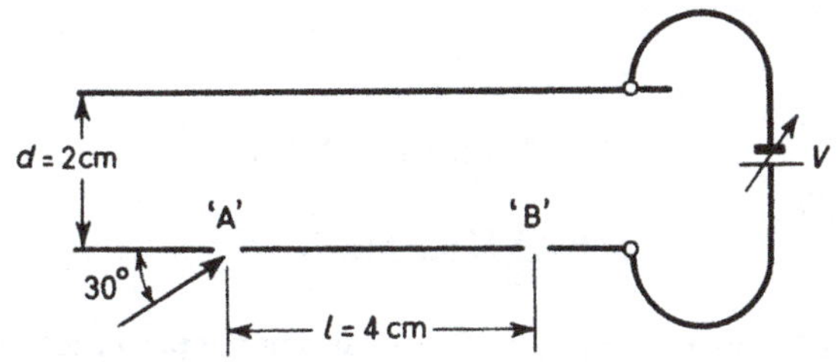

[*Ans.* $V = \dfrac{2dm\,u_o^2 \sin\theta \cos\theta}{el}$ where $\theta = 30^\circ$ in this case and e and m are the charge and mass of the electron respectively; 246 V; $1.4 \times 10^{-3}\,\mathrm{Wbm^{-2}}$]

CHAPTER NINETEEN

MEASUREMENTS

492. A Schering bridge is used for measuring the power loss in dielectrics. The specimens are in the form of discs 3 mm thick and have a dielectric constant of 2.3. The area of each electrode is $3.14 \times 10^{-2}\,\text{m}^2$ and the loss angle is known to be $9'$ for a frequency of 50 Hz. The fixed resistor of the network has a value of 1000 Ω and the fixed capacitance is 50 μμF. Determine the values of the variable resistor and capacitor required.

[*Ans.* 4260 Ω; 0.00196 μF]

493. The diagram shows Anderson's bridge for measuring the inductance L and resistance R of an unknown impedance. Find the values of L and R if balance is obtained when $Q = S = 1000\ \Omega$, $P = 500\ \Omega$, $r = 200\ \Omega$ and $C = 2\ \mu$F.

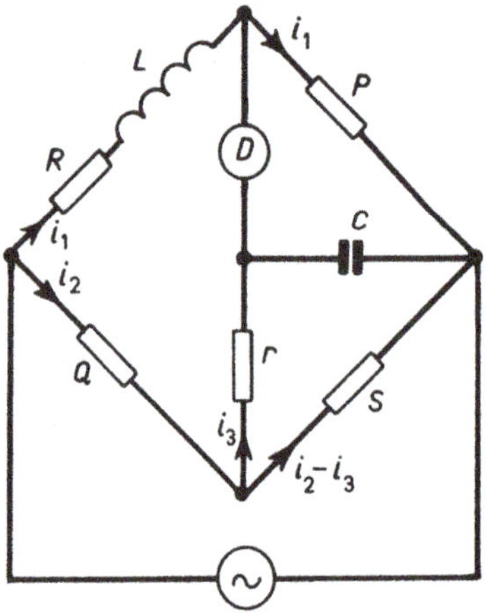

[*Ans.* 1.4 H; 500 Ω]

494. The arms AB, AD of a bridge are of inductances L_1, L_2 and of resistances R_1, R_2 respectively; the arms DC, BC contain capacitors of capacitances C_1, C_2 and are of resistances R_3, R_4 respectively. BD contains the detector and AC a source of alternating voltage. Show that the bridge will not be balanced for all frequencies unless $L_1R_3 = L_2R_4$, $C_1R_2 = C_2R_1$, and either $R_1R_3 = R_2R_4$ or $L_1 = C_1R_2R_4$.

495. The series-resistance bridge network is used for the comparison of capacitances. A capacitor of capacitance C_1 and equivalent series resistance ρ_1 is compared with a standard air capacitor of capacitance 0.023 μF and zero equivalent resistance. When a balance is obtained the resistor in series with C_1 has a value of 11.4 Ω, and that in series with the standard capacitor has a value of 10 Ω. The non-inductive resistors have values of 1000 Ω and 1250 Ω, one end of the latter being connected to one side of C_1. Calculate ρ_1 and C_1.

[*Ans.* 1.1 Ω; 0.0184 μF]

496. The diagram gives the connections of Hay's bridge for the measurement of large self-inductances. L is the inductance to be measured, R_1 its resistance, C is a variable standard capacitor and R_2, R_3 and R_4 are non-inductive resistors. Balance may be obtained by variation of R_2, R_4 and C. Show that, at balance,

$$L = [R_2R_3C/(1 + \omega^2R_4{}^2C^2)]$$

and

$$R_1 = [R_2R_3R_4\omega^2C^2/(1 + \omega^2R_4{}^2C^2)],$$

where $\omega = 2\pi \times$ supply frequency.

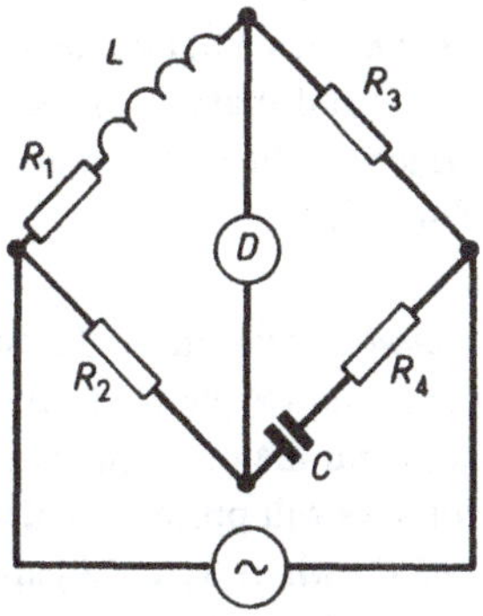

Draw the phasor diagram for the network.

497. One method of measuring a small capacitance C_x is shown in the diagram. C_1 and C_2 are equal high-quality variable air capacitors. C_3 is a fixed high-quality capacitance of much smaller value than the maximum value of C_2 (about 1/10 of C_2). The two following balances are obtained:

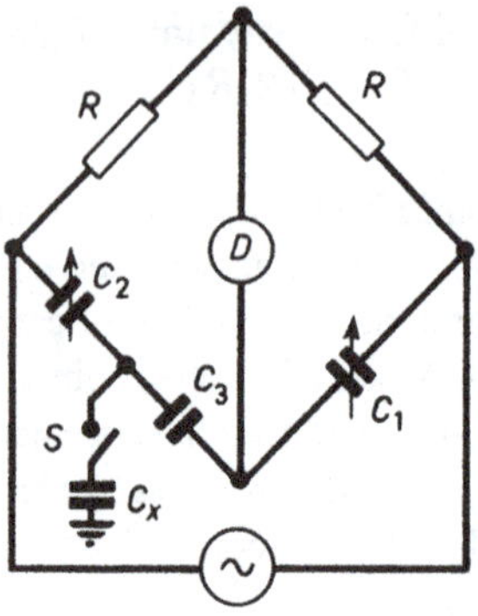

(1) With switch S open, and with C_2 at its maximum value, C_1 is adjusted for balance.

(2) With switch S closed, and C_1 left unaltered, C_2 is adjusted to C_2' to give a new balance.

Prove that

$$C_x = C_3^2(C_2 - C_2')/(C_2'C_2 + C_2'C_3 - C_2C_3).$$

If $R = 1000\ \Omega$, C_1 and C_2 are 1000 $\mu\mu$F and $C_3 = 50\ \mu\mu$F, and assuming the variable capacitors are readable to ± 5 $\mu\mu$F, with what accuracy could a capacitance of 1 $\mu\mu$F be measured?

[*Ans.* ± 3.5 per cent]

498. The voltage across the horizontal deflector plates of a cathode-ray oscillograph is $V_1 \sin(\omega t + \theta_1)$ and that across the vertical plates is $V_2 \sin(\omega t + \theta_2)$. Prove that the trace on the screen is an ellipse, determine its equation and interpret its meaning.

499. The phase-angle between two sinusoidal voltages can be measured by applying one voltage (maximum value V_1) to the vertical deflector plates of a cathode-ray oscillograph and the other (maximum value V_2) to the horizontal plates. These voltages will produce deflections on the screen of the tube $Y = k_1V_1$ and $X = k_2V_2$ where k_1 and k_2 are constants which depend on the sensitivity of the tube. If voltage V_2 leads voltage V_1 by an angle α, an ellipse will result which is bounded by a rectangle with sides $2X$ and $2Y$, as illustrated. Show that the phase-angle can be obtained from the ellipse in two ways; and derive the expressions $\sin\alpha = BC/AD$ and $\sin\alpha = (2a)(2b)/(2X)(2Y)$.

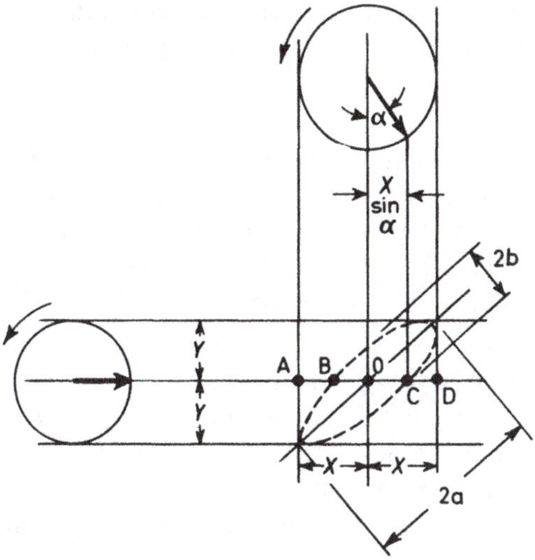

500. In determining phase-angle by the two methods given in the previous problem, an error of ± 0.5 mm may be introduced at either end of each dimension measured. Plot curves showing the resultant phase-angle error, as α varies, for values of AD equal to 40 mm, 70 mm, and 100 mm, suitable for tube screen diameters of about 6 cm, 11 cm, and 21 cm respectively.

501. When harmonics are present in either of the voltage waves of Questions 499 and 500, show that additional errors may be introduced. For both methods plot curves of the error against phase angle when either (*a*) a 5 per cent positive third harmonic is present in the waveform of V_1 or (*b*) a 5 per cent positive third harmonic is present in the waveform of V_2.

502. Two sinusoidal voltages of equal frequency are simultaneously applied to the two pairs of deflector plates in a cathode-ray tube. The co-ordinates (x, y) of the fluorescent spot may be expressed as $x = \sin(\theta + \phi)$ and $y = \sin \theta$. Plot the figures traced on the screen of the tube for the cases $\phi = 0$, $\phi = 30°$, $\phi = 60°$ and $\phi = 90°$ respectively.

503. Two sinusoidal voltages of unequal frequency are simultaneously applied to the two pairs of deflector plates in a cathode-ray tube. The co-ordinates (x, y) of the fluorescent spot may be expressed as $x = \sin(n\theta + \phi)$

and $y = \sin\theta$. Plot the figures traced on the screen of the tube for the cases $\phi = 0$, $\phi = 30^\circ$, $\phi = 60^\circ$ and $\phi = 90^\circ$, respectively, (*a*) when $n = 2$, and (*b*) when $n = 3$.

504. Two sinusoidal voltages of unequal frequency are simultaneously applied to the two pairs of deflector plates in a cathode-ray tube. The co-ordinates (x, y) of the fluorescent spot may be expressed as $x = \sin(3\theta + \phi)$ and $y = \sin 2\theta$. Plot the figures traced on the screen of the tube for the cases $\phi = 0$, $\phi = 30^\circ$, $\phi = 60^\circ$, $\phi = 90^\circ$, $\phi = 120^\circ$ and $\phi = 180^\circ$.

505. Two sinusoidal voltages of unequal frequency are simultaneously applied to the two pairs of deflector plates in a cathode-ray tube. The figure traced out on the screen is illustrated at (*a*). What is the ratio of the frequencies of the two applied voltages?

If the figure traced on the screen is that shown at (*b*), what is then the frequency ratio?

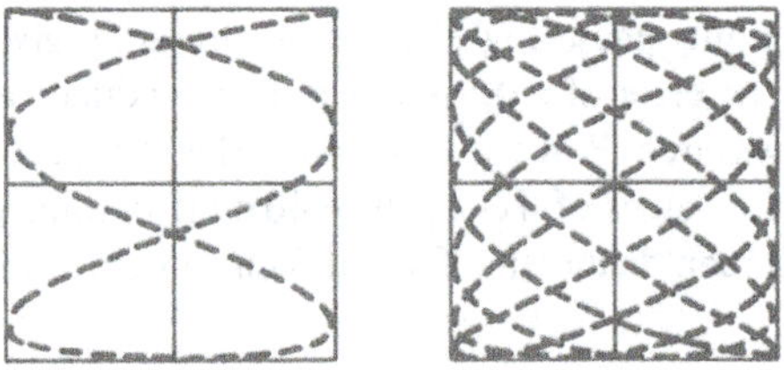

(a) (b)

[*Ans.* (*a*) 5:2; (*b*) 7:4]

506. In the time-base circuit shown the supply frequency is 50 Hz and the capacitance of C is 2 μF. Calculate the resistance of R to give a circular time base for equal sensitivities of the X and Y plates.

Repeat the calculation for sensitivites of the X and Y plates equal to 0.45 and 0.55 mm V^{-1} respectively.

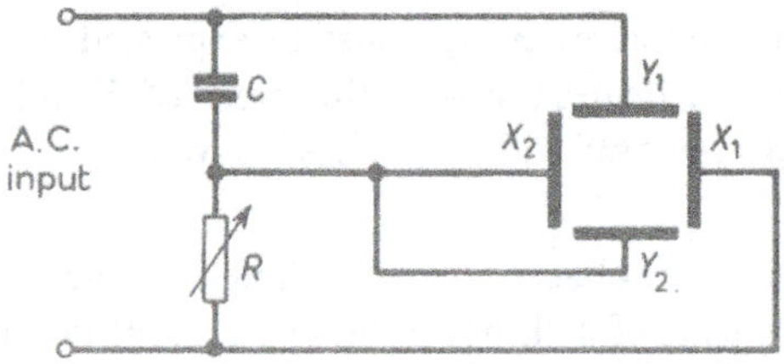

[*Ans.* 1592 Ω; 1946 Ω]

507. In a thyratron time-base circuit the control ratio of the valve is 30, and its extinction voltage is 20 V. The grid bias is set at − 5 V. The capacitor has a capacitance of 0.01 μF and it is charged at a constant rate of 1.5 mA. The output from the circuit is applied to a cathode-ray tube which has a sensitivity of 0.8 mm V^{-1}. Find the length of the time base and the frequency of sweep.

[*Ans.* 0.104 m; 1154 Hz]

ADDITIONAL PROBLEMS

508. The connections of Heaviside's bridge, for the measurement of self-inductance, are shown in the diagram. The primary of a mutual inductometer is in the supply circuit, and the secondary, of self-inductance L_2 and resistance R_2, forms one arm of the bridge. The coil under test, of self-inductance L_1 and resistance R_1, is placed in another arm and non-inductive resistors R_3 and R_4 form the remaining arms. Balance may be obtained by variation of the mutual inductance and the resistors R_3 and R_4. Determine the conditions for balance.

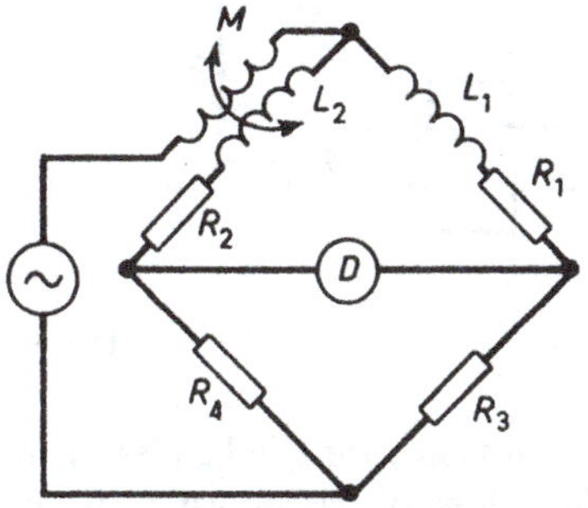

[*Ans.* $R_2R_3 = R_1R_4$ and $R_2(L_2 + M) = R_4(L_1 - M)$]

509. A certain linear time base employs a saturated diode and a thyratron. The striking and extinction voltages of the thyratron are 280 V and 30 V respectively, and the diode charging current is constant at 5 mA. Find the range of capacitance values required for the capacitor if the sweep frequency is to be variable from 20 Hz to 20 kHz.

[*Ans.* 0.001 to 1 μF]

CHAPTER TWENTY

LOGICAL SWITCHING CIRCUITS

510. On a 4-variable Karnaugh map* plot the function f as defined by the circuit below. Minimize this function and draw the minimal circuit using 3-input OR and AND gates.

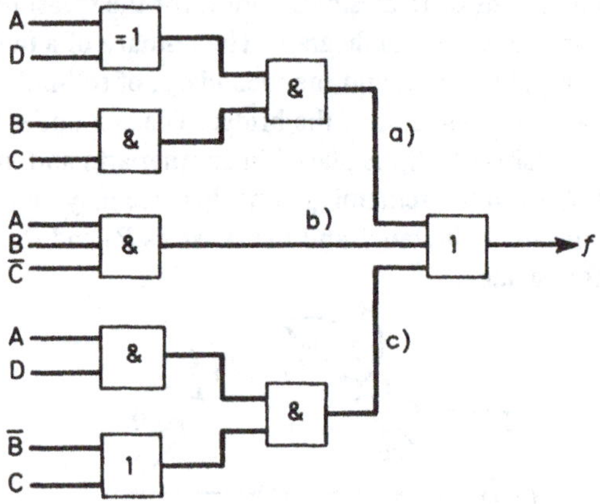

[*Ans.* see the Solution]

511. Draw up the truth table† for a full adder and derive the equations for the two outputs. Show how the circuit can be formed by using two half adders and an OR gate.

[*Ans.* see the Solution]

512. Using the waveforms below, which are applied to the J and K inputs of a J-K flip-flop, derive the output waveform Q.

* The Karnaugh map representation is described in many books, see for example, S. M. Bozic, R. M. H. Cheng and J. D. Parsons, *Electronic and Switching Circuits*, Arnold, 1975, Section 4.7. B. R. Bannister and D. G. Whitehead, *Fundamentals of Digital Systems*, McGraw-Hill, 1973, Section 1.4.

† The truth table is discussed in many books, see for example, B. R. Bannister and D. G. Whitehead, *Fundamentals of Digital Systems*, McGraw-Hill, 1973, Section 1.3, or D. Lewin, *Logical Design of Switching Circuits*, Nelson, 1968, Section 2–6.

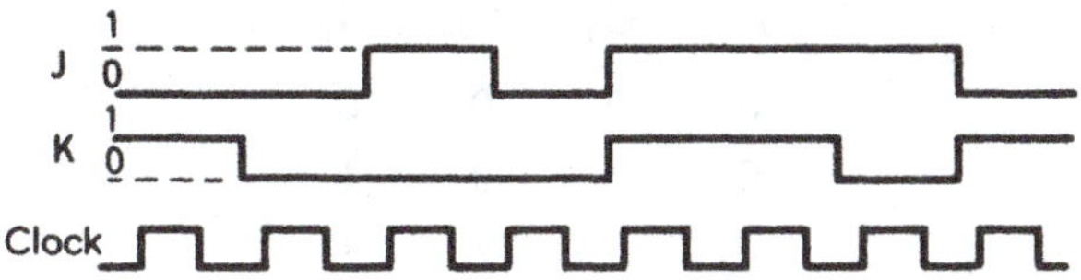

[*Ans.* see the Solution for the output waveform]

513. The diagram below is for a 2-way lamp switching circuit. Each switch can be in either of two positions which are mutually exclusive. Draw a 2-variable Karnaugh map representation of the operation.

Deduce the Karnaugh map for a 3-way switching circuit and sketch the circuit itself.

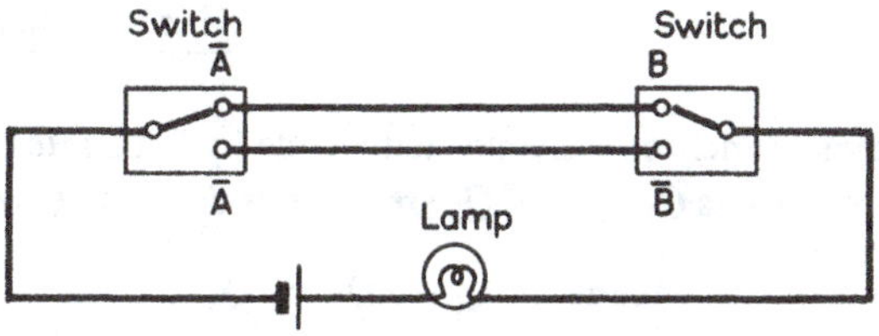

[*Ans.* see the Solution for the maps and circuit]

514. (*a*) Three J-K flip-flops are synchronously clocked and interconnected as follows:

$$J_2 = Q_1, K_2 = \bar{Q}_1, J_3 = Q_2, K_3 = \bar{Q}_2.$$

The input waveform shown below is fed to J_1: and $K_1 = \bar{J}_1$. Assume that the initial condition is $Q_1 = Q_2 = Q_3 = 0$ and draw the output waveforms at Q_1, Q_2 and Q_3 relative to the clock and J_1 waveforms.

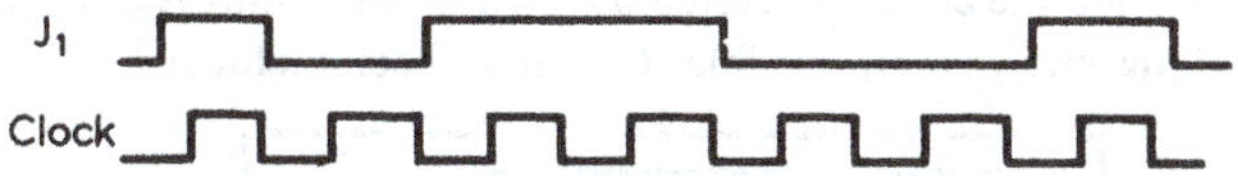

(*b*) What function does this circuit perform?

[*Ans.* (*a*) see the Solution for the waveforms; (*b*) shift register]

515. Design a code converter from the Gray Code below to binary-coded-decimal 7421 ≡ DCBA. This BCD code has the property that it has the least number of 'ones' and thus uses least power.

G_4	G_3	G_2	G_1
0	0	0	0
0	0	0	1
0	0	1	1
0	0	1	0
0	1	1	0
0	1	1	1
0	1	0	1
0	1	0	0
1	1	0	0
1	1	0	1

[*Ans.* see the Solution]

516. Design a synchronously-clocked 'divide-by-5' counter using J-K flip-flops. The outputs Q_1, Q_2 and Q_3 are to be as defined below.

count	Q_1	Q_2	Q_3
0	0	0	0
1	1	0	0
2	0	1	0
3	1	1	0
4	0	0	1
0	0	0	0

[*Ans.* see the Solution]

517. Deduce the codes generated by the feedback shift register shown below making sure that all possible states have been included.

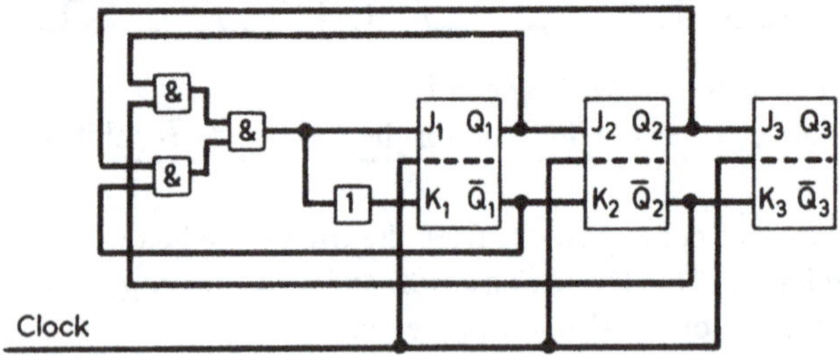

[*Ans.* see the Solution]

518. Analyse the following circuit and draw the waveform timing diagrams showing the sequence of states at the Q outputs and clock input to each stage relative to the square wave input α. Assume $Q_1 = Q_2 = Q_3 = Q_4 = 0$ at the start.

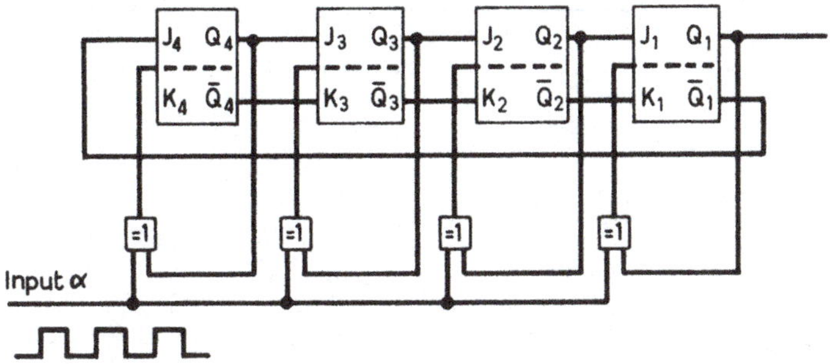

[*Ans.* see the Solution]

ADDITIONAL PROBLEMS

519. It is necessary to convert the inputs VWXYZ (below) to the code ABCDE to use the advantage of the nine's complement. Derive minimal logic expressions for the outputs A, B, C, D and E making full use of 'don't care' states.

Decimal	V	W	X	Y	Z	A	B	C	D	E
0	0	1	1	0	0	0	1	0	1	0
1	1	0	0	0	1	0	1	0	0	1
2	1	0	0	1	0	1	1	0	0	0
3	0	0	0	1	1	0	0	1	1	0
4	1	0	1	0	0	0	0	1	0	1
5	0	0	1	0	1	1	0	1	0	0
6	0	0	1	1	0	0	0	0	1	1
7	1	1	0	0	0	1	0	0	1	0
8	0	1	0	0	1	1	0	0	0	1
9	0	1	0	1	0	0	1	1	0	0

[*Ans.* A = VW + VY + XZ + WZ; B = VY + VZ + XW + WY;
C = VX + WY + YZ + XZ; D = VW + WX + XY + YZ;
E = VX + VZ + WZ + XY]

520. Simplify the following Boolean expressions using a Karnaugh map for each:

(*a*) $F = \bar{A}.\bar{B}.\bar{C}.\bar{D}. + A.\bar{B}.\bar{C}. + A.\bar{B}.C.\bar{D}. + \bar{A}.\bar{B}.C.\bar{D}.$

(*b*) $F = \bar{P}.Q.\bar{R}.\bar{S}. + P.\bar{R}.\bar{S}. + P.\bar{Q}.R.S. + P.R.\bar{S}.$

[*Ans.* (*a*) $F = \bar{B}.\bar{D}. + A.\bar{B}.\bar{C}.$; (*b*) $F = P.\bar{S}. + P.\bar{Q}.R. + Q.\bar{R}.\bar{S}.$]

CHAPTER TWENTY-ONE

MISCELLANEOUS TOPICS

521. What is the skin depth of current penetration in copper at a frequency of 300 MHz? The conductivity of copper is $5.88 \times 10^7 \text{Sm}^{-1}$.

Repeat the calculation for a frequency of 10 000 MHz.

[*Ans.* 3.79×10^{-6} m; 6.56×10^{-7} m]

522. Calculate the inductance of a straight piece of wire 25.4 mm long which has a diameter of 2.54 mm. What is the reactance of this inductance at a frequency of 500 MHz?

[*Ans.* 0.014 μH; 44 Ω]

523. The reflected portion of a plane wave, starting in air and incident normally on a space filled with a loss-free dielectric of relative permittivity 4, is to be eliminated by placing a quarter-wavelength plate between the air and the dielectric. Calculate the required relative permittivity of the material of the plate.

[*Ans.* 2]

524. In the double-diode clipping circuit illustrated $e = 200 \sin \omega t$ volts, $E = 2$ V, and the frequency is 100 kHz. Find the time taken for the output voltage to rise from $-E$ to $+E$.

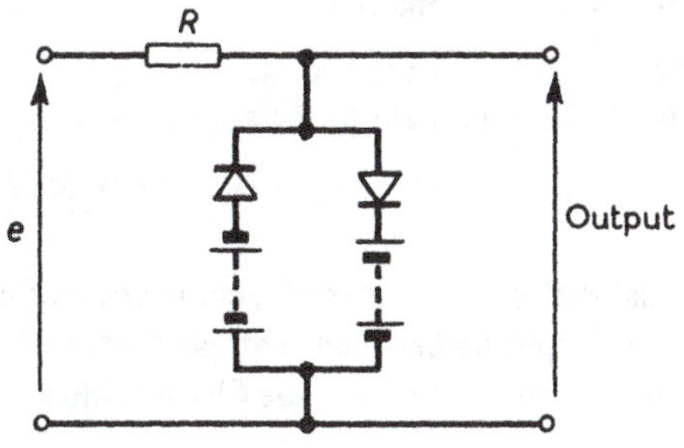

[*Ans.* 0.032 μs]

525. Laplace's equation can be written in cylindrical coordinates as follows:

$$\frac{1}{r}\frac{\partial}{\partial r}\left(r\frac{\partial V}{\partial r}\right)+\frac{1}{r^2}\frac{\partial^2 V}{\partial \theta^2}+\frac{\partial^2 V}{\partial z^2}=0$$

Given that V is independent of z and varies with θ as $\cos 4\theta$ determine the dependence of V on r, given that $V \to 0$ as $r \to \infty$.

If the radial electric field strength at a radius r_0 is E_0, what will its value be at a radius $2r_0$ in the same θ-direction?

[*Ans.* r^{-4}; $E_0/32$]

526. An infinite parallel-plate capacitor is filled with two infinite layers of dielectric each of the same thickness. One of the layers of dielectric has a relative permittivity K and no loss, the other has a relative permittivity also of K and conductivity σ. Show that the composite dielectric appears to have an apparent relative permittivity $2K(K - j\sigma/\omega\epsilon_0)$ where ω is the angular frequency and ϵ_0 is the permittivity of free space.

527. Why is the internal electric field E_i in a solid dielectric not identical to the externally applied field E?

If the internal field can be assumed to be given by

$$E_i = E + P/3\epsilon_0$$

where P is the polarization, derive the Clausius-Mosotti equation for the relative permittivity in terms of the polarizability and number density of atoms in the material.

A solid contains 5×10^{28} identical atoms per cubic metre, each with a polarizability of 2×10^{-40} F m^{-2}. Assuming that the internal field in the solid is given by the above formula find

(*a*) the relative permittivity of the solid,
(*b*) the ratio of the internal field to the applied field.

[*Ans.* (*a*) 2.81; (*b*) 1.6]

528. An artificial dielectric consists of a cubic array of metal spheres 2 mm in diameter. The spacing between centres of adjacent spheres is 4 mm. Calculate the relative permittivity using the Clausius-Mosotti formula.

[*Ans.* 1.21]

529. The relative permittivity of polythene is 2.25. Expanded polythene has a density of only 5 per cent of that of polythene. Find its relative permittivity using the Clausius-Mosotti formula. Neglect the polarizability of the gas in the voids.

[*Ans.* 1.058]

530. (*a*) Show that for photo-electric emission to be possible over the whole visible region, 4000 to 8000 Å, the work function of the photo-sensitive surface must be less than 1.55 eV.

Determine the threshold wavelength in the case of a caesium surface for which the work function is 1.8 eV.

(*b*) Determine the maximum velocity of the emitted photoelectrons when a molybdenum surface, having a work function of 4.3 eV, is irradiated with the mercury line, 2537 Å.

[*Ans.* (*a*) 6890 Å; (*b*) $4.56 \times 10^5 \text{ m s}^{-1}$]

531. A photoelectric cell* has a semi-cylindrical cathode of radius 10 mm and an anode of radius 0.5 mm situated along the axis of the cathode. It is filled with argon at a pressure of 1 torr for which gas the number of ion pairs produced per cm path of an electron is given approximately by $Ape^{-Bp/E}$, where $A = 13.6$, $B/A = 17.3$, p is the pressure in torr and E is the field strength in V cm^{-1}. Show that, neglecting fringing effects in the electrostatic field, the naperian logarithm of the gas amplification factor is given approximately by $(V/52)e^{-35.3/V}$, where V is the voltage between the electrodes.

532. A cylindrical magnetron has a cathode of radius r_c and a coaxial anode of radius r_a which is maintained at a positive potential V with respect to the cathode. A magnetic field is applied parallel to the common axis of the electrodes. The critical flux density for the electrons just to graze the anode is B_c. Assuming that the electrons produced at the cathode have zero initial velocities, prove that the value of B_c is given by

$$B_c = [\sqrt{(8\,Vm/e)}/r_a(1 - r_c^2/r_a^2)],$$

where m and e are the mass and charge of an electron respectively.

533. A schematic diagram of a klystron is shown. The effect of the superimposed buncher alternating voltage on the accelerating voltage V_a is

* Some interesting problems on optoelectronic devices including electroluminescent devices and photocells are given in Chapter 9 by J. W. Allen of the book R. L. Ferrari and A. K. Jonscher (Editors), *Problems in Physical Electronics*, Pion, 1973.

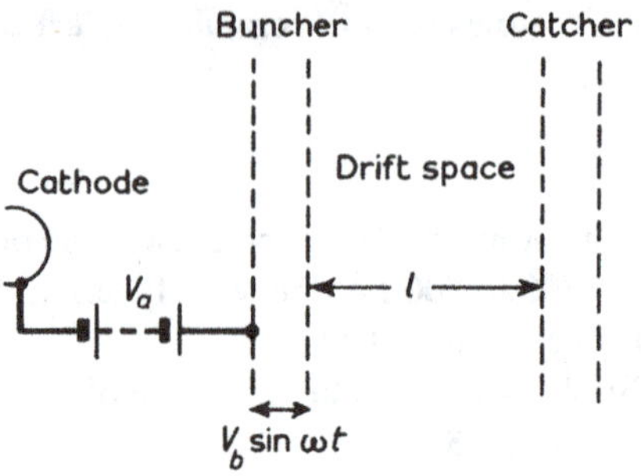

to give the electrons a speed v. Assuming that the buncher grids are very close together show that the velocity of an electron beyond the buncher is given by $v = \sqrt{(2eV_a/m)}(1 + V_b \sin \omega t/V_a)$, and thus that the electrons are velocity modulated at the buncher frequency. m and e are the mass and charge of an electron respectively.

If the time of arrival, at the catcher, of an electron that passed through the buncher at time t_b is t_c, show that

$$\theta_c = [\theta_b + \theta_o - k \sin \theta_b] \text{ radians}$$

where $\theta_b = \omega t_b$ is the departure angle, $\theta_c = \omega t_c$ is the arrival angle, $\theta_o = [\omega l/\sqrt{(2eV_a/m)}]$ and k is the bunching parameter

$$[\omega V_b l/2V_a\sqrt{(2eV_a/m)}]$$

534. An electron beam with an average charge density ρ_0 is moving with a velocity v_o. A wave of small amplitude is superimposed, so that the charge density and velocity may then be written as $\rho = [\rho_o + \rho_1 e^{-Pz+j\omega t}]$ respectively. Show that the possible values for the propagation constant P are $[j(\omega \pm \omega_P)/v_o]$, where ω_P is the electron plasma frequency.

Hence, explain the operation of a klystron amplifier by supposing that a pair of grids, between which there is an alternating voltage of known frequency, is placed at the point $z = 0$ in a uniform electron beam.

535. Voltage breakdown in air at s.t.p. occurs for a field strength $E \simeq 30\,\text{kV cm}^{-1}$. How much power can be carried in 1 cm^2 of air by a uniform plane wave without causing voltage breakdown?

[*Ans.* $1.19 \times 10^6\,\text{W cm}^{-2}$]

ADDITIONAL PROBLEMS

536. What is the skin depth of current penetration in nickel at a frequency of 10 000 MHz, if the effective permeability of the metal is 3 at this frequency?

[*Ans.* 8.9×10^{-7} m]

537. Determine the thickness of a dielectric sheet of relative permittivity 2.25 that will present minimum relection of a circularly-polarized plane wave of frequency 10.6 GHz incident at an angle of 45°.

[*Ans.* 1.07×10^{-2} m]

538. Find the reflection and transmission coefficients at the plane $Z = 0$ of the semi-infinite stratified arrangement shown. The frequency is 10 GHz.*

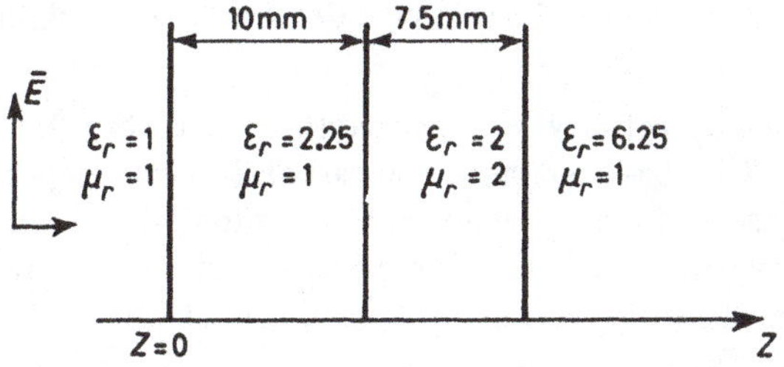

[*Ans.* 0.43; 0.57]

539. Write down and identify Maxwell's equations in a form applicable to an ideal dielectric medium. If the medium is such that its permittivity ϵ is a function of position, show that the electric field **E** satisfies the relationship

$$\nabla^2 \mathbf{E} - \mu\epsilon \frac{\partial^2 \mathbf{E}}{\partial t^2} = -\nabla \left(\mathbf{E}.\frac{\nabla_\epsilon}{\epsilon}\right)$$

What is the corresponding expression for the magnetic field **H**? What would be the effect of a positional dependence of the permeability μ instead of ϵ?

[*Ans.* $\nabla^2 \mathbf{H} - \mu\epsilon \frac{\partial^2 \mathbf{H}}{\partial t^2} = 0$; expressions for **E** and **H** are reversed]

* Propagation of electromagnetic waves through dielectric materials is considered in a book edited by L. Solymar, *Microwaves, Communications and Radar*, volume 4, Chapman and Hall, 1974, Section 1.12.

540. A probe is used to measure the electric field intensity inside a tank of oil, where a 1-GHz uniform plane wave is reflected from a conducting wall. The probe gives readings of 84 at 5 cm from the wall, 2 at 11.7 cm from the wall and 88 at 17.5 cm. What is the relative permittivity of the oil? Obtain also an estimate of the attenuation coefficient in the oil.

[*Ans.* 1.65; $\simeq$ 0.2 neper m^{-1}]

541. A laminated insulating material when dry has a negligible loss tangent and a bulk permittivity of ϵ_m'. If dampness penetrates the uniform air gap between the laminations show that the apparent complex permittivity would be given by:

$$\frac{\epsilon_m'(1+s)(\epsilon_\omega' + j\,\epsilon_\omega'')}{\epsilon_\omega' + s\,\epsilon_m' + j\,\epsilon_\omega''}$$

if the electric field is normal to the laminations. $\epsilon_\omega' + j\,\epsilon_\omega''$ is the complex permittivity of water and s is the volume ratio of water to insulating material.

542. A certain dielectric when subjected to an alternating field of frequency $f_1 = 4$ GHz has a measured real part of the complex permittivity of 2.57. The tangent of the loss angle is measured to be 0.0032. Determine (*a*) the imaginary part of the relative permittivity and (*b*) the power dissipated in the dielectric per unit volume if a field of 100 cos $2\pi f_1 t$ volts per metre is applied.

[*Ans.* (*a*) 0.0082, (*b*) 9.1 Wm^{-3}]

543. If the electrons in the argon atom can be represented by a uniform sphere of charge with radius R and there are N atoms per unit volume, show that the susceptibility is $\chi = 4\pi NR^3$.

The relative permittivity of a sample of argon is 1.000435 and there are 2.7×10^{25} atoms per cubic metre. Find the polarizability of the argon atom and its approximate radius.

[*Ans.* 1.4×10^{-40} Fm^{-2}, 0.11×10^{-10} m]

544. A sealed-off vessel is filled with gas so that there are 2.4×10^{25} molecules per cubic metre. The vessel contains electrodes to measure the relative permittivity of the gas. The relative permittivity is measured to be 1.0067 at 300 K and 1.0059 at 450 K. Find the permanent dipole moment of the molecules.

The polarizability of a permanent dipole is $\mu^2/3kT$ where μ is the permanent dipole moment.

[*Ans.* 3.3×10^{-30} Cm]

545. Assume that the only contribution to the polarizability of germanium atoms arises from electronic effects and a simple spherical cloud model may be adopted. What is the relative permittivity if there are 4×10^{28} atoms per cubic metre and a Lorentz internal field correction can be applied. The atomic radius of germanium is 1.7 Å.

[*Ans.* 14.9]

546. Show that maximum efficiency and maximum output voltage of a reflex klystron cannot be obtained together.

Section 2

SOLUTIONS

SOLUTIONS

1. Resonant frequency $f_r = 1/2\pi\sqrt{(LC)} = \underline{1126 \text{ kHz.}}$

$$Q = \omega_r L/R = 2\pi f_r L/R = \underline{177.}$$

Impedance $Z = R + \mathrm{j}\left(\omega L - \dfrac{1}{\omega C}\right) = R\left[1 + \mathrm{j}\left(\dfrac{\omega L}{R} - \dfrac{1}{\omega CR}\right)\right].$

$\therefore$ the angle ϕ and magnitude $|Z|$ of Z are given by:

$$\tan\phi = \left[\frac{\omega L}{R} - \frac{1}{\omega CR}\right] \text{ and } |Z| = R\sqrt{(1 + \tan^2\phi)},$$

i.e.
$$\tan\phi = Q\left(\frac{\omega}{\omega_r} - \frac{\omega_r}{\omega}\right).$$

$\therefore$
$$\left(\frac{\omega}{\omega_r}\right)^2 - \frac{\tan\phi}{Q}\left(\frac{\omega}{\omega_r}\right) - 1 = 0$$

and $\dfrac{\omega}{\omega_r} = \dfrac{\tan\phi}{2Q} + \sqrt{\left[1 + \left(\dfrac{\tan\phi}{2Q}\right)^2\right]}$; since at resonance $\omega = \omega_r$ and $\tan\phi = 0$, and only the positive sign has meaning. At the upper half-power frequency $\omega = \omega_1$, $\tan\phi = 1$.

$\therefore$
$$\frac{\omega_1}{\omega_r} = \frac{1}{2Q} + \sqrt{\left[1 + \frac{1}{4Q^2}\right]}.$$

At the lower half-power frequency $\omega = \omega_2$, $\tan\phi = -1$.

$\therefore$
$$\frac{\omega_2}{\omega_r} = -\frac{1}{2Q} + \sqrt{\left[1 + \frac{1}{4Q^2}\right]}.$$

In this case, $Q = 177$, so $f_1 = \dfrac{\omega_1}{2\pi} = \underline{1129 \text{ kHz}}$

and
$$f_2 = \frac{\omega_2}{2\pi} = \underline{1122 \text{ kHz.}}$$

2. $I_{max} = 344$ mA so $I_{max}/\sqrt{(2)} = 243$ mA.
Bandwidth at $I_{max}/\sqrt{(2)} = 16$ kHz.

$\therefore Q = f_r/(16 \times 10^3) = 884 \times 10^3/(16 \times 10^3) = \underline{55.25},$
$R = 5/I_{max} = 5 \times 10^3/344 = \underline{14.53\ \Omega},$

$L = RQ/\omega_r = 14.53 \times 55.25/(2\pi \times 884 \times 10^3)\ \text{H} = \underline{144.5\ \mu\text{H}},$

$C = 1/4\pi^2 f_r^{\,2} L = 1/\ 4\pi^2 \times (884 \times 10^3)^2 \times 144.5 \times 10^{-6}\ \text{F}, = \underline{224\ \mu\mu\text{F}}.$

3. Let the resistance, inductance and capacitance be R ohms, L henrys and C farads respectively.

The impedance of the parallel combination

$$Z = \left[\frac{(R + j\omega L)\left(\dfrac{1}{j\omega C}\right)}{R + j\omega L + \dfrac{1}{j\omega C}}\right] = \frac{L}{CR}\left[\frac{1 - jR/\omega L}{1 + j\left(\dfrac{\omega L}{R} - \dfrac{1}{\omega CR}\right)}\right]$$

At what is often taken as resonance, Z is a pure resistance and

$$\left[\frac{-R}{\omega_r L}\right] = \left[\frac{\omega_r L}{R} - \frac{1}{\omega_r CR}\right].$$

$$\therefore \qquad \omega_r = \sqrt{\left(\frac{1}{LC} - \frac{R^2}{L^2}\right)} = 2\pi f_r.$$

$$\text{Thus, } f_r = \frac{1}{2\pi}\sqrt{\left(\frac{1}{88 \times 10^{-6} \times 375 \times 10^{-12}} - \frac{4.8^2}{88^2 \times 10^{-12}}\right)}\ \text{Hz}$$

$= \underline{876.4\ \text{kHz}}.$

4. $$V = I/(1/j\omega L + j\omega C + 1/R).$$

V has a maximum value equal to IR when $\omega C = 1/\omega L$, i.e. when $\omega = 1/\sqrt{(LC)} = \omega_r$ say.

V drops 3 dB from its maximum value when $\omega C - 1/\omega L = \pm\ 1/R$ and the corresponding angular frequencies are ω_1 and ω_2,

where $$\omega_2/\omega_r - \omega_r/\omega_2 = -\ 1/\omega_r CR$$

and $$\omega_1/\omega_r - \omega_r/\omega_1 = +\ 1/\omega_r CR.$$

By comparison with the solution to Problem 1 the Q factor is seen to be $\underline{\omega_r CR = R/\omega_r L}$.

5. Using the solution to Problem 1 it is seen that

$$Q = \omega_r/(\omega_1 - \omega_2).$$

$$\therefore \qquad Q \simeq \omega_r/2(\omega_1 - \omega_r) \simeq \omega_r/2(\omega_r - \omega_2).$$

In this case $Q \simeq 2\pi \times 10^6/2(2\pi \times 5 \times 10^3) = \underline{100}$.

It is easily shown that the parallel resonant impedance $Z = L/CR$, i.e.

$$Z = Q/\omega_r C = 100/(2\pi \times 10^6 \times 200 \times 10^{-12})\ \Omega = \underline{79.6\ \text{k}\Omega}.$$

6. The impedance-frequency curve for the circuit will have a maximum value of R at some frequency. The bandwidth is the difference in hertz between the two frequencies at which the impedance is $R/\sqrt{(2)}$ and can be shown* to be $1/2\pi CR$.

Here bandwidth $= 250 \times 10^3$ Hz, $C = 50 \times 10^{-12}$ F

$$\underline{\text{so } R = 12\,740\ \Omega.}$$

7. In reducing circuits such as (*a*) and (*b*) to that of (*c*) the rules that determine the values of Z_p, Z_s and M are:

(1) Z_p = impedance measured between primary terminals of actual circuit when secondary is opened.

(2) Z_s = impedance measured by opening secondary of actual circuit and determining the impedance between these open points when the primary is open-circuited.

(3) M is determined by assuming a current I flows in the primary circuit. The voltage which appears across an open-circuited secondary is then $\pm\, \text{j}\omega MI$.

For circuit (*a*) applying the above rules:

$$\underline{Z_p = \text{j}\omega(L_1 + L_m),\ Z_s = \text{j}\omega(L_2 + L_m),\ \text{j}\omega L_m I = \text{j}\omega MI.}$$

$$\therefore \qquad \underline{\text{coefficient of coupling} = L_m/\sqrt{[(L_1 + L_m)(L_2 + L_m)]}.}$$

For circuit (*b*):

$$\underline{Z_p = (C_1 + C_m)/\omega C_1 C_m,\ Z_s = (C_2 + C_m)/\omega C_2 C_m,\ \text{j}I/\omega C_m = \text{j}\omega MI.}$$

$$\therefore \qquad \underline{\text{coefficient of coupling} = \sqrt{[C_1 C_2/(C_1 + C_m)(C_2 + C_m)]}.}$$

8. Impedance reflected into the primary circuit from the secondary by mutual coupling $= \omega^2 M^2/Z_s$.

Primary current $I_p = V/(Z_p + \omega^2 M^2/Z_s)$.

Voltage induced in secondary $= -\text{j}\omega M I_p$.

Secondary current $I_s = -\text{j}\omega M I_p/Z_s = -\text{j}\omega M V/(Z_p Z_s + \omega^2 M^2)$.

* E.g. See L. B. Arguimbau and R. B. Adler, *Vacuum Tube Circuits and Transistors*, Wiley, 1956, p. 249.

$$\therefore \quad Z_p = R_p + j(\omega L_p - 1/\omega C_p) = R_p + j\omega L_p(1 - 1/\alpha^2).$$
$$Z_s = R_s + j(\omega L_s - 1/\omega C_s) = R_s + j\omega L_s(1 - 1/\alpha^2).$$
$$\therefore \quad I_s = -j\omega MV/\{R_pR_s - (1 - 1/\alpha^2)^2\omega^2 L_pL_s + \omega^2M^2 + j(1 - 1/\alpha^2)(\omega L_pR_s + \omega L_sR_p)\}.$$

Dividing the numerator and denominator by $\omega^2 L_pL_s$ and noting that $Q_p = \omega L_p/R_p$, $Q_s = \omega L_s/R_s$, $M^2 = k^2 L_pL_s$ and $\omega = \alpha\omega_r$,

$$I_s = -jVk/\alpha\omega_r\sqrt{(L_pL_s)}\{k^2 + 1/Q_pQ_s - (1 - 1/\alpha^2)^2 + j(1 - 1/\alpha^2)(1/Q_p + 1/Q_s)\}$$
$$I_s = -j\omega MV/[\{R_p + j(\omega L_p - 1/\omega C_p)\}\{R_s + j(\omega L_s - 1/\omega C_s)\} + \omega^2M^2].$$

$\therefore$ I_s reaches a maximum value when the circuits are in resonance and $\omega^2M^2 = R_pR_s$.

For maximum I_s, $\omega M = \sqrt{(R_pR_s)} = \omega\sqrt{(L_pL_s)}\sqrt{(Q_pQ_s)}$.

$\therefore$ critical value of $k = 1/\sqrt{(Q_pQ_s)}$.

9. $k = \sqrt{(300 \times 300)}60 = 0.2.$

Primary current $I_p = 10/(Z + \omega^2M^2/Z)$

where

$$Z = j(\omega L - 1/\omega C)$$
$$= j(2 \times 10^6 \times 300 \times 10^{-6} - 10^{12}/2 \times 10^6 \times 10^3) = j100.$$

Secondary current $I_s = -j\omega MI_p/Z = -j0.273$ A.

10. Input impedance $= Z_p + \omega^2M^2/Z_s$

where $Z_p = (j2\pi \times 10^6 \times 200 \times 10^{-6})\ \Omega$

$Z_s = (100 + j2\pi \times 10^6 \times 20 \times 10^{-6})\ \Omega$

and $M = [0.1\sqrt{(200 \times 20 \times 10^{-12})}]$ H.

$\therefore$ $Z_p = (6.1 + j1249.1)\ \Omega.$

11. Effective primary impedance (Z_p)

$$= R_1 + j(\omega L_1 - 1/\omega C_1) + \omega^2M^2/\{R_2 + j(\omega L_2 - 1/\omega C_2)\}.$$

Substituting the given figures Z_p is found to be $(718 + j0)\ \Omega$,

$\therefore$ Effective resistance = 718 Ω

and $\underline{\text{Effective resistance} = 0.}$

$$\text{Primary current} = 100/718 \text{ A} = \underline{0.139 \text{ A.}}$$

$$\text{Secondary current} = \omega M \times 0.139/R_2 = \underline{1.306 \text{ A.}}$$

12. With the secondary open-circuited the impedance of the primary winding is $j\omega L_1 + \dfrac{1}{j\omega C_1}$ and the resonant frequency $f = \omega/2\pi\sqrt{(L_1C_1)}$.

$$\therefore \qquad C_1 = 1/(2\pi \times 500 \times 10^3)^2 \times 1 \times 10^{-3} \text{ F} = 101 \ \mu\mu\text{F}.$$

When the secondary is short-circuited the impedance of the primary is $[j\omega L_1 + 1/j\omega C_2 + \omega^2 M^2/j\omega L_2]$, and the resonant frequency = $\dfrac{1}{2\pi\sqrt{\left[\left(L_1 - \dfrac{M^2}{L_2}\right)C_2\right]}}$, where C_2 is the new capacitance.

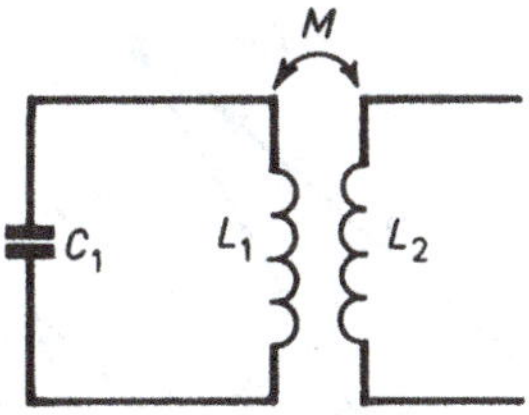

$\therefore$ since the resonant frequencies are the same,

$$(L_1 - M^2/L_2)C_2 = L_1C_1$$

i.e. $$C_2 = \frac{L_1C_1}{L_1 - M^2/L_2} = \frac{10^{-3} \times 101 \times 10^{-12}}{10^{-3}(1 - 0.25)} \text{ F} = 135 \ \mu\mu\text{F}.$$

$\therefore$ The change of capacitance = $(135 - 101)\ \mu\mu\text{F} = \underline{34\ \mu\mu\text{F.}}$

13. The input impedance $= R_1 + j\omega L_1 + 1/j\omega C_1 + \omega^2 M^2/R_2$. When this is purely resistive its value is

$$R_1 + \omega^2 M^2/R_2 = 5 + \frac{(2\pi \times 10^6)^2 \times (10 \times 10^{-6})^2}{20} = \underline{202.4\ \Omega.}$$

14. With the currents as shown the equations for the circuit are:

$$e_1 = (R_1 + j\omega L_1)I_1 - j\omega M I_2$$

and $$e_2 = (R_2 + j\omega L_2)I_2 - j\omega M I_1$$

Now $(R_1 + j\omega L_1) = (60 + j1885 \times 50 \times 10^{-3})\ \Omega$

$$(R_2 + j\omega L_2) = (80 + j1885 \times 70 \times 10^{-3})\ \Omega$$

$$-j\omega M = -(j1885 \times 17.75 \times 10^{-3})\ \Omega$$

$$e_1 = \frac{169.7}{\sqrt{(2)}} \underline{/0^\circ}\ \text{V}$$

and $$e_2 = \frac{141.4}{\sqrt{(2)}} \underline{/45^\circ}\ \text{V}.$$

∴ $$I_1 = (0.835 - j0.819)\ \text{A} = \underline{1.168 \underline{/-45.6^\circ}\ \text{A}}$$

and $$I_2 = (0.874 - j0.212)\ \text{A} = \underline{0.903 \underline{/-13.6^\circ}\ \text{A}}.$$

The phasor diagram is as shown below:

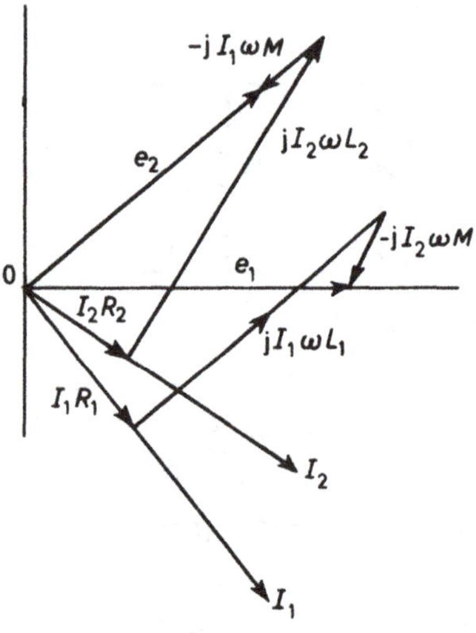

15. The two following equations apply:

$$e = (R_1 + j\omega L_1)I_1 \pm j\omega M I_2$$

and $$e = (R_2 + j\omega L_2)I_2 \pm j\omega M I_1.$$

Writing $Z_1 = R_1 + j\omega L_1$, $Z_2 = R_2 + j\omega L_2$ and $Z_m = \pm j\omega M$,

$$e = Z_1 I_1 + Z_m I_2$$

$$e = Z_m I_1 + Z_2 I_2.$$

∴ $$I_1 = e(Z_2 - Z_m)/(Z_1 Z_2 - Z_m^2)$$

and $$I_2 = e(Z_1 - Z_m)/(Z_1Z_2 - Z_m^2).$$

$\therefore$ $$I = I_1 + I_2 = e(Z_1 + Z_2 - 2Z_m)/(Z_1Z_2 - Z_m^2).$$

Equivalent impedance

$$Z_p = e/I = \underline{(Z_1Z_2 - Z_m^2)/(Z_1 + Z_2 - 2Z_m)}.$$

16. When the coils are in series:

$$L_1 + L_2 + 2M = 2(L + M) = 360 \text{ mH}$$

and $$L_1 + L_2 - 2M = 2(L - M) = 40 \text{ mH}.$$

$\therefore$ $$L = 100 \text{ mH and } M = 80 \text{ mH}.$$

Using the result of the previous solution the equivalent inductance L_e of the two coils in parallel is given by:

$$\omega L_e = \{\omega L_1 \omega L_2 - (\pm\, \omega M)^2\}/\{\omega L_1 + \omega L_2 - (\pm\, 2\omega M\}$$

i.e. $$L_e = (L^2 - M^2)/2(L \pm M) = (100^2 - 80^2)/2(100 \pm 80) \text{ mH}$$
$$= \underline{10 \text{ or } 90 \text{ mH}}.$$

17. Using Thévenin's theorem the circuit to the left of points A and B can be replaced by a single e.m.f. acting in series with a single impedance. The e.m.f. (e) is the voltage between A and B when the network to the right of these points is disconnected. The impedance (Z) is equal to that which would be measured looking to the left at terminals A and B.

If the network is opened at A, B the current I_1 flowing in mesh 1

$$= E/(R_1 + j\omega L_1).$$

$\therefore$ $$e = -j\omega M_1 I_1$$
$$= -j \times 2 \times 10^6 \times 50 \times 10^{-6} \times 6/(40 + j200)$$
$$= -2.94 \underline{/11^\circ\, 19'} \text{ V}.$$

Also $Z = j\omega L_2 + \omega^2 M_1^2/(R_1 + j\omega L_1) = (j\omega L_2 + 9.6 - j48)\ \Omega$.

The original circuit therefore reduces to the following:

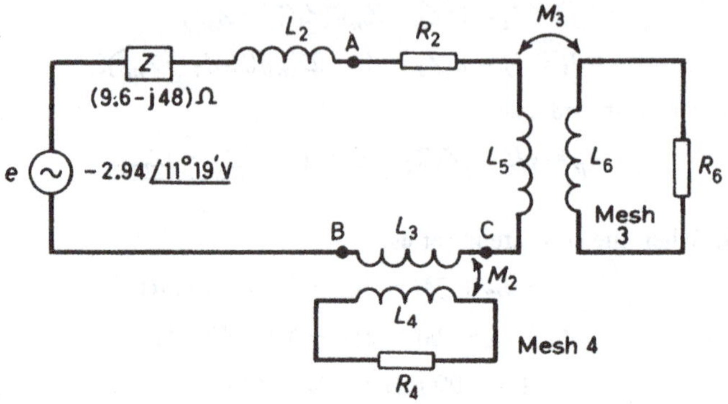

Similarly, mesh 4 can be removed by adding an impedance $\omega^2 M_2^2/(R_4 + j\omega L_4) = (15.1 - j68)\ \Omega$ in series with L_3 as shown in the following figure:

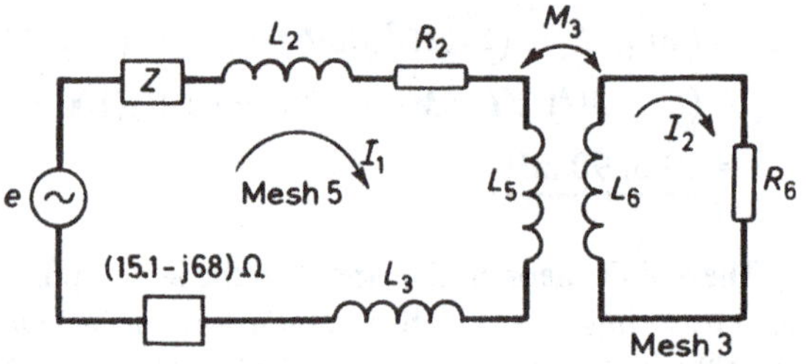

For mesh 5

$e = I_1\{9.6 - j48 + 15.1 - j68 + R_2 + j\omega(L_2 + L_3 + L_5) + j\omega M_3 I_2.$

For mesh 3

$0 = j\omega M_3 I_1 + I_2(R_6 + j\omega L_6).$

From these two equations I_2 is found to be $0.00369\ \angle{-64^\circ 6'}$ A.

18. The total impedance of the primary loop

$= \{(3.4 + 5.1) + j\omega(55 + 725) \times 10^{-6} - j/\omega 7.6 \times 10^{-9}\}\ \Omega$

$= (8.5 - j174)\ \Omega$ since $\omega = 2\pi \times 50 \times 10^3$.

The total impedance of the secondary loop

$= \{(0.5 + 120) + j\omega(106 + 450) \times 10^{-6} - j/\omega C\}\ \Omega$

where

$1/C = 1/C_2 + 1/C_3 = 10^6[1/0.0421 + 1/0.0076]$

i.e. total impedance of secondary loop $= (120.5 - j320)\ \Omega$.

The mutual impedance includes the impedance of the common branch and the mutual impedance resulting from M. It is therefore $j(\omega M + 1/\omega C_3)$

$$= j(2\pi \times 50 \times 10^3 \times 268 \times 10^{-6} + 1/2\pi \times 50 \times 10^3 \times 0.0076 \times 10^{-6})\ \Omega$$

$$= \underline{j503\ \Omega.}$$

The apparent impedance which the voltage source sees is

$$(8.5 - j174) - (j503)^2/(120.5 - j320)\ \Omega$$
$$= \underline{(271 + j522)\ \Omega.}$$

Primary current $(I_p) = 10/(271 + j522) = 10/589\ \underline{/-62.6^\circ}$

$$= \underline{0.017\ /-62.6^\circ\ \text{A}}$$

where e is taken along the real axis.

The current ratio $I_p/I_s = (120.5 - j320)/j503 = 0.679\ \underline{/20.6^\circ}$.

$\therefore$ $I_s = 0.017\ \underline{/-62.6^\circ}/0.679\underline{/20.6^\circ} = \underline{0.0251\ /-83.2^\circ\ \text{A}}.$

19. If two coils having inductances L_1 and L_2 respectively and a mutual inductance M are connected together their joint inductances are:

(*a*) In series aiding $L_1 + L_2 + 2M$.
(*b*) In series opposing $L_1 + L_2 - 2M$.
(*c*) In parallel aiding $(L_1L_2 - M^2)/(L_1 + L_2 - 2M)$.
(*d*) In parallel opposing $(L_1L_2 - M^2)/(L_1 + L_2 + 2M)$.

For (*a*) here joint inductance is therefore 450 μH.

$\therefore$ frequency range is

$$1/2\pi\sqrt{(450 \times 10^{-6} \times 50 \times 10^{-12})}\ \text{Hz}$$

to

$$1/2\pi\sqrt{(450 \times 10^{-6} \times 1000 \times 10^{-12})}\ \text{Hz}$$

which corresponds to a wavelength range of 283 to 1265 m.

Similarly, the other ranges are found to be:

(*b* (*b*) 249 to 1115 m, (*c*) 122 to 546 m and (*d*) 107 to 481 m.

20. The impedance Z of the combination

$$= \{(R + j\omega L)/j\omega C\}/(R + j\omega L + 1/j\omega C)$$
$$= (R + j\omega L)(1 - \omega^2LC - jR\omega C)/\{(1 - \omega^2LC)^2 + \omega^2C^2R^2\}.$$

The effective resistance is therefore

$$R_e = R/\{(1-\omega^2LC)^2 + \omega^2C^2R^2\}$$

and the effective inductance is

$$L_e = \{L(1-\omega^2LC) - R^2C\}/\{(1-\omega^2LC)^2 + \omega^2C^2R^2\}.$$

Substituting $L = 5 \times 10^{-3}$ H, $R = 100\ \Omega$, $C = 5 \times 10^{-12}$ F and $\omega = 2\pi \times 500 \times 10^3$, $\underline{R_e = 177\ \Omega \text{ and } L_e = 6.67 \text{ mH}}$.

21. Let the inductance and self-capacitance of the coil be L and C respectively and let the original frequency be f hertz.

Then $f = 1/2\pi\sqrt{[L(C+C_1)]}$ and $2f = 1/2\pi\sqrt{[L(C+C_2)]}$

where $C_1 = 250\ \mu\mu\text{F}$ and $C_2 = 55\ \mu\mu\text{F}$.

$\therefore\ C_1 - 4C_2 = 3C$ so that $\underline{C = 10\ \mu\mu\text{F}}$.

22. Apparent mutual inductance M_1 is approximately*

$$M\{1 + \omega^2(L_1C_1 + L_2C_2)\}$$

where $L_1 = 50\ \mu\text{H}$, $L_2 = 200\ \mu\text{H}$, $C_1 = 5\ \mu\mu\text{F}$, $C_2 = 7\ \mu\mu\text{F}$, $\omega = 2\pi \times 2 \times 10^6$ and $M = 0.05\sqrt{(50 \times 200)}\mu\text{H}$.

$$\therefore \qquad \underline{M_1 = 6.3\ \mu\text{H}}.$$

23. For circuit (a) the impedance

$$Z_a = \left[\frac{\dfrac{1}{j\omega C} \cdot \dfrac{j\omega L_1 / j\omega C_1}{\dfrac{1}{j\omega C_1} + j\omega L_1}}{\dfrac{1}{j\omega C} + \dfrac{j\omega L_1 / j\omega C_1}{\dfrac{1}{j\omega C_1} + j\omega L_1}}\right] = \left[\frac{1-\omega^2L_1C_1 - \omega^2L_1C}{j\omega C(1-\omega^2L_1C_1)}\right].$$

For circuit (b) the impedance

$$Z_b = \left[\frac{\dfrac{1}{j\omega C'} \cdot \left(j\omega L_2 + \dfrac{1}{j\omega C_2}\right)}{\dfrac{1}{j\omega C'} + \dfrac{1}{j\omega C_2} + j\omega L_2}\right] = \left[\frac{1-\omega^2L_2C_2}{j\omega C_2(1 + C'/C_2 - \omega^2L_2C')}\right].$$

* This is easily proved from first principles but readers may like to look at the following: F. K. Harris, *Electrical Measurements*, Wiley, 1952, pp. 671 and 672; S. Butterworth, 'Capacity and Eddy Current Effects in Inductometers,' *Proc. Phys. Soc.*, **33**, p.312, 1921; L. Hartshorn, 'The Properties of Mutual Inductance Standards at Telephonic Frequencies,' *Proc. Phys. Soc.*, **38**, p. 302, 1926.

If $Z_a = Z_b$,

$$C_2(1-\omega^2L_1C_1-\omega^2L_1C)\left(1+\frac{C'}{C_2}-\omega^2L_2C'\right)$$
$$= C(1-\omega^2L_2C_2)(1-\omega^2L_1C_1).$$

Equating the ω^4 terms gives

$$\underline{C' = CC_1/(C+C_1)} \quad . \quad . \quad . \quad . \quad (1)$$

Equating the ω^2 terms gives

$$L_2 = \frac{L_1}{C_2}\left[\frac{C_1C_2 + C_1C' + CC_2 + CC' - CC_1}{C-C'}\right].$$

Substituting for C' from (1) gives

$$\underline{L_2 = L_1(C_1+C)^2/C^2} \quad . \quad . \quad . \quad (2)$$

Equating the terms which do not contain ω gives

$$C_2 + C' = C$$

Substituting for C' from (1) gives

$$\underline{C_2 = C^2/(C+C_1)} \quad . \quad . \quad . \quad . \quad (3)$$

24. Impedance Z

$$= \{(R+j\omega L)(R+1/j\omega C)\}/\{(R+j\omega L)+(R+1/j\omega C)\}$$
$$= \{R^2 + L/C + jR(\omega L - 1/\omega C)\}/\{2R + j(\omega L - 1/\omega C)\}.$$

$\underline{\text{If } L/C = R^2 \text{ then } Z = R.}$

25.

$$r + j\omega l = Rj\omega L/(R+j\omega L) = (j\omega LR^2 + \omega^2L^2R)/(R^2+\omega^2L^2).$$

Equating real and imaginary parts,

$$r = \omega^2L^2R/(R^2+\omega^2L^2) \text{ and } l = LR^2/(R^2+\omega^2L^2).$$

$\therefore$ $\underline{R = r + (\omega^2l^2/r)}$ and $\underline{L = l + (r^2/\omega^2l)}$.

26. Let the impedance of the source be $Z_s = R_s + jX_s$, the load impedance $Z_L = R_L + jX_L$ and the voltage of the source V. Then the load current $I_L = V/[(R_s + R_L) + j(X_s + X_L)]$.

$\therefore$ the power in the load $(W) = R_L \, . \, V^2/[(R_s+R_L)^2 + (X_s+X_L)^2]$.

If X_L is variable, W is a maximum when $X_L = -X_s$ and W is then $R_L V^2/(R_s + R_L)^2$. This is a maximum when $R_L = R_s$,

i.e. W is a maximum when $Z_L = R_L + jX_L = R_s - jX_s$.

Let the loudspeaker impedance be $(R + jX)\ \Omega$.

Then the total load on the generator $= \dfrac{(R + jX)(-j5)}{R + jX - j5}$.

Conjugate of source impedance $= (3 - j4)\ \Omega$.

$$\therefore \quad \frac{(R + jX)(-j5)}{R + jX - j5} = 3 - j4.$$

Cross-multiplying and equating real and imaginary parts gives:

$$X - 3R = -20 \quad \text{and} \quad 3X + R = 15$$

$$\therefore \quad R = 7.5\ \Omega \quad \text{and} \quad X = 2.5\ \Omega.$$

27. For the series circuit

$$\tan\phi = 1/\omega C\rho,$$

where ϕ is the phase angle between current and voltage.

$$\text{Power factor, } \cos\phi = \rho/\sqrt{(\rho^2 + 1/\omega^2 C^2)} \simeq \omega C\rho.$$

For the parallel circuit

$$\tan\phi = \omega Cr \text{ and } \cos\phi = 1/\sqrt{(1 + C^2\omega^2 r^2)} \simeq 1/\omega Cr$$

$$\therefore \quad 1/\omega Cr = \omega C\rho \text{ or } \omega^2 C^2 \rho r = 1.$$

Here, $\cos\phi = 0.001$, $\omega = 2\pi f$, $C\rho = 25 \times 10^{-10}$ so

$$f = 63.7 \text{ kHz}.$$

28. The phasor diagram for the network is as shown. I is the current through R and C.

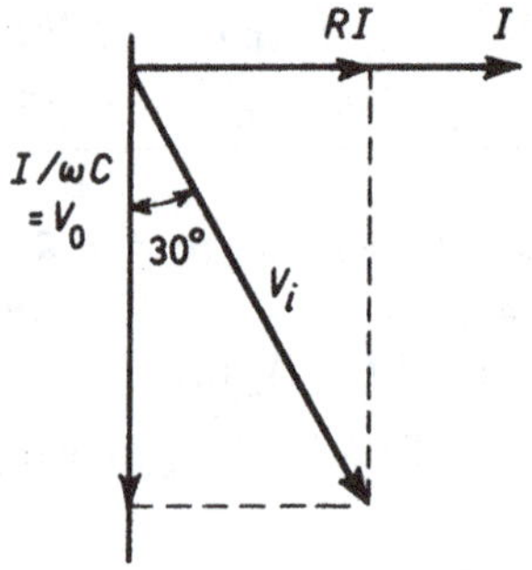

$$(R^2 + 1/C^2\omega^2)^{1/2} = 5000 \quad . \quad . \quad . \quad (1)$$

$$R\omega C = \tan 30^\circ = 1/\sqrt{(3)} \quad . \quad . \quad . \quad (2)$$

$\therefore$ $\underline{R = 2500\ \Omega \text{ and } C = 0.037\ \mu\text{F and } V_o \text{ lags behind } V_i.}$

29. *Mesh analysis.*

The equations for the three loops are:

$$E = (600 + \mathrm{j}600 + 400)I_1 - \mathrm{j}600I_2 - 400I_3 \quad . \quad . \quad (1)$$

$$0 = -\mathrm{j}600I_1 + (900 + \mathrm{j}600 - \mathrm{j}600)I_2 - (-\mathrm{j}600)I_3 \quad . \quad (2)$$

$$0 = -400I_1 - (-\mathrm{j}600)I_2 + (600 + 400 - \mathrm{j}600)I_3 \quad . \quad (3)$$

Currents I_1, I_2 and I_3 can be found from equations (1), (2) and (3) using Cramer's Rule. They are:

$$I_1 = E(83.3 - \mathrm{j}35.7)10^{-5},$$

$$I_2 = E(23.8 + \mathrm{j}23.8)10^{-5},$$

and $$I_3 = E(47.6)10^{-5}.$$

$\therefore$ $$V_1 = E - 600I_1 = \underline{E(0.499 + \mathrm{j}0.214)},$$

$$V_2 = 400(I_1 - I_3) = \underline{E(0.143 - \mathrm{j}0.143)},$$

and $$V_3 = 600I_3 = \underline{E(0.284)}.$$

Nodal analysis

The various admittances in the network are:

$$Y_g = 1/R_g = 1.67 \times 10^{-3}\ \text{S},$$

$$Y_1 = 1/R_1 = 1.1 \times 10^{-3}\ \text{S},$$

$$Y_2 = 1/R_2 = 2.5 \times 10^{-3}\ \text{S},$$

$$Y_3 = 1/X_3 = -\mathrm{j}1.67 \times 10^{-3}\ \text{S},$$

$$Y_4 = 1/X_4 = \mathrm{j}1.67 \times 10^{-3}\ \text{S},$$

$$Y_l = 1/R_l = 1.67 \times 10^{-3}\ \text{S}.$$

The nodal equations are:

$$E/600 = V_1(1.67 \times 10^{-3} + 1.1 \times 10^{-3} - \mathrm{j}1.67 \times 10^{-3})$$
$$- V_2(-\mathrm{j}1.67 \times 10^{-3}) - V_3(1.1 \times 10^{-3}) \quad . \quad . \quad (4)$$

$$0 = -V_1(-\mathrm{j}1.67 \times 10^{-3})$$
$$+ V_2(2.5 \times 10^{-3} - \mathrm{j}1.67 \times 10^{-3} + \mathrm{j}1.67 \times 10^{-3})$$
$$- V_3(\mathrm{j}1.67 \times 10^{-3}) \quad . \quad . \quad . \quad . \quad . \quad . \quad . \quad (5)$$

$$0 = -V_1(1.1\times 10^{-3}) - V_2(j1.67\times 10^{-3}) + V_3(1.67\times 10^{-3}) + 1.1\times 10^{-3} + j1.67\times 10^{-3}) \quad . \quad . \qquad (6)$$

Node voltages V_1, V_2 and V_3 can be found directly from equations (4), (5) and (6). They are:

$$\underline{V_1 = E(0.499 + j0.214),}$$

$$\underline{V_2 = E(0.143 - j0.143),}$$

$$\underline{\text{and } V_3 = E(0.284)}$$

30. The nodal equations are obtained by simply applying Kirchhoff's first law at nodes 1 and 2. Thus:

$$\underline{-E_1 Y_1 + V_1(Y_1 + Y_3 + Y_4 + Y_5) - V_2(Y_4 + Y_5) = 0}$$

and

$$\underline{-E_2 Y_2 + V_2(Y_2 + Y_4 + Y_5 + Y_6) - V_1(Y_4 + Y_5) = 0}$$

31.

$$\begin{aligned} I_1 &= Y_{11}V_1 + Y_{12}V_2 + Y_{13}V_3 + \quad . \quad . \quad + Y_{1n}V_n \\ I_2 &= Y_{21}V_1 + Y_{22}V_2 + Y_{23}V_3 + \quad . \quad . \quad + Y_{2n}V_n \\ I_3 &= . \quad . \quad . \quad . \quad . \quad . \quad . \quad . \quad . \quad . \\ &\quad . \quad . \quad . \quad . \quad . \quad . \quad . \quad . \quad . \quad . \\ &\quad . \quad . \quad . \quad . \quad . \quad . \quad . \quad . \quad . \quad . \\ I_n &= Y_{n1}V_1 + Y_{n2}V_2 + Y_{n3}V_3 + \quad . \quad . \quad + Y_{nn}V_n \end{aligned}$$

$$\therefore V_k = \frac{\begin{vmatrix} Y_{11}\,Y_{12} & . & . & Y_{1k-1}I_1\,Y_{1k+1} & . & . & Y_{1n} \\ Y_{21}\,Y_{22} & . & . & Y_{2k-1}I_2\,Y_{2k+1} & . & . & Y_{2n} \\ . & . & . & . & . & . & . \\ Y_{n1}\,Y_{n2} & . & . & Y_{nk-1}I_n\,Y_{nk+1} & . & . & Y_{nn} \end{vmatrix}}{\Delta}$$

$$\text{where } \Delta = \begin{vmatrix} Y_{11}\,Y_{12}\,Y_{13} & . & . & Y_{1n} \\ Y_{21}\,Y_{22}\,Y_{23} & . & . & Y_{2n} \\ . & . & . & . \\ . & . & . & . \\ Y_{n1}\,Y_{n2}\,Y_{n3} & . & . & Y_{nn} \end{vmatrix}$$

$$\therefore V_k = \frac{A_{1k}I_1}{\Delta} + \frac{A_{2k}I_2}{\Delta} + . \quad . \quad . \frac{A_{jk}I_j}{\Delta} + . \quad . \quad . \frac{A_{nk}I_n}{\Delta}$$

where A_{jk} absorbs the algebraic sign associated with it. If only I_j is present

$$V_k = I_j \frac{A_{jk}}{\Delta} \text{ where } \frac{A_{jk}}{\Delta} \text{ is the open-circuit transfer impedance.}$$

Similarly, the open-circuit input impedance $Z_{11} = \frac{V_1}{I_1} = \frac{A_{11}}{\Delta}$

32.

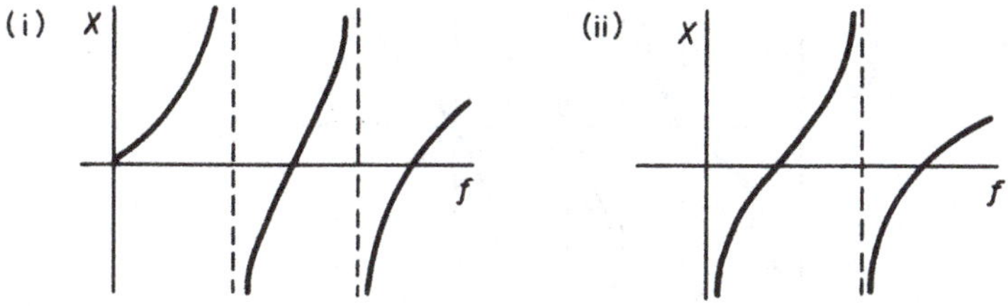

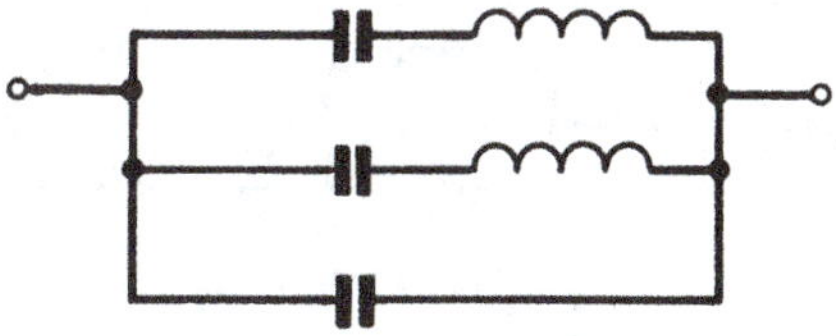

33.

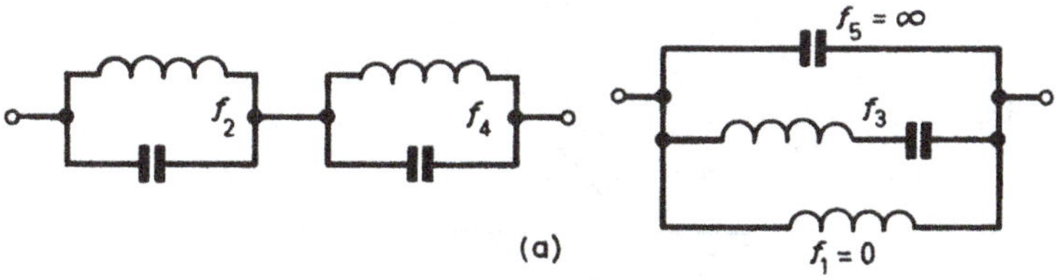

(a)

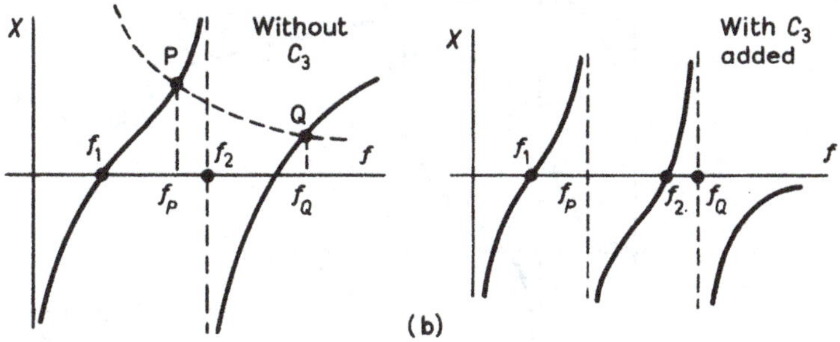

(b)

34.

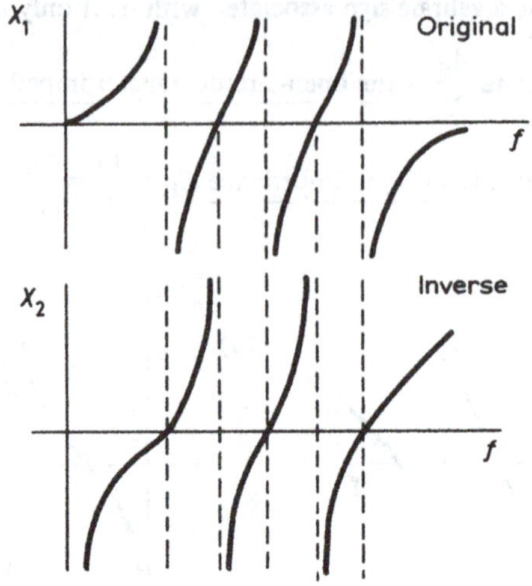

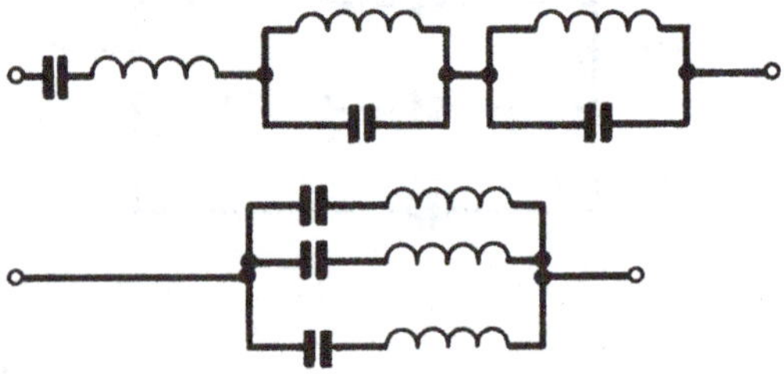

35.

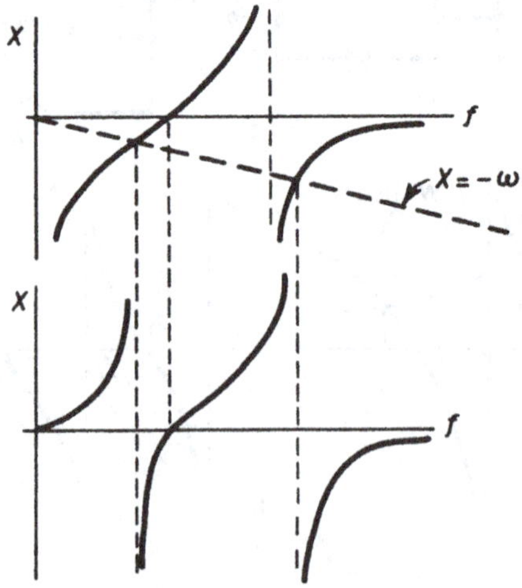

For the part to the right of AA.

For the part to the right of BB.

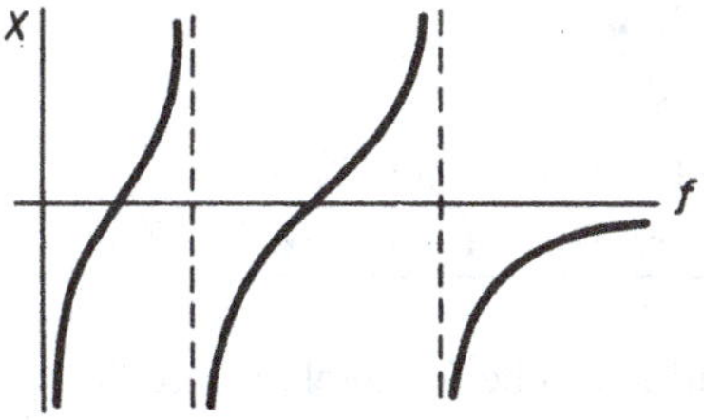

For whole circuit.

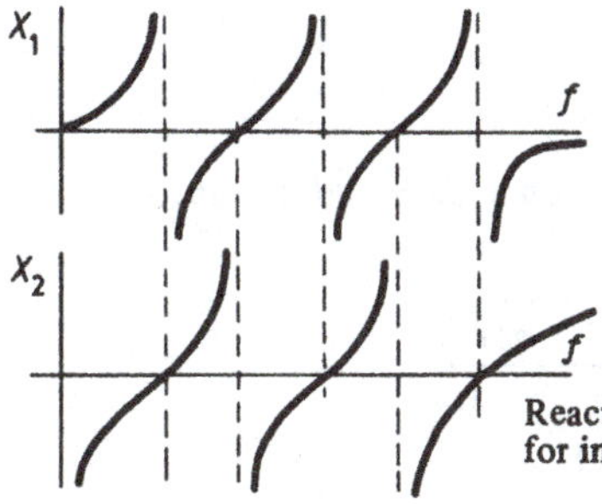

Reactance/f graph for (b)

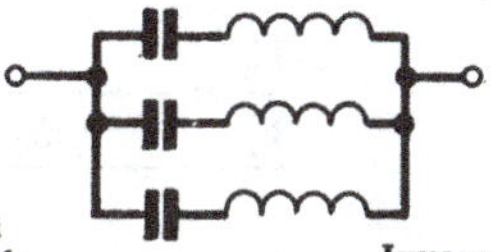

Reactance/f graph for inverse network

Inverse networks

36. (*a*) $t_{11}x_1 + t_{12}x_2 + t_{10}x_0 = 0 \quad . \quad . \quad . \quad . \quad . \quad (1)$

$$\therefore x_1 = -\frac{t_{10}}{t_{11}}x_0 - \frac{t_{12}}{t_{11}}x_2 \quad . \quad . \quad . \quad . \quad . \quad . \quad . \quad (2)$$

$$t_{21}x_1 + t_{22}x_2 + t_{20}x_0 = 0 \quad . \quad . \quad . \quad . \quad . \quad . \quad (3)$$

$$\therefore x_2 = -\frac{t_{20}}{t_{22}}x_0 - \frac{t_{21}}{t_{22}}x_1 \quad . \quad . \quad . \quad . \quad . \quad . \quad . \quad (4)$$

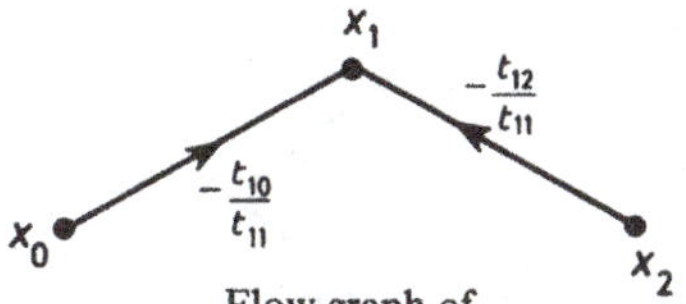

Flow graph of equation (2)

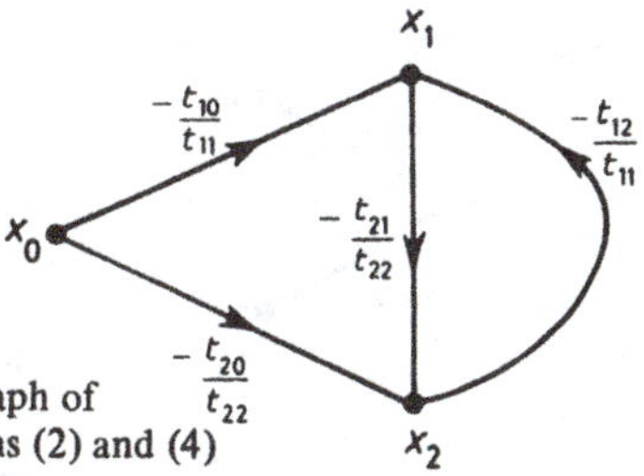

Flow graph of equations (2) and (4)

(*b*) (i) $V_1 = aV_0 + dV_2 \quad . \quad . \quad . \quad . \quad . \quad . \quad (1)$

$$V_2 = cV_1 + eV_2 \quad . \quad . \quad . \quad . \quad . \quad . \quad (2)$$

$$V_3 = bV_1 + fV_2 \quad . \quad . \quad . \quad . \quad . \quad . \quad (3)$$

$$\therefore \frac{V_3}{V_0} = \frac{acf + ab(1-e)}{1-e-cd}$$

(ii) $$G = \Sigma \frac{G_k \Delta_k}{\Delta}$$

$$= \frac{ab\,(1-e)}{1-cd-e} + \frac{acf\,(1)}{1-cd-e}$$

37. (*a*) The solution can be found elsewhere.*

(*b*) Using the general flow-graph equation

$$G = \Sigma_k \frac{G_k \Delta_k}{\Delta}$$

$$G_1 = acd,\ \Delta_1 = 1,\ \Delta = 1-(ab+de+acdf)+abed$$

$$\therefore \frac{V_6}{V_1} = \frac{(acd)\,1}{1-(ab+de+acdf)-abed}$$

38. (i) $V_1 = aV_0 + cV_2$ (1)

$V_2 = bV_1 + dV_2$ (2)

From (2) $V_1 = V_2(1-d)/b$

Substituting in (1) $V_2/V_0 = ab/(1-d-bc)$

(ii) $G_k = ab,\ \Delta = 1-bc-d,\ \Delta_k = 1$

$$\therefore V_2/V_0 = \frac{(ab)\,1}{1-bc-d}$$

39.

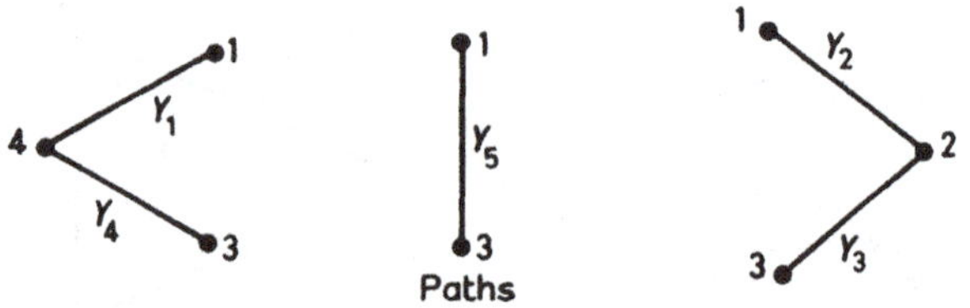

Paths

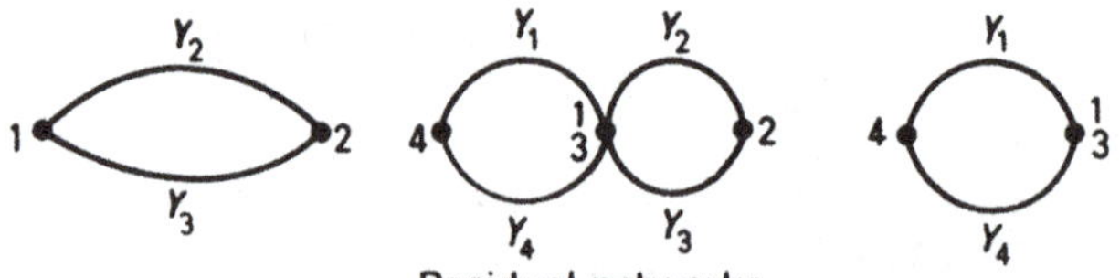

Residual networks

* See F. A. Benson and D. Harrison, *Electric Circuit Theory*, Arnold, 3rd Edition, 1975, pp. 280–281.

Path values and cofactors are:

$\underline{P_1 = Y_1 Y_4}$ $\underline{\Delta_1 = Y_2 + Y_3}$

$\underline{P_2 = Y_5}$ $\underline{\Delta_2 = (Y_1 + Y_4)(Y_2 + Y_3)}$

$\underline{P_3 = Y_2 Y_3}$ $\underline{\Delta_3 = (Y_1 + Y_4)}$

Network determinant Δ

$$= \underline{Y_1 Y_4 (Y_2 + Y_3) + Y_5 (Y_1 Y_2 + Y_1 Y_3 + Y_4 Y_2 + Y_4 Y_3) + Y_2 Y_3 (Y_1 + Y_4)}$$

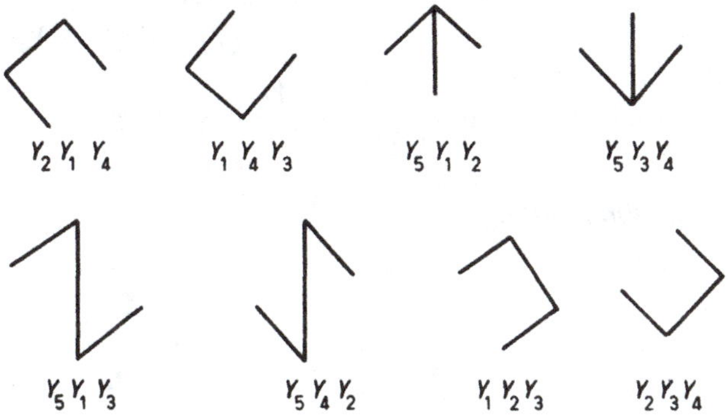

Individual trees

40. Trees are:

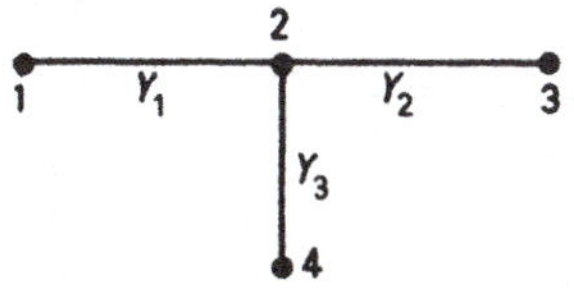

$\underline{\text{Tree value } Y_1 Y_2 Y_3}$

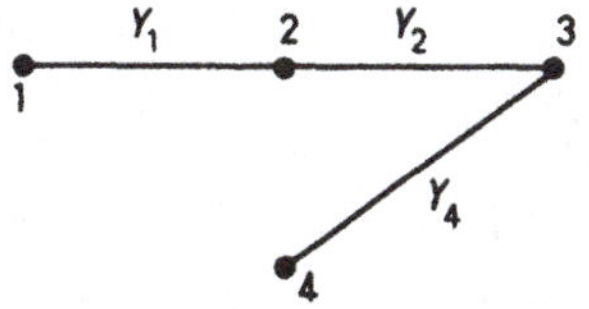

$\underline{\text{Tree value } Y_1 Y_2 Y_4}$

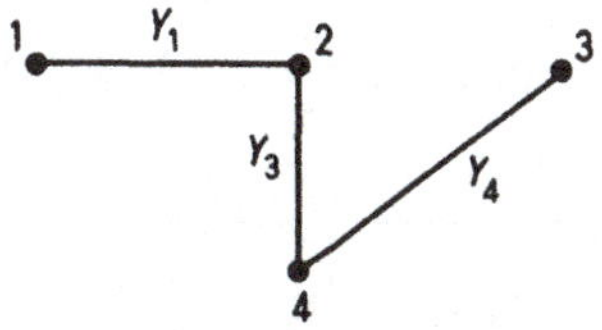

$\underline{\text{Tree value } Y_1 Y_3 Y_4}$

Network determinant $\Delta = Y_1 Y_2 Y_3 + Y_1 Y_2 Y_4 + Y_1 Y_3 Y_4$

$$= \underline{Y_1 (Y_2 Y_3 + Y_2 Y_4 + Y_3 Y_4)}$$

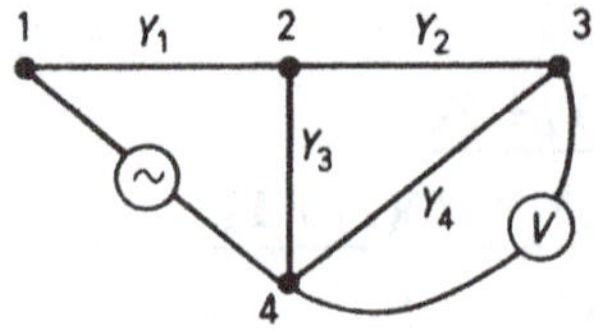

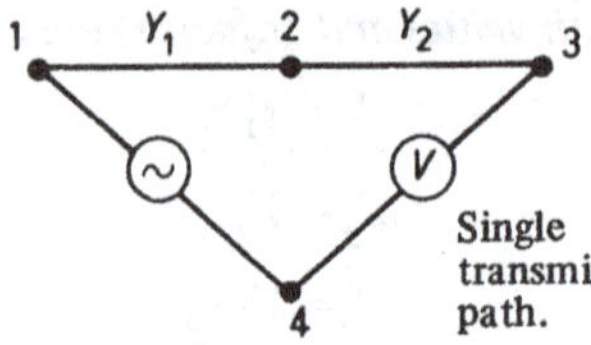

Single transmission path.

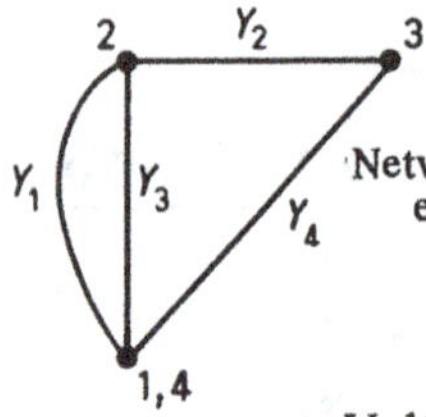

Network for evaluating Δ.

Path value $= Y_1Y_2$

Path cofactor $= 1$

$\Delta = (Y_1 + Y_3)(Y_2 + Y_4) + Y_2Y_4$

$$\therefore \text{ Voltage ratio} = \frac{Y_1Y_2}{(Y_1 + Y_3)(Y_2 + Y_4) + Y_2Y_4}$$

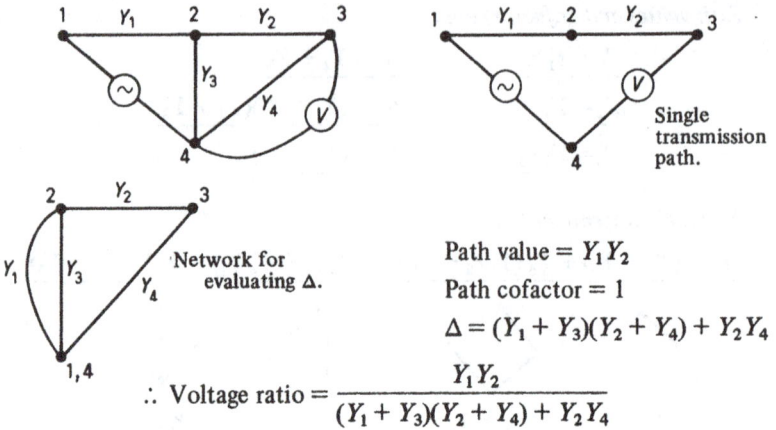

41. *Expansion in paths*

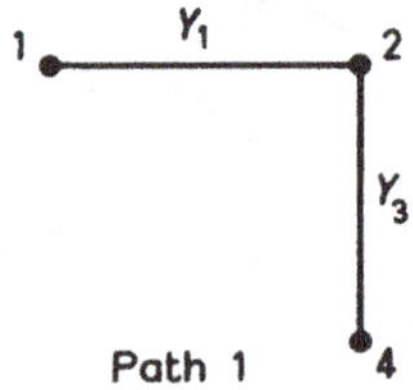

Path 1

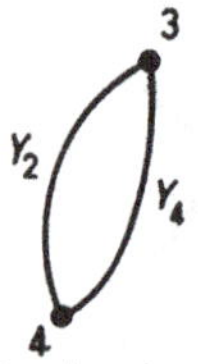

Residual network 1

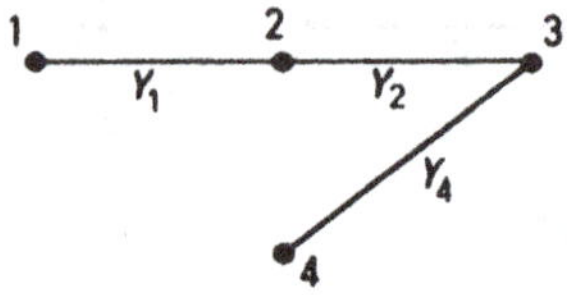

Path 2

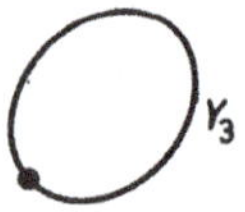

Residual network 2

Path values	*Cofactors*
$P_1 = Y_1Y_3$	$\Delta_1 = Y_2 + Y_4$
$P_2 = Y_1Y_2Y_4$	$\Delta_2 = 1$

Network determinant $\Delta = Y_1Y_3(Y_2 + Y_4) + Y_1Y_2Y_4$

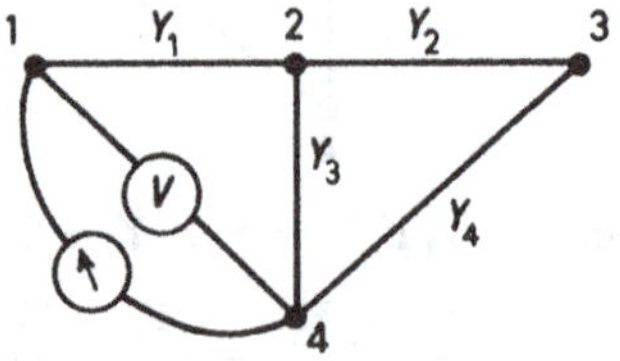

$P' = 1$

When transmission path is collapsed we get the following residual network.

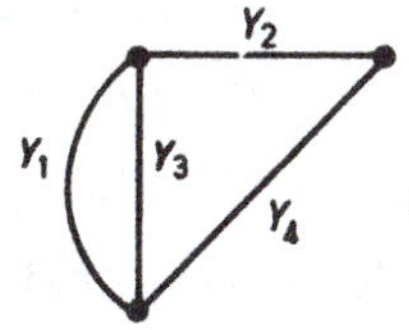

$$\Delta' = (Y_1 + Y_3)(Y_2 + Y_4) + Y_2 Y_4$$

$$\therefore \qquad T = Z_i = \frac{Y_1Y_2 + Y_1Y_4 + Y_3Y_2 + Y_3Y_4 + Y_2Y_4}{Y_1Y_2Y_3 + Y_1Y_3Y_4 + Y_1Y_2Y_4}$$

42. Use s to replace $j\omega$.

The network determinant is:

$$\Delta = \begin{vmatrix} \left(3s \times 10^{-4} + \dfrac{10^8}{3s}\right) & \left(-2s \times 10^{-4} - \dfrac{10^8}{3s}\right) \\ \left(-2s \times 10^{-4} - \dfrac{10^8}{3s}\right) & \left(5s \times 10^{-4} + \dfrac{4 \times 10^8}{3s}\right) \end{vmatrix}$$

$$= \frac{33s^4 \times 10^{-8} + 13s^2 \times 10^4 + 10^{16}}{3s^2}$$

Dividing this expression by $A_{11} = 5s \times 10^{-4} + \dfrac{4 \times 10^8}{3s}$ gives the driving-point impedance $Z(s)$

$$\therefore \qquad Z(s) = \frac{33s^4 \times 10^{-8} + 13s^2 \times 10^4 + 10^{16}}{s(15s^2 \times 10^{-4} + 4 \times 10^8)}$$

Replacing s by $j\omega$ and multiplying top and bottom by 10^8

$$Z(\omega) = \frac{1}{j\omega}\left\{\frac{33\omega^4 - 13\omega^2 \times 10^{12} + 10^{24}}{-15\omega^2 \times 10^4 + 4 \times 10^{16}}\right\}$$

An alternative form is:

$$Z(\omega) = \frac{j\omega\, 2.2 \times 10^{-4}(\omega^2 - 10.48 \times 10^{10})(\omega^2 - 28.9 \times 10^{10})}{\omega^2(\omega^2 - 26.67 \times 10^{10})}$$

43. $$Z(s) = \frac{(sL + 1/sC_2)\,1/sC_1}{sL + 1/sC_2 + 1/sC_1} = \frac{s^2LC_2 + 1}{s\,[s^2LC_1C_2 + (C_1 + C_2)]}$$

Substituting given values:

$$Z(s)=\frac{2s^2+1}{s(2s^2+3)}=\frac{(s-\mathrm{j}1/\sqrt{(2)}(s+\mathrm{j}1/\sqrt{(2)})}{s[s-\mathrm{j}\sqrt{(3/2)}][s+\mathrm{j}\sqrt{(3/2)}]}$$

Zeros occur at $s_1=\mathrm{j}1/\sqrt{(2)}, s_3=-\mathrm{j}1/\sqrt{(2)}$

Poles occur at $s_2=0, s_4=\mathrm{j}\sqrt{(3/2)}, s_6=-\mathrm{j}\sqrt{(3/2)}$

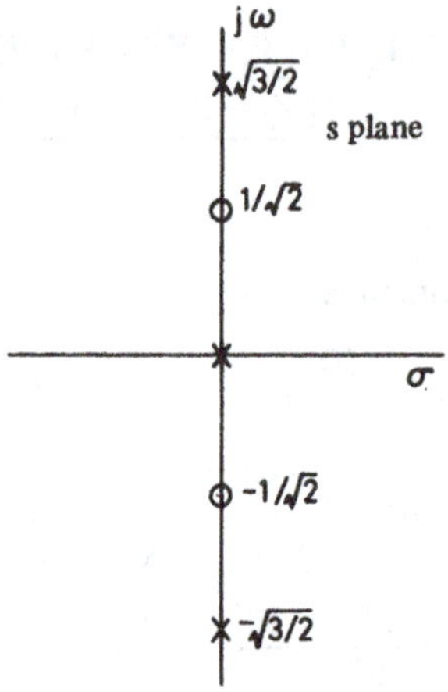

The plot of poles and zeros is illustrated.

$$Z(2)=\frac{1.3\times 2.7}{0.8\times 3.2\times 2.0}$$
$$=\underline{0.68}$$

44.

$$\text{Input impedance } Z(s)=\frac{(sL)\left(\frac{1}{sC}\right)}{sL+\frac{1}{sC}}+R$$

$$=\frac{s^2RLC+sL+R}{s^2LC+1}$$

Substituting numerical values

$$Z(s)=\frac{4s^2+2s+1}{4s^2+1}$$

$$=\frac{[s+\frac{1}{4}+\mathrm{j}\sqrt{(3/4)}][s+\frac{1}{4}-\mathrm{j}\sqrt{(3/4)}]}{(s+\mathrm{j}/2)(s-\mathrm{j}/2)}$$

The poles and zeros are shown in the figure.

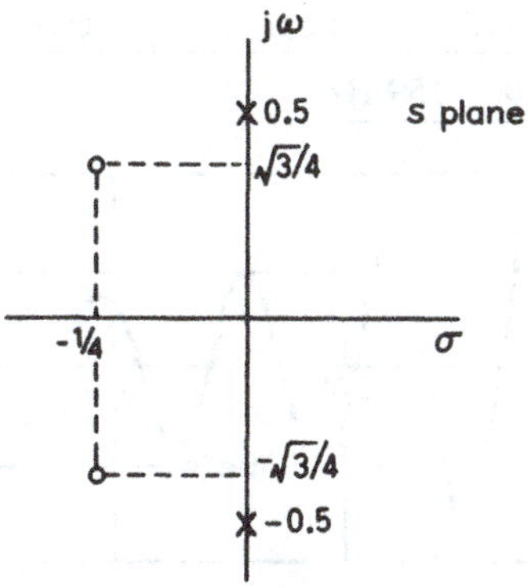

59. The following equation holds for the circuit:

$$L\frac{di}{dt} + Ri + \frac{q}{C} = V$$

where i is the current, V is the applied voltage and q is the charge on the capacitor.

Differentiating $$\frac{d^2i}{dt^2} + \frac{R}{L}\frac{di}{dt} + \frac{i}{LC} = 0.$$

The solution of this equation depends on the relative magnitudes of the constants R, L and C. In this case $\frac{R^2}{4L^2} < \frac{1}{LC}$ and the solution is:

$$i = Ae^{-\frac{Rt}{2L}} \cos\left[\sqrt{\left(\frac{1}{LC} - \frac{R^2}{4L^2}\right)}\ t + B\right]$$

where A and B are constants.

Initially when $t = 0, i = 0$ and $q = 0$.

$$\therefore \qquad A = -V/L\sqrt{\left(\frac{1}{LC} - \frac{R^2}{4L^2}\right)} \text{ and } B = \pi/2.$$

$$\therefore \qquad i = \frac{V}{L\sqrt{\left(\frac{1}{LC} - \frac{R^2}{4L^2}\right)}}\, e^{-\frac{Rt}{2L}} \sin \sqrt{\left(\frac{1}{LC} - \frac{R^2}{4L^2}\right)}\ t \text{ amperes.}$$

Substituting the given circuit values in this expression gives:

$$\underline{i = 40e^{-50t} \sin 1000t \text{ amperes,}}$$

i.e. the current is oscillatory, of gradually decreasing amplitude and of frequency $1000/2\pi$ Hz = 159 Hz.

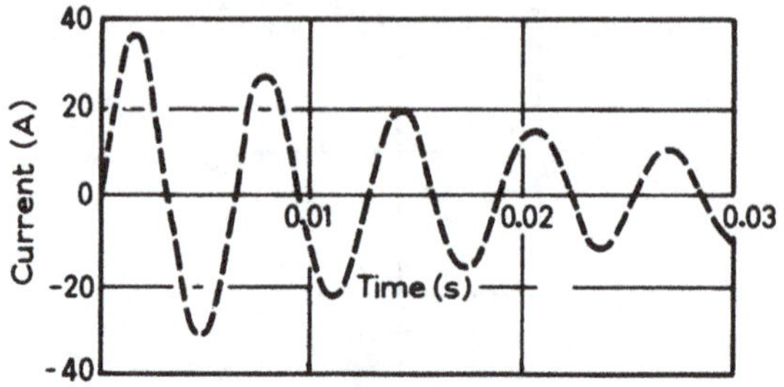

The current/time curve is plotted from the above expression.

When $R = 10\ \Omega$, $\frac{R^2}{4L^2} = \frac{1}{LC}$ and the solution of the above differential equation is:

$$i = (At + B)e^{-\frac{Rt}{2L}}$$

where A and B are constants.

When $t = 0, i = 0$ and $q = 0$.

$$\therefore \qquad A = V/L \text{ and } B = 0.$$

$$\therefore \qquad i = \frac{V}{L}\, t\, e^{-\frac{Rt}{2L}} \text{ amperes.}$$

Substituting the given circuit values in this expression gives:

$$\underline{i = 40\,000t\, e^{-1000t} \text{ amperes.}}$$

The current/time curve is plotted from this expression.

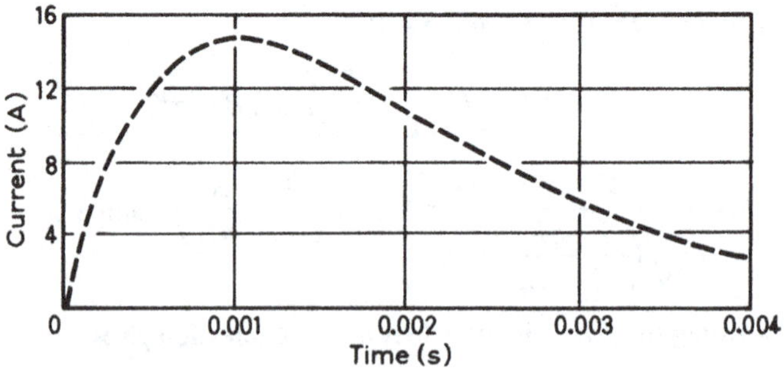

When $R = 20\ \Omega$, $\dfrac{R^2}{4L^2} > \dfrac{1}{LC}$ and the solution of the differential equation is $i = A_1 e^{m_1 t} + B_1 e^{m_2 t}$, where A_1 and B_1 are constants and m_1 and m_2 are the two roots of $m^2 + \dfrac{R}{L}\mathrm{m} + \dfrac{1}{LC} = 0$.

With the same initial conditions as before

$$A_1 = -B_1 = V/L(m_1 - m_2)$$

and
$$i = \frac{V}{L(m_1 - m_2)}(e^{m_1 t} - e^{m_2 t}) \text{ amperes.}$$

Using the given circuit values, $m_1 = -3732$ and $m_2 = -268$.

$\therefore$
$$i = 11.54\,(e^{-268t} - e^{-3732t}) \text{ amperes.}$$

The current/time curve is plotted from this expression.

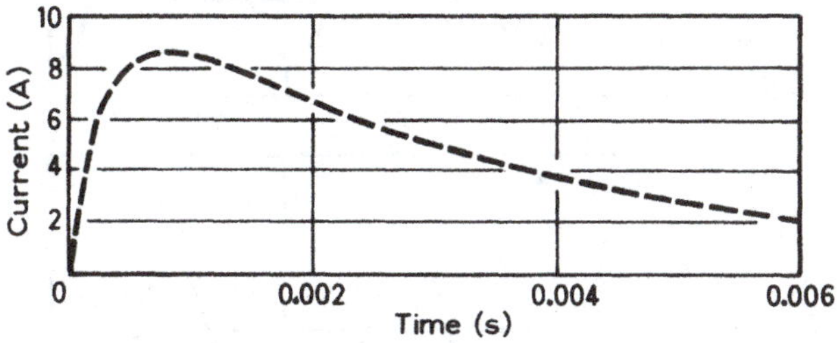

60. At any time t after closing the switch the current in the circuit (i) is given by:

$$L\frac{di}{dt} + Ri = 200 \sin 628t = V \sin \omega t.$$

The solution of this equation is:

$$i = A\,e^{-\frac{Rt}{L}} + V \sin(\omega t - \theta)/\sqrt{(R^2 + \omega^2 L^2)}$$

where A is a constant and $\tan\theta = \omega L/R$.

With the given initial conditions

$$A = V \sin\theta/\sqrt{(R^2 + \omega^2 L^2)}.$$

$\therefore$ the transient current $i_1 = A\,e^{-\frac{Rt}{L}} = V \sin\theta\, e^{-\frac{Rt}{L}}/\sqrt{(R^2 + \omega^2 L^2)}$ and the steady cyclic current $i_2 = V \sin(\omega t - \theta)/\sqrt{(R^2 + \omega^2 L^2)}$.

Substituting the given circuit values in these expressions:

$$i_1 = 15.52\, e^{-100t} \text{ amperes}$$

and
$$i_2 = 15.71 \sin(628t - 81^\circ) \text{ amperes.}$$

Thus i_1, i_2 and i can be plotted against t as shown. It is seen that after a time corresponding to about three complete cycles of the supply voltage i_1 is small.

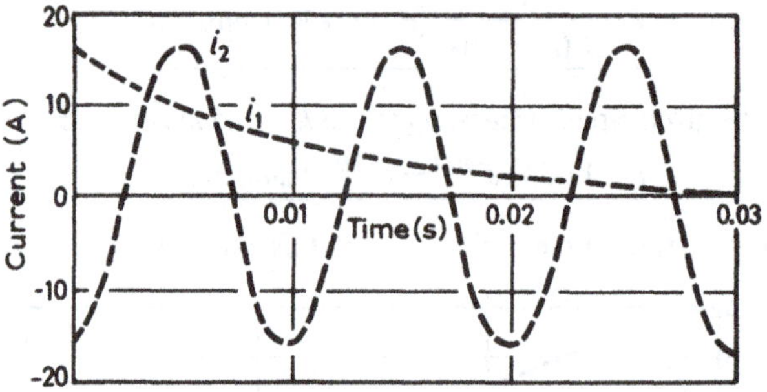

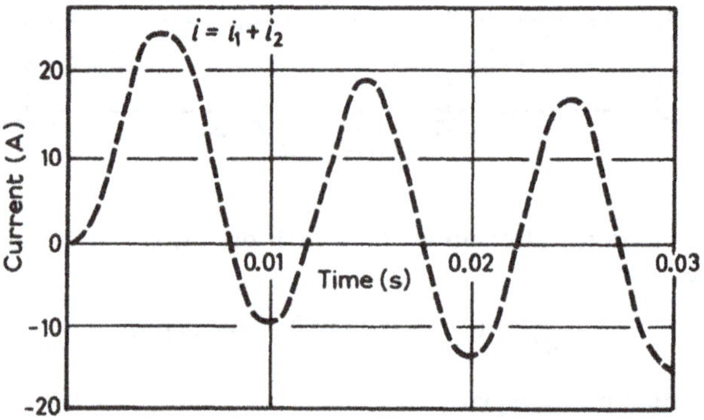

When $R = 0$, $\theta = 90^\circ$, and with the same initial conditions

$$i = V(1 - \cos \omega t)/\omega L,$$

i.e. i never becomes negative; its minimum value is 0. It is also seen that the voltage and current values are zero at the same instant.

61. The following equation holds for the circuit:

$$L\frac{di}{dt} + Ri + \frac{q}{C} = V\cos(\omega t - \theta)$$

where i is the current and q is the charge on the capacitor.

$$\therefore \qquad \frac{d^2i}{dt^2}+\frac{R}{L}\frac{di}{dt}+\frac{i}{LC}=\frac{V\omega}{L}\cos(\omega t-\theta+\pi/2).$$

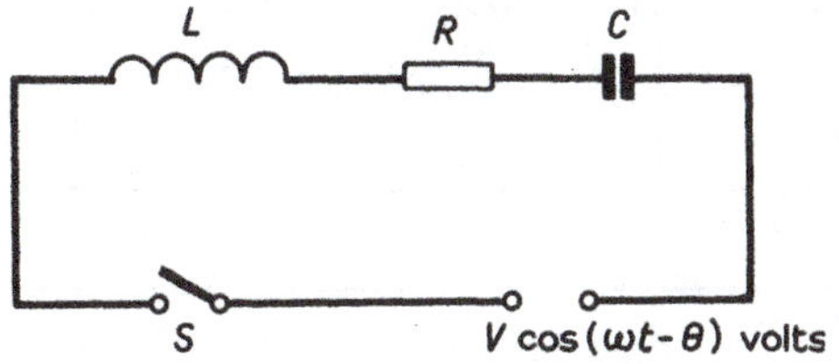

In this case $\frac{R^2}{4L^2}<\frac{1}{LC}$ and the solution is:

$$i=A\,e^{-\frac{Rt}{2L}}\cos\left(\sqrt{\left(\frac{1}{LC}-\frac{R^2}{4L^2}\right)}\,t+\alpha\right)+\frac{\frac{V\omega}{L}\cos\left(\omega t-\theta+\frac{\pi}{2}-\beta\right)}{\sqrt{\left[\left(\frac{1}{LC}-\omega^2\right)^2+R^2\omega^2/L^2\right]}}$$

where $\tan\beta=\frac{R\omega/L}{(1/LC-\omega^2)}$ and A, α and θ are constants determined by the initial conditions that when $t=0$, $i=0$, $q=0$ and the applied voltage is zero.

Using the given circuit values it is found that

$$i=41.5\,e^{-50t}\cos(1000t+173.5^\circ)+41.3\cos(628t-6^\circ)\text{ amperes}$$

$$=i_1+i_2.$$

The first term is the transient and it has a frequency of 159 Hz. It is seen from the graph of this current against time that about 0.05 s after closing S its amplitude is less than 10 per cent of its maximum amplitude of 41.3 A.

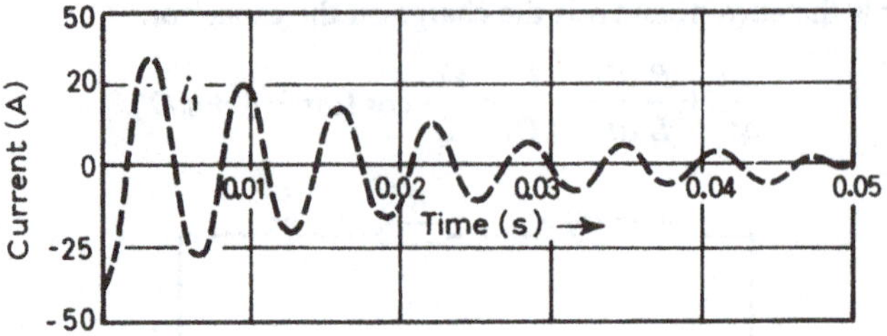

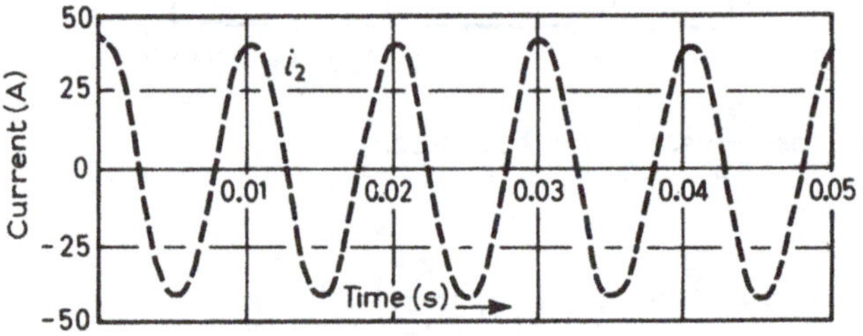

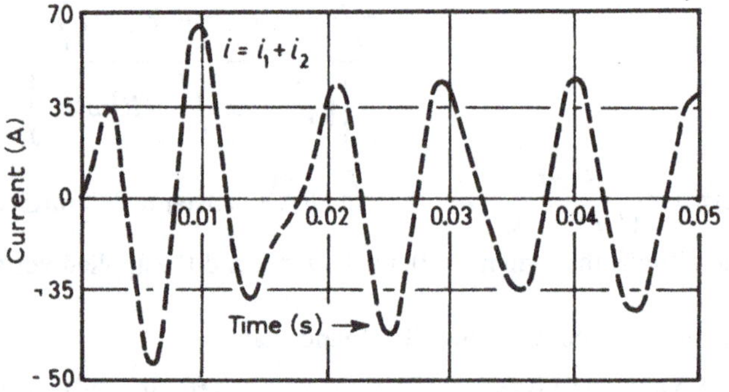

62. In this case $\frac{R^2}{4L^2} < \frac{1}{LC}$ and the natural frequency of the circuit is the same as the frequency of the applied voltage.

Proceeding in the same way as in the previous solution it is found that

$$i = -800\,e^{-25t}\sin 1000t + 800 \sin 1000t \text{ amperes}$$

$$= i_1 + i_2.$$

The i/t, i_1/t and i_2/t curves are plotted from this expression.

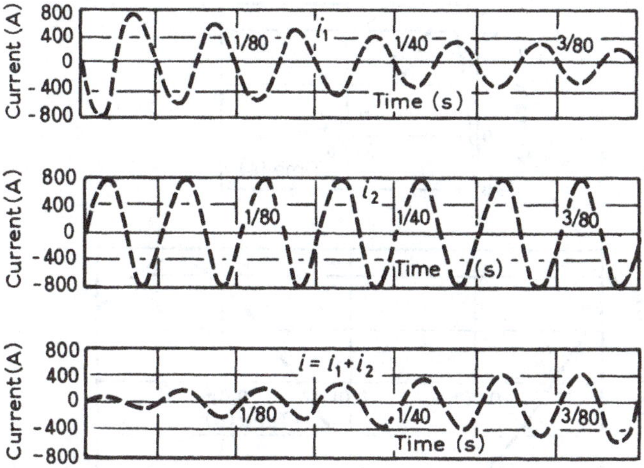

63. In this case $\frac{R^2}{4L^2} > \frac{1}{LC}$ and the solution of the differential equation of Problem 61 is now of the form:

$$i = A\, e^{m_1 t} + B\, e^{m_2 t}$$

$$+ \frac{V\omega}{L} \cos\left(\omega t - \theta + \frac{\pi}{2} - \beta\right) \Big/ \sqrt{\left[\left(R\omega/L\right)^2 + \left(\frac{1}{LC} - \omega^2\right)^2\right]}.$$

Substituting the given circuit values in this expression gives–

$$i = A\, e^{-1151t} + B\, e^{-868t} + 11.4 \cos(314t - \theta + \pi/2 - 35.3^\circ)$$

where A, B and θ are constants depending on the initial conditions.

If when $t = 0, i = 0, q = 0$ and the applied voltage is at its maximum positive value, i.e. $\theta = 0$, it is found that

$$i = -131.6\, e^{-1151t} + 125\, e^{-868t} + 11.4 \cos(314t + 54.7^\circ) \text{ amperes.}$$

The transient current $i_1 = 131.6\, e^{-1151t} + 125\, e^{-868t}$ amperes, the permanent current $i_2 = 11.4 \cos(314t + 54.7^\circ)$ amperes and i can therefore be plotted against t as illustrated.

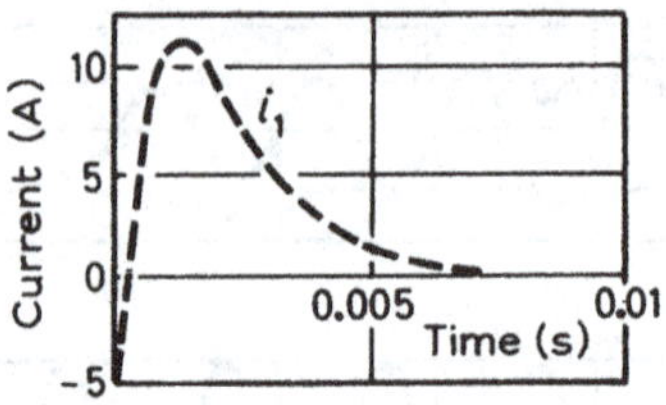

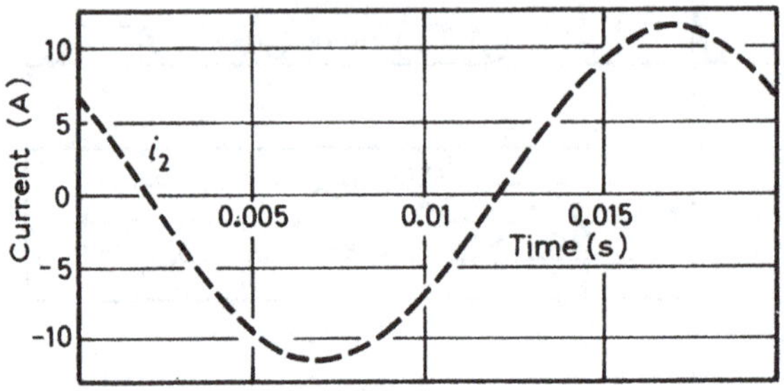

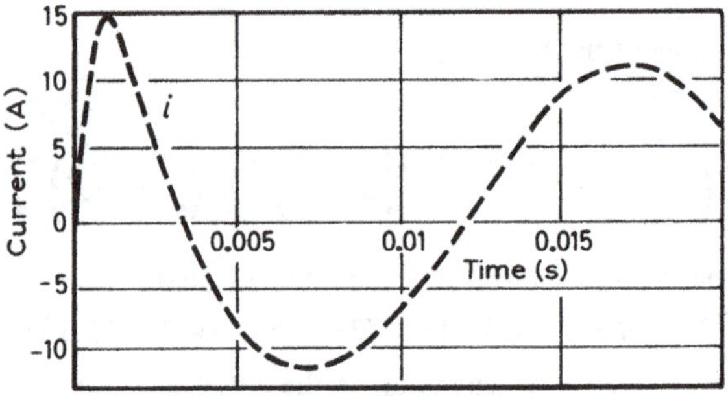

64. The solution to this problem has been given elsewhere.*

65. The solution to this problem has been given elsewhere.†

66. The solution to this problem has been given elsewhere.‡

67. The solution to this problem has been given elsewhere.§

* F. A. Benson and D. Harrison, *Electric Circuit Theory*, Arnold, 3rd Edition, 1975, pp. 260–1.

† *Ibid.*, pp. 249–51. ‡ *Ibid.*, pp. 263–4. § *Ibid.*, pp. 268.

68. Suppose $y(t)$ is a known function of t for values of $t > 0$. Then the Laplace transform $\bar{y}(s)$ of $y(t)$ is defined as

$$\bar{y}(s) = \int_0^\infty e^{-st} y(t)\, dt \quad . \quad . \quad . \quad (1)$$

where s is a number sufficiently large to make the integral convergent.

If a is any number, real or complex, then $\bar{y}(s+a)$ is the Laplace transform of $e^{-at}y(t)$.

Using (1) it is found that if $y(t) = t^{n-1}/(n-1)!$, then $\bar{y}(s) = 1/s^n$.

Thus, the transform of $e^{-at}t^{n-1}/(n-1)!$ is $1/(s+a)^n$. Similarly, using (1) if $y(t) = \sin at$, then $\bar{y}(s) = a/(s^2 + a^2)$.

Thus, the transform of $e^{-bt} \sin at = a/\{(s+b)^2 + a^2\}$.

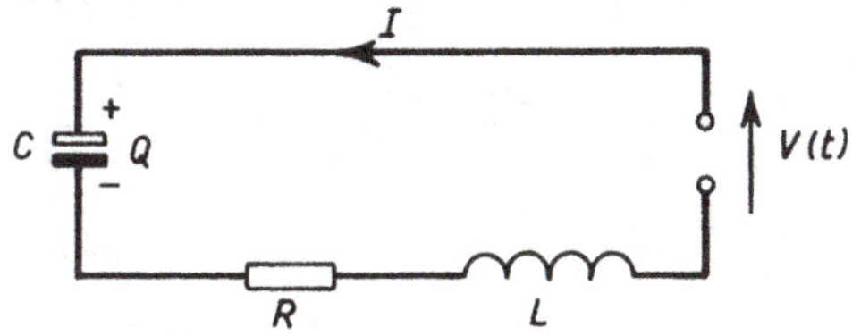

For the circuit illustrated,

$$I = dQ/dt \quad . \quad . \quad . \quad . \quad (2)$$

Also,

$$L\, dI/dt + RI + Q/C = V \quad . \quad . \quad . \quad (3)$$

The problem is to solve (2) and (3) with given initial values,

$$I = I_0, \; Q = Q_0 \text{ at } t = 0 \quad . \quad . \quad . \quad (4)$$

Forming the subsidiary equations for (2), (3) and (4) in the usual way:

$$(Ls + R)\bar{I} + \bar{Q}/C = LI_0 + \bar{V} \quad . \quad . \quad . \quad (5)$$

$$\bar{Q} = \bar{I}/s + Q_0/s \quad . \quad . \quad . \quad . \quad (6)$$

From (5) and (6)

$$(Ls + R + 1/Cs)\bar{I} = \bar{V} + LI_0 - Q_0/Cs \quad . \quad . \quad (7)$$

If a constant voltage E is applied at $t = 0$ and $I_0 = Q_0 = 0$, the subsidiary equation (7) becomes:

$$(Ls + R + 1/Cs)\bar{I} = E/s \quad . \quad . \quad . \quad (8)$$

Thus,

$$\bar{I} = E/L\{(s + \alpha)^2 + \beta^2\} \quad . \quad . \quad . \quad (9)$$

where

$$\alpha = R/2L \quad \text{and} \quad \beta^2 = 1/LC - R^2/4L^2$$

The solution of (9) is $I = Ete^{-\alpha t}/L$, when $R = 2\sqrt{(L/C)}$. Similarly, the transient response of the circuit can be investigated using (7) no matter what the form of the applied voltage.

69. (*a*) The subsidiary equations are:

$$(s^2+2)\bar{x} - s\bar{y} = \frac{1}{s} + sx_0$$

$$s\bar{x} + (s^2+2)\bar{y} = x_0$$

Solving:

$$\bar{x} = \frac{s^4x_0 + s^2(3x_0+1)+2}{s(s^2+1)(s^2+4)} = \frac{1}{2s} + \frac{s(2x_0-1)}{3(s^2+1)} + \frac{s(2x_0-1)}{6(s^2+4)}$$

$$\bar{y} = \frac{2x_0-1}{(s^2+1)(s^2+4)} = \frac{(2x_0-1)}{3}\left(\frac{1}{s^2+1} - \frac{1}{s^2+4}\right)$$

$\therefore$ $$x = \tfrac{1}{2} + \tfrac{1}{3}(2x_0-1)\cos t + \tfrac{1}{6}(2x_0-1)\cos 2t$$

and $$y = \tfrac{1}{3}(2x_0-1)\sin t - \tfrac{1}{6}(2x_0-1)\sin 2t$$

(*b*) The subsidiary equations are:

$$L_1s\bar{i}_1 + Ms\bar{i}_2 = \bar{v}$$

$$Ms\bar{i}_1 + \left(L_2s + R_2 + \frac{1}{C_2s}\right)\bar{i}_2 = 0$$

$\therefore$ $$\bar{i}_2 = \frac{-Ms\bar{v}}{(L_1L_2 - M^2)s^2 + R_2L_1s + L_1/C_2}$$

e.g. if v = a constant V, $\bar{v} = V/s$.

Then, $$\bar{i}_2 = \frac{-MV}{(L_1L_2-M^2)s^2 + R_2L_1s + L_1/C_2}$$

$\therefore$ $$i_2 = \frac{-MV}{\beta(L_1L_2-M^2)}e^{-\alpha t}\sin\beta t$$

where $$\alpha = \frac{R_2L_1}{2(L_1L_2-M^2)} \quad \text{and} \quad \beta^2 = \frac{L_1}{C_2(L_1L_2-M^2)} - \alpha^2$$

70. (*a*) Logarithmic decrement $\delta = \pi R/\omega L = R/2fL$.
The frequency f corresponding to a wavelength of 300 m is 1 MHz.

$\therefore$ $$\delta = 10/(2 \times 10^6 \times 150 \times 10^{-6}) = \underline{0.033}.$$

(*b*) Let the number of oscillations be N.

Then the amplitude of the Nth oscillation, $I_N = I_1 e^{-(N-1)\delta}$, where δ is the logarithmic decrement.

$\therefore$ $$100 = e^{(N-1)0.1} \text{ and } \underline{N = 47}.$$

71. The natural frequency of free oscillations is

$$\frac{1}{2\pi}\sqrt{\left(\frac{1}{LC} - \frac{R^2}{4L^2}\right)} = \underline{478 \text{ kHz}}.$$

To make the discharge non-oscillatory R must be at least equal to $2\sqrt{\frac{L}{C}}$, i.e. $\underline{12.1\ \Omega}$.

77. For any waveform which is cyclic, repeating itself at intervals of 2π,

$$f(\theta) = A + a_1 \sin\theta + \ldots + a_n \sin n\theta + \ldots$$
$$+ b_1 \cos\theta + \ldots + b_n \cos n\theta + \ldots$$

where $$A = \frac{1}{2\pi}\int_0^{2\pi} f(\theta)\, d\theta$$

$$a_n = \frac{1}{\pi}\int_0^{2\pi} f(\theta) \sin n\theta\, d\theta$$

and $$b_n = \frac{1}{\pi}\int_0^{2\pi} f(\theta) \cos n\theta\, d\theta.$$

In the case of a half-wave rectifier $f(\theta) = E \sin\theta$ from 0 to π and $f(\theta) = 0$ from π to 2π.

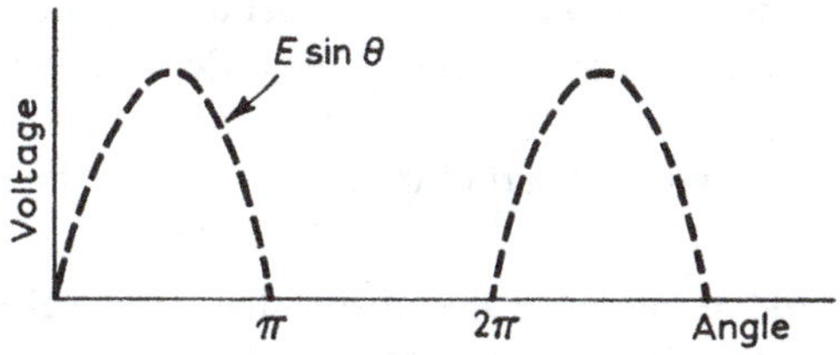

$\therefore$ $$A = \frac{1}{2\pi}\int_0^{\pi} E \sin\theta\, d\theta = E/\pi.$$

$$a_n = \frac{1}{\pi}\int_0^\pi E \sin\theta \sin n\theta \, d\theta$$ which is zero except for $n = 1$ in which case $a_1 = E/2$.

$$b_n = \frac{1}{\pi}\int_0^\pi E \sin\theta \cos n\theta \, d\theta.$$

When n is odd, $b_n = 0$; when n is even $b_n = -2E/\pi(n^2-1)$.

The Fourier expansion is therefore

$$E\left[\frac{1}{\pi}+\frac{1}{2}\sin\theta-\frac{2}{\pi}\sum_{n=2,4,6}\frac{\cos n\theta}{(n^2-1)}\right].$$

The full-wave circuit consists essentially of two half-wave circuits, one circuit operates during one half-cycle and the second operates during the next half-cycle. Also analysing each half-wave separately using the above result it is seen that for the full-wave circuit the component fundamentals cancel out, the negative even cosine harmonics are coincident, and are therefore present with twice the amplitude, and it is evident that the value of the constant term is twice the value for the previous case.

The Fourier expansion for the full-wave case is therefore

$$E\left[\frac{2}{\pi}-\frac{4}{\pi}\sum_{n=2,4,6\ldots}\frac{\cos n\theta}{(n^2-1)}\right].$$

The r.m.s. value $= E\sqrt{[4/\pi^2 + 16/2\pi^2\{(1/3)^2 + (1/15)^2 + \ldots\}]}$
$= E/\sqrt{2}$.

78. The method of solution is the same as that already given for Problem 77 and is therefore not given again here.

79. The method of solution for the first part of the problem is the same as that already given for Problem 77 and is therefore not given again here.

The solution to the second part of the problem can be found elsewhere.*

80. The method of solution is the same as that already given for Problem 77 and is therefore not given again here.

* W. H. Middendorf, *Analysis of Electric Circuits*, Wiley, 1956, Chapter 17.

81. The method of solution is the same as that already given for Problem 77 and is therefore not given again here.

82. The solution to this problem has been given elsewhere.*

83. The formula† for $f(t)$ is:

$$\underline{f(t) = \int_{-\infty}^{\infty} g(\omega) e^{j\omega t}\, d\omega}$$

The relationship between the transform pairs and the Fourier series is discussed in many textbooks.‡

$$g(\omega) = \frac{1}{2\pi} \int_{-\infty}^{+\infty} f(t) e^{-j\omega t}\, dt$$

$$= \frac{1}{2\pi} \int_{0}^{\infty} e^{-(\alpha + j\omega)t}\, dt$$

$$= \frac{1}{2\pi} \left[\frac{e^{-(\alpha + j\omega)t}}{-(\alpha + j\omega)} \right]_0^\infty$$

i.e.

$$\underline{g(\omega) = 1/2\pi(\alpha + j\omega)}$$

For amplifier of complex gain $G(\omega)$ spectrum is $G(\omega)\, g(\omega)$ and output is:

$$F(t) = \mathop{\mathscr{L}}_{\alpha \to 0} \int_{-\infty}^{+\infty} G(\omega) g(\omega) e^{j\omega t}\, d\omega$$

or

$$\underline{F(t) = \mathop{\mathscr{L}}_{\alpha \to 0} \frac{1}{2\pi} \int_{-\infty}^{\infty} \frac{G(\omega)}{(\alpha + j\omega)} e^{j\omega t}\, d\omega}$$

84. The Fourier transform of $f(t)$ is

$$g(\omega) = \int_{-\infty}^{\infty} f(t)\, e^{-j\omega t}\, dt$$

* F. A. Benson and D. Harrison, *Electric Circuit Theory*, Arnold, 3rd Edition, 1975, pp. 202–204

† See Footnote after the Question.

‡ See, for example, R. E. Scott, *Linear Circuits* (complete), Addison Wesley, 1960, Chapter 20.

For (*a*):
$$g(\omega) = \int_{-T/2}^{T/2} e^{-j\omega t}\,dt = \left[\frac{e^{-j\omega t}}{-j\omega}\right]_{-T/2}^{T/2}$$
$$= T\left\{\frac{\sin \omega T/2}{\omega T/2}\right\}$$

For (*b*):
$$g(\omega) = \int_{-T}^{0} (1 + t/T)e^{-j\omega t}\,dt$$
$$+ \int_{0}^{T} (1 - t/T)e^{-j\omega t}\,dt$$
$$= T\left\{\frac{\sin \omega T/2}{\omega T/2}\right\}^2$$

91. $$r_n = \frac{\epsilon_0 h^2 n^2}{\pi m Z e^2}$$
$$= \frac{8.855 \times 10^{-12} \times (6.624 \times 10^{-34})^2 \times 10^{10} n^2}{\pi \times 9.107 \times 10^{-31} \times (1.602 \times 10^{-19})^2 Z} \text{ angstrom units}$$
$$= 0.529\, n^2/Z \text{ angstrom units}$$

$$W_n = -\frac{m e^4 Z^2}{8 \epsilon_0^2 h^2 n^2} \text{ J}$$
$$= -\frac{9.107 \times 10^{-31} \times (1.60 \times 10^{-19})^4 Z^2}{8 \times (8.855 \times 10^{-12})^2 \times (6.62 \times 10^{-34})^2 n^2} \text{ J}$$
$$= -\frac{21.8 \times 10^{-19} Z^2}{n^2} \text{ J}$$
$$= -\frac{21.8 \times 10^{-19} Z^2}{n^2 \times 1.602 \times 10^{-19}} \text{ eV}$$
$$= -13.6 Z^2/n^2 \text{ eV}$$

92. (*a*) The permissible energy levels W_n may be expressed as*:

$$W_n = -(13.6\, Z^2/n^2) \text{ eV} \qquad \text{(see Question 91)}$$

where Z is the atomic number of the atom. For a hydrogen atom $Z = 1$.

The lowest energy state ($n = 1$) for hydrogen is therefore $-$ 13.6 eV.

* See, for example, D. J. Harris and P. N. Robson, *The Physical Basis of Electronics*, Pergamon, 1974.

$$\text{When } n = 2,\ W_2 = -(13.6/4)\text{ eV} = \underline{-3.4\text{ eV}}$$
$$\text{When } n = 3,\ W_3 = -(13.6/9)\text{ eV} = \underline{-1.51\text{ eV}}$$
$$\text{When } n = 4,\ W_4 = -(13.6/16)\text{ eV} = \underline{-0.85\text{ eV}}$$

(*b*) Energy released = (13.6 − 3.4) eV = 10.2 eV

Frequency of radiation (f) is given by:

$$hf = (10.2 \times 1.602 \times 10^{-19})\text{ J}$$

$$\therefore \quad f = \frac{10.2 \times 1.602 \times 10^{-19}}{6.624 \times 10^{-34}}\text{ Hz}$$
$$= \underline{2.465 \times 10^{15}\text{ Hz}}$$

93. $$W_n = \frac{-13.6\,Z^2}{\epsilon^2 n^2}\text{ eV} \qquad \text{(see Problem 91)}$$

For $Z = 1, n = 1, \epsilon = 11.7$

$$W_n = \frac{13.6}{(11.7)^2} = \underline{0.099\text{ eV}}$$

$$r = \frac{\epsilon\epsilon_0 h^2 n^2}{\pi m e^2 Z} \qquad \text{(see Problem 91)}$$
$$= \frac{11.7 \times 8.855 \times 10^{-12} \times (6.62 \times 10^{-34})^2}{\pi \times 9.107 \times 10^{-31} \times (1.602 \times 10^{-19})^2}\text{ m}$$
$$= \underline{6.16\text{ Å}}$$

i.e. the smallest orbit passes outside the nearest neighbour atoms so is essentially in the bulk crystal.

94. Bohr postulate:

$$\text{Angular momentum*} = \frac{nh}{2\pi}$$

For $n = 1, mvr = \dfrac{h}{2\pi}$

$$r = \frac{0.529 n^2}{Z}\text{ angstrom units} \qquad \text{(see Problem 91)}$$

* See D. J. Harris and P. N. Robson, *The Physical Basis of Electronics*, Pergamon, 2nd Edition, 1974, p. 25.

$$= 5.29 \times 10^{-11}\ \text{m}$$

$$\therefore \qquad v = \frac{6.624 \times 10^{-34}}{2\pi \times 5.29 \times 10^{-11} \times 9.107 \times 10^{-31}}\ \text{ms}^{-1}$$

$$= \underline{2.19 \times 10^{6}\ \text{ms}^{-1}}$$

$$\text{Ratio}\ \frac{v}{c} = \frac{2.19 \times 10^{6}}{3 \times 10^{8}} = \underline{7.3 \times 10^{-3}}$$

95. The conductivity σ of a semiconductor is given by*

$$\sigma = e(p\mu_h + n\mu_e)$$

where

n = electron density

p = hole density

μ_e = electron mobility

μ_h = hole mobility

For an intrinsic semiconductor $p = n = n_i$, where n_i is the density of holes and electrons. Therefore the intrinsic conductivity σ_i is given by:

$$\sigma_i = n_i e(\mu_e + \mu_h)$$

$$\therefore \qquad n_i = \frac{1}{0.47 \times 1.602 \times 10^{-19}(0.36 + 0.17)}\ \text{m}^{-3}$$

$$= \underline{2.5 \times 10^{19}\ \text{m}^{-3}}$$

96. Density of donor impurities $= (4.4 \times 10^{28}) \times 10^{-6}\ \text{m}^{-3}$

$$= 4.4 \times 10^{22}\ \text{m}^{-3}$$

The intrinsic density $= 2.5 \times 10^{19}\ \text{m}^{-3}$

$$\therefore \qquad \text{hole density} = \frac{(2.5 \times 10^{19})^2}{4.4 \times 10^{22}} = \underline{1.42 \times 10^{16}\ \text{m}^{-3}}$$

$$\text{Electron density} = \underline{4.4 \times 10^{22}\ \text{m}^{-3}}$$

$$\text{Resistivity} = \frac{1}{4.4 \times 10^{22} \times 1.602 \times 10^{-19} \times 0.36}$$

$$= \underline{4 \times 10^{-4}\ \Omega\text{m}}$$

* See, for example, D. J. Harris and P. N. Robson, *The Physical Basis of Electronics*, Pergamon, 1974, Section 3.4.1.

97. The Einstein relation between mobility μ and diffusion constant D is $D = kT\mu/e$ where k is Boltzmann's constant and T is the absolute temperature.

For electrons, $$D_n = \frac{1.38 \times 10^{-23} \times 300 \times 0.36}{1.602 \times 10^{-19}} = \underline{9.3 \times 10^{-3}\,\mathrm{m^2\,s^{-1}}}$$

For holes, $$D_p = \frac{1.38 \times 10^{-23} \times 300 \times 0.17}{1.602 \times 10^{-19}} = \underline{4.4 \times 10^{-3}\,\mathrm{m^2\,s^{-1}}}$$

98. The conductivity is:

$$\sigma = ne\mu_e + pe\mu_h$$

and $$np = n_i^2$$

$\therefore$ $$\frac{\sigma}{e} = n\mu_e + \frac{n_i^2}{n}\mu_h$$

This is a minimum when $\dfrac{d(\sigma/e)}{d_n} = 0$

i.e. where $$\mu_e - \frac{n_i^2}{n^2}\mu_h = 0$$

or $$\underline{n = n_i\sqrt{\frac{\mu_h}{\mu_e}}}$$

$\dfrac{d^2(\sigma/e)}{dn^2}$ is positive so the turning point is a minimum.

$$p = \frac{n_i^2}{n} = \underline{n_i\sqrt{\frac{\mu_e}{\mu_h}}}$$

Under intrinsic conditions:

$$\begin{aligned}\sigma &= n_i e(\mu_e + \mu_h)\\ &= 2.5 \times 10^{19} \times 1.6 \times 10^{-19}\,(0.57)\,\mathrm{Sm^{-1}}\\ &= \underline{2.28\,\mathrm{Sm^{-1}}}\end{aligned}$$

Under the minimum conductivity condition:

$$\begin{aligned}\sigma &= n_i e\sqrt{(\mu_h\mu_e)} + n_i e\sqrt{(\mu_e\mu_h)}\\ &= 2n_i e\sqrt{(\mu_h\mu_e)}\\ &= 5 \times 10^{19} \times 1.6 \times 10^{-19}\sqrt{(0.38 \times 0.19)}\,\mathrm{Sm^{-1}}\\ &= \underline{2.12\,\mathrm{Sm^{-1}}}\end{aligned}$$

The conductivity is equal to the intrinsic one when:

$$ne\mu_e + \frac{n_i^2}{n} e\mu_h = n_i e(\mu_e + \mu_h)$$

or

$$n^2\mu_e - nn_i(\mu_e + \mu_h) + n_i^2\mu_h = 0$$

i.e.

$$n = \frac{n_i(\mu_e + \mu_h) \pm \sqrt{[n_i^2(\mu_e + \mu_h)^2 - 4\mu_e n_i^2 \mu_h]}}{2\mu_e}$$

$\therefore$

$$n = \frac{n_i}{0.76}(0.57 \pm \sqrt{[(0.57)^2 - 4(0.38)(0.19)]}$$

or

$$n = \frac{n_i}{4}(3 \pm 1)$$

But $n \neq n_i$, so $n = n_i/2 = \underline{1.25 \times 10^{19}\ \text{m}^{-3}}$

Also $p = n_i^2/n = \underline{5 \times 10^{19}\ \text{m}^{-3}}$

99. For the p-type material $\sigma_p = p_p e\mu_h$ where σ_p is the conductivity of the p material and μ_h the mobility of holes.

so

$$p_p = \frac{10^4}{0.17 \times 1.602 \times 10^{-19}} = 3.68 \times 10^{23}\ \text{m}^{-3}$$

For the n-type material

$$n_n = \frac{100}{0.36 \times 1.602 \times 10^{-19}} = 1.75 \times 10^{21}\ \text{m}^{-3}$$

Now

$$p_n = n_i^2/n_n = (2.5 \times 10^{19})^2/1.75 \times 10^{21}$$
$$= 3.57 \times 10^{17}\ \text{m}^{-3}$$

Contact potential

$$V_j = \frac{kT}{e}\ln\left(\frac{p_p}{p_n}\right)$$
$$= \frac{1.38 \times 10^{-23} \times 300}{1.602 \times 10^{-19}}\ln\left(\frac{3.68 \times 10^{23}}{3.57 \times 10^{17}}\right)$$
$$= \underline{0.35\ \text{V}}$$

100. Total saturation current density is given by*

* See D. J. Harris and P. N. Robson, *The Physical Basis of Electronics*, Pergamon 1974, Appendix 3B.

$$J_s = \frac{D_p e p_n}{L_p} + \frac{D_n e n_p}{L_n}$$

where D_p and D_n are the diffusion coefficients and L_p and L_n the diffusion lengths.

From the previous solution

$$p_n = 3.57 \times 10^{17}\,\mathrm{m}^{-3}$$

and $$n_p = n_i^2/p_p = 1.7 \times 10^{15}\,\mathrm{m}^{-3}$$

Also $$-D_p = \frac{kT}{e}\mu_h \quad \text{and} \quad D_n = \frac{kT}{e}\mu_e$$

$$\therefore \quad J_s = (1.38 \times 10^{-23})\, 300 \left\{ \frac{3.57 \times 10^{17} \times 0.17 + 1.7 \times 10^{15} \times 0.36}{1 \times 10^{-3}} \right\}$$

$$= \underline{0.25\ \mathrm{Am}^{-2}}$$

$$\frac{\text{Hole saturation current}}{\text{Electron saturation current}} = \frac{\mu_h p_n}{\mu_e n_p} \text{ since } L_p = L_n$$

$$= \underline{100}$$

101. The solution to this problem can be found elsewhere.*

102. $$J = J_s \left\{ \exp\left(\frac{eV}{kT}\right) - 1 \right\}$$

$$\therefore \quad \exp\left(\frac{eV}{kT}\right) - 1 = \frac{10^5}{0.25} = 4 \times 10^5$$

$$\therefore \quad \frac{eV}{kT} = 12.9$$

so $$V = \frac{12.9 \times 1.38 \times 10^{-23} \times 300}{1.602 \times 10^{-19}}$$

$$= \underline{0.33\ \mathrm{V}}$$

* See, for example, M. V. Joyce and K. K. Clarke, *Transistor Circuit Analysis*, Addison-Wesley, 1961, p. 9, or D. J. Harris and P. N. Robson, *Vacuum and Solid State Electronics*, Pergamon, 1963, pp. 107 and 243.

103. Mean free path $\lambda = 1/N\pi r^2$

where r is the radius of the spherical scattering centre and N is the density.

In this case $\lambda = (1/10^{20} \times \pi \times 25 \times 10^4 \times 10^{-20})$ m

$$= \underline{1.27 \times 10^{-6} \text{ m}}$$

Mean time between collisions is $\tau = \lambda/\bar{c}$ where $\bar{c}$ is the mean electron speed.

Also $\frac{1}{2} m^* (\bar{c})^2 = \frac{3}{2} kT$

$$\therefore \qquad \tau = \lambda \left(\frac{m^*}{3kT}\right)^{\frac{1}{2}}$$

$$= 1.27 \times 10^{-6} \left\{\frac{1.57 \times 9.107 \times 10^{-31}}{3 \times 1.38 \times 10^{-23} \times 300}\right\}$$

$$= \underline{1.36 \times 10^{-11} \text{ s}}$$

Mobility $$\mu = \frac{e\tau}{m^*} = \frac{1.602 \times 10^{-19} \times 1.36 \times 10^{-11}}{1.57 \times 9.107 \times 10^{-31}}$$

$$= \underline{1.52 \text{ m}^2 \text{ V}^{-1} \text{ s}^{-1}}$$

104. The conductivity $\sigma = e(n\mu_e + p\mu_h)$

For intrinsic material $n = p = n_i$

$$\therefore \qquad \sigma_i = n_i e(\mu_e + \mu_h)$$

or $$n_i = \frac{\sigma_i}{e(\mu_e + \mu_h)}$$

At 310 K:

$$n_i = \frac{3.56}{1.602 \times 10^{-19} (0.36 + 0.17)} = 42 \times 10^{18} \text{ m}^{-3}$$

At 273 K:

$$n_i = \frac{0.42}{1.602 \times 10^{-19} (0.36 + 0.17)} = 4.7 \times 10^{18} \text{ m}^{-3}$$

In doped material $(n + p)p = n_i^2$ where n is the ionized donor density = 10^{21} m^{-3}

$$\therefore \qquad n \gg n_i \gg p$$

$$\therefore \qquad n_p \simeq n_i^2$$

At 310 K:

$$p = \frac{n_i^2}{n} = \frac{(42 \times 10^{18})^2}{10^{21}} = 176 \times 10^{16}\ \text{m}^{-3}$$

$$\therefore \quad \sigma = 1.602 \times 10^{-19}(10^{21} \times 0.36 + 176 \times 10^{16} \times 0.17)$$
$$= \underline{57.6\ \Omega^{-1}\ \text{m}^{-1}}$$

At 273 K:

$$p = \frac{n_i^2}{n} = \frac{(4.7 \times 10^{18})^2}{10^{21}} = 2.2 \times 10^{16}\ \text{m}^{-3}$$

$$\therefore \quad \sigma = 1.602 \times 10^{-19}(10^{21} \times 0.36 + 2.2 \times 10^{16} \times 0.17)$$
$$= \underline{57.6\ \Omega^{-1}\ \text{m}^{-1}}$$

105. The conductivity σ of an intrinsic material is given by

$$= n_i e(\mu_e + \mu_n)$$

where n_i is the intrinsic density and μ the mobility. If the mobilities remain constant, n_i is the only term which varies with temperature, T, as follows.

$$n_i = Ne^{-E_g/2kT}$$

where N is some constant.

Hence the resistivity and thus the resistance R varies as n_i^{-1} or

$$R = Ce^{-Eg/2kT}$$

where C is another constant.

At 290 K, $R = 500\ \Omega$ so

$$500 = Ce^{\frac{1.08 \times 1.06 \times 10^{-19}}{2 \times 1.38 \times 10^{-23} \times 290}} = Ce^{21.6}$$

Similarly at 325 K

$$R_2 = Ce^{19.3}$$

Dividing:
$$\frac{500}{R_2} = e^{(21.6-19.3)}$$

which gives
$$\underline{R_2 = 50\ \Omega}$$

106. The derivation of the formula can be found elsewhere.* The formula is:

* See, for example, W. Shockley, *Electrons and Holes in Semiconductors*, D. van Nostrand, 1956, p. 217.

Hall coefficient $\underline{R = (p\mu_p^2 - n\mu_n^2)/e(p\mu_p + n\mu_n)^2}$

(*a*) For intrinsic material, $p = n = n_i$

$$\therefore \quad R = \frac{n_i(\mu_p^2 - \mu_n^2)}{en_i^2(\mu_p + \mu_n)^2}$$

$$\text{i.e.} \quad \underline{R = (\mu_p - \mu_n)/en_i(\mu_p + \mu_n)}$$

(*b*) For the highly-droped *n*-type material, $n \gg p$

$$\therefore \quad R = \frac{1}{e}\left(\frac{-n\mu_n^2}{n^2\mu_n^2}\right) = \underline{-1/ne}$$

107. The conductivity of the semiconductor is

$$\sigma = \frac{l}{RA} = pe\mu_H$$

where l is its length, A its area of cross section, R is its resistance and p the hole concentration, assuming it to be p-type.

Also the Hall coefficient is given by

$$R_H = \frac{1}{pe} = \frac{V_H.d}{IB}$$

where V_H is the Hall voltage and d the sample thickness

$$\therefore \quad \frac{1}{p \times 1.6 \times 10^{-19}} = \frac{5 \times 10^{-3} \times 1 \times 10^{-3}}{10 \times 10^{-3} \times 0.5}$$

which gives $\underline{p = 6.25 \times 10^{21}}$.

Substituting this value in the first equation gives:

$$\mu_H = \frac{l}{RApe} = \frac{30 \times 10^{-3}}{500 \times 6 \times 10^{-6} \times 6.25 \times 10^{21} \times 1.6 \times 10^{-19}}$$

$$= \underline{10^{-2}\ \mathrm{m^2\ V^{-1}\ s^{-1}}}$$

Notice that for constant dimensions, field and current the Hall voltage is proportional to the reciprocal of the carrier density. Hence the Hall voltage with a copper sample, V_{Hc} is:

$$V_{Hc} = V_H \frac{\left(\frac{1}{n}\right)}{\left(\frac{1}{p}\right)} = 5 \times 10^{-3} \times \frac{6.25 \times 10^{21}}{8.5 \times 10^{28}}\ \mathrm{V} = \underline{0.37\ \mathrm{nV}}$$

108. In equilibrium, charge neutrality exists and

$$n + N_a = p + N_d$$

where N_a and N_d are the acceptor and donor concentrations and the impurities are all assumed to be ionized.

(*a*) The net impurity concentration $= N_a - N_d = p - n$

$$= 10^{20} - 2 \times 10^{19} = \underline{8 \times 10^{19}\ \text{m}^{-3}}$$

(*b*) $(N_a - N_d)$ is positive so acceptors are in a majority and the compensated material is *p*-type.

(*c*) The intrinsic density, n_i, is obtained from:

$$n_i^2 = n_p = 10^{20} \times 2 \times 10^{19}$$

or

$$n_i = \underline{4.5 \times 10^{19}\ \text{m}^{-3}}$$

109. The conductivity σ of the intrinsic material is

$$\sigma = \frac{1}{p} = en_i(\mu_h + \mu_e)$$

where the intrinsic density, n_i, varies with temperature as $\exp(-E_g/2kT)$. Hence

$$\frac{1}{p} \alpha \exp\left(-\frac{E_g}{2kT}\right) T^{-\frac{3}{2}}$$

or

$$p = Ce\frac{E_g}{2hT} T^{\frac{3}{2}} \quad \text{where } C \text{ is a constant}$$

or

$$\ln(pT^{-\frac{3}{2}}) = \ln C + \frac{E_g}{2kT}$$

Hence, if the assumptions are correct a graph of $\ln(pT^{-\frac{3}{2}})$ versus $1/T$ should yield a straight line of slope $E_g/2k$. The data for the graph is given in the question and when drawn the graph is a straight line of slope 4670.

The gap energy is then obtained from:

$$\frac{E_g}{2k} = 4670$$

or

$$E_g = 2 \times 4670 \times \frac{1.38 \times 10^{-23}}{1.6 \times 10^{-19}} = \underline{0.8\ \text{eV}}$$

110. The incremental junction capacitance of an abrupt junction, C_j, is given by*:

$$C_j = \left[\frac{\epsilon e N_a N_d}{2(N_a + N_d)}\right]^{\frac{1}{2}} V_j^{-\frac{1}{2}}\ \mathrm{Fm}^{-2}$$

where V_j is the junction voltage and N_a and N_d are the doping levels at either side of the junction. Hence for a particular diode,

$$C_j = \frac{k}{(V + V_0)^{\frac{1}{2}}}$$

where k is a constant, V is the reverse bias voltage and V_0 is the contact potential.

When $V = 2$ V, $C_j = 200\ \mu\mu$F, so

$$k = 200 \times 10^{-12} \times (2 + 0.85)^{\frac{1}{2}} = 3.38 \times 10^{-10}$$

Then, when $C_j = 100\ \mu\mu$F, the reverse bias voltage necessary is found from

$$100 \times 10^{-12} = \frac{3.38 \times 10^{-10}}{(V + 0.85)^{\frac{1}{2}}}$$

or

$$\underline{V = 10.6\ \mathrm{V}}$$

111. The conductivity, σ, of the channel region is given by

$$\sigma = \mu_e e N_d$$

where N_d is the doping concentration and μ_e is the electronic mobility.

Hence

$$N_d = \frac{\sigma}{\mu_e e} = \frac{20.9}{0.13 \times 1.6 \times 10^{-19}} = 10^{21}\ \mathrm{m}^{-3}$$

The pinch-off voltage, V_p, is given by†

$$V_p = \frac{e N_d a^2}{2\epsilon_r t_0}$$

where a is the half width of the channel when the gate voltage, V_g, is zero, so

$$V_p = \frac{1.6 \times 10^{-19} \times 10^{21} \times (2.5 \times 10^{-6})^2}{12 \times 8.85 \times 10^{-12}} = \underline{4.71\ \mathrm{V}}$$

The drain-source resistance, R, can be deduced from†

* See J. Allison, *Electronic Engineering Materials and Devices*, McGraw-Hill, 1971, p. 205.

† See J. Allison, *Electronic Engineering Materials and Devices*, McGraw-Hill, 1971, p. 269.

$$R = \frac{R_0}{1 - (V_g/V_p)^{\frac{1}{2}}}$$

where R_0 is the resistance when $V_g = 0$. When $R = 250\ \Omega$, V_g is given by:

$$250 = \frac{50}{1 - (V_g/4.71)^{\frac{1}{2}}}$$

which leads to $\underline{V_g = 3.01\ \text{V}}$ (negative with respect to the source).

112. The ratio of hole to electron current at a *p-n* junction is approximately equal to the ratio of the conductivities of the *p*- and *n*-type materials which constitute the junction for all bias conditions. Hence

$$\frac{J_h}{J_e} = \frac{\sigma_p}{\sigma_n} = \frac{e\mu_n N_a}{e\mu_e N_d}$$

where N_a is the acceptor concentration and N_d the donor concentration. So, in this case

$$\frac{J_n}{J_e} = \frac{10^{22} \times 0.2}{10^{24} \times 0.4} = \underline{1:200}$$

113. The rectifier equation which both diodes obey is

$$I = I_s\,[\exp\,(eV/kT) - 1]$$

where I_s is the saturation current. So for the germanium diode:

$$100 \times 10^{-3} = 10^{-6} \exp \left\{\frac{1.6 \times 10^{-19}\ V}{1.38 \times 10^{-23} \times 293}\right\}$$

or $$\underline{V = 288\ \text{mV}}$$

A similar calculation for the silicon diode using $I_s = 10^{-8}$ A gives $\underline{V = 407\ \text{mV}}$.

114. The diode current is given by the rectifier equation

$$I = I_0 \left\{\exp\left(\frac{eV}{kT}\right) - 1\right\}$$

where I_0 is the saturation current and V the bias voltage. Hence, since 0.1 V is dropped across the diode:

$$I = 3 \times 10^{-6} \left(\exp \left\{\frac{1.6 \times 10^{-19} \times 0.1}{1.38 \times 10^{-23} \times 293}\right. - 1\right) = 154\ \mu\text{A}$$

the series resistance, R, is then

$$R = \frac{V}{I} = \frac{0.1}{154 \times 10^{-6}} = \underline{650\ \Omega}$$

115. It can be shown* that the transconductance, g_m, can be estimated from:

$$g_m = \frac{\mu_e C_g}{l^2} V_d$$

where C_g is the gate capacitance, l its length, μ_e the electron mobility in the channel and V_d the drain-source voltage at saturation. Now

$$C_g = \frac{\epsilon A}{d} = \frac{3.7 \times 8.854 \times 10^{-12} (0.84 \times 10^{-3} \times 5 \times 10^{-6})}{150 \times 10^{-9}} = 0.917\ \mu\mu\text{F}$$

So $$g_m = \frac{0.02 \times 0.917 \times 10^{-12} \times 10}{(5 \times 10^{-6})^2} = \underline{7.34 \times 10^{-3}\ \text{S}}$$

116. The concentration of acceptors at a depth x and time t, $N(x,t)$ for this limited source diffusion is given by†

$$N(x,t) = \frac{Q}{\sqrt{(\pi D_B t)}} \exp\left\{\frac{-x^2}{4D_B t}\right\}$$

where Q is initial surface concentration of boron atoms.

At the junction ($x = 1\ \mu$m), $N(x,t)$ = background concentration $= 10^{22}$. Hence

$$10^{22} = \frac{Q}{\sqrt{(\pi\ 10^{-16}\ 3600)}} \exp\left\{-\frac{10^{-12}}{4 \times 10^{-16} \times 3600}\right\}$$

which gives $Q = \underline{2.1 \times 10^{16}\ \text{m}^{-2}}$.

144. Let the voltage across the diode be V and the current through the diode I mA,

$$\therefore \qquad V = 200 - 20\left(\frac{V}{60} + I\right), \text{ i.e. } V = 150 - 15I$$

which is the equation of the load line.

* See J. Allison, *Electronic Engineering Materials and Devices*, McGraw-Hill, 1971, p. 278.

† J. Allison, *Electronic Integrated Circuits, their Technology and Design*, McGraw-Hill, 1975, p. 44.

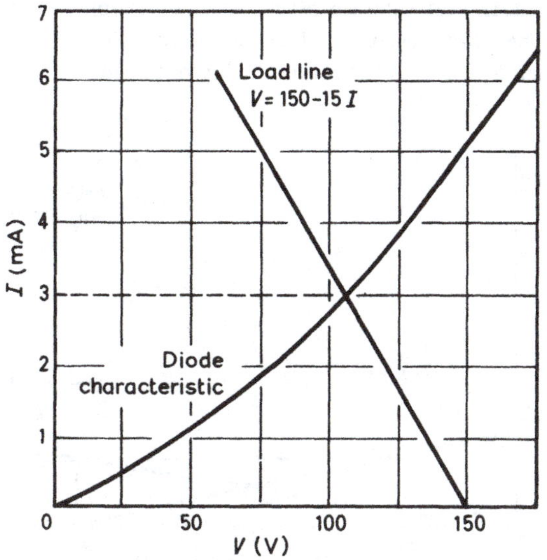

At the point of intersection of the I/V curve and the load line $\underline{I = 3 \text{ mA}}$.

145. The static characteristic has been plotted from the given figures.

$$V_i = V_a + R_l I_a \quad . \quad . \quad . \quad . \quad (1)$$

where $R_l = 2500\ \Omega$.

If (1) is plotted on the same sheet as the static curve a straight line (the load line) results.

A typical load line (for $V_i = 40$ V) is shown. The point of intersection of the load line with the static curve, P, indicates the current flowing. Thus the dynamic curve can be plotted because the current is that corresponding to P when the input voltage is 40 V and so the first point on the dynamic curve is P'.

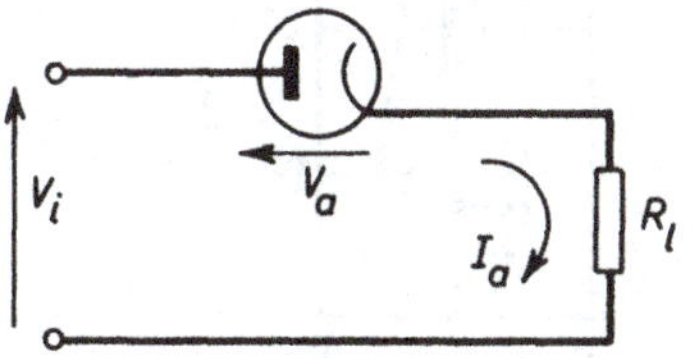

Hence, when the supply voltage is 50 V the load current is $\underline{14.5 \text{ mA}}$. The voltage across the load $= 2500 \times (14.5 \times 10^{-3}) = \underline{36.25 \text{ V}}$.

From the static curve and the 50-V load line the voltage across the diode is 13.75 V. The voltage across the load is therefore (50 − 13.75) V = 36.25 V which agrees with the result already obtained.

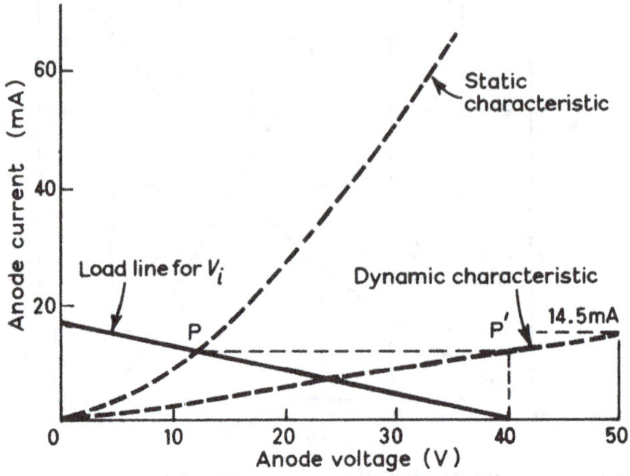

146. The control characteristics are as shown. From these, when V_a = 400 V, the change in critical grid voltage required is seen to be about 2.8 V.

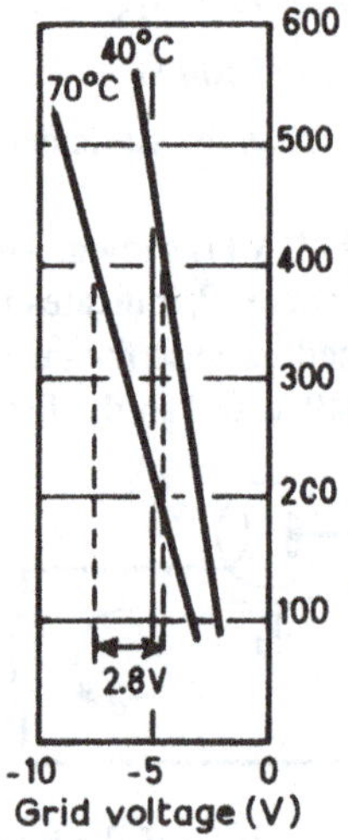

When the temperature is 40°C and $V_g = -4$ V, $V_a = 320$ V. But $V_a = 350 \sin\theta$, therefore $\theta = \sin^{-1}(320/350) = 66° \, 5'$.

When the temperature is 70°C and $V_g = -4$ V, $V_a = 150$ V and

$$\theta = \sin^{-1}(150/350) = \underline{25° 22'}.$$

147. The effective mutual conductance is the sum of the individual mutual conductances since the anode currents add directly, i.e. (2 + 5 + 3) mS = 10 mS.

The equivalent anode resistance is obtained by adding the individual anode resistances as one adds resistances in parallel, i.e.

$$1/(1/5000 + 1/4000 + 1/10\,000)\ \Omega = \underline{1818\ \Omega}.$$

The equivalent amplification factor

$$= 1818 \times 10 \times 10^{-3} = \underline{18.18}.$$

148. Thermionic emission of electrons is in accordance with the expression:

$$I = AT^2 e^{-b/T}\ \text{Am}^{-2},$$

where T is the absolute temperature.

For the thoriated-tungsten filament:

$$85 \times 10^{-3} = 3 \times 10^4 \times (1900)^2\, e^{-30\,500/1900} \times \text{area} \quad . \qquad (1)$$

For the pure-tungsten filament:

$$i \times 10^{-3} = 602 \times 10^3 \times (2500)^2\, e^{-52\,400/2500} \times \text{area} \quad . \qquad (2)$$

Dividing (2) by (1):

$$\frac{i}{85} = \frac{60.2 \times (2500)^2\, e^{-52\,400/2500}}{3 \times (1900)^2\, e^{-30\,500/1900}} \text{ and } \underline{i = 21.8 \text{ mA}}.$$

149. The Child-Langmuir equation for plane-parallel electrodes gives* $J = 2.34 \times 10^{-6}\, V_a^{3/2}/d^2$, where J is the current density (Am^{-2}), V_a is the anode voltage in volts and d is the anode-cathode distance.

Here $V_a = 200$ V, $d = 2 \times 10^{-3}$ m so $\underline{J = 1.65 \times 10^3\ \text{Am}^{-2}}$.

* This equation is proved in many textbooks. For example, see S. Seely, *Electron-tube Circuits*, McGraw-Hill, 2nd Edition, 1958, p. 12, or P. Parker, *Electronics*, Arnold, 1950, pp. 93–6; or K. R. Spangenberg, *Vacuum Tubes*, McGraw-Hill, 1948, pp. 170–1.

150. The current is given by the following expression:*

$$I = 1.47 \times 10^{-5} V_a^{3/2} l/r_a\beta^2 \text{ amperes}$$

where V_a is the anode voltage, l is the active length of the valve, r_a is the anode radius and β^2 is a quantity that is determined from the ratio of anode radius to cathode radius (r_f).†

For the first valve $r_a = 2$ mm, $l = 20$ mm, $r_f = 0.05$ mm and $V_a = 25$ V. Thus $r_a/r_f = 40$ and $\beta^2 = 1.0946$,

$$\therefore \qquad \underline{I = 17 \text{ mA.}}$$

For the second valve $r_f = 0.75$ mm, $r_a/r_f = 2.67$ and $\beta^2 \simeq 0.45$,

$$\therefore \qquad \underline{I = 41 \text{ mA.}}$$

151. The solution to this problem can be found in many textbooks.‡

152. The current I under the condition of an accelerating field of E (Vm^{-1}) at the cathode surface is§ $I_1\, e^{+0.44E^{1/2}/T}$, where I_1 is the zero-field thermionic current and T is the absolute temperature of the cathode.

$$\therefore \qquad \log_{10}(I/I_1) = 0.4343 \times 0.44 \times (10^6)^{1/2}/2600 = 0.07345.$$

thus $I/I_1 = 1.184$, which shows that the Schottky theory predicts an increase of <u>18.4 per cent</u> over the zero-field emission current.

153. (*a*) The amplification factor $\mu = -2\pi a_2/a_g \ln(2 \sin \pi r_w/a_g)$ where a_2 is the grid-anode spacing, a_g is the grid-wire spacing and r_w is the grid-wire radius.||

* For example, see S. Seely, *Electron-tube Circuits*, McGraw-Hill, 2nd Edition, 1958, p. 12, or P. Parker, *Electronics*, Arnold, 1950, pp. 98–9, or K. R. Spangenberg, *Vacuum Tubes*, McGraw-Hill, 1948, p. 176.

† $$\beta = \alpha - \frac{2}{5}\alpha^2 + \frac{11}{120}\alpha^3 - \frac{47}{3300}\alpha^4 + \ldots$$

where $\alpha = \log_e(r_a/r_f)$.

Values of β^2 corresponding to various values of the ratio (r_a/r_f) have been plotted in Parker's book, Fig. 82, and tabulated in Appendix II of that book.

‡ E.g. see K. R. Spangenberg, *Vacuum Tubes*, McGraw-Hill, 1948, pp. 181–2; or P. Parker, *Electronics*, Arnold, 1950, pp. 99–100.

§ For the proof of this expression see J. Millman and S. Seely, *Electronics*, McGraw-Hill, 1951, Section 5–19, pp. 151–6.

|| For the proof of this see, for example, K. R. Spangenberg, *Vacuum Tubes*, McGraw-Hill, 1948, pp. 125–8.

Since a_g is large compared with r_w, $\mu \simeq 2\pi a_2/a_g \ln(a_g/2\pi r_w)$.
Now $a_2 = 1.9 \times 10^{-3}$ m, $a_g = 1.27 \times 10^{-3}$ m and $r_w = 6.4 \times 10^{-5}$ m.

$\therefore$

$$\underline{\mu \simeq 8.}$$

(*b*) The amplification factor $\mu \simeq 2\pi r_g \ln(r_a/r_g)/a_g \ln(a_g/2\pi r_w)$ where r_a is the anode radius, r_g is the radius of the grid-wire circle, r_w is the radius of the grid wire and a_g is the linear distance between the grid-wire centres at radius r_g.*

If $N = 1/a_g$, $\mu \simeq 2\pi N r_g \ln(r_a/r_g)/\ln(1/2\pi N r_w)$.

Here, $\mu = 20$, $r_a = 1.05 \times 10^{-2}$ m, $r_g = 5 \times 10^{-3}$ m and $r_w = 4 \times 10^{-4}$ m, so $N \simeq 3$.

$\underline{\text{Total number of grid wires} = 2\pi N r_g \simeq 10.}$

(*c*) The expressions are:

(*i*) *For plane-electrode triode,*

$$\mu = \{2\pi a_2/a_g - \ln\cosh(2\pi r_w/a_g)\}/\{\ln(\coth 2\pi r_w/a_g)\}$$

where a_2 is the grid-anode distance, a_g is the grid-wire spacing and r_w is the grid-wire radius.

(*ii*) *For cylindrical triode,*

$$\mu = \{2\pi N r_g \ln(r_a/r_g) - \ln(\cosh 2\pi N r_w)\}/\{\ln\coth(2\pi N r_w)\}$$

where the symbols having the same meaning as in the solution to the previous problem.

The derivations of the expressions can be found elsewhere.†

154. The load line passes through the points A (0, 4 mA) and B (6 V, 0). The quiescent working point is at Q. When an input signal fo 40 μA peak current is applied, the peak-to-peak input signal will be 80 μA; the base current will vary between 0 and 80 μA. The extremes of the working range are given by points X and Y.

Peak-to-peak collector-emitter voltage excursion is $X'\,Y' \simeq \underline{4.7\text{ V.}}$

At Q, collector current $\simeq$ 2 mA.

Power supplied by battery = (2 × 6) mW = 12 mW.

* See, for example, K. R. Spangenberg, *Vacuum Tubes*, McGraw-Hill, 1948, pp. 135–7.

† See F. B. Vodges and F. R. Elder, 'Formulas for the Amplification Constant for Three-element Tubes,' *Phys. Rev.*, **24**, pp. 683–9, 1924. W. G. Dow, *Fundamentals of Engineering Electronics*, Wiley, 2nd Edition, 1952, Chapter 4. K. R. Spangenberg, *Vacuum Tubes*, McGraw-Hill, 1948, pp. 142–52.

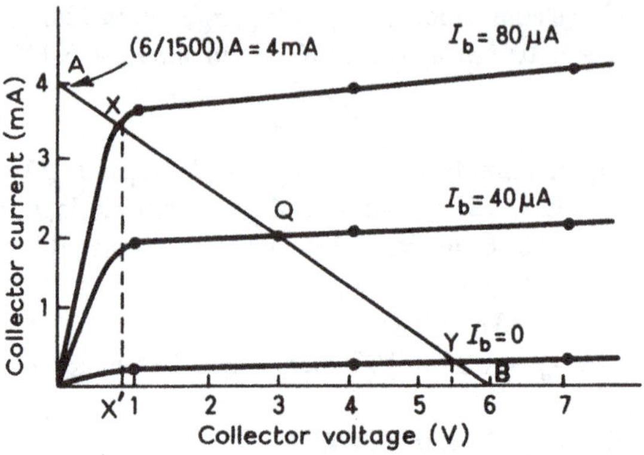

Power dissipated as heat in 1500-Ω load = $(2^2 \times 10^{-6} \times 1500)$ W = 6 mW.

∴ power dissipated in the transistor itself = (12 − 6) mW = 6 mW.

155. Consider first the I_c/V_{cb} characteristics.

With the collector-base voltage constant at − 4 V a change in I_e from 1 mA to 5 mA gives a change in collector current from − 1.03 mA to − 4.95 mA.

Thus,
$$\alpha = -\left\{-\frac{(4.95 - 1.03)}{(5 - 1)}\right\} = \underline{0.98}$$

Consider now the I_c/V_{ce} curves and a constant value of collector-emitter voltage of − 4 V. A change of I_b from − 20 μA to − 80 μA gives a change of collector current from − 1.1 mA to − 4.5 mA.

Thus,
$$\beta = \frac{-(4.5 - 1.1) \,.\, 10^{-3}}{-(80 - 20) \,.\, 10^{-6}} \simeq \underline{57}$$

$$\beta = (\delta i_c/\delta i_b)$$

But
$$\delta i_b = -(\delta i_e + \delta i_c)$$

so
$$\beta = -\delta i_c/(\delta i_e + \delta i_c)$$
$$= -(\delta i_c/\delta i_e)/(\delta i_e/\delta i_e + \delta i_c/\delta i_e)$$

i.e.
$$\underline{\beta = \alpha/(1 - \alpha)}$$

From this expression for β it is seen that:

$$\underline{\alpha = \beta/(1 + \alpha)}$$

This equation can also be obtained directly from the definition of α, substituting $-(\delta i_b + \delta i_c)$ for δi_e and dividing each term in the numerator and denominator by δi_b.

156. Current gain $\beta = \delta I_c/\delta I_b$

When $V_c = -5$ V and $I_b = -70$ μA, $I_c = 2.46$ mA

When $V_c = -5$ V and $I_b = -50$ μA, $I_c = 1.72$ mA

$$\therefore \quad \text{gain} = \frac{(2.46 - 1.72)\,10^{-3}}{(70 - 50)\,10^{-6}} = \underline{37}$$

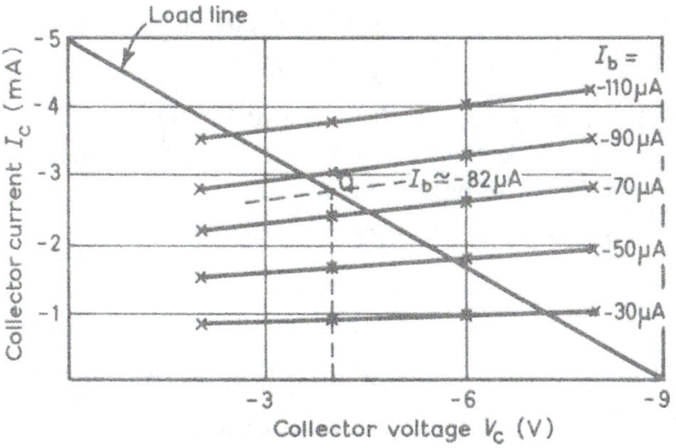

The load line is as shown. It passes through the points $V_c = -9, I_c = 0$ and $V_c = 0, I_c = \dfrac{9 \times 10^3}{1800}$ mA (i.e. $I_c = 5$ mA)

For $V_c = -4$ V, operating point is Q where $I_b \simeq \underline{-82\ \mu\text{A}}.$

157. The equivalent circuit is as shown.

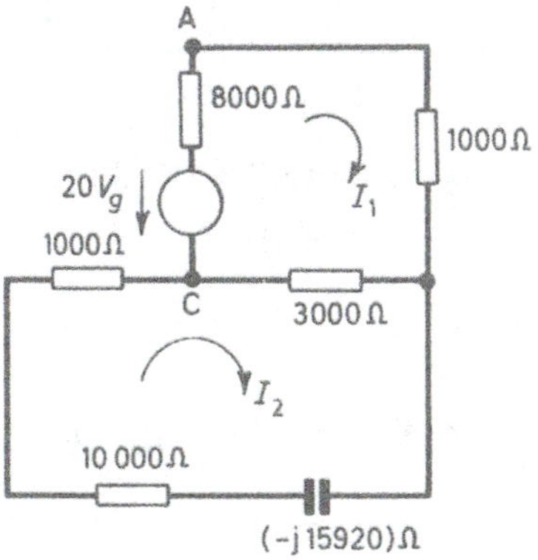

Reactance of capacitance

$$= \frac{1}{2\pi fC} = \frac{10^6}{2\pi \times 2000 \times 0.005} = 15\,920\ \Omega.$$

Let currents I_1 and I_2 in milliamps circulate as shown.

For the I_2 mesh:

$$(10 + 1 + 3 - j15.92)I_2 - 3I_1 = 0 \quad . \quad . \quad (1)$$

For the I_1 mesh:

$$(8 + 1 + 3)I_1 - 3I_2 + 20V_g = 0 \quad . \quad . \quad . \quad (2)$$

Also, $$V_g = 1 + I_2 \quad . \quad . \quad . \quad . \quad (3)$$

From (1), (2) and (3) $I_2 = (-0.1556 - j0.1357)$ mA.

The capacitor blocks the d.c. and the meter reads the product of its resistance and the a.c. through it, i.e. I_2.

$\therefore$ meter reads $10[0.1556^2 + 0.1357^2]^{1/2} = \underline{2.06\ \text{V}}.$

158. The equivalent circuit is as shown. Let the currents I_1, I_2 and I_3 circulate as shown.

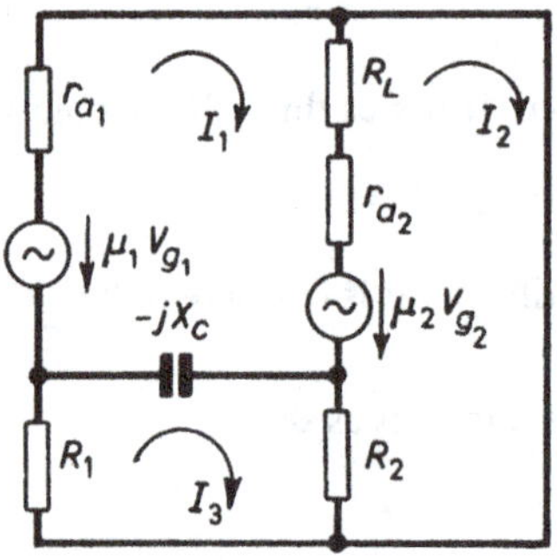

If $$e_1 = 1 + j0$$
$$e_2 = 2\,(\cos 30^\circ + j \sin 30^\circ)$$
$$= 1.73 + j1.$$

For the I_1 mesh:

$$(r_{a_1} + R_L + r_{a_2} - jX_c)I_1$$
$$-(R_L + r_{a_1})I_2 - (-jX_c)I_3 + \mu_1 V_{g_1} - \mu_2 V_{g_2} = 0 \qquad (1)$$

For the I_2 mesh:

$$(R_L + r_{a_2} + R_2)I_2 - (R_L + r_{a_2})I_1 - R_2 I_3 + \mu_2 V_{g_2} = 0 \quad . \qquad (2)$$

For the I_3 mesh:

$$(R_1 - jX_c + R_2)I_3 - (-jX_c)I_1 - R_2 I_2 = 0 \quad . \quad . \qquad (3)$$

Also, $$V_{g_1} = e_1 + R_1 I_3 = 1 + R_1 I_3 \quad . \quad . \quad . \qquad (4)$$

and $$V_{g_2} = e_2 + R_2(I_2 - I_3) = 1.73 + j1 + R_2(I_2 - I_3) \quad . \qquad (5)$$

$\therefore$ I_1, I_2 and I_3 can be found.

159. For a triode, a change δI_a in the anode current I_a can be written

$$\left(\frac{\delta I_a}{\delta V_a}\right)_{V_g \text{ const.}} \delta V_a + \left(\frac{\delta I_a}{\delta V_g}\right)_{V_a \text{ const.}} \delta V_g = \frac{1}{r_a}\delta V_a + g_m \delta V_g.$$

$\therefore$ $$g_m \delta V_g = \delta I_a - \delta V_a / r_a.$$

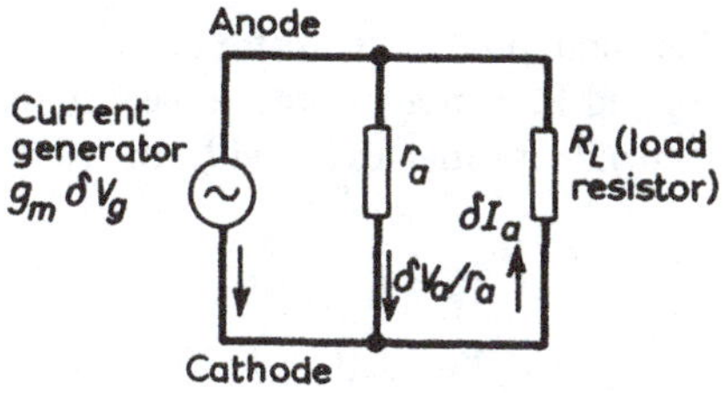

The current-source equivalent circuit shown follows from this expression.

160. The equivalent circuit of the arrangement is as shown.

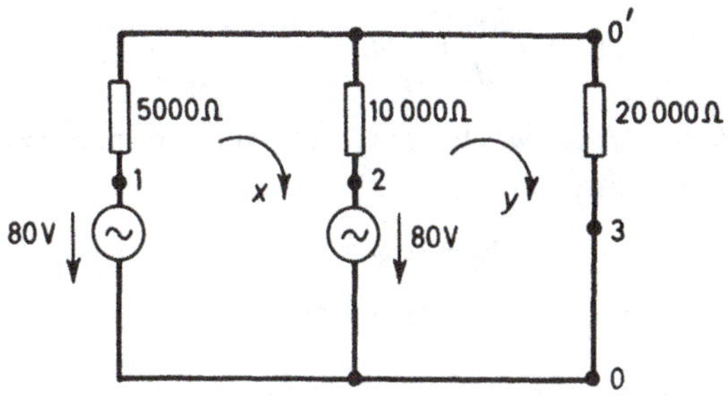

Millman's Theorem* states that

$$V_{00}' = \frac{V_{01}Y_1 + V_{02}Y_2 + V_{03}Y_3}{Y_1 + Y_2 + Y_3}$$

where V_{00}' is the voltage drop from 0 to 0′

V_{01} „ „ „ „ 0 to 1, etc.

In this case $V_{01} = 80$, $V_{02} = 80$, $V_{03} = 0$, $Y_1 = 1/5000$, $Y_2 = 1/10\,000$, $Y_3 = 1/20\,000$.

$\therefore$ $\underline{V_{00}' = 68.6 \text{ V.}}$

Let the currents in the two meshes be x and y mA.

For the x mesh: $5x + 10(x-y) - 80 + 80 = 0$.

„ „ y „ $10(y-x) + 20y + 80 = 0$.

From these equations $x = -2.3$ mA, $y = -3.4$ mA.

The valve currents are $-x = 2.3$ mA and $x - y = 1.1$ mA.

161. Consider the common-base transistor connection. The emitter and collector voltages, V_e and V_c, measured with respect to the base, are functions of the independent variables I_e and I_c, the emitter and collector currents.

i.e. $$V_e = f_1(I_e, I_c) \quad . \quad . \quad . \quad . \quad (1)$$

and $$V_c = f_2(I_e, I_c) \quad . \quad . \quad . \quad . \quad (2)$$

For small-signal variations the voltage variations are given by:

$$\delta V_e = \left(\frac{\delta V_e}{\delta I_e}\right)_{I_c} \delta I_e + \left(\frac{\delta V_e}{\delta I_c}\right)_{I_e} \delta I_c \quad . \quad . \quad (3)$$

and $$\delta V_c = \left(\frac{\delta V_c}{\delta I_e}\right)_{I_c} \delta I_e + \left(\frac{\delta V_c}{\delta I_c}\right)_{I_e} \delta I_c \quad . \quad . \quad (4)$$

If δV_e, δV_c, δI_e and δI_c are written as v_e, v_c, i_e and i_c respectively, these equations may be written as:

$$v_e = r_{11}i_e + r_{12}i_c \quad . \quad . \quad . \quad . \quad (5)$$

$$v_c = r_{21}i_e + r_{22}i_c \quad . \quad . \quad . \quad . \quad (6)$$

* See J. Millman, 'A Useful Network Theorem,' *Proc. I.R.E.*, 28, pp. 413–17, 1940, and F. A. Benson, *Electric Circuit Problems with Solutions*, Chapman and Hall, 2nd Edition, 1975, pp. 183–4.

where the coefficients r_{11}, r_{12}, r_{21} and r_{22} are defined as:

$$r_{11} = \left(\frac{\delta V_e}{\delta I_e}\right)_{I_c} \quad . \quad . \quad . \quad . \quad . \quad (7)$$

$$r_{12} = \left(\frac{\delta V_e}{\delta I_c}\right)_{I_e} \quad . \quad . \quad . \quad . \quad . \quad (8)$$

$$r_{21} = \left(\frac{\delta V_c}{\delta I_e}\right)_{I_c} \quad . \quad . \quad . \quad . \quad . \quad (9)$$

and

$$r_{22} = \left(\frac{\delta V_c}{\delta I_c}\right)_{I_e} \quad . \quad . \quad . \quad . \quad . \quad (10)$$

It is possible to draw several equivalent circuits which satisfy equations (5) and (6). These four-terminal networks are active, not passive, so four independent parameters are needed to specify their performances. In some equivalent circuits the four parameters used are r_e, r_b, r_c and r_m (or α). By comparing the mesh equations for the various networks it is easily shown that*:

$$r_{11} = r_e + r_b \quad . \quad . \quad . \quad . \quad . \quad (11)$$

$$r_{12} = r_b \quad . \quad . \quad . \quad . \quad . \quad . \quad (12)$$

$$r_{21} = r_b + r_m \quad . \quad . \quad . \quad . \quad . \quad (13)$$

$$r_{22} = r_b + r_c \quad . \quad . \quad . \quad . \quad . \quad (14)$$

and

$$\alpha = r_{21}/r_{22} \quad . \quad . \quad . \quad . \quad . \quad (15)$$

Equations (5) and (6) can be re-arranged to give the voltage v_e and current i_c in terms of i_e and v_c. The h parameters (or hybrid parameters) are then defined by these equations as follows:

$$v_e = h_{ib}i_e + h_{rb}v_c \quad . \quad . \quad . \quad . \quad . \quad (16)$$

$$i_c = h_{fb}i_e + h_{ob}v_c \quad . \quad . \quad . \quad . \quad . \quad (17)$$

Similar parameters may be defined for common-emitter and common-collector arrangements. The relationships between the h and r parameters can easily be determined as follows:

From equation (5), $r_{11} = v_e/i_e$ with $i_c = 0$. Under this condition:

$$v_e = h_{ib}i_e + h_{rb}v_c$$

* See, for example, S. Seely, *Electronic Engineering*, McGraw-Hill, 1956, Chapter 16 or L. M. Krugman, *Fundamentals of Transistors*, Rider and Chapman and Hall, 2nd Edition, 1959, or F. A. Benson and D. Harrison, *Electric-Circuit Theory*, Edward Arnold, 3rd Edition, 1975, pp. 342–3.

and $$0 = h_{fb}i_e + h_{ob}v_c$$

Thus, $$r_{11} = v_e/i_e = (h_{ib}h_{ob} - h_{rb}h_{fb})/h_{ob} \quad . \quad . \quad . \quad (18)$$

Similarly, $$r_{21} = v_c/i_e \text{ when } i_c = 0$$

Then, $$0 = h_{fb}i_e + h_{ob}v_c$$

$\therefore$ $$r_{21} = -h_{fb}/h_{ob} \quad . \quad . \quad . \quad . \quad . \quad (19)$$

Also, $$r_{12} = v_e/i_c \text{ with } i_e = 0$$

Then, $$v_e = h_{rb}$$

and $$i_c = h_{ob}v_c$$

so $$r_{12} = h_{rb}/h_{ob} \quad . \quad . \quad . \quad . \quad . \quad (20)$$

Finally, $$r_{22} = v_c/i_c \text{ with } i_e = 0.$$

Then, $$i_c = h_{ob}v_c$$

i.e. $$r_{22} = 1/h_{ob} \quad . \quad . \quad . \quad . \quad . \quad (21)$$

Also, $$\alpha = r_{21}/r_{22} = -h_{fb} \quad . \quad . \quad . \quad . \quad . \quad (22)$$

It follows that:

$$r_e = r_{11} - r_{12} = h_{ib} - h_{rb}(1 + h_{fb})/h_{ob} \quad . \quad . \quad . \quad (23)$$

$$r_b = r_{12} = h_{rb}/h_{ob} \quad . \quad . \quad . \quad . \quad . \quad . \quad (24)$$

$$r_c = r_{22} - r_{12} = (1 - h_{rb})/h_{ob} \simeq 1/h_{ob} \quad . \quad . \quad . \quad (25)$$

and $$r_m = r_{21} - r_{12} = -(h_{fb} + h_{rb})/h_{ob} \quad . \quad . \quad . \quad . \quad (26)$$

In the example given:

$$r_{11} = (35 \times 1 \times 10^{-6} + 7 \times 10^{-4} \times 0.976)/(1 \times 10^{-6}) = \underline{718.2\ \Omega}$$

$$r_{12} = (7 \times 10^{-4})/(1 \times 10^{-6}) = \underline{700\ \Omega}$$

$$r_{21} = \{0.976/(1 \times 10^{-6})\}\Omega = \underline{976\ \text{k}\Omega}$$

$$r_{22} = 1/(1 \times 10^{-6})\Omega = \underline{1\ \text{M}\Omega}$$

$$\alpha = \underline{-0.976}$$

$$r_e = (718.2 - 700) = \underline{18.2\ \Omega}$$

$$r_b = \underline{700\ \Omega}$$

$$r_c = r_{22} \simeq \underline{1\ \text{M}\Omega}$$

$$r_m = (976\,000 - 700)\Omega = \underline{975.3\ \text{k}\Omega}$$

162. The solution to this problem can be found elsewhere.*

163. Consider the two arrangements shown at (*a*) and (*b*).

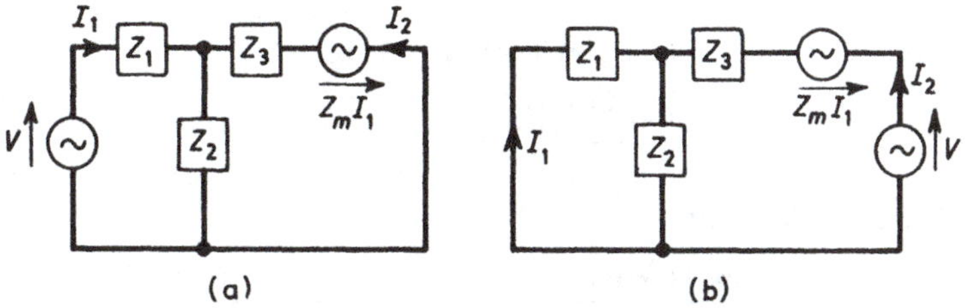

For circuit (*a*)

$$(Z_1 + Z_2)I_1 + Z_2I_2 = V$$
$$(Z_2 + Z_m)I_1 + (Z_2 + Z_3)I_2 = 0$$

$$\therefore I_2 = \frac{\begin{vmatrix} (Z_1 + Z_2) & V \\ (Z_2 + Z_m) & 0 \end{vmatrix}}{\begin{vmatrix} (Z_1 + Z_2) & Z_2 \\ (Z_2 + Z_m) & (Z_2 + Z_3) \end{vmatrix}}.$$

For circuit (*b*)

$$(Z_1 + Z_2)I_1 + Z_2I_2 = 0,$$
$$(Z_2 + Z_m)I_1 + (Z_2 + Z_3)I_2 = V$$

$$\therefore I_1 = \frac{\begin{vmatrix} 0 & Z_2 \\ V & (Z_2 + Z_3) \end{vmatrix}}{\begin{vmatrix} (Z_1 + Z_2) & Z_2 \\ (Z_2 + Z_m) & (Z_2 + Z_3) \end{vmatrix}}.$$

In general, $I_1 \neq I_2$, so the original circuit does not satisfy the reciprocity condition. For the reciprocity condition to be satisfied Z_m must be zero.

164. It is found† that α varies with frequency according to the following expressions:

$$\alpha = \alpha_0 \left\{ \frac{1}{1 + j(f/f_\alpha)} \right\}$$

where α_0 is the low-frequency value of α and f_α, called the alpha cut-off frequency, is that frequency where $\alpha = \alpha_0/\surd(2)$.

Thus, if $\alpha_0 = 0.96$, $f_\alpha = 5$ MHz and $f = 10$ MHz,

$$\alpha = 0.96/\surd(1 + (10/5)^2)$$

* See, for example, S. Seely, *Electronic Engineering*, McGraw-Hill, 1956, Chapter 16. See also, L. M. Krugman, *Fundamentals of Transistors*, Rider and Chapman & Hall, 2nd Edition, 1959, and F. A. Benson and D. Harrison, *Electric-Circuit Theory*, Edward Arnold, 3rd Edition, 1975, Chapter 15.

† R. L. Pritchard, *Frequency Variations of Current-Amplification Factor for Junction Transistors*, Proc. I.R.E., **40**, p. 1476, 1952, and D. E. Thomas, *Transistor Amplifier Cut-off Frequency*, ibid., **40**, p. 1481, 1952.

$$= \underline{0.43}$$

If $\alpha_0 = 0.96$, $\alpha = 0.6$ and $f = 5$ MHz,

$$f = f\sqrt{[(\alpha_0/\alpha)^2 - 1]}$$
$$= (5\sqrt{(0.96/0.6)^2 - 1})\ \text{MHz}$$
$$= \underline{6.25}\ \text{MHz.}$$

165. $\alpha' = \alpha/(1-\alpha)$

$$= \frac{\alpha_0/\{1 + j(f/f_\alpha)\}}{1 - \alpha_0/\{1 + j(f/f_\alpha)\}} = \frac{\alpha_0}{(1-\alpha_0) + j(f/f_\alpha)}$$

The cut-off frequency is defined as that for which the gain falls to $1/\sqrt{2}$ of its original value. This occurs for the common-emitter circuit when the frequency is f_α' such that $f_\alpha'/f_\alpha = 1 - \alpha_0$

i.e. $\underline{f_\alpha' = f_\alpha(1 - \alpha_0)}$

166. The drain current I_D is a function of the gate voltage V_{GS} and drain voltage V_{DS}, i.e.

$$I_D = f(V_{GS}, V_{DS})$$

$\therefore$ $$\delta I_D = (\partial I_D/\partial V_{GS})_{v_{DS}}\,\delta V_{GS} + (\partial I_D/\partial V_{DS})_{v_{GS}}\,\delta V_{DS}$$

or $$i_d = g_m v_{gs} + (1/r_d)\,v_{ds}$$

where δI_D, δV_{GS} and δV_{DS} are written as i_d, v_{gs} and v_{ds} respectively.

$g_m = (\partial I_D/\partial V_{GS})_{v_{DS}}$ is the mutual conductance or transconductance and $1/r_d = (\partial I_D/\partial V_{DS})_{v_{GS}}$ and r_d is the drain resistance.

An equivalent circuit which satisfies the above expression for i_d is shown below.

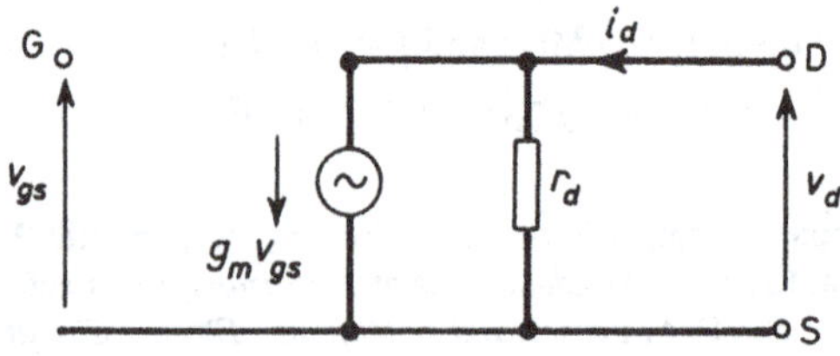

177. (*a*) Mean load current

$$(I_{\text{d.c.}}) = \frac{1}{2\pi}\int_0^\pi \frac{300\sqrt{2}\sin\theta}{(150 + 1000)}\,d\theta = \underline{117\ \text{mA.}}$$

(*b*) Alternating load current

$$(I_{\text{r.m.s.}}) = \left[\frac{1}{2\pi}\int_0^{\pi}\left(\frac{300\sqrt{2}\sin\theta}{1150}\right)^2 d\theta\right]^{1/2} = \underline{184 \text{ mA.}}$$

(*c*) D. C. power supplied to the load $= (I_{\text{d.c.}})^2 \times 1000 = \underline{13.8 \text{ W.}}$

(*d*) Power supplied to the circuit $= (I_{\text{r.m.s.}})^2 \times 1150 = \underline{39.1 \text{ W.}}$

(*e*) Rectification efficiency

$$= \frac{\text{d.c. output power}}{\text{power supplied to the circuit}} \times 100\% = \underline{35.3\%}$$

(*f*) Ripple factor $= [(I_{\text{r.m.s.}}/I_{\text{d.c.}})^2 - 1]^{1/2} = \underline{1.21.}$

178. (*a*) The d.c. load voltage

$$(E_{\text{d.c.}}) = \frac{1}{2\pi}\int_{\theta_1}^{\theta_2}(300\sqrt{2}\sin\theta - 10)\,d\theta$$

where θ_1 and θ_2 are the angles at the striking and extinction points.

Since $300\sqrt{2} \gg 10$, θ_1 may be taken as zero and θ_2 as π.

$$\therefore \qquad E_{\text{d.c.}} = \underline{130 \text{ V.}}$$

(*b*) D.C. power supplied to load $= (E_{\text{d.c.}})^2/1000 = \underline{16.9 \text{ W.}}$

(*c*) Input power to circuit

$$= \frac{1}{2\pi}\int_0^{\pi} 300\sqrt{2}\sin\theta\left(\frac{300\sqrt{2}\sin\theta - 10}{1000}\right) d\theta = \underline{43.7 \text{ W.}}$$

(*d*) Rectification efficiency $= \dfrac{16.9}{43.7} \times 100$ per cent $=$ <u>38.7 per cent.</u>

(*e*) It can be shown* that the ripple factor is

$$\text{approximately } 1.21\left[1 + 0.5 \times \frac{10}{300\sqrt{2}}\right] = \underline{1.225.}$$

179. Mean load voltage $E_{\text{d.c.}} =$ Mean load current $I_{\text{d.c.}} \times R_l$, where R_l is the resistance of the load and $I_{\text{d.c.}} = \dfrac{230\sqrt{2}}{\pi(500 + R_l)}$.

* J. Millman and S. Seely, *Electronics*, McGraw-Hill, 2nd Edition, 1951, p. 350.

$\therefore \qquad E_{d.c.} = 230\sqrt{2}/\pi - 500 I_{d.c.}$

$E_{d.c.}$ changes from 103.5 V when $I_{d.c.} = 0$ to 63.5 V when $I_{d.c.} = 80$ mA, i.e. regulation is (103.5 − 63.5) V = 40 V.

$$\text{Efficiency} = \frac{(I_{d.c.})^2 R_l}{(I_{r.m.s.})^2 (R_l + 500)} \times 100 \text{ per cent} = \frac{40.6}{1 + \dfrac{500}{R_l}} \text{ per cent.}$$

∴ efficiency decreases from 40.6 per cent when $I_{d.c.} = 0$ to 24.9 per cent when $I_{d.c.} = 80$ mA.

Maximum output power is obtained when $R_l = 500\ \Omega$ and the efficiency is then 20.3 per cent.

∴ the current at which maximum power is obtained is given by $20.3 = 40.6[1 - 500 I_{d.c.}/103.5]$.

$\therefore \qquad I_{d.c.} = 103.5$ mA.

180. (*a*) Mean load current $(I_{d.c.}) = \dfrac{2}{\pi}\left(\dfrac{300\sqrt{2}}{500 + 2000}\right) = 108$ mA.

(*b*) Alternating load current $(I_{r.m.s.}) = \dfrac{1}{\sqrt{2}}\left(\dfrac{300\sqrt{2}}{500 + 2000}\right) = 120$ mA.

(*c*) D.C. output power $= (I_{d.c.})^2 \times 2000 = 23.3$ W.

(*d*) Input power $= (I_{r.m.s.})^2 (500 + 2000) = 36$ W.

(*e*) Rectification efficiency $= \dfrac{23.3}{36} \times 100$ per cent = 64.8 per cent.

(*f*) Ripple factor $= [(I_{r.m.s.}/I_{d.c.})^2 - 1]^{1/2} = 0.482$.

(*g*) D.C. output voltage $E_{d.c.} = \dfrac{2}{\pi} \times 300\sqrt{2} - I_{d.c.}\, 500$.

∴ $E_{d.c.}$ changes from 270 V when $I_{d.c.} = 0$ to 216 V when $I_{d.c.} = 108$ mA, i.e. regulation is 54 V.

181. R.m.s. current $= 5\text{ A} = \left[\dfrac{1}{2\pi}\displaystyle\int_0^{\pi} I_m^2 \sin^2\theta \, d\theta\right]^{1/2} = I_m/2$

where I_m is the maximum value of the current.

∴ $$I_m = 10 \text{ A}.$$

Moving-coil ammeter reads $\dfrac{1}{2\pi}\displaystyle\int_0^{\pi} I_m \sin\theta \, d\theta = \dfrac{I_m}{\pi} = \underline{3.18 \text{ A}}.$

For full-wave rectification:

A.C. ammeter reads r.m.s. value $= I_m/\sqrt{2} = \underline{7.07 \text{ A}}.$

Moving-coil ammeter reads mean value $= \dfrac{2}{\pi} I_m = \underline{6.37 \text{ A}}.$

182.

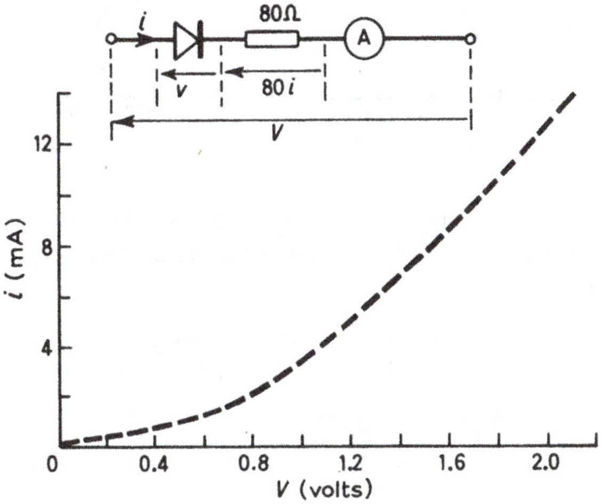

The following table can be drawn up using the rectifier characteristic:

Current i (mA) .	2	4	6	8	10	12	14
$80i$ volts . .	0.16	0.32	0.48	0.64	0.80	0.96	1.12
v volts . . .	0.60	0.76	0.82	0.88	0.93	0.98	1.03
$V = (v + 80i)$ volts .	0.76	1.08	1.30	1.52	1.73	1.94	2.15

The i/V characteristic is drawn. The current wave corresponding to the positive half-cycle of voltage can then be obtained as shown. The current during the negative half-cycle is so small that it can be neglected. The moving-coil ammeter reads the mean current taken over the whole cycle. This is found to be $\underline{3.32 \text{ mA}}$.

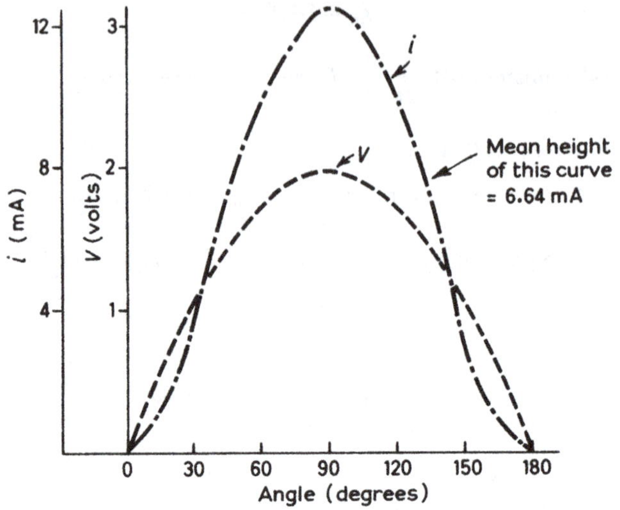

183. Current flows in each cycle for an angle θ, where $\cos\theta/2 = V_R/V$. The current through R is V_R/R which must equal the mean current through the rectifier,

$$\therefore \qquad V_R/R = \frac{1}{2\pi}\int_{-\theta/2}^{\theta/2} \frac{V(\cos\phi - \cos\theta/2)\,d\phi}{10}$$

But θ is given as $2\pi/6$, so $\underline{R = 585\ \Omega.}$

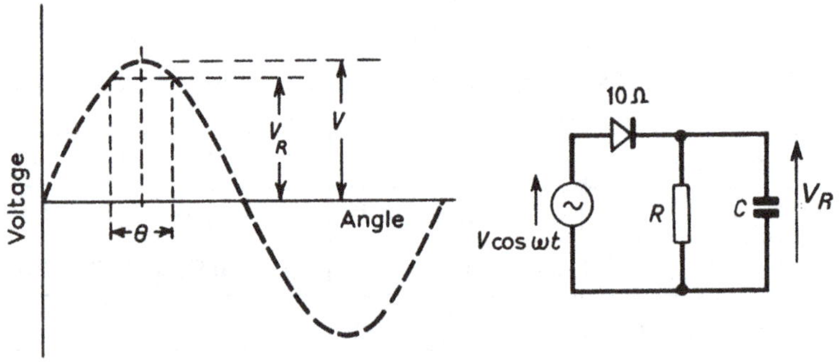

Component of fundamental frequency in the a.c. supply is

$$I_1 = \frac{1}{10\pi}\int_{-\theta/2}^{\theta/2} V(\cos\phi - \cos\theta/2)\cos\phi\,d\phi = 0.0287 \times V/10$$

A.C. power input $= \frac{1}{2} VI_1 = \frac{1}{2} V^2 \times 0.0287/10$

D.C. power output $= (V_R)^2/R = (V \cos\theta/2)^2/R = V^2 \left(\frac{\sqrt{3}}{2}\right)^2 \Big/ 585.$

∴ Efficiency of rectification

$$= \frac{\text{d.c. power output}}{\text{a.c. power input}} \times 100 \text{ per cent} = \underline{89.4 \text{ per cent.}}$$

184. It is evident from the diagram that, since $200\sqrt{2} \gg 10$, conduction may be assumed to continue until the end of each positive half-cycle.

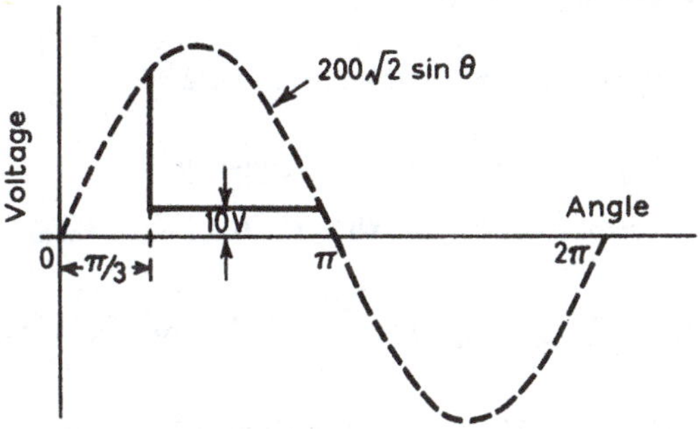

(*a*) R.m.s. load current

$$= \sqrt{\left[\frac{1}{2\pi} \int_{\pi/3}^{\pi} \left(\frac{200\sqrt{2}\sin\theta - 10}{200}\right)^2 d\theta\right]} = \underline{0.63 \text{ A.}}$$

(*b*) R.m.s. value of voltage across valve

$$= \sqrt{\left\{\frac{1}{2\pi}\left[\int_0^{\pi/3} (200\sqrt{2}\sin\theta)^2\, d\theta + \int_{\pi/3}^{\pi} 10^2\, d\theta + \int_{\pi}^{2\pi} (200\sqrt{2}\sin\theta)^2\, d\theta\right]\right\}}$$

$$= \underline{155 \text{ V.}}$$

(*c*) Power

$$= \frac{1}{2\pi} \int_{\pi/3}^{\pi} \left(\frac{200\sqrt{2}\sin\theta - 10}{200}\right) (200\sqrt{2}\sin\theta)\, d\theta = \underline{77 \text{ W.}}$$

185. The filter is shown in the diagram. Any losses in the rectifying elements, transformer and choke will be neglected.

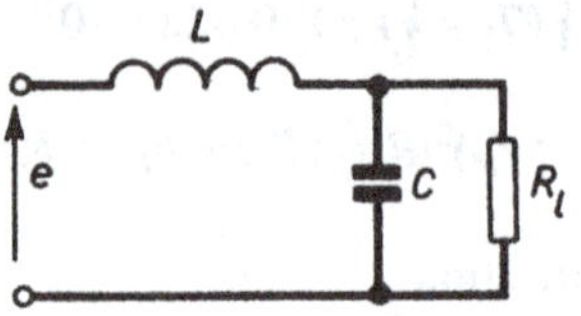

Suppose e is given by the first two terms of the Fourier-series representation of the rectifier output voltage, i.e. $\frac{2E_m}{\pi}\left[1-\frac{2}{3}\cos 2\omega t\right]$ where E_m is the maximum value of the transformer voltage to the centre-tap.

R.m.s. value of $e(e_{\text{r.m.s.}}) = \sqrt{2}\,\frac{E_m}{\pi}\cdot\frac{2}{3}$.

$\therefore$ a.c. through the circuit is approximately $\sqrt{2}\,\frac{E_m}{\pi}\cdot\frac{2}{3}\cdot\frac{1}{X_L} = I_{\text{r.m.s.}}$

where $X_L = 2\pi(2f)L$ and f is the supply frequency.

$\therefore$ ripple voltage across load is approximately $I_{\text{r.m.s.}}X_C = E_{\text{r.m.s.}}$, where $X_C = 1/2\pi(2f)C$.

Ripple factor $= E_{\text{r.m.s.}}/(2E_m/\pi) = \sqrt{2}X_c/3X_L = \sqrt{2}/3(4\pi f)^2LC = 10/300$ in this case.

$\therefore$ when $f = 50$ Hz, $LC = 35.86 \times 10^{-6}$, and when $f = 60$ Hz, $LC = 24.87 \times 10^{-6}$.

If the rectifier is to pass current throughout the whole cycle the peak current delivered must be less than the direct current, i.e. $4E_m/3\pi X_L \leqslant 2E_m/\pi R_l$.

The limiting condition for this is when $L = R_l/6\pi f$.

In this case $R_l = 300/0.12 = 2500\ \Omega$.

$\therefore$ when (a) $f = 50$ Hz, $L = 2.65$H, and when (b), $f = 60$ Hz, $L = 2.21$H.

The above expressions give the minimum values of L and LC that may be used to obtain the required results. Since the minimum value of L = 2.65H for case (a) and 2.21H for case (b) choose a 10-H choke, in both instances. This is a readily available item and its size must be such as to carry the necessary current.

If $L = 10$ H and $f = 50$ Hz, $C = 35.86 \times 10^{-6}/10 = 3.586\ \mu$F.
If $L = 10$ H and $f = 60$ Hz, $C = 24.87 \times 10^{-6}/10 = 2.487\ \mu$F.

$\therefore$ in both cases choose a 4-μF capacitor which is also readily available.

186. (*a*) *Simple inductor filter.*

$$\text{Load current} = \frac{2E_m}{\pi R_l} - \frac{4E_m}{3\pi}\frac{\cos(2\omega t - \phi)}{\sqrt{(R_l^2 + 4\omega^2 L^2}}$$

where the symbols E_m, R_l and L have the same meanings as in the previous solution, and $\tan\phi = 2\omega L/R_l$.

$$\therefore \qquad \text{the ripple factor} = \frac{\dfrac{4E_m}{3\pi\sqrt{2}} \Big/ \sqrt{(R_l^2 + 4\omega^2 L^2)}}{2E_m/\pi R_l}.$$

If $\omega = 100\pi$, $L = 20$ H and $R_l = 2000\ \Omega$.

$\therefore$ the ripple factor $= 0.074$.

If $\omega = 120\pi$, the ripple factor $= 0.062$.

(*b*) *Simple inductor filter.*

When $L = 40$ H, the ripple factor is 0.037 for $f = 50$ Hz and 0.031 for $f = 60$ Hz.

(*c*) *Simple capacitor filter.*

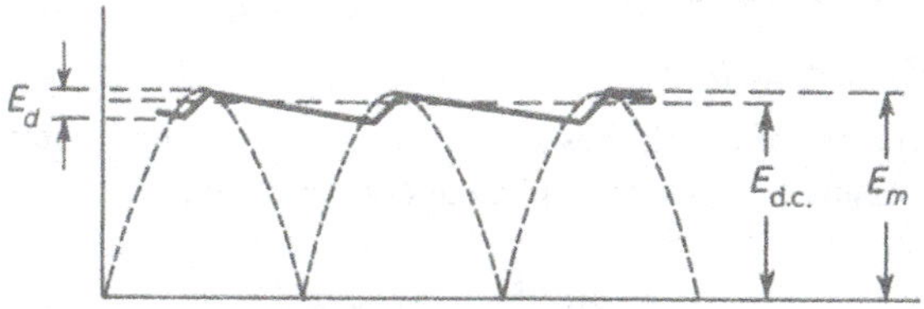

The diagram shows the voltage curves.

The r.m.s. value of the ripple voltage $e_{r.m.s.} = E_d/2\sqrt{3}$.

Assume the capacitor discharge continues for the full half-cycle at a constant rate equal to the average value of the load current $I_{d.c.}$*

In the time for half a cycle $(1/2f)$ the capacitor will lose an amount of charge $I_{d.c.}/2f$ coulombs.

$$\therefore \qquad E_d = I_{d.c.}/2fC.$$

* This gives a ripple factor for a given C which is too large. See J. Millman and S. Seely, *Electronics*, McGraw-Hill, 2nd Edition, 1951, p. 393, and S. Seely, *Radio Electronics*, McGraw-Hill, 1956, pp. 71–3.

The ripple factor $= e_{r.m.s.}/E_{d.c.} = \dfrac{I_{d.c.}/(2fC \cdot 2\sqrt{3})}{I_{d.c.}R_l}$

In this case $C = 16\ \mu F$ and $R_l = 2000\ \Omega$.

$\therefore$ when $f = 50$ Hz, the ripple factor = 0.090, and when $f = 60$ Hz, the ripple factor = 0.075.

(*d*) *Simple capacitor filter.*

When $C = 32\ \mu F$ the ripple factor is 0.045 for $f = 50$ Hz, and 0.0375 for $f = 60$ Hz.

(*e*) *Single L-type filter.*

In the previous solution it has been shown that the ripple factor for a single L-type filter is $\sqrt{2}/3(4\pi f)^2LC$.

Substituting the values of f, L and C it is found that the ripple factor is 0.0037 for $f = 50$ Hz, and 0.0025 for $f = 60$ Hz.

(*f*) *Single L-type filter.*

When $L = 40$ H and $C = 32\ \mu F$ the ripple factor is 0.0009 for $f = 50$ Hz, and 0.0006 for $f = 60$ Hz.

(*g*) *Double L-type filter.*

The reactances of the chokes are much larger than the reactances of the capacitors. Assume reactance of C small compared with R_l.

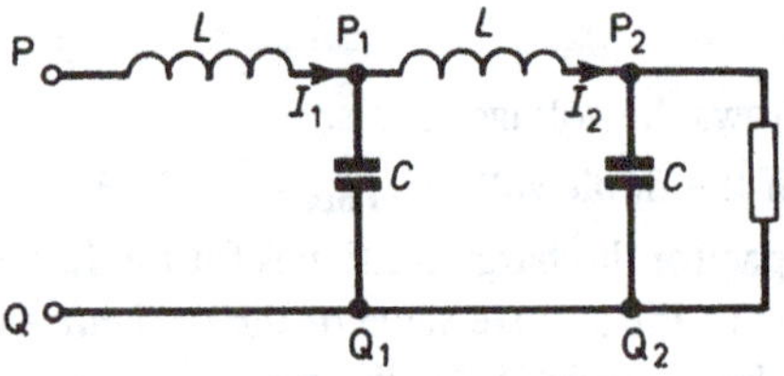

$\therefore$ impedance between P_2 and Q_2 is approximately $X_C = \dfrac{1}{2\pi(2f)C}$

" " P_1 " Q_1 " " X_C

P Q $X_L = 2\pi(2f)L$

Alternating current I_1 is approximately $\dfrac{\sqrt{2}}{3} \cdot \dfrac{2E_m}{\pi} \cdot \dfrac{1}{X_L}$.

Alternating voltage across P_1Q_1 is I_1X_C.

Also $$I_2 = I_1X_C/X_L.$$

$\therefore$ $$\text{Alternating voltages across } P_2Q_2 = I_2X_C = \frac{\sqrt{2}}{3}\cdot\frac{2E_m}{\pi}\left(\frac{X_C}{X_L}\right)^2$$

$\therefore$ $$\text{ripple factor} = \frac{\sqrt{2}}{3}\left(\frac{X_C}{X_L}\right)^2.$$

When $L = 20$ H and $C = 16$ μF the ripple factor is found to be 2.95×10^{-5} for $f = 50$ Hz, and 1.42×10^{-5} for $f = 60$ Hz.

187. An upper limit to the ripple can be found by assuming that cut-out takes place for the entire half-cycle.* The triangular ripple waveform shown in the solution to Question 186 becomes a triangular wave with vertical sides.

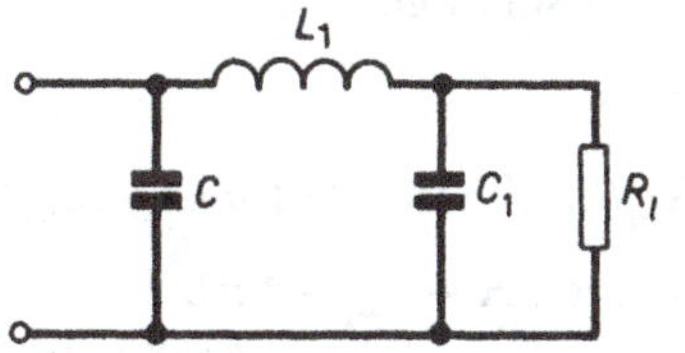

The Fourier analysis of such a waveform gives

$$E_{\text{d.c.}} - \frac{E_d}{\pi}\left(\sin 2\omega t - \frac{\sin 4\omega t}{2} + \frac{\sin 6\omega t}{3} - \ldots\right)$$

where $E_d = I_{\text{d.c.}}/2fC$ as in Question 186. Harmonics greater than the second will be neglected. R.m.s. second-harmonic voltage $E_2 = I_{\text{d.c.}}/2\pi fC\sqrt{2}$ and this is impressed on an L-section filter.

The output ripple is therefore approximately $E_2 \,.\, X_{C_1}/X_{L_1}$

where $$X_{C_1} = 1/2\pi(2f)C_1 \text{ and } X_{L_1} = 2\pi(2f)L_1.$$

Ripple factor $= E_2 \,.\, X_{C_1}/X_{L_1} \,.\, E_{\text{d.c.}} = \sqrt{2}/L_1C_1CR_l(2\pi \,.\, 2f)^3$.

If C and C_1 are in microfarads and $f = 50$ Hz, ripple factor $= 5700/CC_1L_1R_l$.

In this case $R_l = 250 \times 1000/50 = 5000\ \Omega$ and the ripple factor $= 0.01/100$.

$\therefore$ $$\text{if } C_1 = C,\ C^2L_1 = 11\,400.$$

A value for L_1 is usually chosen to be that of a readily available item.

* J. Millman and S. Seely, *Electronics*, McGraw-Hill, 2nd Edition, 1951, p. 402.

For example if $L_1 = 20$ H, $C = 23.9$ μF.

Alternatively, if $L_1 = 40$ H, $C = 16.9$ μF.

The capacitors chosen for these two values of L_1 would need to be not less than the corresponding figures quoted.

Having chosen a suitable choke its d.c. resistance will be known and therefore the d.c. voltage drop across it can be calculated. This gives the voltage drop across the first capacitor from which the peak transformer voltage to the centre-tap can be evaluated.

If C and C_1 are in microfarads and $f = 60$ Hz, ripple factor = $3300/CC_1L_1R_l$. In this case, if $C_1 = C$, $C^2L_1 = 6600$.

If now $L_1 = 20$ H, $C = 18.2$ μF. Alternatively, if $L_1 = 40$ H, $C = 12.8$ μF.

188. A π-section filter with a resistor replacing the inductor may be analysed as in the previous solution.

$\therefore$ the ripple factor is now

$$\sqrt{2}X_C \,.\, X_{C_1}/R_l \,.\, R \text{ instead of } \sqrt{2}X_C \,.\, X_{C_1}/R_l \,.\, X_{L_1}$$

i.e. for the same ripple factor $R = X_{L_1} = 4\pi f L_1$

$= 12\,568\ \Omega$ for 50 Hz, and $15\,082\ \Omega$ for 60 Hz.

When output current = 100 mA, power dissipated is

(*a*) $(0.1)^2 \times 12\,568$ W = 125.7 W.

(*b*) $(0.1)^2 \times 15\,082$ W = 150.8 W.

When output current = 10 mA, power dissipated is (*a*) 1.257 W, (*b*) 1.508 W.

189. (*a*) To obtain the minimum value of R the Zener current I_z must be at an optimum value. This current must satisfy the regulation requirement

$$I_z = 8 + (65 - 15) = 8 + 50 = 58 \text{ mA}$$

If the Zener current is 58 mA it can decrease to 8 mA to allow the load current to go from 15 to 65 mA. If the load current is at the maximum 65 mA the Zener current can take the excess current if the load decreases to 15 mA, for (65 − 15) + 58 = 108 mA which is less than 120 mA.

$$R = (65 - 33)/I$$

$$I = 15 + 58 = 73 \text{ mA}$$

so $$R = 32/73 \times 10^{-3} = \underline{440\ \Omega}.$$

(*b*) From (*a*) $I_z = \underline{58\text{ mA}}$.

(*c*) $V_{max} = (58 + 55)\,10^{-3} \times 440 + 33 = \underline{82.7\text{ V}}$

$V_{max} = (8 + 55)\,10^{-3} \times 440 + 33 = \underline{60.6\text{ V}}$.

190. The solution to this problem can be found elsewhere.*

191. A number of solutions are possible. The following one possibly represents the simplest approach with a minimum of extra components.

Select R_1 to provide 3 mA in the Zener diode (operational amplifier input circuits neglected)

$$\therefore \qquad R_1 = \{(30 - 6.5)/3 \times 10^{-3}\}\Omega = \underline{7.8\text{ k}\Omega}.$$

Assuming the operational amplifier has high gain and low output voltage

$$R_2/R_3 = 6.5/(15 - 6.5) = 6.5/8.5$$

In the absence of further information let a current of 1 mA flow in R_2 and R_3

$$\therefore \qquad R_2 = \underline{6.5\text{ k}\Omega}$$

$$R_3 = \underline{8.5\text{ k}\Omega}$$

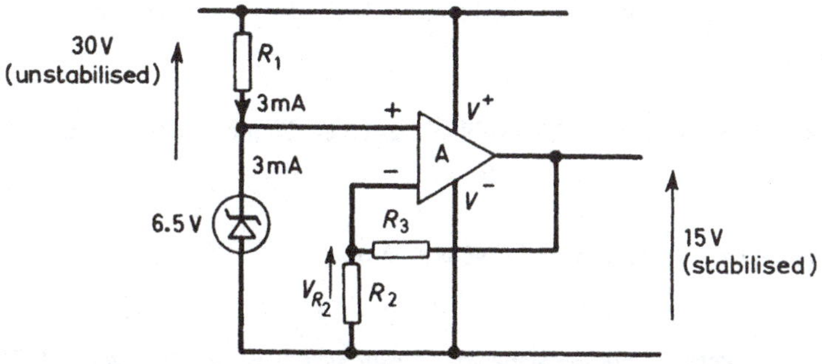

A, R_2 and R_3 effectively form a negative feedback amplifier for which the output resistance R_0' is given by $R_0' = \dfrac{R_0}{1 + \beta A_v}$ where $\beta = R_2/(R_2 + R_3)$

* See R. J. Maddock, *Intermediate Electronics*, Book 2, Butterworths, 1970, pp. 236–9.

and R_0 is the open-loop output resistance of A

$$\therefore \qquad R_0' = \frac{200}{1 + \left(\frac{6.5}{15} \times 3 \times 10^4\right)} \Omega = \underline{15.4 \mathrm{m}\Omega}$$

192. The solution to this problem can be found elsewhere.*

193. Let resistance of series resistor be R ohms.

Current through $R = (20 + 30)$ mA $= 50$ mA.

Voltage across $R = (400 - 200)$ V $= 200$ V.

$$\therefore \qquad R = 200/50 \times 10^{-3} = \underline{4 \text{ k}\Omega.}$$

Since the load current = 20 mA, and the tube current may vary from 10 to 50 mA, the current through R varies from 30 mA to 70 mA.

∴ the voltage across R varies from 120 V to 280 V,

i.e. <u>the input voltage varies from 320 V to 480 V.</u>

Load current can vary from zero to 40 mA (when tube current is at its minimum value of 10 mA),

i.e. <u>load resistance varies from 5 kΩ to ∞, since voltage across load is 200 V.</u>

194. The solution to this problem has been given elsewhere by the author.†

195. The solution to this problem has been given elsewhere by the author.‡

196. The voltage-current curve is as shown.

* See F. A. Benson, 'Voltage Stabilizers,' *Electronic Engineering Monograph*, 1950, pp. 30–2. See also E. W. Titterton, 'Some Characteristics of Glow-discharge Voltage Regulator Tubes,' *J. Sci. Instrum.*, **26**, p. 33, 1949.

† F. A. Benson, 'Voltage Stabilizers,' *Electronic Engineering Monograph*, 1950, Chapter 4.

‡ F. A. Benson and G. V. G. Lusher, 'Voltage Stabilizers for Microwave Oscillators,' *Electronic Engineering*, **26**, p. 106, 1954.

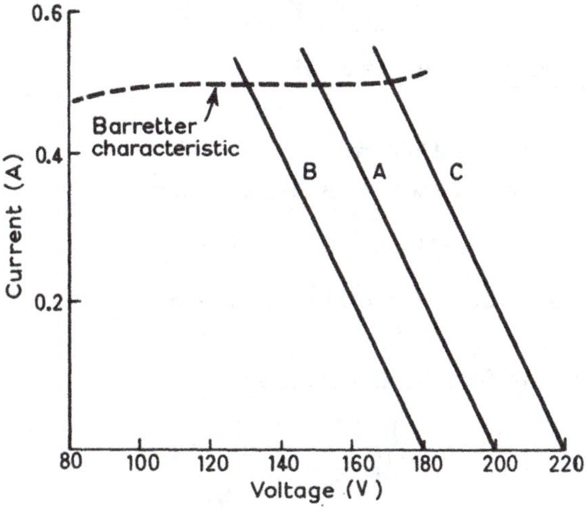

If v is the voltage across the barretter and I the current through it, then for the 200-V input

$$200 = v + 100I.$$

This is the equation of straight line A which cuts the barretter characteristic at 0.5 A.

For 180-V input line B is obtained which cuts the barretter characteristic at 0.5 A.

For 220-V input line C is obtained which cuts the barretter characteristic at 0.504 A.

Current variation if input voltage changes by ± 10 per cent is 0.004 A.

205. Supply voltage = $\{250 + (10 \times 10^3 \times 9 \times 10^{-3})\}$ V = 340 V.

Resistance of load = $(430 - 250)/9 \times 10^{-3}\ \Omega = \dot{2}0$ kΩ.

206. Resistance = $8/(9 \times 10^{-3}) = 889\ \Omega$.

The capacitor should have low reactance compared with 889 Ω. The greater the capacitance the more effective is the capacitor in taking most of the alternating component of the anode current.

Suppose the reactance of the capacitor is chosen to be 1/10 of the resistance. Then at 1000 Hz, $C = 10^6/2\pi \times 1000 \times 88.9\ \mu$F, i.e. $$C = 1.79\ \mu F, \text{ say } 2\ \mu F.$$

At 100 Hz, $C = 17.9\ \mu F$, say $20\ \mu F$.

207. Power input = 1/600 W.

Power output = $10I^2$, where I is the load current.

$$\therefore \quad 10 \log_{10} (10I^2 \times 600) = 60, \text{ so } I = 12.9 \text{ A}$$

$$60 \text{ dB} = 60 \times 0.1151 \text{ nepers} = 6.9 \text{ nepers.}$$

208. The equivalent circuit is as shown.

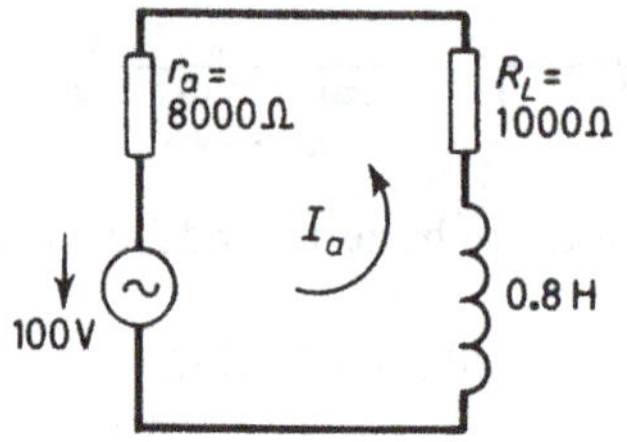

$$I_a = \frac{100}{8000 + 1000 + j(2\pi \times 300 \times 0.8)} \text{ A}$$
$$= (10.81 - j1.81) \text{ mA.}$$

The output voltage

$$V_0 = -(10.81 - j1.81)(1000 + j1508)10^{-3} \text{ V}$$
$$= -(13.54 + j14.49) = 19.61 \angle -133^\circ.$$

$$\text{The gain } A = \frac{19.61 \angle -133^\circ}{5} = 3.92 \angle -133^\circ.$$

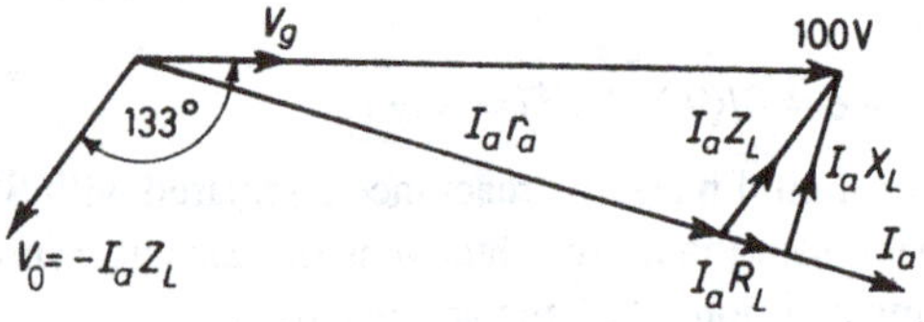

The phasor diagram is therefore as illustrated.

When the frequency is 2000 Hz:

$$I_a = \frac{100}{8000 + 1000 + j(2\pi \times 2000 \times 0.8)} \text{ A} = (4.94 - j5.52) \text{ mA.}$$

The output voltage

$$V_o = -(4.94 - j5.52)(1000 + j10\,060) \times 10^{-3}\ \text{V}$$
$$= 74.87 \underline{/-143.8^\circ}.$$

$\therefore$ the gain $A = \underline{14.97 /-143.8^\circ}.$

The gain at 2000 Hz is greater than the gain at 300 Hz, i.e. frequency distortion is present. The results also show that phase-shift distortion exists in the amplifier.

209. The solution to this problem can be found elsewhere.*

210. The equivalent circuit of the arrangement is as shown.

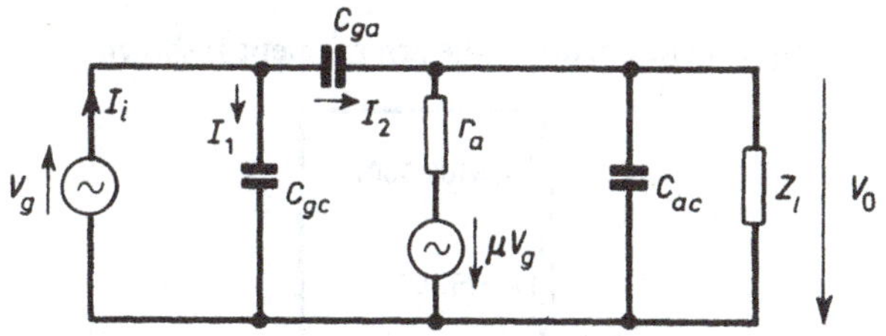

Using the Millman Theorem, $V_o = \dfrac{\mu V_g Y_a - V_g Y_3}{Y_a + Y_l + Y_2 + Y_3}$ where $Y_a = 1/r_a$, $Y_2 = j\omega C_{ac}$, $Y_3 = j\omega C_{ga}$ and $Y_l = 1/Z_l$.

$$\therefore \quad \text{the gain} = -\frac{V_o}{V_g} = \frac{Y_3 - g_m}{Y_a + Y_l + Y_2 + Y_3} = A \text{ say.}$$

In this case, since $\omega = 2\pi \times 10\,000$, $Y_2 = j2.26 \times 10^{-7}$ S, and $Y_3 = j1.88 \times 10^{-7}$ S. Also $Y_l = 1.11 \times 10^{-5}$ S, $Y_a = 2.5 \times 10^{-5}$ S and $g_m = 1.5 \times 10^{-3}$ S.

$$\therefore \quad \text{gain} = \frac{-1.5 \times 10^{-3} + j1.88 \times 10^{-7}}{3.61 \times 10^{-5} + j4.14 \times 10^{-7}}.$$

Thus the j terms which come from Y_2 and Y_3 are negligible. Neglecting these j terms the gain is $\underline{-41.6}$.

Since A is real the input impedance consists of a capacitance of value $C_i = C_{gc} + (1 + A)C_{ga}$

* See, for example, J. D. Ryder, *Engineering Electronics*, McGraw-Hill, 1957.

$$= (3.0 + 42.6 \times 3.0)\ \mu\mu\text{F} = 130.8\ \mu\mu\text{F}.$$

For a two-stage amplifier the input impedance of the second stage acts as a shunt for the load of the first stage. Thus C_i, along with the C_{ac} of the first tube, shunts the load. It should also be remembered that every 1 $\mu\mu$F of stray capacitance between the leads to the anode and grid of the second stage adds effectively 42.6 $\mu\mu$F across the load resistor of the first stage. It is reasonable to assume therefore that the 90 000-Ω load of the first stage is shunted by a capacitance of 200 $\mu\mu$F (a conservative figure).

$$\therefore \qquad Y_l = 1.11 \times 10^{-5} + j1.26 \times 10^{-5}\ \text{S}.$$

$$\therefore \qquad \text{the gain} = \frac{Y_3 - g_m}{Y_a + Y_l + Y_2 + Y_3} \simeq \frac{-g_m}{Y_a + Y_l + Y_2 + Y_3}$$

$$= -36.79 + j13.24 = \underline{\underline{39.1 \angle 160.2^\circ}}.$$

211. The equivalent circuit of the arrangement is shown.

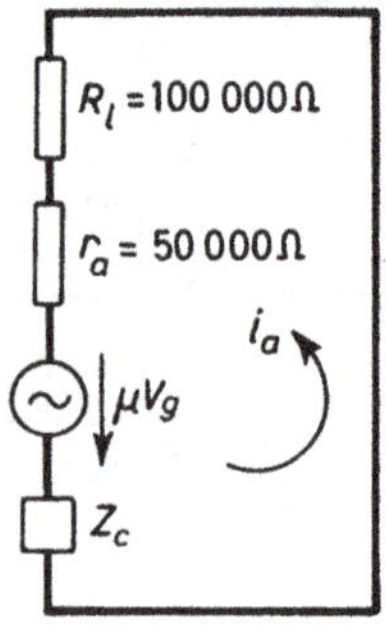

$$V_g = v_i - i_a Z_c \qquad (1)$$

From the equivalent circuit:

$$i_a = \mu V_g/(R_l + r_a + Z_c) \qquad (2)$$

From (1) and (2):

$$i_a = \mu v_i/\{R_l + r_a + Z_c(1 + \mu)\} \qquad (3)$$

Now

$$v_o = -R_l i_a \qquad (4)$$

From (3) and (4),

$$v_o/v_i = -\mu R_l/\{r_a + R_l + Z_c(1 + \mu)\} \qquad (5)$$

But $R_l = 100\,000\ \Omega$, $Z_c = \dfrac{2000/j\omega C}{2000 + 1/j\omega C}$, $r_a = 50\,000\ \Omega$ and $\mu = 80$

$$\therefore \qquad v_o/v_i = 8000 \bigg/ \left\{150 + \frac{162}{1 + 2000\mathrm{j}\omega C}\right\}.$$

$\therefore$ v_o/v_i is a maximum when $\omega \to \infty$ and is 53.3, and v_o/v_i is a minimum when $\omega \to 0$ and is 25.6.

v_o/v_i is equal to 0.707 of its maximum value when the frequency $(\omega/2\pi)$ = 121.2 Hz.

212. The equivalent circuit of one stage is as shown. Applying the Millman Theorem between points O and B:

$$V_{OB} = \frac{V_{OA} Y_C}{Y_C + Y_{Rg} + Y_{Cg}}$$

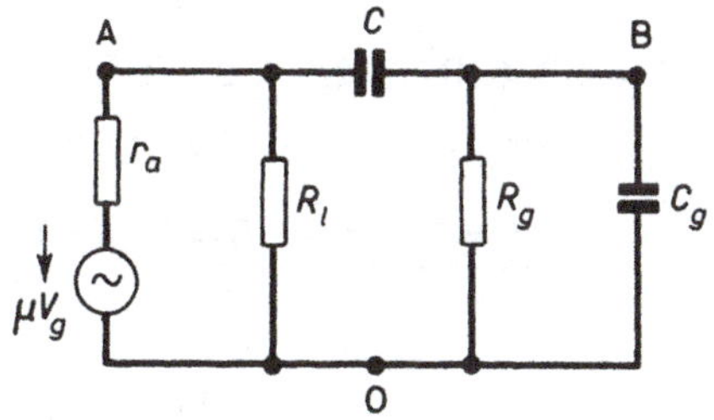

where $\qquad Y_C = \mathrm{j}\omega C,\ Y_{Rg} = 1/R_g$ and $Y_{Cg} = \mathrm{j}\omega C_g$.

Applying the Millman Theorem between points O and A:

$$V_{OA} = \frac{\mu V_g Y_a + V_{OB} Y_C}{Y_a + Y_l + Y_C}, \text{ where } Y_a = 1/r_a \text{ and } Y_l = 1/R_l.$$

$\therefore$ gain $A = -V_{OB}/V_g$

$$= \frac{-\mu Y_a Y_C}{(Y_C + Y_{Rg} + Y_{Cg})(Y_a + Y_l) + Y_C(Y_{Rg} + Y_{Cg})}.$$

At intermediate frequencies where Y_C is large and Y_{Cg} is small,

$$A = A_o = -\mu Y_a/(Y_a + Y_l + Y_{Rg}).$$

At low frequencies the effect of C_g is negligible and

$$A = A_1 = -\mu Y_a Y_C/\{Y_C(Y_a + Y_l + Y_{Rg}) + Y_{Rg}(Y_a + Y_l)\}.$$

$$\therefore \qquad \frac{A_1}{A_o} = \frac{1}{1 - \mathrm{j}f_1/f} \text{ where } f_1 = \frac{Y_{Rg}(Y_a + Y_l)}{2\pi C(Y_a + Y_l + Y_{Rg})}.$$

If the load is a pure resistance f_1 is real and $\dfrac{A_1}{A_o} = \dfrac{1}{\sqrt{[1+(f_1/f)^2]}}$

i.e. f_1 represents that frequency at which the gain falls to $1/\sqrt{2}$ of its intermediate-frequency value.

At high frequencies Y_{Rg} and Y_{Cg} can be neglected in comparison with Y_C and $A = A_2 = -\mu Y_a/(Y_a + Y_l + Y_{Rg} + Y_{Cg})$.

$$\therefore \qquad \frac{A_2}{A_o} = \frac{1}{1 + \mathrm{j}f/f_2}, \text{ where } f_2 = (Y_a + Y_l + Y_{Rg})/2\pi C_g.$$

If the load is a pure resistance f_2 is real and $\dfrac{A_2}{A_0} = \dfrac{1}{\sqrt{[1+(f/f_2)^2]}}$, i.e. f_2 represents that frequency (at the high-frequency end) where the gain falls to $1/\sqrt{2}$ of its intermediate-frequency value.

In this case,

$$Y_a = 1.3 \times 10^{-4}\ \text{S},\ Y_l = 0.2 \times 10^{-4}\ \text{S},$$

and

$$Y_{Rg} = 0.02 \times 10^{-4}\ \text{S}.$$

$$\therefore \qquad \underline{A_o = -17.1, f_1 = 31\ \text{Hz and } f_2 = 121\,000\ \text{Hz}.}$$

$A_0 = -17.1$ so when $A = 14$

$$\text{the minimum gain ratio } \frac{A}{A_o} = \frac{14}{17.1} = 0.8187.$$

If f' is the low frequency where the gain drops to 14 and f'' is the high frequency where the gain drops to 14,

$$\frac{1}{\sqrt{[1+(f_1/f')^2]}} = 0.8187 = \frac{1}{\sqrt{[1+(f''/f_2)^2]}}$$

$$\therefore \qquad \underline{f' = 44\ \text{Hz and } f'' = 84\,960\ \text{Hz}.}$$

213. Gain per stage $= \sqrt{(6000)} = 78$.

Using the symbols introduced in the solution to Problem 212:

$$\left|\frac{A_2}{A_0}\right| = \left[\frac{1}{1+(f/f_2)^2}\right]^{n/2}$$

where n is the number of stages (in this case 2)

$$\therefore \qquad 0.95 = \left[\frac{1}{1+(f/f_2)^2}\right]^{2/2}$$

i.e. $$f/f_2 = 0.223$$

Since $$f = 100 \text{ kHz}, f_2 = 450 \text{ kHz}.$$

Now $$f_2 = 1/2\pi C_g R_l, \text{ where } C_g = 20.5\ \mu\mu\text{F (given)}$$

$$\therefore \quad R_l = 1/(2\pi \times 20.5 \times 10^{-12} \times 450 \times 10^3) = \underline{17\,200\ \Omega}$$

The gain per stage at mid-frequency is

$$-g_m R_l = -5.2 \times 10^{-3} \times 17\,200 = -89.4$$

The overall gain $= 89.4^2 = \underline{7992.}$

214. It is shown in Solution 212 that:

$$A_0 = -\mu Y_a/(Y_a + Y_l + Y_{Rg})$$

With pentodes it is possible to assume that $r_a \gg R_l$. Further, it may be assumed that $R_g \gg R_l$ because R_l must be made small to raise f_2, whereas R_g must be large to lower f_1. With these assumptions $A_0 = -g_m R_l$ and the high-frequency gain becomes:

$$A_2 = -g_m R_l/(1 + j\omega C_g R_l)$$

The gain ratio for a pentode is then

$$\left|\frac{A_2}{A_0}\right| = \left[\frac{1}{1 + (f/f_2)^2}\right]^{\frac{1}{2}}$$

where $f_2 = 1/2\pi C_g R_l$ = bandwidth in hertz since f_1 will be low.

Figure of merit (gain $\times$ bandwidth) $= g_m R_l/2\pi C_g R_l = g_m/2\pi C_g$.

This is constant for a given type of valve. If $C_g = C_{ac} + C_{gc}$ (the irreducible minimum value of C_g for pentodes) $= 9.2\ \mu\mu$F in this case and $g_m = 5.7$ mS:

$$\text{Figure of merit} = 5.7 \times 10^{-3}/(2\pi \times 9.2 \times 10^{-12})$$
$$= \underline{98.6.}$$

215. If an amplifier is made up of n cascaded RC-coupled stages, not necessarily identical, the overall high-frequency gain ratio is:

$$\left|\frac{A_2}{A_0}\right| = \left[\frac{1}{1 + (f/f_2')^2}\right]^{\frac{1}{2}} \left[\frac{1}{1 + (f/f_2'')^2}\right]^{\frac{1}{2}} \cdots$$

If the stages are identical

$$\left|\frac{A_2}{A_0}\right| = \left[\frac{1}{1+(f/f_2)^2}\right]^{n/2}$$

If f_s designates the 3 dB point for the overall amplifier of n stages:

$$1/\sqrt{2} = \left[\frac{1}{1+(f_s/f_2)^2}\right]^{n/2}$$

Similarly, for the three non-identical stages

$$1/\sqrt{2} = \left[\frac{1}{1+(f/f_2')^2}\right]^{\frac{1}{2}} \left[\frac{1}{1+(f/f_2'')^2}\right]^{\frac{1}{2}} \left[\frac{1}{1+(f/f_2''')^2}\right]^{\frac{1}{2}}$$

$$\therefore \quad 1/2 = \left[\frac{1}{1+(f/250)^2}\right]\left[\frac{1}{1+(f/350)^2}\right]\left[\frac{1}{1+(f/550)^2}\right]$$

This expression gives f at the high-frequency end in kHz.

A similar calculation gives the low-frequency limit of the overall bandwidth:

$$\left|\frac{A_1}{A_0}\right| = 1/\sqrt{2} = \left[\frac{1}{1+(100/f)^2}\right]^{\frac{1}{2}} \left[\frac{1}{1+(80/f)^2}\right]^{\frac{1}{2}} \left[\frac{1}{1+(50/f)^2}\right]^{\frac{1}{2}}$$

216. The solution to this problem can be found elsewhere.*

217. The solution to this problem can be found elsewhere.†

218. Consider first the low-frequency equivalent circuit (a) of the amplifier. The secondary of the transformer feeds the grid circuit of the next valve which is assumed to have infinite impedance.

$$\therefore \quad I_p = \mu V_g/(r_a + R_p + j\omega L_p) \qquad (1)$$

$$\text{Voltage across primary} = j\omega L_p I_p \qquad (2)$$

$$= \mu V_g/\{1 - j(r_a + R_p)/\omega L_p\} \qquad (3)$$

* See J. D. Ryder, *Engineering Electronics*, McGraw-Hill, 1957, p. 108.

† See, for example, V. C. Rideout, *Active Networks*, Constable, 1954, pp. 224–7; or S. Seely, *Electron-tube Circuits*, McGraw-Hill, 2nd Edition, 1958, pp. 319–21.

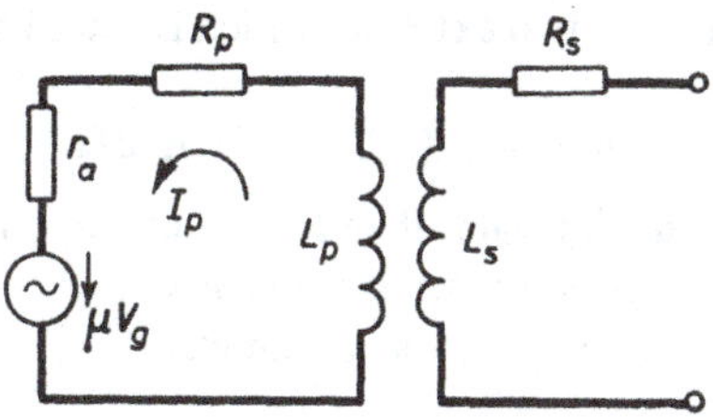

(a)

Voltage across secondary is n times as large as this.

$$\therefore \qquad \text{gain} = \pm n\mu/\{1 - \text{j}(r_a + R_p)/\omega L_p\} \qquad (4)$$

The magnitude of the gain $(A) = n\mu/\sqrt{[1 + \{(r_a + R_p)/\omega L_p\}^2]}$. (5)

When $\omega L_p \gg (r_a + R_p)$, $A = n\mu = 30$ in this case. The gain drops off at low frequencies because ωL_p is not large compared with $(r_a + R_p)$. When $\omega L_p = (r_a + R_p)$ the gain is only 70.7 per cent of its value $n\mu$ approached at higher frequencies. Thus the gain drops to 70.7 per cent of 30, i.e. 21.2 when $f = (8000 + 3500)/(2\pi \times 70) = 26$ Hz.

Now consider circuit (b) which is the high-frequency equivalent circuit.

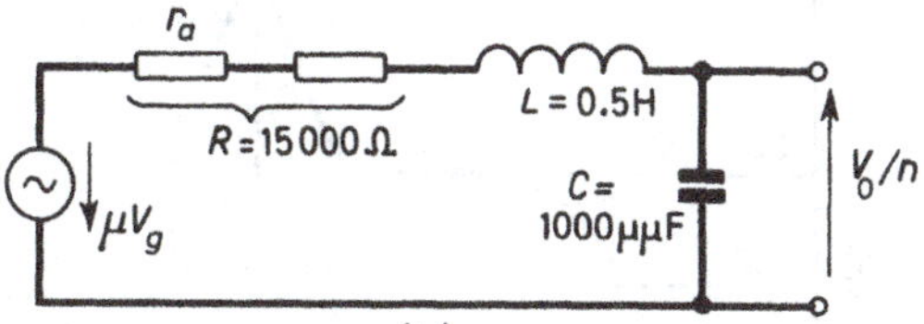

(b)

An analysis of this circuit shows the gain to be

$$\frac{\pm \text{j}n\mu\left(\dfrac{1}{\omega C}\right)}{R + \text{j}\left(\omega L - \dfrac{1}{\omega C}\right)} \qquad (6)$$

The magnitude of the gain $A = \dfrac{n\mu\left(\dfrac{1}{\omega C}\right)}{\sqrt{\left[R^2 + \left(\omega L - \dfrac{1}{\omega C}\right)^2\right]}}$. (7)

At low frequencies, ωL is small and $1/\omega C$ is large, therefore the gain approaches $n\mu$ as already stated. At very high frequencies $1/\omega C$ is small and ωL is large and the gain falls rapidly to zero. The gain passes through a maximum between these two extremes which is found by putting $dA/d\omega = 0$ to occur when

$$1/\omega C = \{2(\omega L)^2 + R^2\}/2\omega L.$$

Since ωL is usually much greater than R, the maximum occurs when $\omega L = 1/\omega C$. This is the condition for series resonance.

In this case the frequency for maximum gain

$$= \frac{1}{2\pi\sqrt{(0.5 \times 1000 \times 10^{-12})}} = 7117 \text{ Hz}.$$

An analysis of the circuit shows that the corresponding gain is

$$\frac{n\mu}{R}\sqrt{\left(\frac{L}{C}\right)} = \frac{30}{15\,000}\sqrt{\left[\frac{0.5}{1000 \times 10^{-12}}\right]} = 44.7.$$

A gain-frequency curve can be plotted by finding other values of gain at the low-frequency end using equation (5) and at the high-frequency end using equation (7). Both expressions give a gain of $n\mu = 30$ for the mid-band frequencies. A sketch of the resulting response curve is shown in diagram (c).

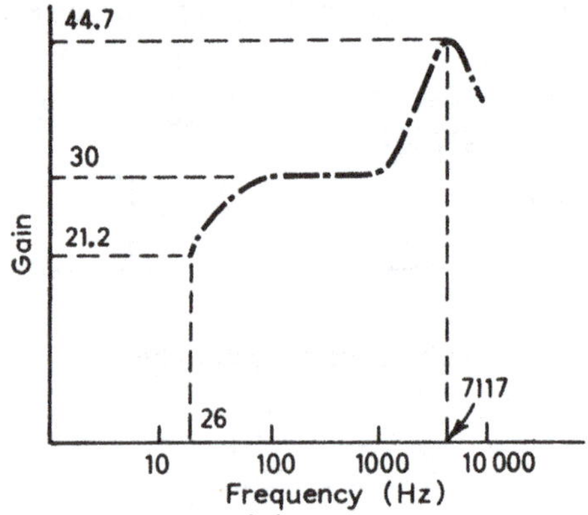

(c)

219. Let the input voltage be sinusoidal and of the form $v_g = V_g \cos \omega t$. The anode current i_a is of the form

$$I_a + B_0 + B_1 \cos \omega t + B_2 \cos 2\omega t \quad . \quad . \quad (1)$$

B_0, B_1, etc., can be found from the characteristic curves of the valve. From the figure when:

$$\omega t = 0, i_a = I_{max}$$

$$\omega t = \pi/2, i_a = I_a$$

$$\omega t = \pi, i_a = I_{min}.$$

Substituting in (1):

$$I_{max} = I_a + B_0 + B_1 + B_2 \quad . \quad . \quad . \quad (2)$$

$$I_a = I_a + B_0 - B_2 \quad . \quad . \quad . \quad . \quad (3)$$

$$I_{min} = I_a + B_0 - B_1 + B_2 \quad . \quad . \quad . \quad (4)$$

From (3), $B_0 = B_2$ . . . . . . (5)

From (2) and (4), $B_1 = (I_{max} - I_{min})/2$ . . . . . . (6)

From (2) and (6), $B_2 = (I_{max} + I_{min} - 2I_a)/4$ . . . . . (7)

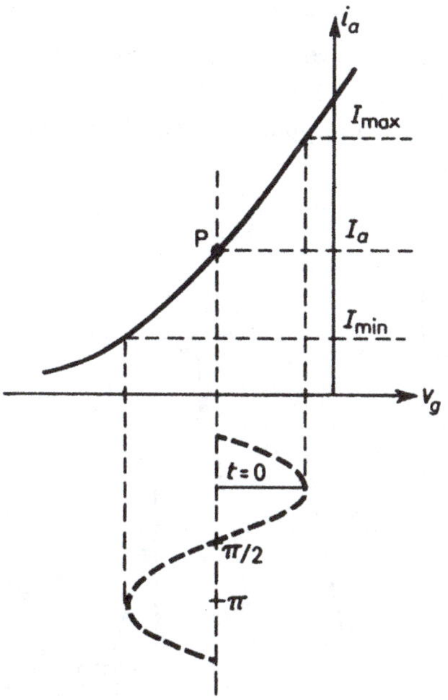

In this case maximum current corresponds to a grid voltage of $(-8 + 6)\text{V} = -2$ V and minimum current corresponds to a grid voltage of $(-8 - 6)\text{V} = -14$ V.

From the characteristic curves and the load line,

$$I_{max} = 21.6 \text{ mA}, I_a = 13.2 \text{ mA and } I_{min} = 6.3 \text{ mA}.$$

$$\therefore \qquad B_2 = B_0 = (21.6 + 6.3 - 26.4)/4 = 0.375 \text{ mA}.$$

Total steady current = (13.2 + 0.375) mA = 13.575 mA.

Peak fundamental current is

$$B_1 = (21.6 - 6.3)/2 \text{ mA} = 7.65 \text{ mA}.$$

$$\text{Peak fundamental output voltage} = \frac{7.65}{1000} \times 8000 = 61.2 \text{ V}.$$

Fundamental gain = 61.2/6 = 10.2.

Percentage of second-harmonic distortion

$$= 100B_2/B_1 = 100 \times 0.375/7.65 = 4.9 \text{ per cent.}$$

220. The quiescent point Q is determined by drawing the load line through the point $I_a = 0$, $V_a = 300$ V with a slope fixed by the resistance R_1 of the choke. Since R_1 is generally small the static load line is almost vertical. Since anode dissipation is 25 W, anode current permissible is 25/300 = 83 mA. This corresponds to a grid bias of about − 20 V.

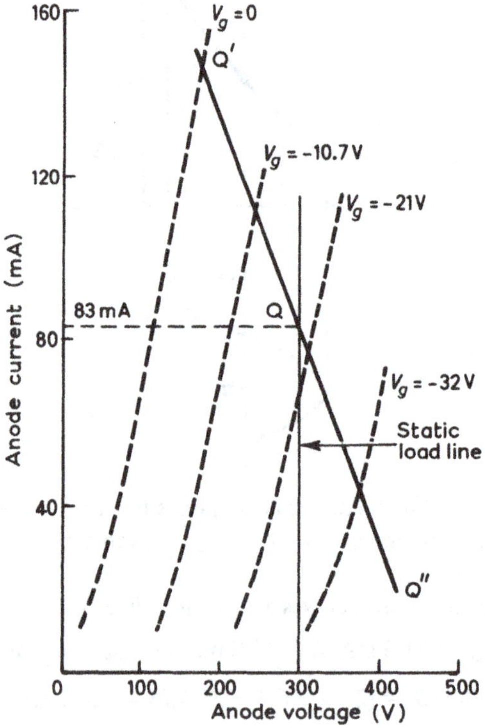

Permissible grid swing is about 20 V peak; distortion occurs from the non-linear parts of the valve characteristics. Thus a minimum anode current of about 20 mA is set where characteristics begin to curve. Therefore, dynamic load line is as shown ($Q'QQ''$). Voltage swing is (425 − 175) V = 250 V. Corresponding current change is (148 − 20) mA = 128 mA. Load resistance = $250/(128 \times 10^{-3})\ \Omega = 1.95\ \text{k}\Omega$.

$$\text{Output power} = (V_{max} - V_{min})(I_{max} - I_{min})/8 = (250 \times 0.128)/8 = \underline{4\ \text{W}}.$$

$$\text{Efficiency} = (4/25) \times 100 \text{ per cent} = \underline{16 \text{ per cent}}.$$

221. (*a*) The analysis required can be found in many textbooks.*

(*b*) The method of determining the composite characteristic consists of inverting the characteristic of valve (2) with the quiescent point P_2 immediately under P_1 and then adding algebraically the corresponding ordinates of the two characteristics.

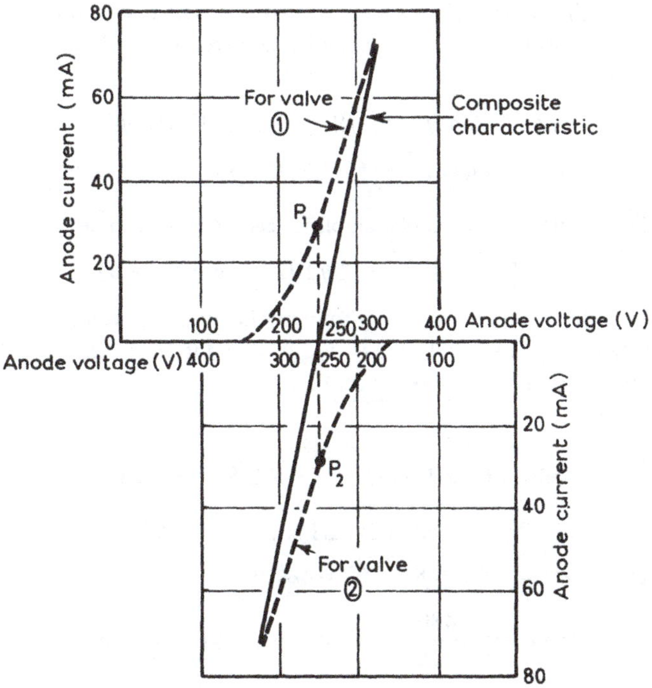

* See, for example, P. Parker, *Electronics*, Arnold, 1950, Section 73; or Cruft Electronics Staff, *Electronic Circuits and Tubes*, McGraw-Hill, 1947, Chapter 13.

At the points P, slopes of characteristics

$$= 1/2000 \text{ S, so } \underline{r_a = 2000\ \Omega.}$$

$$\underline{\text{At } Q, r_a = 1000\ \Omega.}$$

222. (*a*) The solution to this problem can be found in many standard textbooks.*

(*b*) Power output $= \frac{1}{2}V_l I_l$ where V_l and I_l are respectively the peak values of the voltage across, and the current through, one section of the output transformer primary. Now $I_l = I_{max}$ and $V_l = V - V_{min}$ where $V = 500$.

$$\therefore \qquad \text{power output } P_{a.c.} = \tfrac{1}{2}I_{max}(500 - V_{min}).$$

But $V_{min} = 1000 I_{max}$, so $P_{a.c.} = \frac{1}{2}I_{max}(500 - 1000 I_{max})$. This is a maximum when $I_{max} = \frac{1}{4}$A $\underline{\text{when } P_{a.c.} = 31.25 \text{ W}}$.

Power drawn from h.t. supply, $P_{d.c.} = 2I_a V$ where I_a is the mean anode current of either valve (valves assumed identical). The pulses of anode current may reasonably be taken as half sine waves so $I_a = I_{max}/\pi$ and therefore $P_{d.c.} = 2\,V\,I_{max}/\pi$.

$$\text{The efficiency} = P_{a.c.}/P_{d.c.} = \pi(1 - V_{min}/V)/4.$$

In this case the efficiency $= \pi(1 - 250/500)/4 = 0.393 = \underline{39.3 \text{ per cent.}}$

(*c*) The efficiency of a class-C amplifier can be shown to be†

$$(1 - V_{min}/V)(\theta - \sin 2\theta/2)/2\,(\sin\theta - \theta\cos\theta)$$

where 2θ is the angle of flow, V_{min} is the minimum anode voltage and V is the supply voltage. In the ideal case, $V_{min} = 0$ and if 2θ is then $120°$ the efficiency is found to be $\underline{89.6 \text{ per cent.}}$

223. Mean value of anode current $= \dfrac{1}{2} \times 2.5 \times \dfrac{90}{360} = 0.31$ A.

Power supplied by h.t. source is $0.31 \times 2500 = 775$ W.

Output power $= 0.8 \times 0.8 \times 750 = 480$ W

$$\therefore \qquad \text{efficiency} = \frac{480}{775} \times 100 \text{ per cent} = \underline{61.9 \text{ per cent.}}$$

* For example, see P. Parker, *Electronics*, Arnold, 1950, p. 340.

† For the proof of this expression see, for example, P. Parker, *Electronics*, Arnold, 1950, pp. 343–4; or A. T. Starr, *Electronics*, Pitman, 2nd Edition, 1959, p. 272.

At the point where anode current commences to flow, the instantaneous angle voltage is:*

$$V_a = V_{\text{h.t.}} - V_{\text{a.c.}} \cos\theta \text{ (}2\theta\text{ is the angle of flow)}$$
$$= 2500 - 2000 \cos 45^\circ = \underline{1086 \text{ V}}.$$

224. Let Z be the impedance of the parallel resonant circuit shown.

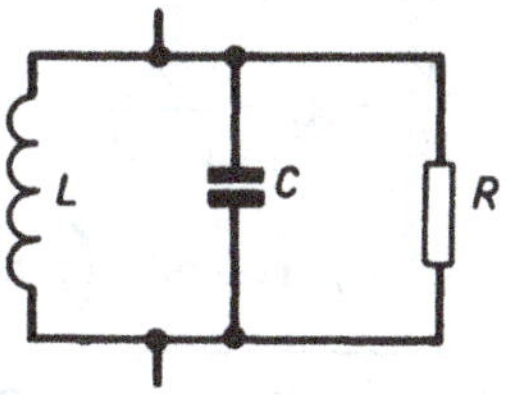

Then $$\frac{1}{Z} = \frac{1}{j\omega L} + \frac{1}{R} + j\omega C.$$

Let $$\omega_0^2 LC = 1 \text{ and } Q = R/\omega_0 L.$$

$\therefore$ $$\frac{1}{Z} = \frac{R(1-\omega^2/\omega_0^2) + j\omega R/\omega_0 Q}{Rj\omega R/\omega_0 Q}$$

$\therefore$ $$Z = R/[1 + jQ(\omega/\omega_0 - \omega_0/\omega)].$$

When ω is near to ω_0 let $\omega = \omega_0 + \Delta\omega$.

Then $$Z = R/[1 + 2jQ\Delta\omega/\omega_0].$$

For the anode load of the valve the voltage across L is

$$v_L = -\mu Z v_g/(Z + r_a).$$

$\therefore$ the voltage across L_2 is $\dfrac{v_L}{j\omega L} \,.\, j\omega M = v_L M/L = v_0$.

$\therefore$ $$v_0 = -\mu Z v_g M/L(Z + r_a)$$
$$= -50 M v_g \Bigg/ \left[L\left\{1 + \frac{30\,000}{15\,000}\left(1 + 2j \,.\, 45 \,.\, \frac{\Delta\omega}{\omega_0}\right)\right\}\right].$$

Now $\dfrac{\Delta\omega}{\omega} = \dfrac{500}{20\,000}$, $v_g = 1$ V, $M = 1$ mH,

* See, for example, J. D. Ryder, *Electronic Fundamentals and Applications*, Pitman, 3rd Edition, 1964, Chapter 12.

$L = R/\omega_0 Q = 15\,000/(2\pi \times 20\,000 \times 45)$.

$\therefore$ $|v_0| = 3.485$ V.

225. Referring to the diagram:

$$V_o = AV_g \quad . \quad . \quad . \quad . \quad . \quad (1)$$

and $$V_g = V_i + \beta V_o \quad . \quad . \quad . \quad . \quad . \quad (2)$$

$\therefore$ $$\frac{V_o}{V_i} = A_f = \frac{A}{1 - \beta A} \quad . \quad . \quad . \quad . \quad . \quad (3)$$

In this case, gain with feedback $A_f = 20 \Big/ \left(1 + \frac{1}{10} . 20\right) = 6.67.$

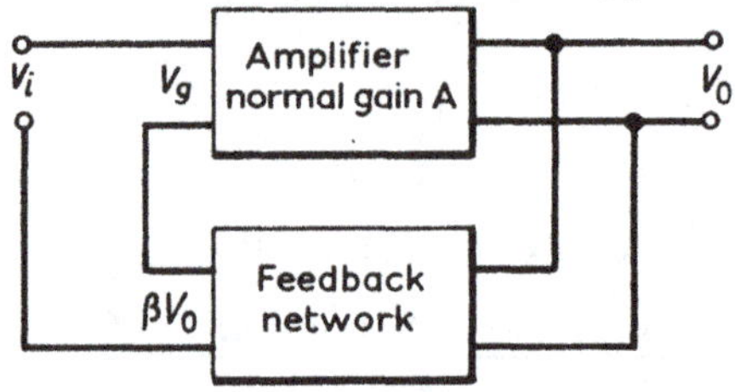

226. Original input voltage = 60/120 = 0.5 V

" distortion " = 10 × 60/100 = 6 V.

The distortion voltage has to be reduced 10 times, therefore:

$1 - \beta \times 120 = 10$, i.e. $\beta = -0.075$ where β is the feedback factor.

The gain will also be reduced by a factor of 10. $A_f = 120/10 = 12$. The added distortionless gain needed ahead of the feedback amplifier is 120/12 = 10, and this amplifier must supply a signal voltage of 60/12 = 5 V.

227. With feedback and normal supply voltage the gain

$$A_{f_1} = 24\,000(1 + 24\,000/1000) = 960.$$

With feedback and a 25 per cent reduction of supply voltage from its normal value the gain $A_{f_2} = 16\,000(1 + 16\,000/1000) = 941$.

228. The gain of each stage $\simeq -g_m R_l \left\{\dfrac{R_g}{R_g + 1/j\omega C}\right\}$

$$\simeq \frac{-j\omega C R_g g_m R_l}{1 + j\omega C R_g}$$

$$\therefore \qquad \text{loop gain of amplifier} = \beta \left\{\frac{-j\omega C R_g g_m R_l}{1 + j\omega C R_g}\right\}^3$$

$$= j\beta \left\{\frac{\omega C R_g g_m R_l}{1 + j\omega C R_g}\right\}^3$$

According to Nyquist's criterion, instability will occur if the loop gain > 1 when there is no phase-shift around the loop, i.e. when $\tan(\omega C R_g) = 30°$ or when $\omega C R_g = 1/\sqrt{3}$.

Under this condition the loop gain is $\beta(g_m R_l)^3/8$. Thus, for stability, $\beta(g_m R_l)^3/8 \ngtr 1$

i.e. $$\underline{\beta \ngtr 8/(g_m R_l)^3}$$

229. The cathode follower has been analysed by many authors.* The output impedance is nearly equal to $1/g_m$. In this case the output impedance $= 10^3/4 = \underline{250\ \Omega}$.

230. The solution to this problem can be found elsewhere.†

231. (*a*) For the solution to this problem see the book by Seely.‡

(*b*) For the solution to this and a similar problem see the book by Rideout.§

232. The input resistance of a common-base amplifier is given by||:

$$R_i = r_e + r_b - r_b(r_b + r_m)/(r_b + r_c + R_l)$$

$$= r_{11} - r_{12}r_{21}/(r_{22} + R_l),$$

* E.g. see S. Seely, *Electron-tube Circuits*, McGraw-Hill, 2nd Edition, 1958, Chapter 5; or A. T. Starr, *Telecommunications*, Pitman, 1954, pp. 232 and 233.

† See S. Seely, *Electron-tube Circuits*, McGraw-Hill, 2nd Edition, 1958, pp. 176–8.

‡ S. Seely, *Electron-tube Circuits*, McGraw-Hill, 2nd Edition, 1958, pp. 164–6.

§ V. C. Rideout, *Active Networks*, Constable, 1954, pp. 175–8.

|| See, for example, S. Seely, *Electronic Engineering*, McGraw-Hill, 1956, Chapter 16; L. M. Krugman, *Fundamentals of Transistors*, Rider and Chapman & Hall, 2nd Edition, 1959; J. D. Ryder, *Engineering Electronics*, McGraw-Hill, 1957, Chapter 12; R. B. Hurley, *Junction Transistor Electronics*, Wiley, 1958.

where $r_b, r_c, r_e, r_m, r_{11}, r_{12}, r_{21}$ and r_{22} are the usual transistor parameters and R_l is the load resistance.

In this case, $R_i = \{550 - 500 \times 1.9 \times 10^6/(2 \times 10^6 + R_l)\}\ \Omega$. Thus, R_i varies from 75 Ω to 550 Ω as R_l changes from 0 to ∞.

The output resistance of the arrangement is given by*:

$$R_0 = r_c + r_b - r_b(r_m + r_b)/(r_b + r_e + R_g)$$
$$= r_{22} - r_{12}r_{21}/(R_g + r_{11}),$$

where R_g is the resistance of the source (zero in this case).

Thus,

$$R_0 = (2 \times 10^6 - 500 \times 1.9 \times 10^6/550)\ \Omega = 2.72 \times 10^5\ \Omega$$

The maximum possible voltage gain*

$$= r_{21}/r_{11} = 1.9 \times 10^6/550 = 3454.$$

233. The solution to this problem can be found elsewhere.†

234. The solution to this problem can be found elsewhere.†

235.

$$r_e = r_{11} - r_{12} = 20\ \Omega$$
$$r_b = r_{12} = 800\ \Omega$$
$$r_c = r_{22} - r_{12} \simeq 2\ \text{M}\Omega$$
$$r_m = r_{21} - r_{12} \simeq 1.98\ \text{M}\Omega$$

Voltage gain (A_v)

$$= \frac{R_l}{r_b + \{(r_b + r_e)(r_c + R_l)/(r_e - r_m)\}}$$

* See, for example, S. Seely, *Electronic Engineering*, McGraw-Hill, 1956, Chapter 16; L. M. Krugman, *Fundamentals of Transistors*, Rider and Chapman & Hall, 2nd Edition, 1959; J. D. Ryder, *Engineering Electronics*, McGraw-Hill, 1957, Chapter 12; R. B. Hurley, *Junction Transistor Electronics*, Wiley, 1958.

† See, for example, S. Seely, *Electronic Engineering*, McGraw-Hill, 1956, Chapter 16; L. M. Krugman, *Fundamentals of Transistors*, Rider and Chapter & Hall, 2nd Edition, 1958; J. D. Ryder, *Engineering Electronics*, McGraw-Hill, 1957, Chapter 12; R. B. Hurley, *Junction Transistor Electronics*, Wiley, 1958; F. A. Benson and D. Harrison, *Electric-Circuit Theory*, Arnold, 3rd Edition, 1975, Chapter 15.

$$\simeq \frac{430}{800 - \{(820)(2 + 10^6 + 430)/(1.98 \times 10^6 - 20)\}}$$

$$\simeq \underline{-15.2.}$$

Current gain (A_i)

$$= \frac{1}{1 + (r_c + R_l)/(r_e - r_m)}$$

$$\simeq \frac{1}{1 - (2 \times 10^6 + 430)/(1.98 \times 10^6 - 20)}$$

$$\simeq \underline{99}$$

Input resistance (R_i)

$$= r_b + \frac{r_e(r_c + R_l)}{(r_c + r_e - r_m + R_l)}$$

$$\simeq 800 + \frac{20(2 \times 10^6 + 430)}{(2 \times 10^6 + 20 - 1.98 \times 10^6 + 430)}$$

$$\simeq \underline{2755\ \Omega}$$

236. The solution to the first part of the Question can be found elsewhere.*

$$\text{Current gain } A_{ie} = \frac{-h_{fe}}{1 + h_{oe}R_l} = \frac{+11.5}{1 + 12.5 \times 10^{-6} \times 16\,000} = \underline{9.6}$$

$$\text{Voltage gain } A_{ve} = \frac{-h_{fe}R_l}{h_{ie}(1 + h_{oe}R_l - h_{re}h_{fe}R_l)}$$

$$= \frac{11.5 \times 16\,000}{500\,(1 + 12.5 \times 10^{-6} \times 16\,000 + 2.5 \times 10^{-4} \times 11.5 \times 16\,000)}$$

$$= \underline{285.}$$

$$\text{Input resistance } R_i = h_{ie} - \frac{h_{re}h_{fe}R_l}{1 + h_{oe}R_l} = \underline{538\ \Omega}$$

Output resistance R_{oe} is found to be

* See, for example, F. A. Benson and D. Harrison, *Electric Circuit Theory*, Arnold, 3rd Edition, 1975, pp. 366–367.

$$\frac{R_g + h_{ie}}{(R_g + h_{ie})h_{oe} - h_{re}h_{fe}}$$

where $R_g = 460\ \Omega$

$\therefore$ $$\underline{R_{oe} = 64.5\ \text{k}\Omega}$$

237. (*a*) *Low frequencies*

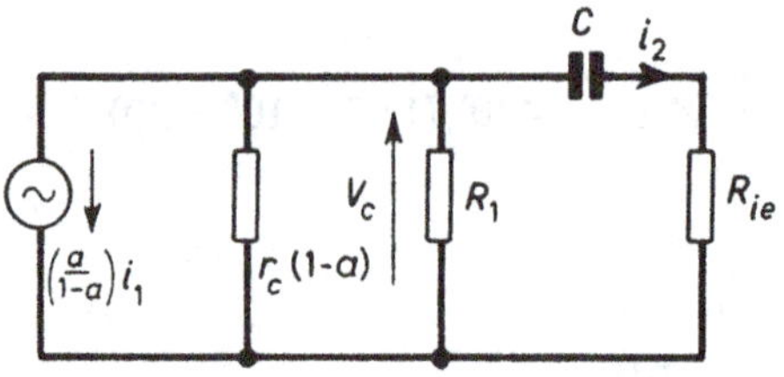

First neglect C to calculate the mid-frequency gain.

Current summation gives:

$$\left(\frac{a}{1-a}\right)i_1 = -V_c\left[\frac{1}{r_c(1-a)} + \frac{1}{R_1} + \frac{1}{R_{ie}}\right]$$

But $V_c = i_2 R_{ie}$

$\therefore$ $$\underline{\frac{i_2}{i_1} = \frac{-a\,r_c R_1}{[R_1 + r_c(1-a)]\left[R_{ie} + \dfrac{R_1 r_c(1-a)}{R_1 + r_c(1-a)}\right]} = A_{ii}}$$

For low frequencies include C

Now $$\left(\frac{a}{1-a}\right)i_1 = -V_c\left[\frac{1}{r_c(1-a)} + \frac{1}{R_1} + \frac{1}{R_{ie} - \text{j}/\omega C}\right]$$

and $V_c = i_2(R_{ie} - \text{j}/\omega C)$

$\therefore$ $$\underline{\frac{i_2}{i_1} = \frac{-a\,r_c R_1}{[R_1 + r_c(1-a)]\left[R_{ie} + \dfrac{R_1 r_c(1-a)}{R_1 + r_c(1-a)} - \dfrac{\text{j}}{\omega C}\right]} = A_{il}}$$

$\therefore$ $$\frac{A_{il}}{A_{ii}} = \frac{1}{1 - \dfrac{\text{j}}{\omega C}\left[\dfrac{1}{R_{ie} + \dfrac{R_1 r_c(1-a)}{R_1 + r_c(1-a)}}\right]} = \frac{1}{1 - \text{j}\,f_1/f}$$

where $$f_1 = \frac{1}{2\pi C}\left[\frac{1}{R_{ie} + \dfrac{R_1 r_c(1-a)}{R_1 + r_c(1-a)}}\right] \simeq \frac{1}{2\pi C}\left\{\frac{1}{R_{ie}+R_1}\right\}$$

High frequencies

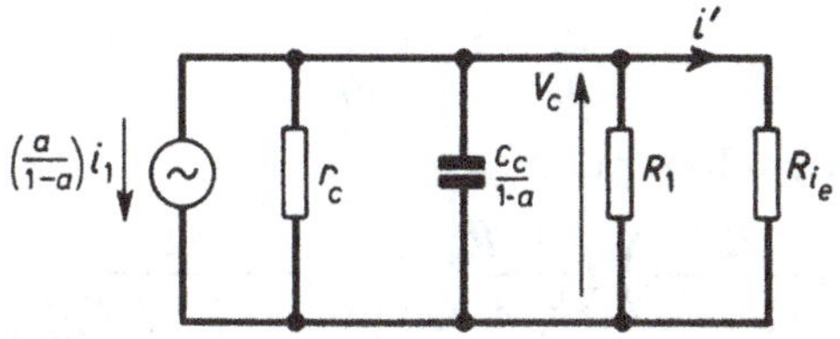

Now $$\left(\frac{a}{1-a}\right)i_1 = -V_c\left[\frac{1}{r_c(1-a)} + \frac{1}{R_1} + \frac{1}{R_{ie}} + \frac{j\omega C_c}{1-a}\right] \text{and } V_c = i' R_{ie}$$

$$\therefore \quad A_{ih} = \frac{i'}{i_1} = \frac{-a\, r_c R_1}{[R_1 + r_c(1-a)]\left[R_{ie} + \dfrac{R_1 r_c(1-a)}{R_1 + r_c(1-a)} + \dfrac{j\omega C_c R_1 r_c R_{ie}}{R_1 + r_c(1-a)}\right]}$$

$$\frac{A_{ih}}{A_{ii}} = \frac{1}{1 + \dfrac{j\omega C_c r_c R_1 R_{ie}}{R_{ie}[R_1 + r_c(1-a)] + R_1 r_c(1-a)}} = \frac{1}{1 + jf/f_2}$$

where $$f_2 = \frac{1}{2\pi C_c}\left[\frac{R_{ie}\{R_1 + r_c(1-a)\} + R_1 r_c(1-a)}{R_1 R_{ie} r_c}\right] \simeq \frac{(1-a)}{2\pi C_c}\left(\frac{1}{R_1} + \frac{1}{R_{ie}}\right)$$

(*b*)

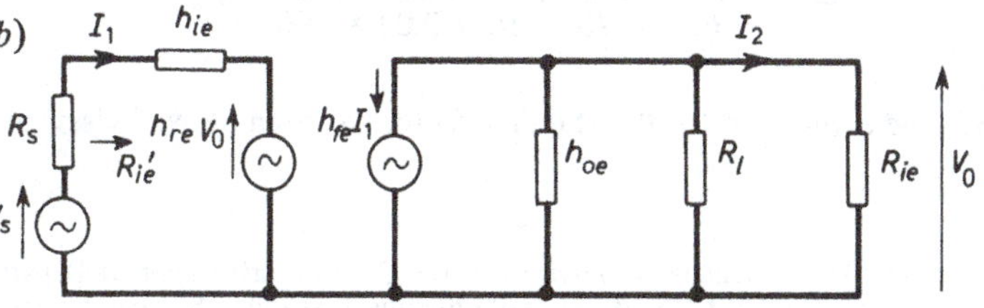

Intermediate-frequency circuit

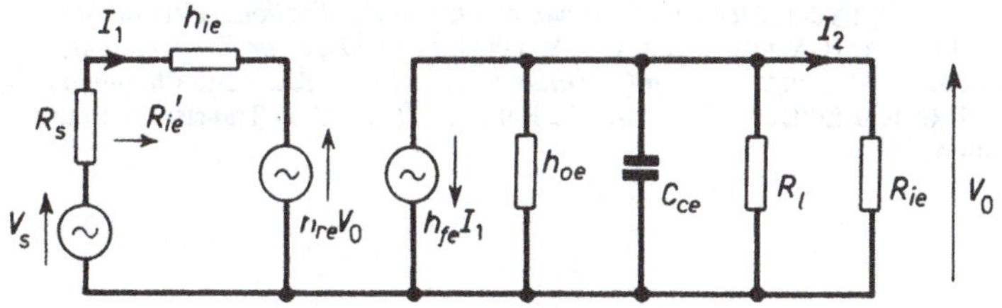

High-frequency circuit

The intermediate-frequency voltage gain $A_{ve_i} = V_0/V_s$

$$= -g_m \left(\frac{R_{ie}'}{R_s + R_{ie}'}\right)\left(\frac{R_p R_{ie}}{R_p + R_{ie}}\right)$$

where
$$g_m = h_{fe}/h_{ie}$$

$$\frac{1}{R_p} = h_{oe} + \frac{1}{R_l}$$

The high-frequency voltage gain A_{veh}

$$= -g_m \left(\frac{R_{ie}'}{R_s + R_{ie}'}\right)\left(\frac{R_p R_{ie}}{R_p + R_{ie}}\right)\left[\frac{1}{1 + j\omega C_{ce}\left(\frac{R_p R_{ie}}{R_p + R_{ie}}\right)}\right]$$

Greatest value of A_{vci} is when $R_s = 0$

Then
$$A_{vei} = -g_m \frac{R_p R_{ie}}{R_p + R_{ie}}$$

Define
$$f_2 = \frac{R_{ie} + R_p}{2\pi C_{ce} R_{ie} R_p}$$

∴
$$A_{vei} \times f_2 = \frac{g_m}{2\pi C_{ce}} = \text{gain-bandwidth product.}$$

238. The expression for the stability factor has been derived elsewhere.*

$$S = \frac{R_b + R_c}{R_c + (1 - \alpha)R_b} = \frac{110}{10 + 0.02 \times 100} = 9.2$$

239. The expression for the stability factor has been derived elsewhere.*

*See, for example, H. Henderson, *Transistors*, B.B.C. Engineering Training Department, Supplement No. 12, 1958. Methods of obtaining bias and stabilizing the operating point are described in many books, e.g., J. D. Ryder, *Engineering Electronics*, McGraw-Hill, 1957. J. D. Ryder, *Electronic Fundamentals and Applications*, Pitman, 3rd Edition, 1964. A. H. Seidman and S. L. Marshall, *Semiconductor Fundamentals*, Wiley, 1963. L. M. Krugman, *Fundamentals of Transistors*, Rider and Chapman and Hall, 2nd Revised Edition, 1958. Mullard Reference Manual on Transistor Circuits, 1st Edition, 1960.

$$S = \frac{R_b + R_e}{R_e + R_b(1-\alpha)} \text{ where } R_b = R_1R_2/(R_1+R_2)$$

Here, $$R_b = (50 \times 20)/70 = 14.3 \text{ k}\Omega$$

so $$S = \frac{14.3 + 2.5}{2.5 + 14.3(0.02)} = \underline{6}.$$

240. Using a constant-voltage source equivalent circuit for the F.E.T. the original circuit can be replaced by the one illustrated here.

Let the loop currents be i_1 and i_2 mA as shown.

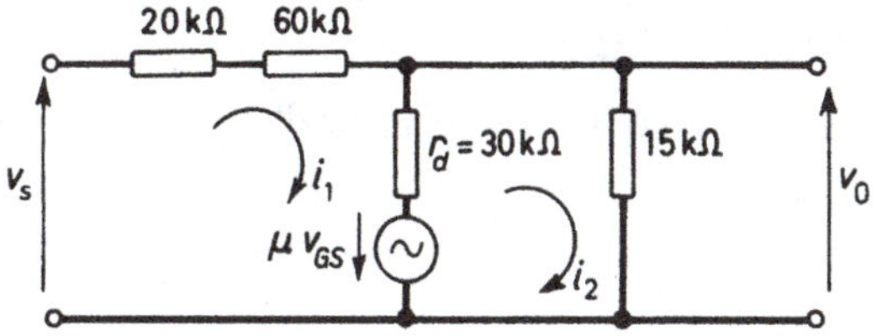

The voltage between G and S

$$v_{GS} = v_s - 20i_1 \quad . \quad . \quad . \quad . \quad (1)$$

Also $$\mu = g_m r_d = 5 \times 10^{-3} \times 30 \times 10^3 = 150$$

For the i_1 loop:

$$v = i_1(20 + 60 + 30) - i_2 30 - \mu v_{GS} \quad . \quad . \quad (2)$$

From equations (1) and (2) and substituting for μ

$$151 v_S = 3110 i_1 - 30 i_2 \quad . \quad . \quad . \quad (3)$$

Now $$v_0 = 15 i_2 \quad . \quad . \quad . \quad . \quad (4)$$

and for the i_1 loop

$$v_s = 80 i_1 + v_0 \quad . \quad . \quad . \quad . \quad (5)$$

From equations (3), (4) and (5)

$$v_0/v_s = \underline{2.7}$$

241. The equivalent circuit is shown below.

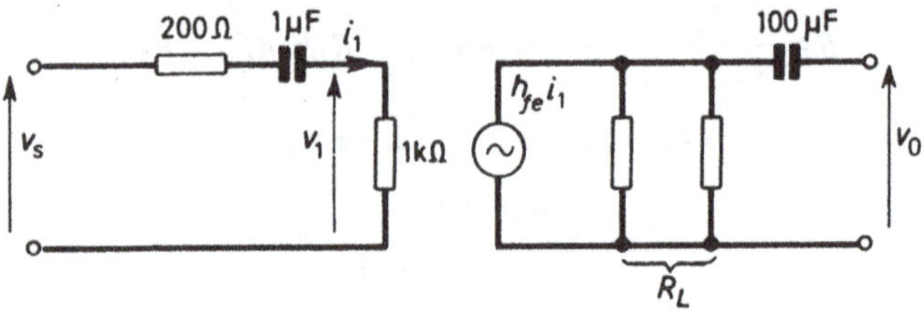

$$\text{Impedance of 1-}\mu\text{F capacitor} = \frac{1}{100\pi \times 10^{-6}}\ \Omega = 3200\ \Omega$$

Impedance of 100-μF capacitor = 32 Ω (negligibly small compared to say R_L)

Also $1/h_{oe} = 10^6/40 = 25$ kΩ.

R_L is made up of the load resistance R_L in parallel with 25 kΩ. i.e. $R_L = \dfrac{25 \times 10}{35} = 7.15$ kΩ.

$$v_1 = h_{ie} i_1$$

$$v_0 = -h_{fe} i_1 R_L$$

$$\therefore \quad \frac{v_0}{v_1} = \frac{-h_{fe} R_L}{h_{ie}} = \frac{-120 \times 7.15}{1} = -860$$

$$\frac{v_1}{v_s} = \frac{1000}{\sqrt{[(1200)^2 + (3200)^2]}} = 0.295$$

Total gain = − 860 × 0.295 = − 254

Output voltage = − 254 × 3 × 10^{-3} = <u>0.76 V</u>

Phase angle between v_1 and v_s is given by $\tan\phi = \dfrac{1200}{3200} = 0.375$ so $\phi = 20.6°$.

Phase from input to output = 180 + 20.6 = <u>200.6°</u>.

242. The solution is similar to that for Problem 236 so will not be repeated here.

243. The solution is similar to that for Problem 236 so will not be repeated here.

244. The solution can be found elsewhere.*

* See, for example, F. A. Benson and D. Harrison, *Electric-Circuit Theory*, Arnold, 3rd Edition, 1975, pp. 367–368.

245. The solution can be found elsewhere.*

246.

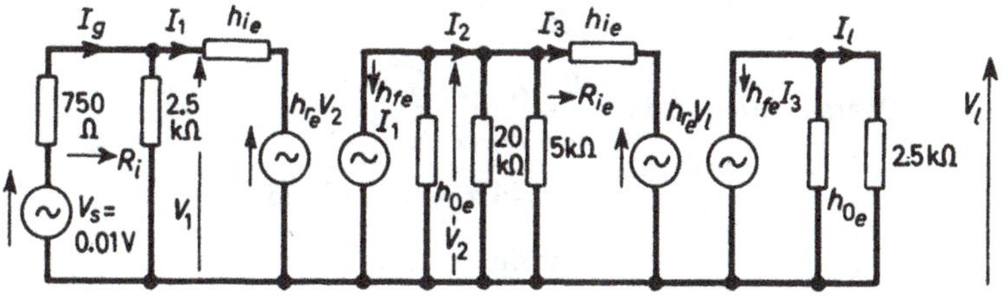

$$A_{i_2} = \frac{I_l}{I_3} = \frac{-h_{fe}}{1 + h_{oe}R_l} = \frac{50}{1 + (45 \times 10^{-6})(2.5 \times 10^3)} = 44.4$$

$$R_{i_2} = h_{ie} - \frac{h_{re}\,h_{fe}R_l}{1 + h_{oe}R_l} = 2400 - \frac{(2.5 \times 10^{-4})(-50)(25 \times 10^3)}{1 + 0.1125}$$

$$= 2680\ \Omega.$$

I_2 is divided between 20 kΩ, 5 kΩ and R_{i_2} in parallel. Let the equivalent resistance of these three be R_e(kΩ)

$$\therefore \qquad \frac{1}{R_e} = \frac{1}{20} + \frac{1}{5} + \frac{1}{2.68} \quad \text{i.e: } R_e = 1.6\ \text{k}\Omega$$

Voltage drop across each parallel branch = $1600\,I_2$ and $I_3 = 1600\,I_2/2680 = 0.597\,I_2$

$$\therefore \qquad I_3/I_2 = 0.597$$

R_e, through which I_2 flows, is the load R_{l_1} on the first stage

$$\therefore \qquad A_{i_1} = \frac{I_2}{I_1} = \frac{-h_{fe}}{1 + h_{oe}R_{l_1}} = \frac{24}{1 + (20 \times 10^{-6})(1.6 \times 10^3)} = 23.2$$

$$R_{i_1} = h_{ie} - \frac{h_{re}h_{fe}R_{l_1}}{1 + h_{oe}R_{l_1}} = 800 - \frac{(8 \times 10^{-4})(-24)(1.6 \times 10^3)}{1 + (20 \times 10^{-6})(1.6 \times 10^3)}$$

$$= 830\ \Omega.$$

The 2.5-kΩ bias resistor is paralleled by R_{i_1} so not all the generator current enters the transistor.

* See P. K. Yu and C. Y. Suen, 'Analysis of the Darlington Configurations', *Electronic Engrg.*, **40**, 38, January, 1968.

$$I_1 = \frac{2500\, I_g}{2500 + 830} \qquad \therefore I_1/I_g = 0.752$$

$$R_i = \frac{2500\, R_{i_1}}{2500 + R_{i_1}} = \underline{623\ \Omega}$$

$$\text{Overall current gain} = \frac{I_l}{I_g} = \frac{I_l}{I_3} \cdot \frac{I_3}{I_2} \cdot \frac{I_2}{I_1} \cdot \frac{I_1}{I_g}$$

$$= 44.4 \times 0.597 \times 23.2 \times 0.752$$

$$= \underline{463}$$

247. The solution to this problem can be found elsewhere.*

248. Maximum power in load $= \left(\frac{30}{\sqrt{2}}\right)^2 \times \frac{1}{8} = \underline{56\ \text{W}}$

Now $P_{o\,max}$ occurs when $I_p = \dfrac{2\,V_{cc}}{\pi R_L}$

and $$P_c = P_{dc} - P_{ac}$$

$\therefore$ $$P_c = \frac{2 I_p}{\pi} V_{cc} - \frac{I_p^2 R_L}{2}$$

$$P_{c\,max} = \frac{4\,V_{cc}^2}{\pi^2 R_L} - \frac{2\,V_{cc}^2}{\pi^2 R_L} = \frac{2\,V_{cc}^2}{\pi^2 R_L}$$

Hence if R_L is reduced to 4Ω and $P_{c\,max} = 30$ W

$$30 = \frac{2\,V_{cc}^2}{\pi^2 \times 4}$$

so $$\underline{V_{cc} = 24.4\ \text{V}}$$

284. The solution to this problem can be found elsewhere.†

* J. D. Ryder, *Electronic Fundamentals and Applications*, Pitman, 4th Edition, 1970, Chapter II.

Readers will probably find the following reference useful: J. K. Skilling, Pulse and Frequency Response, The General Radio Experimenter, **42**, Nos. 11, 12, 3, Nov.–Dec. 1968.

† S. Seely, *Electron-tube Circuits*, McGraw-Hill, 2nd Edition, 1958, Chapter 8.

285. This circuit and modifications of it have been analysed by many authors so the solution can be found elsewhere.*

286–288. For the solution see the books by Seely.†

289–290. The solutions to these problems can be found elsewhere.‡

293. The condition for maintenance of oscillation in a tuned-anode oscillator is $M = (L + r_a RC)/\mu$, where M is the mutual inductance between the two coils.

With the higher anode voltage

$$M = (175 + 220 \times 10^{-6} \times 18 \times 9000)/9\ \mu\text{H} = 23.4\ \mu\text{H}.$$

The coefficiency of coupling

$$= 23.4/\sqrt{(175 \times 60)} = \underline{0.228.}$$

With the lower anode voltage

$$M = (175 + 220 \times 10^{-6} \times 18 \times 11\,000)/9\ \mu\text{H} = 24.3\ \mu\text{H}.$$

The coefficient of coupling

$$= \frac{24.3}{\sqrt{(175 \times 60)}} = \underline{0.237.}$$

294. The frequency of oscillation of a tuned-anode oscillator is given by

$$\frac{1}{2\pi}\sqrt{\left(\frac{r_a + R}{r_a LC}\right)},$$

where R, L and C are the usual constants of the anode coil.

$$\therefore \qquad 25 = \frac{1}{2\pi}\sqrt{\left(\frac{1800 + 11}{1800 \times 0.6 \times C}\right)} \quad \therefore C = 67.9 \times 10^{-6}\ \text{F}.$$

* See for example, S. Seely, *Electronic Circuits*, Holt, Rinehart and Winston, 1968, Chapter 5. J. F. Pierce, *Transistor Circuit Theory and Design*, Merrill Books Inc., 1963, Section 6.8. F. C. Fitchen, *Transistor Circuit Analysis and Design*, Van Nostrand, 1960, p. 213. R. J. Maddock, *Intermediate Electronics*, Book 1, Butterworths, 1969, pp. 158–161.

† S. Seely, *Electron-tube Circuits*, McGraw-Hill, 2nd Edition, 1958, Chapter 8, and S. Seely, *Electronic Circuits*, Holt, Rinehart and Winston, 1968, Chapter 5.

‡ S. Seely, *Electron-tube Circuits*, McGraw-Hill, 2nd Edition, 1958, Chapter 8.

The condition for maintenance of oscillation is given in the previous solution.

$$\therefore \qquad M = (0.6 + 67.9 \times 10^{-6} \times 11 \times 1800)/5 = 0.389 \text{ H}.$$

M must have at least this value for oscillation.

The maximum mutual inductance available is

$$0.32 \times 0.6 = 0.192 \text{ H}$$

∴ the circuit will not oscillate.

From the maintenance condition the value of C corresponding to the mutual inductance 0.192 H is found to be 18.2 μF.

This capacitance gives a frequency of oscillation of 48.3 Hz.

295. The expressions for the frequency of oscillation and the condition for maintenance of oscillation are identical with those for the tuned-anode oscillator given in the previous two solutions.

296. The tuned-collector oscillator has been analysed by many authors so the solution can be found elsewhere.*

297. The condition for maintenance of oscillation in a tuned-grid circuit is:

$$\frac{\mu M}{C}\left\{1 - \frac{M}{\mu L}\right\} = Rr_a$$

where M is the mutual inductance between the grid and anode coils.

$$\therefore \qquad M \text{ must be as large as } \frac{\mu L}{2} - \quad \left[\left(\frac{\mu L}{2}\right)^2 - Rr_a LC\right]$$

$$= \left[\frac{9 \times 180}{2} - \sqrt{\left\{\left(\frac{9 \times 180}{2}\right)^2 - 26 \times 11\,000 \times 180 \times 0.0012\right\}}\right] \mu\text{H}$$

$$= 39 \ \mu\text{H}.$$

But the maximum available M is $0.3\sqrt{(180 \times 50)} = 28.5\ \mu$H.

∴ the circuit will not oscillate.

* See for example, J. R. Abrahams and G. J. Pridham, *Semiconductor Circuits: Worked Examples*, Pergamon, 1966, pp. 163–164.

298. The theorem is well known and will not be proved here. The equivalent circuit of the tuned-anode oscillator is shown.

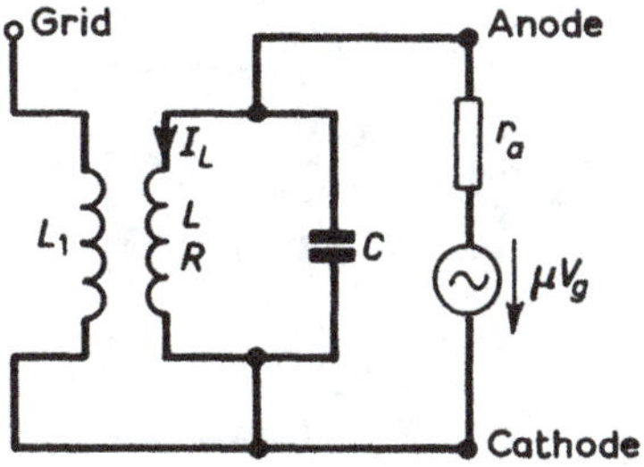

$$Z = \frac{(R + j\omega L)\dfrac{1}{j\omega C}}{R + j\omega L + \dfrac{1}{j\omega C}}$$

$$I_L = V_a/(R + j\omega L).$$

$\therefore$ $$V_g = -j\omega M \,.\, V_a/(R + j\omega L).$$

$\therefore$ $$N = -j\omega M/(R + j\omega L).$$

Substitution of the expressions for Z and N in $Z + r_a/(1 + \mu N) = 0$, equating real and imaginary parts and rearranging gives:

(*a*) the frequency of oscillation $f = \dfrac{\omega}{2\pi} = \dfrac{1}{2\pi}\sqrt{\left(\dfrac{r_a + R}{r_a LC}\right)}$,

and (*b*) the maintenance condition $M = (L + r_a RC)/\mu$.

299. The frequency of oscillation* $= 1/2\pi\sqrt{[(C(L_1 + L_2 + 2M)]} = f$. If $M = 0, f = 1/2\pi\sqrt{(0.1 \times 10^{-6} \times 40 \times 10^{-3})} = 2517$ Hz.

In the second case, $2000 = 1/2\pi\sqrt{[0.1 \times 10^{-6}(40 + 2M)10^{-3}]}$, where M is in mH.

$\therefore$ $$M = 11.67 \text{ mH}.$$

The coefficient of coupling $= 11.67/20 = 0.584$.

* See solution to Question 300.

300. The equivalent circuit is as shown.

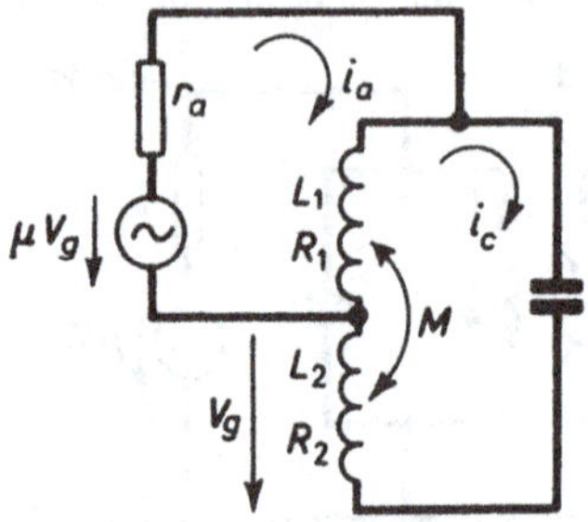

The voltage across the bottom coil is

$$V_g = (R_2 + j\omega L_2)i_c + j\omega M(i_c - i_a) \quad . \quad . \quad (1)$$

Applying Kirchhoff's second law to the i_a and i_c loops:

$$i_a(r_a + R_1 + j\omega L_1) = i_c\{R_1 + j\omega(L_1 + M)\} - \mu V_g \quad . \quad (2)$$

and $$i_a(R_1 + j\omega L_1) = i_c(R_1 + j\omega L_1 + j\omega M + 1/j\omega C) + V_g \quad . \quad (3)$$

Substituting (1) in (2) and (3) and then dividing (2) and (3)

$$\frac{r_a + R_1 + j\omega L_1 - \mu j\omega M}{R_1 + j\omega L_1 + j\omega M} = \frac{R_1 - \mu R_2 + j\omega(L_1 + M) - j\omega(L_2 + M)\mu}{R_1 + R_2 + j\omega L_1 + j\omega L_2 + 2j\omega M + 1/j\omega C} \quad (4)$$

Simplifying, and equating the imaginary terms, gives:

$$\omega^2 = \frac{1 + R_1/r_a}{C\left[(L_1 + L_2 + 2M) + \dfrac{(R_1L_2 + R_2L_1)(1 + \mu)}{r_a}\right]} = (2\pi f)^2$$

where f is the frequency of oscillation.

Equating the real terms gives:

$$(r_a + R_1)(R_1 + R_2) - \omega^3(L_1 - \mu M)(L_1 + L_2 + 2M) + (L_1 - \mu M)/C$$
$$= R_1(R_1 - \mu R_2) - \omega^2(L_1 + M)(L_1 + M - \mu L_2 - \mu M).$$

301. The equivalent circuit is as shown.

$$V_g = i_c/j\omega C_2 \quad . \quad . \quad . \quad . \quad (1)$$

Applying Kirchhoff's second law to the i_a and i_c loops:

$$i_a/j\omega C_1 = i_c(R + j\omega L + 1/j\omega C_1 + 1/j\omega C_2) \quad . \quad . \quad (2)$$

and

$$i_a(r_a + 1/j\omega C_1) = i_c(1/j\omega C_1 - \mu/j\omega C_2) \quad . \quad . \quad (3)$$

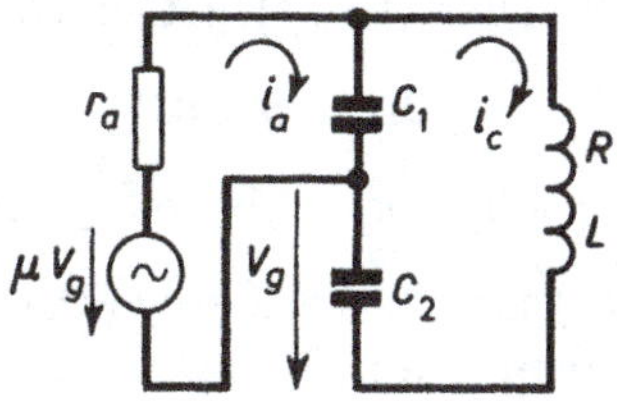

Dividing (2) and (3), simplifying, and equating imaginary and real terms, as in the previous solution gives:

$$\omega^2 = \frac{1}{L}\left\{\frac{1}{C_2} + \frac{1}{C_1}(1 + R/r_a)\right\} = (2\pi f)^2$$

where f is the frequency of oscillation.

$(1 + \mu)/\omega^2 C_1 C_2 = r_a R + L/C_1$ which is the condition for maintenance of oscillations.

302. The solution to this problem can be found elsewhere.*

303. The method of solution is the same as that for Problem 302 so is not given here.

304. The equivalent circuit is shown.

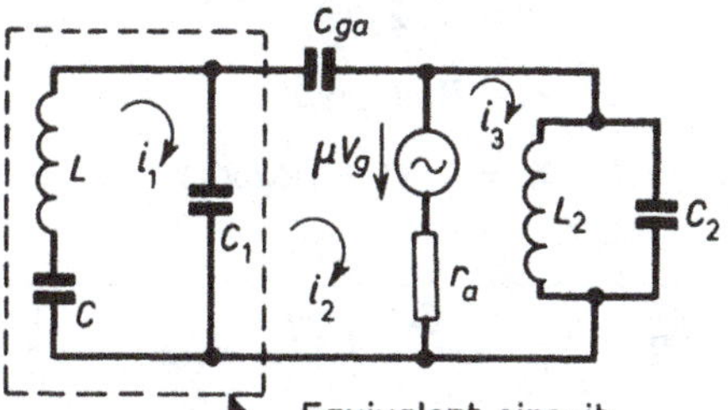

* See J. D. Ryder, *Engineering Electronics*, McGraw-Hill, 1957, Chapter 12.

$$V_g = -i_1(\text{j}\omega L + 1/\text{j}\omega C) \quad . \quad . \quad . \qquad (1)$$

Applying Kirchhoff's second law to the three meshes in turn:

$$i_1(\text{j}\omega L + 1/\text{j}\omega C + 1/\text{j}\omega C_1) = i_2/\text{j}\omega C_1 \quad . \quad . \qquad (2)$$

$$i_1(\text{j}\omega L\mu + \mu/\text{j}\omega C - 1/\text{j}\omega C_1) + i_2(1/\text{j}\omega C_1 + 1/\text{j}\omega C_{ga} + r_a) = i_3 r_a \qquad (3)$$

and

$$i_1(\text{j}\omega L\mu + \mu/\text{j}\omega C)$$
$$+ i_2 r_a - i_3\{r_a + \text{j}\omega L_2/(1 - \omega^2 L_2 C_2)\} = 0 \quad . \quad . \qquad (4)$$

Eliminating i_3 from (3) and (4), dividing by (2), cross-multiplying and equating the imaginary terms gives:

$$\omega^2 = \frac{1}{LC}\left[\frac{1 + (1 + C_1/C_{ga} + C/C_{ga})/\mu}{1 + (1 + C_1/C_{ga})/\mu}\right] = (2\pi f)^2$$

where f is the frequency of oscillation.

305. The feedback network is shown in the diagram.

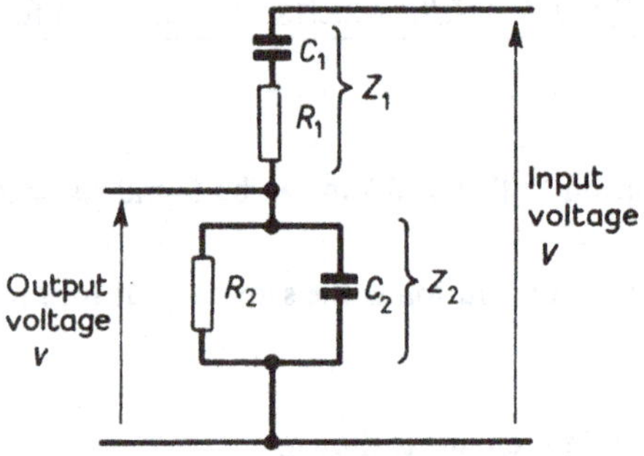

$$v = E\,.\,Z_2/(Z_1 + Z_2)$$

$$Z_1 = R_1 + 1/\text{j}\omega C_1$$

$$Z_2 = R_2/(1 + \text{j}R_2\omega C_2)$$

$$\therefore \qquad v = \frac{R_2 V}{\left(R_2 + R_1 + \dfrac{R_2 C_2}{C_1}\right) + \text{j}\left(R_1 R_2 \omega C_2 - \dfrac{1}{\omega C_1}\right)}.$$

$\therefore$ v will be in phase with V at a frequency given by:

$$\omega^2 = \frac{1}{C_1 C_2 R_1 R_2} \text{ or } f = \frac{1}{2\pi\sqrt{(C_1 C_2 R_1 R_2)}}$$

The system will then oscillate at this frequency if the associated amplifier gain is greater than $1 + R_1/R_2 + C_2/C_1$.

If $C_1 = C_2 = 0.001\ \mu\text{F}$ and $R_1 = R_2 = 120\ \text{k}\Omega$,

$$\underline{f = 1326\ \text{Hz}.}$$

306. The phase-shift network is as shown.

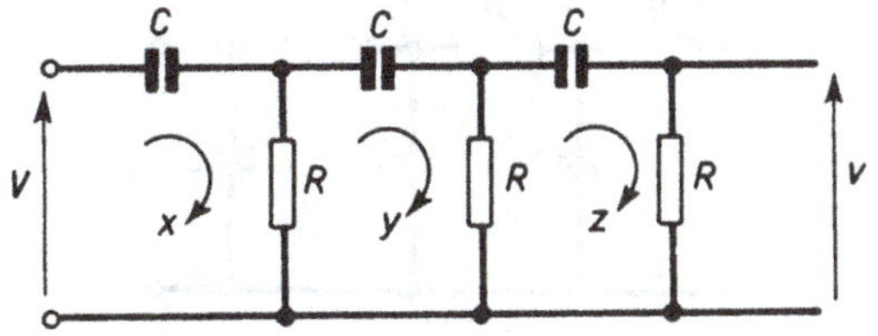

Let currents x, y and z circulate as shown:

Then
$$\left(R + \frac{1}{j\omega C}\right) x - Ry = V \quad . \quad . \quad . \quad (1)$$

$$\left(2R + \frac{1}{j\omega C}\right) y - Rx - Rz = 0 \quad . \quad . \quad . \quad (2)$$

and
$$\left(2R + \frac{1}{j\omega C}\right) z - Ry = 0 \quad . \quad . \quad . \quad (3)$$

From (3)
$$y = \left(2R + \frac{1}{j\omega C}\right) z/R \quad . \quad . \quad . \quad (4)$$

From (1) and (4)
$$x = \frac{V + \left(2R + \frac{1}{j\omega C}\right) z}{R + \frac{1}{j\omega C}} \quad . \quad . \quad . \quad (5)$$

Substituting (4) and (5) in (2) gives:

$$z\left(R^3 + \frac{6R^2}{j\omega C} - \frac{5R}{\omega^2 C^2} - \frac{1}{j\omega^3 C^3}\right) = VR^2 \quad . \quad . \quad (6)$$

There is no j term when $\dfrac{6R^2}{\omega C} = \dfrac{1}{\omega^3 C^3}$, i.e. when $\omega^2 = 1/6R^2C^2$,

i.e. when $f = \dfrac{1}{2\pi RC\sqrt{6}}$.

At this frequency $z(-29R^3) = VR^2 \therefore v = Rz = -V/29$, i.e. the attenuation ratio of the network is 29, and the total phase shift is 180° when $f = 1/2\pi RC\sqrt{6}$.

In this case, $f = 1/2\pi \times 10^5 \times 0.0005 \times 10^{-6}\sqrt{6} = 1300$ Hz.

307. The phase-shift network is as shown.

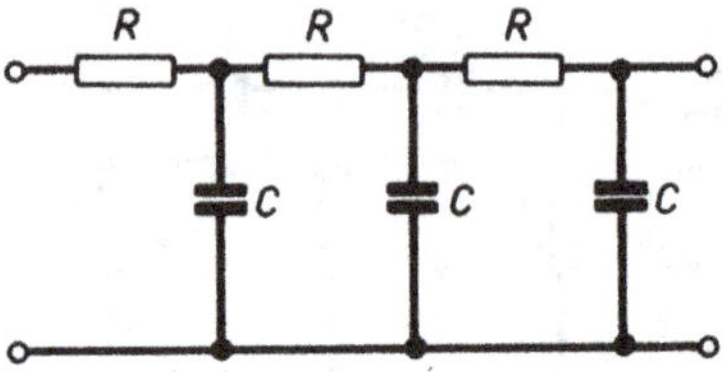

Proceeding with the analysis as in the previous solution it is found that the frequency f at which the network produces 180° phase shift is $\sqrt{6}/2\pi CR$.

In this case $f = \sqrt{6}/2\pi \times 10^5 \times 0.0005 \times 10^{-6} = 7800$ Hz.

The attenuation ratio of the network is again 29.

308. Let currents x, y, z and p circulate as shown.

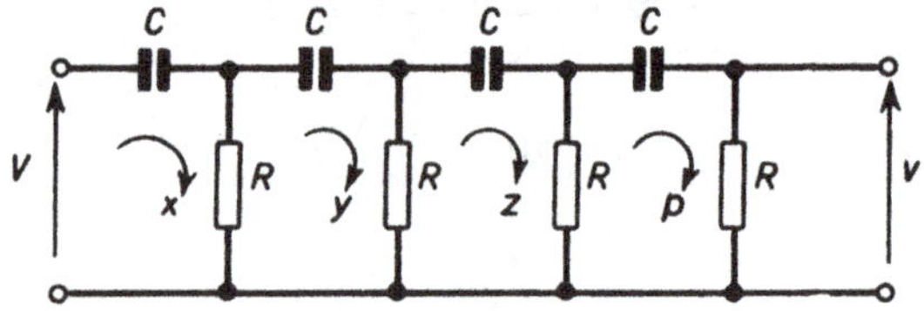

Then
$$\left(R + \frac{1}{j\omega C}\right)x - Ry = V \quad . \quad . \quad . \quad (1)$$

$$\left(2R + \frac{1}{j\omega C}\right)y - Rx - Rz = 0 \quad . \quad . \quad (2)$$

$$\left(2R + \frac{1}{j\omega C}\right)z - Ry - Rp = 0 \quad . \quad . \quad (3)$$

and
$$\left(2R + \frac{1}{j\omega C}\right)p - Rz = 0 \quad . \quad . \quad . \quad (4)$$

From (4)
$$z = \left(2R + \frac{1}{j\omega C}\right)p/R \quad . \quad . \quad . \quad (5)$$

From (3) and (5)

$$y = (3R^2 + 4R/j\omega C - 1/\omega^2C^2)p/R^2 \quad . \quad . \qquad (6)$$

From (2), (5) and (6),

$$x = (4R^3 + 10R^2/j\omega C - 6R/\omega^2C^2 - 1/j\omega^3C^3)p/R^3 \quad . \qquad (7)$$

From (1), (6) and (7),

$$p\left[R^4 + \frac{10R^3}{j\omega C} - \frac{15R^2}{\omega^2C^2} - \frac{7R}{j\omega^3C^3} + \frac{1}{\omega^4C^4}\right] = ER^3 \quad . \quad . \qquad (8)$$

There is no imaginary term when $\omega^2 = 0.7/R^2C^2$.

At this frequency, $pR = v = -V/18.39$,

i.e. the attenuation ratio of the network is 18.39.

In this case

$f = \sqrt{(0.7)}/2\pi RC = \sqrt{(0.7)}/2\pi \times 10^5 \times 0.0005 \times 10^{-6} = 2663$ Hz.

309. When S is closed, the voltage across C rises exponentially as shown until it reaches V_s. C is then suddenly discharged until the voltage across it falls to V_e.

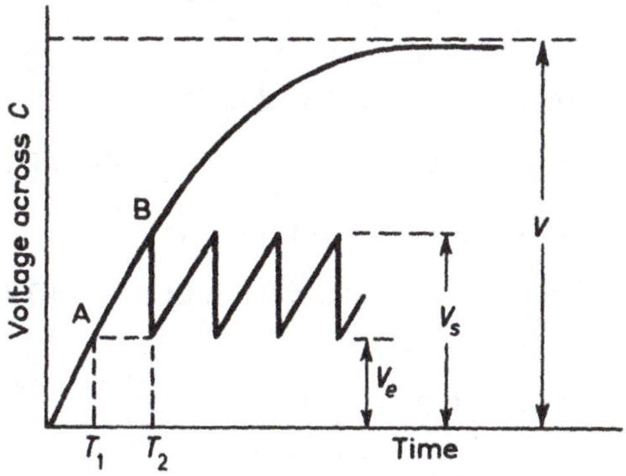

The voltage across $C(V_c)$ at any time t after closing S is given by

$$V_c = V(1 - e^{-t/CR})$$

$\therefore$ at points A and B $\qquad V_e = V(1 - e^{-T_1/CR})$

and $\qquad V_s = V(1 - e^{-T_2/CR})$

∴ period of oscillation

$$T = T_2 - T_1 = CR \ln \{(V - V_e)/(V - V_s)\}.$$

310. Using the solution to Question 309 and the same symbols,

$$T = 0.01 \times 10^{-6} \times 500 \times 10^3 \ln \{230/(250 - V_s)\}.$$

Also $V_s - V_e = 100$ V, so that

$$V_s = 120 \text{ V and } T = 2.83 \times 10^{-3} \text{ s.}$$

Since control ratio is 30, $V_g = (-120/30)$ V $= -4$ V.

311. An expression for the period of oscillation of a multivibrator has been developed by Seely.* For a symmetrical multivibrator the expression can be reduced to:

$$T = 2CR_g \ln \left[\frac{V_1 - V_s}{V_g}\right]$$

where here $R_g = 50 \times 10^3\,\Omega$, $C = 0.005\,\mu$F, $V_s = 250$ V, $V_1 = 110$ V and $V_g = -20$ V.

∴ $$f = 1/T = 1027 \text{ Hz.}$$

312. The frequency of a 300-m signal is 1 MHz.

∴ beat frequency = (1.3 − 1) MHz = 300 kHz.

The frequency of a 400-m signal is 0.75 MHz.

∴ new oscillator frequency = (750 + 300) kHz = 1050 kHz.

313. (*a*) For feedback type of oscillator,

$$\frac{C_{max}}{C_{min}} = \left(\frac{10\,000}{50}\right)^2 = 4 \times 10^4.$$

(*b*) For beat-frequency oscillator,

$$\frac{C_{max}}{C_{min}} = \left(\frac{100 + 10}{100 + 0.05}\right)^2 = 1.2.$$

* See S. Seely, *Electron-tube Circuits*, McGraw-Hill, 2nd Edition, 1958, p. 429.

314.

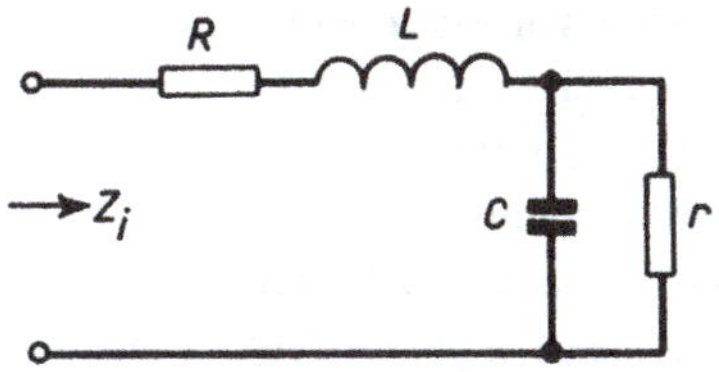

$$Z_i = R + j\omega L + \frac{r/j\omega C}{r + 1/j\omega C}$$

$$= \left(R + \frac{r}{1 + \omega^2 C^2 r^2}\right) + j\omega\left(L - \frac{Cr^2}{1 + \omega^2 C^2 r^2}\right)$$

The real term is zero when

$$R + \frac{r}{1 + \omega^2 C^2 r^2} = 0$$

or
$$\omega = \pm \frac{1}{Cr}\sqrt{\left[-\left(1 + \frac{r}{R}\right)\right]}$$

Since r is negative

$$f_R = \frac{1}{2\pi Cr}\sqrt{\left(\frac{|r|}{R} - 1\right)}$$

The quadrature component is zero when

$$L - \frac{Cr^2}{1 + \omega^2 C^2 r^2} = 0$$

or
$$f_X = \frac{1}{2\pi\sqrt{(LC)}}\sqrt{\left(1 - \frac{L}{Cr^2}\right)}$$

with values given
$$f_R = \underline{504 \text{ MHz}}$$
$$f_X = \underline{186 \text{ MHz}}$$

f_X – impedance is negative resistance and reactance is zero – corresponds to natural frequency of oscillation of circuit.

f_R – at frequencies $< f_R$ input impedance has a negative resistance component. This is the upper frequency limit for which the circuit is capable of oscillating with additional series capacitance.

324. The thermal agitation noise voltage is given by

$$E^2 = 4kT\int_{f_1}^{f_2} R\, df$$

where E is the r.m.s. noise voltage in volts.
T „ „ absolute temperature.
R „ „ resistance in ohms.
f „ „ frequency in hertz.
f_1 and f_2 are the limits of the frequency band.
When the integration is carried out over the band,

$$E = \sqrt{[4kTR(f_2 - f_1)]} \text{ volts.}$$

In this case

$$E = \sqrt{[4 \times 1.38 \times 10^{-23} \times 290 \times 1000(10^7)]} \text{ V} = \underline{12.66\ \mu\text{V.}}$$

The effect of thermal-agitation noise may be expressed either as an e.m.f. in series with the resistor considered noiseless, or as a constant-current generator in parallel with the resistor considered noiseless, as shown.

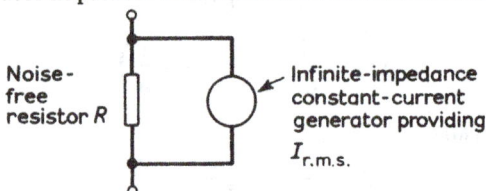

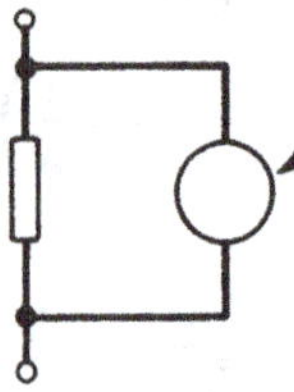

The output current of the generator is obtained by dividing the expression for the r.m.s. noise voltage, given in the previous solution, by R.

$$\therefore \qquad I_{r.m.s.} = \sqrt{\left(\frac{4kT(f_2 - f_1)}{R}\right)} \text{ amperes.}$$

In this case $\underline{I_{r.m.s.} = 12.66 \times 10^{-9} \text{ A.}}$

325. The r.m.s. value of the noise-current components in a bandwidth $(f_2 - f_1)$ hertz is given by

$$(i_{r.m.s.})^2 = 2\,eI(f_2 - f_1) \text{ amperes}^2$$

where I is the average current in amperes.

$$\therefore \quad i_{r.m.s.} = \sqrt{(2 \times 1.602 \times 10^{-19} \times 10^{-3} \times 2 \times 10^4)} = \underline{2.53 \times 10^{-9} \text{ A.}}$$

326. The mean square of the fluctuation components of the current depends only on the magnitude of the emission current I_0 and the frequency bandwidth.

$$I_{\text{r.m.s.}} = \sqrt{\{2\,eI_0(f_2 - f_1)\}} \text{ amperes}$$
$$= \sqrt{(2 \times 1.59 \times 10^{-19} \times 10 \times 10^{-3} \times 20 \times 10^3)} \text{ A}$$
$$= \underline{7.98 \times 10^{-9} \text{ A.}}$$

327. As in the solution to Question 324 the thermal-agitation noise voltage is given by

$$E^2 = 4kT \int_{f_1}^{f_2} R\,df.$$

The impedance of the parallel combination is

$$(R_1 - jR_1^2\omega C)/(1 + R_1^2\omega^2C^2)$$

$\therefore$
$$R = R_1/(1 + \omega^2C^2R_1^2)$$

$\therefore$
$$E^2 = 4kT \int_0^\infty R_1\,df/(1 + 4\pi^2f^2C^2R_1^2) = kT/C$$

$\therefore$
$$E = \sqrt{(kT/C)}.$$

328. The value of the noisy resistor is approximately $2.5/g_m$* ohms = $2.5/2.6 \times 10^{-3} = \underline{961\ \Omega.}$

329. The equivalent resistor is $\dfrac{2.5}{g_m}\left(\dfrac{I_a}{I_a + I_s}\right)\left(1 + \dfrac{8I_s}{g_m}\right)$ *† ohms

$$= \frac{2.5}{9 \times 10^{-3}}\left(\frac{10}{12.5}\right)\left(1 + \frac{8 \times 2.5 \times 10^{-3}}{9 \times 10^{-3}}\right) \text{ ohms} = \underline{716\ \Omega.}$$

330. The equivalent resistance ‡ = $(20R_g^2 + 4 \times 10^4 I_a/g_m^3)I$ ohms where R_g is the shunt resistance of the grid circuit in ohms, and I is the control-grid current in amperes.

* See W. A. Harris, 'Space Charge Limited Current Fluctuations in Vacuum Tube Amplifiers and Input Systems,' *R.C.A. Review*, 5, 505, 1941 and 6, 114, 1941.
K. R. Spangenberg, *Vacuum Tubes*, McGraw-Hill, 1st Edition, 1948, Chapter 12.
L. B. Arguimbau and R. B. Adler, *Vacuum Tube Circuits and Transistors*, Wiley, 1956, Chapter 15.

† D. O. North, 'Fluctuations in SpaceCharge Limited Currents in Multi-collectors,' *R.C.A. Review*, 5, 244, 1940.

‡ See K. R. Spangenberg, *Vacuum Tubes*, McGraw-Hill, 1st Edition, 1948, Chapter 12.

$\therefore$ the resistance

$$= \{20 \times 10^{10} + 4 \times 10^4 \times 10^{-3}/(5 \times 10^{-3})^3\}0.01 \times 10^{-6}\ \Omega$$

$$= \underline{2003.2\ \Omega.}$$

331. Current through R due to V_1 with V_2 short-circuited

$$= \frac{R_2}{R + R_2}\left\{\frac{V_1}{R_1 + RR_2/(R + R_2)}\right\}$$

$$= R_2V_1/(RR_1 + R_2R_1 + RR_2)$$

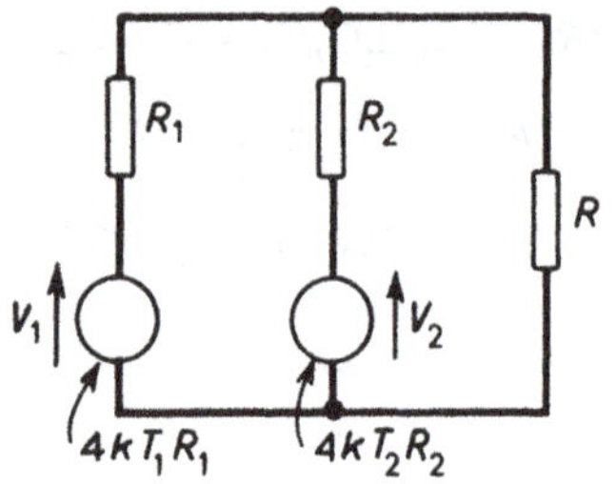

Similarly, current through R due to V_2 with V_1 short-circuited

$$= R_1V_2/(RR_1 + R_2R_1 + RR_2)$$

The Johnson formula for thermal noise generated in a resistor R_3 is:

$$\overline{V_n^2} = 4kTR_3df$$

therefore total mean-square noise current through R per unit bandwidth

$$= \frac{4k(T_1R_1R_2^2 + T_2R_2R_1^2)}{(RR_1 + R_2R_1 + RR_2)^2}$$

$$= \frac{4kR_1R_2(T_1R_2 + T_2R_1)}{(RR_1 + R_2R_1 + RR_2)^2}$$

$$\text{Noise power } P = \frac{4kR_1R_2(T_1R_2 + T_2R_1)R}{\{(R_1 + R_2)R + R_1R_2\}^2}$$

This is a maximum when $\underline{R = R_1R_2/(R_1 + R_2)}$

$$\therefore \qquad P_{\text{max.}} = \frac{4kR_1R_2(T_1R_2 + T_2R_1)R_1R_2}{(R_1 + R_2)\{R_1R_2 + R_1R_2\}^2}$$

$$= \underline{k(T_1R_2 + T_2R_1)/(R_1 + R_2)}$$

332. (*a*) For two resistors R_1 and R_2 in series, total resistance

$$= R_1 + R_2$$

∴ per unit bandwidth

$$4kT_1R_1 + 4kT_2R_2 = T_{\text{eff.}}\,4k(R_1 + R_2)$$

where $T_{\text{eff.}}$ is the effective noise temperature.

$$\therefore \qquad T_{\text{eff.}} = \frac{T_1R_1 + T_2R_2}{(R_1 + R_2)}$$

Using the statement, $T_{\text{eff.}} = \dfrac{T_1R_1}{(R_1+R_2)} + \dfrac{T_2R_2}{(R_1+R_2)} = \dfrac{T_1R_1 + T_2R_2}{(R_1+R_2)}$

(*b*) When the resistors are in parallel

$$\frac{4kT_1R_1R_2^2}{(R_1+R_2)^2} + \frac{4kT_2R_2R_1^2}{(R_1+R_2)^2} = T_{\text{eff.}}\frac{R_1R_2}{(R_1+R_2)}$$

$$\therefore \qquad T_{\text{eff.}} = \frac{T_1R_2 + T_2R_1}{(R_1 + R_2)}$$

Using the statement, $T_{\text{eff.}} = \dfrac{T_1\left(\dfrac{1}{R_1}\right)}{\dfrac{1}{R_2} + \dfrac{1}{R_1}} + \dfrac{T_2\left(\dfrac{1}{R_2}\right)}{\dfrac{1}{R_2} + \dfrac{1}{R_1}}$

$$\therefore \qquad T_{\text{eff.}} = \frac{T_1R_2 + T_2R_1}{(R_1 + R_2)}$$

Thus, the statement has been verified for the two cases.

Using the statement:

$T_{\text{eff.}} = T_1\{1 - \exp(-2\alpha l)\} + T_2 \exp(-2\alpha l)$ (see diagram)

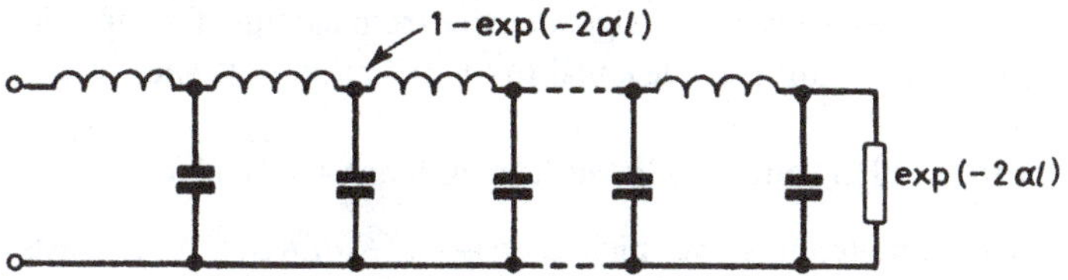

333. Open-circuit voltage due to R_1 with sources of e.m.f. in R_2 and R_3 branches short-circuited

$$= \frac{4kT_1R_1}{\left\{R_1 + \dfrac{R_2R_3}{(R_2+R_3)}\right\}^2}\left\{\frac{R_2R_3}{(R_2+R_3)}\right\}^2$$

$$= \frac{4kT_1R_1R_2^2R_3^2}{(R_1R_2+R_1R_3+R_2R_3)^2}$$

By repeating this calculation for the other two resistors and adding the results the total voltage

$$= \frac{4kR_1R_2R_3(T_1R_2R_3 + T_3R_1R_2 + T_2R_3R_1)}{(R_1R_2+R_1R_3+R_2R_3)^2}$$

For single resistor at temperature T this voltage squared would be

$$\frac{4kTR_1R_2R_3}{(R_1R_2+R_1R_3+R_2R_3)}$$

because for the three resistors in parallel

$$\underline{R = \frac{R_1R_2R_3}{R_1R_2+R_1R_3+R_2R_3}}$$

$$\therefore \qquad \underline{T = \frac{T_1R_2R_3 + T_3R_1R_2 + T_2R_3R_1}{R_1R_2+R_1R_3+R_2R_3}}$$

When the resistors are in series:

$$\underline{R = R_1 + R_2 + R_2}$$

and $4kT_1R_1 + 4kT_2R_2 + 4kT_3R_3 = 4kT(R_1+R_2+R_3)$

$$\therefore \qquad \underline{T = \frac{T_1R_1 + T_2R_2 + T_3R_3}{(R_1+R_2+R_3)}}$$

334. To receive maximum signal power from antenna the input impedance of the circuit is made equal to the radiation resistance of the antenna.

In bandwidth df power radiated from antenna $= d\overline{V_n^2}/4R_l$

$\therefore$ thermal radiation power picked up $= 4kTR_l df/4R_l = \underline{kTdf \text{ watts}}$

If P is the noise power generated in the receiver and G is the power gain

$$2(Gk\,300 + P) = Gk\,900 + P$$

$$\therefore \qquad P = 300\,Gk$$

Noise figure = 10 $\log_{10} X$

$$\left\{\frac{\text{Output noise power from actual receiver at room temperature}}{\text{Output noise power from a perfect receiver that introduced no noise}}\right\}$$

$$\therefore \qquad \text{noise figure} = 10 \log_{10}\left\{\frac{300\,Gk + P}{300\,Gk}\right\} = 10 \log_{10} 2 \simeq \underline{3 \text{ dB.}}$$

335. Let calibration of signal generator read a power of P watts.

Then voltage generated in signal generator = V where $V^2/(4 \times 500) = P$ or $V^2 = 2 \times 10^3 P$.

Signal on grid of triode = $(V \times 1000)/1500 = V/1.5$.

Signal output from receiver $\propto (V/1.5)^2$.

Noise output power produced by a 500-Ω resistor in parallel with a 1000-Ω resistor $\propto \overline{V_n}^2$, i.e. $4kT\dfrac{1000}{3} \cdot \Delta f$ since $1/500 + 1/1000 = 3/1000$.

$$4kT\frac{1000}{3}\Delta f = 4 \times 1.38 \times 10^{-23} \times \frac{1000}{3} \times 300 \times 10^4$$

$$= 5.52 \times 10^{-14}$$

$$\therefore \qquad (V/1.5)^2 = 5.52 \times 10^{-14}$$

$$\therefore \qquad V^2 = 5.52 \times 10^{-14} \times 1.5^2 = 2 \times 10^3 P$$

$$\underline{\text{so } P = 6.2 \times 10^{-17}\,W}$$

336. The mean-square deflection $\bar{\theta}^2$ is given by:

$$\frac{1}{2}C\bar{\theta}^2 = \frac{kT}{2}$$

where C is the specific couple of the suspension

$$\therefore \qquad \bar{\theta}^2 = \frac{kT}{C} = \frac{1.38 \times 10^{-23} \times 300}{10^{-10}} = 41.4 \times 10^{-12}$$

i.e. $\qquad \bar{\theta} = \sqrt{(41.4 \times 10^{-12})} = 6.44 \times 10^{-6}$ radian.

Thus, r.m.s. deflection = 2 × (optical arm length) × $\sqrt{\theta^2}$

$$= 2 \times 1000 \times 10^{-6} \times 6.44 \text{ mm} = \underline{0.0129 \text{ mm.}}$$

Minimum detectable current $= \dfrac{0.0129}{75} \times 1000\ \text{m}\mu\text{A} = \underline{0.172\ \text{m}\mu\text{A.}}$

337.

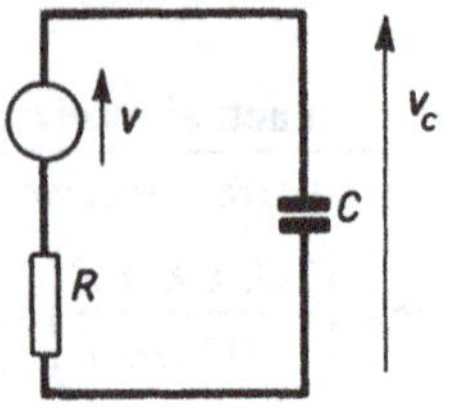

$$V_c = \frac{v}{1 + j\omega CR}$$

where $\omega = 2\pi f$.

$$\text{Mean square output voltage} = 4kTRG^2 \frac{1}{2\pi} \int_{\omega=0}^{1/CR} \frac{d\omega}{1 + \omega^2 C^2 R^2}$$

Put $\omega CR = x$

$$\text{Mean square output voltage} = \frac{4kTRG^2}{2\pi CR} \int_0^1 \frac{dx}{1 + x^2}$$

$$= \frac{kTG^2}{2C}$$

343. $R + j\omega L = 10.4 + j5000 \times 3.67 \times 10^{-3} = 10.4 + j18.35$

$$= 21.08 \,\underline{/60^\circ\,27'}\ \Omega$$

$$G + j\omega C = 0.8 \times 10^{-6} + j5000 \times 0.00835 \times 10^{-6}$$

$$= (0.8 + j41.75)10^{-6} = 41.76 \,\underline{/88^\circ\,55'} \times 10^{-6}\,\text{S}.$$

Characteristic impedance

$$Z_0 = \sqrt{\left(\frac{R + j\omega L}{G + j\omega C}\right)} = 711 \,\underline{/-14^\circ\,14'} = (689 - j175)\ \Omega.$$

Propagation constant $P = \sqrt{[(R + j\omega L)(G + j\omega C)]} = \alpha + j\beta$, where α is the attenuation constant and β is the wavelength or phase constant.

$\therefore$ $P = 0.0297 \,\underline{/74^\circ\,41'} = 0.00785 + j0.0287$

$\therefore$ $\alpha = 0.00785$ neper/km^{-1}

and $\beta = 0.0287$ rad km^{-1}

The wavelength

$$\lambda = 2\pi/\beta = 219 \text{ km}.$$

Velocity of propagation

$$v = f\lambda = \omega/\beta = 5000/0.0287 = 174\,300 \text{ km s}^{-1}.$$

344. Since the line is terminated by Z_0 the input impedance is also Z_0. Input current when connected to generator (i_1)

$$= 2/(600 + 689 - j175)\ \text{A} = \underline{0.001539\ \angle 7^\circ 44'\ \text{A}}.$$

Current at receiving end (i_2)

$$= i_1 e^{-Pl} \text{ where } l \text{ is 300 km} = \underline{0.0001458\ \angle -485^\circ 16'\ \text{A}.}$$

Voltage across load $= i_2 Z_0 = \underline{0.1036\ \angle -499^\circ 30'\ \text{V}}.$

345. In this case

$$R + j\omega L = 10.4 + j18.35 + (7.3 + j5000 \times 0.246)/7.88$$

$$= 11.32 + j174.35 = 174.35\ \angle 86^\circ 18'\ \Omega$$

$$G + j\omega C = 41.76\ \angle 88^\circ 55' \times 10^{-6}\ \text{S}.$$

$$Z_0 = \sqrt{\left(\frac{R + j\omega L}{G + j\omega C}\right)} = \underline{2038\ \angle -1^\circ 19'\ \Omega}$$

$$\underline{P = 0.0036 + j0.0850} = \alpha + j\beta$$

$$\lambda = 2\pi/\beta = \underline{74\ \text{km}}$$

$$v = \omega/\beta = \underline{58\,800\ \text{km s}^{-1}}.$$

346. $Z_0 = 689 - j175 = 711\ \angle -14^\circ 14'\ \Omega$

$$\alpha = 0.00785 \quad \therefore \alpha l = 0.785 \text{ and } e^{\alpha l} = 2.192$$

$$\beta = 0.0287 \quad \therefore \beta l = 2.87 \text{ radians} = 164^\circ 20'.$$

Load impedance $= 500\ \angle 45^\circ = (353.5 + j353.5)\ \Omega = Z_r$.

Assume the initial voltage at the sending end is $1 \angle 0$ V $= E_s$. Then the receiving-end voltage due to this is $E_r = (1/2.192)\ \angle -164^\circ 20'$

$$= 0.456\ \angle -164^\circ 20' = (-0.440 - j0.123)\ \text{V}.$$

Reflected-wave voltage at receiving-end is

$$E_r' = E_r(Z_r - Z_0)/(Z_r + Z_0)$$

$$E_r' = 0.270\ \angle -51^\circ 36' = (0.168 - j0.211)\ \text{V}.$$

Voltage at receiving end due to E_r' is

$$E_r'' = \frac{0.270 \angle -51^\circ 36'}{2.192 \angle 164^\circ 20'} = 0.123 \angle -215^\circ 56' = (-0.10 + j0.072)\text{ V.}$$

Let I_s be the component of the sending-end current due to E_s, then

$$I_s = 1/(711 \angle -14^\circ 14') = 1.407 \times 10^{-3} \angle 14^\circ 14'$$

$$= (1.364 + j0.347)10^{-3}\text{ A.}$$

If I_s'' is the component of the sending-end current due to E_r'', then

$$I_s'' = \frac{0.123 \angle -215^\circ 56'}{711 \angle -14^\circ 14'} \times 1\angle 180^\circ = 0.173 \times 10^{-3} \angle -21^\circ 42'$$

$$= (0.161 - j0.064)10^{-3}\text{ A.}$$

Sending-end voltage is

$$E_s + E_r'' = 1 - 0.10 + j0.072 = (0.9 + j0.072)$$

$$= 0.9\angle 4^\circ 35'\text{ V.}$$

Sending-end current is

$$I_s + I_s'' = (1.364 + j0.347)10^{-3} + (0.161 - j0.064)10^{-3}$$

$$= (1.525 + j0.283)10^{-3} = 1.55\angle 10^\circ 30'\text{ A.}$$

Receiving-end voltage is

$$E_r + E_r' = (-0.440 - j0.123) + (0.168 - j0.211)$$

$$= (-0.272 - j0.334) = 0.431 \angle 230^\circ 52'\text{ V.}$$

Input impedance of line

$$Z_i = \frac{0.9 \angle 4^\circ 35'}{1.55 \angle 10^\circ 30'}\,\Omega = 580 \angle -5^\circ 55'\,\Omega$$

$$= (576 - j60)\,\Omega.$$

Actual sending-end voltage $= \left| \frac{2 \times Z_i}{600 + Z_i} \right| = 0.986$ V.

Since the original assumption that $E_s = 1\angle 0$ gave a value of sending-end voltage of 0.9 V,

$$|E_r + E_r'| = \frac{0.431 \times 0.986}{0.9} = \underline{0.472\text{ V} = \text{receiving-end voltage}}$$

and $$|I_r| = \frac{|E_r + E_r'|}{|Z_r|} = \left(\frac{0.472}{500}\right) \text{ A} = \underline{944 \text{ mA.}}$$

347.

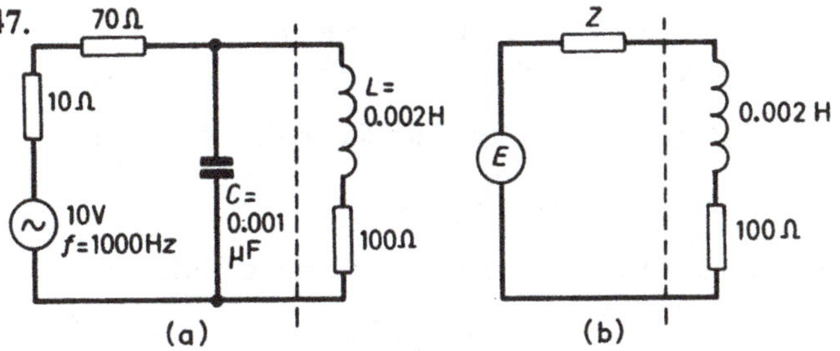

The actual circuit (*a*) can be replaced, using Thévnin's theorem by the one at (*b*).

$$\therefore \qquad E = \left[\frac{10 \times \dfrac{1}{j\omega C}}{\left(10 + 70 + \dfrac{1}{j\omega C}\right)}\right] = \frac{-j1592}{80 - j159.2}$$

$$Z = \frac{1}{j\omega C} \times 80 \Big/ \left(\frac{1}{j\omega C} + 80\right) = -80(j159.2)/(80 - j159.2)$$

$$\therefore \qquad \text{load current} = E/(Z + 100 + j\omega L) = \underline{0.71 \text{ mA.}}$$

348.
$$-\frac{\partial v}{\partial x} = Ri + L\frac{\partial i}{\partial t}$$

$$-\frac{\partial i}{\partial x} = Gv$$

$$-\frac{\partial^2 v}{\partial x^2} = R\frac{\partial i}{\partial x} + L\frac{\partial^2 i}{\partial x \partial t}$$

$$-\frac{\partial^2 i}{\partial x \partial t} = G\frac{\partial v}{\partial t}$$

$$\therefore \qquad -\frac{\partial^2 v}{\partial x^2} = -RGv - LG\frac{\partial v}{\partial t}$$

Assume $V = V_0 \sin(\pi x/l)e^{-\gamma t}$

$$\frac{\partial^2 V}{\partial x^2} = -\frac{\pi^2}{l^2}V; \frac{\partial V}{\partial t} = -\gamma V$$

$\therefore$ $$\pi^2/l^2 = -RG + \gamma LG$$

so $$\underline{\gamma = R/L + \pi^2/LGl^2}$$

349. The line must be half a wavelength long.
In free-space the wavelength corresponding to 20 MHz is 15 m.

$\therefore$ if ϵ is the permittivity of the dielectric $5 = 7.5/\sqrt{\epsilon}$,

i.e. $$\underline{\epsilon = 2.25.}$$

For a short-circuited line of length l the input impedance

$$Z_1 = Z_0 \tanh Pl.$$

For an open-circuited line of length l the input impedance

$$Z_2 = Z_0 \coth Pl$$

$\therefore$ $$Z_1Z_2 = Z_0^2.$$

In this case $$Z_0 = \sqrt{(4.61 \times 1390)} = \underline{80\ \Omega.}$$

Also, $Z_1/Z_2 = \tanh^2 Pl$, $\therefore \tanh Pl = \sqrt{\left(\frac{4.61}{1390}\right)} = 0.05758.$

The attenuation constant $= 0.05758/5$ nepers $\text{m}^{-1} = \underline{0.1\ \text{dB}\,\text{m}^{-1}}$.

Velocity of propagation = velocity of light$/\sqrt{\epsilon} = \underline{2 \times 10^8\ \text{ms}^{-1}}$.

350. If a line with a characteristic impedance Z_0 is terminated by an impedance Z_L the voltage reflection coefficient $\rho e^{j\theta}$ is $(Z_L - Z_0)/(Z_L + Z_0)$.

Let the voltage of the wave travelling towards the load be $V \cos \omega(t + x/v)$ at a distance x from the load. Then the voltage at the load due to this wave is $V \cos \omega t$. Thus, at a distance x from the load, the reflected wave is $\rho V \cos \{\omega(t - x/v) + \theta\}$. The total voltage at distance $x = V_x = V \cos \omega \left(t + \frac{x}{v}\right) + \rho V \cos \{\omega(t - x/v) + \theta\}$. The amplitude of $V_x = |V_x| = V\sqrt{[1 + \rho^2 + 2\rho \cos (\theta - 2\omega x/v)]}$.

Voltage standing-wave ratio (as a quantity > 1)

$$= r = \frac{|V_x|_{max}}{|V_x|_{min}} = \frac{1+\rho}{1-\rho}.$$

Also, position of first voltage maximum is given by $\theta - 2\omega x/v = 0$, i.e. when $\theta = 4\pi x/\lambda$.

In this case

$$r = 2 \qquad \therefore \rho = (r-1)/(r+1) = 1/3$$

$$x = \lambda/12 \quad \therefore \theta = \pi/3.$$

$$(Z_L - Z_o)/(Z_L + Z_o) = \rho e^{j\theta}$$

$$\therefore \qquad Z_L/Z_o = \frac{1+\rho e^{j\theta}}{1-\rho e^{j\theta}} = \frac{1+\dfrac{e^{j\pi/3}}{3}}{1-\dfrac{e^{j\pi/3}}{3}} = \frac{8+j3\sqrt{3}}{7}.$$

$$\therefore \qquad Z_L = 70(8+j3\sqrt{3})/7 = \underline{80 + j52\ \Omega.}$$

351. The solution to this problem can be found elsewhere.*

352. Normalized terminating impedance

$$= (37.5 + j52.5)/75 = 0.5 + j0.7.$$

This point (A) can be located on either the Cartesian or Smith Charts (not shown).

On the Cartesian Chart, at A the values of u and v are:

$$u_0 = 0.325,\ v_0 = 0.11\lambda.$$

At the input B: $u_1 = 0.325$ since there is no loss and

$$v_1 = 0.11\lambda + 0.30\lambda = 0.41\lambda.$$

B corresponds to $z = 0.42 - j0.55$.

Hence, input impedance $= 75(0.42 - j0.55) = \underline{(31.5 - j41.2)\ \Omega}$.

On the Smith Chart the value of u need not be found since the u circles are all centred at the origin of the chart. Hence, movement of point A on the circle centred at the origin through a distance 0.3λ towards the generator locates point B. Again B corresponds to $z = 0.42 - j0.55$ and so the input impedance is $\underline{(31.5 - j41.2)\ \Omega}$.

The Cartesian diagram will now be used to find the input impedance when the loss in the line is 1.15 dB.

* See W. Jackson, *High Frequency Transmission Lines*, Methuen, 3rd Edition, 1958, Chapter 6.

$$1.15 \text{ dB} = 1.15/8.686 = 0.132 \text{ neper}.$$

Hence, input impedance is located at a point B' for which $v_1' = v_0 + 0.30\lambda = 0.41\lambda$ and $u_1' = u_0 + 0.132 = 0.457$. Point B' gives $z = (0.56 - j0.48)$, i.e. input impedance $= \underline{(42 - j36)\ \Omega}$.

In using the Smith Chart to solve this part of the problem the value of u_0 can be read off the pre-calibrated cursor to be 2.85 dB. Then $u_1' = u_0 + 1.15 \text{ dB} = 4.0$ dB. Point B' is then located at the intersection of the 4 dB circle and the 0.41λ line.*

The voltage standing-wave ratio existing in the line is equal to the intercept of the u circle on the resistive axis, i.e. $\underline{0.315}$.

353. The input impedance (Z_1) of a finite short-circuited line of length l is $Z_0 \tanh Pl$, where $P = \alpha + j\beta$ is the propagation constant.

If $l = n\lambda/4$ where n is an odd integer and λ is the wavelength, $Z_1 = Z_0/\tanh \alpha l$ which is approximately $Z_0/\alpha l$.

Now α is approximately $R/2Z_0$.

$$\therefore \qquad Z_1 = 8Z_0^2/Rn\lambda$$

$$R = 41.6\sqrt{f}[1/a + 1/b]10^{-9}\ \Omega\text{m}^{-1}$$

$$Z_0 = 138 \log_{10}(b/a)\ \Omega$$

$\therefore$ if $n = 1$, in this case, $\underline{Z_1 = 248600\ \Omega}$.

354. The selectivity of a parallel tuned circuit may be expressed in terms of the 'Q' of the coil; and, by analogy, an expression for the 'Q' of a resonant line may be obtained.

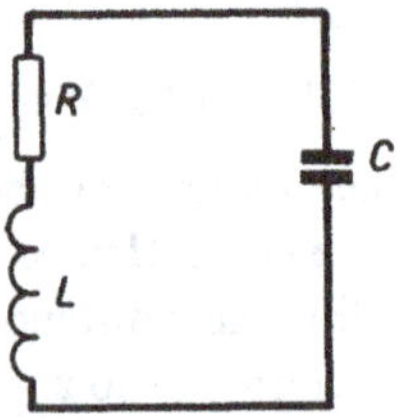

* Further information on transmission-line charts can be found in: W. Jackson and L. G. H. Huxley, 'The Solution of Transmission Line Problems by Use of the Circle Diagram of Impedance,' *J.I.E.E.*, 91, Part III, 105, 1944, and P. H. Smith, 'Transmission Line Calculator,' *Electronics*, 12, 29, January, 1939.

Consider the parallel tuned circuit shown. Its impedance

$$Z = \frac{R + j\omega L}{1 - \omega^2 LC + j\omega CR} \quad . \quad . \quad . \quad (1)$$

At resonance $\omega_R{}^2 LC = 1$ and $Q = \omega_R L/R$ is large compared with 1, hence

$$Z_R \text{ is approximately } L/CR \quad . \quad . \quad . \quad (2)$$

Now the impedance at $\omega_R + \delta\omega$ near resonance is

$$Z = jL(\omega_R + \delta\omega)/[j(\omega_R + \delta\omega)CR - 2\omega_R \delta\omega LC] \quad . \quad (3)$$

$$\therefore \quad Z = Z_R(1 - j2Q\delta\omega/\omega_R) \quad . \quad . \quad . \quad (4)$$

The impedance of a short-circuited $\lambda/4$ line at resonance is $Z_R = Z_0/\alpha l$, as mentioned in the previous solution, and its impedance in general is $Z = Z_0 \tanh{(\alpha + j\beta)l}$, where $\beta = 2\pi f/c = \omega_R/c$ and c is the velocity of light.

When operation is at $\omega_R + \delta\omega$,

$$\beta = (\omega_R + \delta\omega)/c = 2\pi/\lambda + \delta\omega/c$$

$$\therefore \quad \beta l = \pi/2 + l\,.\,\delta\omega/c.$$

$$\therefore \quad Z = Z_0 \tanh{(\alpha l + j\delta\omega\,.\,l/c + j\pi/2)} \quad . \quad . \quad (5)$$

Since αl and $\delta\omega\,.\,l/c$ are small:

$$Z = Z_R[1 - j2(\omega_R/2c\alpha)\delta\omega/\omega_R] \quad . \quad . \quad (6)$$

Now equations (4) and (6) are of the same form so the Q of the resonant line is

$$\omega_R/2c\alpha = \pi f/\alpha c = 2\pi f Z_0/Rc \quad . \quad . \quad . \quad (7)$$

Substituting for Z_0 and R and putting in the values of the constants gives:

$$\underline{Q = 1468.}$$

355. For a short-circuited line $Z_1 = Z_0 \tanh{(\alpha l + j\beta l)}$, where α is the attenuation constant and β is the phase constant.

Expanding and manipulating:

$$Z_1 = Z_0\{\sinh 2\alpha l + j \sin 2\beta l\}/\{\cosh 2\alpha l + \cos 2\beta l\}$$

But, as αl is small, $\cosh 2\alpha l \simeq 1$ and $\sinh 2\,\alpha l \simeq 2\alpha l$

$$\therefore \quad Z_1 = Z_0\{\alpha l/\cos^2 \beta l + j \tan \beta l\}.$$

Now $\alpha \simeq R/2Z_0$ so,

$$\underline{Z_1 = Rc(l/\lambda)/2f\cos^2 2\pi(l/\lambda) + jZ_0 \tan(2\pi l/\lambda).}$$

In the case of ordinary reactances, the change of reactance ΔX produced by a fractional change of frequency $\Delta f/f$ is $\Delta X = X \,.\, \Delta f/f$.

In the case of the above line, $X = Z_0 \tan(2\pi l/\lambda) = Z_0 \tan(2\pi f l/c)$

$$\therefore \qquad dX = 2\pi(l/\lambda)Z_0(df/f)/\cos^2(2\pi l/\lambda).$$

Multiplying both numerator and denominator by $\tan(2\pi l/\lambda)$ and reducing gives

$$dX = 4\pi(l/\lambda)(df/f)X/\sin(4\pi l/\lambda)$$

$$\frac{\text{Selectivity factor of line reactance}}{\text{Selectivity factor of lumped reactance}} = \frac{4\pi l/\lambda}{\sin(4\pi l/\lambda)}.$$

<u>When $l/\lambda = 0.2$ this ratio is 4.28.</u>

356. The attenuation in a coaxial line is given by Jackson* as:

$$\alpha = 9.95 \times 10^{-6}\sqrt{(f\epsilon/\epsilon_0)}\ \ 1/a\sqrt{\sigma_a} + 1/b\sqrt{\sigma_b}\ /\log_{10}(b/a)$$
$$+ 9.10 \times 10^{-8}\sqrt{(\epsilon/\epsilon_0 f)}\tan\delta \text{ dB m}^{-1}$$

where f is the frequency in hertz, ϵ/ϵ_0 is the ratio of the permittivity of the line dielectric to that of air, a and b are the radii of the inner and outer conductors respectively in metres, σ_a and σ_b are the conductivities of the inner and outer conductors in siemens per metre cube and $\tan\delta$ is the power factor of the dielectric.

Here $\sigma_a = 5.62 \times 10^7$ siemens per metre cube, $\sigma_b = 1.54 \times 10^7$ siemens per metre cube, $a = 5.65 \times 10^{-4}$ m, $b = 3.97 \times 10^{-3}$ m, $\epsilon/\epsilon_0 = 1$, and $\tan\delta = 0$.

$$\therefore \qquad \underline{\alpha = 0.331 \text{ dB m}^{-1}.}$$

The characteristic impedance of a coaxial line is also given by Jackson† as:

$$Z_0 = 138\sqrt{(\epsilon_0/\epsilon)}\log_{10}(b/a) \text{ ohms} = \underline{117\ \Omega.}$$

* See W. Jackson, *High Frequency Transmission Lines*, Methuen, 3rd Edition, 1958, p. 50.

†ibid, p. 46.

357. Using the expression quoted in the previous solution and remembering that $\epsilon/\epsilon_0 = 2.25$ and $\tan\delta = 0.0004$ it is found that,

$$\underline{\alpha = 0.977 \text{ dB m}^{-1}} \text{ and } \underline{Z_0 = 78\ \Omega.}$$

358. The formulae for calculating the characteristic impedance Z_0 and the attenuation α are given by Blackband and Brown.*

$$\alpha = 8.686 \tanh^{-1}\sqrt{(g_{min}/g_{max})} \text{ dB.}$$

From the circle (given with the problem),

$$g_{min} = 0.489, g_{max} = 1.202, \underline{\text{so } \alpha = 6.55 \text{ dB.}}$$

$Z_0 = Z_0'\sqrt{(g_{min} \cdot g_{max})}$, where Z_0' is the characteristic impedance of the measuring line.

$$\therefore \qquad Z_0 = 75/\sqrt{(0.489 \times 1.202)} = \underline{97.8\ \Omega.}$$

359. The zero-susceptance points are seen from the circle (given with the problem) to be $g'_{min} = 0.492$ and $g'_{max} = 1.198$.

α and Z_0 are now calculated as in the previous solution.

$$\underline{\alpha = 6.60 \text{ dB.}}$$

$$\underline{Z_0 = 97.7\ \Omega.}$$

360. A quarter-wavelength section of line of characteristic impedance $Z_0 = \sqrt{(150 \times 75)}\ \Omega$, i.e. $\underline{106\ \Omega}$ provides the desired transformation, eliminating a reflected wave on the 75-Ω line.

361. The admittance of the load $= 1/(100 + j100)$ S.
$= (1 - j)/200$ S.

Susceptance of load is thus $(-j/200)$ S, so that of the stub must be $(+j/200)$ S. The conductance of the load is then $(1/200)$ S, i.e. the load resistance $= 200\ \Omega$. To match this load to a line of characteric impedance $500\underline{/0^\circ}\ \Omega$, the quarter-wave line must have an impedance of $\sqrt{(500 \times 200)}\Omega = \underline{316\ \Omega.}$

* W. T. Blackband and D. R. Brown, 'The Two-point Method of Measuring Characteristic Impedance and Attenuation of Cables at 3000 Mc/s,' *J.I.E.E.*, 93, Part IIIA, p. 1383, 1946.

The susceptance of a short-circuited line of characteristic impedance Z_0 and length l is

$$-\mathrm{j}/Z_0 \tan \beta l = -\mathrm{j}/Z_0 \tan (2\pi l/\lambda).$$

Thus, $$-\mathrm{j}/Z_0 \tan (2\pi l/\lambda) = \mathrm{j}/200.$$

$\therefore$ $$\tan (2\pi f l/c) = -200/Z_0 = -200/316 = 0.6328$$

$\therefore$ $$2\pi f l/c = 2.578 \text{ radians.}$$

Now $f = 100 \times 10^6$ Hz, $c = 3 \times 10^8$ ms^{-1}, so the minimum length of line l is $2.578 \times 3 \times 10^8/2\pi \times 10^8 = 1.23$ m.

362. For the explanation asked for see the book by Kraus.*

363. The mesh equations are:

$$V_1 = 60I_1 - 50I_3 \quad . \quad . \quad . \quad . \quad (1)$$

$$90I_3 = 50I_1 + 20I_4 \quad . \quad . \quad . \quad . \quad (2)$$

$$80I_4 = 20I_3 + 10I_2 \quad . \quad . \quad . \quad . \quad (3)$$

$$V_2 = 10(I_4 - I_2) \quad . \quad . \quad . \quad . \quad (4)$$

If I_3 and I_4 are eliminated two equations remain which can be put in the form:

$$V_1 = AV_2 + BI_2 \quad \text{and} \quad I_1 = CV_2 + DI_2$$

where $A = 20.8, B = 179\ \Omega, C = 0.68$ S and $D = 5.9$.

364. Let the network be represented by the T-section shown. If the image impedance Z_i is connected across terminals 3 and 4 the impedance measured between 1 and 2 is also Z_i.

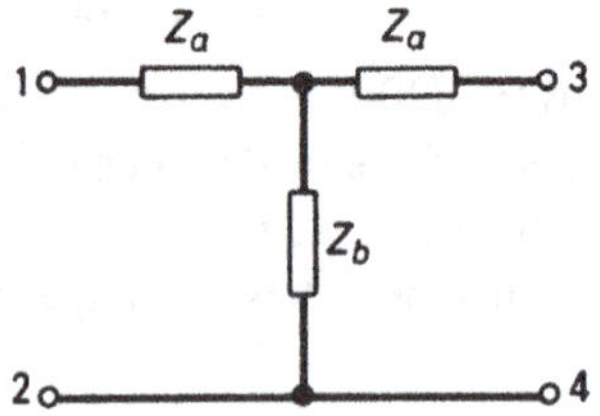

* J. D. Kraus, *Electromagnetics*, McGraw-Hill, 1953, pp. 439–441.

$\therefore \qquad Z_i^2 = Z_a^2(1 + 2Z_b/Z_a) \quad . \quad . \quad . \quad (1)$

If the current flowing into 1, 2 is i_1 and the current flowing out of 3, 4 is i_2, the image transfer constant is given by

$$e^{+\theta} = i_1/i_2 \quad . \quad . \quad . \quad . \quad (2)$$

Voltage across terminals 3 and 4 $= i_2 Z_i$

Voltage across Z_b $= i_2(Z_i + Z_a)$

$\therefore \qquad$ Current in $Z_b = i_2(Z_i + Z_a)/Z_b = i_1 - i_2 \quad . \quad (3)$

From (2) and (3),

$$\frac{Z_i}{Z_b} = e^\theta - 1 - \frac{Z_a}{Z_b} = \frac{Z_i}{Z_a} \cdot \frac{Z_a}{Z_b} \quad . \quad . \quad . \quad (4)$$

$\therefore$ from (1) and (4),

$$Z_i^2 = Z_a^2\{1 + 2(Z_i/Z_a + 1)/(e^\theta - 1)\} \quad . \quad . \quad (5)$$

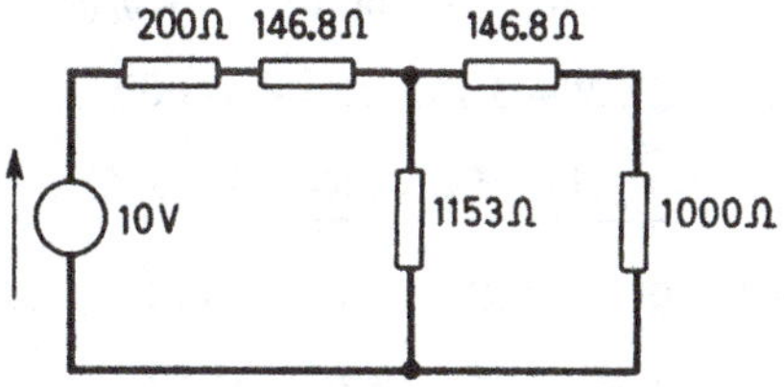

In this case $\theta = 0.5$ and $Z_i = 600\ \Omega \quad \therefore Z_a = 146.8\ \Omega$.

Also $\qquad Z_b = Z_a(Z_i/Z_a + 1)/(e^\theta - 1) = 1153\ \Omega$.

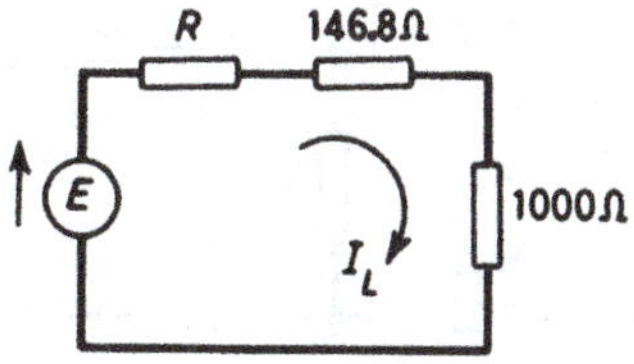

Using Thévenin's Theorem, the network can be replaced by the one shown where

$$E = 10 \times 1153/(1153 + 200 + 146.8) = 7.68\ \text{V}$$

and $\qquad R = 1153 \times 346.8/(1153 + 346.8) = 266\ \Omega$.

$\therefore \qquad I_L = 7.68/(266 + 146.8 + 1000) = \underline{5.44\ \text{mA}}.$

365. The conditions for zero output are:*

$$\omega^2 = 1/R_3C_1C_2(R_1 + R_2) \text{ and } \omega^2 = (C_1 + C_2)/(C_1C_2R_1R_2).$$

In this case $f = \omega/2\pi = \underline{1240 \text{ Hz.}}$

366. (*a*) With the output short-circuited,

$$Z_{sc} = R_1 + R_1R_2/(R_1 + R_2)$$

" " " open-circuited, $Z_{oc} = R_1 + R_2$

$$\therefore \quad Z_i^2 = Z_{oc}Z_{sc} = R_1^2 + 2R_1R_2$$

and $$\tanh^2 \theta = Z_{sc}/Z_{oc} = (R_1^2 + 2R_1R_2)/(R_1 + R_2)^2.$$

It follows that $R_2 = Z_i/\sinh \theta$ and $R_1 = Z_i \tanh(\theta/2)$.

If N is the voltage ratio $= e^{\theta}$,

$$R_1 = Z_i(N - 1)/(N + 1) \text{ and } R_2 = 2NZ_i/(N^2 - 1).$$

When the loss is 10 dB, $N = 3.162$; also $Z_i = 600\ \Omega$

$$\therefore \quad \underline{R_1 = 311.8\ \Omega} \text{ and } \underline{R_2 = 421.6\ \Omega}.$$

When the loss is 20 dB, $N = 10$; also $Z_i = 600\ \Omega$

$$\therefore \quad \underline{R_1 = 491\ \Omega} \text{ and } \underline{R_2 = 121\ \Omega}.$$

(*b*) Let the elements of the attenuator have resistances $(R_1/2)$ and R_2 as illustrated.

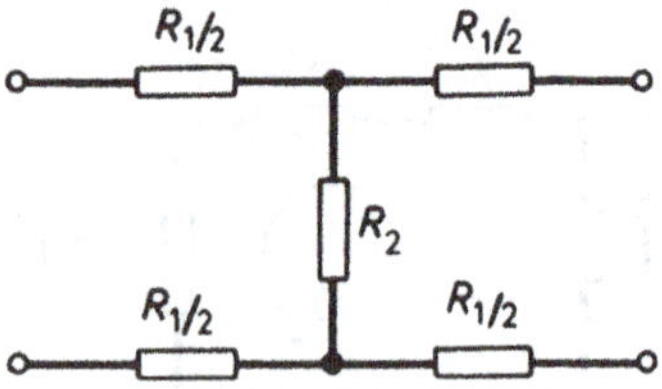

Then, $$600 = \sqrt{[R_1(R_1 + 2R_2)]} \quad . \quad . \quad . \quad (1)$$

and $$\alpha = \cosh^{-1}(1 + R_1/R_2) \quad . \quad . \quad . \quad (2)$$

From (1), $600 = 480(480 + R_2)$

$$\therefore \quad \underline{R_2 = 135\ \Omega}$$

* A. T. Starr, *Electronics*, Pitman, 2nd Edition, 1959, pp. 155–6.

From (2) $\alpha = \cosh^{-1}(1 + 480/135)$ nepers = 19.1 dB.

367. With terminals 3 and 4 open-circuited:

$$Z_a + Z_c = (250 + j100)\ \Omega \qquad (1)$$

With terminals 3 and 4 short-circuited:

$$Z_a + Z_b Z_c/(Z_b + Z_c) = (400 + j300)\ \Omega \qquad (2)$$

With terminals 1 and 2 open-circuited:

$$Z_b + Z_c = 200\ \Omega \qquad (3)$$

From (1), (2) and (3): $Z_a = (150 + j300)\ \Omega$, $Z_b = (100 + j200)\ \Omega$, $Z_c = (100 - j200)\ \Omega$.

368. The solution to this problem has been given elsewhere.*

369. The equation relating the input voltage V_1 and current I_1 with the output voltage V_2 and current I_2 are:

$$V_1 = AV_2 + BI_2 \qquad (1)$$

$$I_1 = CV_2 + DI_2 \qquad (2)$$

For circuit (*a*),

$$V_1 = V_2 + ZI_2 \qquad (3)$$

and

$$I_1 = I_2 \qquad (4)$$

Comparing equations (1) and (3), also (2) and (4),

$$A = 1,\ B = Z \text{ ohms},\ C = 0,\ D = 1.$$

The transfer matrix $[A]$ is there $\begin{bmatrix} 1 & Z \\ 0 & 1 \end{bmatrix}$.

For circuit (*b*),

$$V_1 = V_2 \qquad (5)$$

and

$$I_1 = YV_2 + I_2 \qquad (6)$$

Comparing equations (1) and (5), also (2) and (6),

$$A = 1,\ B = 0,\ C = Y \text{ siemens},\ D = 1.$$

* F. A. Benson and D. Harrison, *Electric Circuit Theory*, Arnold, 2nd Edition, 1963, p. 128.

The transfer matrix $[A]$ is therefore $\underline{\begin{bmatrix} 1 & 0 \\ Y & 1 \end{bmatrix}}$.

The transfer matrix of the network and load in cascade is

$$[A] = \begin{bmatrix} A & B \\ C & D \end{bmatrix} \cdot \begin{bmatrix} 1 & 0 \\ 1/Z_l & 1 \end{bmatrix} = \underline{\begin{bmatrix} A + B/Z_l & B \\ C + D/Z_l & D \end{bmatrix}}.$$

Thus, the input impedance

$$Z_{11} = \frac{A + B/Z_l}{C + D/Z_l} = \frac{AZ_l + B}{CZ_l + D}$$

and the voltage gain

$$= \frac{1}{A + B/Z_l}$$

For the common-base transistor:

$$[Z] = \begin{bmatrix} r_{11} & r_{12} \\ r_{21} & r_{22} \end{bmatrix}$$

so

$$[A] = \begin{bmatrix} \dfrac{r_{11}}{r_{21}} & \dfrac{|Z|}{r_{21}} \\ \dfrac{1}{r_{21}} & \dfrac{r_{22}}{r_{21}} \end{bmatrix}$$

where

$$|Z| = r_{11}r_{22} - r_{12}r_{21}$$

$\therefore$

$$\text{voltage gain} = \frac{1}{r_{11}/r_{21} + |Z|/r_{21}R_l}$$

$$= \underline{\frac{r_{21}R_l}{r_{11}R_l + r_{11}r_{22} - r_{12}r_{21}}}$$

$$\text{The input resistance} = \frac{r_{11}R_l/r_{21} + |Z|/r_{21}}{R_l/r_{21} + r_{22}/r_{21}}$$

$$= \underline{r_{11} - r_{12}r_{21}/(r_{22} + R_l)}$$

370. Circuit (*a*) consists of a series impedance and a shunt admittance in cascade. Therefore, using the results of the previous solution, the transfer matrix $[A]$ is:

$$\begin{bmatrix} 1 & Z \\ 0 & 1 \end{bmatrix} \cdot \begin{bmatrix} 1 & 0 \\ Y & 1 \end{bmatrix} = \underline{\begin{bmatrix} (1 + ZY) & Z \\ Y & 1 \end{bmatrix}}$$

Circuit (*b*) consists of a shunt admittance and a series impedance in cascade. Thus,

$$[A] = \begin{bmatrix} 1 & 0 \\ Y & 1 \end{bmatrix} \cdot \begin{bmatrix} 1 & Z \\ 0 & 1 \end{bmatrix} = \underline{\begin{bmatrix} 1 & Z \\ Y & (1+ZY) \end{bmatrix}}.$$

Circuit (*c*) can be considered as a series impedance, a shunt admittance and a series impedance in cascade. Therefore:

$$[A] = \begin{bmatrix} 1 & Z_1 \\ 0 & 1 \end{bmatrix} \cdot \begin{bmatrix} 1 & 0 \\ 1/Z_{12} & 1 \end{bmatrix} \cdot \begin{bmatrix} 1 & Z_2 \\ 0 & 1 \end{bmatrix}$$

$$= \underline{\begin{bmatrix} (1+Z_1/Z_{12}) & (Z_1+Z_2+Z_1Z_2/Z_{12}) \\ 1/Z_{12} & (1+Z_2/Z_{12}) \end{bmatrix}}.$$

Similarly for circuit (*d*),

$$[A] = \begin{bmatrix} 1 & 0 \\ 1/Z_1 & 1 \end{bmatrix} \cdot \begin{bmatrix} 1 & Z_{12} \\ 0 & 1 \end{bmatrix} \cdot \begin{bmatrix} 1 & 0 \\ 1/Z_2 & 1 \end{bmatrix}$$

$$= \underline{\begin{bmatrix} (1+Z_{12}/Z_2) & Z_{12} \\ \{1/Z_1 + (1+Z_{12}/Z_1)(1/Z_2)\} & (1+Z_{12}/Z_1) \end{bmatrix}}.$$

371. The transfer matrix for the first network excluding the load is:

$$[A] = \begin{bmatrix} 1 & j\omega L \\ 0 & 1 \end{bmatrix} \cdot \begin{bmatrix} 1 & 0 \\ j\omega C & 1 \end{bmatrix} \cdot \begin{bmatrix} 1 & j\omega L \\ 0 & 1 \end{bmatrix} \cdot \begin{bmatrix} 1 & 0 \\ j\omega C & 1 \end{bmatrix}$$

$$= \begin{bmatrix} (1-3\omega^2LC+\omega^4L^2C^2) & (2j\omega L - j\omega^3L^2C) \\ (2j\omega C - j\omega^3LC^2) & (1-\omega^2LC) \end{bmatrix}.$$

The transfer matrix of a network which has general parameters A, B, C and D, and a load Z_l in cascade is:

$$\begin{bmatrix} A+B/Z_l & B \\ C+D/Z_l & D \end{bmatrix}.$$

Thus, $V_2/V_1 = 1/(A+B/Z_l)$.

Here $\quad A = 1-3\omega^2LC+\omega^4L^2C^2,$

$\quad B = 2j\omega L - j\omega^3L^2C,$

and $\quad Z_l = \sqrt{(L/C)} + j\omega L/2.$

$$\therefore \quad V_2/V_1 = \underline{\frac{1}{1-3\omega^2LC+\omega^4L^2C^2 + j\omega L(2-\omega^2LC)/(\sqrt{(L/C)}+j\omega L/2)}}$$

The transfer matrix for the second network excluding the load is:

$$[A] = \begin{bmatrix} (1-\omega^2LC) & (2j\omega L - j\omega^3L^2C) \\ (j\omega C) & (1-\omega^2LC) \end{bmatrix}$$

$$\therefore \qquad V_2/V_1 = \frac{R_l}{(1-\omega^2LC)R_l + (2j\omega L - j\omega^3L^2C)}$$

372. (*a*)

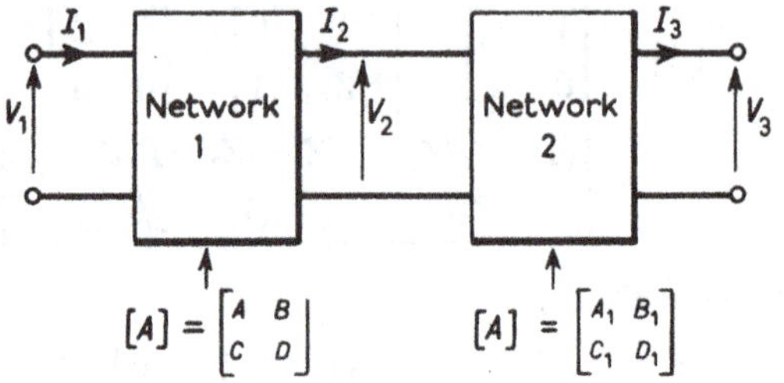

For network 1:

$$V_1 = AV_2 + BI_2$$

$$I_1 = CV_2 + DI_2$$

For network 2:

$$V_2 = A_1V_3 + B_1I_3$$

$$I_2 = C_1V_3 + D_1I_3$$

$$\therefore \qquad V_1 = (AA_1 + BC_1)V_3 + (AB_1 + BD_1)I_2$$

$$I_1 = (CA_1 + DC_1)V_3 + (CB_1 + DD_1)I_3$$

For the combined network, therefore,

$$[A] = \begin{bmatrix} (AA_1 + BC_1) & (AB_1 + BD_1) \\ (CA_1 + DC_1) & (CB_1 + DD_1) \end{bmatrix} = \begin{bmatrix} A & D \\ C & D \end{bmatrix} \cdot \begin{bmatrix} A_1 & B_1 \\ C_1 & D_1 \end{bmatrix}$$

(*b*) When the two networks are connected in order 1, 2 the transfer matrix of the combination is the product of the original transfer matrices, i.e.

$$[A_{1,2}] = [A_1] \cdot [A_2] = \begin{bmatrix} 1.50 & 11 \\ 0.25 & 2.5 \end{bmatrix} \cdot \begin{bmatrix} 1.66 & 4 \\ 1 & 3 \end{bmatrix} = \begin{bmatrix} 13.5 & 39.0 \\ 2.92 & 8.5 \end{bmatrix}.$$

The Y parameters of the networks are as follows:

	Network 1	Network 2
$Y_{11} = D/B$	2.5/11	3/4
$Y_{12} = -\|A\|/B$	−1/11	−1/4
$Y_{21} = 1/B$	1/11	1/4
$Y_{22} = -A/B$	−1.5/11	−1.66/4

The admittance matrix of the networks in parallel is

$$[Y_{1,2}] = [Y_1] + [Y_2]$$

$$= \begin{bmatrix} 2.5/11 & -1/11 \\ 1/11 & -1.5/11 \end{bmatrix} + \begin{bmatrix} 3/4 & -1/4 \\ 1/4 & -1.66/4 \end{bmatrix}$$

$$= \underline{\begin{bmatrix} 43/44 & -15/44 \\ 15/44 & -73/132 \end{bmatrix}}.$$

373. The mesh equations for the circuit are:

$$Z_2(I_1 - i) + Z_1(I_1 - i + I_2') = V_1 \quad . \quad . \quad (1)$$

$$Z_2(i - I_2') - Z_1(I_1 - i + I_2') = V_2 \quad . \quad . \quad (2)$$

$$Z_1 i + Z_2(i - I_2') = Z_1(I_1 - i + I_2') + Z_2(I_1 - i) \quad . \quad (3)$$

From (3), $$i = (I_1 + I_2')/2 \quad . \quad . \quad . \quad . \quad (4)$$

Substituting (4) in (1) and (2) there results:

$$Z_2(I_1 - I_2') + Z_1(I_1 + I_2') = 2V_1 \, . \quad . \quad . \quad (5)$$

$$Z_2(I_1 - I_2') - Z_1(I_1 + I_2') = 2V_2 \, . \quad . \quad . \quad (6)$$

Thus, the $[Z]$ matrix is seen to be

$$\underline{\begin{bmatrix} (Z_1 + Z_2)/2 & (Z_2 - Z_1)/2 \\ (Z_2 - Z_1)/2 & (Z_1 + Z_2)/2 \end{bmatrix}}.$$

Equations (5) and (6) can be re-arranged to give the A, B, C and D parameters of the $[A]$ matrix. Alternatively,

$$A = Z_{11}/Z_{12} = Z_{22}/Z_{12} = D = (Z_1 + Z_2)/(Z_2 - Z_1),$$

$$B = (Z_{11}Z_{22} - Z_{12}^2)/Z_{12} = 2Z_1Z_2/(Z_2 - Z_1),$$

and $C = 1/Z_{12} = 2/(Z_2 - Z_1)$.

$$\therefore \quad [A] = \begin{bmatrix} (Z_1+Z_2)/(Z_2-Z_1) & 2Z_1Z_2/(Z_2-Z_1) \\ 2/(Z_2-Z_1) & (Z_1+Z_2)/(Z_2-Z_1) \end{bmatrix}.$$

374. The transfer matrices are:

For Z_1, $\begin{bmatrix} 1 & Z_1 \\ 0 & 1 \end{bmatrix}$, (see Solution 369)

For Y, $\begin{bmatrix} 1 & 0 \\ Y & 1 \end{bmatrix}$, (see Solution 369)

For Z_2, $\begin{bmatrix} 1 & Z_2 \\ 0 & 1 \end{bmatrix}$, (see Solution 369)

For the transformer, $\begin{bmatrix} n & 0 \\ 0 & 1/n \end{bmatrix}$, (for a transformer $V_1 = nV_2$ and $I_1 = I_2/n$)

$\therefore$ Transfer matrix for whole arrangement is:

$$\begin{bmatrix} 1 & Z_1 \\ 0 & 1 \end{bmatrix} \cdot \begin{bmatrix} 1 & 0 \\ Y & 1 \end{bmatrix} \cdot \begin{bmatrix} n & 0 \\ 0 & 1/n \end{bmatrix} \cdot \begin{bmatrix} 1 & Z_2 \\ 0 & 1 \end{bmatrix}$$

$$= \begin{bmatrix} n(1+Z_1Y) & nZ_2(1+Z_1Y)+Z_1/n \\ nY & nZ_2Y+1/n \end{bmatrix}$$

375. For the π network $[A] = \begin{bmatrix} 3 & 2R \\ 4/R & 3 \end{bmatrix}$

For the lattice network $[A] = \begin{bmatrix} 3 & 4R \\ 2/R & 3 \end{bmatrix}$

For the T network $[A] = \begin{bmatrix} 3/2 & 5R/2 \\ 1/2R & 3/2 \end{bmatrix}$

$\therefore$ for the whole network

$$[A] = \begin{bmatrix} 3 & 2R \\ 4/R & 3 \end{bmatrix} \cdot \begin{bmatrix} 3 & 4R \\ 2/R & 3 \end{bmatrix} \cdot \begin{bmatrix} 3/2 & 5R/2 \\ 1/2R & 3/2 \end{bmatrix}$$

$$= \begin{bmatrix} 57/2 & 119R/2 \\ 79/2R & 165/2 \end{bmatrix}$$

$$\text{Input impedance } Z_{11} = \frac{A + B/Z_l}{C + D/Z_l} = \frac{AZ_l + B}{CZ_l + D}$$

$$= \underline{\frac{57R_l + 119R}{79R_l/R + 165}}$$

$$\frac{V_{\text{out}}}{V_{\text{in}}} = \frac{1}{A + B/Z_l} = \underline{\frac{2R_l}{57R_l + 119R}}$$

376.

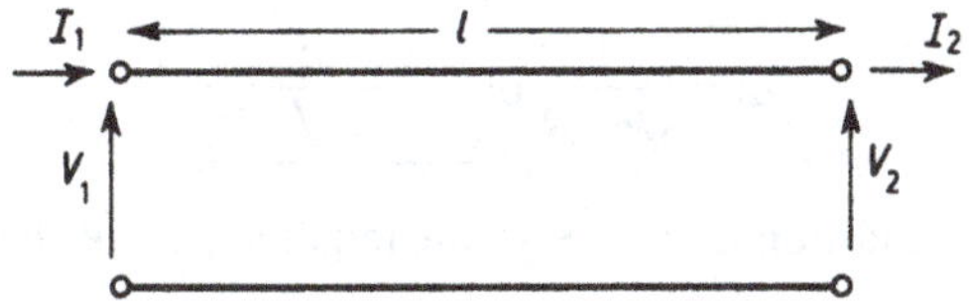

$$V_1 = V_2 \cosh \gamma l + I_2 Z_0 \sinh \gamma l$$

$$I_1 = V_2 Y_0 \sinh \gamma l + I_2 \cosh \gamma l$$

where $\gamma l = \theta$ and $Y_0 = 1/Z_0$.

$$\therefore \quad [A] = \begin{bmatrix} \cosh \theta & Z_0 \sinh \theta \\ Y_0 \sinh \theta & \cosh \theta \end{bmatrix}$$

For the T network

$$[A] = \begin{bmatrix} 1 & Z_1 \\ 0 & 1 \end{bmatrix} \cdot \begin{bmatrix} 1 & 0 \\ 1/Z_2 & 1 \end{bmatrix} \cdot \begin{bmatrix} 1 & Z_1 \\ 0 & 1 \end{bmatrix}$$

$$= \begin{bmatrix} (1 + Z_1/Z_2) & \dfrac{Z_1(Z_1 + 2Z_2)}{Z_2} \\ 1/Z_2 & (1 + Z_1/Z_2) \end{bmatrix}$$

Equating the two $[A]$ matrices it is found that

$$\underline{Z_1 = Z_0(\cosh \theta - 1)/\sinh \theta}$$

and $\underline{Z_2 = Z_0/\sinh \theta}$

377.

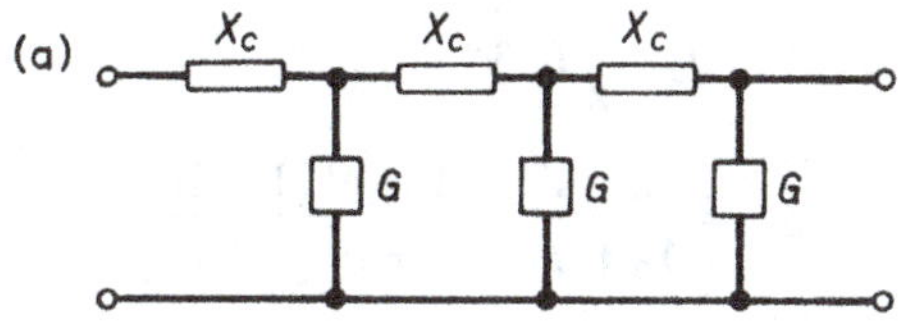

$X_c = 1/\text{j}\omega C$

$G = 1/R$

$$[A] = \begin{bmatrix} 1 & X_c \\ 0 & 1 \end{bmatrix}\begin{bmatrix} 1 & 0 \\ G & 1 \end{bmatrix}\begin{bmatrix} 1 & X_c \\ 0 & 1 \end{bmatrix}\begin{bmatrix} 1 & 0 \\ G & 1 \end{bmatrix}\begin{bmatrix} 1 & X_c \\ 0 & 1 \end{bmatrix}\begin{bmatrix} 1 & 0 \\ G & 1 \end{bmatrix}$$

The A element only is required

this is $$1 + 6X_cG + 5X_c^2G^2 + X_c^3G^3$$

or $$1 - \frac{5}{\omega^2C^2R^2} + \frac{6}{j\omega CR} - \frac{1}{j\omega^3C^3R^3}$$

There is no j term when $6\omega^2C^2R^2 = 1$

i.e. $$\omega = \frac{1}{\sqrt{6}CR} \text{ or } f = \frac{1}{2\pi\sqrt{6}CR}$$

Under this condition $A = -29$ so the required gain of the amplifier is ≥ 29.

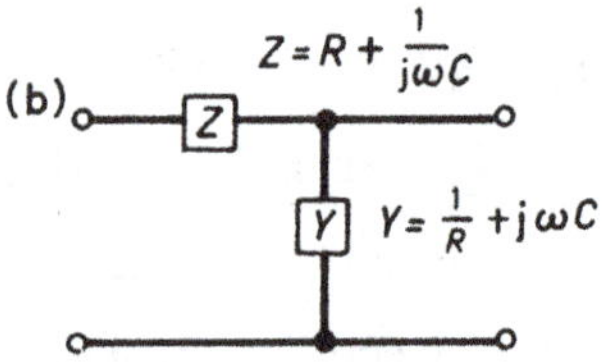

$$[A] = \begin{bmatrix} 1 & Z \\ 0 & 1 \end{bmatrix} \cdot \begin{bmatrix} 1 & 0 \\ Y & 1 \end{bmatrix} = \begin{bmatrix} (1+ZY) & Z \\ Y & 1 \end{bmatrix}$$

$$\text{Transfer function} = 1/(1+ZY)$$

$$= \frac{1}{3 + j\left(\omega CR - \dfrac{1}{\omega CR}\right)}$$

The j term is zero when $\omega = 1/RC$ i.e. $f = 1/2\pi RC$.

Gain of amplifier required is then 3.

378. $$\left.\begin{aligned} V_2 &= n\,V_1 \\ I_2 &= \frac{1}{n} I_1 \end{aligned}\right\} \therefore Y_2 = \frac{1}{n^2} Y_1$$

(i) $$S_{11} = \frac{Y_0 - Y_L}{Y_0 + Y_L} = \frac{1 - n^2[1 + jB]}{1 + n^2[1 + jB]}$$

$$= \frac{1 - n^2 - jn^2 B}{1 + n^2 + jn^2 B} = \frac{(1-j)}{3+j} \text{ (given)}$$

∴ Equating real and imaginary parts

$$\underline{n = \sqrt{2}} \quad \underline{B = 0.5}$$

Check:

$$S_{22} = \frac{1 - [1/n^2 + jB]}{1 + [1/n^2 + jB]}$$

$$= \frac{(n^2 - 1) - jn^2 B}{(n^2 + 1) + jn^2 B} = \frac{1-j}{3+j} \text{ (given)}$$

∴

$$\underline{n = \sqrt{2}} \quad \underline{B = 0.5}$$

(ii)

$$S_{12} = \frac{V_1^-}{V_2^+} \text{ when } V_1^+ = 0 = \frac{1}{n} = \underline{\frac{1}{\sqrt{2}}}$$

391. The solution to this problem can be found in certain standard textbooks.*

392. The solution to this problem can be found in certain standard textbooks.*

393. Critical wavelength $\lambda_c = 2 \times 0.0762 = \underline{0.1524 \text{ m}}.$

Guide wavelength λ_g is given by $1/\lambda_g^2 = 1/0.1^2 - 1/0.1524^2$, since a wavelength of 0.1 m corresponds to the frequency of 3000 MHz

∴

$$\underline{\lambda_g = 0.133 \text{ m}}.$$

394. The solution to this problem can be found in certain standard textbooks.†

395. It can be shown that the attenuation in nepers per unit length of a guide carrying an evanescent mode is given by: ‡

* E.g., see H. R. L. Lamont, *Wave Guides*, Methuen, 3rd Edition, 1950, Chapter 1.

† E.g., see H. R. L. Lamont, *Wave Guides*, Methuen, 3rd Edition, 1950, Chapter 2.

‡ See, for example, H. M. Barlow and A. L. Cullen, *Microwave Measurements*, Constable, 1950, p. 245; or L. G. H. Huxley, *A Survey of the Principles and Practice of Waveguides*, Cambridge U.P., 1947, p. 57.

$$\alpha = 2\pi\sqrt{[1-(\lambda_c/\lambda)^2/\lambda_c]}.$$

Here $\lambda_c = 2.61a$, where a is the cylinder radius* and $\lambda = 0.3$ m. Also $\alpha =$ 1000 dB m^{-1} = 1000 × 0.115 nepers m^{-1}.

$\therefore$ $$\underline{a = 0.0206 \text{ m.}}$$

396. A general formula for calculating the attenuation in a waveguide caused by losses in the wall metal has been given by Kuhn.† For the case of the H_{01} mode in a rectangular waveguide the attenuation α is given by the following expression:

$$\alpha = \left[\frac{c}{\sigma}\cdot\frac{\mu_1}{\mu}\left(\frac{\epsilon}{\mu}\right)^{1/2}\right]^{1/2}\frac{1}{b^{3/2}}\cdot\frac{1}{\left[\frac{\lambda_e}{\lambda_{cr}}\left(1-\frac{\lambda_e^2}{\lambda_{cr}^2}\right)\right]^{1/2}}\left(\frac{1}{2}\right)^{1/2}\left[\frac{\lambda_e^2}{\lambda_{cr}^2}+\frac{b}{2a}\right] \quad . \quad (1)$$

where a and b are the short and long internal dimensions of the guide respectively, λ_e is the wavelength in the unbounded dielectric, λ_{cr} is the critical wavelength of the guide, σ is the conductivity of the wall metal, μ_1 is the permeability of the wall metal, ϵ and μ are the dielectric constant and relative permeability of the dielectric respectively, and c is the velocity of electromagnetic waves. In the case of an air-filled copper guide with resistivity 1.7 × 10^{-8} Ωm the factor $\left[\frac{c}{\sigma}\cdot\frac{\mu_1}{\mu}\cdot\left(\frac{\epsilon}{\mu}\right)^{1/2}\right]^{1/2} = 0.2065$, if α is measured in dB m^{-1}, the guide dimensions and wavelengths being in centimetres.

Expression (1) gives α in a form in which the ratio λ_e/λ_{cr} is the only parameter involving wavelength. An alternative expression is:

$$\alpha = \left[\frac{c}{\sigma}\cdot\frac{\mu_1}{\mu}\cdot\left(\frac{\epsilon}{\mu}\right)^{1/2}\right]^{1/2}\frac{\lambda_g}{b(\lambda_e)^{3/2}}\left[\frac{\lambda_e^2}{\lambda_{cr}^2}+\frac{b}{2a}\right] \quad . \quad . \quad (2)$$

where λ_g is the guide wavelength and

$$\frac{1}{\lambda_g^2} = \frac{1}{\lambda_e^2} - \frac{1}{\lambda_{cr}^2} \quad . \quad . \quad . \quad . \quad (3)$$

* See Problem No. 392.

† S. Kuhn, 'Calculation of Attenuation in Waveguides,' *J. Instn. Electrical Engrs.*, 3, Part IIIA, 663–78, 1946.

Consider the case where $\lambda_e = 3.1$ cm,

$$b = 2.54 \text{ cm}, b/a = 2, \lambda_{cr} = 2b = 5.08 \text{ cm}$$

$$\therefore \qquad \frac{1}{\lambda_g^2} = \frac{1}{3.1^2} - \frac{1}{5.08^2}, \text{ i.e. } \lambda_g = 3.92 \text{ cm.}$$

From (2),

$$\alpha = \frac{0.2065 \times 3.92}{2.54\ (3.1)^{3/2}} \times \left[\frac{(3.1)^2}{(5.08)^2} + 1\right] \text{ dB m}^{-1} = \underline{0.0801 \text{ dB m}^{-1}}.$$

Similarly if $\lambda_e = 3.2$ cm, α is found to be $\underline{0.0814 \text{ dB m}^{-1}}$.

397. The losses due to the wall metal can be calculated from equation (2) of the solution to Question 396. It should be remembered, however, that the constant 0.2065 previously used for $\left[\frac{c}{\sigma}.\frac{\mu_1}{\mu}\left(\frac{\epsilon}{\mu}\right)^{1/2}\right]^{1/2}$ should now be multiplied by $(2.55)^{1/4}$ since $\epsilon = 2.55$.

In this case $\lambda_e = 10/\sqrt{2.55} = 6.318$ cm, $\lambda_{cr} = 2b = 9.6$ cm, so $\lambda_g = 8.391$ cm. Further $b/a = 3$,

$$\therefore \qquad \alpha = 0.05543 \text{ dB m}^{-1}.$$

A formula for calculating the loss in the dielectric of a waveguide has been given by Kuhn.* The attenuation constant α_d in dB m^{-1} is given by:

$$\alpha_d = \frac{2726}{\lambda_e}\ [\tan\delta] \Big/ \left[1 - \left(\frac{\lambda_e}{\lambda_{cr}}\right)^2\right]^{1/2}.$$

In this case, $\lambda_e = 6.318$ cm, $\tan\delta = 0.0006$ and $\lambda_{cr} = 9.6$ cm.

$$\therefore \qquad \alpha_d = 0.3438 \text{ dB m}^{-1}.$$

The total value of the attenuation in this guide is

$$(0.05543 + 0.3438) \text{ dB m}^{-1} = \underline{0.399 \text{ dB m}^{-1}}.$$

398. The guide wavelength $\lambda_g = 2(5.731 - 3.749) \times 10^{-2}$ m = $\underline{0.03964 \text{ m}}$.

*S. Kuhn, 'Calculation of Attenuation in Waveguides,' *J. Instn. Electrical Engrs.*, **93**, Part IIIA, 663–78, 1946.

The voltage standing-wave ratio is*†

$$r = [K^2 - \cos^2(\pi w/\lambda_g)]^{\frac{1}{2}}/\sin(\pi w/\lambda_g) = \underline{15.25}$$

[For high voltage standing-wave ratios $r \simeq \sqrt{(K^2-1)}\lambda_g/\pi w$, i.e. $r \simeq 15.17$, i.e. less than 0.5 per cent error.]

The loss in the component

$$\alpha = 10 \log_{10} [(r+1)/(r-1)] \text{ dB} = \underline{0.581 \text{ dB}}.$$

402. The cut-off frequency f_c‡ $= 1/\pi\sqrt{(LC)} = 1000$ Hz . (1)

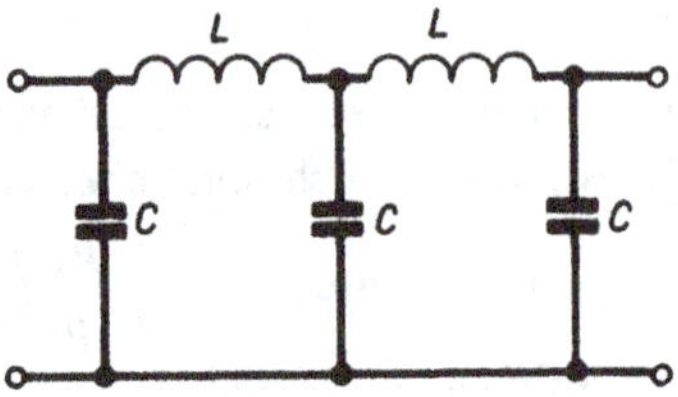

Now load resistance $= \sqrt{(L/C)} = 50\ \Omega$. . . . . . (2)

From (1) and (2), $\underline{C = 6.37\ \mu\text{F}}$ and $\underline{L = 15.92 \text{ mH}}$.

Attenuation constant α (per section)

$$= \cosh^{-1}(-1)(1 + Z_1/2Z_2)$$

where $Z_1 = j\omega L$, and $Z_2 = 1/j\omega C$,

$$= \cosh^{-1}(-1)(1 - 2f^2/f_c^2)$$

$$\therefore \qquad \alpha = \cosh^{-1}(-1)\left\{1 - 2\left(\frac{9}{4}f_c^2\right)\Big/ f_c^2\right\} = \underline{1.928.}$$

* See S. Roberts and A. von Hippell, 'A New Method of Measuring Dielectric Constant and Loss in the Range of Centimetric Waves,' *J. App, Phys.*, 17, 610, 1946; or H. M. Barlow and A. L. Cullen, *Microwave Measurements*, Constable, 1950, Chapter 5; or F. A. Benson, 'Waveguide Attenuation and its Correlation with Surface Roughness, *Proc. I.E.E.*, **100**, Part III, 85, 1953.

† Here the voltage standing-wave ratio is measured as a quantity greater than unity.

‡ See, for example, L. C. Jackson, *Wave Filters*, Methuen, 3rd Edition, 1960, Chapter 2.

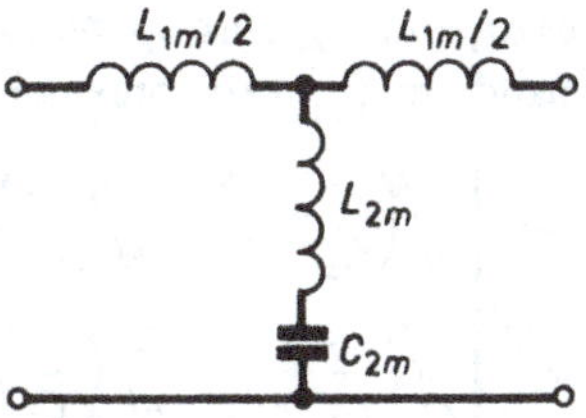

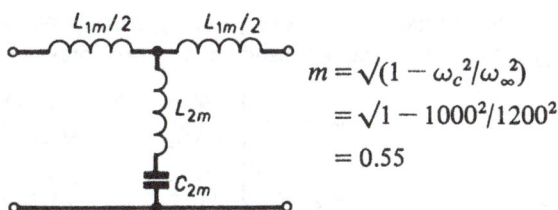

$$m = \sqrt{(1 - \omega_c^2/\omega_\infty^2)}$$
$$= \sqrt{1 - 1000^2/1200^2}$$
$$= 0.55$$

$$L_{1m} = mL = 0.55 \times 15.92 = \underline{8.8 \text{ mH}}$$

$$L_{2m} = (1 - m^2)L/4m = 5 \text{ mH}$$

$$C_{2m} = mC = 0.55 \times 6.37 = \underline{3.52\ \mu\text{F}}$$

$$\alpha_m = 2 \sinh^{-1} \left\{ \frac{m\omega/\omega_c}{2\sqrt{(\omega^2/\omega_\infty^2 - 1)}} \right\}$$

When $\omega = \omega_c$, $\alpha_m = \underline{1.51}$.

403. (*a*) The frequencies f_1 and f_2 at the ends of the pass band are given by:*

$$f_1 = f_c \left[\sqrt{\left(\frac{C_1}{C_2} + 1 \right)} - \sqrt{\left(\frac{C_1}{C_2} \right)} \right]$$

and

$$f_2 = f_c \left[\sqrt{\left(\frac{C_1}{C_2} + 1 \right)} + \sqrt{\left(\frac{C_1}{C_2} \right)} \right]$$

where f_c is the resonant frequency of both arms = 1000 Hz, C_1 is the capacitance in the series arm and C_2 is the capacitance in the shunt arm.

$\therefore$ $$f_1 = 1000[\sqrt{1.01} - \sqrt{0.01}] = 905 \text{ Hz}$$

and $$f_2 = 1000[\sqrt{1.01} + \sqrt{0.01}] = 1105 \text{ Hz}$$

$\therefore$ $$\underline{\text{bandwidth} = (f_2 - f_1) = 200 \text{ Hz.}}$$

(*b*) The *T*-section is illustrated in the figure.

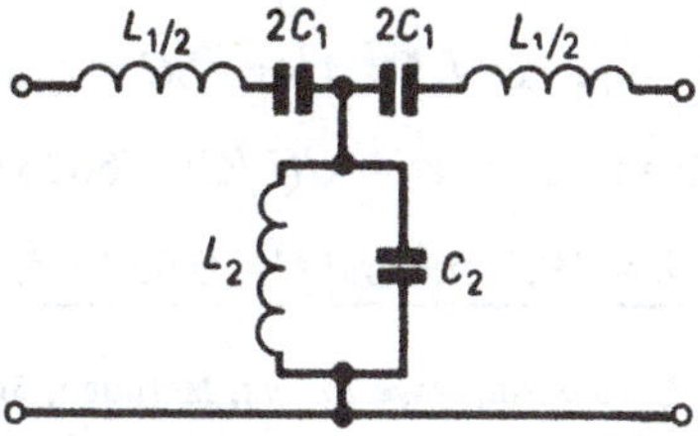

* See, for example, L. C. Jackson, *Wave Filters*, Methuen, 3rd Edition, 1960, Chapter 2.

The angular frequencies ω_1 and ω_2, corresponding to frequencies f_1 and f_2 at the ends of the pass band are, from the previous solution:

$$\omega_1 = \omega_c \left[\sqrt{\left(\frac{C_1}{C_2}+1\right)} - \sqrt{\left(\frac{C_1}{C_2}\right)}\right]$$

and
$$\omega_2 = \omega_c \left[\sqrt{\left(\frac{C_1}{C_2}+1\right)} + \sqrt{\left(\frac{C_1}{C_2}\right)}\right]$$

where
$$\omega_c^2 = 1/L_1C_1 = 1/L_2C_2$$

The iterative impedance*

$$Z_0 = R\sqrt{\left[1 - \frac{\left(\frac{\omega}{\omega_c} - \frac{\omega_c}{\omega}\right)^2}{\left(\frac{\omega_1}{\omega_c} - \frac{\omega_c}{\omega_1}\right)^2}\right]}$$

where
$$R = \sqrt{(L_1/C_2)} = \sqrt{(L_2/C_1)}$$

From these equations and assuming $Z_0 = R$:

$$L_1 = 2R/(\omega_2 - \omega_1) = 2 \times 600/3000 \times 2\pi = 63.6 \times 10^{-3}\ \text{H}$$

$\therefore$ each series inductance = 31.8 mH

$$C_2 = L_1/R^2 = (63.6 \times 10^{-3} \times 10^6)/600^2\ \mu\text{F} = 0.177\ \mu\text{F}$$

$$L_2 = (\omega_2 - \omega_1)R/2\omega_2\omega_1$$
$$= (3000 \times 2\pi \times 600 \times 10^6/2 \times 2\pi \times 120 \times 2\pi \times 123 \times 10^6)\mu\text{H}$$
$$= 9.7\ \mu\text{H}$$

$$C_1 = L_2/R^2 = (9.7 \times 10^{-6} \times 10^{12}/600^2)\ \mu\mu\text{F} = 26.95\ \mu\mu\text{F}$$

$\therefore$ each series capacitance = 53.9 $\mu\mu$F.

404. The cut-off frequency $f_c{}^* = 1/4\pi\sqrt{LC} = 2500$ Hz . (1)

Now load resistance $= \sqrt{(L/C)} = 600\ \Omega$ . . (2)

$\therefore$ $L = 19.1$ mH and $C = 0.053\ \mu$F.

* See, for example, L. C. Jackson, *Wave Filters*, Methuen, 3rd Edition, 1960, Chapter 2.

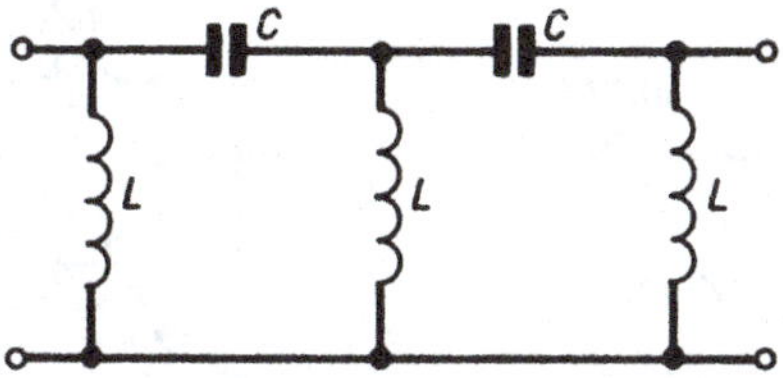

405. The solution to this problem can be found elsewhere.*

406. The solution to this problem can be found elsewhere.†

407. The solution to this problem can be found elsewhere.‡

408. The solution to this problem can be found elsewhere.§

409. Cut-off frequency|| $f_c = 1/\pi\sqrt{(LC)} = 796$ Hz.
Terminating impedance|| $= \sqrt{(L/C)} = 600\ \Omega$.

It follows that $L = 240$ mH and $C = 0.666\ \mu$F. A T-section would therefore be constructed from two 120-mH ($L/2$) series inductors and a 0.666-μF capacitor in the shunt arm.

For a π-section there would be a 240-mH series inductor with two 0.333 μF ($C/2$) capacitors as shunt elements.

410. The series-derived *T*-section is shown in diagram (*a*) and the shunt-derived π-section in diagram (*b*).

Here $$Z_1 = \omega L \text{ and } Z_2 = 1/\omega C$$

$\therefore$ for (*a*) each series inductance

$$= mL/2 = 0.6 \times 120 \text{ mH} = \underline{72 \text{ mH.}}$$

Also, inductance in shunt arm

$$= (1 - m^2)240/2.4 \text{ mH} = \underline{64 \text{ mH.}}$$

* See, for example, L. C. Jackson, *Wave Filters*, Methuen, 3rd Edition, 1960, pp. 12 and 13.

† *ibid.*, pp. 27 to 30. See, also, the Solution to Problem 410.

‡ *ibid.*, p. 32.

§ *ibid.*, p. 43.

|| *ibid.*, pp. 15–17.

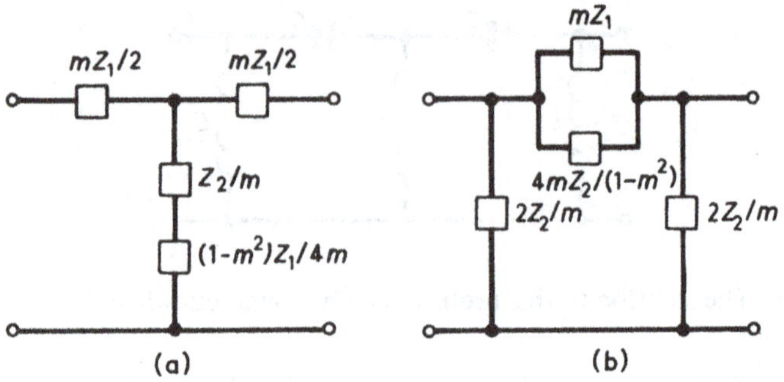

Capacitance in shunt arm

$$= 0.666 \times 0.6\ \mu\text{F} = \underline{0.4\ \mu\text{F}}.$$

Similarly, for π-section, inductance in series arm

$$= 0.6 \times 240\ \text{mH} = \underline{144\ \text{mH}}.$$

Also, capacitance in series arm

$$= 0.666 \times (1 - m^2)/4m\ \mu\text{F} = \underline{0.178\ \mu\text{F}}.$$

Capacitance of each shunt arm

$$= 0.333 \times 0.6\ \mu\text{F} = \underline{0.2\ \mu\text{F}}.$$

411. The limits of the pass band are given by:

$$\frac{Z_1}{4Z_2} = 0 \text{ or } -1 \text{ where } Z_1 = 1/j\omega_c C \text{ and } Z_2 = j\omega_c L$$

i.e.

$$-1/4\omega_c^2 LC = 0 \text{ or } -1$$

$$\omega_c = \infty \text{ or } 1/2\sqrt{(LC)}$$

$$f_c = \infty \text{ or } \underline{1/4\pi\sqrt{(LC)}}$$

$$Z_0 = \sqrt{[Z_1 Z_2 (1 + Z_1/4Z_2)]} = \sqrt{\left[\frac{L}{C}\ 1 - \frac{1}{4\omega^2 LC}\right]} = \underline{\sqrt{\left[\frac{L}{C}\left(1 - \frac{\omega_c^2}{\omega^2}\right)\right]}}$$

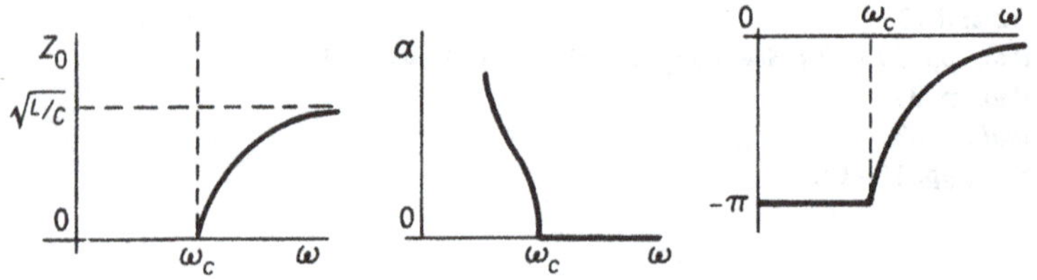

412. (i) section has $f_\infty = 1.05\, f_c$
(ii) section has $f_\infty = 2\, f_c$
(iii) section has $f_\infty = \infty$
(iv) section has $f_\infty = 1.25\, f_c$

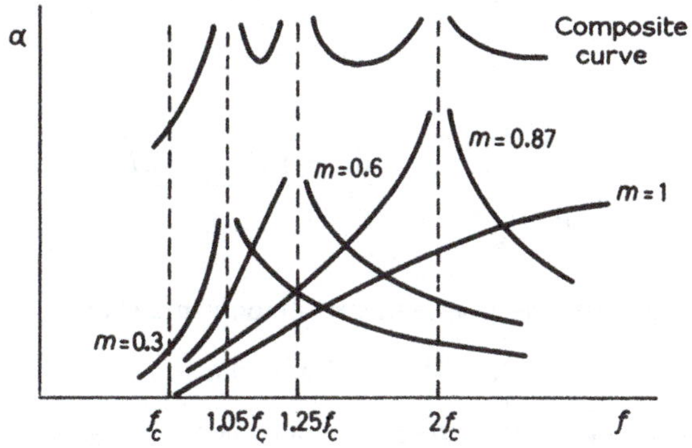

413. Magnitude function is:*

$$|N(j\omega)| = \frac{1}{[1 + \epsilon^2 C_n^2(\omega)]^{\frac{1}{2}}}$$

The tolerance band edge is unity

$$\therefore \qquad |N(j1)| = \frac{1}{(1 + \epsilon^2)^{\frac{1}{2}}}$$

For allowable 0.5 dB tolerance $N(j1) = 0.945$

$$\therefore \qquad \epsilon = 0.347$$

Parameter n (no. of poles) given from

$$|N(j2)| = \frac{1}{(1 + \epsilon^2 \cosh^2 n \cosh^{-1} 2)^{\frac{1}{2}}} = 0.125$$

$$\therefore \qquad n = 2.94$$

n must be an integer so take n to be 3.

Knowing n and ϵ

$$\nu = \frac{1}{3} \sinh^{-1} 1/\epsilon = 0.593$$

* Modern filter theory is discussed in the books F. R. Connor, *Networks*, Arnold, 1972, Chapter 6 and J. D. Ryder, *Introduction to Circuit Analysis*, Prentice-Hall, 1973, Section 10.8.

$x = \frac{\pi}{2n}(2k+1)$ which gives location of poles in left-hand plane

Poles are found to be

$$s_1 = -0.628$$
$$s_2 = -0.314 + j\,1.022$$
$$s_3 = -0.314 - j\,(1.022)$$

$$\therefore \qquad N(s) = \frac{K}{s^3 + 1.256s^2 + 1.549s + 0.72}$$

where K is a constant.

416. The radiation resistance of a small loop antenna* is

$$R = 31\,171\,(A/\lambda^2)^2 \text{ ohms}$$

where A is the area of the loop (m^2) and λ is the wavelength (m).

Here $\qquad A = \pi(\lambda/4\pi)^2/4$ and $\underline{R = 0.77\ \Omega}$.

417. The radiation resistance R of a short dipole is† $80\pi^2(l/\lambda)^2$ ohms where l/λ is the line length in wavelengths.

In this case,

$$R = 80\pi^2 \times (1/12)^2\ \Omega = \underline{5.5\ \Omega}.$$

The directivity is defined as the ratio of the maximum radiation intensity to the average radiation intensity. For a short dipole this is‡ 1.5.

418. It is often useful to consider that a receiving antenna possesses an aperture, or equivalent area, over which it extracts energy from a radio wave.

The aperture A is given by§ $D\lambda^2/4\pi$ where D is the directivity and λ is the wavelength.

In this case $\qquad A = 90 \times 4/4\pi\ \text{m}^2 = \underline{28.6\ \text{m}^2}.$

* See J. D. Kraus, *Electromagnetics*, McGraw-Hill, 1953, pp. 486–9; or S. Ramo and J. R. Whinnery, *Fields and Waves in Modern Radio*, Wiley, 2nd Edition, 1953, 189–190 and 457–8.

† See J. D. Kraus, *Electromagnetics*, McGraw-Hill, 1953, 500–1.

‡ *ibid.*, 502–4.

§ *ibid.*, 504–7.

419. The field strength due to a distant transmitting station is, neglecting absorption, given by*:

$$E = 377(hI/\lambda d)\ \mathrm{Vm^{-1}}$$

where h = effective height of transmitting antenna in metres,

d = distance in metres,

λ = wavelength in metres

and I = antenna current in amperes.

The power radiated from an antenna* $W = 1.58h^2I^2/\lambda^2$ kW.

$$\therefore \qquad E = 300\sqrt{(W)}\mathrm{d}\ \mathrm{Vm^{-1}}.$$

Here $W = 100, d = 100 \times 10^3$ m, so $E = \underline{0.03\ \mathrm{Vm^{-1}}}$.

420. Using the expression for W in the previous solution and noting that $h = 100$ m, $I = 450$ A and $\lambda = 7.5 \times 10^3$ m, W is found to be $\underline{56.9\ \mathrm{kW}}$.

$$\text{Radiation resistance*} = 1580 \times h^2/\lambda^2 \text{ ohms}$$

$$= 15.8/7.5^2\ \Omega$$

$$\text{Efficiency} = 15.8/(7.5^2 \times 1.12) = 0.251 = \underline{25.1 \text{ per cent.}}$$

421. In an antenna array with finite spacing, the total field in a direction at an angle θ with the normal to the array is*

$$E = E_1 \sin(N\alpha/2)/\sin(\alpha/2),$$

where E_1 is the field due to one antenna,

N is the number of vertical antennas,

and α is the phase difference between the radiations of consecutive antennas in the given direction.

Also $$\alpha = (2\pi a/\lambda)\sin\theta \pm \phi,$$

where a is the antenna spacing,

λ is the wavelength,

and ϕ is the phase difference between the currents in adjacent antennas.

* See, for example, *Admiralty Handbook of Wireless Telegraphy*, Vol. II, 1938, Section R.

E is zero when $N\alpha/2 = \pi, 2\pi$, etc.

If the antenna currents are in phase, as in the present problem, $\phi = 0$ and the first zero occurs when $\sin\theta = \lambda/Na$. In this case,

$$\sin\theta = \lambda/(10\lambda/2) = 1/5.$$

The angular width of the broadside beam $= 2\theta = 23^\circ\,4'$.

422. The voltage received in a frame antenna in the plane of propagation of the wave is* $2\pi EAN/\lambda$ volts, where A is the frame area in m^2, N is the number of turns, E is the field strength in Vm^{-1} and λ is the wavelength in m.

Here $E = 0.01, A = 1, N = 12$ and $\lambda = 300$, so the voltage received $= 25.14 \times 10^{-4}$ V.

423. The solution to this problem can be found elsewhere.†

424. The radiation pattern, $E(\sin\theta)$, of a finite aperture distribution $E(y)$ is given by‡

$$E(\sin\theta) = \int_{-a/2}^{a/2} E(y)\exp(jky\sin\theta)\,dy$$

For regions in the vicinity of boresight, $\sin\theta \simeq \theta$ and for uniform illumination, $E(y) = 1$.

$$\therefore \qquad E(\theta) = \int_{-a/2}^{a/2} \exp(jky\theta)\,dy = \left[\frac{\exp(jky\theta)}{jk\theta}\right]_{-a/2}^{a/2}$$

$$= a\,\frac{\sin(\pi\theta a/\lambda)}{(\pi\theta a/\lambda)}$$

The nulls occur when $E(\theta) = 0$, i.e. $\pi\theta_n a/\lambda = n\pi, n = 1, 2, 3 \ldots$

or
$$\theta_n = \frac{n\lambda}{a}$$

When $f = 10$GHz, $\lambda = 3$ cm and

$$\theta_1 = 1.91^\circ \quad \theta_2 = 3.82^\circ \quad \theta_3 = 5.73^\circ$$

* See, for example, *Admiralty Handbook of Wireless Telegraphy*, Vol. II, 1938, Section T.

† F. R. Connor, *Antennas*, Arnold, 1972, Section 2.1.

‡ L. Thourel, *The Antenna*, Chapman and Hall, 1960, 222.

The sidelobe maxima occur at the maxima and minima of $E(\theta)$, i.e. when $\pi\theta a/\lambda = n\pi/2, n = 3, 5, 7 \ldots$ The first sidelobe maximum relative to the main beam amplitude is

$$E_1 = \left| \frac{a \sin(3\pi/2)}{(3\pi/2)} \bigg/ a \frac{\sin(0)}{(0)} \right| = \frac{2}{3\pi}$$

$$\therefore \qquad E_1 = \underline{-13.46 \text{ dB}}$$

425. If E_2 and E_1 are the received field strengths with and without the presence of the blockage, then at any point in the radiation pattern

$$E_1 = a \frac{\sin(\pi\theta a/\lambda)}{(\pi\theta a/\lambda)} \quad \text{and*} \quad E_2 = E_1 - b \frac{\sin(\pi\theta b/\lambda)}{(\pi\theta b/\lambda)}$$

(*a*) $\theta = 0°$

$$E_1 = 0.9 \quad E_2 = 0.9 - 0.1 = 0.8$$

$$\therefore \qquad \text{Change} = 20 \log_{10} \frac{E_2}{E_1} = 20 \log_{10} \left(\frac{8}{9}\right) = \underline{-1.038 \text{ dB.}}$$

(*b*) $\theta = 2.865° \quad \therefore \pi\theta a/\lambda = 3\pi/2, \pi\theta b/\lambda = 0.1667\pi$

$$E_1 = -\frac{0.9 \times 2}{3\pi} = -19.1 \times 10^{-2}$$

$$E_2 = \left(-19.1 - \frac{0.1 \times 0.5}{0.523}\right) \times 10^{-2} = -28.67 \times 10^{-2}$$

$$\text{Change} = 20 \log_{10} \frac{E_2}{E_1} = 20 \log_{10} \left(\frac{28.67}{19.1}\right) = \underline{+3.52 \text{ dB.}}$$

426. Input noise power at 300 K

$$= 1.38 \times 10^{-23} \times 300 \times 5 \times 10^6 = 2.07 \times 10^{-14} \text{ W}$$

$$\text{Receiver noise level} = 10 \log_{10} (2.07 \times 10^{-14}) + 10 \simeq -133 \text{ dBW}$$

$$\text{Wavelength } \lambda = 3 \times 10^6 / 1.2 \times 10^{10} = 0.025 \text{ m}$$

$$\text{Path loss} = 20 \log_{10} \left\{ \frac{4\pi \times 4 \times 10^7}{0.025} \right\} = -206 \text{ dB}$$

$$100 \text{ kw effective radiated power} = +50 \text{ dBW}$$

* S. Silver, *Microwave Antenna Theory and Design*, McGraw-Hill, 1949, 190.

$\therefore$ receiver signal level $= -206 + 50 = -156$ dBW

If receiver signal-to-noise level is to be +20 dB the antenna must supply x dB.

$$\therefore \quad -156 - (-133) + x = 20$$

so $$x = \underline{46 \text{ dB}}$$

431. The carrier frequency

$$f_c = \frac{1}{2\pi\sqrt{(LC)}} = \frac{1}{2\pi\sqrt{(50 \times 10^{-6} \times 0.001 \times 10^{-6})}} = 712 \text{ kHz}.$$

$\therefore$ sidebands are of frequencies 712 ± 10 kHz,

<u>i.e. frequency range occupied is 702 to 722 kHz.</u>

432. Let the amplitude of carrier current $= I$, then sidebands each have amplitude $mI/2$.

Power in carrier $\propto I^2 = kI^2$ say.

$$\text{Power in sidebands} = k\left(\frac{m^2 I^2}{4}\right) \times 2.$$

$$\therefore \text{ total power radiated} = (\text{carrier power})\left(1 + \frac{m^2}{2}\right),$$

i.e. $$8.93^2 = 8^2\left(1 + \frac{m^2}{2}\right).$$

$\therefore$ <u>$m = 0.7$ and percentage modulation = 70 per cent.</u>

Let new antenna current be I_1 when $m = 0.8$.

Then $$I_1^2 = 8^2\left(1 + \frac{0.8^2}{2}\right), \text{ i.e. } I_1 = \underline{9.19 \text{ A.}}$$

433. As in the previous solution, total power radiated

$$= (\text{carrier power})\left(1 + \frac{m^2}{2}\right).$$

$$\therefore \quad 10.125 = 9\left(1 + \frac{m^2}{2}\right), \text{ i.e. } \underline{m = 0.5.}$$

$$\text{Radiated power} = 9\left(1+\frac{(0.5)^2}{2}+\frac{(0.4)^2}{2}\right) = \underline{10.845\ \text{kW.}}$$

434. Let the values of m for the several frequencies be m_1, m_2, m_3, etc. Then $m_1 + m_2 = m_3 +$, etc., must not exceed unity otherwise over-modulation will occur.

Total power of all sidebands

$$= \text{Carrier power}\left(\frac{m_1^2}{2}+\frac{m_2^2}{2}+\frac{m_3^2}{2}+, \text{etc.}\right).$$

If $m_1 + m_2 + m_3 + \ldots$, etc., does not exceed unity then $m_1^2 + m_2^2 + m_3^2 +$, etc., is less than unity.

∴ $\underline{\text{total power of all sidebands} < \tfrac{1}{2} \times \text{carrier power.}}$

435. Let $I = A + aV + bV^2$.

Let $V = E_s \sin \omega_s t + E_c \sin \omega_c t.$

$$\therefore\quad I = A + a(E_s \sin \omega_s t + E_c \sin \omega_c t) + b(E_s \sin \omega_s t + E_c \sin \omega_c t)^2$$

$$= A + \frac{b}{2}(E_c^2 + E_s^2) + aE_s \sin \omega_s t + aE_c \sin \omega_c t - \frac{b}{2}E_c^2 \cos 2\omega_c t - \frac{b}{2}E_s^2 \cos 2\omega_s t + bE_sE_c \cos(\omega_c - \omega_s)t - bE_sE_c \cos(\omega_c + \omega_s)t.$$

Substituting the given values:

$$\underline{I_a = 10.2725 + 3 \sin \omega_s t + 10 \sin \omega_c t - 0.25 \cos 2\omega_c t - 0.0225 \cos 2\omega_s t + 0.15 \cos(\omega_c - \omega_s)t - 0.15 \cos(\omega_c + \omega_s)t\ \text{mA.}}$$

where $\underline{\omega_s = 1000t \text{ and } \omega_c = 4 \times 10^6 t.}$

The carrier has an amplitude of 10 mA and the sidebands have amplitudes of 0.15 mA.

$$\therefore \qquad m = (2 \times 0.15)/10 = \underline{0.03}.$$

436. If f_m is the highest modulating frequency the highest sideband frequency is $f_c + f_m$, where f_c is the carrier frequency, and the lowest sideband frequency is $f_c - f_m$.

$\therefore$ bandwidth of transmission is $(f_c + f_m) - (f_c - f_m)$

$$= 2f_m = 2 \times 3.4 \text{ kHz} = \underline{6.8 \text{ kHz}}$$

The upper sideband will extend from (104 kHz + 300 Hz) to (104 kHz + 3.4 kHz), i.e. from 104.3 kHz to 107.4 kHz.

The lower sideband will extend from (104 kHz − 300 Hz) to (104 kHz − 3.4 kHz), i.e. from 103.7 kHz to 100.6 kHz.

These frequencies will be present in the transmitted wave in addition to the carrier frequency of 104 kHz.

437. Total sideband power is given by*

$$P_{sb} = P_c\,[2\overline{f(t)} + \overline{f^2(t)}]$$

Now

$$\overline{f(t)} = \frac{1}{T_m}\int_0^{T_m} f(t)\,dt = 0$$

$$\overline{f^2(t)} = \frac{1}{T_m}\int_{-\frac{T_m}{2}}^{\frac{T_m}{2}} \left(\frac{2t}{T_m}\right)^2 dt = \frac{4}{T_m^{\,3}}\left[\frac{t^3}{3}\right]_{-\frac{T_m}{2}}^{\frac{T_m}{2}} = 0.333$$

$$\therefore \qquad \underline{\text{Total sideband power} = 0.333\,P_c}$$

The modulation index for the fundamental component of $f(t)$ is

$$m_1 = \frac{E_1}{E_c} = \frac{2/\pi}{1} = 0.637$$

Similarly

$$m_2 = \frac{2}{2\pi} = 0.318$$

* A. Bruce Carlson, *Communication Systems*, McGraw-Hill, 1968, 171.

$$m_3 = \frac{2}{3\pi} = 0.212$$

$$m_4 = \frac{2}{4\pi} = 0.159$$

Now $P_{sb_1} = P_c \dfrac{m_1^2}{2} = \underline{0.203\,P_c}$ $P_{sb_2} = P_c \dfrac{m_2^2}{2} = \underline{0.051\,P_c}$

$P_{sb_3} = P_c \dfrac{m_3^2}{2} = \underline{0.0225\,P_c}$ $P_{sb_4} = P_c \dfrac{m_4^2}{2} = \underline{0.0126\,P_c}$

438. Let the carrier voltage be $E_c \sin \omega_c t$ and the audio-frequency voltage be $E_a \sin \omega_a t$.

At the input to the first non-linear element there is a voltage $(E_a \sin \omega_a t + E_c \sin \omega_c t)$.

At the input to the second element there is a voltage $(E_c \sin \omega_c t - E_a \sin \omega_a t)$.

$$\therefore \quad I_1 = I + a(E_a \sin \omega_a t + E_c \sin \omega_c t) + b_1(E_a \sin \omega_a t + E_c \sin \omega_c t)^2$$

and

$$I_2 = I + a(E_c \sin \omega_c t - E_a \sin \omega_a t) + b_2(E_c \sin \omega_c t - E_a \sin \omega_a t)^2.$$

In the output $I_1 - I_2$ results

i.e. $\underline{2aE_a \sin \omega_a t + \dfrac{b_1 - b_2}{2}(E_c^2 + E_a^2)}$

$$\underline{-\left(\frac{b_1 - b_2}{2}\right)(E_c^2 \cos 2\omega_c t + E_a^2 \cos 2\omega_a t)}$$

$$\underline{+ (b_1 + b_2)E_a E_c \{\cos(\omega_c - \omega_a)t - \cos(\omega_c + \omega_a)t\}.}$$

Therefore the carrier frequency is suppressed.

439. The circuit arrangement of the anode-modulated Class-C amplifier is shown below.

$$e_a = E_a + e_l = E_a + E_l \sin \omega_l t \quad . \quad . \quad . \quad (1)$$

The amplitude of the r.f. current is directly proportional to the anode-supply voltage. This proportionality may be expressed as

$$I_t = ke_a \text{ where } k \text{ is a constant} \quad . \quad . \quad . \quad (2)$$

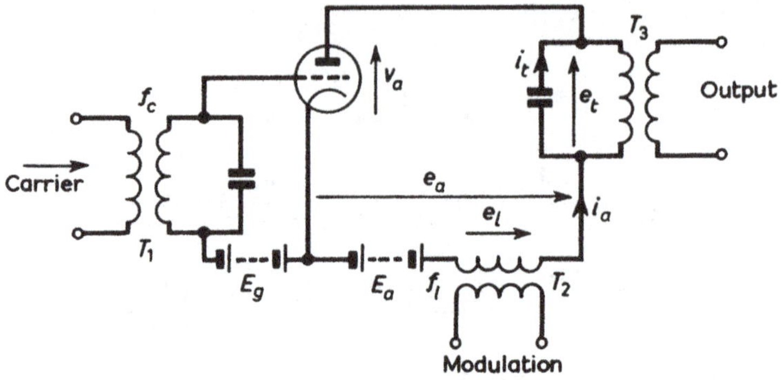

From (1) and (2)

$$I_t = kE_a(1 + m \sin \omega_l t) \qquad (3)$$

where

$$m = E_l/E_a \qquad (4)$$

The instantaneous r.f. current

$$i_t = I_t \sin \omega_c t = kE_a(1 + m \sin \omega_l t) \sin \omega_c t \qquad (5)$$

which is of the usual form.

The r.f. voltage across the tank circuit is also proportional to the total anode-supply voltage, or

$$E_t = k' E_a(1 + m \sin \omega_l t) \text{ where } k' \text{ is a constant} \qquad (6)$$

Voltage v_a is the algebraic sum of E_a, $E_l \sin \omega_l t$ and e_t. The maximum value of e_t is $k'(E_a + E_l)$ as seen from equation (6). In practice k' is about 0.9. With $m = 1$ therefore the voltage v_a can reach the value 3.8 E_a.

With no modulation the power developed in the tank circuit is the carrier power

$$P_c = (E_t)^2/2R_l \text{ since } E_t \text{ is the peak value} \qquad (7)$$

With modulation the power delivered is

$$P = P_c \left(1 + \frac{m^2}{2}\right) = (k' E_a)^2 \left(1 + \frac{m^2}{2}\right) \Big/ 2R_l \qquad (8)$$

Assume that the anode-supply current $i_a = k'' e_a$ where k'' is a constant.

$$\therefore \qquad i_a = k''(E_a + E_l \sin \omega_l t) \qquad (9)$$

Average power from d.c. source is

$$E_a \bar{I_a} = k'' E_a^2 \text{ using (9)} \qquad (10)$$

Average power delivered by modulating transformer

$$= \tfrac{1}{2}E_l(k''E_l) = \tfrac{1}{2}k''m^2E_a^2 \quad . \quad . \quad . \quad (11)$$

Total average power supplied by anode-supply source is

$$P_a = k''E_a^2 + k''m^2E_a^2/2 \quad . \quad . \quad . \quad (12)$$

$$\text{Anode-circuit efficiency} = P/P_a = (k')^2/2k''R_l \quad . \quad (13)$$

In the problem under consideration:
(*a*) $m = E_l/E_a = 1400/2000 = \underline{0.7}$.

(*b*) Maximum value of $v_a = (E_a + E_l)(1 + k') = 3400(1.9) = \underline{6460 \text{ V}}$.

(*c*) Power delivered by d.c. supply

$$= E_a\bar{I}_a = 2000 \times 200/1000 = \underline{400 \text{ W}}.$$

(*d*) Power delivered by modulation transformer $= E_l^2k''/2$. From equation (10) $k''E_a^2 = 400$ W, so $k'' = 400/(2000)^2$.

∴ power delivered by transformer = $\underline{98 \text{ W}}$.

(*e*) R.f. output power without modulation $= 0.8 \times 400 = \underline{320 \text{ W}}$.

(*f*) R.f. output power with modulation $= 320(1 + m^2/2) = \underline{398 \text{ W}}$.

(*g*) The modulating voltage E_l causes the anode-supply current to have a component of amplitude $k''E_l$ in phase with E_l. Thus the load on the modulation transformer is effectively a resistor whose resistance is $E_l/k''E_l$, i.e. $E_a/k''E_a = E_a/\bar{I}_a$. In this case the resistance = 2000/0.2 = 10 000 Ω.

440. The solution to this problem can be found in certain standard textbooks.*

441. The solution to the previous problem gives*

$$\begin{aligned} i = I[J_0(M) \sin ct &+ J_1(M)\{\sin (c + a)t - \sin (c - a)t\} \\ &+ J_2(M)\{- \sin (c + 2a)t + \sin (c - 2a)t\} \\ &+ J_3(M)\{\sin (c + 3a)t - \sin (c - 3a)t\} \\ &+ J_4(M)\{- \sin (c + 4a)t + \sin (c - 4a)t\} \\ &+ \ldots]. \end{aligned}$$

* See, for example, L. B. Arguimbau and R. B. Adler, *Vacuum Tube Circuits and Transistors*, Wiley, 1956, Chapter 12, Section 11.

In this case $M = 50/5 = 10$ so that, disregarding signs

$$J_0(M) \simeq 0.24, J_1(M) \simeq 0.05, J_2(M) \simeq 0.26, J_3(M) \simeq 0.05, \text{ etc.,}$$

as are readily found from graphs of these functions.*

$\therefore$ carrier amplitude $= 240 \times 10^{-6}\ \text{Vm}^{-1}$ and sideband amplitudes are $50 \times 10^{-6}\ \text{Vm}^{-1}$, $260 \times 10^{-6}\ \text{Vm}^{-1}$, $50 \times 10^{-6}\ \text{Vm}^{-1}$, etc.

442. $C = K_1 V^{-\frac{1}{2}}$ and $f_r = 1/2\pi\sqrt{(LC)}$

so
$$f_r = K_2 V^{\frac{1}{4}} \text{ and } K_2 = \frac{50 \times 10^6}{16^{\frac{1}{4}}} = 25 \times 10^6$$

$$\delta f_r = \tfrac{1}{4} K_2 V^{-\frac{3}{4}} \delta V = \frac{25 \times 10^6 \times 0.1}{4 \times 16^{\frac{3}{4}}} = 78\,125 \text{ Hz}$$

$$= 78.125 \text{ kHz.}$$

$\therefore$
$$M = \frac{\delta f_r}{f_m} = \frac{78.125}{10} \simeq 7.8$$

$$f_r = K_2 V^{\frac{1}{4}} = K_2 \{16 + 0.1 \sin 2\pi \times 10^4 t\}^{\frac{1}{4}}$$

$$= K_2 \,.\, 16^{\frac{1}{4}} \left\{1 + \frac{0.1}{16} \sin 2\pi \times 10^4 t\right\}^{\frac{1}{4}}$$

$$= 2K_2 \left\{1 + \tfrac{1}{4} \frac{0.1}{16} \sin 2\pi \times 10^4 t + \frac{\frac{1}{4}(-\frac{3}{4})}{2} \left(\frac{0.1 \sin 2\pi \times 10^4 t}{16}\right)^2 + \ldots\right\}$$

$$= 2 \times 25 \times 10^6 \left[1 + \frac{0.1}{64} \sin 2\pi \times 10^4 t - \frac{3}{32}\left(\frac{0.1}{16}\right)^2 \tfrac{1}{2} (1 - \cos 4\pi \times 10^4 t) + \ldots\right]$$

$$\text{Second-harmonic distortion} = \frac{\frac{3}{32}\left(\frac{0.1}{16}\right)^2 \frac{1}{2}}{\left(\frac{0.1}{64}\right)} = 0.117 \text{ per cent.}$$

* See, for example, L. B. Arguimbau and R. B. Adler, *Vacuum Tube Circuits and Transistors*, Wiley, 1956, Chapter 12, Section 11.

443. When the carrier is at its first zero the modulation index, $m_f =$ 2.405.

The modulator conversion factor is defined as

$$k_f = \frac{m_f f_m}{E_m} = \frac{2.405 \times 3 \times 10^3}{3.46} = \underline{2085 \text{ Hz V}^{-1}}$$

For the modulating signal 2.11 sin 4000 πt

$$m_f = \frac{k_f E_m}{f_m} = \frac{2085 \times 2.11}{2000} = 2.2$$

From tables of Bessel functions the significant sideband amplitudes, $J_N(m_f)$, are found and the spectrum is drawn as follows:

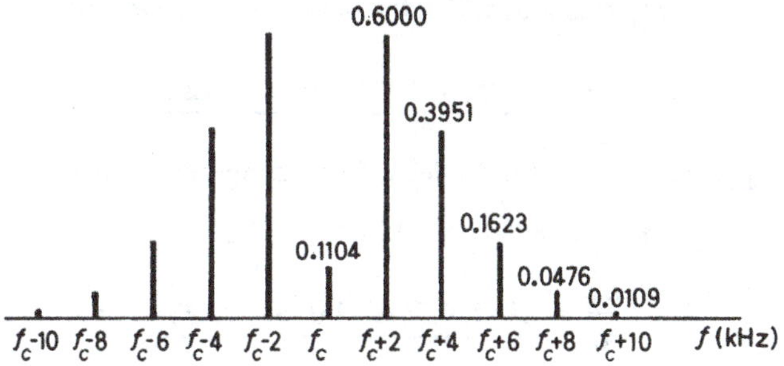

444. $$\left(\frac{S}{N}\right)_{\text{A.M.}} = 20 \text{ dB} = 100 = \frac{P_c}{2\eta B_r}$$

where P_c is the transmitter power, B_r is the receiver bandwidth and η is the noise power spectral density.

$$\left(\frac{S}{N}\right)_{\text{F.M.}} = 12 \text{ dB} = \frac{P_c}{\eta B_t} = 16.$$

$\therefore$ $$200\, B_r = 16\, B_t$$

$\therefore$ $$B_t = \left(\frac{200 \times 3}{16}\right) \text{kHz} = 37.5 \text{ kHz}$$

But $B_t = 6 f_m + 2.13\, f_{fm}$

$\therefore$ $$f_{fm} = \left\{\frac{37.5 - (6 \times 3)}{2.13}\right\} \text{kHz} = \underline{9.1 \text{ kHz}}$$

Now $\left(\frac{S_0}{N_0}\right)_{\text{F.M.}} = 3\left(\frac{f_{fm}}{B_r}\right)^2 \frac{P_c}{2\eta B_r} = 3\left(\frac{9.1}{3}\right)^2 100 = 2750 = 34.4 \text{ dB}$

$\therefore$ Improvement $= 34.4 - 18 = \underline{16.4 \text{ dB}}$

445. The modulation index, $m_p = k_p E_m = 3$ rad. Therefore,* the number of significant sideband pairs, $S_p = 6$ and the maximum value of f_m is given by:

$$f_m = \frac{\text{Bandwidth}}{2S_p} = \frac{40}{12} = \underline{3.33 \text{ kHz}}$$

For suppression of the carrier component, $J_0(m_p) = 0$

i.e. $m_p = 2.405, 5.520, 8.654, 11.792 \ldots$ rad

$\therefore$ $E_m = \frac{m_p}{k_p} = \underline{2.405, 5.520, 8.654, 11.792 \ldots \text{V}}$

For suppression of the third sideband pair component, $J_3(m_p) = 0$

i.e. $m_p = 6.380, 9.761, 13.015, 16.223 \ldots$ rad

$\therefore$ $E_m = \frac{m_p}{k_p} = \underline{6.380, 9.761, 13.015, 16.223 \ldots \text{V}}$

446. The solution to this problem can be found in certain standard textbooks.†

447. Problem 80 gives the answer to the first part of this question and the method of solution is the same as that already given for Problem 77 so will not be dealt with here. The final expression for the P.A.M. train follows directly from the other expressions given in the Question.

448. The maximum permissible value for the time constant of a diode detector RC circuit is given by:‡

$$RC \leqslant \sqrt{(1 - m^2)}/(2\pi f)m.$$

* Goodyear, C.C. *Signals and Information*, Butterworths, 1971, 142.

† For example, see K. R. Sturley, *Radio Receiver Design*, Part 2, Chapman & Hall, 1954, 250 and F. R. Connor, *Modulation*, Arnold, 1973, 34 and 94.

‡ J. D. Ryer, *Electronic Fundamentals and Applications*, Pitman, 3rd Edition, 1964, 493–4.

In this case, $220 \times 10^3 \times 100 \times 10^{-12} \leqslant \sqrt{(1-m^2)}/(2\pi \times 6000)\,m$.

i.e. $\underline{m \leqslant 0.77.}$

449. The solution to this problem can be found elsewhere* in the case of a valve as the device but the I_a/V_g relationship for a valve having two control grids is stated without any discussion of why the relationship should hold. The reader can find such a discussion, however, in the book *Thermionic Valve Circuits*, by E. Williams.† Readers may also wish to read about dual-gate MOS field-effect transistors.‡

450. The oscillator frequency = 700 + 465 = 1165 kHz.

Let $I = a_0 + a_1 V + a_2 V^2 + a_3 V^3$ and assume $V = (E_s \cos \omega_s t - E_h \cos \omega_h t)$ where s refers to the signal and h to the oscillator. The expansion of the $a_3 V_g^3$ terms shows that there are eight frequencies in the output, namely $f_s, 3f_s, f_h, 3f_h, 2f_s + f_h, 2f_s - f_h, 2f_h + f_s, 2f_h - f_s$.

Undesired-signal frequencies of 351, 816, 1867 and 2797 kHz produce 2 kHz whistles because:

$$1165 - 2 \times 351 = 463 \text{ kHz}$$
$$2 \times 816 - 1165 = 467 \text{ kHz}$$
$$2 \times 1165 - 1867 = 463 \text{ kHz}$$
$$2797 - 2 \times 1165 = 467 \text{ kHz.}$$

451. (*a*) The oscillator circuit is as shown, where L is the tuning inductance, C_o the coil self capacitance and C_p the padding capacitance.

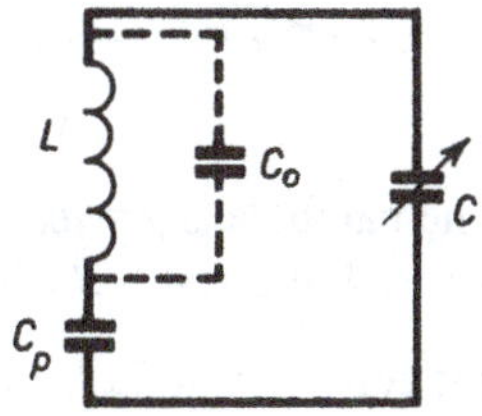

* K. R. Sturley, *Radio Receiver Design*, Part 1, Chapman & Hall, 3rd Edition, 1965, 430.

† E. Williams, *Thermionic Valve Circuits*, Pitman, 4th Edition, 1961, 270–2.

‡ See H. M. Kleinman, *Application of Dual-Gate MOS Field-Effect Transistors in Practical Radio Receivers*, R.C.A. Publication ST-3486, reprinted from IEEE Transactions on Broadcast and T.V. Receivers, July 1967.

The oscillator frequency

$$f_h = 1/2\pi\sqrt{\left[L\left(C_o + \frac{C_pC}{C_p + C}\right)\right]} \quad . \quad . \quad (1)$$

This equation can be satisfied simultaneously for any two values f_{h_1} and f_{h_2} by a suitable choice of L and C_p. Suppose that for these two frequencies C has values C_1 and C_2.

Then $$\frac{1}{(2\pi f_{h_1})^2} = L\{C_o + C_pC_1/(C_p + C_1)\} \quad . \quad . \quad (2)$$

and $$\frac{1}{(2\pi f_{h_2})^2} = L\{C_o + C_pC_2/(C_p + C_2)\} \quad . \quad . \quad (3)$$

From these two equations L and C_p can be found. Let f_{h_1} and f_{h_2} correspond to signal frequencies f_{s_1} and f_{s_2}. The most suitable values of f_{s_1} and f_{s_2} are those giving the least error over the frequency band and to find them the shape of the error/frequency curve must be known. Assume the error/frequency curve is parabolic and that there are equal errors at the ends and centre of the range as illustrated. Let frequency be represented by x and let $x = -1$ when $f = f_a$ the lowest frequency of the range and let $x = +1$ when $f = f_b$ the highest frequency of the range. The maximum error is d kHz.

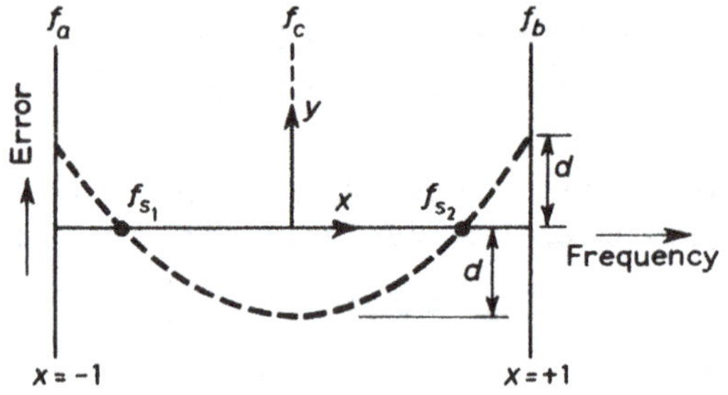

The general equation of the parabola is $y = ax^2 + bx + c$, but $dy/dx = 0$ when $x = 0$, $y = d$ when $x = \pm 1$ and $y = -d$ when $x = 0$.

$\therefore$ the equation is $y = d(2x^2 - 1)$.

Thus the frequencies for zero error are given by $x = \pm 1/\sqrt{2}$.

$$\therefore \quad f_{s_1} = f_c - 0.707(f_c - f_a)$$
$$f_{s_2} = f_c + 0.707(f_b - f_a).$$

In this case, $f_c = 1025$ kHz, $f_a = 550$ kHz and $f_b = 1500$ kHz.

$\therefore$ $f_{s_1} = 689$ kHz and $f_{s_2} = 1361$ kHz.

The capacitance required to tune the signal coil at these two frequencies can easily be calculated since the inductance is given as 156 μH. Not all this tuning capacitance is found in the tuning capacitor itself. It is reasonable to assume that about 40 $\mu\mu$F is due to stray capacitance (of range switch, wiring, self-capacitance of coil, trimmer). Hence the actual value of tuning capacitance is found by subtracting 40 $\mu\mu$F from the calculated figures. Similarly assume the oscillator tuning circuit has 20 $\mu\mu$F stray capacitance (there is no trimmer here).

The value of C at a signal frequency of 689 kHz is therefore the calculated value 342 $\mu\mu$F $-$ 40 $\mu\mu$F + 20 $\mu\mu$F = 322 $\mu\mu$F = C_1.

Similarly $C_2 = 67.6$ $\mu\mu$F.

Assume $C_0 = 10$ $\mu\mu$F.

Also $f_{h_1} = (f_{s_1} + 465)$ kHz and $f_{h_2} = (f_{s_2} + 465)$ kHz.

From equations (2) and (3),

$$\underline{C_p = 288\ \mu\mu\text{F and } L = 117.3\ \mu\text{H}.}$$

(*b*) The oscillator circuit is as shown, where C_p is the trimmer capacitance. In the equations below C_t represents the total capacitance across L, including self and stray capacitances. The method of solution is similar to that of (*a*).

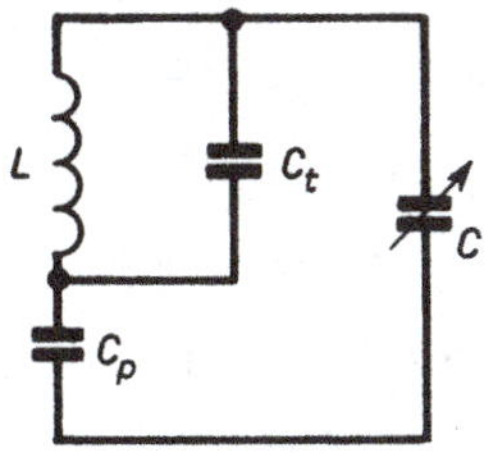

Zero error can now be obtained at three oscillator frequencies f_{h_1}, f_{h_2} and f_{h_3} corresponding to signal frequencies f_{s_1}, f_{s_2} and f_{s_3}. Suppose that for these frequencies C has values C_1, C_2 and C_3 respectively.

Then
$$\frac{1}{(2\pi f_{h_1})^2} = L\left[C_t + \frac{C_pC_1}{C_p + C_1}\right] \quad . \quad . \quad . \quad (1)$$

$$\frac{1}{(2\pi f_{h_2})^2} = L\left[C_t + \frac{C_pC_2}{C_p + C_2}\right] \quad . \quad . \quad . \quad (2)$$

and
$$\frac{1}{(2\pi f_{h_3})^2} = L\left[C_t + \frac{C_pC_3}{C_p + C_3}\right] \quad . \quad . \quad . \quad (3)$$

From these equations L, C_p and C_t can be found. Proceeding as before we can now assume the error/frequency curve is cubic of the form illustrated

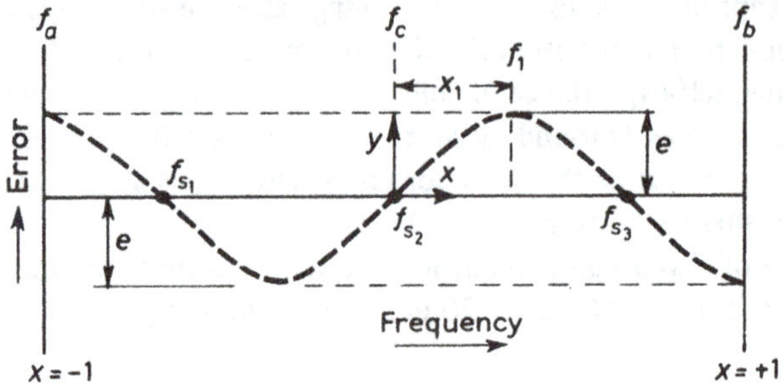

The general equation of the curve is

$$y = ax^3 + bx^2 + cx + d \quad . \quad . \quad . \quad (4)$$

When $x = 0, y = 0$ and when $x = \mp 1, y = \pm e$ so the equation reduces to

$$y = ax^3 + cx \quad . \quad . \quad . \quad . \quad (5)$$

and

$$(a + c) = -e \quad . \quad . \quad . \quad . \quad (6)$$

At frequency f_1 where $x = x_1$, $dy/dx = 0$.

$\therefore$

$$x_1 = +\sqrt{(-c/3a)} \quad . \quad . \quad . \quad . \quad (7)$$

From (7), (5) and (6), since $y = e$ at $x = x_1$

$$c = -3a/4 \quad . \quad . \quad . \quad . \quad (8)$$

From (5) and (8), $\qquad y = ax(x^2 - 3/4)$

$\therefore$ for zero error $\qquad x = 0$ or $\pm\sqrt{(3/4)}$

i.e.

$$f_{s_2} = f_c$$

$$f_{s_1} = f_c - \sqrt{(\tfrac{3}{4})}(f_c - f_a)$$

and

$$f_{s_3} = f_c + \sqrt{(\tfrac{3}{4})}(f_b - f_c).$$

In this case, $f_a = 550$ kHz, $f_b = 1500$ kHz and $f_c = 1025$ kHz, so $f_{s_1} =$ 614 kHz, $f_{s_2} = 1025$ kHz and $f_{s_3} = 1436$ kHz.

Making the same assumptions as in (*a*)

$$C_1 = 410.5\ \mu\mu\text{F},\ C_2 = 134.58\ \mu\mu\text{F and } C_3 = 58.74\ \mu\mu\text{F}.$$

Now $\qquad f_{h_1} = (f_{s_1} + 465)$ kHz, $f_{h_2} = (f_{s_2} + 465)$ kHz and $$f_{h_3} = (f_{s_3} + 465)\ \text{kHz}.$$

∴ from equations (1) to (3),

$$\underline{C_p = 601\ \mu\mu\text{F},\ C_t = 36.5\ \mu\mu\text{F and } L = 77.4\ \mu\text{H}.}$$

457. Number of possible combinations for a given increment $= 64 \times 16 = 2^{10}$ i.e. 10 bits per increment.

There are $5 \times 10^5 \times 100$ increments per second i.e. 5×10^7.

$$\text{Number of bits per second} = 5 \times 10^7 \times 10 = \underline{5 \times 10^8}$$

The Hartley-Shannon law is:

$$C = B \log_2 \left(1 + \frac{S}{N}\right)$$

$$\frac{S}{N} = 30\ \text{dB} = 10^3$$

∴ $$B = \frac{C}{\log_2 10^3} = \frac{5 \times 10^8}{3.32 \log_{10} 10^3}$$

since $\log_2 x = 3.32 \log_{10} x$

i.e. $$B = 5 \times 10^8/9.96 \simeq \underline{50\ \text{MHz}}.$$

458. $H(\omega) = \exp(-a\omega^2 - jb\omega)$

$$\text{Impulse response } h(t) = \int_{-\infty}^{\infty} \exp(-a\omega^2 - jb\omega) \exp(j\omega t)\, df.$$

where $\omega = 2\pi f$.

so $$h(t) = \frac{1}{2\pi} \int_{-\infty}^{\infty} \exp\{j\omega(t - b)\} \exp(-a\omega^2)\, d\omega$$

∴ $$h(t) = \frac{1}{2\sqrt{(\pi a)}} \exp\left\{-\frac{(t-b)^2}{4a}\right\}$$

<u>Thus resulting output signal reaches its maximum at $t = b$.</u>

The signal falls to $1/e$ of the maximum value when $(t - b)^2 = 4a$

i.e. when $$t - b = \pm 2\sqrt{a}$$

or $$t = b \pm 2\sqrt{a}$$

The width $= 2(2\sqrt{a}) = \underline{4\sqrt{a}}.$

459. Entropy $= \frac{1}{4}\log_2 4 + \frac{3}{4}\log_2 \frac{4}{3}$

$= 0.812$

Group	Probability	Bits	
AA	9/16	1	9/16
AB	3/16	2	6/16
BA	3/16	3	9/16
BB	1/16	3	3/16
			27/16

∴ 27/32 bits per symbol on average = 0.845

Efficiency = 0.812/0.845 = 96 per cent.

460. The solution to the first part of the Question can be found in many books.*

Entropy $= -(0.5\log 0.50 + 0.15\log 0.15 + \ldots)$

$= 2.21$ bits per symbol.

Symbol	P	N	NP
A	0.5	1	0.5
B	0.15	001	0.45
C	0.12	011	0.36
D	0.10	010	0.30
E	0.04	00011	0.20
F	0.04	00010	0.20
G	0.03	00001	0.15
H	0.02	00000	0.10
			Σ 2.26

* See, for example, F. R. Connor, *Signals*, Arnold, 1972, Section 6.1.

Efficiency = 2.21/2.26 = 97.7 per cent.

Code

A	000
B	001
C	010
D	011
E	100
F	101
G	110
H	111

Efficiency = 2.21/3 = 73.5 per cent.

461. C = channel capacity
B = bandwidth
S = signal power on reception
N = noise power on reception.

[Readers may like to consult books by F. R. Connor and C. C. Goodyear.* Connor shows that the relationship is plausible.]

S/N is increased by a factor of 2

$\therefore$ C is increased by $B \log_2 2 = B = 10^7$ bits per second.

467. $\frac{1}{2} m\bar{v}^2 = \frac{3}{2} kT$

Thus, when $T = 273$ K,

$$\bar{v}^2 = \frac{3 \times 1.38 \times 10^{-23} \times 273}{2 \times 14 \times 1.67 \times 10^{-27}}$$

i.e. $$\bar{v} = 492 \text{ ms}^{-1}$$

When $T = 373$ K,

$$\bar{v}^2 = \frac{3 \times 1.38 \times 10^{-23} \times 373}{2 \times 14 \times 1.67 \times 10^{-27}}$$

i.e. $$\bar{v} = 575 \text{ ms}^{-1}.$$

468. The fractional number of particles having velocities in the range v to $v + dv$ is given by:

* F. R. Connor, *Signals*, Arnold, 1972, Section 6.2, C. C. Goodyear, *Signals and Information*, Butterworths, 1971, Section 9.6.

$$\frac{dN_v}{N} = 4\pi \left(\frac{m}{2\pi kT}\right)^{3/2} v^2 \, e^{-\frac{mv^2}{2kT}} \, dv$$

The most probable velocity $v_p = \sqrt{\left(\frac{2kT}{m}\right)}$

When $v = v_p$:

$$\frac{dN_v}{N} = 4\pi \left(\frac{m}{2\pi kT}\right)^{3/2} \left(\frac{2kT}{m}\right) e^{-1} \, dv$$

$$= \frac{4}{\sqrt{(2\pi)}} \left(\frac{m}{kT}\right)^{\frac{1}{2}} e^{-1} \, dv$$

In this case $dv = \frac{2}{100} \sqrt{\left(\frac{2kT}{m}\right)}$

$$\therefore \qquad \frac{dN_v}{N} = \frac{4}{\sqrt{2\pi}} \left(\frac{m}{kT}\right)^{\frac{1}{2}} e^{-1} \, \frac{2}{100} \sqrt{\left(\frac{2kT}{m}\right)} = \underline{0.0166.}$$

469. $$\frac{dN_{xyz}}{N} = \left(\frac{m}{2\pi kT}\right)^{3/2} e^{-\frac{m}{2kT}(v_x^2 + v_y^2 + v_z^2)} \, dv_x \, dv_y \, dv_z$$

so

$$dN_x = N \left(\frac{m}{2\pi kT}\right)^{3/2} e^{-\frac{mv_x^2}{2kT}} \, dv_x \int_{-\infty}^{\infty} e^{-\frac{mv_y^2}{2kT}} \, dv_y \int_{-\infty}^{\infty} e^{-\frac{mv_z^2}{2kT}} \, dv_z$$

Now $$\int_{-\infty}^{\infty} e^{-\beta s^2} \, ds = \sqrt{(\pi/\beta)}$$

$$\therefore \qquad \int_{-\infty}^{\infty} e^{-\frac{mv_y^2}{2kT}} \, dv_y = \sqrt{(2kT\pi/m)}$$

and $$\int_{-\infty}^{\infty} e^{-\frac{mv_z^2}{2kT}} \, dv_z = \sqrt{(2kT\pi/m)}$$

$$\therefore \qquad dN_x = N \left(\frac{m}{2\pi kT}\right)^{3/2} e^{-\frac{mv_x^2}{2kT}} \, dv_x \, (2kT\pi/m)$$

$$= \underline{N \left(\frac{m}{2\pi kT}\right)^{\frac{1}{2}} e^{-\frac{mv_x^2}{2kT}} \, dv_x}$$

Now $$v_p = (2kT/m)^{\frac{1}{2}}$$

$$\therefore \qquad dN_x = N\left(\frac{m}{2\pi kT}\right)^{\frac{1}{2}} e^{-v_x^2/v_p^2}\, dv_x$$

$$= \frac{N}{\sqrt{\pi}}\left(\frac{1}{v_p}\right) e^{-v_x^2/v_p^2}\, dv_x$$

Let $\qquad \omega = v_x/v_p$

Then $\qquad d\omega = dv_x/v_p$

$$\therefore \qquad \underline{dN_x = N e^{-\omega^2}\, d\omega/\sqrt{\pi}}$$

470. First find the number of molecules with velocity v perpendicular to the wall of the box that strike the wall in unit time.

Let the wall be perpendicular to v_x. In unit time distance moved is v_x.

$$\therefore \qquad \text{number striking unit area of wall} = dN_x\, v_x$$

so number with velocity greater than v is

$$\int_v^\infty dN_x\, v_x = \frac{N}{\sqrt{\pi}} \int_{v/v_p}^\infty e^{-\omega^2}\, d\omega\, v_p\, \omega$$

$$= \frac{Nv_p}{\sqrt{\pi}}\left[\frac{e^{-\omega^2}}{2}\right]_{v/v_p}^\infty = \frac{Nv_p}{2\sqrt{\pi}}\, e^{-(v/v_p)^2}$$

$$\underline{= N\, v_p\, e^{-\omega^2}/2\sqrt{\pi}}$$

471. Number striking unit area of wall per second $= v_x\, dN_x$.
Partial pressure $= (2mv_x)\, v_x\, dN_x$

$$\therefore \qquad \text{total pressure } p = 2mN\left(\frac{m}{2\pi kT}\right)^{\frac{1}{2}} \int_0^\infty e^{-\frac{mv_x^2}{2kT}}\, v_x^2\, dv_x$$

Put $mv_x^2/2kT = s^2$, i.e. $v_x = s\sqrt{(2kT/m)}$

$$\therefore \qquad p = 2mN\left(\frac{m}{2\pi kT}\right)^{\frac{1}{2}} \frac{2kT}{m} \cdot \sqrt{\frac{2kT}{m}} \int_0^\infty (e^{-s^2})\, s^2\, ds$$

$$= \frac{4NkT}{\sqrt{\pi}} \int_0^\infty (e^{-s^2})\, s^2\, ds$$

Now $\qquad \displaystyle\int_{-\infty}^\infty e^{-\beta s^2}\, ds = \sqrt{(\pi/\beta)}$

$$\therefore \qquad \int_{-\infty}^{\infty} s^2 \, e^{-\beta s^2} \, ds = \frac{\sqrt{(\pi)}(\frac{1}{2})}{\beta\sqrt{\beta}}$$

When $\beta = 1$,

$$\int_0^{\infty} s^2 e^{-s^2} \, ds = \sqrt{\pi}/4$$

$$\therefore \qquad \underline{p = NkT.}$$

472. The electrons which escape in unit time are those with a velocity v_x such that $\frac{1}{2}mv_x^2 > \phi$, i.e. $v_x^2 > 2\phi/m$

$$\therefore \qquad \text{number} = \frac{Nv_p}{2\sqrt{\pi}} \, e^{-\omega^2} = \frac{Nv_p}{2\sqrt{\pi}} \, e^{-v_x^2/v_p^2}$$

$$= \frac{Nv_p}{2\sqrt{\pi}} \, e^{-2\phi/mv_p^2}$$

where

$$v_p^2 = 2kT/m$$

$$\therefore \qquad \text{number} = \frac{N}{2\sqrt{\pi}} \sqrt{\left(\frac{2kT}{m}\right)} \, e^{-2m\phi/m2kT}$$

$$= \frac{N}{2\sqrt{\pi}} \sqrt{\left(\frac{2k}{m}\right)} \sqrt{(T)} \, e^{-\phi/kT}$$

$$= \underline{A \sqrt{(T)} \, e^{-\phi/kT}}$$

where

$$A = \frac{N}{2\sqrt{\pi}} \sqrt{\left(\frac{2k}{m}\right)}$$

473.

$$dN_E = 2\pi N \left(\frac{1}{\pi kT}\right)^{3/2} E^{1/2} \, e^{-E/kT} \, dE$$

$$\text{Mean energy} = 2\pi \left(\frac{1}{\pi kT}\right)^{3/2} \int_0^{\infty} E^{3/2} \, e^{-E/kT} \, dE$$

Put $E/kT = x^2$, then $dE/kT = 2x \, dx$ and $E^{3/2} = (kT)^{3/2} x^3$

$$\therefore \qquad \text{mean energy} = 2\pi \left(\frac{1}{\pi kT}\right)^{3/2} (kT)^{3/2} \int_0^{\infty} x^3 \, e^{-x^2} 2x dx (kT)$$

$$= 4\pi \left(\frac{1}{\pi}\right)^{3/2} kT \int_0^{\infty} x^4 \, e^{-x^2} \, dx$$

But $$\int_0^\infty x^4 e^{-x^2}\, dx = 3\sqrt{\pi}/8$$

$\therefore$ $$\underline{\text{mean energy} = 3kT/2}$$

$E^{1/2} e^{-E/kT}$ is a maximum for most probable energy.

Write $y = E^{1/2} e^{-E/kT}$.

Then $\dfrac{dy}{dE} = E^{1/2} e^{-E/kT} \left(-\dfrac{1}{kT}\right) + \frac{1}{2}E^{-1/2} e^{-E/kT} = 0$ for maximum

$\therefore$ $$E/kT = -1/2$$

$\therefore$ $$\underline{\text{most probable energy} = kT/2}$$

$$3kT/2 = 1.602 \times 10^{-19}$$

$\therefore$ $$T = \frac{1.602 \times 10^{-19} \times 2}{3 \times 1.38 \times 10^{-23}} = \underline{7740\ \text{K}}$$

474. (i)

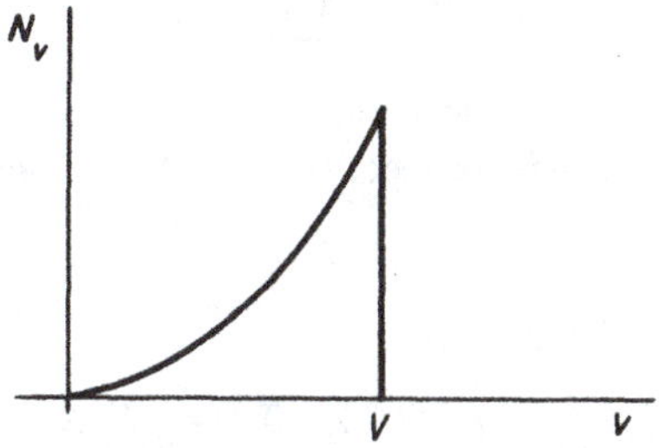

(ii) $$N = \int_{v=0}^{v=\infty} dN_v = K \int_0^V v^2\, dv = \frac{kV^3}{3}$$

$\therefore$ $$\underline{K = 3N/V^3}$$

(iii) Average speed $$\bar{v} = \frac{\int_0^\infty v\, dN_v}{\int_0^\infty dN_v} = \frac{K \int_0^V v^3\, dv}{K \int_0^V v^2\, dv} = \frac{3V^4}{4V^3}$$

$\therefore$ $$\underline{\bar{v} = 3V/4}$$

Mean square speed $$\bar{v}^2 = \frac{\int_0^\infty v^2\, dN_v}{\int_0^\infty dN_v}$$

$$= \frac{K \int_0^V v^4\, dv}{K \int_0^V v^2\, dv} = \frac{3V^5}{5V^3}$$

$\therefore$ r.m.s. speed $\sqrt{(\bar{v}^2)} = \underline{\sqrt{(3)}\, V/\sqrt{5}}$

Most probable speed $= \underline{V}$

475. (*a*) The kinetic energy $\frac{1}{2}mv^2 = Ve$.

$$\therefore \quad \tfrac{1}{2} \times 9.107 \times 10^{-31} \times v^2 = 11.6 \times 1.602 \times 10^{-19}$$

where v is in m s^{-1}.

$$\therefore \quad \underline{v = 2.02 \times 10^6 \text{ m s}^{-1}.}$$

(*b*) Excess energy

$$= \tfrac{1}{2} \times 9.107 \times 10^{-31} \times (2.02 \times 10^6)^2 - 10.4 \times 1.602 \times 10^{-19}$$

$$= 9.107 \times 10^{-31} v^2.$$

$$\therefore \quad \underline{v = 0.459 \times 10^6 \text{ m s}^{-1}.}$$

(*c*) Let the field strength be x Vm^{-1}. Then the acceleration imparted to the electron is xe/m. If v is the electron velocity acquired in a distance s m,

$$v^2 = 2xes/m$$

But $\quad v^2 = 21.5 \times 2 \times e/m.$

$$\therefore \quad x = 21.5/s = 21.5/7.9 \times 10^{-4} = \underline{2.72 \times 10^4 \text{ Vm}^{-1}.}$$

(*d*) If an electron falls from an energy level W_1 to another level W_2, then $W_1 - W_2 = hf$ where h is Planck's constant and f is the frequency of the emitted radiation. The wavelength of the emitted radiation is in Å given by $12\,400/(W_1 - W_2)$.

In this case the two wavelengths λ_1 and λ_2 are given by:

$$\lambda_1 = 12\,400/(7.93 - 6.71) \text{ and } \lambda_2 = 12\,400/6.71$$

i.e. $\quad \underline{\lambda_1 = 10\,160 \text{ Å}}$ and $\underline{\lambda_2 = 1848 \text{ Å}.}$

476. Suppose n_0 electrons per second are released from the cathode by external means. Consider a plane distant x from the cathode.

Number of electrons crossing this plane per second $(n) = n_0 +$ number produced in x.

The n electrons produce in a further distance dx an additional number of electrons $dn = \alpha\, ndx$, where α is Townsend's first ionization coefficienct. Hence,

$$\int_{n_0}^{n} \frac{dn}{n} = \alpha \int_0^x dx$$

i.e.

$$n = n_0 e^{\alpha x}.$$

Thus, the value of the current i for a given point on the current/x characteristic $= i_0 e^{\alpha x}$, where i_0 is the current produced at the cathode by external means.

Experimentally it is found that a log plot of i against x does not give a straight line but increases faster than exponentially with x. This is attributed nowadays to secondary emission from the cathode. The theory above works well, however, for small currents.

Now let n_a = the number of electrons to the anode per second;

n_+ = the number of electrons released from the cathode per second by positive-ion bombardment;

and γ = secondary emission coefficient at the cathode, i.e. the number of electrons from the cathode per incident ion.

Thus, $n_a = (n_0 + n_+)e^{\alpha d}$

where d is the anode-cathode spacing.

Also, $n_+ = \gamma\{n_a - (n_0 + n_+)\}$.

$$\therefore \qquad n_a = n_0 e^{\alpha d}/\{1 - \gamma(e^{\alpha d} - 1)\},$$

or

$$i_a = i_0 e^{\alpha d}/\{1 - \gamma(e^{\alpha d} - 1)\}.$$

Here, from a plot of $\ln I$ against x, for $0 < x < 0.8$ cm, the slope $\alpha = 3\ \text{cm}^{-1}$.

Also, $\ln i_0 = 0$, so $i_0 = 1 \mu\mu$A.

If $d = 1.6$ cm, from the above expression for i_a:

$$200 = e^{4.8}/\{1 - \gamma(e^{4.8} - 1)\}.$$

$$\gamma = 0.0033.$$

From the above expression for current i_a it is seen that $i_a \to \infty$ if $\gamma(e^{\alpha d} - 1) = 1$, or if $e^{\alpha d} = (\gamma + 1)/\gamma$. Usually $\gamma \ll 1$, so for breakdown $\gamma e^{\alpha d} \simeq 1$. Here $0.0033\, e^{3d} \simeq 1$, so $d \simeq 1.91$ cm.

477. At breakdown, $\gamma\ \mathrm{e}^{\alpha d} = 1$

so $$0.02\ \mathrm{e}^{0.5\alpha} = 1$$

i.e. $$0.5\ \alpha = \log_e 50$$

$\therefore$ $$\underline{\alpha = 7.82\ \mathrm{cm}^{-1}}$$

At 200 V, with $d = 2.5$ mm, α is the same since E is unaltered

$\therefore$ $$\text{multiplication} = \frac{\mathrm{e}^{7.82\times0.25}}{1 - 0.02(\mathrm{e}^{7.82\times0.25} - 1)} = \underline{8.06}.$$

478. The theory of probes and details of probe measurements can be found in many textbooks.*

The electron current I_e, corresponding to a probe current I_p, is given by:

$$I_e = I_p + I_i = I_p + 0.08,$$

where I_i is the saturation value of the positive-ion current.

The slope of the $\log_e I_e/V_p$ graph is found to be 0.65 V^{-1} and this equals e/kT_e, where k is Boltzmann's constant and T_e is the electron temperature.

Thus, in this case,

$$T_e = 1.602 \times 10^{-19}/0.65 \times 1.38 \times 10^{-23} = \underline{17\,800\ \mathrm{K}}$$

The random electron current density

$$J_e = I_e/A = 36.4/0.033 = 1100\ \mathrm{mA/cm^{-2}} = 1.1 \times 10^4\ \mathrm{A/m^{-2}}.$$

Therefore, $$1.1 \times 10^4 = eN_e\sqrt{(kT_e/2\pi m)},$$

where N_e is the electron concentration and m is the electron mass, i.e.
1.1×10^4

$$= N_e \,.\, 1.602 \times 10^{-19}\sqrt{(1.38 \times 10^{-23} \times 17\,800/2\pi \times 9.107 \times 10^{-31})}$$

$\therefore$ $$\underline{N_e = 3.3 \times 10^{17}/\mathrm{m}^{-3}}.$$

Plasma potential $= -11$ V, so $E = (11 - 5)/12 = \underline{0.5\ \mathrm{V/cm^{-1}}}$, where E is the voltage gradient.

The drift current density $= 1.1/6\ \mathrm{A\ cm^{-2}} = 0.18\ \mathrm{A\ cm^{-2}}$.

* For example, see J. Millman and S. Seely, *Electronics*, McGraw-Hill, 2nd Edition, 1951, 286–9; P. Parker, *Electronics*, Arnold, 1950, 637–44; and F. G. Spreadbury, *Electronics*, Pitman, 1947, 93–8.

Mobility of electrons $= 0.18/N_e eE$

$= 0.18/3.3 \times 10^{11} \times 1.602 \times 10^{-19} \times 0.5$

$= \underline{6.8 \times 10^6 \text{ cm}^2 \text{ V}^{-1} \text{ s}^{-1}}$.

479. The current I at any point x can be represented by

$$I = I_0 e^{-Ax} = I_0(1 - Ax \ldots),$$

where I_0 is the current at $x = 0$ and $A = QN$. N is the number of particles per unit volume and Q is the total collision cross-section. Here, $Ax = 1/10$ and $x = 20$ cm, so $A = 1/200$. $N = 2.7 \times 10^{19}\ (p/760)$, where p is the gas pressure in torr.

$\therefore \qquad 1/200 = 10^{-16} \times 2.7 \times 10^{19}(p/760)$ so $\underline{p = 1.405 \times 10^{-3}}$.

480. $$f_0 = \sqrt{\left(\frac{ne^2}{\pi m}\right)} \text{ Hz.}$$

At 8 mm, $f_0 = 3.75 \times 10^{10}$ Hz, so $n = 1.75 \times 10^{13}$ cm^{-3}.
At 3 cm, $f_0 = 10^{10}$ Hz, so $n = 1.24 \times 10^{12}$ cm^{-3}.
If concentration is n_0 at $t = 0$, then at time t:

$$n = n_0/(1 + n_0 \alpha t)$$

$\therefore \qquad 1.75 \times 10^{13} = n_0/(1 + n_0 \alpha\, 5.7 \times 10^{-6})$

and $\qquad 1.24 \times 10^{12} = n_0/(1 + n_0 \alpha\, 81 \times 10^{-6})$

$\therefore \qquad \underline{\alpha \simeq 10^{-8}}$

485. Choose axes as shown.

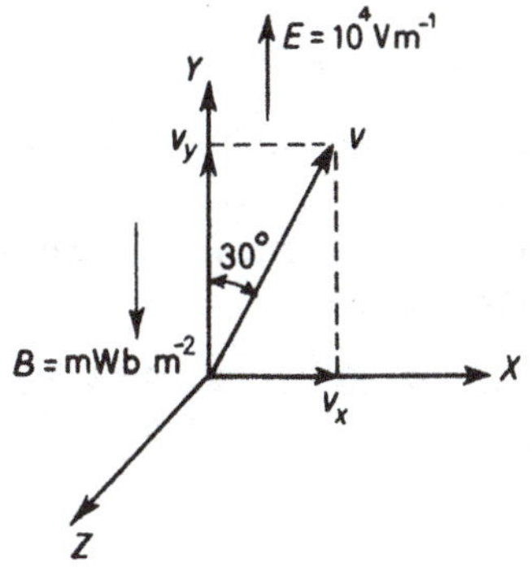

If the initial velocity of the electron was directed along the fields the magnetic field would exert no force on the electron. The electron would then move in a direction parallel to the fields with constant acceleration. If the initial velocity has a component perpendicular to the magnetic field, as in the present case, this component together with the magnetic field, will give rise to circular motion. Because of the field E the velocity along the fields changes with time so the resultant path of the electron is helical.

The velocity v can be resolved into two components v_x and v_y.

$$v_x = 1.19 \times 10^7 \sin 30° = 5.95 \times 10^6 \text{ ms}^{-1}$$
$$v_y = 1.19 \times 10^7 \cos 30° = 1.03 \times 10^7 \text{ ms}^{-1}.$$

The acceleration along the

$$-Y \text{ direction} = a = eE/m = 1.759 \times 10^{15} \text{ ms}^{-2}.$$

The projection of the electron path on the XZ plane is a circle of radius

$$r = mv_x/eB = 5.95 \times 10^6/1.759 \times 10^{11} \times 5 \times 10^{-3} = 0.00677 \text{ m}.$$

The velocity along the fields is not constant but is given by

$$v_y' = 1.03 \times 10^7 - 1.759 \times 10^{15} t \text{ ms}^{-1}$$

and y, the distance moved $= 1.03 \times 10^7 t - \frac{1}{2} \times 1.759 \times 10^{15} t^2$.

The electron begins to move in the $+Y$ direction but because the acceleration is along the $-Y$ direction, it will gradually come to rest and will then reverse its motion in the Y direction. This reversal will occur after a time t' for which $v_y' = 0$.

i.e. $$t' = 1.03 \times 10^7/1.759 \times 10^{15} = 5.86 \times 10^{-9} \text{ s}.$$

The distance travelled in the $+Y$ direction in this time t' is

$$y' = 1.03 \times 10^7 \times 5.86 \times 10^{-9}$$
$$- \tfrac{1}{2} \times 1.759 \times 10^{15} \times (5.86 \times 10^{-9})^2 = 0.03 \text{ m}.$$

After the reversal of motion the electron continues moving in the $-Y$ direction and does not reverse again. There is, of course, no reversal of the direction in which the electron traverses the circular component of its path.

The angular velocity is constant.

$$= \omega = Be/m = 1.759 \times 10^{11} \times 5 \times 10^{-3} = 8.8 \times 10^8 \text{ rad s}^{-1}.$$

The periodic time $T = 2\pi/\omega = 7.14 \times 10^{-9}$ s.

486. The force on an electron due to E is directed along the $+X$ axis. Any force due to the field B is always at right angles to B. Thus there is no component of force along the Y direction.

The two following equations therefore hold:

$$m\frac{dv_x}{dt} = eE - ev_zB \quad . \quad . \quad . \quad . \quad (1)$$

$$m\frac{dv_z}{dt} = ev_xB \quad . \quad . \quad . \quad . \quad . \quad (2)$$

From (1) $\dfrac{d^2v_x}{dt^2} = -\dfrac{eB}{m}\dfrac{dv_z}{dt} = -\omega\dfrac{dv_z}{dt} = -\omega^2 v_x$ from (2) . . (3)

where $\omega = Be/m.$

The solution of equation (3) is of the form

$$v_x = P\cos\omega t + Q\sin\omega t \quad . \quad . \quad . \quad (4)$$

where P and Q are constants determined by the initial conditions that $v_x = v_z = 0$ when $t = 0$

$\therefore$ $P = 0.$

From (1) when $t = 0$ $\dfrac{dv_x}{dt} = \dfrac{eE}{m}$

and from (4) when $t = 0$ $\dfrac{dv_x}{dt} = Q\omega$

$\therefore$ $Q = \dfrac{eE}{m\omega} = \dfrac{E}{B} = u$ say.

Thus, $v_x = u\sin\omega t$ . . . . . (5)

Using this in equation (1),

$$v_z = u - \frac{1}{\omega}\frac{dv_x}{dt} = u - u\cos\omega t \quad . \quad . \quad . \quad (6)$$

From (5) $x = \int v_x\,dt = \int u\sin\omega t\,dt = -\dfrac{u}{\omega}\cos\omega t + \text{constant.}$

Since $x = 0$ when $t = 0$, constant $= \dfrac{u}{\omega}$.

From (6)

$$z = \int v_z\,dt = \int(u - u\cos\omega t)\,dt = ut - \frac{u}{\omega}\sin\omega t + \text{constant.}$$

Since $z = 0$ when $t = 0$, constant $= 0$.

Thus $$x = \frac{u}{\omega}(1 - \cos \omega t) \text{ and } z = ut - \frac{u}{\omega} \sin \omega t.$$

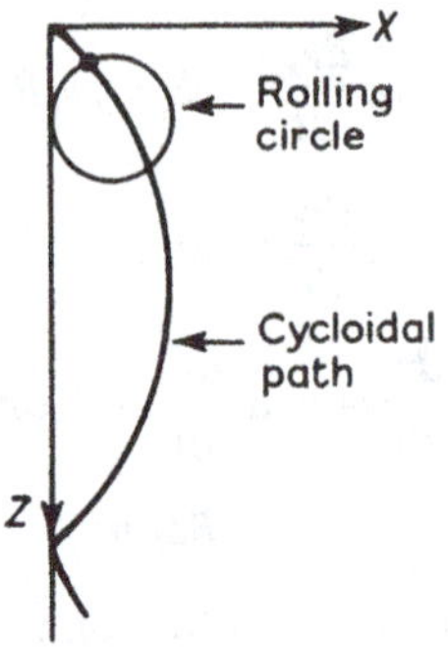

The electron path is a common cycloid, the path generated by a point on the circumference of a circle of radius u/ω which rolls along a straight line, the Z axis, as shown.

487. The axes are chosen as in Question 486.

As shown in the previous solution the electron path is cycloidal in the XZ plane. The electron travels with constant velocity along the Y axis.

Referring to the previous solution:

$$\omega = eB/m = 1.759 \times 10^9 \text{ rad s}^{-1}$$
$$u = E/B = 10^6 \text{ ms}^{-1}.$$

The time t for which the electron is in the region between the plates $= 0.02/10^6 = 2 \times 10^{-8}$ s.

Angle θ turned through in this time t

$$= \omega t = (1.759 \times 10^9)(2 \times 10^{-8}) = 35.18 \text{ rad}$$
$$= (31.42 + 3.76) \text{ radians} = (10\pi + 3.76) \text{ rad}.$$

i.e. the electron enters upon its sixth revolution before leaving the plates.

Referring to the previous solution and noting 3.76 rad = 215°:

$$x = \frac{u}{\omega}(1 - \cos \omega t) = 0.0569 \times 10^{-2}(1 - \cos 215^\circ)$$
$$= 1.035 \times 10^{-3} \text{ m}$$

$$z = \left(ut - \frac{u}{\omega}\sin \omega t\right) = 0.0569 \times 10^2(35.18 - \sin 215°)$$

$$= 2.034 \times 10^{-2}\ \text{m}.$$

∴ distance from axis when electron leaves the region between the plates is $\sqrt{(x^2 + z^2)} = \underline{2.04 \times 10^{-2}\ \text{m}}$.

488. The electric field E has two components $E_x = E \sin 20°$ and $E_y = -E \cos 20°$.

It follows that the equations of motion are those given as (1) and (2) in the solution to Question 486 where E is replaced by $-E \sin 20°$ but the force in the Y direction is no longer zero but is $e(E \cos 20°)$. The equations for x and z are then those given at the end of the solution to Question 486 with E replaced by $-E \sin 20°$ and the expression for y is $v_{0y}t + \dfrac{1}{2}\dfrac{e(E\cos 20)t^2}{m}$, where v_{0y} is the initial velocity in the Y direction.

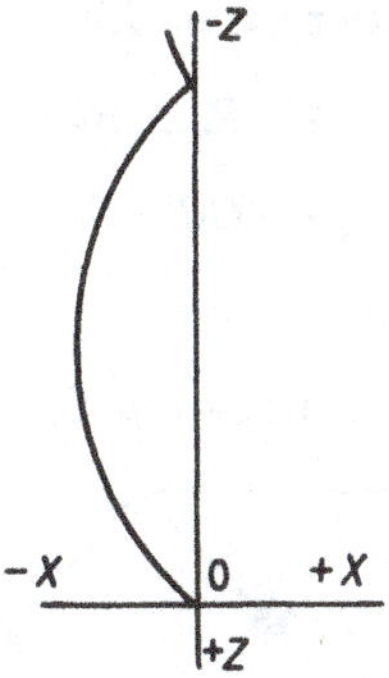

Thus, again, the projection of the path in the XZ plane is a common cycloid as shown. The equation of the cycloid is given by:

$$-x = \frac{u}{\omega}(1 - \cos \omega t)$$

and

$$-z = \frac{u}{\omega}(\omega t - \sin \omega t)$$

$$u = \frac{E \sin 20°}{B} = \frac{5 \times 10^3 \times \sin 20°}{10^3} = \underline{1.71 \times 10^6\ \text{ms}^{-1}}$$

$$\omega = eB/m = \underline{1.759 \times 10^8\ \text{rad s}^{-1}}.$$

489. The deflection at the screen* $= Vl(l/2 + L)/2Ed = \delta$, where $l =$ 1.5 cm, $d = 0.3$ cm, $L = 20$ cm, $E = 1500$ volts and V is the voltage applied to the deflector plates.

$$\therefore \quad V/\delta = 2 \times 1500 \times 0.3/1.5 \times 20.75 = \underline{28.9 \text{ V cm}^{-1}}.$$

490. The deflection at the screen† $= Hl\sqrt{(e/2mE)}[l/2 + L] = \delta$, where $l = 0.015$ m, $L = 0.2$ m, $E = 1500$ V and H is the magnetic field produced by the poles.

$$\therefore H/\delta = 1/0.015 \times 0.2075\sqrt{(1.759 \times 10^{11}/3000)} = \underline{0.042 \text{ Wb m}^{-2} \text{ per metre.}}$$

492. The Schering bridge circuit is shown in the diagram.
At balance:

$$\frac{1/j\omega C_1}{\rho_2 + 1/j\omega C_2} = \frac{1/(1/R_4 + j\omega C_4)}{R_3} \quad . \quad . \quad . \quad (1)$$

Equating real and imaginary parts of this equation gives:

$$C_2 = R_4 C_1/R_3 \quad . \quad . \quad . \quad . \quad (2)$$

and

$$\rho_2 = C_4 R_3/C_1 \quad . \quad . \quad . \quad . \quad (3)$$

The loss angle δ_2 is given by

$$\tan \delta_2 = \omega \rho_2 C_2 \quad . \quad . \quad . \quad . \quad (4)$$

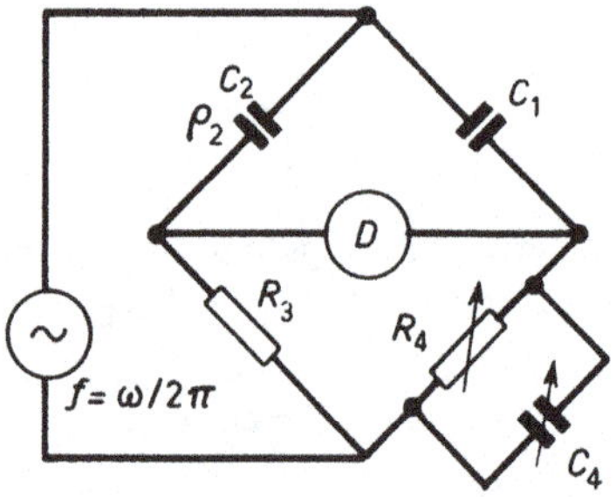

In this case, $C_2 = \epsilon\epsilon_0 A/t$ farads, where ϵ is the dielectric constant, $\epsilon_0 =$ 8.855×10^{-12}, A is the area of the plates in sq. metres and t is the distance between the plates in metres.

* See F. A. Benson, *Electrical Engineering Problems with Solutions*, Spon, 1954, 219–20.

† *ibid.*, 220–1.

$\therefore$ $$C_2 = 0.000213\ \mu\text{F}.$$

From (2) therefore

$$\underline{R_4 = 4260\ \Omega.}$$

From (4) $\tan 9' = (2\pi \times 50)\rho_2 \times 0.000213 \times 10^{-6}$

i.e. $$\rho_2 = 39\,200\ \Omega.$$

$\therefore$ from (3) $$\underline{C_4 = 0.00196\ \mu\text{F}.}$$

493. At balance the following equations are obtained:

$$i_1(R + j\omega L) = i_2 Q + i_3 r \quad . \quad . \quad . \quad (1)$$

$$i_1 P = i_3/j\omega C \quad . \quad . \quad . \quad (2)$$

and $$i_3 r + i_3/j\omega C = (i_2 - i_3)S \quad . \quad . \quad . \quad (3)$$

From (1), (2) and (3), eliminating i_1, i_2 and i_3:

$$\{(R + j\omega L)/j\omega CP - r\}S = Q(r + S + 1/j\omega C) \quad . \quad (4)$$

Equating real and imaginary parts of (4):

$$R = PQ/S \text{ and } L = CP(rQ + SQ + rS)/S.$$

In this case, $R = 500 \times 1000/1000 = \underline{500\ \Omega}$

and $L = 2 \times 10^{-6} \times 500(200 + 1000 + 200)10^3/1000 = \underline{1.4\ \text{H}}.$

494. At balance the following equation holds:

$$(R_1 + j\omega L_1)/(R_2 + j\omega L_2) = (R_4 - j/\omega C_2)/(R_3 - j/\omega C_1) \quad . \quad (1)$$

Equating the real and imaginary parts of (1):

$$R_1R_3 + L_1/C_1 = R_2R_4 + L_2/C_2 \quad . \quad . \quad . \quad (2)$$

and $$-R_1C_2 + \omega^2 L_1C_1R_3C_2 = -R_2C_1 + \omega^2 L_2C_2C_1R_4 \quad . \quad (3)$$

From (3) it follows that $L_1C_1R_3C_2$ must equal $L_2C_2C_1R_4$.

i.e. $$\underline{L_1R_3 = L_2R_4} \quad . \quad . \quad . \quad . \quad (4)$$

<u>Also from (3) R_1C_2 must equal R_2C_1</u>

From (2) it follows that if $R_1R_3 = R_2R_4$, L_1/C_1 must equal L_2/C_2.

From (4) and (5) $L_1/C_1 = \dfrac{L_2}{C_2} \cdot \dfrac{R_2R_4}{R_1R_3} = L_2/C_2$ when $R_1R_3 = R_2R_4$.

Similarly, if $L_1 = C_1R_2R_4$ it follows from (2) that R_1R_3 must equal L_2/C_2.

From (4) and (5) $R_1R_3 = \dfrac{R_2C_1}{C_2} \cdot \dfrac{L_2R_4}{C_1} = \dfrac{L_2}{C_2}$ when $L_1 = C_1R_2R_4$

$\therefore$ either $R_1R_3 = R_2R_4$ or $L_1 = C_1R_2R_4$.

495. The network is shown in the diagram.

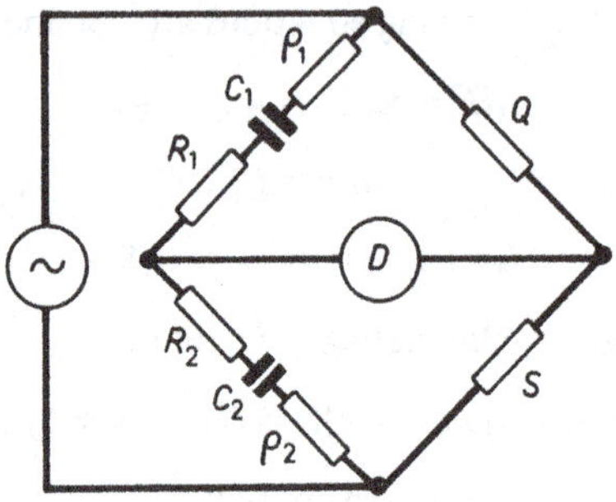

At balance:

$$Q/S = (R_1 + \rho_1 + 1/j\omega C_1)/(R_2 + \rho_2 + 1/j\omega C_2) \quad . \quad (1)$$

Equating real and imaginary parts of (1):

$$Q/S = (R_1 + \rho_1)/(R_2 + \rho_2) = C_2/C_1 \quad . \quad . \quad (2)$$

Here $R_1 = 11.4\ \Omega$, $\rho_2 = 0$, $R_2 = 10\ \Omega$, $C_2 = 0.023\ \mu F$

$\therefore$ from (2) $\rho_1 = 1.1\ \Omega$ and $C_1 = 0.0184\ \mu F$.

496. Let the currents and voltages be as shown on the diagram.

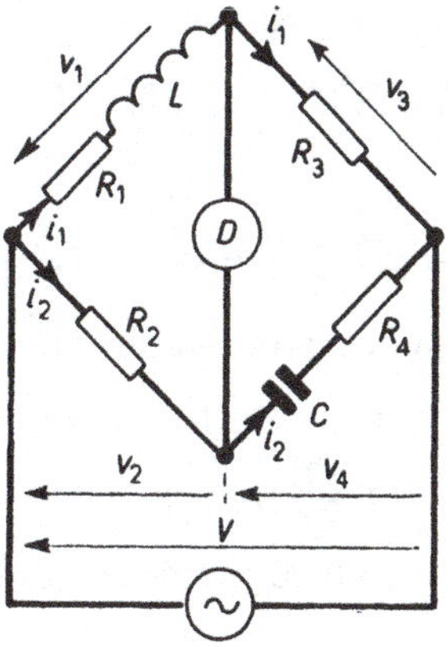

At balance:

$$(R_1 + j\omega L)i_1 = R_2 i_2 \quad . \quad . \quad . \quad . \quad (1)$$

$$R_3 i_1 = (R_4 + 1/j\omega C)i_2 \quad . \quad . \quad . \quad (2)$$

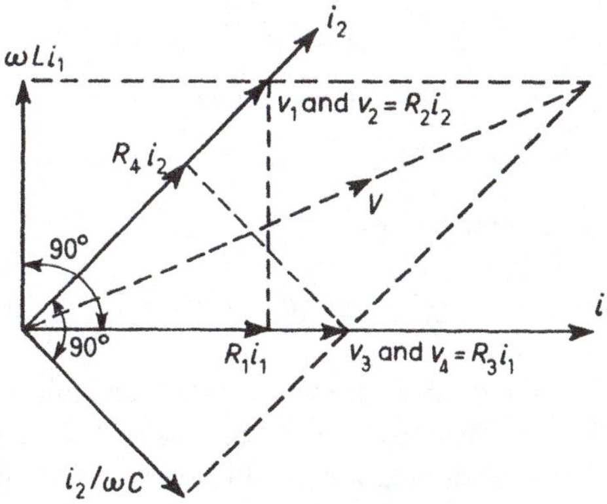

Dividing (1) and (2) and equating real and imaginary parts gives two equations in terms of L and R_1 from which:

$$\underline{L = R_2 R_3 C/(1 + \omega^2 R_4^2 C^2)}$$

and

$$\underline{R_1 = R_2 R_3 R_4 \omega^2 C^2/(1 + \omega^2 R_4^2 C^2).}$$

The phasor diagram for the network is as shown.

497. With S open the balance condition is:

$$C_1 = C_2 C_3/(C_2 + C_3) \quad . \quad . \quad . \quad . \quad (1)$$

With S closed the balance condition is:

$$C_1 = C_2'(C_3 + C_x)/(C_2' + C_3 + C_x) \quad . \quad . \quad (2)$$

From (1) and (2),

$$\underline{C_x = C_3^2(C_2 - C_2')/(C_2'C_2 + C_2'C_3 - C_2C_3).}$$

With S open and with C_1 adjusted then at balance

$$C_1 = 1000 \times 50/1050 = 47.6\ \mu\mu\text{F}.$$

With S closed, $47.6 = C_2' \times 51/(C_2' + 51)$ $\therefore$ $C_2' = 714\ \mu\mu\text{F}$.

Thus $\qquad C_2 - C_2' = (1000 - 714)\ \mu\mu\text{F} = 286\ \mu\mu\text{F}$.

There are two readings, one at the maximum setting of C_2 and the other at $C_2 = 286\ \mu\mu$F, so the reading error is $\pm\ 10 \times 100/286$ per cent = $\underline{\pm\ 3.5 \text{ per cent}}$.

498. Let $V_x = V_1 \sin(\omega t + \theta_1)$ and $V_y = V_2 \sin(\omega t + \theta_2)$.

$\therefore$
$$V_x = V_1 (\sin \omega t \cos \theta_1 + \cos \omega t \sin \theta_1) \quad . \quad . \quad (1)$$

and
$$V_y = V_2 (\sin \omega t \cos \theta_2 + \cos \omega t \sin \theta_2) \quad . \quad . \quad (2)$$

From (1) and (2) eliminating ωt gives:

$$\frac{V_x^2}{V_1^2} + \frac{V_y^2}{V_2^2} - \frac{2V_xV_y}{V_1V_2}\cos(\theta_1 - \theta_2) = \sin^2(\theta_1 - \theta_2).$$

This is the equation of an ellipse whose major and minor axes coincide with the x and y axes respectively when $(\theta_1 - \theta_2) = \pi/2$. In general, the trace gives an ellipse the orientation of which depends on the phase difference between the two voltage waves.

499. The solution to this problem can be found elsewhere.*

500. The solution to this problem can be found elsewhere.*

501. The solution to this problem can be found elsewhere.*

* F. A. Benson and A. O. Carter, 'A Critical Survey of Some Phase-angle Measurements Using a Cathode-ray Tube,' *Electronic Engineering*, **22**, 238–42, 1950.

502.

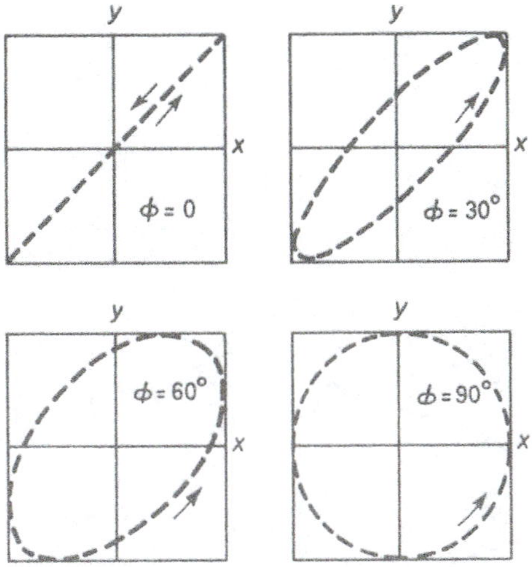

503.

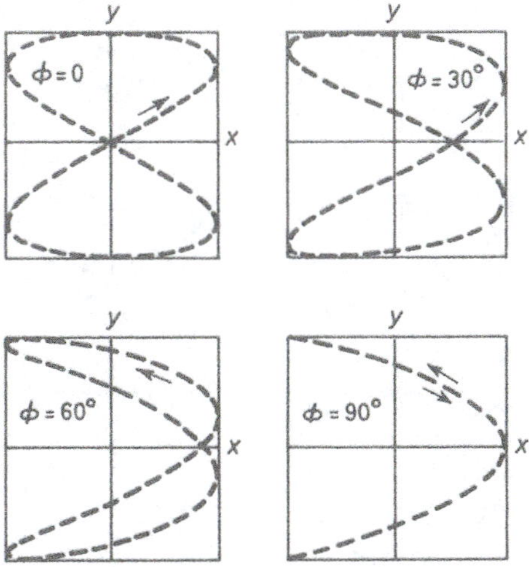

$n = 2$

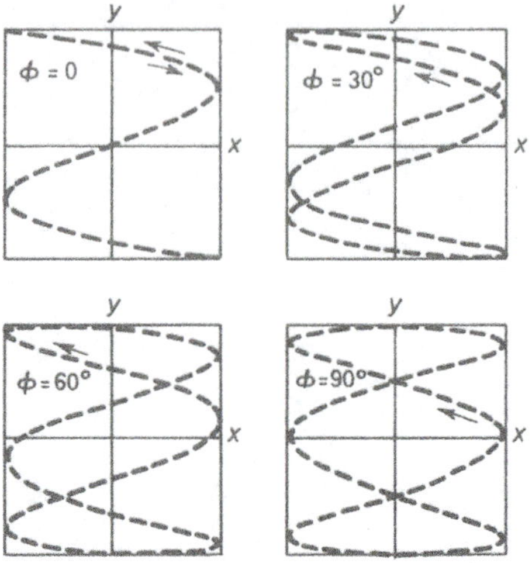
y
x
$\phi = 0$
$\phi = 30°$
$\phi = 60°$
$\phi = 90°$

$n = 3$

504.

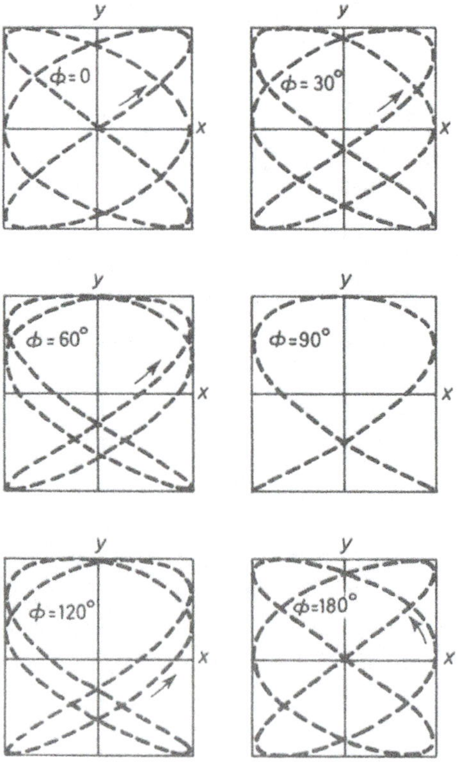
y
x
$\phi = 0$
$\phi = 30°$
$\phi = 60°$
$\phi = 90°$
$\phi = 120°$
$\phi = 180°$

505. One method of finding the frequency ratio is as follows: draw a line parallel to the x-axis, which does not pass through any intersections of different parts of the curve, and count the number of points where the line intersects the curve; repeat this procedure with a line drawn parallel to the y-axis. It should be noted that the lines must not be part of the boundary rectangle. The ratio of the two numbers so found will be the required frequency ratio. The number of intersections on the line parallel to the x-axis is proportional to the frequency of the y-variation, and vice versa.*

506. For equal sensitivities

$$R = 1/\omega C = 1/2\pi \times 50 \times 2 \times 10^{-6}\ \Omega = \underline{1592\ \Omega.}$$

For differing sensitivities

$$R = 1592 \times 0.55/0.45 = \underline{1946\ \Omega.}$$

507. Voltage range = (5 × 30 − 20) = 130 V.

Length of time base = 130 × 0.8 mm = $\underline{0.104 \text{ m.}}$

If T is the time of the sweep,

$$0.01 \times 10^{-6} \times 130 = 1.5 \times T \times 10^{-3}.$$

$$\therefore \qquad \text{Frequency } f = 1/T = \underline{1154 \text{ Hz.}}$$

510. Tabulate all values of ABCD as below.

ABCD	a)	b)	c)	f
0000	0	0	0	0
0001	0	0	0	0
0010	0	0	0	0
0011	0	0	0	0
0100	0	0	0	0
0101	0	0	0	0
0110	0	0	0	0
0111	1	0	0	1

* For further information see G. Parr and O. H. Davie, *The Cathode-Ray Tube and its Applications*, Chapman & Hall, 3rd Edition, 1959, Chapter 6. See also, F. E. Terman, *Radio Engineer's Handbook*, McGraw-Hill, 1943, 955.

ABCD	a)	b)	c)	f
1000	0	0	0	0
1001	0	0	1	1
1010	0	0	0	0
1011	0	0	1	1
1100	0	1	0	1
1101	0	1	0	1
1110	1	0	0	1
1111	0	0	1	1

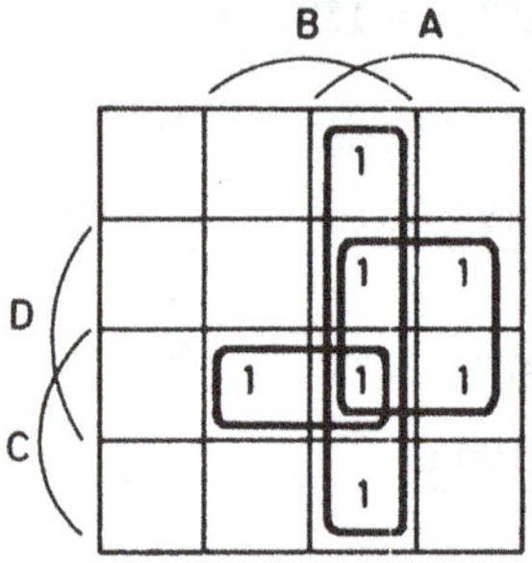

$f = AB + AD + BCD$

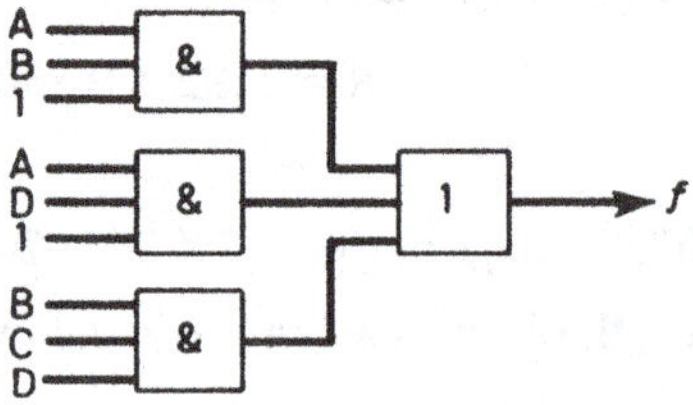

511.

Inputs			Outputs	
A	B	P	S	C
0	0	0	0	0
0	0	1	1	0
0	1	0	1	0
0	1	1	0	1
1	0	0	1	0
1	0	1	0	1
1	1	0	0	1
1	1	1	1	1

P = previous carry

S = sum

C = carry

$$S = \bar{A}B\bar{P} + A\bar{B}\bar{P} + \bar{A}\bar{B}P + ABP$$
$$= \bar{P}(\bar{A}B + A\bar{B}) + P(\bar{A}\bar{B} + AB)$$
$$= P(\bar{A}B + A\bar{B}) + P\overline{(\bar{A}B + A\bar{B})}$$
$$= PS' + P\bar{S}'$$

where S′ is sum of half adder

$$
\begin{aligned}
C &= AB\bar{P} + \bar{A}BP + A\bar{B}P + ABP \\
&= P(\bar{A}B + A\bar{B}) + AB(P + \bar{P}) \\
&= PS' + AB \\
&= PS' + C'
\end{aligned}
$$

where C′ is carry of half adder.

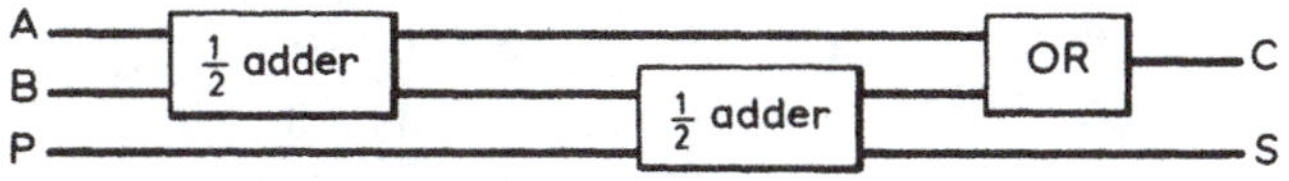

512.

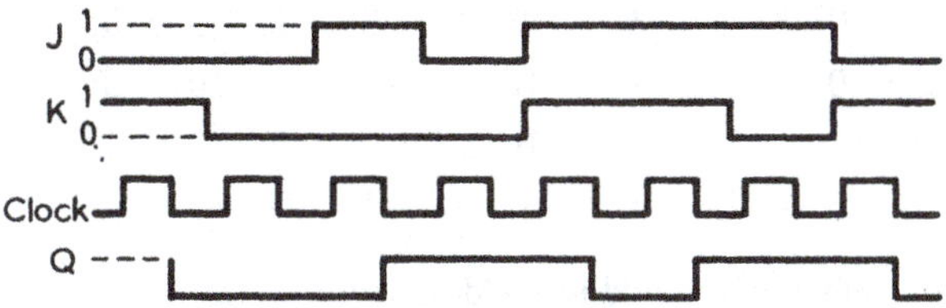

513.

	A	$\bar{A}$
B	1	0
$\bar{B}$	0	1

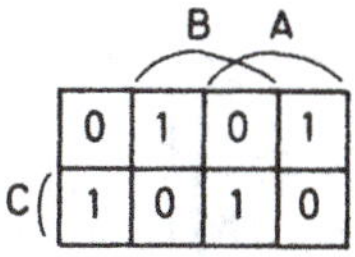

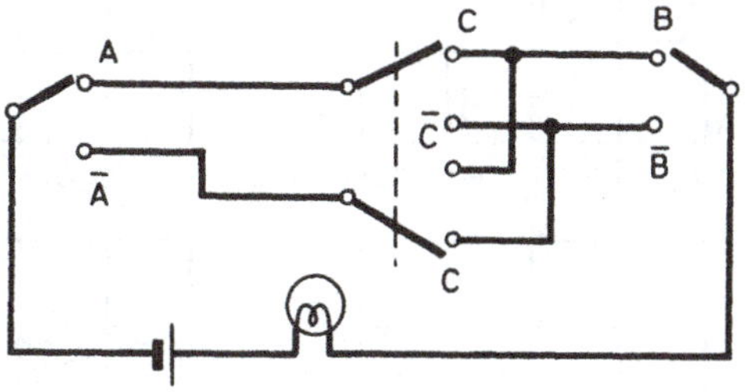

514. (*a*)

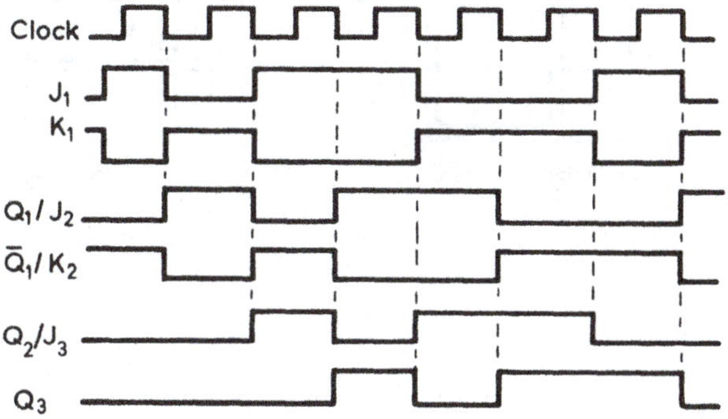

(*b*) Shift register.

515.

G_4	G_3	G_2	G_1	D	C	B	A
0	0	0	0	0	0	0	0
0	0	0	1	0	0	0	1
0	0	1	1	0	0	1	0
0	0	1	0	0	0	1	1
0	1	1	0	0	1	0	0
0	1	1	1	0	1	0	1
0	1	0	1	0	1	1	0
0	1	0	0	1	0	0	0
1	1	0	0	1	0	0	1
1	1	0	1	1	0	1	0

By Karnaugh Map method using 'don't care' states.

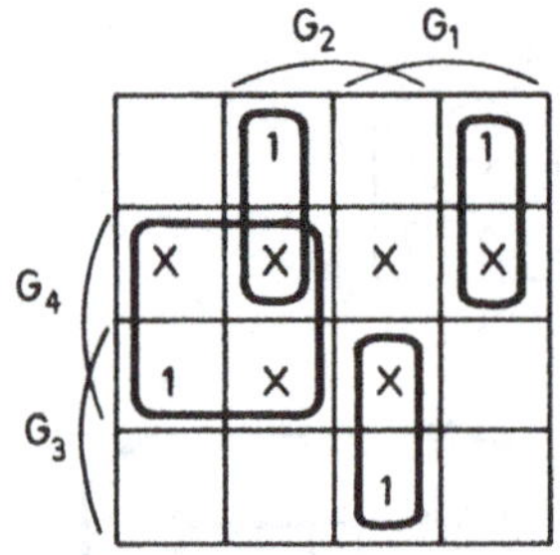

$A = \bar{G}_1 G_4 + \bar{G}_1 G_2 \bar{G}_3 + G_1 G_2 G_3 + G_1 \bar{G}_2 \bar{G}_3$

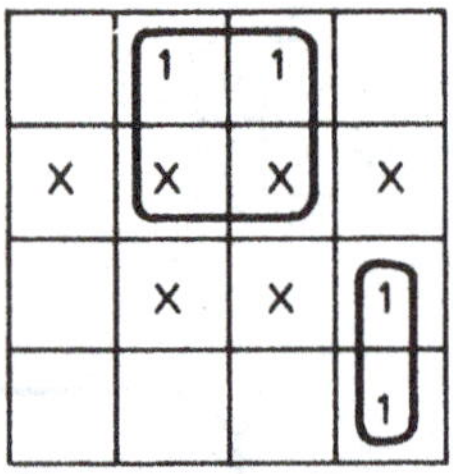

$B = G_2 \bar{G}_3 + G_1 \bar{G}_2 G_3$

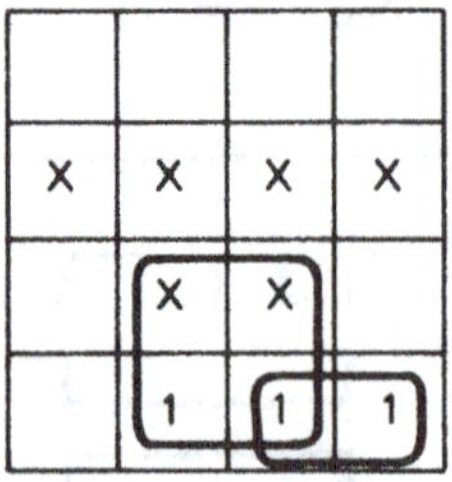

$C = G_2 G_3 + G_1 G_3 \bar{G}_4$

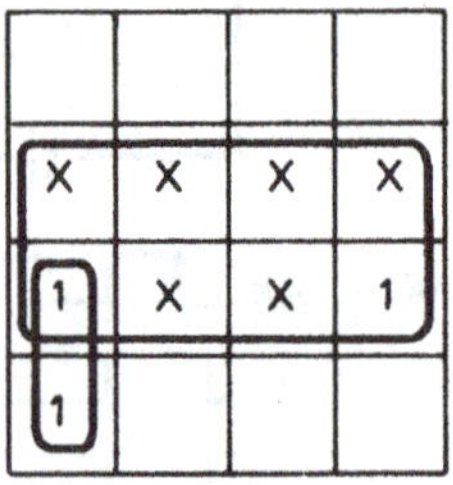

$D = G_4 + \bar{G}_1 \bar{G}_2 G_3$

516.

Count	J_1	K_1	Q_1	J_2	K_2	Q_2	J_3	K_3	Q_3
0	1	X	0	0	X	0	0	X	0
1	X	1	1	1	X	0	0	X	0
2	1	X	0	X	0	1	0	X	0
3	X	1	1	X	1	1	1	X	0
4	0	X	0	0	X	0	X	1	1
0	1	X	0	0	X	0	0	X	0

The equations below will satisfy the above table.

$$J_1 = \bar{Q}_3 \quad J_2 = Q_1 \quad J_3 = Q_1Q_2$$

$$K_1 = 1 \quad K_2 = Q_1 \quad K_3 = 1$$

517. Decimal column is $Q_1Q_2Q_3$ in binary.
J_1 is the exclusive or function of Q_1 and Q_2.

Decimal	Clock	J_1	K_1	Q_1/J_2	$\bar{Q}_1/K_2$	Q_2/J_3	$\bar{Q}_2/K_3$	Q_3
0	0	0	1	0	1	0	1	0
				terminates				
1	0	0	1	0	1	0	1	1
0	1	0	1	0	1	0	1	0
				terminates				
2	0	1	0	0	1	1	0	0
5	1	1	0	1	0	0	1	1
6	2	0	1	1	0	1	0	0
3	3	1	0	0	1	1	0	1
5	4	1	0	1	0	0	1	1
				continuous $5 \to 6 \to 3 \to 5$				
4	0	1	0	1	0	0	1	0
6	1	0	1	1	0	1	0	0
3	2	1	0	0	1	1	0	1
5	3	1	0	1	0	0	1	1
6	4	0	1	1	0	1	0	0
				continuous $6 \to 3 \to 5 \to 6$				

Decimal	Clock	J_1	K_1	Q_1/J_2	$\bar{Q}_1/K_2$	Q_2/J_3	$\bar{Q}_2/K_3$	Q_3
7	0	0	1	1	0	1	0	1
3	1	1	0	0	1	1	0	1
5	2	1	0	1	0	0	1	1
6	3	0	1	1	0	1	0	0
3	4	1	0	0	1	1	0	1

continuous $3 \rightarrow 5 \rightarrow 6 \rightarrow 3$

Entry at 0 and 1 terminates in 0
All other entries lead to loop sequence $3 \rightarrow 5 \rightarrow 6 \rightarrow 3$.

518.

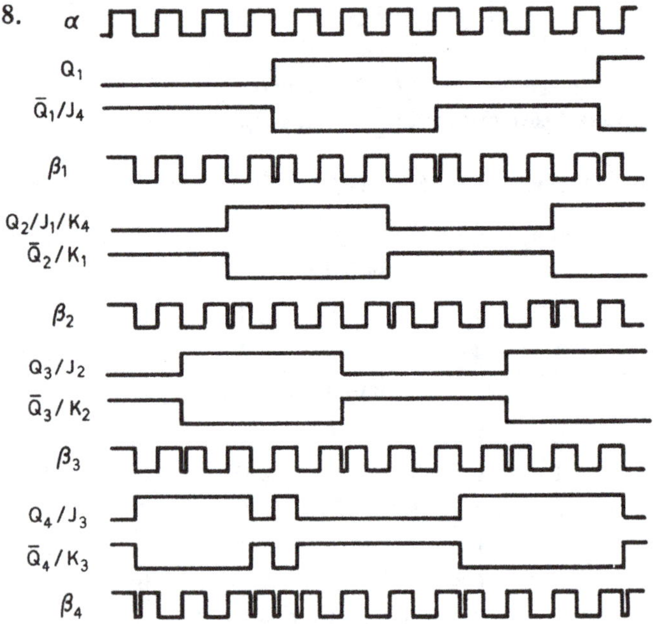

521. The skin depth $\delta = 1/\sqrt{(\pi\mu f\sigma)}$

where σ is the conductivity, μ the permeability and f the frequency.*

* See, for example, J. C. Slater, *Microwave Transmission*, McGraw-Hill, 1942, 114; or R. A. Bailey, 'A Resonant-cavity Torque-operated Wattmeter for Microwave Power,' *Proc. I.E.E.*, Part C, **103**, 60, 1956.

For copper,

$$\delta = 1/\sqrt{(\pi \times 4\pi \times 10^{-7} \times f \times 5.88 \times 10^{7})}\ \text{m}$$

When $f = 300$ MHz, $\underline{\delta = 3.79 \times 10^{-6}\ \text{m.}}$

When $f = 10\,000$ MHz, $\underline{\delta = 6.56 \times 10^{-7}\ \text{m.}}$

522. The inductance of a straight piece of wire at very high frequencies is:*

$$L = 0.002/(2.303 \log_{10} 4l/d - 1 + d/21)\ \mu\text{H},$$

where l is the length of the wire in centimetres and d is the wire diameter in centimetres.

In this case, $l = 2.54$ cm and $d = 0.0254$ cm so $\underline{L = 0.014\ \mu\text{H.}}$

At 500 MHz the reactance

$$= 2\pi \times 500 \times 10^{6} \times 0.014 \times 10^{-6}\ \Omega = \underline{44\ \Omega.}$$

523. The intrinsic impedance of the plate $Z_0 = \sqrt{(Z_1 Z_2)}$,

where Z_1 = intrinsic impedance of air

and Z_2 = intrinsic impedance of dielectric medium.

Now $Z_1 = \sqrt{(\mu_0/\epsilon_0)} = 377\ \Omega$ and $Z_2 = 377/\sqrt{4}\ \Omega = 188\ \Omega$

∴ $Z_0 = \sqrt{(377 \times 188)}\ \Omega = 266\ \Omega.$

$\underline{\text{The relative permittivity required} = (377/266)^2 = 2.}$

524. The output voltage is as shown in the diagram.

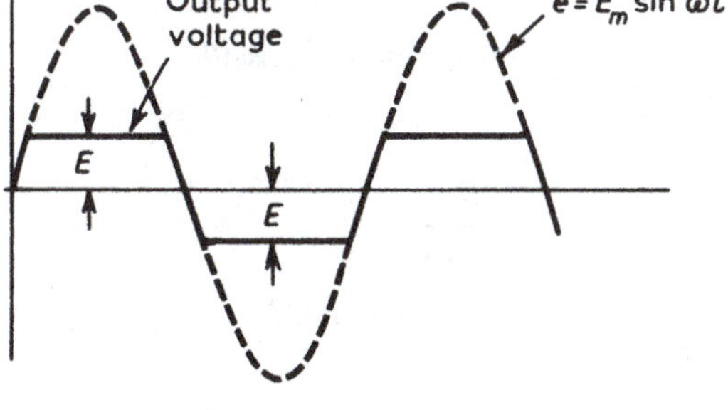

* See K. R. Spangenberg, *Vacuum Tubes*, McGraw-Hill, 1948, 477.

Rate of rise of waveform $= \dfrac{de}{dt} = \omega E_m \cos \omega t \simeq \omega E_m$.

Time taken to rise from $-E$ to $+E$ is $\delta T \simeq 2E/\omega E_m$,

i.e. $$\delta T = 2 \times 2/(2\pi \times 10^5 \times 200)\ \text{s} = \underline{0.032\ \mu\text{s}.}$$

525. If V is independent of z:

$$\frac{1}{r}\frac{\delta}{\delta r}\left(r\frac{\delta V}{\delta r}\right) + \frac{1}{r^2}\frac{\delta^2 V}{\delta \theta^2} = 0$$

Let $V = f(r) \cos 4\theta$

$\therefore$ $$\frac{1}{r}\frac{\delta}{\delta r}\left(r\frac{\delta f}{\delta r}\right)\cos 4\theta - \frac{16f}{r^2}\cos 4\theta = 0$$

or $$r\frac{\delta}{\delta r}\left(r\frac{\delta f}{\delta r}\right) = 16f$$

Suppose $f = r^n$

$$\frac{df}{dr} = nr^{n-1} \quad \text{and} \quad r\frac{df}{dr} = nr^n$$

$\therefore$ $$r\frac{d}{dr}\left(r\frac{df}{dr}\right) = n^2 r^n = n^2 f$$

$\therefore$ $$n^2 = 16 \quad \text{or} \quad n = \pm 4$$

i.e. $$f(r) = r^4 \quad \text{or} \quad r^{-4}$$

<u>The solution is r^{-4} since $V \to 0$ as $r \to \infty$</u>

$$E_r = -\frac{\delta V}{\delta r}$$

$$V = Ar^{-4} \cos 4\theta$$

so $$E_r = -4Ar^{-5} \cos 4\theta$$

$$\frac{E_{(2r_0)}}{E_{(r_0)}} = \frac{(2r_0)^{-5}}{(r_0)^{-5}} = 2^{-5}$$

i.e. $$\underline{E_{(2r_0)} = E_0/32.}$$

526. For the first layer: capacitance $= A\epsilon_0 K/d$

For the second layer: capacitance $= A\epsilon_0 K/d$

conductance $= A\sigma/d.$

$$\text{Total impedance} = \frac{d}{j\omega A\epsilon_0 K} + \frac{\dfrac{d}{A\sigma}\cdot\dfrac{d}{j\omega A\epsilon_0 K}}{\dfrac{d}{A\sigma}+\dfrac{d}{j\omega A\epsilon_0 K}}$$

$$= \frac{d}{j\omega A\epsilon_0 K}\left\{1+\frac{1}{1+\sigma/j\omega\epsilon_0 K}\right\}$$

For the composite dielectric impedance $= 2d/j\omega A\epsilon_0 K'$

$$\therefore \qquad \frac{2}{K'} = \frac{1}{K}\left\{1+\frac{1}{1+\sigma/j\omega\epsilon_0 K}\right\}$$

or $$\underline{K' = 2K(K - j\sigma/\omega\epsilon_0)/(2K - j\sigma/\omega\epsilon_0).}$$

527. The electric field at an atom site is the sum of that due to the external field and that due to all the induced electric dipoles in the material. The latter will be proportional to the electric polarization.

Here $$E_i = E + P/3\epsilon_0 \quad . \quad . \quad . \quad . \quad (1)$$

The relative permittivity ϵ_r is related to the susceptibility χ by:

$$\epsilon_r = 1 + \chi = 1 + P/\epsilon_0 E \quad . \quad . \quad . \quad (2)$$

But $$P = N\alpha E_i \quad . \quad . \quad . \quad . \quad (3)$$

where N is the atomic number density and α is the atomic polarizability.

Eliminating E_i from (1) and (3) gives:

$$P = N\alpha E + N\alpha P/3\epsilon_0$$

or $$P/\epsilon_0 E = \frac{N\alpha/\epsilon_0}{(1 - N\alpha/3\epsilon_0)}$$

From (2) therefore,

$$\epsilon_r = 1 + \frac{N\alpha/\epsilon_0}{(1 - N\alpha/3\epsilon_0)}$$

or $$\underline{\frac{N\alpha}{3\epsilon_0} = \frac{\epsilon_r - 1}{\epsilon_r + 2}}$$

which is the Clausius-Mosotti relationship.

(*a*) $$\frac{N\alpha}{\epsilon_0} = \frac{5 \times 10^{28} \times 2 \times 10^{-40}}{8.855 \times 10^{-12}}$$

$$\therefore \qquad \epsilon_r = 1 + \frac{N\alpha/\epsilon_0}{(1 - N\alpha/3\epsilon_0)} = \underline{2.81}$$

$$(b) \qquad \frac{E_i}{E} = 1 + \frac{P}{3\,\epsilon_0 E} = 1 + \frac{1.81}{3} = \underline{1.6.}$$

528. The Clausius-Mosotti relationship* is:

$$\frac{\epsilon_r - 1}{\epsilon_r + 2} = \frac{N\alpha}{3\epsilon_0}$$

To calculate the polarizability α of a sphere:

$$\text{Dipole moment} = 4\pi\epsilon_0 r^3 E$$

where E is the electric field and r the sphere radius.

$$\therefore \qquad \alpha = 4\pi\epsilon_0 r^3$$

$$= 4\pi \times \frac{10^{-9}}{36\pi} \times (10^{-3})^3$$

$$= 10^{-18}/9$$

$$\therefore \qquad N = \left(\frac{1}{4/1000}\right)^3 = 10^9/64.$$

Thus,

$$\frac{\epsilon_r - 1}{\epsilon_r + 2} = \frac{10^9}{64} \cdot \frac{10^{-18}}{9} \cdot \frac{36\pi}{3 \times 10^{-9}}$$

$$\therefore \qquad \underline{\epsilon_r = 1.21.}$$

529. The Clausius-Mosotti relation is:

$$\frac{\epsilon_r - 1}{\epsilon_r + 2} = \frac{N\alpha}{3\epsilon_0}$$

$$\therefore \qquad \frac{N\alpha}{3\epsilon_0} = \frac{1.25}{4.25}$$

For the expanded polythene,

$$\frac{N\alpha}{3\epsilon_0} = \left(\frac{1.25}{4.25}\right) \frac{5}{100} = 0.0148$$

* See, for example, B. I. Bleaney and B. Bleaney, *Electricity and Magnetism*, Oxford, 1957, 493, also the previous Solution.

$$\therefore \qquad \frac{\epsilon_r - 1}{\epsilon_r + 2} = 0.0148$$

i.e.

$$\underline{\epsilon_r = 1.058.}$$

530. (*a*) Light is considered as composed of particles of energy hf so that electron emission is possible only if the frequency of the impinging light is greater than the 'threshold' value $f_c = e\phi/h$; where ϕ is the work function in electron volts, e is the charge on the electron and h is Planck's constant.

Corresponding threshold wavelength, $\lambda_c = \dfrac{ch}{e\phi} = \dfrac{12\,400}{\phi}$ Å.

In this case ϕ must be less than $12\,400/8000 = \underline{1.55 \text{ eV}.}$

For caesium, $\lambda_c = (12\,400/1.8)$ Å $= \underline{6890 \text{ Å}.}$

(*b*) The electron-volt equivalent of the energy of the incident photons is 12 400/2537, i.e. 4.89 eV.

According to Einstein* the maximum energy of the emitted electrons is $4.89 - 4.3 = 0.59$ eV.

The maximum velocity

$$v = \sqrt{\left(2\frac{e}{m}E\right)} = 5.93 \times 10^5 \sqrt{E} \text{ ms}^{-1}$$

$$= 5.93 \times 10^5 \sqrt{0.59} \text{ ms}^{-1} = \underline{4.56 \times 10^5 \text{ ms}^{-1}.}$$

531. If the charge per unit length of electrode is Q, then

$$E = Q/2\pi r\epsilon_0 \quad \text{and} \quad V = \int_a^b E\,dr = Q \ln (b/a)/2\pi\epsilon_0,$$

where a and b are the anode and cathode radii respectively and r is any radius between a and b.

$$\therefore \qquad E = V/r \ln (b/a)$$

Let the number of ion pairs be n at any point. Then,

$$dn/n = Ape^{-Bp \ln (b/a) r/V}\,dr$$

* A. Einstein, 'Über einen die Erzeugung und Verwandlung des Lichtes betreffenden heuristischen Gesichtspunkt,' *Ann. Physik.*, 17, 32, 1905.

Here $A = 13.6, \quad B = 17.3 \times 13.6 \simeq 235, \quad b/a = 20,$

so $\ln(b/a) \simeq 3 \quad \text{and} \quad p = 1$

$\therefore$ $dn/n = 13.6\, e^{-235 \times 3r/V}\, dr,$

and $$\ln(n/n_0) = 13.6 \int_a^b e^{-705r/V}\, dr$$

Write $705r/V = s$, then $705\, dr/V = ds$, so

$$\ln(n/n_0) = 13.6 \int_{705/20V}^{705/V} e^{-s}(V/705)\, ds$$

$$= (13.6\, V/705)\{e^{-705/20V} - e^{-705/V}\}$$

$$\simeq \underline{(V/52)e^{-35.3/V}}.$$

532. The solution to this problem can be found elsewhere.*

533. The solution to this problem can be found elsewhere.†

534. The solution to this problem can be found elsewhere.‡

535. $$E_{max} = 3 \times 10^4 \text{ V cm}^{-1}$$

$$H_{max} = E_{max}/120\pi$$

$$P = \tfrac{1}{2} \int_0^1 \int_0^1 (E^2/Z_0)\, dx\, dy = E^2/2Z_0$$

i.e. $$P = 9 \times 10^8/2 \times 120\pi = \underline{1.19 \times 10^6 \text{ W cm}^{-2}}.$$

* See, for example, P. Parker, *Electronics*, Arnold, 1950, 50–3 and 980–2; or R. Latham, A. H. King, L. Rushforth, *The Magnetron*, Chapman & Hall, 1952, Section 6.4.2.

† See, for example, J. Millman and S. Seely, *Electronics*, McGraw-Hill, 1951, 80–2. See also, P. Parker, *Electronics*, Arnold, 1950, Section 107.

‡ See W. W. Harman, *Fundamentals of Electronic Motion*, McGraw-Hill, 1953, 207–15.

INDEX

Page numbers are given first, followed by problem numbers set in bold and in parentheses.